ROMAN AND MEDIEVAL EXETER AND THEIR HINTERLANDS

ROMAN AND MEDIEVAL EXETER AND THEIR HINTERLANDS

FROM *ISCA* TO *EXCESTER*

Edited by

STEPHEN RIPPON AND NEIL HOLBROOK

with contributions from

JOHN ALLAN, PAUL BIDWELL, DELPHINE FRÉMONDEAU,
DAVID GOULD, ROBERT HIGHAM, NEIL HOLBROOK,
MARK MALTBY, GUNDULA MÜLDNER AND STEPHEN RIPPON

EAPIT

Exeter:
A Place in Time

EXETER: A PLACE IN TIME 1/EXETER ARCHAEOLOGICAL REPORT 7

OXBOW | books
Oxford & Philadelphia

Published in the United Kingdom in 2021 by
OXBOW BOOKS
The Old Music Hall, 106–108 Cowley Road, Oxford, OX4 1JE

and in the United States by
OXBOW BOOKS
1950 Lawrence Road, Havertown, PA 19083

Hardcover Edition: 978-1-78925-615-4
Digital Edition: 978-1-78925-616-1 (epub)

A CIP record for this book is available from the British Library

Library of Congress Control Number: 2020951525

Printed in Malta by Melita Press

Typeset by Versatile PreMedia Service (P) Ltd.

For a complete list of Oxbow titles, please contact:

UNITED KINGDOM
Oxbow Books
Telephone (01865) 241249
Email: oxbow@oxbowbooks.com
www.oxbowbooks.com

UNITED STATES OF AMERICA
Oxbow Books
Telephone (610) 853-9131, Fax (610) 853-9146
Email: queries@casemateacademic.com
www.casemateacademic.com/oxbow

Oxbow Books is part of the Casemate Group

This monograph was published with the aid of a grant from Historic England.

Historic England

Title page image: The Common Seal of Exeter. Made *c.* 1200 and still used in the early 20th century, this large silver seal matrix is the earliest example of a civic seal surviving in Britain. The inscription reads '+SIGILLUM CIVITATIS EXONIE' – the seal of the city of Exeter. The reverse records the maker named Luke and the donor, the wealthy Exeter citizen William Prudum.

Front cover: Excavation in 1972 of the fortress baths and the later remains of the basilica and forum, looking south-west from the West Front of the Cathedral (Exeter Archaeology archive, © Exeter City Council)

Back cover: Obverse of a penny of Cnut's *Quatrefoil* issue, struck by the moneyer Isegod at Exeter *c.* 1017–23, illustrating the distinctive local style of Exeter coins of this issue with their hooped drapery.

Contents

List of Figures

List of Tables

List of Appendices

Online material can be found at https://doi.org/10.24378/exe.1983

List of Abbreviations

ADS	Archaeology Data Service
BL	Bodleian Library
BSE	back scattered electron images
D&C	Dean and Chapter deeds, court rolls, and account rolls, in Exeter Cathedral Library and Archive
EA	Exeter Archaeology
EAACR	Exeter Archaeology Advisory Committee Report
EAAP	Exeter Archaeology Archive project
EAPIT	Exeter: A Place in Time project
EAR	Exeter Archaeological report
ECC	Exeter City Council
EMAFU	Exeter Museums Archaeological Field Unit
EOL	extra applied outer layer of clay
FH	Friernhay Street
HER	Historic Environment Record (maintained by Exeter City Council)
H/FL	hearth/furnace lining
MY	Mermaid Yard
NISP	Number of identified specimens
OSL	Optically Stimulated Luminescence
PAS	Portable Antiquities Scheme
PPG16	Planning Policy Guidance note 16
pXRF	portable X-Ray Fluorescence
RAMM	Royal Albert Memorial Museum
RIB	Roman Inscriptions of Britain
RS	Rack Street
RSRB	Rural Settlement of Roman Britain Project (see Smith *et al.* 2016)
SEM-EDS	Scanning Electron Microscopy-Energy Dispersive X-Ray Spectroscopy
SS	South Street
TS	Trichay Street
VC	Vicars Choral deeds, court rolls, and account rolls, in Exeter Cathedral Library and Archive
XRF	X-Ray Fluorescence

List of Contributors

John Allan is the Consultant Archaeologist of Exeter Cathedral, Archaeological Adviser to Glastonbury Abbey, President of the Devonshire Association, a past President of the Devon Archaeological Society, and former Joint Editor of the journal *Post-Medieval Archaeology*. For twenty years (1984–2004) he was Curator of Antiquities of Exeter City Museums. He has published about 180 papers on different aspects of the medieval and later archaeology of South-West England including ceramics, church architecture, numismatics, domestic buildings and cultural links to Brittany.

Paul Bidwell retired as Head of Archaeology and a Senior Manager of Tyne and Wear Archives and Museums in 2013, after excavating and publishing widely on the archaeology of Hadrian's Wall. He also led the development of the archaeological parks at the Roman forts of South Shields and Wallsend. He was appointed OBE in 2012. Until 1980 he worked for Exeter Museums Archaeological Field Unit, supervising and publishing the excavations on the fortress baths and the basilica and forum. He also wrote a general account of Roman Exeter and, together with Neil Holbrook, a comprehensive survey of Roman pottery from the fortress and town (*Roman Finds from Exeter*, 1991).

Delphine Frémondeau is a zooarchaeologist specialising in the study of animal husbandry practices using stable isotope analysis. She developed a reference dataset for the study of seasonality of birth and diet in pigs and published several papers on the pastoral economy of Late Iron Age and Early Byzantine societies. Delphine was one of two Post-Doctoral Research Assistants on the EAPIT project, based at the University of Reading, where she continues to be an Honorary Research Fellow. She is currently based at the Institute of Archaeology, University College London.

David Gould was one of two Post-Doctoral Research Assistants on the EAPIT project, based at the University of Exeter. His PhD, funded by the Universities of Exeter and Bristol, investigated the landscapes and history of medieval and post-medieval rabbit warrens across South-West England, and journal articles on this work have been published in *Landscape History*, *Landscapes* and *Cornish Archaeology*. He has also published an investigation of a Cold War weapons-testing facility in *Landscapes*.

Dr Robert Higham was formerly Senior Lecturer in Archaeology at the University of Exeter, where he is now an Honorary Fellow. He was a co-founder of the Castle Studies Group, a council member of the International Castles Institute (Europa Nostra), a Vice-President of the Royal Archaeological Institute and President of the Devon Archaeological Society. Published work includes: excavations at Okehampton castle, in Devon and Hen Domen, in Powys; books on castles, urban defences and *Making Anglo-Saxon Devon*; and articles on many south-western subjects including medieval Exeter.

Neil Holbrook is Chief Executive of Cotswold Archaeology. He worked for the Exeter Museums Archaeological Field Unit between 1986 and 1989 and is the co-author with Paul Bidwell of *Roman Finds from Exeter* (1991). He was the co-director of the Roman Rural Settlement Project with Michael Fulford and joint series editor of the three monographs in the *New Visions of the Countryside of Roman Britain* series (2016–18). He also co-edited a volume examining the contribution of developer-led archaeology to knowledge of Roman towns in Britain (2015). He was president of the Bristol and Gloucestershire Archaeological Society for 2017–18.

Mark Maltby is Professor of Archaeology at Bournemouth University. He is a zooarchaeologist, who began his career by examining animal bones from Exeter at the University of Sheffield. He became a Research Fellow at the University of Southampton before going to Bournemouth in 1990. He has studied many bone assemblages from England and Europe. His publications include *Faunal*

Studies and Urban Sites: the Animal Bones from Exeter (1979); *Feeding a Roman Town: Environmental Evidence from Excavations in Winchester, 1972–1985* (2010) and, with co-author, Mark Brisbane, *Animals and Archaeology in Northern Medieval Russia: Zooarchaeological Studies in Novgorod and its Region* (2020).

Gundula Müldner is Associate Professor of Bioarchaeology at the University of Reading. She is a specialist in stable isotope analysis of humans and animals for the study of diet, mobility and animal husbandry. She has a special interest in the historical periods and has published widely in areas relating to social differentiation and diachronic change in medieval British diet and migration in Roman Britain.

Stephen Rippon is Professor of Landscape Archaeology at the University of Exeter. He was Principal Investigator on the AHRC-funded *Exeter: A Place in Time* project, and has recently completed excavating the Iron Age, Roman and early medieval settlement at Dainton Elms Cross, in Ipplepen (Devon). He has published a series of studies of regional variation in landscape character covering the Roman and medieval periods including *Beyond the Medieval Village* (2008), *Making Sense of an Historic Landscape* (2012), *The Fields of Britannia* (2015) and *Kingdom, Civitas and County* (2018). He is current President of the Society for Medieval Archaeology, and past President of the Medieval Settlement Research Group and Somerset Archaeological and Natural History Society.

Preface

This is the first of two volumes that present the results of the *Exeter: A Place in Time* project. Exeter is one of Britain's major historic cities, and at times in its near 2,000 year history it was one of the most important places in these islands. The 19th and 20th centuries did not always treat the city well, and extensive bombing during the Second World War and redevelopment in the 1950s to 1970s led to large parts of its historic fabric being destroyed. Exeter was, however, fortunate in having strong links with archaeologists at its University – with the first appointment being that of Lady Aileen Fox in 1945 – and in seeing the City Council establish its own archaeology unit in 1971 (the Exeter Museums Archaeological Field Unit) under their dynamic new Museum Director, Patrick Boylan (latterly Professor Emeritus of City University, London). This led to a remarkably long history of archaeological excavation in Exeter, although in common with so many British cities a very large backlog of unpublished work had built up by the time that the unit (then called Exeter Archaeology) closed in 2012. Prior to the closure of Exeter Archaeology English Heritage (now Historic England) and Exeter City Council funded them to produce a 'Guide to the Archives of Archaeological Projects Carried Out in Exeter 1970–1990' (Leverett *et al.* 2011), and subsequently they funded Cotswold Archaeology to produce the 'Exeter Archaeology Archive Project' that made some archive material freely available online (https://archaeologydataservice.ac.uk/archives/view/exeter_parent_2015/index.cfm). But otherwise there seemed little prospect of actually publishing any of these backlog sites.

In 2014 Neil Holbrook and Stephen Rippon first discussed an idea to try and publish some of the excavation backlog. It was clear that a substantial amount of funding would be required, and that it was unlikely that this could all come from a single source. They also recognised an opportunity to not just write up old excavations, but to use modern scientific techniques to analyse some of the artefacts that had been carefully curated in Exeter's Royal Albert Memorial Museum. The Iron Age, Roman and medieval archaeology of South-West England has also been somewhat neglected compared to other parts of southern Britain, and so there was also a need to try and place the development of Exeter within its wider landscape context.

And so it was that the *Exeter: A Place in Time* project (EAPIT) was born, from which two volumes have been published. In this, the first, a series of authors present the overall results of the project starting with introductory discussions of the region as of whole – based upon the historic (*i.e.* pre 1974) counties of Cornwall, Devon, Dorset and Somerset – that cover the physical landscape and its various '*pays*' (districts), and the development of the landscape during the later Iron Age, Roman and medieval periods. There follow discussions of the Roman fortress and *civitas* capital (*Isca Dumnoniorum*), the re-emergence of urbanism in the Late Saxon period (when Exeter was referred to as *Escanceaster* in the Anglo-Saxon Chronicle), and the development of the city during the later medieval period (when it was known as *Excester*). The second volume – *Studies in the Roman and Medieval Archaeology of Exeter* (EAPIT 2) – comprises a series of specialist papers that present the various strands of detailed research that formed a key part of the EAPIT project.

From the start, in 2016, this was a collaborative project whose success was dependent on a large team of partner organisations and researchers drawn from the worlds of higher education, commercial archaeology, heritage management and public engagement. It was led by the University of Exeter and Cotswold Archaeology, who worked in collaboration with Exeter City Council and the Royal Albert Memorial Museum, Historic England, and the University of Reading. The project was generously funded by the Arts and Humanities Research Council, Historic England and the University of Exeter (who funded two PhD studentships). The Principal Investigators were Stephen Rippon (University of Exeter) and Neil Holbrook (Cotswold Archaeology), with Andrew Pye leading for Exeter City Council, Thomas Cadbury for the Royal Albert Memorial Museum, and Gundula Müldner for the University of Reading. Invaluable advice and support were given throughout by the project's consultants – John Allan and Paul Bidwell – who were also major contributors to the research. The two AHRC-funded research assistants were David Gould (University of Exeter) and Delphine Frémondeau (University of Reading), and the two University of Exeter-funded PhD students were Mandy Kingdom (human bone) and Malene Lauritsen (animal bone).

The writing-up of four key unpublished excavations – Trichay Street, Goldsmith Street III, 196–7 High Street and Rack Street – was undertaken by staff at Cotswold Archaeology, with the full reports appearing in the second EAPIT volume (EAPIT 2, Chapters 5–8). In order to enhance Exeter's Historic Environment Record summaries have also been produced for all of the excavations within Exeter and its immediate vicinity (EAPIT 2, Chapter 2), with gazetteers of the evidence for Roman streets and buildings (EAPIT 2, Chapter 3).

EAPIT was also able to commission programmes of scientific analysis on various categories of material. The Roman and medieval pottery from Exeter's 1970s excavations has been published in full (Allan 1984; Holbrook and Bidwell 1991) but the origin of some of the fabrics remained unidentified and so as part of EAPIT John Allan and Paul Bidwell led a programme of scientific analyses with the specific aim of trying to establish where these fabrics were produced, with key contributions from Kamal Badreshany (University of Durham), Hugo Blake, Alejandra Gutiérrez (University of Durham), Michael Hughes and Roger Taylor (EAPIT 2, Chapters 12, 17 and 18). The animal bones from some of Exeter's excavations in the 1970s were the subject of a pioneering study by Mark Maltby (Bournemouth University), with further work carried out by Bruce Levitan (English Heritage), but many key assemblages remained unstudied and so these were the subject of Malene Lautritsen's University of Exeter PhD thesis (EAPIT 2, Chapter 9). Gundula Müldner and Delphine Frémondeau undertook a programme of isotopic analysis of Exeter's faunal remains with the aim of establishing where the animals had been grazing before they were slaughtered (summarised in Chapters 3 and 4 of this volume). One of Exeter's most important excavations – in the Cathedral Close – revealed an extensive medieval cemetery associated with the late Saxon minster and later cathedral, and Mandy Kingdom's University of Exeter PhD examined the human skeletal material both from these cemeteries and several monastic sites in and around Exeter (EAPIT 2, Chapter 19). Historic England specialists also re-assessed two categories of material from Exeter: David Dungworth (with Carlotta Gardner from University College London) applied modern scientific techniques to the archaeometallurgical debris (EAPIT 2, Chapter 10), while Cathy Tyers reviewed the evidence from Exeter's dendrochronological sequences (EAPIT 2, Chapter 11).

Over the course of the project several other researchers agreed to contribute new studies of various categories of material. Two of these papers – Andrew Brown and Sam Moorhead's study of the Roman coins from Devon (EAPIT 2, Chapter 16), and Ruth Shaffrey's analysis of the querns (EAPIT 2, Chapter 14) – sprung from Stephen Rippon's excavations at the Romano-British roadside settlement at Dainton Elm's Cross in Ipplepen, and a conference and exhibition that Torquay Museum hosted about the site. Robert Kenyon has also contributed a paper on the Claudian coins from Exeter (EAPIT 2, Chapter 15). Sara Machin and Peter Warry undertook a major programme of analysis of the Roman tile found both in Exeter and across Devon (EAPIT 2, Chapter 13). Although EAPIT focused on the archaeological evidence for Exeter's past, John Allan was able to undertake a pioneering study of the documentary sources for one parish – St Pancras (EAPIT 2, Chapter 4) – that has seen some of the most important excavations within the city (including three of those written up in EAPIT 2, Chapters 5–7). Robert Higham also agreed to contribute a paper on his work identifying three high status enclaves within late Saxon Exeter (see Chapter 7, this volume).

Acknowledgements

This project would not have been possible without the generous financial support of the Arts and Humanities Research Council (award reference AH/N001931/1) and Historic England (project 6902), and help-in-kind from Historic England (through the contributions of Cathy Tyers and David Dungworth), Exeter City Council (most notably through its Principal Project Manager (Heritage) Andrew Pye), and the Royal Albert Memorial Museum (RAMM, most notably through the help of its Assistant Curator Thomas Cadbury). The Historic England elements of the project were managed by Karen Walker of Cotswold Archaeology, and we are grateful for the assistance and support of Kath Buxton, Rebecca Garrett and Michael Russell of Historic England. Neil Holbrook and Karen Walker thank Tom Cadbury of the RAMM for facilitating access to the archives and Andrew Pye of Exeter City Council for access to its Historic Environment Record GIS. The stratigraphic analysis of the excavations at Trichay Street, 196–7 High Street, and Rack Street was undertaken by Nicky Garland, while that for Goldsmith Street Area III was prepared by Jonathan Hart. The illustrations in EAPIT 2 Chapters 5–8 were produced by Lesley Davidson, Aleks Osinska and Charlotte Patman. We are particularly grateful to John Allan who significantly enhanced and improved the text relating to the medieval periods of these four sites. His first-hand personal knowledge has proved invaluable and has avoided some fundamental misinterpretations of the medieval evidence. Paul Bidwell kindly commented in detail on the text of the Roman periods to telling effect.

We would like to thank all of the members of the project's Advisory Board, chaired by Michael Fulford, and thank Christopher Dyer, Michael Fulford and Bob Higham for reading earlier drafts of both EAPIT volumes. Their detailed feedback was extremely useful but the views expressed here reflect those of the individual chapter authors. The individual authors of the EAPIT 1 chapters wish to acknowledge the following assistance they received in writing them, and with the project generally:

Stephen Rippon and David Gould wish to thank John Allan, Paul Bidwell, Christopher Dyer, Michael Fulford, Bob Higham and Neil Holbrook for reading through earlier drafts of their chapters, and for the feedback that they provided. For supplying unpublished information, and their general advice, they also thank Andrew Pye (Exeter City Council), Andy Jones (Cornwall Archaeology Unit), Bill Horner (Devon County Council), Cain Hegarty (Devon County Council), Charlotte Coles (AC Archaeology), Chris Smart (University of Exeter), Duncan Coe (Cotswold Archaeology), Gareth Chaffey (Wessex Archaeology), Jenny Durrant (formerly RAMM), John Davey (formerly University of Exeter), John Salvatore (formerly EMAFU), John Valentin (AC Archaeology), Karen Walker (Cotswold Archaeology), Naomi Payne (AC Archaeology), Neil Holbrook (Cotswold Archaeology), Oliver Creighton (University of Exeter), Peter Warry, Sarah Wyles (Cotswold Archaeology), Stephen Armstrong (University of Exeter), Stuart Blaylock, and Thomas Cadbury (RAMM).

Paul Bidwell is in debt to the other contributors to this volume, especially John Allan, Neil Holbrook and Stephen Rippon, for much discussion and information, together with David Gould who not only prepared the illustrations but found and cross-checked the information on which some are based. At the same time the achievements of colleagues at Exeter with whom he worked some five decades ago are gratefully acknowledged, particularly those of John Salvatore and the late Christopher Henderson without whose efforts much less would be known about the legionary fortress and its environs. The main contributors to this volume, together with Michael Fulford, Andrew Pye and John Salvatore, commented on earlier drafts of Chapter 5, much to its benefit. Andrew Passmore, Andrew Pye, Marc Steinmetzer and John Valentin are warmly thanked for information about various excavations in advance of their publication.

Neil Holbrook thanks John Allan, Paul Bidwell, Michael Fulford and Stephen Rippon for their helpful comments on an earlier draft of Chapter 6. They do not necessarily agree with all that is said there, but their knowledge has helped the author avoid some obvious errors.

For answering queries and supplying unpublished information John Allan wishes to thank Nat Alcock (vernacular building), Peter Bath (Caen stone), Stuart Blaylock (city wall, Exeter-style roofs, bellfounding, Bishop's Palace, etc), Stewart Brown (St Stephen's church; Fox's wellpool), Brian and Mora Gittos (Purbeck marble), Tom Greeves (Dartmoor tin), Roland Harris (Beer stone at the Tower of London), Graham Langman (pottery), Nicholas Orme (medieval churches), Richard Parker (later medieval houses), Naomi Payne (medieval pottery), Christopher Pickvance (late medieval chests), and Tim Tatton-Brown (Caen and other building stones).

For permission to reproduce illustrations in EAPIT 1 we thank AC Archaeology, A.H. Baldwin & Sons, Alex Woodcock, British Library, Cornwall Council, Cotswold Archaeology, David Garner, Dean and Chapter of Exeter Cathedral, Devon and Exeter Institution, Devon County Council, Devon Heritage Centre, Downes Estate, Exe Estuary Management Partnership, Exeter City Council (as residual copyright holder of the EMAFU/EA archive), Gary Young, Henrietta Quinnell, Historic England, John Thorp, Portable Antiquities Scheme, Richard Parker, Römisch-Germanisches Museum, Royal Albert Memorial Museum and Art Gallery (who hold the copyright for all images given as ©RAMM), and Substrata. Ordnance Survey maps are reproduced under Cotswold Archaeology's map licence.

From its formation in 1972 the staff of Exeter Museums Archaeology Field Unit (EMAFU) – that was later renamed Exeter Archaeology (EA) – worked hard to record the archaeology of Exeter prior to its destruction by development, and particular credit must go to the two Unit Directors, Michael Griffiths (1972–5) and Christopher Henderson (1975–1999). Henderson especially devoted innumerable hours to the archaeology of the city and was energetic in reacting to opportunities for archaeological investigation in advance of construction, and indeed in some cases he proactively created the chance to elucidate important aspects of the city's past development. He was a particularly skillful excavator and meticulous recorder, and his enquiring mind spurred him to interpret each and every new discovery and place it within an overall picture of Exeter's past, both topographically and chronologically (see Anon 2001 for an obituary). It is a considerable regret that so little of his insight ever made it into print, although his influence on his colleagues was profound.

The EMAFU/EA was fortunate that it employed many other talented individuals who made considerable contributions to the archaeology of the city over many decades. Their expertise and passion in unravelling the complex stratigraphy of Exeter puts the work of the Unit on a par with that of the best efforts of other urban field units operating at the time. Particularly notable contributions were made by former EMAFU employees John Allan, Paul Bidwell, Shirley Blaylock, Stuart Blaylock, Stewart Brown, Richard Parker, John Salvatore, Marc Steinmetzer and John Thorp. Too much of their work has not been formally disseminated, although progress has been made in publication over the last decade thanks to the dedication of the individuals involved, and more reports will appear in the next few years.

Summary

This is the first of two volumes that report on the work of the *Exeter: A Place in Time* (EAPIT) project. EAPIT explored how the Roman fortress/town and medieval city of Exeter developed over time in a region that at times did not show the same patterns of socio-economic development as seen further east. This was achieved through four strands of research: the writing up of key unpublished excavations; analysis of the faunal assemblages in order to understand Exeter's meat supply; work on various categories of material culture (most notably the pottery, but also the archaeometallurgical debris, dendrochronological samples, Roman ceramic tile, querns and coins, and medieval human burials); and the writing of a synthesis that describes the evolution of Exeter and how it developed within its local, regional, national and international contexts. The synthesis is presented in this the first of two books to be published, with the other – *Studies in the Roman and Medieval Archaeology of Exeter* (Exeter: A Place in Time 2) – containing a series of specialist contributions that underpin the discussion presented here.

Exeter began life as a Roman legionary fortress in *c.* AD 55 whereupon for around two decades it was one of the most important places in Roman Britain until it was abandoned in the early AD 80s. The cumulative result of many city-centre excavations is that Exeter has the most complete plan of a Claudio-Neronian fortress in Britain. It was soon converted into the only major town within the Dumnonian *civitas*, and the size of its forum/basilica and the area enclosed by its later 2nd-century AD defences suggest that the civil authorities had high hopes for its development. These hopes were, however, never realised as Exeter itself and its rural hinterland failed to develop to the same extent as areas further east. The town appears to have become largely deserted in the early 5th century, although two burials radiocarbon dated to somewhere in the 5th to early 7th centuries hint at the presence of a church before it is first documented in the late 7th century. Exeter's Roman defences saw it become a *burh* and mint under King Alfred in the late 9th century, although there is no sign of renewed urban life until the 10th century when its growth was rapid. In part this expansion appears to have been due to its role in the exploitation of Devon's rich mineral resources, as well as its development as a port. Exeter maintained its high ranking within English towns into the 11th and 12th centuries, although a decline in tin production on Dartmoor led to a fall in its prosperity. Its fortunes were, however, restored during the 15th century through the rapid growth in East Devon's woollen cloth production and by the early 16th century Exeter was the 6th wealthiest and most populous city in England.

Résumé

Ceci est le premier de deux volumes qui constituent le compte rendu des travaux de *Exeter: Un Lieu en son Temps* (EAPIT). Le projet EAPIT a exploré comment la forteresse/ville romaine et la cité médiévale d'Exeter se sont développées au fil du temps dans une région qui, à certains moments n'a pas révélé les mêmes caractéristiques de développement socio-économique que celles observées plus à l'est. Ceci a été obtenu grâce à quatre branches de recherches: le rapport d'analyse de fouilles clés non publiées; l'analyse des assemblages de faune de manière à comprendre l'approvisionement en viande d'Exeter; des travaux sur différentes catégories de culture matérielle, (plus notablement la poterie mais aussi sur des débris archéométallurgiques; des échantillons dendrochronologiques, des tuiles en céramique romaines, des moulins à bras et des pièces de monnaie et des inhumations humaines médiévales) et la rédaction d'une synthèse qui décrit l'évolution d'Exeter et comment elle s'est développée dans le cadre de ses contextes locaux, régionaux, nationaux et internationaux. Cette synthèse est présentée dans ce premier de deux livres qui doivent être publiés avec l'autre - *Etudes de l'archéologie romaine et médiévale d'Exeter* (Exeter un lieu en son Temps 2) qui contient une série de contributions de spécialistes qui étayent la discussion présentée ici.

La vie d'Exeter commença avec la forteresse d'une légion romaine en env. 55 ap. J.-C. après quoi pour environ deux décennies elle fut l'une des plus importantes places de la Grande-Bretagne romaine avant qu'elle ne soit abandonnée dans les débuts des années 80 ap. J.-C. Les résultats cumulés de nombreuses fouilles du centre ville font qu'Exeter a le plan le plus complet de forteresse claudio-néronienne de Grande-Bretagne. Elle a peu de temps après été convertie en la seule ville importante à l'intérieur de la *civitas* Dumnonienne et la taille de son forum/basilique et la surface enclose par ses dernières défences du deuxième siècle ap. J.-C. donnent à penser que les autorités civiles avaient de grandes espérances pour son expansion. Ces espérances ne furent toutefois jamais réalisées car Exeter elle-même et son arrière pays rural ne parvinrent pas à s'agrandir au même degré que d'autres régions plus à l'est. La ville semble avoir été en grande partie désertée au début du 5ième siècle bien que deux inhumations datées au C^{14} quelque part entre le 5ième et le 7ième siècle suggèrent la prèsence d'une église avant qu'elle ne soit mentionée à la fin du 7ième siècle. Les fortifications romaines d'Exeter l'ont vue devenir un bourg et un hôtel de la monnaie sous le roi Alfred, à la fin du 9ième siècle, bien qu'aucun signe n'indique un renouveau de la vie urbaine avant le dixième siècle quand elle s'agrandit rapidement. Cette expansion semble avoir été due en partie à son rôle dans l'exploitation des riches ressources minières du Devon ainsi que son développement en tant que port. Exeter a conservé son rang élevé parmi les villes anglaises au cours des 11ième et 12ièmes siècles bien qu'un déclin dans la production d'étain de Dartmoor a conduit à une baisse de sa prospérité. Elle retrouva cependant sa fortune au cours du 15ième siècle grâce à la rapide croissance de la production de tissu de laine dans l'est du Devon et venu le début du 16ième siècle Exeter était la sixième plus prospère et plus peuplée cité d'Angleterre.

Zusammenfassung

Dies ist der Erste von zwei Bänden, mit denen die im Projekt *Exeter: A Place in Time* (EAPIT) durchgeführten Arbeiten vorgelegt werden. Im Rahmen von EAPIT wurde untersucht, wie sich das römische Lager/Stadt und die mittelalterliche Stadt Exeter im Laufe der Zeit in einer Region entwickelte, die phasenweise nicht die gleichen sozioökonomischen Entwicklungsmuster aufwies, wie sie weiter östlich erkennbar sind. Dies wurde durch vier Forschungsansätze erreicht: der Aufarbeitung wichtiger, bislang unveröffentlichter Ausgrabungen; der Analyse der Tierknochenfunde zum Verständnis der Fleischversorgung Exeters; der Bearbeitung verschiedener Kategorien der materiellen Kultur (vor allem der Keramik, aber auch von archäometallurgischen Abfallprodukten, dendrochronologischen Proben, römischen Keramikfliesen, Mahlsteinen und Münzen sowie von mittelalterlichen Bestattungen); und die Ausarbeitung einer Zusammenschau, die die Geschichte der Stadt Exeter und ihrer Entwicklung in ihrem lokalen, regionalen, nationalen und internationalen Umfeld beschreibt. Diese Synthese wird mit diesem, dem ersten von zwei Bänden vorgelegt, während der andere – *Untersuchungen zur römischen und mittelalterlichen Archäologie von Exeter* (Exeter a Place in Time 2) – eine Reihe von Fachbeiträgen enthält, die die hier vorgestellte Diskussion untermauern.

Exeter begann ca. 55 n. Chr. als römisches Legionslager und war dann etwa zwei Jahrzehnte lang einer der wichtigsten Orte im römischen Britannien, bis es Anfang der 80er-Jahre n. Chr. aufgegeben wurde. Als kumulatives Ergebnis der zahlreichen Stadtkerngrabungen kann Exeter mit dem vollständigsten Grundriss eines claudisch-neronischen Lagers in ganz Britannien aufwarten. Es entwickelte sich bald zur einzigen größeren Stadt innerhalb der dumnonischen *civitas*, und die Größe seines Forums/Basilika sowie des von den Verteidigungsanlagen des späten 2. Jahrhunderts umschlossenen Areals legen nahe, dass die zivile Stadtverwaltung große Hoffnungen in seine zukünftige Entwicklung gesetzt hatte. Diese Hoffnungen erfüllten sich jedoch nie, da sich weder Exeter selbst noch sein ländliches Hinterland im gleichen Maße wie die weiter östlich gelegenen Gebiete entwickeln konnten. Die Stadt scheint zu Beginn des 5. Jahrhunderts weitgehend verlassen zu sein, obwohl zwei Bestattungen, die grob in das 5. bis 7. Jahrhundert radiokarbon-datiert wurden, auf die Existenz einer Kirche vor ihrer ersten urkundlichen Erwähnung im späten 7. Jahrhunderten schließen lassen. Dank der römischen Befestigungsanlagen wurde Exeter unter König Alfred im späten 9. Jahrhundert *burh* und Münzstätte, obwohl es bis zum 10. Jahrhundert, als die Stadt rasch wuchs, keine Anzeichen für eine Wiederbelebung des städtischen Lebens gibt. Diese Expansion scheint teilweise auf Exeters Rolle bei der Ausbeutung der reichen Bodenschätze der Grafschaft Devon sowie auf seine Entwicklung als Hafen zurückzuführen zu sein. Exeter behielt seinen hohen Stellenwert innerhalb der englischen Städte bis ins 11. und 12. Jahrhundert hinein, obwohl ein Rückgang der Zinnproduktion im Dartmoor einen Wohlstandsverlust nach sich zog. Die wirtschaftliche Prosperität erholte sich jedoch im 15. Jahrhundert durch das rasche Wachstum der Wolltuchproduktion in Ost-Devon wieder, und zu Beginn des 16. Jahrhunderts war Exeter die sechstreichste und -bevölkerungsreichste Stadt Englands.

Übersetzung: Jörn Schuster
(ARCHÆOLOGICALsmallFINDS)

1

Introduction: Roman and Medieval Exeter and their Hinterlands – From *Isca* to *Excester*

Stephen Rippon and Neil Holbrook

Towns and their hinterlands

Today, we see the diverse character of the British landscape as one of its most treasured features. Britain's richly varied geology, topography and soils have combined with its pivotal location on Europe's western seaboard, and a complex history of invasions and migrations, to create a series of countrysides and townscapes whose character vary enormously from region to region. Exeter lies at the heart of one of the most distinctive landscapes in Britain – the South-West Peninsula – although its location (remote from London) and the character of its archaeological record (that does not conform to that seen across much of lowland Britain) has led many to regard it in less than positive terms. The eminent Romanist Francis Haverfield, for example, suggested that Exeter was an 'outpost of Romanization in the far west', and that the territory west of the River Exe 'presented none of the normal features of Romano-British life' (Haverfield 1924a, 214; 1924b, 2). It certainly is true that neither Exeter nor the countryside around it looked much like London and the South-East during the Roman period, but was this because the region was backward and poorly developed, or a reflection of how the communities living there chose to adopt subtly different identities compared to those in South-East Britain? Although Romanists were somewhat slow to recognise and understand the diversity that is evident within the landscapes of Britain, this is thankfully now changing (*e.g.* Mattingly 2006; Rippon 2008a; 2012a; Smith *et al.* 2016) with the regional boundaries that are starting to emerge being remarkably similar to those that have long been recognised during the medieval period (Gray 1915; Rackham 1986; Roberts and Wrathmell 2000; 2002; Rippon *et al.* 2015; Rippon 2018a).

The development of urban centres was crucial to the wider social and economic character of any region, and the evolution of a town can only be understood within the context of its wider landscape. Urban centres were on the whole agriculturally non-productive settlements, although Domesday records that Exeter's burgesses had land for 12 ploughteams *extra civitatem* [outside the city] suggesting that a large area of arable – perhaps over a thousand acres – was cultivated by people living there (Allan *et al.* 1984, 406). In the well-documented medieval period we know that towns will have had a variety of hinterlands ranging from the immediately adjacent countryside that produced food consumed by the townsfolk and the raw materials used by its craftsmen, through to more distant places with which its merchants traded. These different urban hinterlands can be thought of as a series of zones that surrounded a town, although variations in topography, ease of communication, and a wide range of socio-economic factors will have led these zones to be rather irregular in shape. The innermost hinterland was the local area that both supplied a town with its day-to-day needs, and to which in turn the town provided basic services. This inner hinterland is likely to be the area of a day's walk from the town, something that in the case of medieval Exeter is borne out by a variety of documentary sources (Kowaleski 1995). In the medieval period at least Exeter was, however, part of a hierarchy of towns that included a series of smaller centres about 20 km away, and for their day-to-day needs people living more than 10 km from Exeter will probably have visited one of those other local markets for goods and services that were in regular demand.

There were, however, more specialised items that people required far less frequently such that only a major town – with a regional-scale catchment – would generate sufficient custom for a trader to be able to make a living. In the case of Exeter this included precious metal working

– there is still a road called Goldsmith Street – as well as being a regional centre for services such as secular and ecclesiastical administration. Exeter's international significance started when it was a Roman legionary fortress that, along with its port at Topsham, was part of an important trade route for goods from mainland Europe that were supplied to the army in western Britain. Exeter was refounded as a civilian town (*Isca Dumnoniorum*) whereupon it became the largest settlement in the South-West Peninsula, although the extent to which it functioned as a town in the medieval sense will need further discussion (see Chapters 6 and 9). Following a period of post-Roman desertion that was common to most British towns, the revival of urbanism in *Escanceaster* (as Exeter was described in the *Anglo-Saxon Chronicle*) saw it rapidly re-establish itself in the 10th century as a town of regional standing, with an important mint and ceramic assemblages suggesting that international trade had resumed by the early 10th century.

The need to study Exeter in the wider context of its multiple hinterlands was a major theme of the *Exeter: A Place in Time* project (EAPIT), and as such this book is about not just Exeter but the South-West region generally (Fig. 1.1). Exeter, and the wider South-West, provide a particularly distinctive area to study due to their liminality within both Roman Britain and Anglo-Saxon England, yet they have seen far less archaeological research than many other parts of Britain (both before and after the routine introduction of development-led archaeology in 1990). Exeter and the South-West do, however, possess great potential for research. The large backlog of unpublished excavations within the city, alongside the extensive collections of artefacts in the Royal Albert Memorial Museum (RAMM) – much already catalogued and published (Allan 1984a; Holbrook and Bidwell 1991; 1992) – provide an excellent opportunity for new work to be carried out, and in particular for the application of modern scientific techniques. The geologically varied landscape of the South-West also makes it ideal for the use of stable isotope (EAPIT 1, Chapters 3 and 4) and petrological analysis of pottery (EAPIT 2, Chapters 12, 17 and 18) and tile (EAPIT 2, Chapter 13).

Exeter is located at the head of the Exe Estuary, one of the major sheltered tidal inlets on Britain's South-West coast (Figs 1.1 and 1.2). It was located at the river's lowest crossing point (using bridge-building technology available in both the Roman and medieval periods), although there were fording-places further downstream such as at Countess Weir (where an 18th-century bridge now stands). Although the river may have been navigable by small boats as far upstream as Exeter, its main port in both the Roman and medieval periods was established downstream at Topsham. Exeter's immediate hinterland was the agriculturally rich farmland of the Eastern Devon Lowlands – sometimes called 'Red Devon' due to the colour of its soils – that also provided iron-rich clays that were used for making pottery and tiles. The South-West Peninsula also has a range of other minerals that at various times were crucial to the economy of Exeter, such as the Blackdown Hills – *c.* 30 km to the east of the city – that supported another important pottery industry as well as the production of iron and quern stones. To the west of Exeter lay the granite uplands of Dartmoor and Cornwall that were rich in a range of metals, most notably tin, lead and silver, that were also exploited during the Roman and medieval periods, as well as being a source of summer grazing.

Whilst Exeter's location was ideal for exploiting these rich natural resources, as well as engaging in international trade, it was often liminal to the places of power, wealth and cultural influence in Roman and medieval Britain. After a brief period when it was central to the Roman invasion and conquest, the civic authorities appear to have had ambitious plans for Exeter to become a substantial civilian town, which is reflected in it having the 7th largest forum in Britain for which we have evidence. The development of the town was, however, slow and the limited uptake of Roman-style architecture and material culture in the countryside suggest that Dumnonian society was rather lukewarm when it came to *Romanitas*, especially in the Early Roman period. As Britain ceased to be part of the Roman Empire the South-West lay beyond the areas that were then subject to Anglo-Saxon immigration, and although from the late 7th century Exeter and its immediate hinterland – what was to become the county of Devon – was drawn into the West Saxon kingdom it remained peripheral to centres of secular and political authority (reflected, for example, in the choice of Sherborne as the episcopal seat). The South-West Peninsula does, however, appear to have experienced the same intensification in landscape exploitation around the 8th century that was seen across southern Britain, and with the revival of urbanism in the 10th century Exeter soon became one of the wealthiest cities in England (and briefly its fifth most productive mint).

Table 1.1 provides the information we have for the population of Exeter at different times, and its national ranking. These figures must be taken with a huge pinch of salt – especially for the Roman period as so little of Exeter's peripheral areas have been excavated – and there are also very great dangers in comparing population figures derived from archaeological evidence for the density of buildings, and documentary sources that provide a series of different numerators such as heads of household and taxpayers, from which populations have to then be assumed. What seems clear, however, is that Exeter's highest population during the Roman and medieval periods was when it was a legionary fortress with its associated civilian settlements; that the population of the civilian town was far lower, but may have doubled in size over the course of the late 1st to 4th centuries AD when it may have been comparable to that of the Late Saxon city;

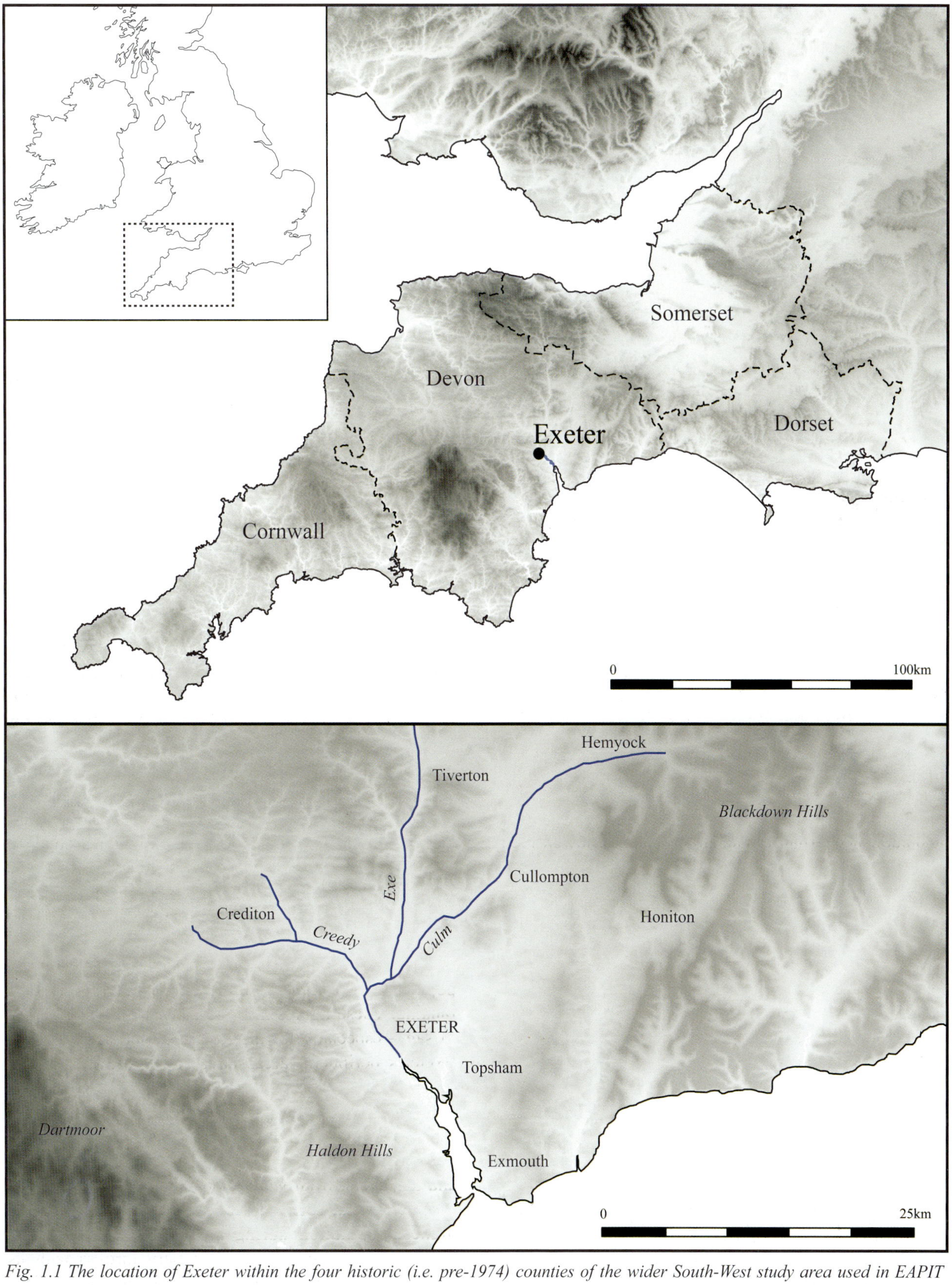

Fig. 1.1 The location of Exeter within the four historic (i.e. pre-1974) counties of the wider South-West study area used in EAPIT (drawn by David Gould)

Fig. 1.2 The head of the Exe Estuary with Topsham in the foreground (with key excavations discussed in Chapters 5 and 6) looking north-west towards Exeter (photo: © Exe Estuary Management Partnership; transcription drawn by Stephen Rippon)

that its population then at least doubled before being cut back by the Black Death, although this was a slow rate of growth compared to other English towns; but that it then rapidly increased from the late 15th century as Exeter's cloth trade flourished such that it became the 6th wealthiest city in England (Table 1.1).

History of archaeological work in Exeter

Early antiquarians such as Geoffrey of Monmouth, John Leland and William Camden were all aware of Exeter's Roman origins, and from the 17th century there are accounts of labourers finding numerous antiquities (Bidwell 1980, 1–5). Of particular note are the observations

Table 1.1 Exeter's estimated population and rankings amongst other English towns (based upon the evidence discussed towards the end of this Chapter, and in Chapters 5–8 below)

Date	*Source*	*Evidence*	*Population*	*Ranking*	*Reference*
c. AD 55/60–75/80 (fortress)	archaeological excavations and analogy with other legionary fortresses, and associated civilian settlements		*c.* 10,000	one of four legionary fortresses in Britain at that time	see below
late 1st to 2nd century AD (town)	archaeological excavations, and the density of occupation that they reveal		< *c.* 1,000	7th largest forum in Britain for which we have evidence, suggesting that the civil authorities aspired to Exeter being a major town	Holbrook and Bidwell 1991, 18; Bidwell 1979, 80, table 6
4th century AD (town)	archaeological excavations, and the density of occupation that they reveal		*c.* 2,000–5,000	13th largest defended town in Britain that once again may reflect civil aspirations	Holbrook and Bidwell 1991, 18; Millett 1990, 152–3
Æthelred II (978–1016)	% of estimated coins produced	the time of highest proportion of national output, *c.* 985–91	n/a	5th	Metcalf 1998
Æthelred II (978–1016)	% of known moneyers		n/a	7th	Hill 1981, 130
973–1066	% of estimated coins produced	overall standing in the lists of mints	n/a	8th	Metcalf 1998
1086	Domesday	399 houses	*c.* 2,000+	18th??	Welldon Finn 1967, 280–1; Dyer 2000, 752
1129–30	aids and tallages	tax paid	n/a	joint 6th	Biddle 1976b, 501
1158–9				3rd	
1160–1				7th	
1167–9				5th	
1172–3				10th	
1176–7				7th	
1213–14				6th	
1334	Lay Subsidy	tax paid	n/a	27th/28th	Donkin 1973, 134; Glasscock 1973, 184; Dyer 2000, 755–6

(Continued)

Table 1.1 Exeter's estimated population and rankings amongst other English towns (based upon the evidence discussed towards the end of this Chapter; and in Chapters 5–8 below) (Continued)

Date	*Source*	*Evidence*	*Population*	*Ranking*	*Reference*
c. 1340	based on assumption that the Black Death killed a third of the population, that had not recovered significantly by 1377		*c.* 5,000		For 1377 population see below
1377	Poll Tax	tax payers	*c.* 3,101	23rd	Hoskins 1984, 277; Kowaleski 1995, 371; Dyer 2000, 758
1377	Murage Tax	tax payers	*c.* 2,525		Kowaleski 1995, 374
1524–5	Lay Subsidy	tax payers	*c.* 8,000	6th	Baker 1973, 243; Hoskins 1984, 278; Dyer 2000, 761
		taxable wealth	n/a	6th	Dyer 2000, 766
1660	Poll Tax	tax payers	*c.* 12,000		MacCaffrey 1958, 12
1662	Hearth Tax	hearths taxed	n/a	6th	Hoskins 1984, 278

made by Captain W.T.P. Shortt between 1832 and 1855 (Shortt 1841a; b; and see Goodchild 1947), while in 1928 the Exeter Excavation Committee was established by the newly founded Devon Archaeological Excavation Society. Several excavations were carried out between 1931 and 1938 that included the discovery of the *piscina* of the public baths and several investigations of the town's defences (Montgomerie-Neilson and Montague 1933; 1934; Goodchild 1946). Further systematic excavations were carried out in 1945–7 by Lady Aileen Fox within parts of the city destroyed by German bombing during the Second World War, and although elements of the legionary fortress were in fact uncovered they were not recognised as such at the time due to the relatively small size of the areas that were excavated (*e.g.* Fig. 1.3). In 1948 Lady Fox was appointed to teach courses on Romano-British and Anglo-Saxon archaeology at the University College of the South-West (predecessor of the University of Exeter) which was then located in Gandy Street (Fox 2000, 111–12). Lady Fox remembers that 'I sensed that there was something wrong because, in comparison with the adjoining counties, the prehistoric and early civilisations in Devon had been so little studied' (Fox 2000, 113), but over the coming decades she carried out extensive research across Devon. During the 1950s and 1960s these included several small-scale excavations in Exeter, including work at the South Gate in 1964 when a short length of what was interpreted at the time as a Roman military ditch was discovered (although in fact this was just a stretch of roadside ditch: Site 36; all of the significant excavations in and around Exeter have been given a unique 'Site Number' each of which has a set of key information, including references and a summary of what was found in EAPIT 2, Chapter 2).

The work of Lady Fox started a very long association between the City and the University, that in 1970 saw the appointment of John Collis (see below) and then a series of other staff who carried out research across the South-West Peninsula including Henrietta Quinnell's (2004) large-scale excavations at Trethurgy, Valerie Maxfield's (1991) work at Bolham Roman fort in Tiverton, Malcolm Todd's excavations at Rudge, Bury Barton and Hembury (Todd 1998; 2002; 2007a), Robert Higham's research into Okehampton Castle (Higham 1977; Higham *et al.* 1982), and Stephen Rippon's work on medieval silver mining in the Tamar Valley and the South-West's distinctive landscape character (Rippon 2008a; Rippon *et al.* 2009; Rippon 2012). Important historical research into medieval Exeter included Nicholas Orme's studies of its ecclesiastical institutions (*e.g.* Orme 2014; 2015a; 2015b; 2016).

Whereas some other British towns – such as Cirencester and Winchester – saw the establishment of rescue archaeology committees during the 1960s, Exeter's provision remained in Lady Fox's hands, but she only had very limited time and resources. In 1970, however, John

Fig. 1.3 Lady Fox's excavations in South Street Area 1 in 1945–6 (Site 15 in EAPIT 2 Chapter 2), showing the remains of timber buildings (with white upright posts in the post pipes of the major postholes) that we now know were structures within the legionary fortress, and the earliest phase of Roman road with the range pole laid across the central road ditch (© RAMM)

Collis was appointed to the History Department at the University, and as the pace of redevelopment in Exeter's historic centre increased he undertook excavations at Goldsmith Street (Sites I and II) in advance of the construction of the Guildhall Shopping Centre (Collis 1972; Fox 2000, 130, 144). In 1971 the City Council and their new Museum Director Patrick Boylan (latterly Professor Emeritus of City University, London) created the Exeter Museums Archaeological Field Unit (EMAFU), that was overseen by the Exeter Archaeological Advisory Committee that included representatives from the city council, museum and University. After the 1974 reorganisation of local government Exeter consistently paid more per capita for its museum service (which included archaeology) than any other city in England (John Allan pers. comm.), and a strong sense of pride in the museum – with a relatively high level of financial support from the Council – remains a feature of the city. The EMAFU's initial excavations included further work at the Guildhall Shopping Centre including Goldsmith

Fig. 1.4 Excavations at Trichay Street in 1972–4 (Site 42), in advance of the construction of the Guildhall Shopping Centre, showing how close to the surface the medieval remains were (© RAMM)

Street III (Site 37–39), Trichay Street (Site 42; Fig. 1.4) and 196–7 High Street (Site 43) (Collis 1972) – all finally published in EAPIT 2 – that together revealed the first evidence for a fortress associated with the *legio II Augusta* (Second Augustan Legion) including barrack blocks and a *fabrica*, as well as a complex sequence relating to the Roman and medieval town. A particularly significant early excavation was on the site of St Mary Major church in the Cathedral Close, whose importance as the potential site of the Late Saxon minster was brought to Lady Fox's attention by W.G. Hoskins, a resident of Exeter. Lady Fox recalls how 'I shall never forget seeing, in one of the first cuttings, the monumental flight of stone steps belonging to the town's basilica, overlying the red tile pillars of the hypocaust of the military baths' (Fox 1979, v; Fox 2000, 144; see Figs 1.5 and 6.4, and Bidwell 1979 for the full excavation report). The excavated sequence beneath St Mary Major church included the Roman legionary bath-house, civilian basilica, an early medieval cemetery and minster church (Site 40). The redevelopment of Exeter's centre continued – with the loss of many historic buildings (*e.g.* Fig. 1.6) – and other important early excavations included the medieval bridge across the River Exe (recently published: Brown 2019), the Roman and medieval defences, areas of suburban development, and several of the medieval monasteries.

Although the Cathedral Close excavations were published with commendable speed (Bidwell 1979) the relentless destruction of archaeological sites in the city, and a focus on fieldwork as opposed to post-excavation and publication, soon led to a backlog of unpublished work (as was so often the case in other major British cities). Progress was, however, made with the analysis of the ecofactual and artefactual material from the 1970s, with Mark Maltby's (1979) seminal study of the faunal remains found between 1971 and 1975, Bruce Levitan's (1987) work on the animal bones from a series of medieval sites, John Allan's (1984a) analysis of the

Fig. 1.5 The monumental flight of stone steps belonging to the town's basilica, overlying the rubble infill and red tile pillars of the hypocaust of the military baths, published by Paul Bidwell (1979) and described by Lady Fox in a visit during 1971 (Fox 1979, v) (© RAMM)

medieval and post-medieval finds, and Neil Holbrook and Paul Bidwell's (1991) report on the Roman finds. Indeed, the publication of these two finds volumes – and the associated spot-dating of contexts that was carried out – was one of the factors that made the writing up of four excavations as part of EAPIT far easier than it would otherwise have been. There were, however, also major gaps in these specialist analyses – notably the human remains from a series of medieval cemeteries, and a number of large animal bone assemblages – while most of the excavations themselves went unpublished (but now see EAPIT 2, Chapters 5–8, 9 and 19). Unfortunately, almost no plant macrofossil assemblages were recovered, and this gap will need to be filled through future work.

The EMAFU made most progress with Exeter's legionary fortress. Typescript reports – with distinctive green covers – were produced for all excavations where military evidence was found (*e.g.* Salvatore 1992; Bedford and Salvatore 1992; Salvatore and Simpson 1992; Bedford and Salvatore 1993), although these were never published (they are now available online: https://doi.org/10.5284/1035173). Less progress was made on pulling together the evidence for the Roman town and medieval city, and for this reason the four sites that are published as part of EAPIT all have well-preserved medieval as well as Roman sequences. A major problem was that the preservation of structural evidence for the medieval period was often poor, and so – as with the Roman civil phase – less sense could be made of it than for the Roman military period. From the very start, however, the EMAFU was committed to paying equal attention to the medieval and post-medieval archaeology of Exeter, and David Crossley (1990, 77) comments that 'In Friernhay Street, Exeter there have been excellent examples of tenements where a complete record of stratification has survived and where buildings can be related to features within the curtilages' (and see Cherry 1982, 218–20). Eyebrows were raised at the time when the unit excavated and carefully recorded 18th- and 19th-century buildings and deposits, and retained the animal bones and pottery. John Allan's (1984a) volume on the *Medieval & Post-Medieval Finds from Exeter 1970–80* included everything up to 1750, at a time when some other units excluded post-1550 or post-1600 material (the

Fig. 1.6 The demolition of 38 North Street in May 1972. For an account of this important building see Thorp 2012 (photo: Nigel Cheffers-Heard; © Exeter City Council)

post-medieval animal bones were recently studied in Malene Lauritsen's (2019) thesis; EAPIT 2, Chapter 9). In the face of demolition (*e.g.* Fig. 1.6) the Unit also undertook major standing building recording projects on medieval and post-medieval structures at a time when this was not common practice, and John Allan recalls that they had to hide the building recording from English Heritage visitors as they would not fund such work! Exeter could, indeed, be regarded as a stronghold of medieval and post-medieval archaeology at that time, and Christopher Henderson (director of the unit between 1975 and 1999: Anon. 2001) and John Allan often spoke to regional and national societies on this theme.

The EMAFU's first director – Michael Griffiths – was clearly influenced by the pioneering work in other major British cities such as York, while John Collis and Chris Henderson followed the strongly interdisciplinary approach being developed in Norwich and Winchester that integrated below ground archaeology with the study of standing structures and historical sources (see Chapter 8 below). This built upon earlier work to record Exeter's important medieval standing buildings (*e.g.* Portman 1966), and the city saw some of the earliest dendrochronological investigations across the whole of the South-West Peninsula (see EAPIT 2, Chapter 11). Another distinctive feature of the EMAFU's work was its use of historical sources. Exeter has a particularly large collection of medieval documents – 'probably the finest collection of medieval civic records outside the City of London' (Hoskins 1960, 32) – although the traditional view suggested that it was impossible to identify the precise location of the tenements recorded. In a remarkable piece of interdisciplinary research carried out as part of EAPIT, and which continues this tradition started by the EMAFU, John Allan has for the first time been able to reconstruct the medieval tenurial geography of an Exeter parish (EAPIT 2, Chapter 4).

During the 1990s the pace of redevelopment within Exeter city centre declined, and the introduction of Planning Policy Guidance Note 16 (PPG16) in 1990, which created a commercial market for development-led archaeology, led to the EMAFU being renamed Exeter Archaeology. In 2006–6 large scale excavations were carried out in advance of the redevelopment of Princesshay (Site 156) and within Rougemont Castle (Site 193), but it was another decade before further significant excavations were carried out (*e.g.* 23–27 Mary Arches Street and Quintana Gate: Site 169). At the time of writing a new military site to the north of the legionary fortress is being uncovered at St Sidwell's Point (Site 189), a reminder that any overview of a city's development such as this can only reflect our understanding at a snap-shot in time. The location of all of these excavations are shown on Figures 1.7 and 1.8, and listed in Table 1.2. Summaries of what was found on each site are given in EAPIT 2, Chapter 2.

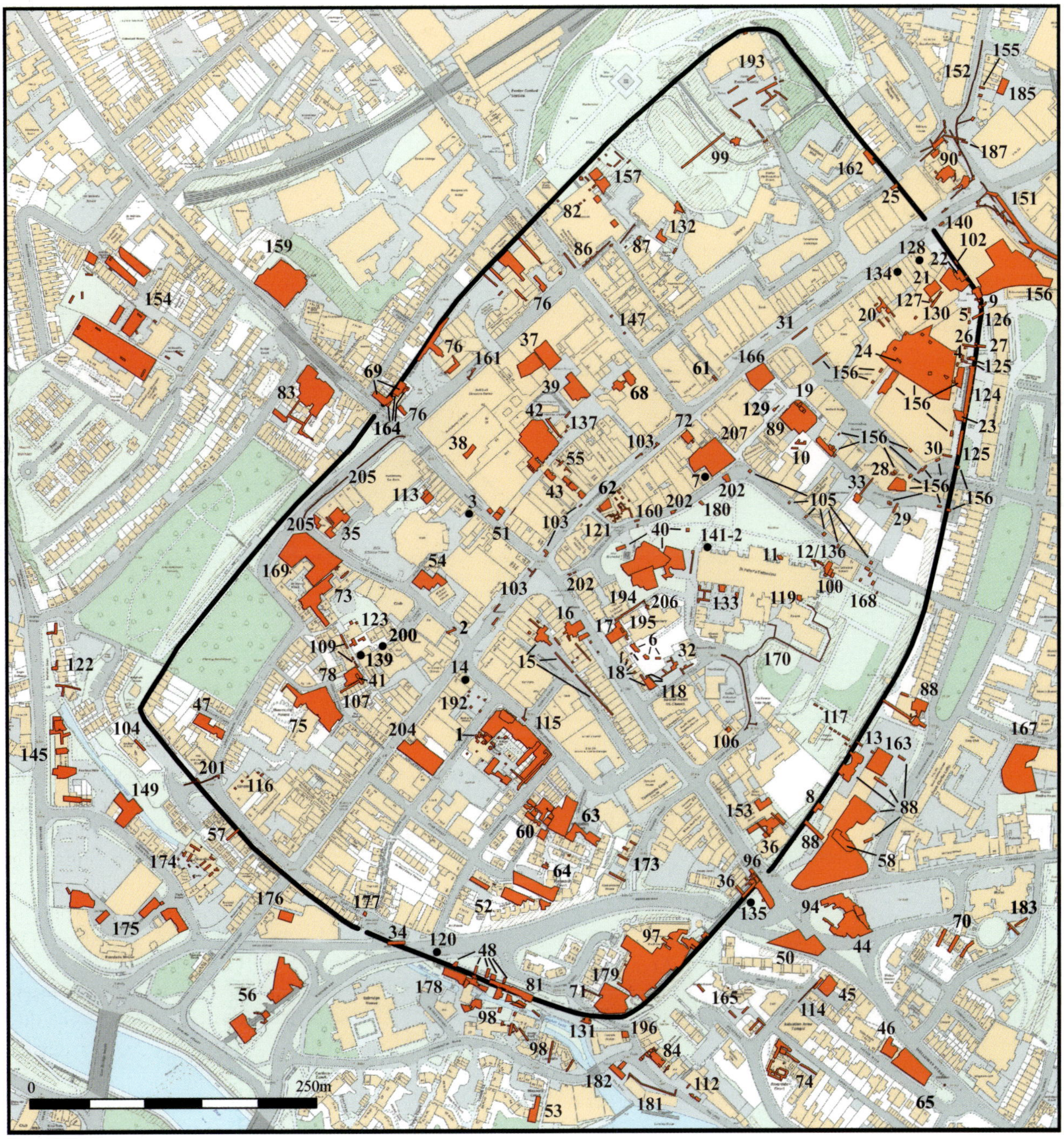

Fig. 1.7 Excavations within the historic core of Exeter: see Table 1.2 for site names (drawn by David Gould)

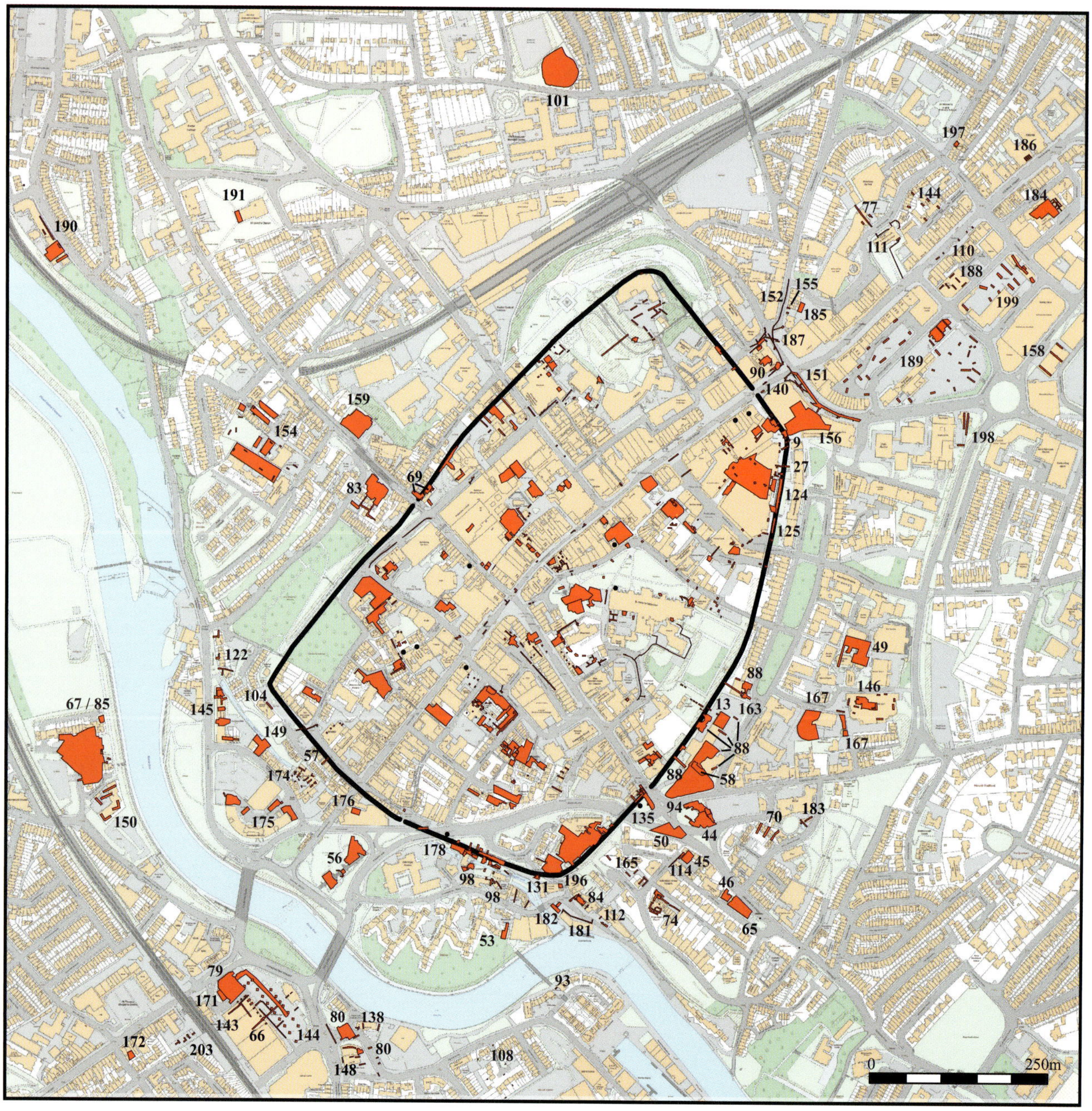

Fig. 1.8 Excavations within the immediate hinterland of Exeter: see Table 1.2 for site names (drawn by David Gould)

The *Exeter: a Place in Time* project (EAPIT)

In 2012 the EMAFU (by then renamed Exeter Archaeology) – who had undertaken all of the significant excavations within the city – closed down, with most of their city centre excavations still unpublished. English Heritage and Exeter City Council funded Exeter Archaeology to prepare *A Guide to the Archives of Archaeological Projects Carried out in Exeter, 1970–90* (Leverett *et al.* 2011), and they then funded a further project – undertaken by Cotswold Archaeology – to get certain key elements of the EMAFU archive online covering the 63 principal pre-PPG 16 excavations in the Exeter district (https://archaeologydataservice.ac.uk/archives/view/exeter_parent_2015/index.cfm; site numbers 37–99 in EAPIT 2, Chapter 2). Post-excavation analysis of the Exe Bridge site was sufficiently advanced for it to be seen through to publication (Brown 2019), and work outside the South Gate at Lower Coombe Street (Site 97) and nearby sites has been worked up for inclusion in a future Devon Archaeological Society monograph on Roman Exeter (Salvatore, Steinmetzer and Quinnell forthcoming) along with several other major Roman-period sites including Dinham Road (Site 154), Princesshay (Site 156) and St Loye's College. The detailed structural recording at Bowhill, 38 North Street (Fig. 1.6) and Great Moor Farm in Sowton have also been published (Blaylock

Table 1.2 Numbered list of excavations in and around Exeter (see EAPIT 2, Chapter 2 for summaries of what was found at each site)

EAPIT Site No.	*Site name*	*Years*
1	Smythen Street	1931
2	Mary Arches Street, Golden Ball Inn	1931
3	North Street Gaummont Cinema	1931
4	St John's School Orchard	1932
5	St John's School Kiln (Bedford Garage)	1935
6	Old Deanery Garden	1932
7	16 Cathedral Yard	1932
8	Palace Gate Convent Garden	1932; 1999
9	St John's School (St John's Bastion)	1933
10	5 Cathedral Close (Annuellar's College)	1933
11	Cathedral, St Andrew's Chapel	1936
12	Cathedral, outside of Speke Chapel	1936
13	11–13 Trinity Street	1936
14	93–94 Fore Street	1938
15	South Street (Fox 1952 Area I)	1945–6
16	South Street (Fox 1952 Area II)	1945–6
17	11–12 South Street (Fox 1952 Area III)	1946
18	20–21 South Street (Fox 1952 Area IV)	1946
19	Catherine Street, Annuellar's College (Fox 1952 Area V)	1945–7
20	28 Catherine Street (Fox 1952 Area VI)	1945–7
21	St John's School, Bedford Garage (Fox 1952 Area VII)	1945–7
22	High Street (former General Post Office) (Fox 1952 Area VIII)	1945–7
23	Post Office Street (Fox 1952 Area IX)	1950
24	9 Bedford Circus (Fox 1952 Trench 12)	1945–7
25	Rougemont (Fox 1952 Trench 13)	1945–7
26	St John's School Garden (Fox 1952 Trench 14)	1945–7
27	39 Southernhay (Fox 1952 Trench 15)	1945–7
28	17 Bedford Circus/Chapel Street (Fox 1952 Trench 16)	1945–7
29	Chapel Street, Abbot's Lodge (Fox 1952 Trench 17)	1945–7
30	14 Bedford Circus (Fox 1952 Area IX)	1950
31	High Street Underground Passages	1950
32	3–8 Bear Street	1953
33	10 Cathedral Close	1955
34	Western Way	1961–2
35	10–18 Bartholomew Street East	1959
36	South Gate	1964–5
37	Goldsmith Street I–II	1971
38	North Street	1971
39	Goldsmith Street III	1971–2
40	Cathedral Close (St Mary Major, War Memorial, Cathedral Yard, Cathedral Green)	1971–6
41	St Nicholas Priory	1971
42	Trichay Street	1972–4
43	196–197 High Street	1972–3

(Continued)

Table 1.2 Numbered list of excavations in and around Exeter (see EAPIT 2, Chapter 2 for summaries of what was found at each site) (Continued)

EAPIT Site No.	*Site name*	*Years*
44	Valiant Soldier	1973–4
45	Friars Gate	1973–4
46	Friars Walk	1973
47	Bartholomew Street West	1974
48	Cricklepit Street	1974
49	Southernhay Gardens	1974
50	Holloway Street	1974
51	45–46 North Street	1973–4
52	Rack Street	1974–5
53	Shilhay	1975
54	Mary Arches Street	1975
55	198 High Street	1975
56	Exe Bridge	1975–9
57	Beedles Terrace	1976
58	Magdalen Terrace	1976
59	Polsloe Priory (St Katherine's Priory)	1976–9; 1991; 2009
60	Preston Street	1976–7
61	228 High Street	1975
62	High Street, NatWest Bank	1977
63	Mermaid Yard	1977–8
64	Rack Street	1977–8
65	Holloway Street	1978
66	Albany Road	1978
67	Flowerpot Lane	1978
68	Queen Street, 22 Goldsmith Street and 211–19 High Street	1978
69	North Gate	1978
70	Good Shepherd Hospital	1979
71	Lower Coombe Street	1979
72	41–42 High Street	1980
73	Bartholomew Street East	1980–1
74	Lucky Lane/Colleton Crescent/Friars Gate	1980–1
75	Friernhay Street	1981
76	Paul Street	1981–5
77	King William Street	1983
78	St Nicholas Priory	1983–4
79	Albany Road	1984
80	Alphington Street/Shooting Marsh Stile	1984
81	Cricklepit Street	1987–9
82	Bradninch Place	1985
83	Exe Street	1985–6
84	The Quay House	1985–6
85	Flowerpot Lane	1986–7
86	Upper Paul Street	1986
87	Castle Ditch and Bradninch Place	1986

(Continued)

Table 1.2 (Continued)

EAPIT Site No.	Site name	Years
88	Magdalen Street	1986–8
89	St Catherine's Almshouses	1987–8
90	ABC Cinema	1987–8
91	Bowhill House, Dunsford Hill	1987–93
92	Guy's Allotments	1988; 1996
93	Haven Banks	1988
94	Acorn Roundabout	1988–9
95	St Loyes Chapel	1988–90
96	South Gate	1988–9
97	Lower Coombe Street	1989–90
98	Cricklepit Mill	1989
99	Castle Gardens	1990
100	Cathedral School	1991
101	Danes Castle	1992–3
102	City Wall, Princesshay	1992
103	Fore Street/High Street British Gas	1980; 1994
104	Paradise Place	1994
105	Cathedral Close	1994
106	5–7 Palace Gate	1994
107	Friernhay Street/Knapmans Yard/The Mint	1994
108	Haven Road, Kapps site	1994
109	St Nicholas Priory	1992
110	161–179 Sidwell Street	1991
111	St Sidwell's Churchyard	1991
112	Exeter Quay	1988–9
113	18–19 North Street	1991; 1999; 2006
114	Friars Walk Sewer	1979
115	Market Street/Smythen Street	1995; 1998; 2001–2; 2012–14
116	51 Bartolomew Street West	1995
117	Bishop's Palace Garden	1939
118	Deanery South Street	1950
119	Bishop's Garden Palace Well Spring	1951–2
120	West Street	1962
121	2 Broadgate (Tinleys)	1994–5
122	18 Bonhay Road	1996
123	21 The Mint	1998
124	Blackfriars Conduit	1950; 1954
125	St John's School Trenches 2 and 3	1933
126	St John's School Trench 1	1935
127	St John's School Trench 4	1935
128	St John's School Trial Trenches	1935
129	Catherine Street	1950
130	Princesshay/Catherine Street Conduit	1950
131	Cricklepit Street	1986–7

(Continued)

Table 1.2 Numbered list of excavations in and around Exeter (see EAPIT 2, Chapter 2 for summaries of what was found at each site) (Continued)

EAPIT Site No.	*Site name*	*Years*
132	Exeter and Devon Arts Centre (EDAC) Redevelopment	1998
133	Cathedral Cloisters	1998
134	Berni's Restaurant, High Street	1935
135	James Street	1962
136	Vicinity of St Peter's Cathedral Church	1843
137	Waterbeer Street (Police Station)	1887
138	Shooting Marsh Stile	1999
139	St Nicholas Priory	1842
140	East Gate	1953
141	Excavations in or near St Edmund's Chapel, Exeter Cathedral	1896
142	St Edmund's Chapel, Exeter Cathedral	1936–7
143	Cowick Street	1999–2000
144	Acland Road	2000
145	Bonhay Road	2000; 2001
146	Southernay East Car Park	2001; 2002–3
147	Queen Street	2001-2
148	Northcott Warehouse	2001-2
149	Tudor Street	2003
150	Victoria Nurseries	2003
151	Paris Street/High Street	2003–44
152	Longbrook Street	2004
153	George's Meeting House, South Street	2004
154	Dinham Road	2005; 2007–9
155	30–32 Longbrook Street	1994; 2015
156	Princesshay	1991; 1997–2006
157	Royal Albert Memorial Museum/Bradninch Place	1994; 2001; 2003; 2008–9
158	Carnegie House	2008
159	28–29 Lower North Street	2011
160	Cathedral Yard	2012–14
161	Paul Street	2012–14
162	Timepiece Nightclub, Little Castle Street	2006–7
163	Southgate Hotel, Southernhay	2009
164	North Gate Court	2010
165	Friar's Green	2011
166	St Stephen's Church	2011–12
167	Dean Clarke House, Southernhay	2013
168	Exeter Cathedral School	2004; 2013
169	23–27 Mary Arches Street and Quintana Gate, Bartholomew Street West	2017
170	Cathedral Green/Palace Gate/Bishops Palace (Gas Main Replacement)	2012–14
171	Exe Bridges Retail Park, Cowick Street	2011
172	31 Cowick Street	2016
173	Western Way	2011
174	Eagle Yard, Tudor Street	2014

(Continued)

Table 1.2 (Continued)

EAPIT Site No.	*Site name*	*Years*
175	Renslade House, Tudor Street	2017–19
176	176 Frog Street (former Radmore and Tucker site)	2018
177	West Street	2015
178	Cricklepit Mill	2002; 2006
179	Quay Hill	2008; 2019
180	Cathedral Close	2010
181	The Quay Antiques Centre	2014
182	Exeter Quay Flood Defences	2014
183	Bull Meadow Road, former Eye Hospital	2010
184	Verney Street	2011; 2016
185	1–11 Sidwell Street (John Lewis), rear of	2011
186	69–73 Sidwell Street	2012
187	Underground Passages	2012
188	1 Cheeke Street	2017
189	St Sidwell's Point	2010; 2018–19
190	Brunel Close	2007
191	St David's Church	2017
192	95–96 Fore Street, rear of	2017
193	Exeter Castle	2006
194	Kalendarhay	2018
195	Exeter Cathedral School (Kalendar Hall)	2013
196	Custom House	2007
197	Well Street	2014
198	Honiton Inn, Paris Street	2018
199	Belgrave Road	2019
200	The Mint	1812; 1837
201	Bartholomew Street West	2012–14
202	Cathedral Yard	2006
203	St Thomas Court	2017–18
204	City Arcade	2019
205	Mama Stones	2019
206	The Deanery	2005–6
207	Royal Clarence Hotel	2016–19

2004; Thorp 2012; Thorp and Adcock 2019), as has the long-running programmes of interdisciplinary research into Exeter's city walls and water supply (Stoyle 2003; 2014). Staff at the EMAFU, such as Paul Staniforth, also transcribed large numbers of key documents – work that has underpinned John Allan's research into the parish of St Pancras (EAPIT 2, Chapter 4), and Jannine Crocker's (2016a; b) work on the Elizabethan Inventories and Wills of the Exeter Orphan's Court has been published by the Devon and Cornwall Records Society. Despite these achievements, for large numbers of the pre-1990 excavations there seemed little prospect of publication.

There have also been relatively few syntheses of Exeter's archaeology. The early overviews by Lady Fox (1952; 1966) brought together the evidence before the rapid redevelopment of Exeter's city centre, and Wacher's (1974) *Towns of Roman Britain* reflected how the EMAFU's early excavations had transformed our understanding of its origins. Bidwell's (1980) *Roman Exeter: Fortress and Town* was the first detailed overview for the Roman period, while this was updated in Henderson's (1988) paper on the fortress. The medieval period was less well served although Allan, Henderson and Higham's (1984) paper on 'Saxon Exeter' brought together the evidence for the minster church and urban revival in the late 9th and 10th centuries. Higham's (2008) *Making Anglo-Saxon Devon* is important in not just describing the origins of Exeter but also placing it within its wider context. Unfortunately, archaeological evidence for later medieval Exeter has not previously been summarised, although there have been studies of its architecture (*e.g.* Portman 1966; Gray and Jackson 2017), city walls (Stoyle 2003), water supply (Stoyle 2014) and economic history (*e.g.* Hoskins 1960; Carus-Wilson 1963; Kowaleski 1995). Henderson's (1999a) contribution 'The city of Exeter from AD 50 to the early nineteenth century' in the *Historical Atlas of South-West England* (Kain and Ravenhill 1999) is the most recent overview – now over 20 years out-of-date – but some elements of his phase plans have proved to be somewhat speculative and are updated in the chapters below.

Although Exeter did see the creation of an English Heritage (now Historic England) sponsored Urban Archaeological Database in the 1990s – that now forms the basis of the HER – it never went on to achieve a published Urban Archaeological Assessment, the first example of which was Cirencester (Darvill and Gerrard 1994) and that now includes Bristol (Baker *et al.* 2018) and Winchester (Ottaway 2017). These Urban Archaeological Assessments adopted a common methodology and had a similar objective – to present the current state of knowledge of the archaeology of a given town – and as such were essentially designed as background documents for archaeological organisations working in a historic town for the first time. EAPIT, however, was not an attempt to create an Urban Archaeological Assessment for Exeter, but instead was a research project which aimed to:

1. **Explore how the Roman fortress and town, and medieval city of Exeter developed over time in a region that does not show the same patterns of socio-economic development as seen further east.** This was achieved through writing up the four most important unpublished excavations alongside the synthesis of the development of Exeter and its hinterland that forms the core of this volume.
2. **Investigate how Exeter was supplied with meat during the Roman and medieval periods.** This was achieved through analysing the previously unpublished animal bone assemblages (EAPIT 2, Chapter 9), using multi-isotopic analysis of faunal remains to investigate where livestock was being brought to Exeter from (Müldner and Frémondeau in Chapters 3 and 4 below), and synthesising all of the faunal data from Exeter including that from the recent development-led work at Princesshay and the South-West more widely (Chapters 3–4, and Maltby in Chapters 5–8, below).
3. **Improve our understanding of manufacturing and trade in and around Exeter.** This was achieved through provenancing major Roman and medieval ceramic fabrics whose sources were not previously known (EAPIT 2, Chapters 12, 17–18), re-analysis of the Roman and medieval archaeometallurgical debris (EAPIT 2, Chapter 10), and studies of the Roman ceramic tile, querns and coins (EAPIT 2, Chapters 13–16).

In order to make the project achievable within its time and financial constraints EAPIT did need parameters. The chronological cut-off was the mid 16th century, which was a significant moment in the history of Exeter as it saw the dissolution of its monastic houses and soon after the production of the first map of the city (by John Hooker in 1587: Oliver *et al.* 2019; Fig. 1.9). Another factor that was undoubtedly important to the success of EAPIT was its clear focus on being selective. Of the 63 significant excavations carried out in Exeter during the pre-PPG16 era, just four were chosen to be written up. Three of these were undertaken before the construction of the Guildhall Shopping Centre in central Exeter: Goldsmith Street III, 1971–2 (Site 39), Trichay Street, 1972–4 (Site 42), and 196–7 High Street, 1972–3 (Site 43). The other site – Rack Street, 1974–5 (Site 52) – lay in the south-eastern part of the city and afforded the opportunity to explore developments in a more peripheral area. A strong case could have been made for several other major excavations – most notably the Saxon minster church – but to have included these would have stretched the available resources beyond the point where successful completion of the project could be assured.

One central part of EAPIT was the production of two particular sets of illustrations. The first is a set of maps covering the wider South-West (the historic pre-1974 counties of Cornwall, Devon, Dorset and Somerset) that show Exeter in its regional context (Chapters 2 to 4 below). These cover both the natural environment (geology, topography, soils, etc) and different aspects of the cultural landscape including the urban hierarchy at different points in time. The second set of maps is a series of phase plans of Exeter itself that present our current understanding of the layout of the Roman legionary fortress, and the Early Roman, Late Roman, Late Saxon, Norman and the later medieval town/city (Chapters 5 to 8 below).

A major theme in EAPIT was the application of scientific techniques that had not even been thought of when the archaeological collections – now stored at the RAMM – were first dug up in the 1970s. No attempt was made at a comprehensive reassessment, and indeed some categories of data that are now standard items in excavations reports – notably plant macrofossils – are noticeably absent as this material was either not collected or not retained in Exeter during the 1970s and 80s. Instead, the decision was taken to focus resources on areas where Exeter has large, well-dated collections that had the

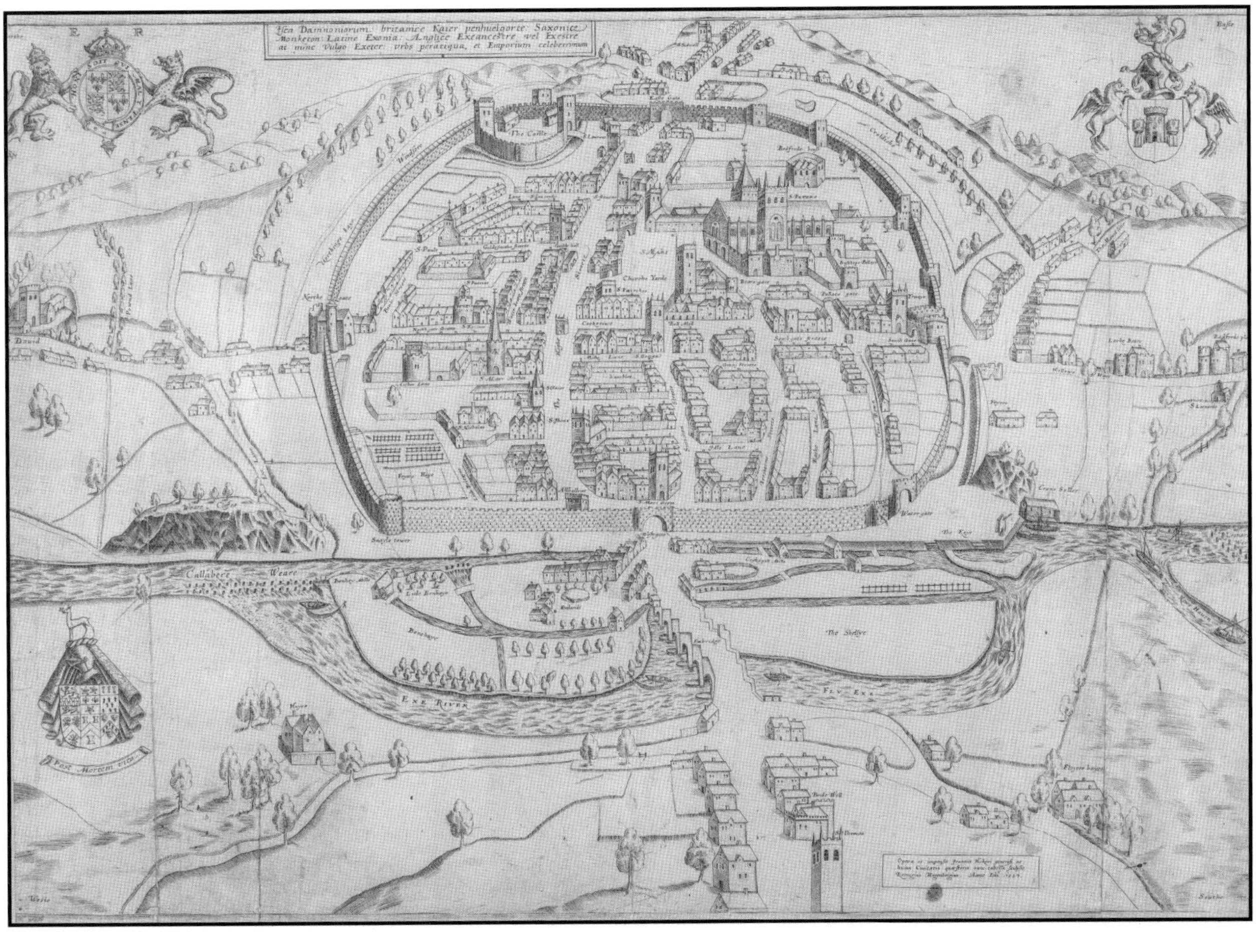

Fig. 1.9 John Hooker's map of Exeter, 1587 (© RAMM)

greatest potential to yield significant new information. The analysis of the faunal remains included an extensive programme of isotopic analysis in order to establish where the animals had been grazing before they were driven to Exeter on the hoof, and whether there was transhumant movement between the fertile lowlands of Devon and uplands such as Dartmoor (that is well documented in the later medieval period). In order to establish the provenance of key ceramic fabrics two techniques were used: an extensive programme of ICP-MS (Inductively Coupled Plasma Mass Spectrometry) as well as more traditional petrology. A twin-track approach was also used in the study of Roman tile through portable x-ray fluorescence (pXRF) and thin sectioning. The archaeometalurgical debris was examined using pXRF and scanning electron microscopy with energy dispersive spectrometry (SEM-EDS).

The writing up of excavations carried out back in the 1970s presented a series of challenges, although the quality of the records produced by EMAFU were generally found to be very good. That said, there were the inevitable issues of working with written and drawn material produced almost 50 years ago. EMAFU adopted a highly interpretative approach to rescue archaeology which stands in contrast to the supposedly more objective philosophy of single-context recording which came into vogue in London and elsewhere (Roskams 2001). However, much telling and incisive interpretation was, sadly, never written down and we cannot underestimate the value during the writing up of the four sites excavated in the 1970s of having access to the personal recollections of John Allan and Paul Bidwell who were both employed by EMAFU during this period and have remained research-active ever since. In particular, John Allan's unrivalled knowledge of the medieval archaeology of Exeter was instrumental in the realisation of the correct interpretation of the medieval deposits reported for the four sites in EAPIT 2 (Chapter 5–8). Without him the post-excavation work on these phases could have gone seriously awry, and our experience does serve to demonstrate just how difficult it will be to revisit these archives in the future without the guidance of individuals with first-hand knowledge of the sites in question. Note that the four excavation reports in EAPIT 2 do not have accompanying finds reports because these assemblages have already been studied and published (Allan 1984; Holbrook and Bidwell 1991).

The project was only possible through collaborative funding, with major awards from the Arts and Humanities Research Council (£640,969, application AH/N001931/1), Historic England (£105,831, project 6802), and the University of Exeter (who funded two PhD studentships for Mandy Kingdom's study of the human bones from the medieval cemeteries, and Malene Lauritsen's analysis of the previously unstudied faunal assemblages). Historic England, Exeter City Council and the Royal Albert Memorial Museum all provided invaluable help-in-kind (worth £104,568) that included Cathy Tyers' reassessment of the dendrochronological evidence (EAPIT 2, Chapter 11), and David Dungworth and Carlotta Gardner's analysis of the archaeometallurgical debris (EAPIT 2, Chapter 10). Key to the success of EAPIT was its partnership-working involving institutions within the higher education sector (led by Stephen Rippon of the University of Exeter who was Principal Investigator on the AHRC-funded project, with Gundula Müldner (Co-Investigator) of the University of Reading undertaking the isotopic analysis of faunal remains), an archaeological contractor (Cotswold Archaeology, led by Neil Holbrook who ran the Historic England funded component of the project), and the local authority curatorial (Exeter City Council, led by Andrew Pye) and museum sectors (Royal Albert Memorial Museum, led by Thomas Cadbury). The project would also not have been possible without the contributions of three consultants – John Allan, Paul Bidwell and Neil Holbrook – who all used to work for EMAFU/Exeter Archaeology. The project also attracted a series of independently funded programmes of research into previously neglected categories of Roman material culture from Exeter and across Devon: Sara Machin and Peter Warry studied the ceramic tile (EAPIT 2, Chapter 13), Ruth Shaffrey the Roman stone querns (EAPIT 2, Chapter 14), Robert Kenyon the copies of Claudian coins (EAPIT 2, Chapter 15), while Andrew Brown and Sam Moorhead examined the Roman coinage as a whole (EAPIT 2, Chapter 16).

This volume – containing a series of discursive chapters that explore the development of Exeter in its wider context – is one of several publications arising from EAPIT. The second volume – *Studies in the Roman and Medieval Archaeology of Exeter* (EAPIT 2) – includes a series of more specialist contributions including: short accounts of all the main excavations within Exeter; a detailed account of the Roman fortress plan, and gazetteers of the evidence for Roman streets and civil buildings; excavation reports for Trichay Street, High Street, Goldsmith Street III and Rack Street; reports on Roman and medieval pottery, archaeometallurgical debris, dendrochronology, Roman tile, Roman querns, and Roman coins; and summaries of Mandy Kingdom's and Malene Lauritsen's theses on the medieval cemeteries and animal bones (the full theses are available online). Summaries of the isotopic analysis of the Roman and medieval faunal remains appear in Chapters 3 and 4 below, with the detailed data published separately in series of journal papers with the raw data deposited with the ADS (Müldner *et al.* 2020: https://doi.org/10.5284/1075876). Two of the out-of-print Exeter Archaeological reports series – Mark Maltby's (1979) study of the faunal remains from excavations carried out between 1971 and 1975, and John Allan's (1984a) report on the medieval and post-medieval finds – are now freely available on the EAPIT website, along with a previously unpublished report on the Roman pottery from the Smythen Street excavations; an inventory of Roman pottery excavated between 1980 and 1989, and the *Guide to the Archives of Archaeological Projects Carried out in Exeter, 1970–90* (https://humanities.exeter.ac.uk/archaeology/research/projects/place_in_time/resources/reports/).

The other project outcomes included improving the summaries of all the significant excavations carried out in Exeter and which appear in the Historic Environment Record managed by Exeter City Council. There was also a programme of public engagement activities managed by the RAMM including a series of 13 improvements to the displays of RAMM's 'Making History' gallery each highlighting one particular aspect of the EAPIT project's results such as how an individual piece of archaeological science has resulted in new insights into Exeter's past. Each of these upgrades is badged up as resulting from the EAPIT project, and stretch from the Roman through to the Tudor displays. There are also ones related to the Hedgeland Model of 18th-century Exeter (see Bhanji 2013) that will link RAMM's displays with three new Minecraft maps that EAPIT funded and which were designed to draw in a very broad audience (worldwide). They are not designed to be detailed reconstructions of Exeter in the past but rather be a created place to explore and play, and there will be opportunities to link through to RAMM's collections and the EAPIT findings by coming across 'hotspot' on the maps.

A family-orientated public event during half-term in February 2020 enabled RAMM's 783 visitors that day to 'Meet the Experts' and find out about EAPIT and Exeter's archaeology more generally, while 350 visitors attended a 'RAMM Late' event featuring the results of EAPIT (organised by the RAMM's Youth Panel, many of whom are students at the University). These evening events are aimed at an adult audience, when the museum is open late and there is music and a bar. They are extremely popular as they allow an interested audience, who often cannot get to RAMM during the day due to work pressures, to come and see the museum in a relaxed, informal atmosphere. When the new displays are fully installed there will be a further programme of childrens' holiday activities where some of the characters, imagined from EAPIT, will be recreated, such as a Roman Dartmoor shepherd and a Roman military Quartermaster, or even the family who ate the first turkey dinner in Britain. The planned *Exeter: A Place in Time* conference at the University of Exeter, planned for April 2020, had to be postponed due to the Cornavirus Crisis.

The development of Exeter, and structure of this volume

Figure 1.10 summarises the development of Exeter during the Roman and medieval periods, while Table 1.1 provides the information we have for the population of Exeter at different times, and its national ranking. **Chapter 2** below introduces the wider landscape context of Exeter across a study area used throughout this volume that covers the historic (*i.e.* pre-1974) counties of Cornwall, Devon, Dorset and Somerset. This was a region of very varied geology, topography and soils, resulting is a series of highly distinctive districts – or *pays* – that offered a wide variety of natural resources including some good arable land, rich pastures, and valuable minerals and stone sources.

Chapter 3 explores this wider South-West from the later Iron Age through to the Roman period. A clear division within the character of the landscape existed either side of the Blackdown and Quantock Hills, with a more centralised Iron Age society to the east – in what was to become the Durotrigian *civitas* – that was capable of building large hillforts, minting coins, and developing a distinctive type of pottery ('Durotrigian Ware') – in contrast to a more fragmented society to the west that chose to construct far smaller hillforts, never minted its own coins, and – in Devon – had a poorly developed ceramic tradition. Within the South-West Peninsula there are also signs of division between an eastern district (broadly modern Devon) – as far west as the Tamar Valley or the high ground of Bodmin Moor and Kit Hill to the west – and a western district that broadly corresponds to Cornwall. These differences in society continue and indeed become clearer during the Roman period, with areas to the east of the Blackdown and Quantock Hills seeing greater change than those to the west. Once again, there are differences between the eastern and western districts of the South-West Peninsula with the former – especially around Exeter – showing greater change.

Chapter 4 continues this overview into the medieval period. During the 5th and 6th centuries AD the South-West Peninsula lay outside the area affected by Anglo-Saxon immigration, and certain communities in Cornwall, Devon and Somerset had access to pottery imported from the Mediterranean. In the mid 7th century the West Saxon kingdom expanded into first Somerset and then Devon, and there is evidence that the region shared in the 8th-century agricultural intensification seen across many parts of southern Britain. After the disruptions caused by Viking raids, a series of fortresses (*burhs*) were established by King Alfred and his successors, several of which – including Exeter – went on to become towns. Following the Norman Conquest there was a proliferation of urban centres and expansion of rural settlement across the wider South-West. Following a dramatic decline in population associated with the Black Death and the subsequent outbreaks of plague, the late medieval period saw growing regional specialisation in agricultural production that in the case of eastern Devon saw a growing focus on wool production (that in turn became a major part of the economy in Exeter).

Chapter 5 discusses the fortress of the *legio II Augusta* at Exeter that now has the most extensively explored plan of any Claudio-Neronian fortress in the Roman World (and see EAPIT 2, Chapter 3 Section 1 for a more detailed discription). It appears to have been constructed in the mid AD 50s at the lowest crossing point of the River Exe. It was occupied at full strength until the mid AD 70s when its garrison was gradually transferred to Caerleon, being finally abandoned in the late AD 70s/early 80s (the likely date for the foundation of the fortress at Caerleon is AD 74 during the Governorship of Sextus Julius Frontinus). The legionary fortress at Exeter was part of a series of military establishments that included a probable cavalry fort just outside the fortress at Princesshay and a port at Topsham (the highest navigable point on the Exe Estuary). An impressive building at Dinham Road may have been the residence of an important Imperial official, while occupation outside the South Gate may have been the *canabae* (a settlement immediately outside a fortress and entirely dependent on it). Another civilian settlement appears to have developed at St Loye's College roughly halfway along the road between Exeter and its port at Topsham.

The population of Exeter at this time is difficult to calculate as parts of the legion may have been posted elsewhere. Paul Bidwell suggests that for periods when the whole legion was at Exeter this would have amounted to 4,800 troops (or 5,300 if the first cohort was at double strength), along with senior officers, members of their households and supernumeraries that altogether may have amounted to another 200 people; there may have been as many as 1,000 slaves, giving a population of 6,000 to 6,500. In addition there was an auxiliary fort at Princesshay, just outside the fortress, that may have accommodated 500, and the civilian *canabae* outside the South-East Gate (in most cases such a settlement would occupy an area at least as extensive as that of the legionary fortress, albeit with less densely-packed buildings). At Exeter, this was south-east of the fortress, between Southernhay Gardens and Lower Coombe Street, and a population equivalent to at least 50% to the military numbers would seem reasonable. Altogether this would give a total population for Exeter in the legionary period in the order of 10,000 (excluding the Dinham Road building, St Loye's College settlement and the port at Topsham), although not all of the troops will necessarily

Fig. 1.10 The development of Exeter during the Roman and medieval periods (drawn by David Gould)

have been based at Exeter as some cohorts may have been campaigning elsewhere in Britain or in other provinces.

Chapter 6 explores the Roman town and *civitas* capital of the Dumnonii. The Early Roman town developed within the defences of the abandoned legionary fortress and the framework provided by its street grid. Construction of the basilica and forum probably started around AD 90, but domestic occupation appears to have developed slowly. The size of the forum – the 7th largest in Britain for which we have evidence – (Bidwell 1979, 80, tab. 6; Holbrook and Bidwell 1991, 18) – suggest that the civic authorities had ambitious plans for Exeter to become a major city, although archaeological evidence for the extent and density of occupation within the early city suggest a population perhaps as low as *c.* 1,000.

Around AD 160/80 the city authorities more than doubled the enclosed area from 16.6 ha to 37.5 ha through the construction of a new circuit of earthwork defences, to which a masonry wall was added perhaps in the early 3rd century AD. Some elements of the street grid were extended across the newly enclosed area, and gradually occupation appears to have expanded beyond the line of the early town's defences. Based upon the defended area, Exeter was the 13th largest town in Roman Britain.

There is no reliable or accurate basis upon which to base an estimate of the population of the Roman town. Frere (1987, 252–3) suggested populations in the order of 2–3,000 for smaller *civitas* capitals like Exeter through a consideration of archaeological evidence and the known populations of medieval towns still enclosed by their Roman walls. More recent studies have used calculations of population density derived from towns in other pre-industrial societies and extrapolation from the well-preserved plans of classical cities of the Mediterranean (summarised by Swain and Williams in their estimates of the population of Roman London; Swain and Williams 2008; more recent work includes McIntyre 2015; Hanson and Orton 2017). The suggested population densities vary from 100 people per hectare (to include allowance for public buildings and undeveloped areas within the walls) to more than double this figure (Hanson and Orton 2017, table 4, for instance uses a density of 183 people per ha as a basis for an estimate of the population of later Roman *Verulamium*).

Taking the lowest estimate of 100 people per hectare favoured by Woolf (1998, 137–8) provides a total of 1,660 for the 16.6 ha occupied by the early town of Exeter. But even this seems too high given the sizeable area occupied by the forum and baths (some 9% of the total defended area) and the absence to date in excavations of intensive, densely-packed, residential buildings. The estimate for a population of the early town of less than 1,000 therefore still feels appropriate (Holbrook and Bidwell 1991, 18). For the later town the defended area enclosed 37.5 ha, to which we can add a small amount of suburban occupation outside the South Gate to suggest a total settlement area of *c.* 40 ha. Use of the Woolf's low estimate of 100 people per ha provides a population of 4,000 which probably lies towards the upper end of the range considering the medieval populations of Exeter. A range of 2,000–5,000 ought not to be wildly wrong for the later Roman town.

Chapter 7 discusses early medieval Exeter and its urban revival. There is little evidence for 5th- to mid 7th-century occupation in Exeter when it lay within the British kingdom of Dumnonia. The context of a small cemetery on the site of the Roman basilica is unclear, although the way that it lay beneath a Middle Saxon cemetery and Late Saxon minster (in what was to become the Cathedral Close) is suggestive of an early pre-Augustinian church. Around the 670s eastern Devon was absorbed within the kingdom of the West Saxons, and by the 680s there appears to have been an Anglo-Saxon monastery in Exeter where the young St Boniface is said to have studied. Other than a small number of coins and other metal finds from the Cathedral Close – presumably associated with this ecclesiastical community – there is virtually no evidence for occupation within Exeter. A stretch of the Roman town wall in the north corner of the town was rebuilt in the Late Saxon period, although it is unclear whether this was just to protect a royal enclave at Rougemont, or was part of a wider programme of work to restore the Roman defences around the entire *burh* under Alfred (871–99) or – as William of Malmesbury suggests – under Æthelstan (924–39). By the 10th century there is fairly widespread evidence for occupation within central Exeter, based upon a network of streets that were largely unrelated to those of the Late Roman town: peripheral parts of the walled area, however, appear to have been largely unoccupied. There were at least five parish churches in addition to the minster and later cathedral. At its height in the early years of the reign of King Æthelred II (978–1016) Exeter was the 5th most productive mint in England, suggesting that it was a sizeable town. Domesday records 399 houses in Exeter suggesting a population of about 2,000 people (Welldon Finn 1967, 280–1). Key historical dates are (and see Higham 2008):

- 680s — Wynfrith (later known as Boniface) educated in the church at Exeter under abbot Wulfhard (Orme 2009, 2).
- 875 and 876 — the *Anglo-Saxon Chronicle* records that a Viking army occupied the *faestan* – a fortress or refuge – at *Escanceaster* (Swanton 1996, 75).
- 890s — King Alfred grants Asser his church in Exeter (Orme 2009, 5).
- 893 — the *Anglo-Saxon Chronicle* records that the Vikings besieged the *burh* at Exeter which held out until the arrival of the West Saxon army led by King Alfred, and in 894 the Viking army that had besieged Exeter sailed east (Swanton 1996, 87).
- *c.* 895–9 — earliest evidence for a mint at Exeter (see Chapter 7 below).
- 909 — Crediton, rather than Exeter, was chosen as the episcopal centre of the newly

created diocese of Devon (Orme 2009, 6–7; 2011, 6–8).

- *c.* 914–17 Exeter is listed in the *Burghal Hidage*.
- 924 Æthelstan's Second Law Code issued at a Council in Exeter, suggesting the presence of a significant royal vill (Whitelock 1955, 386–7).
- 928 Æthelstan issued a charter from his 'royal fortress' (*arce regis*) of Exeter (Sawyer 1968, no. 399).
- 932 Æthelstan refounded the minster, and held a meeting of nobles, bishops and Welsh princes at Exeter (Finberg 1964, nos 229–30; Sawyer 1968, no. 418a; Orme 2009, 7–10).
- 1003 The *Anglo-Saxon Chronicle* records that Exeter was destroyed by a Viking raid (Swanton 1996, 134; Orme 2009, 12).
- 1050 Bishop Leofric moves the seat of the bishop from Crediton to Exeter, presumably being based in Æthelstan's refounded minster (Orme 2009, 6–12).
- 1068 The *Anglo-Saxon Chronicle* describes how King William's army besieged Exeter for 18 days (Swanton 1996, 201; Higham 2013). Domesday tells us that 'In this city 48 houses have been destroyed since the King has come to England' (Thorn and Thorn 1985, C3), and although traditionally this has been seen as the result of the construction of the royal castle at Rougemont in 1068, Higham (see Chapter 7 below) has argued that this area was already a royal enclave.
- 1114 Work began on the new Norman cathedral.

Chapter 8 discusses later medieval Exeter. From the 12th through to the 16th century it remained the major town in the South-West Peninsula, serving local and regional markets alongside a flourishing international trade (reflected in its particularly rich ceramic assemblage). Manufacturing industries included metalworking – gold, pewter or other lead/tin alloys, the manufacturing of bells, and the forging of coins – pottery and tile production, sophisticated carpentry and associated building trades (including glazing), horn working, leather working and textiles. Large parts of the intra-mural area were taken up by series of high status enclaves including the castle, cathedral close, and a series of new monastic foundations. Within the remaining urban areas the high status districts appear to have been along the High Street, with the main area of population growth being the West Quarter (that in the pre-Conquest period had seen relatively little occupation). There was also an expansion of settlement into extra-mural areas during the 13th century.

The Black Death appears to have killed at least a third of Exeter's population, but from the late 14th century it started rising again (Table 1.1). Early estimates of Exeter's population at the time of the 1377 Poll Tax were based on the 1,560 taxpayers in Exeter and 106 on Exe Island – placing it 23rd in England (Hoskins 1984, 277) – which Kowaleski (1995, 371) has estimated a population of *c.* 3,101. The Murage Tax Roll of the same year suggests a population of 2,525 (Kowaleski 1995, 372–4). During the 15th century Exeter prospered, particularly through the cloth trade, with its population in the 1520s estimated to be about 7,000 making it the 6th ranked town in England. Key historical dates are:

- *c.* 1190–1230 building of Exe Bridge (Brown 2019, 10)
- 1205 first recorded mayor (Rowe and Cochlin 1964)
- 1222 creation of parishes (Orme 2014, 28–34)
- 1232 arrival of Dominicans (Orme 2014, 96–9)
- 1240 arrival of Franciscans (Orme 2014, 101–4)
- *c.* 1270–1350 rebuilding of cathedral (Kelly 1991; Orme 2009, 42–54)
- 1346–9 building of first underground conduited water supply to Cathedral (Stoyle 2014, 51–61)
- 1348 Black Death (Kowaleski 1995, 86–7)
- 1420–30 new city water supply built (Stoyle 2014, 51–61)
- 1468 rebuilding of Guildhall (Blaylock 1990
- 1511–14 rebuilding of East Gate (Stoyle 2003, 72–4)
- 1536–8 Dissolution of monastic houses (Youings 1952)
- 1549 Prayer Book Rebellion (Stoyle 2017)
- 1550 Exe Island granted to the city (MacCaffrey 1920).

Notes on nomenclature: Exeter's gates and quarters, other terminology, and county boundaries

The axes of Exeter – based upon the major roads that run between its four gates – run NE to SW and NW to SE (Fig. 1.11). An historical anomaly is, however, that the medieval gates were – and still are – called North, East, South and West (and so – for example – the gate on the SE side of the city was and is called the South Gate as opposed to the South-East Gate: *e.g. Hooker's Chronicle* for the years 1308 and 1328, and *Hooker's Antique Description*, 52, 55, 59). To complicate matters further, when the Roman legionary fortress was discovered archaeologists named its gates according to their correct orientation which means that the 'North-West Gate' of the Roman fortress and early town is just 40 m from what in the medieval period was called the 'North Gate'. As all the existing literature on Exeter uses these terminologies it is, however, retained here. Figure 1.11 also shows the four 'quarters' that Exeter is divided into.

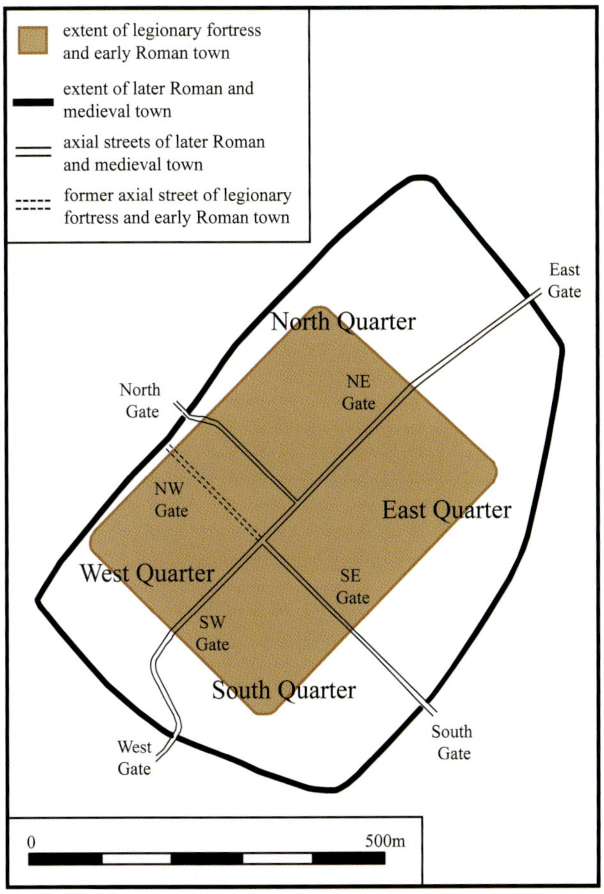

Fig. 1.11 The nomenclature used for the different phases of Exeter's gates and its quarters (drawn by David Gould)

A series of six previous volumes on Exeter's archaeology have been published as 'Exeter Archaeological Reports': these are generally referenced by their authors, although in places they are abbreviated to EAR with their volume number. EAPIT 1 and 2 are Exeter Archaeological Reports 7 and 8.

The county boundaries used throughout EAPIT are those of the historic pre-1974 counties.

Accessing unpublished reports

The two EAPIT volumes make extensive use of unpublished material. The primary excavation archives (written records, plans, black and white negatives and colour slides) and artefacts from excavations undertaken by the EMAFU – later renamed Exeter Archaeology – have been deposited with the RAMM with the exception of the Princesshay (Site 156) and St Loye's College sites for which the RAMM has the artefacts (and related records) while the rest of the archives are digitised and will be deposited with the Archaeology Data Service (ADS).

Archives relating to the EMAFU's documentary and standing buildings research have been deposited with the Devon Heritage Centre with the exception of:

- archives relating to the cathedral and the houses of Cathedral Close that are held at the Exeter Cathedral Library & Archive
- the Bowhill (Site 91) archive which is held at the Historic England Archive in Swindon.

The Exeter Archaeology database, including its digital image collection and digital records of projects, are held by Exeter City Council's Historic Environment Record.

Some pre-1990 archives have been digitised as part of the 'Exeter Archaeology Archive Project' that is available through the ADS (https://doi.org/10.5284/1035173). These include typescript reports prepared for the Exeter Archaeology Advisory Committee (that contain interim reports on many excavations and sometimes include a plan), a set of typescript reports on the Roman military phase in each of the excavations where it was uncovered, a set of reports on the fabric of the city wall, and a Site List of each of the major excavations carried out by the EMAFU between 1970 and 1990. Subsequent post-1990 archives have been generated by development-led archaeology, and have been undertaken by a number of different archaeological contractors including AC Archaeology and Cotswold Archaeology, as well as Exeter Archaeology prior to its closure and Exeter City Council thereafter. Their archives are variously deposited in the RAMM, ADS or are held by the contractor prior to deposition. Online summaries exist in OASIS, and summary reports and HER entries are held at the City and County HERs. Several excavations undertaken after 1990 have been published or are shortly to appear, usually in the *Proceedings of the Devon Archaeological Society* as a condition of planning permission.

The EAPIT webpage includes three further archive reports (http://humanities.exeter.ac.uk/archaeology/research/projects/place_in_time/):

- the Smythen Street Roman Pottery Report
- an *Inventory of Pottery from Sites Excavated 1980–1989* that complements the inventory for earlier excavations that was published on microfiche in Holbrook and Bidwell's (1991) *Roman Finds from Exeter*
- *A Guide to the Archives of Archaeological Projects Carried out in Exeter, 1970–90* (Leverett *et al.* 2011).

Two of the Exeter Archaeological Reports series are now out of print and those volumes have now been digitised and are also available through the EAPIT webpage (http://humanities.exeter.ac.uk/archaeology/research/projects/place_in_time/resources/reports/):

- **Volume 2:** Mark Maltby's *Faunal Studies on Urban Sites: the Animal Bones from Exeter, 1971–1975 (1979,* University of Sheffield, Department of Prehistory and Archeology)
- **Volume 3:** John Allan's *Medieval and Post-Medieval Finds from Exeter, 1971–1980* (1984, Exeter City Council and the University of Exeter).

2

Exeter's Local and Regional Hinterlands: The Landscape of South-West Britain

Stephen Rippon and David Gould

Introduction

Exeter lies at the heart of a region that is extremely diverse in terms of both its physical topography and cultural history. The South-West Peninsula itself – comprising the pre-1974 historic counties of Cornwall, Devon and the western parts of Somerset – is best known for its series of uplands including Exmoor, Dartmoor and Bodmin Moor, but is also characterised by extremely fertile lowlands such as those in the vicinity of Exeter. To the east lay the Blackdown and Quantock Hills that separate the South-West Peninsula from the areas further east that included most of the historic counties of Dorset and Somerset. This eastern region was also topographically diverse and included extensive chalk downland, clay vales and the wetlands of the Somerset Levels. The Blackdown and Quantock Hills also appear to have marked an important division in the region's cultural history. To the east Romano-British and medieval society was broadly typical of central southern England: in the Roman period the landscape contained large numbers of villas, rural temples and a hierarchy of towns, while in the medieval period the countryside came to be characterised by villages and open fields. To the west of the Blackdown and Quantock Hills in contrast – across the South-West Peninsula itself – there is far less cultural change evident in the Romano-British landscape, with just a single town (Exeter) and a few very modest villas, while in the medieval period landscapes were characterised by far more dispersed settlement patterns and diverse field systems. This and the following two chapters will therefore explore that local and regional context within which Exeter developed during the Roman and medieval periods starting with an introduction to the physical landscape.

Topography: a region of contrasts

Compared to the gently undulating chalk downland of central-southern England, and the vast tracts of monotonous low-lying clayland that dominate eastern regions, the wider South-West is extremely varied in its topography, geology and soils. Traditionally, a major dividing line within the topography of Britain is seen as running through two areas of high ground – the Blackdown and Quantock Hills – that divided the 'Lowland Zone' to the east from the 'Highland Zone' to the west. This simplification of the British landscape was first popularised by Cyril Fox's (1932) *Personality of Britain*, and persists in the modern literature (*e.g.* Rackham 1986, fig. 1.3; Jones and Mattingly 1990, map 1.3), but it gives a misleading impression of the character of the South-West Peninsula.

The topography of Cornwall, Devon, Dorset and Somerset is extremely varied, ranging from desolate windswept uplands, through to extensive areas of hospitable lowland (Fig. 2.1). The mostly rugged coastline is punctured by a series of estuaries that provided sheltered natural harbours for shipping, and a series of major medieval towns which developed at the lowest crossing points of the major rivers that flowed into them. These included Exeter that lies in the centre of lowland eastern Devon between the Blackdown Hills to the east, the moderately high ground of the Culm Measures to the north, and Dartmoor to the west. Dartmoor is one of a series of granite uplands (the other major outcrops being Bodmin Moor, the St Austell Moors, Carnmenellis and West Penwith), that protrude through the gently undulating lowlands of southern Devon and Cornwall. The Blackdown Hills separate the lowlands of eastern Devon from those of the Vale of Taunton Deane and central Somerset to the north. The latter two areas form a low-lying basin surrounded by high ground on three sides – the Blackdown Hills to the south, the Jurassic Limestone Hills to the east, and Mendip to the north – with the basin itself dominated by the extensive wetlands of the Somerset Levels. To the east of the Jurassic Limestone Hills the landscape opens out into the extensive low-lying claylands of the Blackmore Vale beyond which lay the chalk downlands of Dorset.

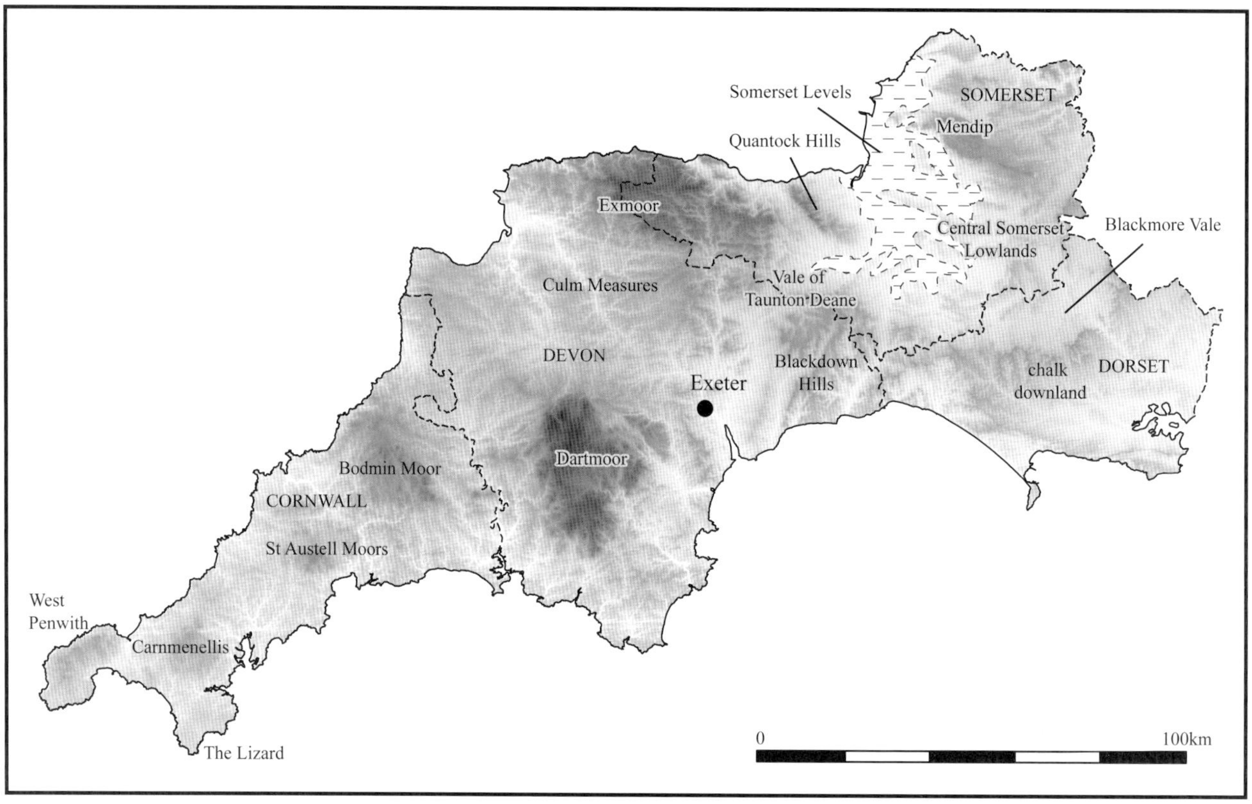

Fig. 2.1 Topography of the wider South-West, comprising the four historic counties of Cornwall, Devon, Dorset and Somerset (drawn by David Gould)

The underlying solid geology

The solid geology of south-western Britain is extremely complex (Fig. 2.2), which accounts for the region's rich mineral deposits (see below) and its wide range of good-quality building stone (discussed in Chapters 7 and 8). This very varied geology and soils also result in different isotopic levels within the plants that grow on them, that in turn affects the isotopic levels within the animals that graze on those plants, and this has allowed a programme of chemical analysis of the faunal remains excavated in Exeter to determine where the livestock were grazing before being taken to Exeter for slaughtering during the Roman and medieval periods (see below, Chapters 3 and 4). Apart from an outcrop of Pre-Cambrian igneous rocks in the Lizard (southern Cornwall), most of lowland Cornwall and southern Devon, as well as the far north of Devon and west of Somerset (Exmoor), comprise rocks of the Devonian period's 'Old Red Sandstone' formation that consist of interbedded slates, shales, sandstones and limestones. Across the far north of Cornwall and central/western Devon these are overlain by shales and sandstones of the Carboniferous 'Culm Measures' that extend as far east as the Exe Valley. Around 290 million years ago – at the start of the Permian period – the intrusion of molten rocks led to the formation of what have become the granite uplands of Dartmoor, Bodmin Moor, St Austell, Carnmenellis and West Penwith. The intrusion of the granite also led to surrounding country rocks being affected by metamorphic processes that included the formation of minerals such as tin, copper, lead and silver that were to become very important in the economic history of the region (see below).

To the east of Dartmoor, the Culm Measures, and Exmoor lie the lowlands of eastern Devon formed from breccias, sandstones and mudstones of the Lower Permian 'New Red Sandstones' and Triassic sandstones. East of Exeter these are overlain by Triassic silty mudstones (formerly known as the 'Keuper Marl') which are capped by the Cretaceous Upper Greensand that forms the Blackdown Hills, while to the north – in Somerset – they underlie the Vale of Taunton Deane and other lowlands around the Quantock Hills. The lowlands of central Somerset are formed from limestones and shales of the Lower Jurassic 'Lias' formations, large parts of which are sealed beneath recent wetland sediments of the Somerset Levels. Further east the Lias is overlain by Middle Jurassic oolitic limestones that form a range of hills running through western Dorset, eastern Somerset and up into Gloucestershire (where they form the Cotswolds). To the east lies the low-lying Blackmore Vale – formed of the Upper Jurassic Oxford, Kimmeridge and Ampthill Clays – beyond which lies the Upper Cretaceous chalk of the Dorset Downs and Cranborne Chase. The south-eastern corner of Dorset is dominated by more recent Eocene sands and gravels, and Tertiary London Clay.

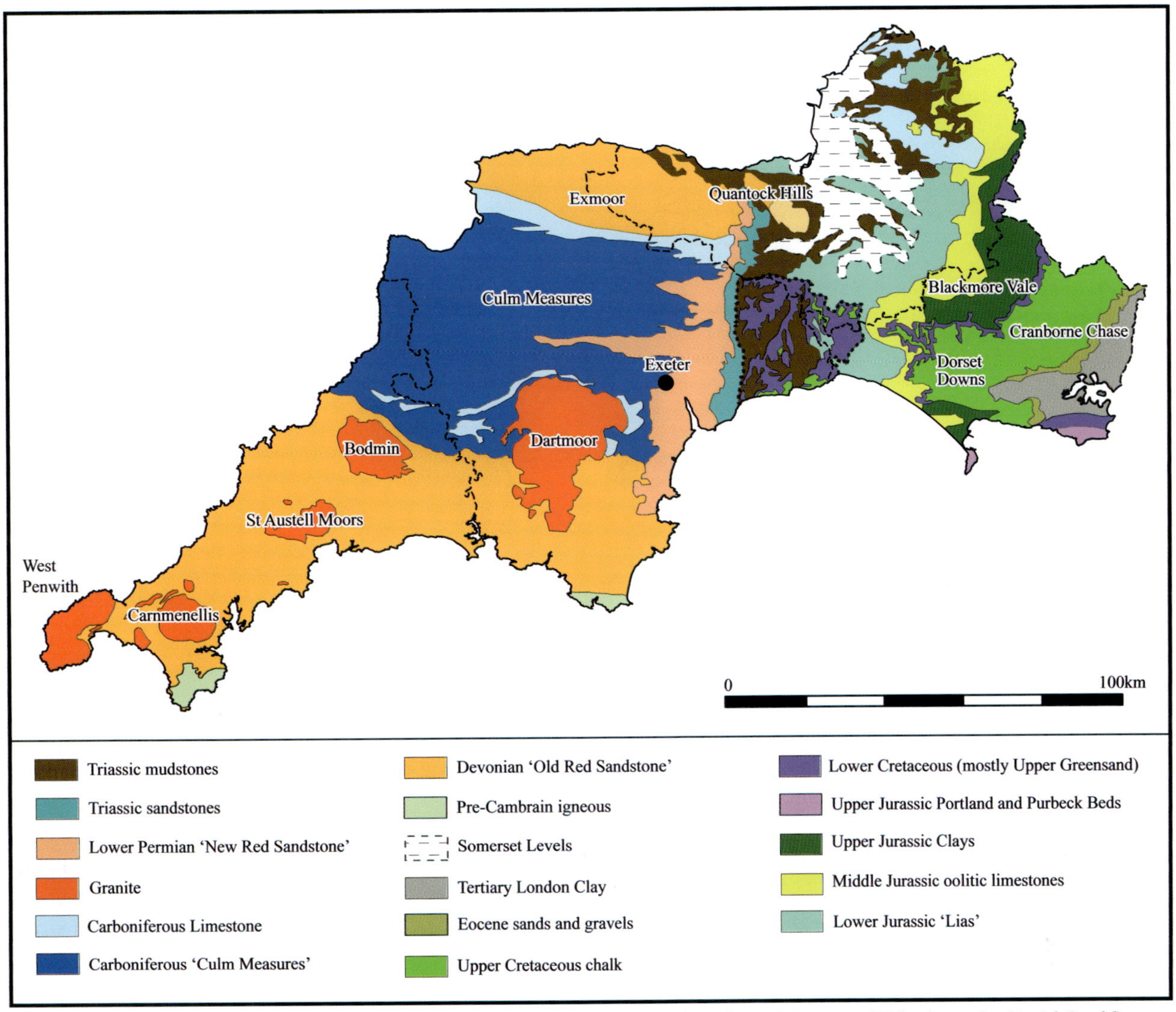

Fig. 2.2 Solid geology underlying the wider South-West (after Institute of Geological Sciences 1979; drawn by David Gould)

The overlying drift geology

Relatively few areas of south-western Britain have significant superficial drift deposits masking the underlying solid geology (Fig. 2.3). The most extensive are the alluvium and peat of the Somerset Levels, while river floodplains comprise a mixture of alluvium and other terrace deposits such as sands and gravels. The highest areas of Bodmin Moor, Dartmoor and Exmoor are capped with areas of peat, while parts of the Blackdown Hills are covered in clay-with-flints. Low-lying areas of south-eastern Dorset lie beneath superficial sand.

Soils

The varied geology and topography of south-western Britain has given rise to an extremely complex series of soils that are shown in a simplified way in Fig. 2.4. The Blackdown Hills mark an important division between that region with non-calcareous and often acidic soils to the west, and calcareous soils to the east (that is of profound importance to the isotopic analysis of faunal remains carried out as part of EAPIT: see Chapters 3–4) Across most of lowland Cornwall, Devon and western Somerset there are various non-calcareous loamy Brown Earths which on higher ground are 'podzolic' (*i.e.* have an iron-rich black or dark brown sub-surface horizon formed through weathering processes under acidic conditions). The flatter interfluvial areas of the Culm Measures have heavier, slowly permeable and seasonally waterlogged clayey stagnogleyic soils (Pelo-Stagnogleys), while further east – in the lowlands of eastern Devon, the Blackdown Hills and Vale of Taunton Deane – there are predominantly loamy soils over clay (Stagnogleyic Argillic Brown Earths). Further east, the soils are mostly calcareous: the lowlands of central Somerset, the Jurassic Limestone Hills and chalk downland have very light soils on the

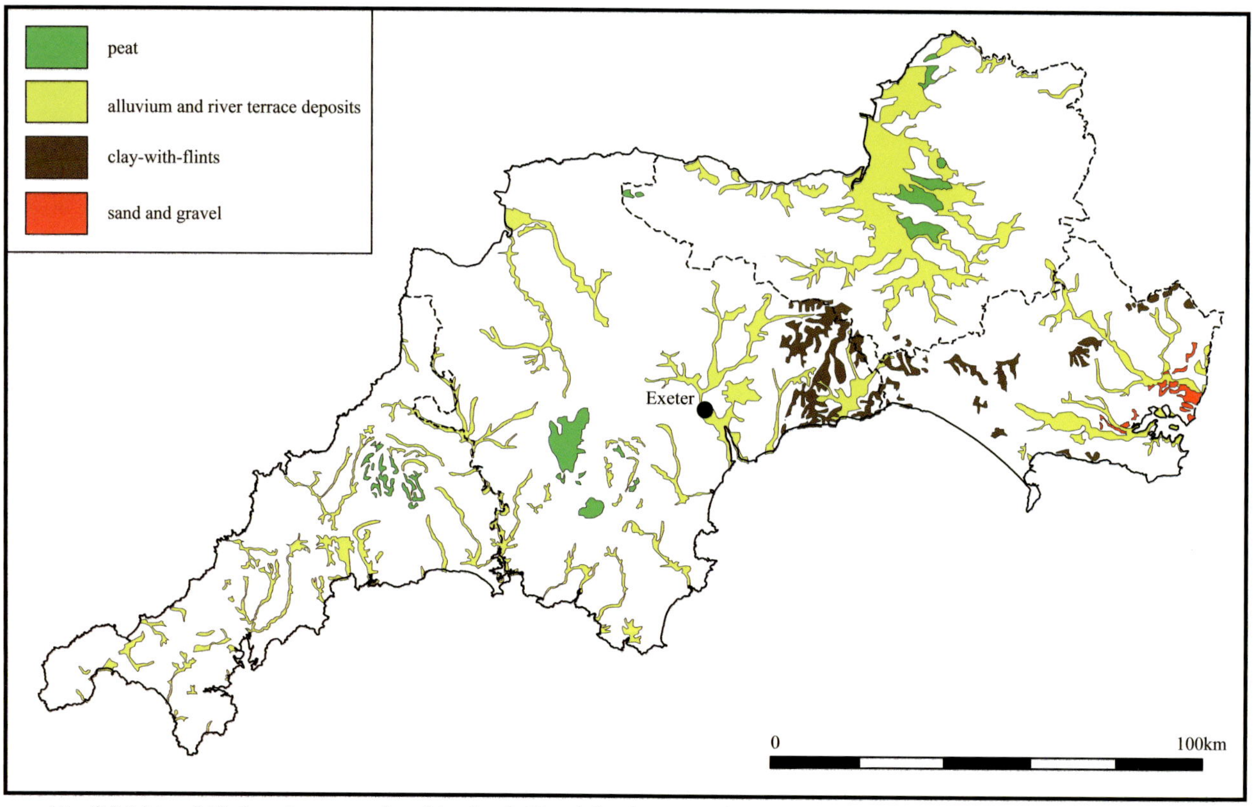

Fig. 2.3 Major drift deposits across the wider South-West (after Institute of Geological Sciences 1977; drawn by David Gould)

higher ground (Brown Rankers and Brown Rendzinas) and more clayey Calcareous Pelosols and Stagnogleyic Argillic Brown Earths in the valleys. The low-lying claylands of the Blackmore Vale have more poorly drained Stagnogleyic soils, while the sandy heathlands of South-East Dorset have Typical Gley Podzols.

Natural resources

The South-West of Britain is particularly rich in mineral resources, with Strabo – writing in the late 1st century BC (*Geography* 4, 199) – stating that gold, silver and iron were exported from Britain, and Tacitus – writing *c.* AD 98 (*Agricola* 12,6) – indicating that Britain's mineral wealth was one reason why it was conquered. While important deposits of silver, lead, iron and copper are found in various places across the greater South-West (Fig. 2.5) – all of which were exploited during the Roman and/or the medieval periods – the region was most important for its deposits of tin.

Tin is found around the various granite outcrops, and documentary sources suggest that it was exported to mainland Europe long before the Roman Conquest. There has been much debate over the *Cassiterides* ('tin islands') that various classical writers refer to as lying out in the ocean at the edge of the World, although whether they actually existed is unclear, and if they did they appear to have been in the ocean between Spain and Britain. Herodotus, who lived *c.* 484 – *c.* 425 BC, is the first to refer to these islands from which tin came although he states that 'concerning the farthest western parts of Europe I cannot speak with exactness … nor have I knowledge of tin-islands' (*Histories* III, 115; Rivet and Smith 1979, 68; Cunliffe 2001, 302). In *c.* 30 BC Diodorus Siculus tell us that there were tin mines on the islets in the ocean near Spain called the *Cattiterides*, and that much tin was also conveyed from the *Prettanic* Island [Britain] to Gaul implying that the *Cattiterides* and Britain were separate places (Rivet and Smith 1979, 63; Cunliffe 2001, 305). The Greek writer Poseidonius, who lived *c.* 135 BC–*c.* 51 BC, similarly stated that tin was produced by the barbarians who live in the *Cattiterides* Islands and that it was brought from the *Prettanic* (a variant of *Brettanic*) Islands to Massalia [Marseille] (Strabo, *Geography* III, 2, 9). In the late 1st century BC to early 1st century AD Strabo places the *Cattiterides* in the sea off Spain, describing how when travelling north of the people called the Artabrians [modern Galicia in north-western Spain] 'you have Lusitania on your right hand side and then the headlands of the Pyrenees that abut the ocean', and that 'the westerly parts of Britain lie opposite these headlands towards the north, and in like manner the islands called *Cattiterides* situated in the open sea approximately in the latitude of Britain, lie opposite to, and north of, the Artabrians' (*Geography* II, 5, 15; II, 5, 30; Rivet and Smith 1979, 90; Cunliffe 2001, 304). Strabo goes on

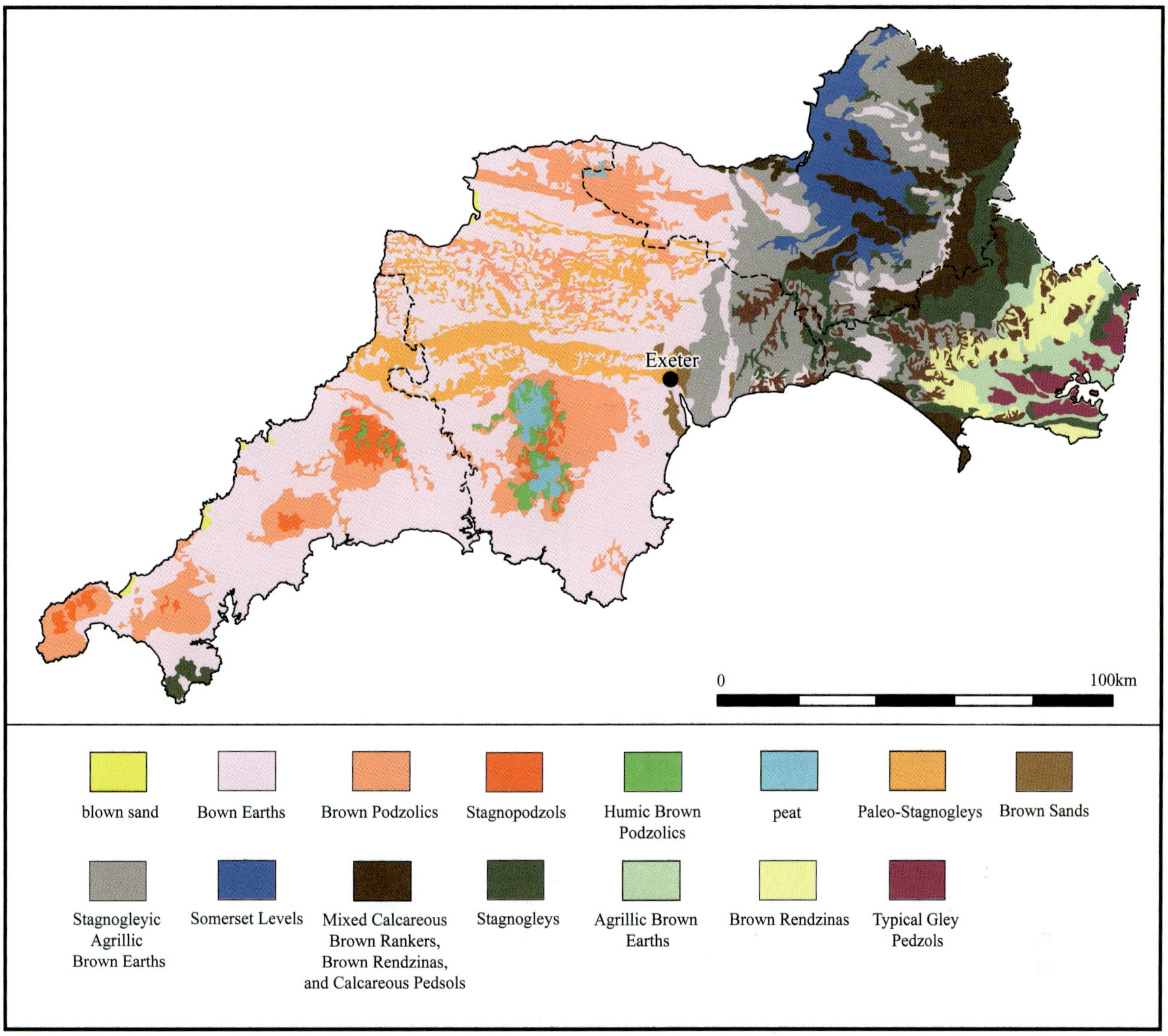

Fig. 2.4 Major soil types across the wider South-West (after Mackney et al. *1983; drawn by David Gould)*

to tell us that the *Cattiterides* were ten in number, and that first the Phoenicians and then the Romans had been involved in the tin trade (Rivet and Smith 1979, 90). It is difficult to know what to make of all this but two clear conclusions can be drawn: firstly, that the *Cassiterides/Cattiterides* – if they actually existed – may have been separate from Britain, and secondly, that there was clearly a trade in tin between Britain and the Mediterranean by the 1st century BC.

Archaeological evidence for the exploitation of tin in Cornwall and on Dartmoor during the later prehistoric, Roman and medieval periods is summarised elsewhere (*e.g.* Penhallurick 1986; Gerrard 2000, 21–3; Newman 2011; Lawson-Jones 2013; Greeves 2017; Quinnell 2017b). The large number of Late Roman coin hoards from the South-West Peninsula's stream deposits, the expansion of the pewter industry both here and around Bath, and elevated tin levels in the Erme Valley south of Dartmoor, all suggest an increase in production just as the Roman Empire's major tin mines in Spain were becoming exhausted, and then another peak in production around the 13th century (Threipland 1956, 52; Penhallurick 1986, 173–224; Holbrook 2001, 154; Thordycraft *et al.* 2002; 2004). The analysis of atmospheric lead deposited in rain-red peat bogs on Bodmin Moor and Dartmoor shows sporadic peaks in the later prehistoric period but then very marked increases during the Roman period (from *c.* AD 100 to 400) and early medieval periods (starting *c.* AD 700 and ceasing *c.* AD 1000) with lower levels and just sporadic minor peaks during the High Middle Ages (Meharg *et al.* 2012).

Silver was largely a by-product of mining lead, of which the most important deposits were on Mendip. There is some evidence for the extraction of lead during the Iron Age, with extensive exploitation in the Roman period including the remarkably well-preserved earthworks at

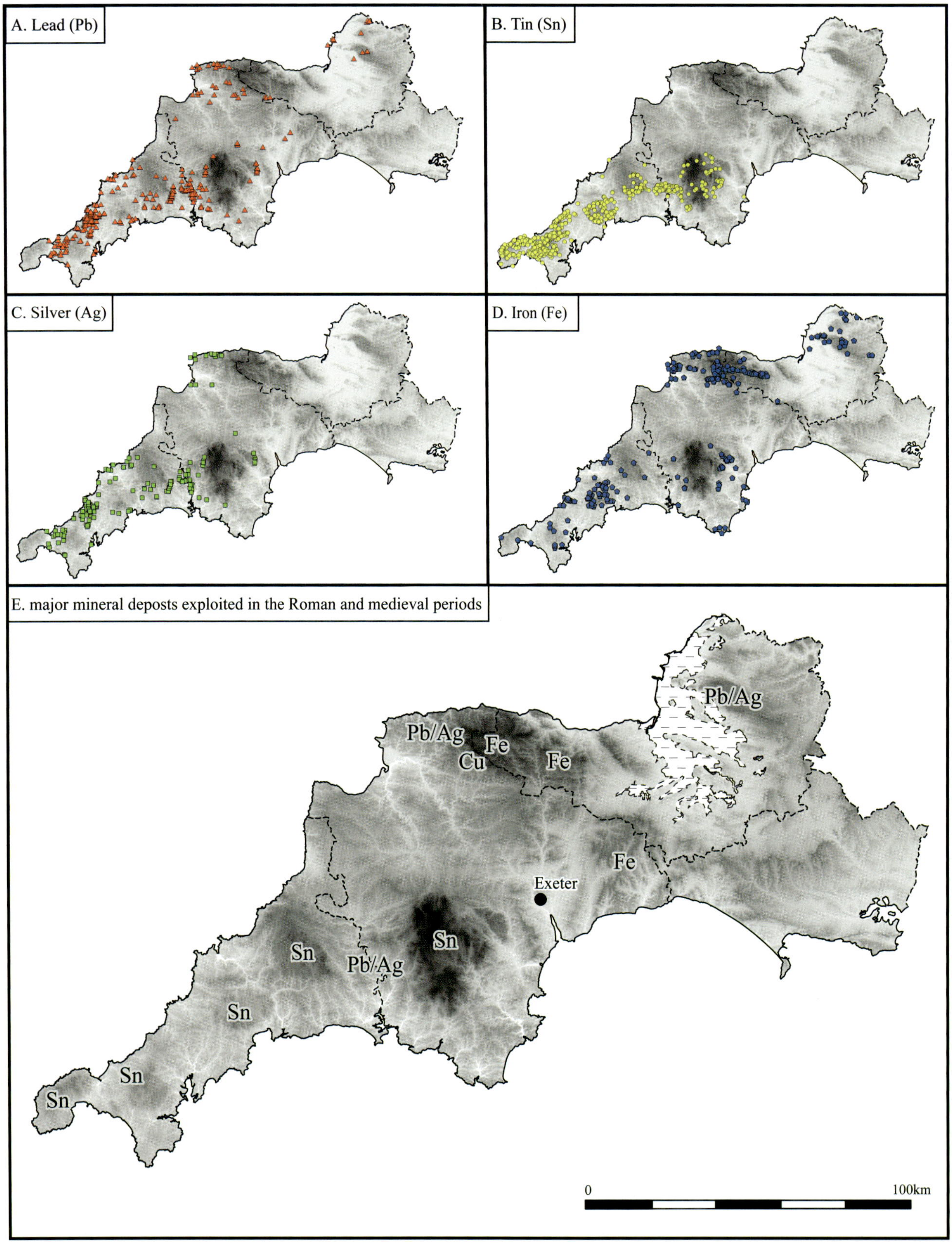

Fig. 2.5 Maps A–D show mineral deposits based on the British Geological Survey's Mineral Occurrence Database that includes the location of known deposits and mines from all historical periods (sourced from the BGS's online Geoindex mapping). What this database does not include is archaeological evidence for undocumented mineral workings, and so these are included in the summary Map E (drawn by David Gould)

Charterhouse and a series of stamped lead ingots, the earliest of which is dated to AD 49 (Todd 2007b; Jamieson 2015, 112–18). The production of lead – and indeed iron and zinc – on Mendip was presumably under the supervision of the *legio II Augusta* that by *c*. AD 55 was based at Exeter, although by the early Flavian period (AD 69–96) military control appears to have been replaced by leasing out to individuals named on some of the ingots (Mattingly 2006, 507; Todd 2007b, 65–6). A concentration of sites with evidence for the production of pewter (an alloy of lead and tin) around Bath reflects one region where South-Western tin production was combined with lead output from Mendip (Beagrie 1989; Mattingly 2006, 508–9; Lee 2009), although two stone mould fragments for a pewter dish from Springfield in Ugborough suggests that it was also going on south of Dartmoor (Mudd and Joyce 2014, 102, 117). There were also lead-silver deposits at Combe Martin and Bere Ferrers in Devon, and to a lesser extent near Dulverton on the southern fringes of Exmoor, and while it is clear that these were worked in the medieval period it is not known whether they were mined during the Roman period (Rippon *et al.* 2009). It is striking, however, that all three Roman forts discovered in Cornwall – Calstock, Restormel and Nanstallon – were in areas rich in metal ores, and at Nanstallon a single droplet of silver-rich slag was found on a crucible fragment (Fox and Ravenhill 1972, 108–10). During both the period of military occupation and subsequent civilian control, Exeter therefore lay at a pivotal location in the landscape between the rich tin deposits to the south, and the rest of Roman Britain to the north and east.

Economically viable iron deposits occur across the wider South-West including on Mendip (Jamieson 2015, 112, 115), the Blackdown Hills (Griffith and Wedell 1996; Smart 2018), Exmoor (Riley and Wilson-North 2001, 78–81), the lowlands of eastern Devon (*e.g.* Reed *et al.* 2006; Farnell 2015a), Dartmoor (Newman 2011, 85; Quinnell 2017b, 24), and across Cornwall (Edmonds *et al.* 1975, 98). The later medieval exploitation of the South-West's iron resources is relatively well-known, but of particular significance is the growing evidence from the Roman and early medieval periods. In Devon, for example, iron ore and smelting slag was recovered at Bolham fort near Tiverton (Maxfield 1991), while the character of the Early Roman pottery assemblages at Upottery on the Blackdown Hills may have started during the legionary phase at Exeter (Griffith and Weddell 1996, 33–4; Riley and Wilson-North 2001, 80–1). There was another important iron industry on Exmoor whose origins lay during the Late Iron Age or Early Roman period, with activity continuing into the 2nd and 3rd centuries AD (Riley and Wilson-North 2001, 80–1, Appendix 2; Paul Bidwell pers. comm.). In Cornwall, the Roman fort at Nanstallon lies just *c*. 1.6 km from an iron lode and excavations produced both iron ore and smelting slag, while the fort at Restormel is just 300 m from a prominent iron lode and a surface scatter of smelting slag has been found nearby (Fox and Ravenhill 1972, 108–9; Hartgroves and Smith 2008, 239; Nicholas and Hartgroves 2018, 184). There is also a growing list of sites with early medieval iron production in Devon. Kestor on Dartmoor now has a mid 5th- to mid 7th-century AD radiocarbon date (Quinnell 2017b, 24), while at Dunkeswell and nearby Hemyock, on the Blackdown Hills, and Burlescombe in the lowlands of eastern Devon, it is dated to the mid 7th to late 9th centuries AD (Griffith and Weddell 1996, 33–4; Orellana and Evans 2018; Orellana and Massey 2019; Reed *et al.* 2006; Smart 2018). For a region best known for its tin production, it is the diversity of metals that were exploited during the Roman and medieval periods that is actually most striking.

Pays

Based upon its topography, geology and soils the landscape of the wider South-West can be divided up into a series of discrete and unique districts – or *pays* – each with its own distinctive character (Fig. 2.6). A wide range of documentary evidence shows that since at least the 11th century many of these *pays* saw significant differences in their population densities and patterns of land-use (detailed in Appendix 2.1), and the perceptive descriptions of past agricultural and travel writers show how these differences in agricultural productivity were evident at the time (see Brayshay 1996 for background on these writers). Some *pays* have also produced archaeological evidence for past agricultural practices in the form of animal bones and charred cereal remains, and these are discussed in Chapters 3 and 4.

Eastern Devon lowlands: Exeter lies at the heart of an extensive area of lowland – mostly below 100 m OD – dominated by the River Exe and its tributaries including the Lowman, Culm, Creedy and Clyst. The underlying geology of Permian breccias, sandstones and mudstones give rise to well-drained loamy soils of the Crediton and Neath Associations, the distinctive colour of which has led to this district being called 'Red Devon' (*e.g.* Welldon Finn 1967, fig. 66). These various deposits have given rise to some excellent clays used for producing pottery and tiles during the Iron Age, Roman and medieval periods (see EAPIT 2, Chapters 12, 13 and 17), as well as the distinctive 'Heavitree Stone' which became a common building material from the late medieval period (Chapter 8 below). As with all *pays* there are some local variations, such as the seasonally flooded river floodplains that will have provided rich meadowland, and localised areas of well-drained sandy brown earths overlying soft Permian Sandstones immediately east of Exeter that historically were heathland. Documentary sources from the 11th century onwards consistently show that the eastern Devon lowlands had a relatively high population density and mixed agricultural regimes including a high proportion of the land put down to arable. Early writers viewed this district very favourably with John Leland, writing *c*. 1540,

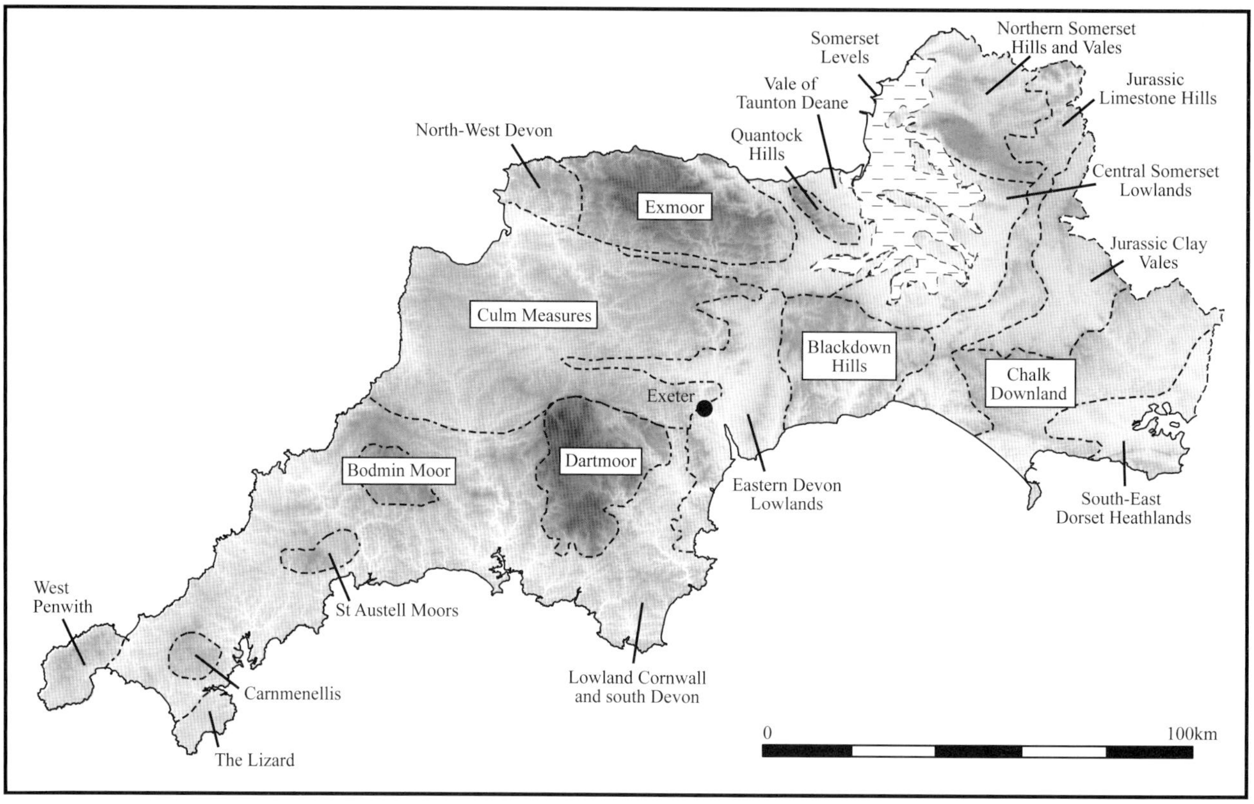

Fig. 2.6 The pays *of the wider South-West (drawn by Stephen Rippon)*

describing it as producing exceptionally fine corn and grass (Toulmin Smith 1964, 239). In 1586 William Camden said that the Exe Valley had 'pretty rich grounds' (Gibson 1695, 30), while in 1724–7 Daniel Defoe described the area as having 'a fat, strong soil, of a deep-red colour, intermixed with veins of different kinds of loam, [that] produce very great crops of corn, and peas of the best kind, not to be excelled in the whole island. Neither doth it fall behind in meadow ground, and pasturage, and turnips; as is evident to a person who goes through any of the markets, and beholds the fine, well fed beef and mutton, with which they are plentifully stored' (Defoe 1742a, 305). Richard Polwhele (1797, 46–7) described the soils as the 'best tillage ground' in Devon. The growing season today is over 275 days (Caseldine 1999, map 1.11), and overall, the inherent characteristics of the physical landscape, and the consistent way that it was perceived so positively by early travellers and agricultural writers, shows that this was a core agricultural area.

Culm Measures: to the west of the Eastern Devon Lowlands lay the low plateau – mostly around 100–200 m OD – of the 'Culm Measures'. These complex interbedded sandstones, siltstones, slates and shales give rise to well-drained fine loamy soils of the Neath and Denbigh Associations on sloping ground, but slowly permeable and seasonally waterlogged clayey soils of the Hallsworth Association on the flatter interfluvial areas. Historical sources from the 11th century onwards record the area as having a low population density and predominantly pastoral farming, with only limited arable. Leland said the area was characterised by 'morische ground but very good for broode [breeding] of catelle' (Toulmin Smith 1964, 172–3). Tristan Risdon (*c*. 1630, 5–6) was unimpressed, reporting that 'the land is more lean and barren, except about towns, where the husbandman, by improvement, hath inforced fertility … otherwhere, so churlish and unthankful to the husbandman's labour that it hardly affords rye and oats for the moors and hills are untractable to tillage'. Such 'improvements' are described by Camden (1623, 31) who notes that the soils of Devon are 'poor and lean' but could make a good return for the husbandman through the application of sea sand, marl, lime and burnt turf. In the 1660s Samuel Colepresse, described the Culm Measures as 'a cold, weepeing, clayie ground' (Stanes 1964), while Defoe (1742b, 305a) described:

> very course, moory or fenny soil, very barren in its nature; in some places productive of nothing but a dwarf kind of furze [gorse, *Ulex europaeus*: see Riley *et al*. (2005, 20) for how poorly valued 'furze' was] of little or no value. In other places, grow nothing but rushes, or a course, sour [land was regarded as 'sour' if it had acidic soil and was in need of marling; Williamson 2002, 67] kind of pasture, which the cattle will not feed upon … the soil here is generally a stiff clay, through which the waters cannot soak away: this renders it very unhealthy especially to sheep, which in those parts are a small kind, and very subject to the rot which (in wet seasons especially) destroys them in great numbers.

On the very highest ground the growing season today dips below 275 days, and overall, both the inherent physical characteristics of this landscape, and the perceptions of early writers, suggest that the Culm Measures were an environmentally marginal landscape.

***Exmoor*:** north of the Culm Measures the ground rises up steeply to the uplands of Exmoor the highest parts of which are over 400 m OD. The underlying solid geology of Devonian slates, mudstones, siltstones, sandstones and limestones give rise to thin silty soils of the Manod Association with areas of blanket peat on the higher areas. There are several iron-bearing deposits that were exploited during both the Roman and medieval periods, and lead/silver deposits at Combe Martin that were mined during the middle ages. Historical sources from the 11th century onwards record the area as having a very low population (large areas were completely unoccupied) with very little arable. Leland described it as 'baren and morisch ground, wher ys store and breading of young catelle, but little or no corne or habitation' (Toulmin Smith 1964, 168), and with a growing season under 225 days, this will always have been a physically marginal landscape for agriculture.

***North-West Devon*:** the geology of north-western Devon is the same as that which underlies the uplands of Exmoor to the east, but a lower elevation – giving rise to a growing season of around 275 days – and a predominance of well-drained coarse silty soils of the Denbigh Association on all but the highest areas, meant that this was a district well-suited to agriculture. This is reflected in the historical sources from the 11th century onwards that record average to high population densities and mixed farming, with Leland describing the area as 'hilly ground, having much enclosures for pasture and corne' (Toulmin Smith 1964, 169).

***Dartmoor*:** the centre of Devon is dominated by the granite massif of Dartmoor that rises to over 400 m OD. This is an area rich in minerals, notably tin, that were an important part of the South-West's economy during the Roman and medieval periods (see below, Chapters 6–8). Granite was also used for producing Roman quern stones (see EAPIT 2, Chapter 14). The thin, gritty and often peaty soils of the Moretonhampstead and Moor Gate Associations that cover the fringes of Dartmoor, and a growing season of under 225 days, makes this a physically marginal landscape for agriculture, while the higher areas are covered with peat and can only support rough grazing. Risdon (*c.* 1630, 6), for example, described how the soils consisted of 'a blackish earth, both rocky and heathy, called, by a borrowed name of its barreness, Dartmoor, richer in its bowels than in the face thereof' [the 'bowels' referring to its rich tin reserves]. Agriculturally, this is the most physically marginal landscape in the wider South-West, although during the medieval period it was used for transhumant grazing (Fox 2012), and an indication of the high regard in which these pasture were held is Camden's (1623, 35) statement that Dartmoor supported 100,000 sheep. Isotopic analysis of faunal remains from Exeter suggest that increasing use was made of animals that had been grazing on Dartmoor over the course of the Roman and medieval periods (see below, Chapters 3 and 4).

***Lowland Cornwall and South Devon*:** to the south and west of Dartmoor the majority of the land lies below 100 m OD and comprises gently rolling hills and valleys. Mineral-rich veins that were extruded into the areas around the granite intrusions are found in many of the lowland areas including important lead/silver deposits in the Tamar Valley (Rippon *et al.* 2009), while stream deposits in the valleys surrounding the granite uplands were an important source of tin. The underlying geology of Lower and Middle Devonian slates, siltstones, sandstones and limestones give rise to well-drained fine loamy and silty soils of the Denbigh and Neath Associations. Domesday records average population densities in Devon but low in Cornwall, although they were average to high by the 16th century (the higher values again being in Devon). Mixed farming generally predominated, although Domesday records a very low density of ploughteams across lowland Cornwall (as the soils and topography in southern Devon and lowland Cornwall were the same, there must be a suspicion that population and ploughteams in Cornwall were under recorded in Domesday). Leland described the area in generally favourable terms with phrases such as 'enclosed ground metely fruteful of corne but exceedingly baren of wood', 'good corne ground', and 'plentiful ground of corn and grasse', although there were also areas of 'hilly and hethy ground' (Toumin Smith 1964, 175, 177, 178, 207, 208). The growing season in all areas was over 275 days, and in the southern coastal areas over 325 days.

***Bodmin Moor, St Austell Moors, Carnmenellis and West Penwith*:** to the west of Dartmoor a series of smaller granite outcrops extend down the spine of the South-West Peninsula as far as Land's End in West Penwith. These were also rich in minerals, notably tin. The thin, gritty and often peaty soils of the Moretonhampstead and Moor Gate Associations, along with some areas that are cloaked in peat, means that – like Dartmoor – these are physically very marginal landscapes.

***Blackdown Hills*:** to the east of Exeter and the Eastern Devon Lowlands lie the Blackdown Hills that comprise an extensive flat-topped plateau at *c.* 250 m OD formed of Cretaceous Greensand – often sealed by superficial deposits of clay-with-flints – and which is heavily dissected by a series of river valleys that cut down into the underlying Triassic mudstones. Various deposits are rich in iron, and clays both on the western side of the Blackdown Hills (*e.g.* around Hemyock) and to the east (*e.g.* around the Neroche Forest) formed the basis of important potting industries (see EAPIT 2, Chapter 17). During the Roman period the Upper Greensand was also used for making Roman quern stones (see EAPIT 2, Chapter 14), while stratigraphically lower rocks such as

Bere Stone – exposed on the coast – were quarried during the medieval period (see below, Chapters 7–8). Soils in the valleys are predominantly fine loamy, silty and clayey soils of the Whimple Association, whereas the higher interfluvial areas had more poorly-drained fine silty and clay soils of the Batcombe Association; some areas are so poorly drained that peaty soils of the Hense Association have formed.

Historical sources from the 11th century onwards record the area as having a relatively low population and predominantly pastoral farming, with only limited arable. The valleys were, however, viewed quite favourably by early writers, with Leland describing the area around Honiton as having good arable and pasture with some woodland, while areas towards the coast are described as 'meatly good ground' (Toulmin Smith 1964, 245). The higher ground, in contrast, was seen as an inhospitable landscape (*e.g.* Risdon *c.* 1630, 4) with Polwhele (1797, 2, 45–6) saying of the Blackdown Hills – 'a name to which the dreariness of their aspect may justly entitle them' and that their soils consisted of a 'blackish mould' (reflecting the high organic content of these soils). The growing season today is 225–75 days, lower than on the Culm Measures, and overall this *pays* should be seen as consisting of two contrasting areas: the gentle-sided valleys that were hospitable places with good soils, and the hill-top plateaus that were bleak and of little value.

Vale of Taunton Deane: to the north of the Blackdown Hills lies the Tone Valley, an area widely known as the Vale of Taunton Deane. The Triassic mudstones give rise to fine loamy, silty and clayey soils of the non-calcareous Whimple Association, with some areas of more slowly permeable clayey soil of the Worcester Formation. This lowland basin mostly lies below 100 m OD, and to the east the Tone floodplain joins the extensive wetlands of the Somerset Levels. Historical sources from the 11th century onwards record the area as having a relatively high population and mixed farming. In 1587 Camden described the area as 'beautified with green meadows [and] abounds in delightful orchards' (Gibson 1695, 30). John Billingsley (1797, 165) said that the climate was particularly mild, the soils highly productive, and 'the eye is agreeably relieved by a judicious mixture of arable and pasture'. The growing season today is over 275 days, and overall, this must always have been a fertile agricultural area.

Central Somerset Lowlands: east of the Vale of Taunton Deane lay the Central Somerset Lowlands that were bounded by the Blackdown Hills to the south-west, the Jurassic Limestone Hills to the south-east and east, and Mendip to the north, while the Somerset Levels occupied its low-lying western areas. This lowland basin, mostly below 100 m OD, is underlain by limestones and shales of the Jurassic Lias Formation that give rise to loamy and clayey calcareous soils (*e.g.* of the Evesham, Badsey, Oxpasture and Curtisden Associations). Historical sources from the 11th century onwards record relatively high populations and mixed farming, with the adjacent wetlands providing excellent pasture. Leland described it as 'very fair and fruteful champain' [*i.e.* 'champion' or open field landscape], although elsewhere 'all this way the pastures and feeldes be much enclosed with hegge rowes of elmes' with 'good pasture and corne ground' (Toulmin Smith 1964, 150, 155–6). Billingsley (1797, 165) describes the area as exceedingly fertile both in corn and pasture, abounding in good orchards and fine luxuriant meadows, and was 'altogether as well cultivated and as productive as most parts of the kingdom'. The growing season today is over 275 days, and overall this must always have been another core agricultural area.

North Somerset Hills and Valleys: to the north of the Central Somerset Lowlands lay the Carboniferous limestone hills of Mendip – that rise to *c.* 260 m OD – along with a series of other hills and intervening valleys cut down into Triassic Mudstones. The hills have very shallow, loamy, calcareous soils of the Crwbin Association, whereas the valleys have loamy and sometimes slowly permeable soils of the Hodnet and Whimple Associations. Historical sources from the 11th century onwards typically record relatively high populations, although over time there was shift from extensive arable to predominantly pastoral farming.

Somerset Marshlands: the landscape of central Somerset is dominated by the extensive wetlands of the Somerset Levels that in the Roman period supported an important salt industry. In the coastal alluvial areas the calcareous clayey soils of the Newchurch Association are very prone to waterlogging, but in Domesday they supported an average density of both population and ploughteams showing that extensive arable was possible if a well-designed drainage system was properly maintained. In contrast, the inland backfens – known historically as the 'moors' – were very poorly drained and dominated by peat: these areas could be grazed by livestock in the summer but settlement was restricted to a small number of bedrock islands.

Jurassic Limestone Hills: the landscape of eastern Somerset and western Dorset was dominated by the Jurassic Limestone Hills that in places reach over 100 m OD and which were capped by a mixture of fine, loamy, calcareous soils of the Elmton and South Petherton Associations, and slowly permeable clayey soils of the Evesham Association. Historical sources from the 11th century and later typically record relatively high populations, but varying proportions of arable and pasture. Leland described the areas around Castle Carey, South Cadbury and Sherborne as 'a very fair and fruitful champain' [*i.e.* open field landscape] (Toulmin Smith 1964, 150), while Billingsley (1797, 165) describes high sheepwalks with corn as the main forms of husbandry, and where folding was unremittingly pursued with wheat seldom sown without two foldings and fallowing every four or five years. The analysis of excavated faunal remains shows that these soils supported distinctive patterns of agriculture during both the Roman and medieval periods.

Jurassic Clay Vales: to the east of the Limestone Hills lies the Jurassic Clay Vale of eastern Somerset and north-western Dorset (the Blackmore Vale) that lies below 100 m OD. The underlying Oxford Clay gives rise to slowly permeable seasonally waterlogged clayey soils that historically supported average population densities but predominantly pastoral farming. Defoe (1742b, 35) described it as 'low and flat, being a rich, inclosed country, full of rivers and towns, and infinitely populous'.

Chalk Downland: the central and eastern parts of Dorset are dominated by chalk downland that gives rise to shallow, well-drained calcareous silty soils of the Andover Association. Historical sources from the 11th century onwards record average population densities and mixed farming, with the balance between arable and pasture fluctuating over time. Celia Fiennes describes the chalk downland of Wiltshire as 'most champion and open … its husbandry is mostly corn and sheep' and where the short grass feed was 'sweet' and 'produces the finest wool and sweet meat' (Morris 1984, 42, 214). Defoe (1742b, 35) described the chalk downland as 'all hilly, spreading themselves far and wide in plains and grassy downs, for breeding and feeding vast flocks of sheep'. The analysis of excavated faunal remains shows that these soils supported distinctive patterns of agriculture during both the Roman and medieval periods.

South-East Dorset Heathlands: the south-eastern parts of Dorset were covered by low-lying sandy heathland (that continued into the New Forest in south-western Hampshire). They surrounded the natural embayment of Poole Harbour around which there developed important pottery and salt industries from the Late Iron Age (the 'Durotrigian Ware' and South-East Dorset Black Burnished Ware (BB1) industries; see below, Chapter 3, and EAPIT 2, Chapter 12). Areas of dry acidic sandy soils are difficult to cultivate and since the 11th century this district supported low populations and predominantly pastoral land-use.

A maritime region?

The popular perception of South-West England is that its landscape and society was essentially a maritime one (*e.g.* Cunliffe 2001; Tompsett 2014; Borlase 2018), and it is true that a large proportion the Peninsula is within one day's walk of the sea (Fig. 2.7). This is very much a notional distance as how far a person can travel in a day will depend on the topography, what they are carrying, whether they are on foot or horseback, or accompanied by a packhorse, ox- or horse-drawn cart. The Antonine Itinerary suggests that many Romano-British *mansiones* were around 12 to

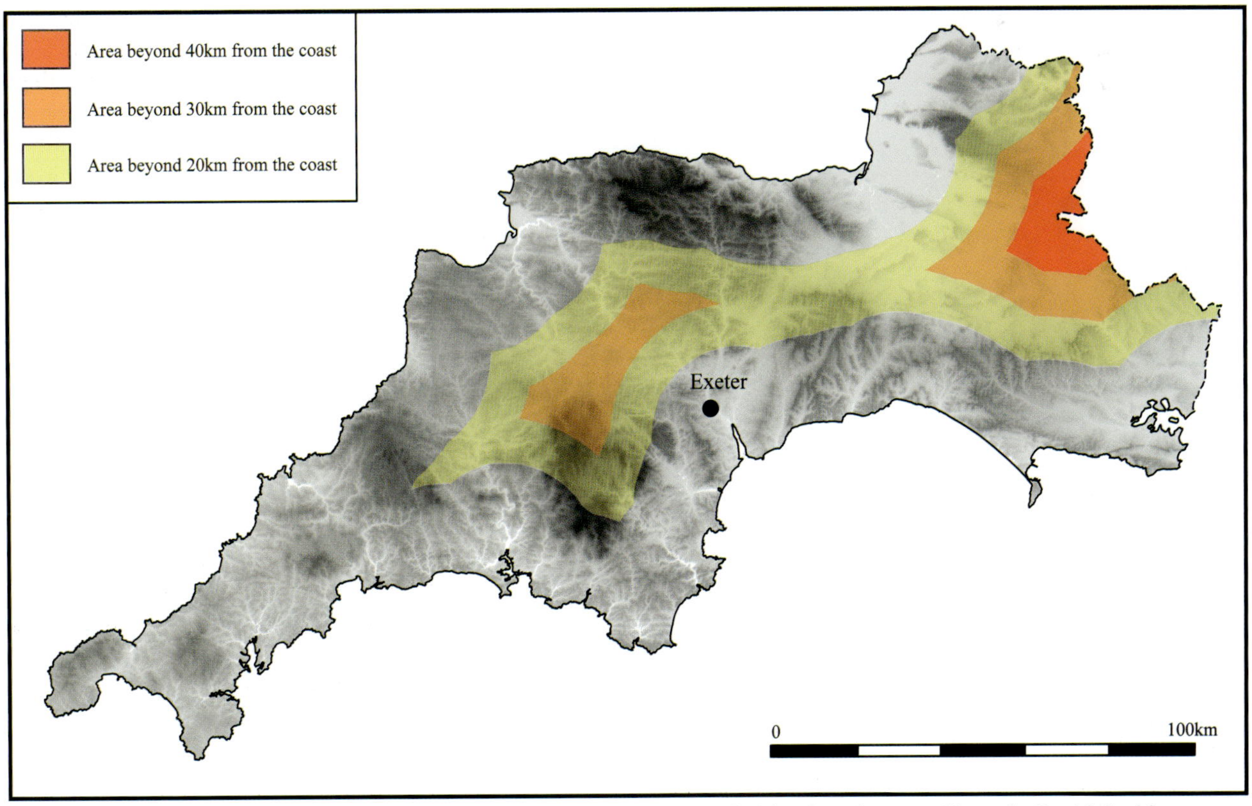

Fig. 2.7 Areas of the South-West that lie more than 20 km, 30 km, and 40 km from the coast (drawn by David Gould)

15 Roman miles apart (18–22 km: Jones and Mattingly 1990, map 2.8), while in 19th-century Devon it was said that people would travel up to six miles to get to a market town in a day (*i.e.* a round trip of 12 miles [19 km]).

Cunliffe (2010, fig. 4.2) includes the South-West Peninsula in his 'Atlantic Zone' on the basis that 'the sea provided an essential means of communication which, on the one hand, bound the south and east coasts of Britain to the Continent through an intricate network of exchange systems while on the other it provided a broad corridor of communication linking the Atlantic-facing communities of the island'. It is indeed true that in recent centuries the coast has been a hive of activity following the development of specialised fishing villages, and it is also clear that the sheltered estuaries were the preferred locations for ports in late prehistoric (*e.g.* Mount Batten beside Plymouth Sound: Cunliffe 1988), Roman (*e.g.* Topsham near Exeter), early medieval (*e.g.* Bantham and Mothecombe in South Devon), and late medieval periods (*e.g.* Exeter).

There is, however, a growing range of evidence that the economy, landscape and society of inland districts within the South-West were not as maritime as is often assumed. The location of medieval churches in parishes that lie adjacent to the coast are invariably positioned well inland at the heart of their agricultural – not maritime – resources, and the coastal fishing villages that today are so characteristic of the South-West Peninsula are no older than the late medieval period (Fox 2001). Maritime activities 'barely affected the distribution or success of fairs in medieval Devon', and 'the influence of the sea mattered little away from the coast' (Kowaleski 1995, 48). The waters around the far South-West are also extremely difficult to navigate, and various studies have postulated terrestrial trade routes that avoided the need to sail around Cornwall (*e.g.* Allen and Fulford 1996; Borlase 2018). While there was, undoubtedly, important coastal trade around the South-West Peninsula this may have been irrelevant for most farming communities living across inland areas.

Conclusions

The landscape of the wider South-West – the historic counties of Cornwall, Devon, Dorset and Somerset – was extremely rich and varied in its character, and while not wishing to return to the dogmatic environmental determinism of the past, it is clear that local variations in geology, topography and soils did help shape the character of the cultural landscape. Exeter lay at the heart of one of the most agriculturally productive districts, and close to the Blackdown Hills that marked the boundary between landscapes and communities that developed in very different ways during the Iron Age, Roman and medieval periods. It is the character of these cultural landscapes that we will now turn to in Chapter 3.

Appendix 2.1: Historical evidence for past land-use in the pays *of the wider South-West*

	Domesday	*1250–1349*	*1350–1449*	*1500–1640*	*1640–1750*	*Early to mid 19th century*	*1930s Land Utilisation Survey*
District/ Sources	Darby and Welldon Finn's (1967) *The Domesday Geography in South West England* contains maps showing the density of population and ploughteams, the distribution of woodland, meadow and pasture, and the distribution of demesne sheep (but unfortunately not cattle or goats).	For **population in 1327–32**, the Lay Subsidies of 1327, 1332 and 1334 are individually incomplete but can be combined to provide a national coverage (Campbell and Bartley 2006, 313–49). For **assessed wealth**, data from these Lay Subsidies are mapped by Glasscock (1975). For **population in 1377–81**, the Poll Tax records both the number of tax payers and the tax they paid in the areas in which records have survived (Fenwick 1998; 2001; 2005). For **agriculture**, *Inquisitions post mortem* and surveys/ account rolls have been synthesised by Campbell (2000) and Campbell and Bartley (2006).		**Population** is based on Sheail's (1972; 1998) analysis of the Lay Subsidies of 1524–5. **Land-use** is based on Thirsk's (1967a; 1984a; 1987) farming regions, based on probate inventories		1801: Crop Returns (Turner 1982a; 1982b; 1982c; 1983a; 1983b; 1984; 1986; Williams 1969)* *c.* 1840: Tithe Files (Kain 1979; 1986)	county reports (*e.g.* Somerset: Stuart Menteath 1938), and summary map (http://www.visionofbritain.org.uk/maps/index.jsp)
eastern Devon lowlands	average to high population density (high in the Exe Valley); high density of ploughteams; moderate amounts of pasture, moderate numbers of sheep; abundant meadow; relatively little woodland	average to high population density; high assessed wealth; roughly equal proportions of arable and pasture (slightly less arable in Culm Valley); oats dominant, with some wheat, rye and barley; cattle dominant amongst livestock; abundant meadow	wheat and oats with some rye; sheep with some cattle	very high population density; mixed farming (corn and stock)	arable dominant: corn and livestock with special enterprises (*e.g.* horses, pigs, fruit, vegetables)	*c.* 1840: pasture dominant but with up to 40% arable (wheat and barley the major crops, with some oats)	arable (predominantly wheat with some oats, barley and potatoes), and pasture (particularly for dairying) in roughly equal proportions, with some heathland
Culm Measures	low to average population density; low density of ploughteams; moderate amounts of pasture, moderate numbers of sheep; deficient in meadow; some extensive areas of woodland	low population density; low assessed wealth; roughly twice as much arable as pasture; wheat and oats dominant; cattle and sheep both important; deficient in meadow	very limited data on cropping suggests oats and rye dominant, with some wheat; sheep with some cattle	average population density; pasture dominant (cattle and sheep rearing)	pasture dominant: subsistence arable with cattle rearing and sheep keeping	*c.* 1840: pasture dominant but with up to 40% arable (wheat the major crop, with some barley and oats)	predominantly pasture for rearing livestock, with some arable (dominated by oats), and rough pasture and moorland

(Continued)

Appendix 2.1: Historical evidence for past land-use in the ***pays*** *of the wider South-West (Continued)*

	Domesday	*1250–1349*	*1350–1449*	*1500–1640*	*1640–1750*	*Early to mid 19th century*	*1930s Land Utilisation Survey*
Exmoor	large areas were unoccupied; the remaining areas – mostly around the fringes – had low population density; very low density of ploughteams; abundant pasture; low numbers of sheep; some extensive areas of woodland	low population density; low assessed wealth; pasture dominant	no data on cropping or livestock	low population density; pasture dominant (cattle and sheep rearing)	pasture dominant: subsistence arable with cattle rearing and sheep keeping		predominantly heathland, moorland and rough pasture, with some improved pasture
North-West Devon	average population density; average to high density of ploughteams; moderate amounts of pasture and meadow; abundant sheep; small amounts of woodland	average to high population density; high assessed wealth; arable dominant	wheat, oats and rye; sheep with some cattle	high population density; mixed farming (corn and stock)	pasture dominant: subsistence arable with cattle rearing and sheep keeping		arable and pasture in roughly equal proportions
Dartmoor	large areas were unoccupied; the remaining areas – mostly around the fringes – had low population density; very low density of ploughteams; abundant pasture; low numbers of sheep; very limited meadow abundant woodland	low population density; low assessed wealth; pasture dominant	no data on cropping or livestock	low population density; pasture dominant (cattle and sheep rearing)	pasture dominant: subsistence arable with cattle rearing and sheep keeping		predominantly heathland, moorland and rough pasture, with some improved pasture

(Continued)

Appendix 2.1: (Continued)

	Domesday	*1250–1349*	*1350–1449*	*1500–1640*	*1640–1750*	*Early to mid 19th century*	*1930s Land Utilisation Survey*
Lowland Cornwall and South Devon	low (in central and western Cornwall) to average (in eastern Cornwall and Devon) population density; very low (in eastern and central Cornwall) but low to average (in eastern Cornwall and south Devon) density of ploughteams; average to abundant amounts of pasture; small amounts of meadow; moderate amounts of woodland	average to high population density; average to high assessed wealth; arable dominant; wheat and oats dominant; sheep and cattle	wheat and oats dominant, with some barley and rye; sheep with some cattle	very high population density in southern Devon, but average across lowland Cornwall; mixed farming (corn and stock) in the coastal areas of southern Devon, but pasture dominant (cattle and sheep rearing) elsewhere	arable dominant in southern areas: corn and livestock with special enterprises (*e.g.* horses, pigs, fruit, vegetables); pasture dominant across rest of lowland Cornwall: subsistence arable with cattle rearing and sheep		arable and pasture (particularly dairying) in roughly equal proportions
Bodmin Moor, St Austell Moors, Carnmenellis and West Penwith	these small upland areas do not produce meaningful patterning on the *Domesday Geography* maps	mapped as having average to high population and assessed wealth (though probably reflecting mining); no data on cropping or livestock	oats dominant	Bodmin Moor had a low population density, but it was average across West Penwith; pasture dominant (cattle and sheep rearing)	pasture dominant: subsistence arable with cattle rearing and sheep keeping		predominantly heathland, moorland and rough pasture, with some improved pasture
Blackdown Hills	low to average population density; low density of ploughteams (though close to average in the south); abundant pasture, small numbers of sheep; deficient in meadow (except in Culm and Axe valleys); some extensive areas of woodland	low to average population density; average to high assessed wealth; roughly equal proportions of arable and pasture; wheat with some oats; cattle and sheep both important; low to average amounts of meadow	wheat and oats, with some rye; no data on livestock	average population density; pasture dominant (cattle and sheep rearing)	arable dominant: corn and livestock with special enterprises (*e.g.* horses, pigs, fruit, vegetables)	1801: wheat and oats, with some barley, turnip, rape, peas and beans. *c.* 1840: pasture dominant but with up to 40% arable (wheat and oats the major crops, with a little barley)	predominantly pasture (mostly for dairying), with some arable (wheat and oats), and rough pasture and moorland

(Continued)

Appendix 2.1: Historical evidence for past land-use in the ***pays*** *of the wider South-West (Continued)*

	Domesday	*1250–1349*	*1350–1449*	*1500–1640*	*1640–1750*	*Early to mid 19th century*	*1930s Land Utilisation Survey*
Vale of Taunton Deane	densely populated; average density of ploughteams (higher than in central Somerset lowlands); moderate amounts of pasture, small numbers of sheep; abundant meadow; relatively little woodland	high population density; high assessed wealth; roughly equal proportions of arable and pasture; wheat and oats; working animals dominate the livestock; abundant meadow	wheat and oats with some barley; sheep and cattle	high population density; mixed farming (corn and stock variously combined)	arable dominant: corn and cattle with substantial dairying	1801: wheat and barley, with some turnips, rape, peas and beans. *c.* 1840: arable and pasture in roughly equal amounts (predominantly wheat)	arable and pasture (particularly dairying) in roughly equal proportions
Central Somerset Lowlands	densely populated; average density of ploughteams; moderate amounts of pasture, small numbers of sheep; abundant meadow; some extensive areas of woodland to the south-west	high population density; high to very high assessed wealth; roughly twice as much arable as pasture; wheat and oats; cattle dominant amongst livestock; abundant meadow	wheat, oats and barley; cattle and sheep	no population data; pasture dominant: cattle (dairying) and pig-keeping	arable dominant: corn and cattle with substantial dairying	1801: wheat, with barley, turnips, rape, peas and beans. *c.* 1840: arable and pasture in roughly equal amounts (wheat and pulses major crops, with some oats and barley)	arable and pasture (particularly dairying) in roughly equal proportions
North Somerset Hills and Valleys	average to high population density; average to high density of ploughteams; average amounts of pasture and abundant meadow, large numbers of sheep; average amounts of woodland	average to high population density; high assessed wealth; wheat and barley or oats; cattle dominant amongst livestock; average amounts of meadow	no data on cropping or livestock	average to high population density; pasture dominant (cattle and sheep rearing)	pasture dominant: subsistence corn with cattle rearing, dairying and/or grazing	1801: wheat, with oats, barley, potatoes and peas. *c.* 1840: pasture dominant (up to 80%) but with up to 40% arable (wheat the major crop with some oats)	predominantly pasture with rough grazing on the higher areas

(Continued)

Appendix 2.1: (Continued)

	Domesday	*1250–1349*	*1350–1449*	*1500–1640*	*1640–1750*	*Early to mid 19th century*	*1930s Land Utilisation Survey*
Somerset Marshlands (settled coastal claylands)	average population density (on the settled coastal claylands); average density of ploughteams on the settled coastal claylands; abundant pasture and meadow, small numbers of sheep; no woodland	average to high population density; high to very high assessed wealth; more pasture than arable; wheat and oats with some barley; cattle dominant; abundant meadow	no data on cropping or livestock	no population data; pasture dominant (stock fattening, with horse-breeding and dairying)	pasture dominant: subsistence corn, with cattle rearing and sheep keeping	1801: wheat, with peas and beans. *c*. 1840: pasture dominant with up to just 20% arable (wheat the major crop and pulses)	almost wholly pasture (for dairying)
Jurassic Limestone Hills	average to high population density; average density of ploughteams; small amounts of pasture recorded, large numbers of sheep; average amounts of meadow; relatively little woodland	high population density; high assessed wealth; roughly twice as much arable as pasture; wheat and oats with some barley; sheep dominant amongst livestock; average amounts of meadow	no data on cropping or livestock	no population data; pasture dominant: cattle (dairying) and pig-keeping	arable dominant: corn and cattle with substantial dairying	1801: wheat, oats and barley, with some turnips, rape, peas and beans. *c*. 1840: arable and pasture in roughly equal amounts (wheat major crop, with some barley)	arable and pasture in roughly equal proportions
Jurassic Clay Vales (Blackmoor Vale, etc.)	average population density; low density of ploughteams; small amounts of pasture (data on livestock not recorded); average amounts of meadow; some extensive areas of woodland	high population density; high assessed wealth; roughly equal proportions of arable and pasture in demesnes; wheat with a small amount of oats and rye; cattle dominant amongst livestock; abundant meadow	no data on cropping or livestock	high population density; pasture dominant (cattle (dairying) and pig-keeping)	arable dominant: corn and cattle with substantial dairying	*c*. 1840: predominantly pasture with some arable (wheat, barley and oats the major crops)	predominantly pasture (for dairying) with some arable
Chalk Downland	average population density; low density of ploughteams; abundant pasture, large numbers of sheep; average to abundant amounts of meadow; relatively little woodland	high population density; high assessed wealth; roughly equal proportions of arable and pasture; wheat, oats and barley; sheep dominant amongst livestock; deficient in meadow	wheat and barley, with some oats; cattle and sheep	average to high population density; mixed farming (sheep and corn)	arable dominant: corn and sheep	*c*. 1840: pasture dominant but with up to 40% arable (wheat and barley the major crops)	arable and pasture (for sheep) in roughly equal proportions

(Continued)

Appendix 2.1: Historical evidence for past land-use in the ***pays*** *of the wider South-West (Continued)*

	Domesday	*1250–1349*	*1350–1449*	*1500–1640*	*1640–1750*	*Early to mid 19th century*	*1930s Land Utilisation Survey*
South-East Dorset Heathlands	low population density; low density of ploughteams; average amounts of pasture, relatively few sheep; relatively little meadow; relatively little woodland	low to average population density; average assessed wealth; no data on cropping; cattle dominant amongst livestock; average amounts of meadow	no data on cropping or livestock	low population density; pasture dominant (livestock rearing and fattening)	pasture dominant: subsistence corn, with cattle rearing and sheep keeping	*c*. 1840: arable and pasture in roughly equal amounts, but relatively large amounts of common land (wheat and oats the major crops)	predominantly rough grazing
	population density (persons/mile^2): low = 2.5–4.9 average = 5–9 high = 10–15 **ploughteam density** low = 1.0–2.4/mile^2 average = 2.5–3.5/mile^2 high = over 3.5/mile^2	**population density** (taxpayers/mile^2): low = <50 average = 50–74 high = >74 **assessed wealth** (per mile^2): low: <£5 average: £5–9 high: £10–19 very high: >£19		**population density** (taxpayers/mile^2): low = 0–4 average = 5–9 high = 10–14 very high = 15+			

3

Regional Identities in the Roman Period: Dumnonia and the Wider South-West of Britain

Stephen Rippon and David Gould

with a contribution by Gundula Müldner and Delphine Frémondeau

Introduction

Roman and medieval Exeter lay at the heart of a region that was often very different in character to the rest of lowland Britain. During the later Iron Age there are few signs of the centralisation within society that led to the development of large complex settlements and the minting of coins that was so characteristic of South-East Britain at that time, while during the Roman period communities living in the South-West Peninsula chose to adopt different identities compared to those further east. Following the collapse of Roman rule the South-West Peninsula lay beyond the areas affected by Anglo-Saxon immigration in the 5th and 6th centuries AD, and the region's assimilation into the West Saxon kingdom during the 7th century was one of political conquest not mass folk migration. In common with large parts of southern Britain, from around the 8th century AD the wider South-West did see an increased intensity in landscape exploitation, but settlement patterns and field systems were never transformed into villages and open fields to anything like the same extent as was seen within England's 'Central Province' to the east of the Blackdown and Quantock Hills. Before discussing the development of Exeter itself, it is therefore important to understand this wider landscape context of the Roman fortress and town (in this chapter), and the medieval city (in Chapter 4).

The Dumnonii

On the eve of the Roman invasion communities living across much of Britain appear to have coalesced into a series of regional groupings. Written sources tell us the names of several of those Late Iron Age communities in South-East Britain, but of the wider South-West these documents are silent. It has long been assumed that the names of Romano-British *civitates* were those of the pre-Roman peoples (*e.g.* Cunliffe 2010, fig. 8.1) although the two South-Western examples – the Dumnonii and Durotriges – are first documented by Ptolemy as late as the mid 2nd century AD (although much of his *Geography* is derived from earlier writers including Marinus of Tyre who appears to have produced a map of the known world in *c.* AD 100 but whose own sources may have pre-dated *c.* AD 75: Rivet and Smith 1979, 103–6, 339, 342, 352). Note that the tribe called the Durotriges by Ptolemy may actually have been known as the Durotraces (Tomlin 2018, 247). The earliest surviving reference to the Dumnonii may be the tombstone of one Aemilius, son of Saen[i]ius, found in Cologne, Germany, which records that he was a sailor in the Roman fleet and a 'tribesman of the Dumnonii' (Fig. 3.1). It dates to the last decade of the 1st century AD or the 2nd century AD and while Maxfield (1984) questioned whether it refers to the Dumnonii of the South-West Peninsula or a people that Ptolemy refers to as the *Damnonii* in southern Scotland (that was briefly part of the Roman empire), Birley (1979, 104) and Tomlin (2018, 302) are confident that it refers to the South-West Peninsula.

Assuming that Aemilius' Dumnonii were in the South-West, it is unclear whether the term referred to the whole of the Peninsula or just its eastern half that became Devon. This is because Ptolemy also records a group known as the Cornovii, the name of which was derived from the British *corn-, meaning 'horn' which place-name scholars have taken to mean 'peninsula' (Rivet and Smith 1979, 324–5). It is generally assumed that the Cornovii were therefore

Fig. 3.1 Late 1st- or early 2nd-century AD tombstone, found in Cologne, Germany, that Tomlin (2018, 302) translates as 'To Aemilius son of Saenus, soldier of the German Fleet Dutiful and Loyal, in the crew of Captain Evodius, a tribesman of the Dumnonii, aged ....' (©Römisch-Germanisches Museum/ RheinischesBildarchiv Köln, Anja Wegner I)

located in Cornwall (*e.g.* Thomas 1966b, 86), the modern name being derived from the Old English *Cornwalas*, 'the *Corn*-Welsh', in which Corn- comes from the name of the Cornovii and was added to the Old English *w(e)alh* meaning 'a foreigner, a Welshman' (Watts 2004, 158). What is also not clear, however, is whether the terms Cornovii, Dumnonii and Durotriges were of pre-Roman origin, and corresponded to communities with discrete identities before the conquest, or if they were created by the Roman authorities in order to provide names for their new administrative districts. In what was to become the Durotrigian *civitas*, for example, Papworth (2011) has shown some variation within Iron Age settlement patterns and burial practices suggesting that there were a series of communities living within discrete territories that coalesced into the wider group later known as the Durotriges.

It is increasingly clear, however, that Iron Age landscapes and material culture in what were to become Devon and Cornwall were significantly different to each other, and they were different to areas east of the Blackdown and Quantock Hills. During the Middle and Late Iron Age, for example, settlement patterns within the area that became the Durotrigian *civitas* were dominated by large, heavily defended hillforts – suggesting a degree of centralisation within society – while across the South-West Peninsula the hillforts were far smaller and more lightly defended (Cunliffe 2010, figs 4.3; Griffith and Wilkes 2011). The area that went on to become the Durotrigian *civitas* also had a distinctive range of material culture including a sequence of Iron Age pottery styles that is very different to that found in the South-West Peninsula (Cunliffe 2010, figs 5.3–5.5). During the Middle Iron Age there was a highly decorated group of ceramics found right across the wider South-West – South-West Decorated Ware (formerly known as 'Glastonbury Ware') – although petrological analysis suggests separate production areas in Cornwall (based on the gabbroic clays in the Lizard), Devon (based on the Permian deposits around Exeter), and Somerset (based upon the Old Red Sandstone and Carboniferous Limestone of Mendip and Jurassic Limestone Hills: Peacock 1969; Cunliffe 2010, fig. 18.17). The Devonian variant was made at various locations the most important being the Ludwell Valley east of Exeter (Taylor 2016; 2017; and see Taylor 2012 for production in the Creedy Valley).

During the Late Iron Age separate ceramic traditions developed in Cornwall, Devon and Dorset/southern Somerset. In Cornwall South-West Decorated Ware evolved into Cordoned Ware that was still made in the gabbroic fabric (Quinnell 1986, 119; 2004, 110; 2011, 237–9). The form and decoration of Cordoned Ware may reflect influences from northern Gaul, with two vessels that appear to have been imported from there having been found at Mount Batten on the banks of Plymouth Sound. Although Cunliffe (1988, 40) suggests that they reached Mount Batten via the port at Hengistbury Head – that appears to have been the focus for cross-Channel trade at that time – the possibility of a direct connection between the South-West Peninsula and Brittany cannot be ruled out. Dorset and southern Somerset, meanwhile, saw the development of handmade 'Durotrigian' Ware that was produced around Poole Harbour and which is found as far west as the Blackdown Hills (Cunliffe 2010, 117, 178–89, fig. 5.6; *e.g.* Honeyditches, in Seaton: Miles 1977a; Silvester 1981a). The evidence for a Late Iron Age pottery tradition in the area between Cornwall and Dorset/Somerset – modern Devon – has until recently been virtually non-existent, but recent work has shown that this lack of evidence was a reflection of how few sites had been excavated as a distinctive Late Iron ceramic tradition is now being identified. The vessel forms of this 'Late Iron Age Plain Ware' are similar to the 'Durotrigian' ones – notably simple bead-rimmed jars (that lack the carination seen in many Cornish Cordoned Ware vessels) – but it lacks decoration and is made from local clays (*e.g.* Gatcombe Ash, in Seaton, that used clays derived from the Upper Greensand of the Blackdown Hills; and St Loye's College and Old Park, in Pinhoe, both near Exeter, that used clays from the Ludwell Valley: Quinnell and Reed 2012, 101; Quinnell 2015, 121; Farnell 2018b, 90–101). This Late Iron Age Plain Ware ceramic tradition therefore suggests some contact with communities using pottery of the 'Durotrigian' tradition – reflected in the similar forms – but a desire to retain a distinctive identity by not copying the decoration.

Another distinctive feature of Late Iron Age material culture in Dorset and southern Somerset is the production and circulation of the 'South-Western Group' of coins, traditionally linked to the Durotriges (although their name does not actually appear on them: Haselgrove 1987, 53, 237–9; Creighton 2000, 33). This coin production suggests that a cohesive socio-political entity was emerging in the Dorset area but this was not the case in the South-West Peninsula where very few Late Iron Age coins – all imported from outside the region – have been found, mostly from Mount Batten and coastal districts of Cornwall (Thomas 2018, 249, figs 7.8 and 7.9). Just two have been found in Exeter – an Armorican stater (unstratified) and copper alloy Durotrigian issue (from a pre-Flavian buried soil) – that have been interpreted as casual losses (Quinnell 2017a, 18–19). There was no 'Dumnonian' coinage equivalent to the South-Western Group (*i.e.* probably Durotrigian issues), and along with the absence of *oppida* or substantial hillforts this suggests that society in the South-West Peninsula was less centralised than in central-southern and south-eastern Britain.

One site of great importance was Mount Batten, a promontory below Stamford Hill on the eastern side of Plymouth Sound. Although much of the Iron Age material is unstratified (Cunliffe 1988) South-Western Decorated Ware and Cornish Cordoned Ware demonstrate occupation from the Middle to Late Iron Age. The amount of pottery is highly unusual for Devon, as is the large number of Iron Age coins including two hoards and perhaps as many as 18 isolated finds (that include Armorican, Dobunnic and Durotrigian issues). Finds from the Stamford Hill cemetery include three bronze mirrors – one dating to the first half of the 1st century AD – pottery vessels, and a wide range of other metalwork including armlets and brooches many of which are clearly post-conquest but which include some native items that could have been deposited earlier. Overall, it appears that Mount Batten (and Plymouth Sound generally) was an important coastal location and the obvious place for a port serving the tin-rich areas of the South-West Peninsula. Its contacts with the outside world are reflected in a large assemblage of pottery and the coins, and there is evidence for bronze working in the 8th to 6th centuries BC, the importation of metal objects from Brittany and further field during the 5th and 6th centuries BC, and possibly the local copying of continental material (*e.g.* 'Iberian style' brooches). The role that Mount Batten played in this Middle Iron Age trade is, however, unclear and while Cunliffe (1988, 104) suggests it was secondary to Hengistbury Head in Dorset, it remains quite possible that there was direct contact with the continent.

During the Late Iron Age Mount Batten appears to have become more peripheral as the South-West lay outside Cunliffe's (2010, 70–71) 'Channel Zone' which saw increasingly strong links between south-eastern Britain and mainland Europe reflected in the widespread circulation of Gallo-Belgic coins, the adoption of a new form of burial (cremation) and other facets of the 'Aylesford-Swarling' package. The South-West, in contrast, sees almost no Gallo-Belgic coins, the only Late Iron Age cremation burials are in the very far east of Dorset, and there were no *oppida* (Cunliffe 2010, figs 6.2–6.5, 7.6). There was some continued trade between coastal and elite communities in the first half of the 1st century BC, but this was focussed in the far east of Dorset with its ports-of-trade at Hengistbury Head and around Poole Harbour that were central to the distribution of Dressel 1A amphora (Cunliffe 2010, figs 17.26 and 17.28; Fitzpatrick 2013). It therefore appears that the primary point of contact in this Late Iron Age cross-Channel trade was central-southern England, where most of the imported goods remained, while the South-West Peninsula was now a peripheral region within which numerous small-scale social groups supplied resources such as tin (although it is unclear what they got in return: Cunliffe 2001, fig 9.27; 2010, fig. 17.27).

The Roman interlude in the South-West

The traditional view of the South-West Peninsula during the Roman period is not a positive one. Lady Fox (1952, 3), for example, argued 'the land that is "attributed" [by Ptolemy] to Isca was mainly highland … much of it must have been poor soil, unsuited in character and elevation to arable cultivation and hence to intensive settlement'. Fox (1952, 4) goes on to argue that 'romanisation appears to have been ineffectual', that 'it would appear that in general the Dumnonii must have lived on in their native settlements with little change in their mode of life', and that 'it is to be expected that the poverty and backwardness of the hinterland will be reflected in some way in its capital city'. At the start of his seminal paper 'The character and origins of Roman Dumnonia', Charles Thomas (1966b) provided an entertaining account of how A.L.F. Rivet described the conference paper upon which it was based as 'the clearest account of the Early Iron Age in the south-west that we have yet heard' (even though Thomas had been describing society in the Roman period). Henrietta Miles (1977a, 127) summarised perceptions in the 1970s as the 'general cultural poverty of Dumnonia'.

Recent decades, however, have seen an impressive increase in the amount of predominantly development-led fieldwork across the South-West Peninsula, for example on the eastern fringes of the modern city of Exeter (that in the Roman period lay *c.* 5 km beyond the Roman town). As a result, archaeologists have increasingly recognised that the character of Romano-British landscape and society across the South-West Peninsula differed to that east of the Blackdown and Quantock Hills (*e.g.* Mattingly

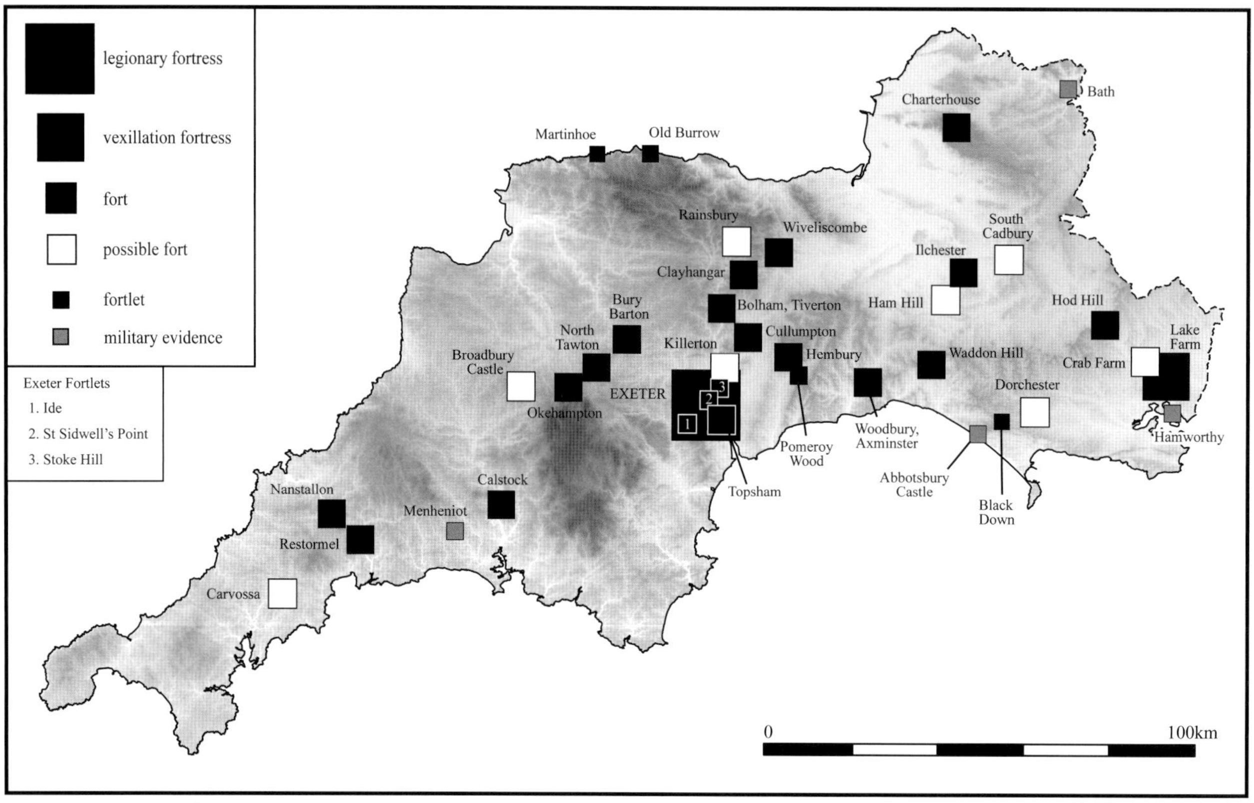

Fig. 3.2 Roman military installations (excluding marching camps) established in the Claudio-Neronian period across the wider South-West with many of the sites continuing in occupation until c. *AD 75–80 (drawn by David Gould)*

2006; Rippon 2006a; 2008a; 2012), and that there were also intra-regional differences between what were to become Devon and Cornwall (*e.g.* Quinnell 1986; 1993; 2004). Recognition that the Blackdown and Quantock Hills marked a major boundary in landscape character has an extremely long history (Rippon 2012, fig. 2.1), and it was therefore no surprise that the Rural Settlement of Roman Britain Project (RSRB) also identified this as a significant boundary in landscape character. Similar regional variation in landscape character has long been recognised across Britain (*e.g.* Roberts and Wrathmell 2000a; 2002; Rippon *et al.* 2015) including the West Midlands and East Anglia (*e.g.* Thomas 1966, 83; Roberts and Wrathmell 2000b; Williamson 2003; 2006; Martin 2007; Martin *et al.* 2008; Rippon 2007; 2008a; 2012), although the RSRB project chose to use Natural England's 'Natural Areas' to delimit their regions (Smith *et al.* 2016, fig. 15) which results in some differences compared to these previous studies whose boundaries were based upon the character of the cultural landscape in the past.

While the RSRB was an extremely impressive achievement in providing a national overview, 'big-data' projects such as this – including, it must be acknowledged, the author's own (Rippon *et al.* 2015) – do have their problems. The RSRB was a broad-brush overview and as such there was not time to explore all of the previously published literature for each region. It was also a review of the excavated evidence for Romano-British rural settlement as opposed to the evidence in total (which means that some important South-Western sites revealed through other means are omitted). Important discoveries have also been made since the RSRB's data collection phase – that ended in 2013 – and this is especially the case immediately east of Exeter.

The Roman invasion, conquest and occupation

The military occupation of the South-West was a relatively brief episode in its history, but one that has left tangible traces within the landscape most notably the establishment of Exeter itself. Figure 3.2 presents our current understanding of permanently occupied military sites in the period *c.* AD 55–75/80. While the identification of most Roman forts is relatively straightforward – where there is good cropmark or geophysical evidence for the plan and/or excavations that have confirmed the site's character and date – there are some places for which the evidence could at best be described as slim. Some examples have, in the past, been identified purely on the basis of partial cropmarks or earthworks while other forts have been mapped on the basis that there logically should have been one there (these are not included on Fig. 3.2). Four potential forts – Bath (Somerset), Abbotsbury Castle (Dorset), Hamworthy (Dorset) and Menheniot (Cornwall) – have, however, been included as their location and significant amounts of Claudio-Neronian material culture suggests some sort of military occupation.

There are very few documentary sources that describe the Roman conquest of south-western Britain, the main one being Suetonius' account of Vespasian's command of the *legio II Augusta*. There is, however, good archaeological evidence for the progress of the Roman army through central-southern England such as the attacks on the hillforts at Maiden Castle and Hod Hill, and the construction of a fort within Hod Hill (Todd 1987, 189–91; 2007a, 115). A small number of Roman military lead slingshots from outside Hawkesdown Hill hillfort near Axmouth, in eastern Devon, could also relate to a military operation (Holbrook 1989). The most westerly hillfort to have seen the construction of a Roman fort was at Hembury – on the western fringes of the Blackdown Hills 22 km to the west of Exeter – where the military occupation appears to have started *c*. AD 55 (Todd 2007a, 117).

It has traditionally been thought that the Roman invasion and conquest of areas west of the Blackdown Hills also dates to the mid AD 50s, with the legionary fortress at Exeter being established around AD 55 during the governorship of Aulus Didius Gallus (Salway 1981, 107–9; see Chapter 5 below). Exeter then lay at the centre of a military landscape that included several extra-mural compounds, a settlement at St Loye's College, a fort and port at Topsham at the head of the Exe Estuary, two small 'fortlets' at Ide and Stoke Hill, as well as a network of forts within Exeter's wider hinterland including Hembury, Cullompton and Bolham in Tiverton. After a few years the army appears to have expanded west when the forts at Bury Barton, North Tawton and Okehampton to the north of Dartmoor, as well as Calstock, Restormel and Nanstallon in Cornwall, were established (see Chapter 5 below).

There are, however, several strands of evidence suggesting an earlier military presence to the south of Dartmoor (Fig. 3.3). A series of sites identified through the Portable Antiquities Scheme have produced Claudian *sestertii* which – unlike copies of Claudian coins in places such as Exeter – did not stay in circulation for very long (EAPIT 2, Chapter 15; Reece 1987a, 39). Andrew Brown and Sam Moorhead suggest (in EAPIT 2, Chapter 16) that these Claudian *sestertii* relate to military activity, and perhaps what we are seeing is evidence for sea-borne expeditions in advance of the land-based army. There is also a potential Roman marching camp south-east of Dartmoor, but this is not closely dated. At Twinyeo Quarry, on the banks of the River Teign near Chudleigh Knighton, one of four ovens of military type has produced a radiocarbon date of 2000+/- 35 BP (100 cal. BC – cal. AD 80: Farnell 2015a). These ovens were positioned parallel with and inside a ditch with a well-defined V-shaped profile and intermittent vertical-sided slot. The ditch was traced for *c*. 100 m, and it formed two sides of a rectilinear enclosure with a rounded corner. Other dating

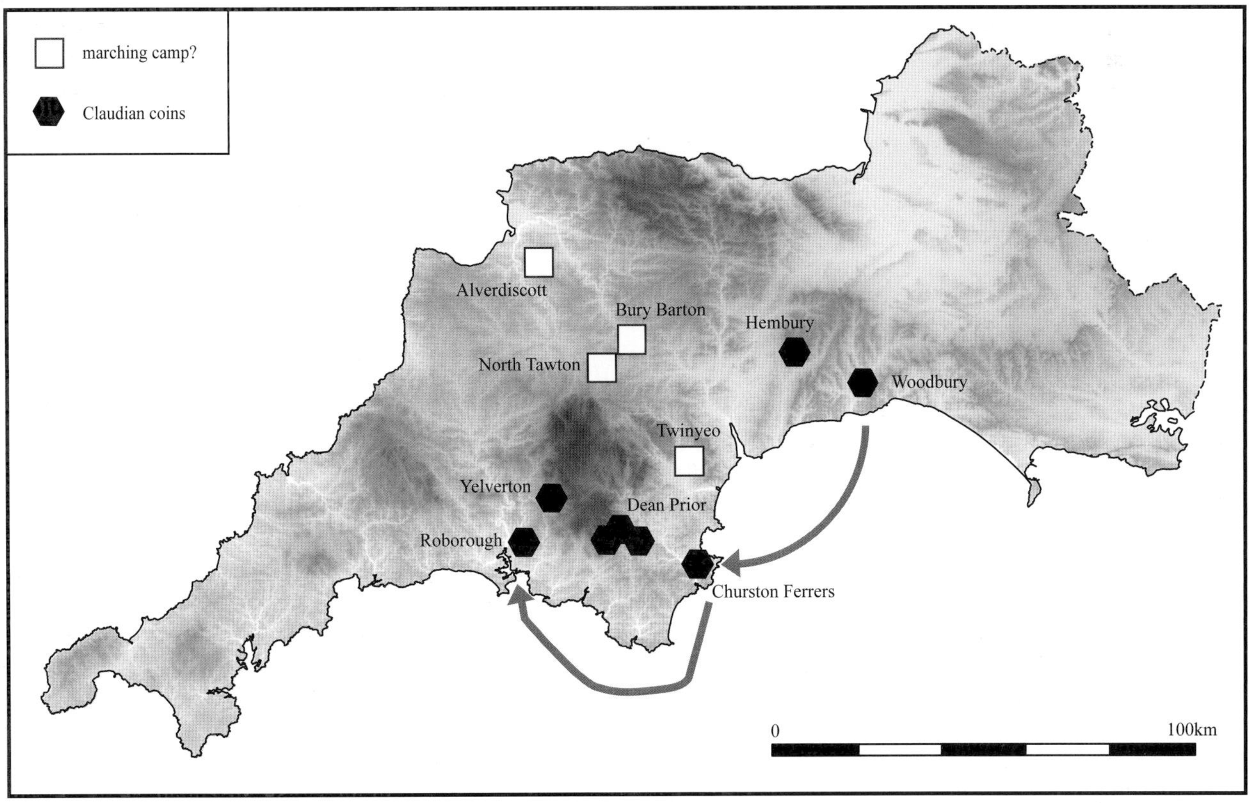

Fig. 3.3 Possible evidence for Claudian activity in the wider South-West (drawn by Stephen Rippon)

evidence was scarce: two Middle Iron Age sherds were recovered from the uppermost fill of the ditch, whereas 86 sherds of Romano-British South Devon Ware were recovered from its middle fill. Most of the latter were a distinctive variant of South Devon Ware only previously found in a late 4th-century AD context at Cadbury Castle (Wilkes *et al.* 2012), while the other Romano-British pottery from Twinyeo Quarry is 2nd to 4th-century AD in date. The published report interprets this ditch as a Middle to Late Iron Age enclosure – seemingly on the basis that there were Middle Iron Age features inside it – whereas it is surely a strong contender for a Roman marching camp (that just happened to have been built over an abandoned Middle Iron Age farmstead). Whether its date is Claudian as opposed to Neronian is, however, unclear, and the Roman pottery presumably represents later occupation of site.

Overall, it seems possible that there were three phases of military campaigning in the South-West Peninsula. The putative earliest phase, under Claudius, appears – based upon the current coin distribution – to have occurred south of Dartmoor, and may simply have been a brief exploratory expedition; the second, in the mid AD 50s, then led to the establishment of a legionary base at Exeter and an associated series of forts in eastern Devon; and the third, in the AD 60s, involved pushing west into central/western Devon and Cornwall. Many of these forts were located in strategic positions so that they could supervise activity in the landscape: most are on major roads and overlooking potential river crossings, while the three Cornish forts – Calstock, Restormel and Nanstallon – were in areas rich in minerals. The military occupation of the South-West Peninsula only lasted until the late AD 70s or early 80s, whereupon the *legio II Augusta* was transferred to Caerleon in South Wales (see Chapter 5 below).

The Roman road network

The legionary fortress and later town at Exeter lay at the centre of five Roman roads, although as with elsewhere in Roman Britain producing a map of these is far from straightforward, and previously published versions are remarkably inconsistent with some roads seemingly included simply because it is assumed that there must have been one linking two places (Fig. 3.4). Figure 3.5 is based upon a re-assessment of this evidence and identifies roads as definite, probable and possible. The network of roads to the east of the Blackdown and Quantock Hills is relatively well known, and the line of the one heading west from Dorchester (*Durnovaria*) to Exeter (*Isca Dumnoniorum*) via Woodbury, in Axminster, and Pomeroy Wood, in Honiton, has now been established (Margary 1955, road 4f; Toller 2014). A postulated southern, coastal, line for this road that appears on many published maps (Margary 1955, road 49) – for which there is actually almost no evidence – can now be dismissed. It is striking, however, how few Roman roads have been identified across the rest of the South-West Peninsula. One headed south-east from Exeter to its port at Topsham (Margary 1955, road 490). Another (that has only recently been identified) headed north of Exeter: a stretch of road surface outside Exeter's East Gate was recorded at 161–79 Sidwell Street (EAPIT 2, Chapter 2 Site 110) and there are several antiquarian accounts of cremation burials in the vicinity (Fox 1952, 103). The alignment of Sidwell Street is continued by the Old Tiverton Road as far as Mincinglake Bridge from where its line can be traced northwards using LiDAR and features within the historic landscape past the possible fort at Killerton (Devon HER MDV29190) and along the Culm valley to the fort at Cullompton (Devon HER MDV124645 and MDV125780). The existence of this road is supported by the distribution of Early Roman coinage and a settlement at Shortlands Lane in Cullompton whose ceramic assemblage is suggestive of a roadside settlement (Thomas 2018, 47, fig. 7.10, 7.13, 7.14). The road presumably then continued north up the Spratford Valley towards the forts (and rich iron deposits) of Clayhanger and Wiveliscombe in western Somerset.

The road that headed west from Exeter – through North Tawton and around the northern side of Dartmoor – has been excavated in several locations of which the most westerly point is Sourton Down near Okehampton (Margary 1955, road 492; Salvatore and Knight 1991; Weddell and Reed 1997; Brennan and Leivers 2013; Salvatore *et al.* 2019). That it then headed west down the spine of Cornwall is logical, but its line has never been confirmed (a short stretch of metalling through the entrance of the enclosed settlement at Carvossa (Carlyon 1987) is insufficient to identify it as a long-distance Roman road).

A road heading south from Exeter, through Kennford and over Haldon Hill towards Kingsteignton and Newton Abbot (the lowest crossing point of the River Teign in the medieval period) appears on most previously published maps, based upon a long alignment of extant roads and tracks (Margary 1955, road 491; Devon HER10067). A possible earthwork in woodland on Haldon Hill interpreted as the road by Woolner and Woolner (1954) has been excavated but produced no evidence for metalling (Miles 1977b, 43–4). The steepness of Haldon Hill, however, means that it is very likely that ancient trackways will have bifurcated, and the overall alignment between Exeter and the River Teign remains convincing. It is noteworthy that there is a concentration of Roman finds discovered through metal detecting on the banks of the Teign just below where this putative road passed over the river at its lowest crossing point before it broadens into the Teign Estuary (Read 1988, 24–5). The relatively straight line taken by the modern A381 between Newton Abbot and Totnes (the lowest crossing point of the Dart) is suggestive of a continuation of this route (Devon HER MDV118358), and recent excavations at Dainton Elms

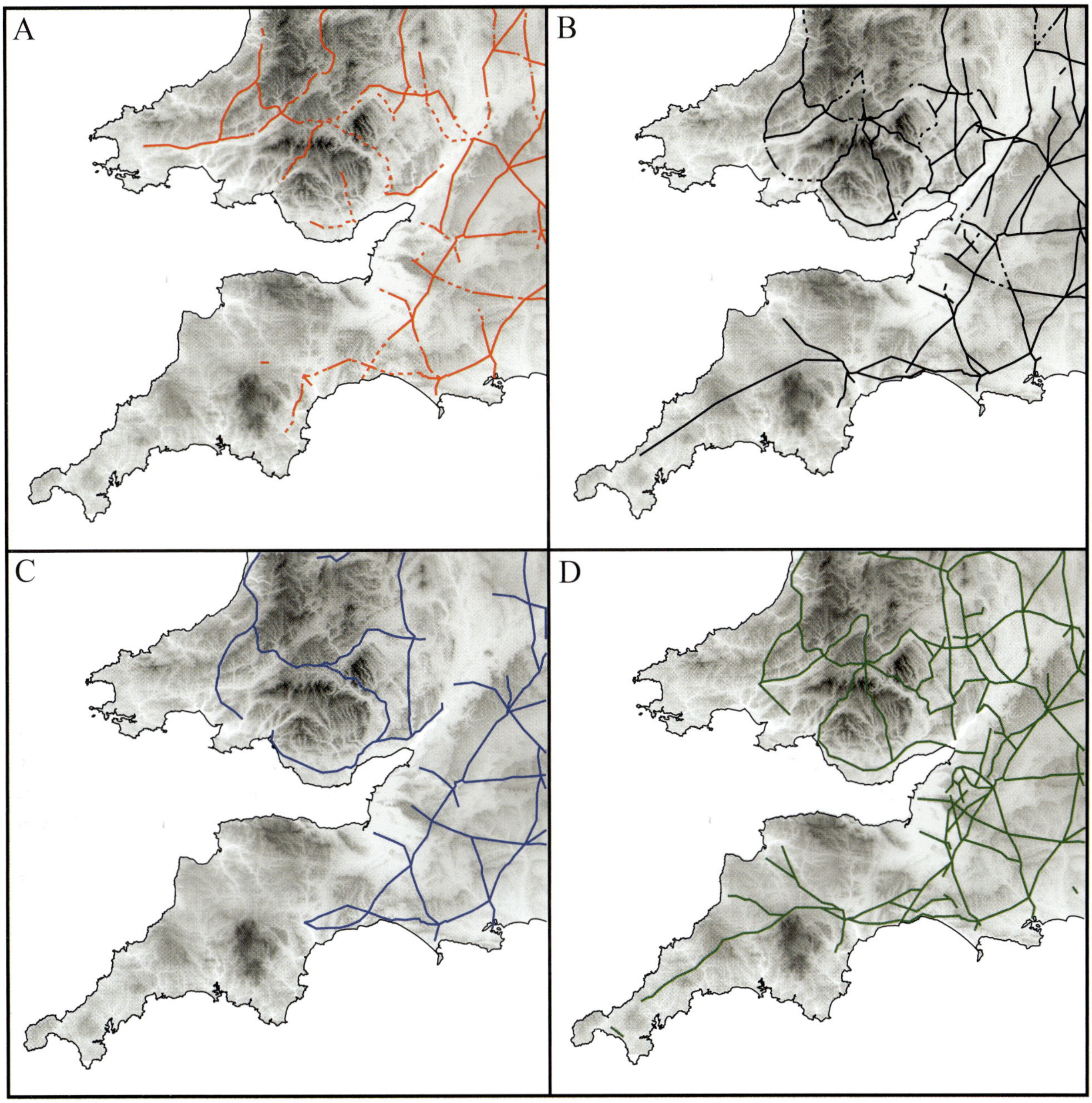

Fig. 3.4 Previous attempts at mapping Roman roads across the wider South-West, showing how inconsistent they are. (A) Ordnance Survey Map of Roman Britain (2010); (B) Margary's Roman Roads in Britain *(1955; 1957; 1967); (C) the* Digital Atlas of Roman Britain *(http://dare.ht.lu.se/); (D) Rural Settlement of Roman Britain's 'Roman Roads' layer on their interactive map (Allen* et al. *2015) (drawn by David Gould)*

Cross, in Ipplepen, have indeed revealed a substantial road with three subsequent resurfacings. The line that it took beyond Totnes is unknown, although logically it will have headed south around Dartmoor towards the sheltered harbour at Plymouth Sound.

The *civitates* of the Dumnonii and the Durotriges

Roman administration in the North-West provinces was based upon districts known as *civitates*, with Dorset and southern Somerset lying within that of the Durotriges (Rivet and Smith 1979, 352). Eagles (2018, fig. 4) has recently suggested that its western boundary followed the rivers Parrett and Brill (13 km east of the present Dorset-Devon border), although the character of the landscape and material culture found on the higher ground to the west – the Blackdown and Quantock Hills – suggests that these areas also lay within the Durotrigian *civitas* (Rippon 2008a; 2012). Durotrigian society soon developed in ways that were typical of lowland Roman Britain. There emerged a hierarchy of urban centres, a highly stratified

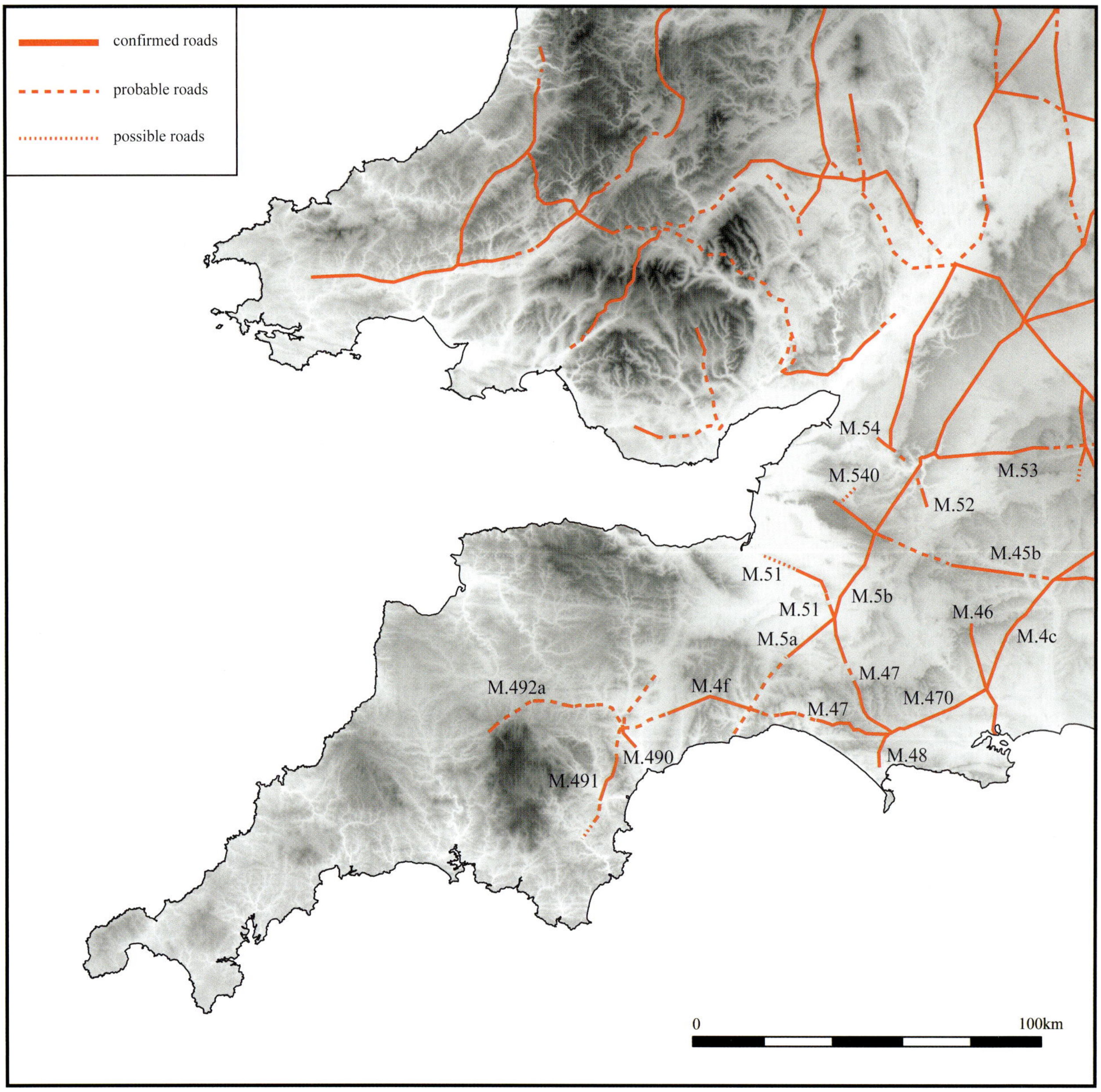

Fig. 3.5 The Roman roads across the wider South-West for which there is some actual evidence, and their Margary numbers (drawn by David Gould)

rural society reflected in the large numbers of villas and lower-status settlements associated with Roman-style architecture and abundant material culture, while religion was practiced in temples with the typical Romano-Celtic layout of a *cella* and ambulatory. The pace of this, what has traditionally been regarded as, 'Romanisation', may not have been quite as fast as in the South-East of Britain, but the direction of travel was the same.

The traditional view is that whole of the South-West Peninsula lay within a single *civitas* – that of the Dumnonii – with Exeter (*Isca Dumnoniorum*) as its *civitas* capital (Fox 1964, 143; Rivet and Smith 1979, 378; Bidwell 1980). This would mean that the Dumnonian *civitas* was one of the largest in Britain – on a par with the Corieltauvi but smaller than the Brigantes – but there is no other major Roman settlement west of Exeter that could have been the capital of another *civitas*. Quinnell (2004, 217) and Mattingly (2006, 407, fig. 10), however, have argued that western parts of the South-West Peninsula – perhaps occupied by the Cornovii (see above) – show only limited evidence for Roman cultural influence, suggesting that they therefore lay outside the Dumnonian *civitas* and instead had some other status, perhaps an imperial estate or *ager publicus*. It has even been suggested that five mid 3rd to early 4th-century AD 'milestones' found in Cornwall were boundary markers for imperial mining regions (Collingwood and Wright 1965, nos 2230–5; Jones and Mattingly 1990, map 5.23; Mattingly 2006,

407, fig. 10). One strand of evidence that the whole of the South-West Peninsula was part of a single Dumnonian *civitas* is Ptolemy's double place-name *Dumnonium sive Ocrinum Promontorium* ('promontory of the Dumnonii, or *Ocrinum* promontory': Rivet and Smith 1979, 135, 429). Mattingly's (2006, 403) suggestion that it was a double place-name – with the 'promontory of the Dumnonii' being somewhere in the vicinity of Prawle Point in South Devon – does not fit with the order in which Ptolemy describes the landmarks on the southern shores of the South-West Peninsula with *Dumnonium sive Ocrinum Promontorium* lying west of the River *Cenio* [Fal?], the River *Tamarus* [Tamar], and the River *Isca* [Exe]). It appears, therefore, that Ptolemy's perception – possibly based upon imperfect sources – was that Dumnonia did extend right down into Cornwall, but this does not preclude there having been several communities within that region, or small parts of it having lain outside the civilian-run *civitas*.

Until recently there has been far less evidence for the character of the Romano-British landscape in the South-West Peninsula, but what seems clear is that it developed somewhat differently to the Durotrigian *civitas* with just a single town – the *civitas* capital at Exeter – and very few villas. In recent years, however, palaeoenvironmental research has demonstrated that the South-West Peninsula was extensively cleared of woodland and used for both arable and pasture. This in turn implies that it was extensively settled (*e.g.* Fyfe and Rippon 2004; Rippon *et al.* 2006), and development-led archaeology is now starting to reveal increasing numbers of Roman-period farmsteads (*e.g.* see below for a discussion of the landscape east of Exeter). It would be easy to assume from this that the South-West Peninsula was not, after all, very different to the rest of Roman Britain but such an assumption would be wrong: it was a well-populated region, but one in which communities appear to have developed subtly different identities compared to those living to the east of the Blackdown and Quantock Hills.

The urban hierarchy

From the late 1st century AD a series of towns started to develop across the wider South-West. In addition to the *civitas* capitals – at Exeter (*Isca Dumnoniorum*) and Dorchester (*Durnovaria*) – Ilchester (*Lendiniae* or *Lindinis*) may have been promoted to this status in the Late Roman period as two inscriptions from Hadrian's Wall refer to a tribal detachment from *civitas Durotragum Lendiniensis* suggesting that the Durotrigian *civitas* had been divided in two (Wacher 1995, 324; Fulford 2006; cf. Putnam 2007, 72).

Over time a series of smaller settlements developed that have traditionally been seen as developing urban characteristics (*e.g.* Millett 1990, 143–56), for which a wide range of terms have been used including *vici*, small towns, roadside settlements and local centres, and which were both defended and undefended. Smith and Fulford (2019, 112) have recently rejected the term 'small town' and suggested instead that they should be regarded as 'defended villages' though 'with the understanding that such sites were far removed from the medieval and modern concepts of the village.' Millett (2016, 708) is, however, correct in his assertion that 'we should be cautious even in referring to [Roman period] nucleated sites as villages', just as Gerrard (2016, 853) is right to regard the use of the term village in the Roman period as 'anachronistic'. It is surely confusing for the term 'village' to mean one thing in the Roman period and another in the medieval period, and so more traditional nomenclature is retained here. In order to map the major settlements across the wider South-West (Fig. 3.6) the character of each site and how it functioned within the wider landscape was examined with each example placed into one of the following categories (after Rippon 2018a):

- **Major towns:** very extensive defended settlements with dense occupation fronting onto a planned grid of streets (suggesting official involvement in their laying out) that includes public buildings, shops and market places, other service provision such as bath-houses, manufacturing and administrative functions. The two examples in the wider South-West are the *civitas* capitals at Exeter and Dorchester.
- **Small towns:** extensive settlements that may or may not have been defended, and whose characteristics may include some areas of dense occupation fronting onto an irregular network of streets that appear to have developed in a piecemeal fashion; evidence for manufacturing and other commercial activity; and some service provision. The three examples in the wider South-West are Ilchester, Shepton Mallet and Bath in Somerset, with Exeter's port at Topsham potentially falling into this category.
- **Local centres**: substantial roadside settlements of varying size and character, but which have evidence for an agricultural and a non-agricultural economic base that included manufacturing and service provision.

Within the hinterland of Exeter we see the development of several local centres, with two – Woodbury, in Axminster (Silvester and Bidwell 1984; Simpson 1993a; Weddell *et al.* 1993), and Pomeroy Wood, in Honiton (Fitzpatrick *et al.* 1999b) – on the Dorchester to Exeter road. In both cases the 2nd to 4th-century AD roadside occupation was located next to a mid 1st-century AD fort, and the settlements spread for *c.* 400–500 m alongside the road and may have covered *c.* 8 ha. Geophysical survey suggests there was a *mansio* at Woodbury at the junction of the Dorchester to Exeter road with the Fosse Way (Cole and Linford 1993).

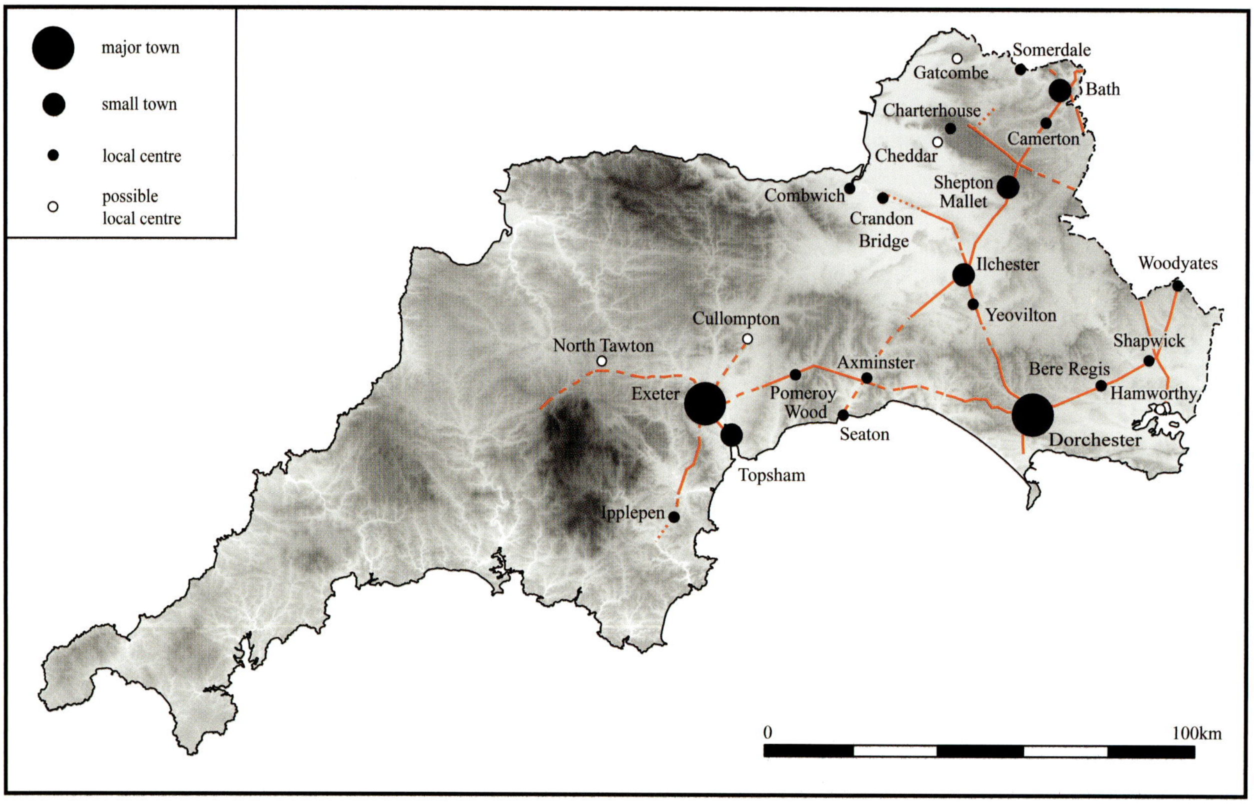

Fig. 3.6: Romano-British towns and local centres across the wider South-West (drawn by David Gould)

Another substantial – but ill-understood – settlement between Dorchester and Exeter lay at the southern end of the Fosse Way on the East Devon coast at Seaton besides the Axe Estuary which is one of very few substantial sheltered inlets between Poole Harbour and the Exe Estuary. That the Fosse Way appears to have ended here itself suggests that it was a significant invasion-period port, although no direct evidence for this has been found. A series of stone buildings at Honeyditches have been variously interpreted as a villa or a *mansio*, with fragmentary traces of occupation spread across at least *c*. 1 ha (Pollard 1972; Miles 1977a; Silvester 1981a; Holbrook 1987). Cropmarks of a rectilinear enclosure *c*. 300 m to the south-west, at Churston Rise on Bramble Hill, have been interpreted as a fort, although small-scale trenching failed to reveal any archaeological features (Simpson 1990). Antiquarian references to a separate rectangular enclosure covering *c*. 1.2 ha and associated with masonry walls built of squared stones at Couchill, *c*. 300 m south of Churston Rise and *c*. 500 m south-west of Honeyditches, could be a second fort. A possibly 2nd or 3rd-century AD *pila* tile stamped LEG II AVG is said to have been found at Seaton in the 19th century on the land of Sir Walter Trevelyan who owned both Honeyditches and Couchill, and while there have been concerns over its authenticity a detailed reassessment by Peter Warry (EAPIT 2, Chapter 13.3) has confirmed that it is indeed genuine, and its morphology suggests it is of military origin. A 3rd-century AD military vulvate stud – from a cavalry harness fitting – also supports a military presence at Seaton long after the invasion/conquest period (Fernandez 1996, 101–2; Bishop and Coulston 2006, fig 124, No. 14; Alex Croom pers. comm., reinterpreting Silvester 1981a, fig. 14, No. 12). Seaton has been one of the places identified as *Moridunum* that the Antonine Itinerary records as lying 35 Roman miles from Dorchester and 15 miles from Exeter, although this was when it was assumed that the Dorchester to Exeter road took a coastal route (Margary 1955, road 49). Having accurately mapped the Dorchester to Exeter road for the first time, however, Toller (2014) has shown that it ran through Woodbury and Pomeroy Wood with the latter corresponding to the distances from Dorchester and Exeter for *Moridunum* (Margary 1955, road 4f). This leaves Seaton as a settlement of unknown character with a bath-house at the end of the Fosse Way, overlooking a sheltered estuary, possibly with a fort, and which may have included a *mansio*, *statio* or similar official centre with a small detachment of soldiers. Exeter's port at Topsham is discussed by Neil Holbrook in Chapter 6.

To the south of Exeter only one substantial Romano-British settlement is currently known: the roadside

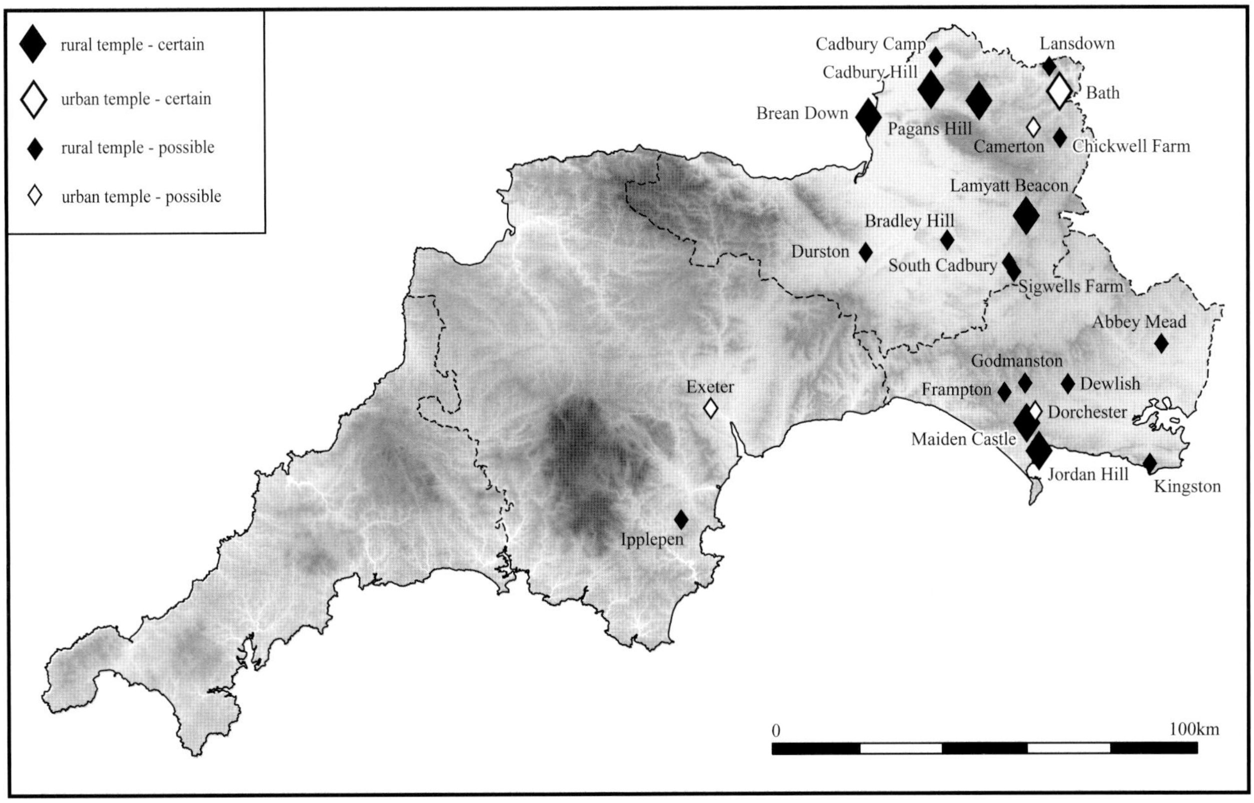

Fig. 3.7 Romano-Celtic temples across the wider South-West (drawn by David Gould)

settlement at Dainton Elms Cross, in Ipplepen. Cropmarks, geophysical survey, artefacts recovered through systematic metal detecting, and trial trenching suggest that this extensive settlement (covering *c.* 6 ha) lay either side of a major Roman road, and should be regarded as a local centre. It has been suggested that there was another roadside settlement west of Exeter, at North Tawton. This substantial cropmark complex (Griffith 1984), that has also recently seen extensive geophysical survey (Chris Smart pers. comm.), includes a complex of military installations including a legionary-sized marching camp and two forts. Small-scale excavation within a rectangular enclosure nearby produced some 2nd to 4th-century AD pottery (Passmore 2005). It has been suggested that this may have been the location of the *mansio* or other official centre of **Nemetostatio* in the Ravenna Cosmography – partly based on a cropmark that has been interpreted as a bath-house (Griffith 1984, 24) – although others have argued that it was at Bury Barton (Rivet and Smith 1981, 424–5; Todd 1987, 199; 2002). The distance between Exeter and North Tawton (26 km) is similar to Pomeroy Wood (24 km) and Dainton Elms Cross, in Ipplepen (26 km), but its identification as a local centre is yet to be confirmed. There is another possible roadside settlement north of Exeter, at Shortlands Lane in Cullompton. Although Morris (2014) interprets this as an enclosed farmstead, Thomas (2018, 47) has made the case for it being a series of regularly arranged ditched tenement plots associated with a pottery assemblage containing a relatively high proportion of imports.

Romano-Celtic temples and shrines

That the landscape to the east of the Blackdown and Quantock Hills saw greater cultural change following the Roman conquest than that to the west is also seen in the distribution of Romano-Celtic temples (Fig. 3.7). Across Dorset and all but the far west of Somerset these were a common feature of both the urban and the rural landscape, but until recently none had been found within the Dumnonian *civitas*, although an example of timber construction has recently been excavated on the edge of the local centre at Dainton Elms Cross. There were, however, ritual places of different character across the South-West Peninsula. Two sites have features interpreted as 'ritual shafts' – Cadbury Castle, north of Exeter (Wilkes *et al.* 2012) and Bosence, in St Irth, Cornwall (Thomas 2018, 43) – and while both could have been dug as wells, the character of the material culture that was dumped into them suggests that they may have been associated with religious sites. The over 300 brooches – some of continental manufacture – from Nornour, in the Isles of

Scilly, point towards a coastal shrine visited by passing ships (Butcher 2014).

Villas: architecture and identity amongst the land-owning

An indication of a community's attitude towards *Romanitas* was whether they adopted new forms of architecture and engaged with the market economy in order to procure building materials and the skills of specialised builders/craftsmen. The most obvious indication of this is the construction of villas, although mapping their distribution is far from easy. This is reflected in the way that Jones and Mattingly's (1990) map 7.6 and Millett's (1990) figure 48 – published in the same year – are so different. The problem is that one archaeologist's 'villa' is another's 'substantial building', and some have had a pretty low evidential threshold (*e.g.* Scott 1993). The criteria used here – that a villa was a residential building of Roman design, stone construction, and with a minimum of mortared floors, plastered walls and a tiled roof (Rippon 2018a, 140–7) is pitched in the middle ground: it acknowledges that buildings could be regarded as a villa even if they lacked under-floor heating and mosaic pavements, but they should be more than simply a stone-built farmhouse. Some previous attempts at mapping villas acknowledge these problems by distinguishing certain from probable sites (*e.g.* Millett 1990, fig. 48), and in this study an attempt is made to differentiate certain, probable and possible villas. This is one reason why Fig. 3.8 is somewhat different to the RSRB's mapping (Brindle 2016, fig. 10.4), others being that the latter only includes the two examples excavated before 2015, whereas Fig. 3.8 includes sites that have seen more recent excavation or have been revealed through survey.

The distribution of villas in Fig. 3.8 is based upon a reassessment of the primary data, and sites that have previously been called villas have not been accepted uncritically. There are 243 sites in Cornwall, Devon, Dorset and Somerset that in the past have been classed as villas although a reassessment of the evidence suggests that only 52 of these can be regarded as certain (that have seen large-scale excavation or have a very clear plan from cropmarks or geophysical survey), 41 probable (based upon evidence for a high-status building in the Roman architectural tradition, with elements that are indicative of a villa but which have only been investigated to a limited extent), and 39 possible, giving a total of 132: based upon present evidence the rest should be regarded simply as substantial buildings.

Figure 3.8 shows a very marked regional variation in the distribution of villas, with large numbers as far west as the Blackdown and Quantock Hills but very few examples further west with just a small number in the hinterland of

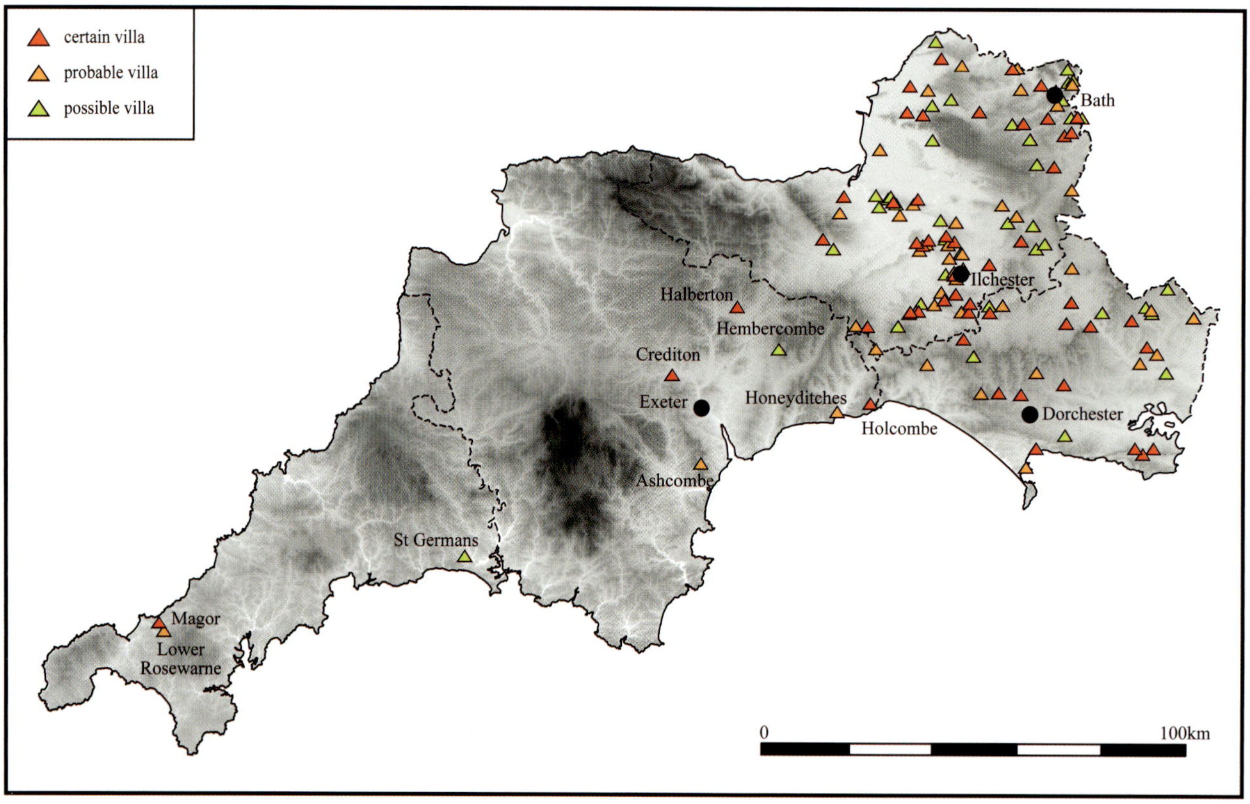

Fig. 3.8 Romano-British villas across the wider South-West (drawn by David Gould)

Exeter including definite examples at Crediton (Fig. 3.9; Griffith 1988) and Halberton (unpublished), and a probable example at Ashcombe near Dawlish (where unstratified scatters of *tesserae* and tile have been found through fieldwalking: Devon HER MDV29550). An antiquarian reference to a 'mosaic pavement' found in 1730 at Hembercombe in Broadhembury may be related to another villa, on the western flanks of the Blackdown Hills. There are three potential sites in Cornwall, although only one of these – Magor (O'Neil 1933) – is certain. At Lower Rosewarne, *tesserae* attached to 'concrete' [mortar?] were found in the garden of a cottage during the digging of a trench for a water pipe in 1980. Although just 1.8 km from Magor, contemporary references make it clear that this was an entirely separate site, and it was subsequently reported that in the 1970s a chunk of tessellated floor, loose *tesserae*, samian pottery and a Roman coin were found in the nearby garden of 40 Tehidy Road just 50 m away (CornHER 26671; Mattingly 2006, 406). The other potential site is at St Germans in south-eastern Cornwall where an early history of Cornwall describes how 'several years ago a tesselated pavement about ten feet square, was found about fifty yards from the present east window of the church; portions of it are still preserved there' (Polsue 1868, 60; Pastscape monument no. 436627).

Any archaeological distribution map will be incomplete, and new villas are occasionally discovered such as Sandy Lane, in Cannington (Hart and Mudd 2018), Yarford (King and Grande 2015) and Lopen (Cosh and Neal 2005, 247–52), all in Somerset, and Halberton in Devon. While the discovery of a Roman limekiln at Whitehill, near Newton Abbot, is suggestive of a major Roman building of unknown character (Randall and Hughes 2020), the fact remains that there are very few villas in the South-West Peninsula compared to Dorset and Somerset. It is also significant that many of the Roman villas were first recorded by antiquarians, and it is difficult to see how this could have led to such a skewed distribution as there were just as many well-educated and well-travelled gentlemen living in Devon and Cornwall – who were busy recording plenty of other archaeological finds (Cobley 2016) – as there were elsewhere. Overall, as Cornwall, Devon, Dorset and Somerset have seen similar levels of antiquarian activity, as well as similar amounts of modern archaeological survey/excavation (*e.g.* Smith *et al.* 2016, figs 4.3 and 10.3), the very different densities of Roman villas on either side of the Blackdown Hills and Quantock Hills does appear to reflect a genuine difference in the character of their Romano-British settlement patterns.

There is nothing about these villas to suggest that they were anything other than country houses and estate centres of the landowning elite, with distinct clusters around towns such as Bath and Ilchester. This clustering of villas around towns is very common across Roman Britain and could be accounted for in a variety of ways. It may reflect a geographical-economic relationship with their proximity to a market centre and its associated road network making it easier for landowners to sell surplus agricultural produce

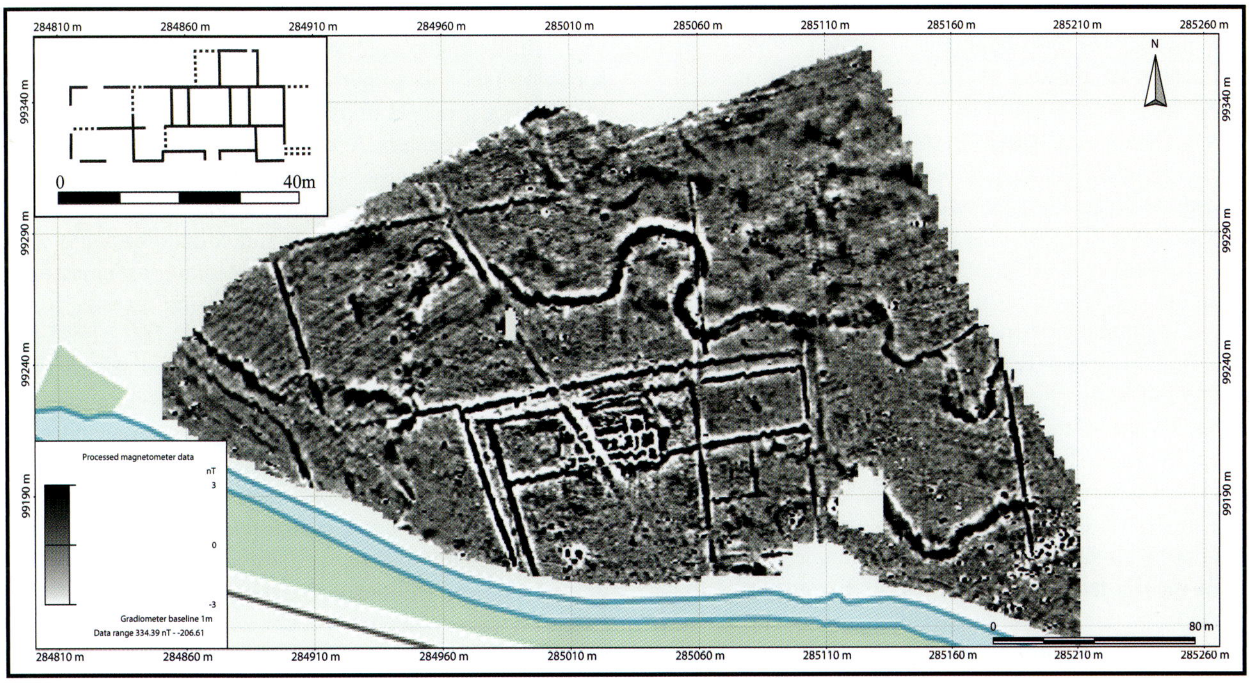

Fig. 3.9 Geophysical survey of the villa south of Downes, near Crediton (© Substrata and Devon County Council; also reproduced with kind permission of the Downes Estate and Historic England), and transcription of the plan of the main building from aerial photographs (Griffith 1988, fig. 1)

to the non-agricultural urban population and then employ the craftsmen and materials required for the construction of villas (*e.g.* Branigan and Miles 1989). The small number of villas, and other relatively (in the context of Devon; see below) wealthy farmsteads around Exeter, may also reflect this. Another possibility is that villas clustered around towns because they were the rural residences of those involved in civic administration (Millett 2016, 704), just as medieval towns contained urban houses of the aristocracy who otherwise resided in their various rural castles.

Further south and west of Exeter, however, the picture appears to have been somewhat different with the only certain villa being the mid 2nd-century AD structure at Magor, near Cambourne (O'Neil 1933). It has a winged-corridor plan in which the portico had a tessellated pavement and other floors were of *opus signinum*, while some walls were decorated with painted plaster; no rooms had under-floor heating. Such a structure elsewhere in Roman Britain would be regarded as a villa, and a geophysical survey has apparently shown that it lies within a ditched enclosure (Griffith 1988, 139; Mattingly 2006, 406; Thomas 2018, 36) which is typical of native farmsteads whose occupants went on to create small villas (*e.g.* Yarford, in Kingston St Mary, and Sandy Lane, in Cannington, both in western Somerset: King and Grande 2015; Hart and Mudd 2018; and Holcombe in eastern Devon: Pollard 1974). Its isolated location – some 95 km south-west of Exeter – has, however, led to speculation that it may have been the residence of an imperial official, lessee or contractor associated with overseeing the tin industry (*e.g.* Todd 1987, 221–2; Mattingly 2006, 407).

There are other places in Devon that have produced small amounts of Roman tile, and while some of this may have been from rural buildings with tiled roofs, several of the sites are military in origin and so the tile may have come from a bath-house (*e.g.* the forts at Bury Barton, North Tawton and Okehampton). Elsewhere the tile is from secondary contexts which suggest that it had been transported from elsewhere such as the box-flue tile from Totnes Castle (Rigold 1954, 250): roof tile has also been found at nearby Dartington (Bidwell 1980, 58, n. 49) and it should not be a surprise to find a major building close to this important crossing point of the River Dart. Roofing and flue tile from reclaimed land within Plymouth's harbour at Sutton Pool (Bidwell 1980, 58, n. 49; Barber 1986) and the motte at Okehampton Castle (Bidwell 1982) has also clearly been transported from elsewhere, in the case of the latter presumably the nearby fort (movement of Roman tile during the medieval period also occurred within the hinterland of Exeter, for example where it has been incorporated into the fabric of Exminster church: Allan *et al.* 2009; and see EAPIT 2, Chapter 13.3). In sum, there is very little Roman tile beyond the immediate hinterland of Exeter that is not either from a known military site, a major roadside settlement, or in a secondary context, and it appears, therefore, that the landed elite living in these more distant areas did not embrace Roman styles of architecture to the same extent as their neighbours in the hinterland of Exeter.

Lower-status rural settlement

The RSRB project identified three types of lower-status settlement across the wider South-West: open, enclosed farmsteads, and complex farmsteads (Smith *et al.* 2016; Allen *et al.* 2017). It was argued that within their dataset 'open farmsteads are almost exclusively a later Iron Age phenomenon' (Allen and Smith 2016, 21), but this settlement type is surely under-represented in the archaeological record as they do not show up as well through aerial photography and geophysical survey. Enclosed farmsteads are 'settlements where all, or the majority, of domestic and associated activity was contained within one or two enclosures and where internal space was not further sub-divided' (Allen and Smith 2016, 23) and this appears to have been the dominant tradition across the South-West Peninsula throughout the Roman period (*e.g.* Figs 3.10–3.11). Enclosed farmsteads were also common in southern and central Britain during the Late Iron Age and Early Roman period, although here they were replaced by 'complex farmsteads' that the RSRB defines as 'settlements where there appears to be significant differentiation of space, either as a system of conjoined enclosures or as a principal outer enclosure with many internal sub-divisions' (Allan and Smith 2016, 28, *e.g.* Fig. 3.12).

Possible complex farmsteads in the hinterland of Exeter

The shift from enclosed to complex farmsteads was seen across Dorset and Somerset (Fig. 3.14A), but the RSRB identified just one example in the South-West Peninsula: the 2nd to 4th-century AD enclosure at Shepherd's Lane, in Teignmouth (Haines 2013). This site plan was, however, derived from geophysical survey and it was only subject to limited evaluation trenching and so the phasing of the different elements of the enclosure complex could not be established with confidence: if all the features were contemporary it could indeed be a complex farmstead, but some of the elements may be sequential. Another characteristic of a true complex farmstead is their relative abundance of artefacts, and this was not seen at Shepherd's Lane (Tom Brindle pers. comm.). It does, however, appear to be different to the simple square enclosures that are otherwise so common in Devon (cf. Figs 13.10 and 13.13), and so it is regarded here as a 'possible complex farmstead' until further excavations have taken place.

Shepherd's Lane lies 18 km south of Exeter in an area with other settlements that, for Devon, are relatively high status including the probable villa at Ashcombe (see above) and another possible complex farmstead at Aller Cross, in Kingskerswell (Fig. 3.13). Aller Cross

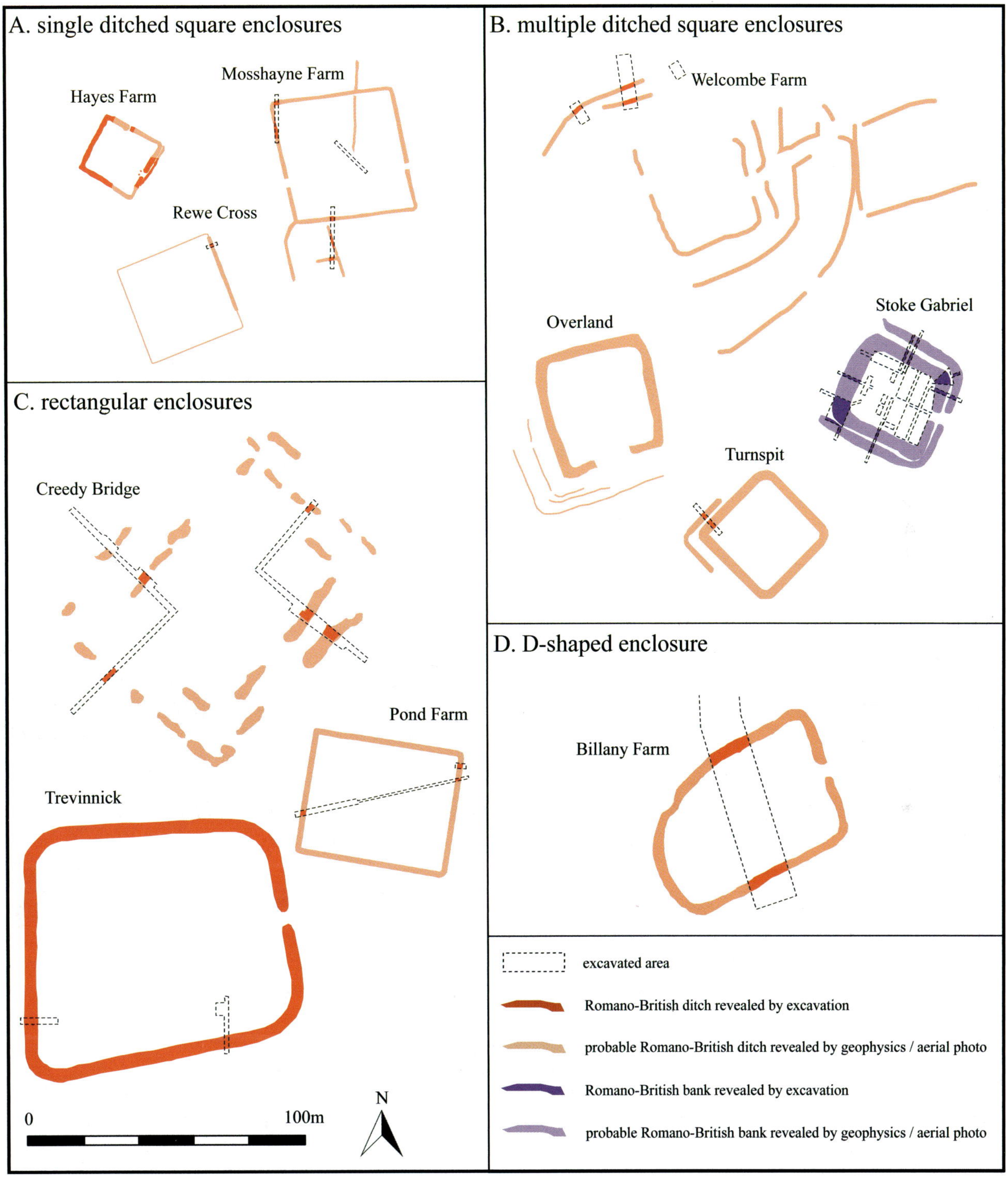

Fig. 3.10 Examples of rectilinear farmstead enclosures (Hayes Farm: Simpson et al. *1989; Hart* et al. *2014; Mosshayne Farm: Ellis 2015b; Rewe Cross: Uglow 2000; Welcombe Farm: Cunningham 2009; Overland: Uglow 2000; Stoke Gabriel: Masson Phillips 1965; Turnspit: Uglow 2000; Creedy Bridge: Caine and Rainbird 2017; Pond Farm: Jarvis 1976; Trevinnick: Fox and Ravenhill 1969; Billany Farm: Mudd and Joyce 2014) (drawn by David Gould)*

was excavated in a series of stages, with the site severely truncated by a modern road, pipeline and quarrying (Hughes 2015). The settlement originated as a later Iron Age enclosed farmstead that continued into the Early Roman period, and during the 3rd century AD a series of additional ditched enclosures were added. The interior of the main enclosure had been quarried away meaning that there is little direct evidence for the character of its buildings, although a large amount of tile, including fragments of a chimney pot, as well as the pottery, vessel

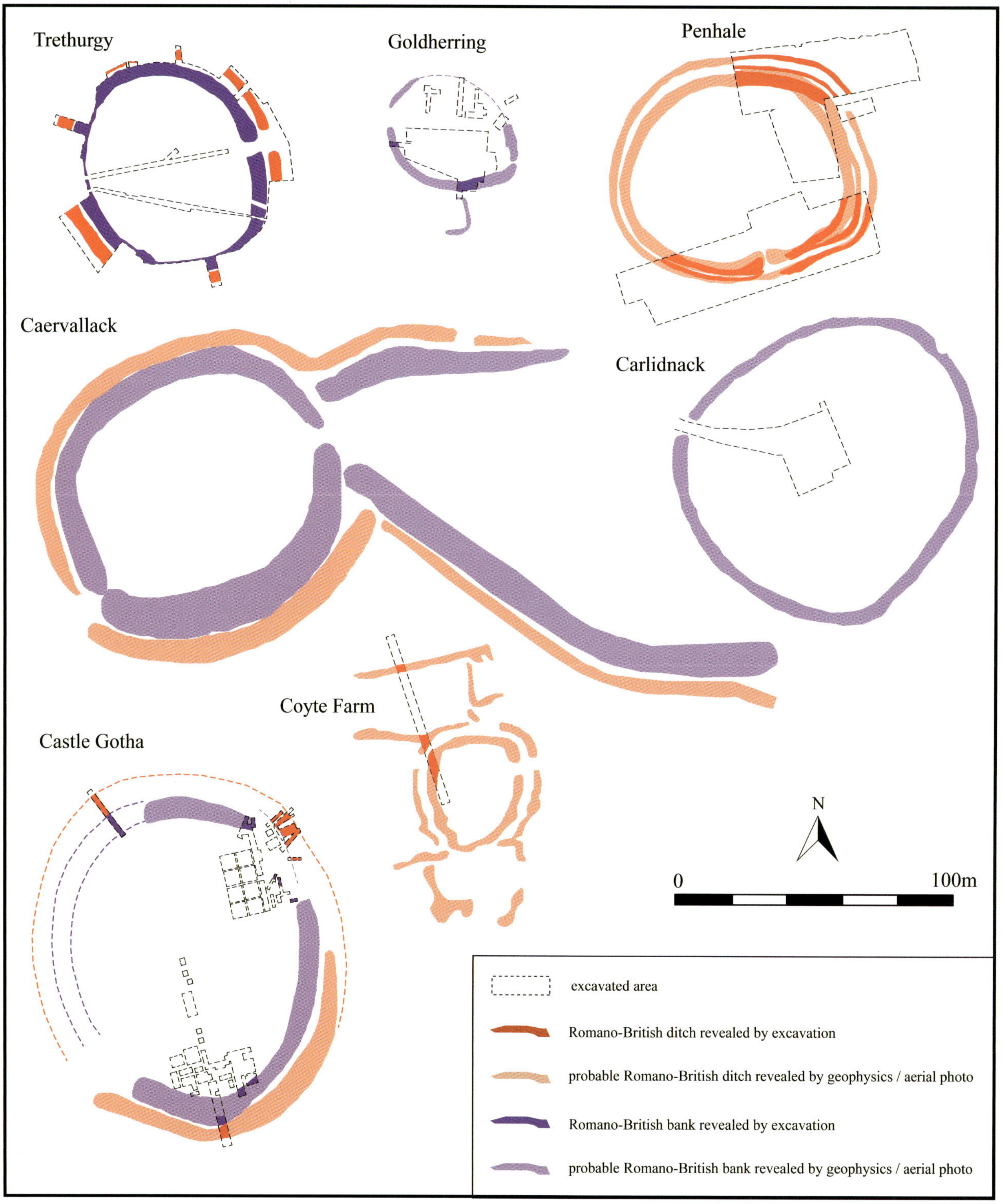

Fig. 3.11 Examples of curvilinear farmstead enclosures (Trethurgy: Quinnell 2004; Goldherring: Guthrie 1969; Penhale: Johnston et al. *1989–90; Caervallack: Edwards and Kirkham 2008; Carlidnack: Harris and Johnson 1976; Castle Gotha: Saunders and Harris 1982; Coyte Farm: Thacker 2012) (drawn by David Gould)*

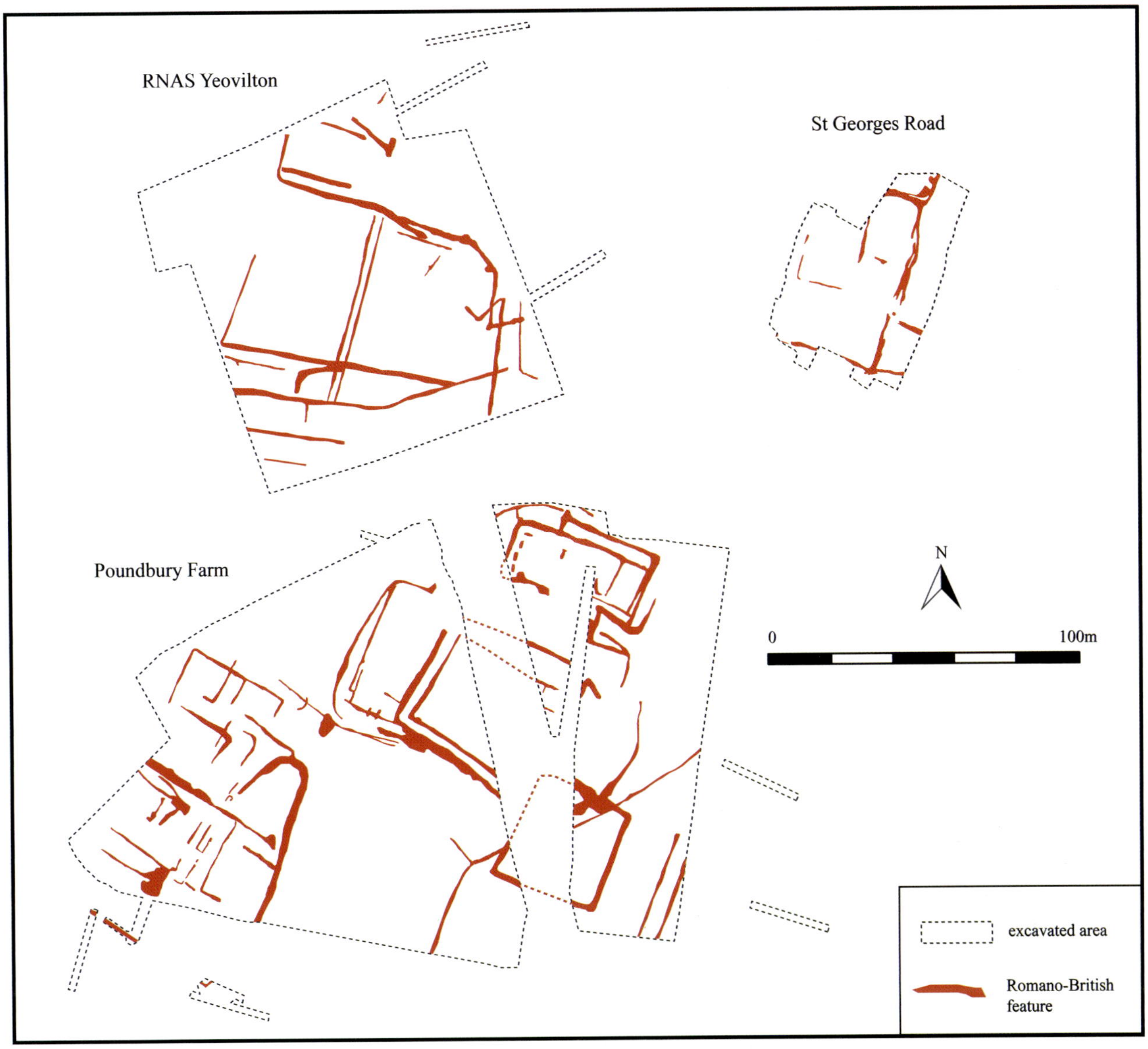

Fig. 3.12 Examples of complex farmsteads, at RNAS Yeovilton in Somerset (Lovell 2006), and St Georges Road (Smith et al. *1997) and Poundbury Farm (Dinwiddy and Bradley 2011) both near Dorchester in Dorset (drawn by David Gould)*

glass and metal objects, suggest a relatively high-status structure. There was, however, no evidence for *tesserae* or wall plaster.

There are two other sites – excavated after the RSRB's data collection – that may be more complex in their layout compared to the simple enclosed farmsteads that are typical of Devon. At Tithe Barn Green, in Monkerton (Fig. 3.13; Good and Massey 2017) – *c.* 5 km east of Exeter – only the western part of a late 1st to 2nd-century AD settlement was excavated (the rest having been destroyed by a cutting for the M5 motorway). The shared alignment of two small enclosures, possible sub-division of the space within the southern enclosure, the possible trackway between them, and associated ditches are all characteristic of a complex farmstead, but as with Shepherd's Lane it is unclear whether all of the features were contemporary; there is similarly a scarcity of finds (although this could reflect that the excavations occurred on the periphery of the site). The final example of a possible complex farmstead is the 1st to 3rd-century AD settlement at nearby Hill Barton, in Pinhoe (Fig. 3.13; Garland 2016a; Mudd *et al.* 2019). A series of enclosures, and their associated internal sub-divisions, are on the same orientation but once again a scarcity of finds means that it is unclear whether they are contemporary or sequential.

Overall, these sites – all within 20 km of Exeter – do not fulfil the criteria of true complex farmsteads as defined by the RSRB project, but are clearly differentiated from the simple enclosed farmsteads found elsewhere in Devon. They are regarded here as 'possible complex

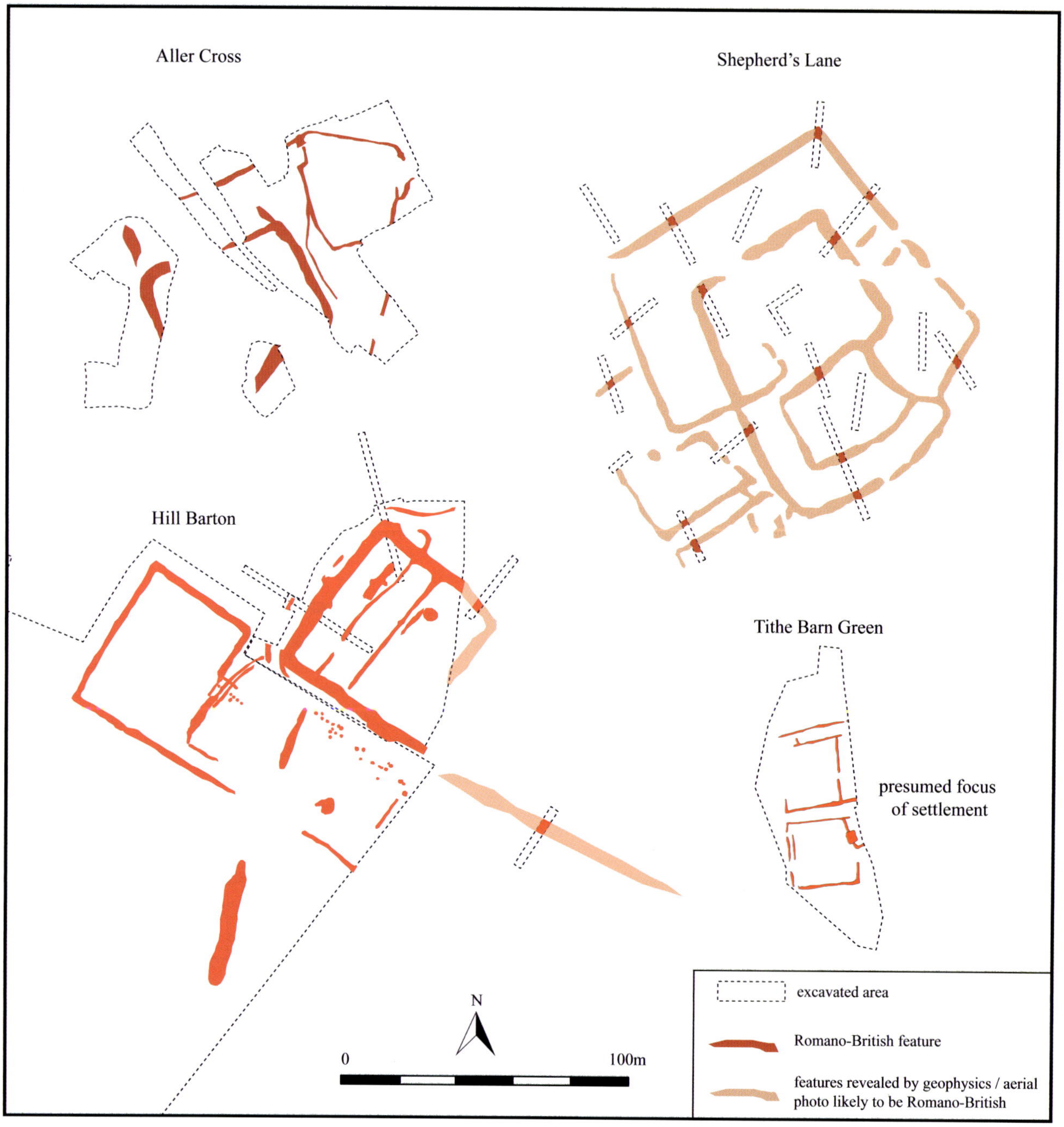

Fig. 3.13 Some possible complex farmsteads in the immediate hinterland of Exeter (Aller Cross: Hughes 2015; Shepherd's Lane: Haines 2013; Hill Barton: Farnell 2018a; Mudd et al. *2019; Tithe Barn Green: Good 2016) (drawn by David Gould)*

farms', and may be a reflection of the greater changes in landscape and society seen within the immediate hinterland of Exeter.

The morphology of settlement enclosures

Our understanding of Romano-British settlement morphology across the South-West Peninsula is largely restricted to eastern and southern Devon where rectilinear enclosures predominate, and central and western Cornwall where the majority are curvilinear, and in this the initial mapping by the RSRB project (Allen and Smith 2016, fig. 2.8) is borne out by subsequent work (Figs 3.10, 3.11 and 3.14). In Devon there are now several further rectilinear enclosures that have been excavated, with the majority being square and *c.* 30–40 m across. In other cases – where just part of the enclosure can be mapped – all that can be said is that they are rectilinear as opposed to curvilinear. This predominant rectiliniarity

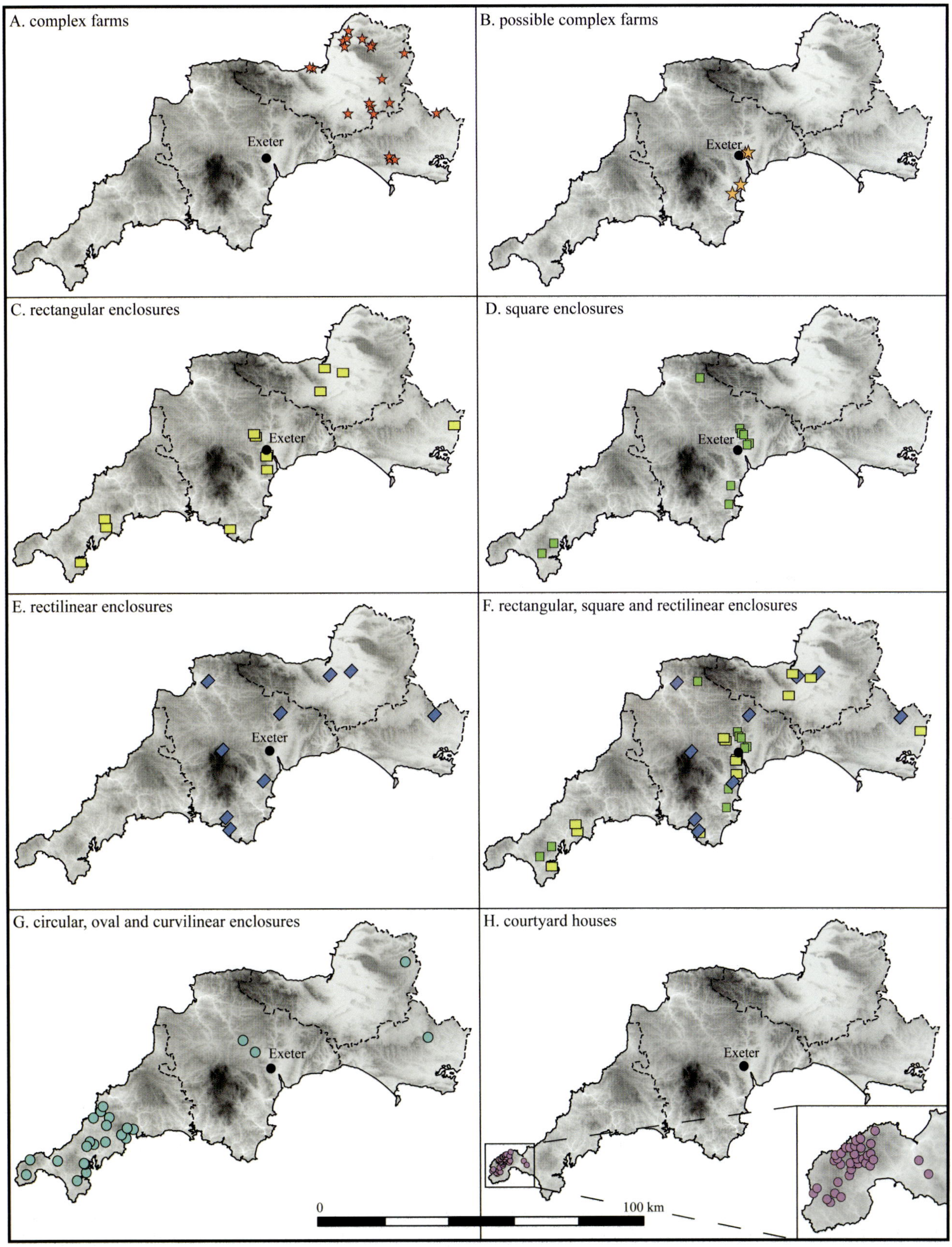

Fig. 3.14 The distribution of different lower-status rural settlement forms across the wider South-West (for villas see Fig. 3.8 above) (drawn by David Gould)

seen in the eastern region – the hinterland of Exeter – is a continuation of the pre-Roman Iron Age tradition when some enclosures were square (*e.g.* Blackhorse, in Clyst Honiton: Fitzpatrick *et al.* 1999a). Other pre-Roman enclosures in this area had some right-angled corners and some curving ones (*e.g.* Holcombe: Pollard 1974; Nether Exe: Uglow *et al.* 1985), a tradition that also continued into the Roman period in southern Devon at least (*e.g.* Billany Farm, in Dartington: Mudd and Joyce 2014, 88–94; Fig. 3.10D).

In the western part of the South-West Peninsula – modern Cornwall – the picture is very different with the majority of enclosures being curvilinear in plan – hence their local name 'rounds' (*e.g.* Trethurgy: Fig. 3.15; Quinnell 2004) – although there are a few examples of rectilinear or even polygonal enclosures. In the far west of Cornwall – the West Penwith Peninsula – there is a distinctive form of settlement associated with 'courtyard houses' that are predominantly Romano-British but which may have had Late Iron Age origins in some cases (Fig. 3.14H; Nowakowski 2016, 171–8). This is one of a series of differences in the Romano-British landscape and material culture of Cornwall that suggests that there may indeed have been two distinct communities with their own identities: the Dumnonii in the east and the Cornovii in the west.

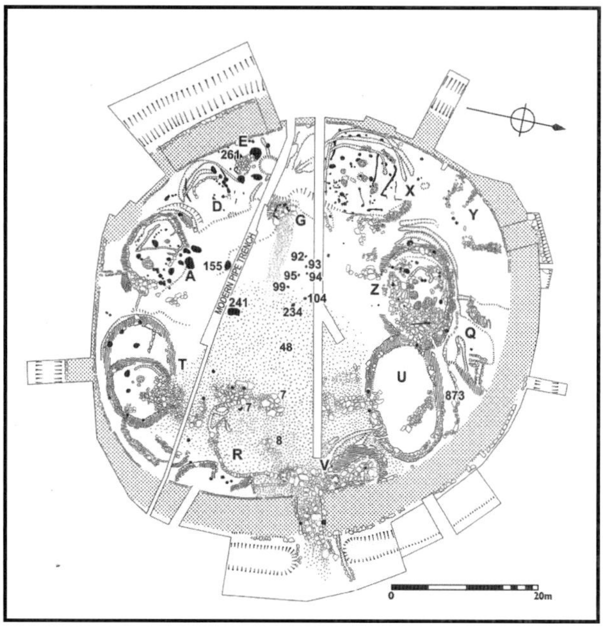

Fig. 3.15 Period 5 at Trethurgy Round, in Cornwall, constructed in the mid 2nd century AD (Quinnell 2004, fig. 5; © Cornwall Council and Henrietta Quinnell)

The expansion and contraction of rural settlement over time

An important contribution of the RSRB project has been to show regional differences in the expansion and contraction of the number of settlements in existence at any one time. In Devon, the profile is broadly similar to many parts of lowland Roman Britain, with an increase from the later Iron Age through to the first half of the 2nd century AD and then a steady decline, which contrasts with Cornwall where the high point was in the later Iron Age with a steady decline thereafter (Brindle 2016, fig. 10.8). There was a distinct cluster of new farmsteads established in the immediate vicinity of Exeter in the 2nd century AD, followed by a marked phase of abandonment during the later 3rd century (*e.g.* Overland, Rewe Cross and Turnspit, in the Exe Valley: Uglow 2000; Hayes Farm: Simpson *et al.* 1989; Old Park Farm, in Pinhoe: Mudd and Weavill 2017), whereas across other parts of Devon and indeed Cornwall there was far greater continuity into the 3rd and 4th centuries AD. This is an important piece of analysis – supported by more recently excavated sites to the east of Exeter (*e.g.* Bishops Court Extension: Govier 2017; Cranbrook water main: Hughes and Rainbird 2016; Hill Barton: Garland 2016a; Mudd *et al.* 2019; Tithe Barn Green: Good 2016; Good and Massey 2017) – but the suggested reason for the abandonment of these farmsteads – that they 'typically occupy low-lying terrain in the Exe Valley, raising the possibility that settlements in the area were adversely affected by an episode of climatic instability that appears to have begun at around the turn of the third century' (Brindle 2016, 340–2) – is simply untenable. The sites lay above areas that will have been liable to flood (*e.g.* Overland lies at 84 m OD whereas the adjacent River Exe floodplain lies at 34 m OD; Rewe Cross lies at 37 m OD whereas the adjacent River Exe floodplain lies at 23 m OD), and surely the appearance and abandonment of these sites clustered around Exeter must be related to the growth and decline of the town, and the demand for food from its non-agriculturally productive population.

Regional and intra-regional variation in domestic architecture

The evidence for individual Romano-British buildings across the South-West Peninsula has also been summarised by the RSRB (Brindle 2016; Smith 2016a) although their use of the catch-all term 'circular' is unfortunate as it disguises another important difference between the eastern and western parts of the region (Fig. 3.16). To the east – in the hinterland of Exeter – there are circular roundhouses, including at the roadside local centres at Pomeroy Wood (Fitzpatrick *et al.* 1999) and Dainton Elms Cross. In the western part of the region, however, the houses are often not circular but oval (*e.g.* Trethurgy: Fig. 3.15; Castle Gotha, near St Austell: Saunders and Harris 1982; Grambla, in Wendron: Saunders 1972; Penhale, in Fraddon: Johnson *et al.* 1998–9; Nowakowski and Johns 2015; Reawla, in Gwinear: Appleton-Fox 1992). Such oval houses are found throughout Cornwall (Smith 2016a, fig. 3.6), with the most easterly possible example being at Sherford, near Plymouth in south-western Devon (Wessex Archaeology 2018).

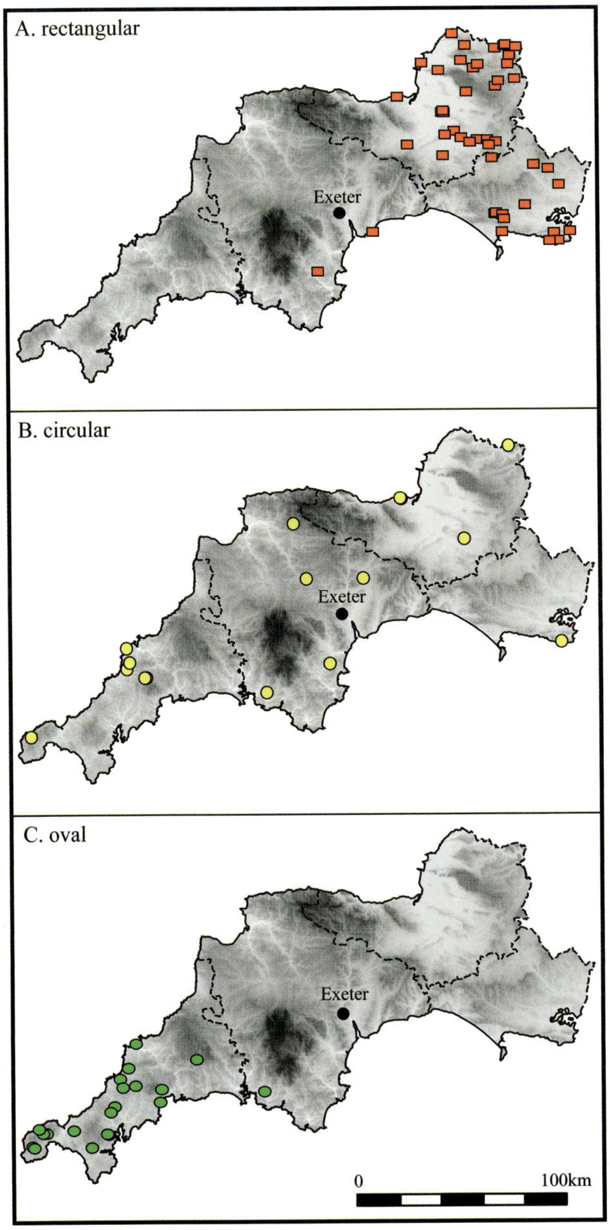

Fig. 3.16 The distribution of different rural domestic building morphologies across the wider South-West (drawn by David Gould)

Once again, therefore, in lower status rural settlements we see important variations across the wider South-West. Firstly, there are major differences between the South-West Peninsula as a whole and the areas east of the Blackdown and Quantock Hills reflected for example in the retention of traditional forms of enclosed farmsteads and non-rectangular buildings across the South-West Peninsula, and the small number of certain and potential villas being largely restricted to the immediate hinterland of Exeter. Secondly, within the South-West Peninsula there are subtle but significant intra-regional differences in the temporal development of settlement patterns such as the morphology of the enclosures (greater rectiliniarity in the east, and curviliniarity in the west), and the style of buildings (circular in the east, and oval in the west).

Romano-British farming and its pre-Roman antecedents

The population of Exeter will have been supplied with food produced in the surrounding countryside. While broad patterns of land use – the extent to which a landscape was wooded, and the balance between improved and unimproved pasture, and arable – can be reconstructed through studying pollen sequences, in order to understand which crops were being grown, and the types of animal that were grazing, we must study animal bones and charred cereals. An initial analysis of the Romano-British and medieval animal bones and charred cereals from Cornwall, Devon, Dorset and Somerset was published in *Making Sense of an Historic Landscape* (Rippon 2012) and expanded in *The Fields of Britannia* (Rippon *et al.* 2015) – that contain the basic methodology used here – and the discussion below is a development of that earlier work. The RSRB has subsequently examined Romano-British arable (Brindle 2016; Lodwick 2017) and pastoral (Allen 2017) farming but this was a broad-brush study whose focus was at a regional level, and the analysis below differs in several important ways: it covers the Iron Age, Roman and medieval periods, is a more fine-grained analysis (where possible at a *pays* level), and uses some different methodologies.

The traditional approach within palaeobotanical and zooarchaeological studies is only to use large assemblages, and when interpreting individual sites this is indeed essential. One welcome result of development-led archaeology has been an increase in palaeoenvironmental sampling although many of the resulting plant macrofossil and faunal assemblages are small. If the minimum sample size used for analysing individual assemblages — say 100 specimens — had been adopted here then many of these smaller assemblages would have been rejected. Rather than consigning these data to the spoil heap, however, such assemblages can provide useful information if sites within the same *pays* or region are aggregated. An example is the Romano-period assemblages from the 'North Somerset Hills and Vales' *pays* where there are very few assemblages of over 100 cattle, sheep/goat and pig bones, but if all the smaller assemblages from this one *pays* are combined then a far larger sample size is created (Table 3.1).

Reconstructing arable regimes through the analysis of charred cereals

Unfortunately, only one assemblage of plant macrofossils from the pre-PPG16 excavations within Exeter has been analysed and published: waterlogged deposits dating to *c.* AD 80–120 within the former fortress ditch at Friernhay Street (Straker *et al.* 1984). Although no cereal grains

Table 3.1 The aggregation of individually small animal bone assemblages from the North Somerset Hills and Valleys pays

		Unphased Roman							*Early Roman*							*Late Roman*							*All Roman*						
		Cattle		*Sheep*		*Pigs*		*Total*	*Cattle*		*Sheep*		*Pigs*		*Total*	*Cattle*		*Sheep*		*Pigs*		*Total*	*Cattle*		*Sheep*		*Pigs*		*Total*
		No.	*%*	*No.*	*%*	*No.*	*%*		*No.*	*%*	*No.*	*%*	*No.*	*%*		*No.*	*%*	*No.*	*%*	*No.*	*%*		*No.*	*%*	*No.*	*%*	*No.*	*%*	
Faulkland, Hemington	Hart 2016b; Hart and McSloy 2018								38	*31*	80	*65*	5	*4*	123	1	*33*	2	*67*	0	*0*	3	39	*31*	82	*65*	5	*4*	126
Herriots Bridge, North Widcombe	Rahtz and Greenfield 1977	62	*71*	22	*25*	4	*5*	88															62	*71*	22	*25*	4	*4*	88
Inns Court, Knowle	Jackson 2007								27	*47*	20	*35*	11	*19*	58	55	*51*	43	*40*	10	*9*	108	82	*49*	63	*38*	21	*12*	166
Kings of Wessex Academy, Cheddar	Zochowski and Holt 2018	7	*32*	14	*64*	1	*5*	22															7	*32*	14	*64*	1	*5*	22
	Green 2016	44	*47*	42	*45*	7	*8*	93															44	*47*	42	*45*	7	*8*	93
Touring Park, Cheddar	Tutt 2006	10	*48*	8	*38*	3	*14*	21															10	*48*	8	*38*	3	*14*	21
Totals		**123**	***55***	**86**	***38***	**15**	***7***	**224**	**65**	***36***	**100**	***55***	**16**	***9***	**181**	**56**	***50***	**45**	***41***	**10**	***9***	**111**	**244**	***47***	**231**	***45***	**41**	***8***	**516**

were preserved, there were 114 fragments of chaff, all except one being from wheat (of which 51 could be identified as coming from emmer or spelt, and 11 as spelt). Unfortunately the large-scale excavations at Princesshay produced few plant macrofossil assemblages, although 'a burnt layer associated with tile production (3556) included abundant wheat grains including spelt (*Triticum spelta*) alongside barley and oat grains, and a quarry pit (3557) yielded abundant hulled wheat grains, with some barley and oat grains' (Steinmetzer, Stead, Pearce, Bidwell and Allan forthcoming): it is frustrating that this assemblage was not examined beyond the assessment stage.

Thankfully, there is significantly more data on arable farming from outside Exeter and a comparative analysis of the charred grain assemblages shows that there were very different arable regimes in Cornwall, Devon and Dorset/Somerset. The approach here has been to analyse charred cereal grain numbers, which contrasts with the RSRB's analysis (Smith *et al.* 2016; Lodwick 2017) that was based simply on the presence/absence of a particular cereal on a site. This author feels that approach is deeply flawed as if there are a series of sites where *c.* 10% of the grain is barley, and *c.* 90% is wheat, the presence/absence approach will lead to all sites appearing in the analysis as simply having barley and wheat present, with no recognition that wheat was clearly the dominant crop.

Lodwick (2017, 13) also includes assemblages from corn driers despite acknowledging that this is 'likely to over-represent those crops processed in these structures', citing Rippon *et al.*'s (2015, 81) clear evidence that this is indeed the case (in the Early Roman period, for example, 95% of the grain the corn driers studied was from wheat, compared to 66% from general domestic assemblages). This means that in the RSRB's analyses wheat in particular will be over-represented, and the resultant under-representation of other crops is a particular problem in regions such as the South-West Peninsula where non-wheat cereals were particularly important. In this study, therefore, charred cereals from corn driers are not included.

Another problem with the RSRB is the inconsistent way that it discusses data across its regions. For example, figs 4.61–4.63 in Smith *et al.*'s (2016) discussion of their 'South' region present quantified analyses of animal bones and cultivated plants, but there is no equivalant analysis for the 'South-West' region. Instead, we are told that 'the meagre evidence indicates that the principal crops of the region were spelt wheat and barley in equal measure, followed by emmer wheat, with free-threshing wheat, oats and rye also occasionally present', and that 'there appears to have been little difference between Cornwall and Devon' (Smith *et al.* 2016, 354). This narrative is presumably based upon the presence/absence form of analysis, but based upon the dataset used in this study, when the 1,701 Roman grains in Devon are counted 70% are wheat and 23% oats, compared to the assemblage of 11,165 grains in Cornwall where 24% are wheat, 26% oats and 50% barley: surely this represents a significant difference between Devon and Cornwall?

One last problem with Lodwick's (2017, 18–19) analysis is that she excludes oats on the basis that they were simply weeds. She argues that this author's suggestion, that 'a higher abundance of oats in one region [the South-West] indicates that more oats were being cultivated (Rippon *et al.* 2014, 211)' overlooks the issue that different cultivation practices causes different proportions of specific weeds (Lodwick 2017, 19). Cool (2006, 71) is equally dismissive of rye and oats, suggesting that although they are recovered from Romano-British sites 'they tend to form small parts of the assemblages' and that 'it is often open to question as to whether they had been deliberately grown or were just present as weeds'. This author is not, however, the first to suggest that oats were a deliberately cultivated crop in the Roman period (*e.g.* Jones 1989, 133; Van der Veen 2016, 808), and what Lodwick chooses to overlook is the indisputable documentary evidence that oats were grown in large amounts in the South-West during the medieval period. Fox (1991, tab. 3.20), for example – the paper cited in Rippon *et al.* 2014 – has shown that during the late medieval period 62% of demesne land (the area cultivated by the lord of the manor themselves) in eastern Devon was sown with oats, with only slightly lower figures in South Devon (49%), the Cornish Coastlands (48%) and Mid- and North-Devon (42%). Campbell (2000, tab. 6.01 and fig. 6.07) has similarly shown that a series of demesnes across the South-West Peninsula during the period 1250–1349 adopted his Type 7 arable regime in which oats (67%) were the dominant cropping type. The archaeological evidence from the medieval period is also very clear, with oats forming (52%) of the charred cereal assemblages on excavated later medieval settlements across Devon (see below Chapter 4, Table 4.2). Fox (1991b, 303) argues that there was an element of cultural choice in these arable regimes, observing that the emphasis upon the coarse grains of oats and rye in the South-West 'was not a backward husbandry constrained simply by soils and by climatic conditions, for in later centuries barley and wheat became as important in Devon and Cornwall as rye and oats were in the middle ages. Lying behind the persistence of oats and rye was preference for the two crops in bread and beer, old and well established already, by the 14th century, and very slow to change'. What these crop growing preferences across the South-West Peninsula mean is that the communities living there had a different diet compared to their wheat-growing neighbours. In the medieval period, for example, it is well-documented that barley and rye were used for making bread, while oats were used in pottage (a thick soup or stew); oats were the most common grain used to make ale until it was later replaced by barley (Fox 1991b, 304).

Of course, we do not have documentary sources recording crop preferences for the Roman period, and it is possible that this indisputable dominance of oats in the later medieval period across the South-West Peninsula was an entirely new phenomenon. But in the light of this medieval evidence, surely the fact that oats are present in higher proportions in Roman-period assemblages across the South-West Peninsula than elsewhere in Roman Britain is significant. It is therefore argued here that we should not ignore oats when studying charred cereal assemblages, and along with the use of grain counts (rather than presence/absence), the exclusion of dumps of charred cereals associated with corn driers, and the inclusion of a far larger number of sites, this does mean that the analysis presented below differs from that of the RSRB project.

Iron Age charred cereals (Table 3.2; online Appendix 3.1)

In order to assess the impact on farming of Britain becoming part of the Roman world, we must start by characterising the Iron Age assemblages. As some of the sample sizes are so small, assemblages dated as Middle Iron Age, Middle to Late Iron Age, and Late Iron Age have been combined, although the period specific data is included in Table 3.2. Across the wider South-West barley accounts for 27% of the grain although this overall figure is heavily skewed by some marked regional variation. It is noteworthy that oats are present in only very small amounts (3%) although the highest figure is in Cornwall (6%) which may reflect the start of a trend seen more clearly in later periods (see below). Wheat ranged from 97% on the Dorset chalklands to just 38% in Cornwall (another trend seen in later periods). Across the wider South-West as a whole half the wheat grains are identified by type, of which 3% is emmer, 2% spelt, 95% emmer or spelt, with just 0.4% free-threshing (bread-type) wheat. Bearing in mind the very small numbers of grains identified as either emmer or spelt, it appears that the former may have been more common in Cornwall and the latter more common in Devon.

Romano-British charred cereals (Table 3.3; online Appendix 3.2)

While it is desirable to compare Early and Late Roman arable regimes, most of the specifically Early Roman material comes from Somerset making it difficult to assess the extent of change over time elsewhere. In Dorset there are sizable assemblages of charred grain from two distinctive *pays* – the chalk downland and sandy heathlands – and in both cases barley was a major crop (64% and 62% respectively) suggesting that the very light character of these soils was shaping the crop choices of local farmers. As barley was just 2% during the Middle to Late Iron Age this represents a major specialisation during the Roman period. Somerset, in contrast, saw a major shift towards wheat that rose from 57% in the Middle to Late Iron Age to 92% in the Roman period, in contrast to Cornwall where it fell from 38% to 24%, and in Devon where it declined from 93% to 70%. The far greater significance of wheat in Roman Devon compared to Cornwall may be yet another indication of the different socio-economic conditions in the two halves of the South-West Peninsula. That the boundary between these sub-regions was the Tamar Valley (or its western watershed) is supported by the charred cereal assemblage at Sherford, near Plymouth, where the as yet unquantified charred cereal assemblage is dominated by spelt (Wessex Archaeology 2018, 61). The distinctiveness of arable regimes across the South-West Peninsula is also seen in the rise in oats from 6% in Cornwall and 2% in Devon during the Iron Age to 26% and 23% respectively in the Roman period. These marked regional variations in arable regimes across the wider South-West probably reflect a combination of farmers' understanding of their local environment, the extent to which they took an active part in the market economy in which wheat appears to have been favoured, and local cultural preferences and traditions (as we know was the case in the medieval period).

Reconstructing animal husbandry through the study of faunal remains

Previous studies have suggested that there were significant variations in animal husbandry during the Roman period across the South-West (*e.g.* Rippon 2012; Rippon *et al.* 2015), and that work can now be updated. The methodology used here follows that outlined in these previous studies: attention focuses on the major domesticates (cattle, sheep/goat and pig), and the quantification is based upon NISP (Number of Identified Specimens) as this is the only data available for the vast majority of assemblages (and is the approach used in the RSRB: Smith *et al.* 2016; Allen 2017). Unfortunately, some important sites including Butcombe (Fowler 1968; 1970), Catsgore 1970–3 (Leech 1982) and Gatcombe (Branigan 1977), all in Somerset, had to be excluded as they use MNI (Minimum Number of Individuals) and the several different ways of calculating this – that themselves produce different results (Lambacker *et al.* 2016) – cannot be compared directly to NISP. Whilst individual assemblages are only discussed if they contain over a hundred cattle, sheep/goat and pig bones, smaller assemblages are used where they can be combined with others of the same date, from sites of the same socio-economic status, and from the same *pays*. Animal burials are excluded, and it is frustrating that some reports do not disaggregate these from the general domestic refuse when providing fragment counts as it leads to those sites having to be removed from this analysis too. Bone preservation varies enormously across different *pays*: on the chalk downland and limestone hills that dominate the eastern region preservation is excellent, whereas across the South-West Peninsula acidic soils mean that there are

Table 3.2 Iron Age cereals from across the wider South-West, excluding wetland sites and material from corn driers, etc.(based on the sites listed in Appendix 3.1)

Site	Oats		Barley		Rye		Emmer wheat		Spelt wheat		Emmer or spelt		Free-threshing wheat		Total identified wheat		Total unidentified wheat		Total wheat		Total
	No.	%	No.	%	No.	%	No.	%	No.	%	No.	%	No.	%	No.	%	No.	%	No.	%	
Early Iron Age (800 BC – 300 BC)																					
Cornwall	10	*3*	15	*4*	0	*0*	0	*0*	0	*0*	253	*100*	0	*0*	253	*70*	107	*30*	360	*94*	385
Devon	3	*9*	10	*29*	0	*0*	1	*5*	0	*0*	21	*95*	0	*0*	22	*100*	0	*0*	22	*63*	35
Somerset							No data for this period														
Dorset chalkland	20	*16*	17	*13*	0	*0*	0	*0*	0	*0*	85	*96*	4	*4*	89	*98*	2	*2*	91	*71*	128
TOTALS	**33**	***6***	**42**	***8***	**0**	***0***	**1**	***0***	**0**	***0***	**359**	***99***	**4**	***1***	**364**	***77***	**109**	***23***	**473**	***86***	**548**
Middle Iron Age (300 BC – 100 BC)																					
Cornwall	0	*0*	391	*71*	0	*0*	21	*13*	7	*4*	131	*81*	3	*2*	162	*100*	0	*0*	162	*29*	553
Devon	0	*0*	16	*29*	0	*0*	0	*0*	0	*0*	28	*97*	1	*3*	29	*73*	11	*28*	40	*71*	56
Somerset	8	*5*	70	*46*	0	*0*	9	*47*	6	*32*	0	*0*	4	*21*	19	*25*	57	*75*	76	*50*	154
Dorset chalkland	0	*0*	14	*<0.1*	0	*0*	0	*0*	0	*0*	0	*0*	0	*0*	0	*0*	6146	*100*	6146	*99.9*	6160
TOTALS	**8**	***<0.1***	**491**	*7*	**0**	***0***	**30**	***14***	**13**	***6***	**159**	***76***	**8**	***4***	**210**	***3***	**6214**	***97***	**6424**	***93***	**6923**
Middle to Late Iron Age																					
Cornwall	10	*28*	5	*14*	0	*0*	0	*0*	0	*0*	20	*95*	1	*5*	21	*100*	0	*0*	21	*58*	36
Devon	7	*5*	1	*1*	0	*0*	9	*26*	18	*52*	0	*0*	8	*22*	35	*28*	88	*72*	123	*94*	131
Somerset	422	*4*	4581	*40*	0	*0*	121	*2*	3	*0*	6129	*98*	1	*0*	6254	*96*	280	*4*	6534	*57*	11537
Dorset chalkland	17	*6*	96	*34*	1	*0*	17	*23*	47	*64*	3	*4*	6	*8*	73	*43*	97	*57*	170	*60*	284
TOTALS	**456**	***4***	**4683**	***39***	**1**	***<0.1***	**147**	***2***	**68**	***1***	**6152**	***96***	**16**	***0***	**6383**	***93***	**465**	***7***	**6848**	***57***	**11988**
Late Iron Age (100 BC+)																					
Cornwall	32	*22*	16	*11*	0	*0*	0	*0*	0	*0*	0	*0*	0	*0*	0	*0*	95	*100*	95	*66*	143
Devon	3	*1*	8	*3*	0	*0*	0	*0*	20	*7*	256	*93*	0	*0*	276	*100*	0	*0*	276	*96*	287
Somerset	1	*5*	1	*5*	0	*0*	3	*18*	0	*0*	14	*82*	0	*0*	17	*100*	0	*0*	17	*89*	19
Dorset chalkland	10	*15*	27	*40*	0	*0*	0	*0*	4	*100*	0	*0*	0	*0*	4	*13*	27	*87*	31	*46*	68
TOTALS	**46**	***9***	**52**	***10***	**0**	***0***	**3**	***1***	**24**	***8***	**270**	***91***	**0**	***0***	**297**	***71***	**122**	***29***	**419**	***81***	**517**

(Continued)

Table 3.2 Iron Age cereals from across the wider South-West, excluding wetland sites and material from corn driers, etc.(based on the sites listed in Appendix 3.1) (Continued)

Site	Oats		Barley		Rye		Emmer wheat		Spelt wheat		Emmer or spelt		Free-threshing wheat		Total identified wheat		Total unidentified wheat		Total wheat		Total
	No.	%	No.	%	No.	%	No.	%	No.	%	No.	%	No.	%	No.	%	No.	%	No.	%	
All M–LIA Iron Age combined																					
Cornwall	42	*6*	412	*56*	0	*0*	21	*11*	7	*4*	151	*83*	4	*2*	183	*66*	95	*34*	278	*38*	732
Devon	10	*2*	25	*5*	0	*0*	9	*3*	38	*11*	284	*84*	9	*3*	340	*77*	99	*23*	439	*93*	474
Somerset	431	*4*	4652	*40*	0	*0*	133	*2*	9	*0*	6143	*98*	5	*0*	6290	*95*	337	*5*	6627	*57*	11710
Dorset chalkland	27	*0*	137	*2*	1	*0*	17	*22*	51	*66*	3	*4*	6	*8*	77	*1*	6270	*99*	6347	*97*	6512
TOTALS	**510**	***3***	**5226**	***27***	**1**	***<0.1***	**180**	***3***	**105**	***2***	**6581**	***95***	**24**	***0.4***	**6890**	***50***	**6801**	***50***	**13691**	***70***	**19428**

Table 3.3 Romano-British cereals from across the wider South-West, excluding wetland sites and material from corn driers, etc.(based on the sites listed in Appendix 3.2)

Site	Oats		Barley		Rye		Emmer wheat		Spelt wheat		Emmer or spelt		Free-threshing wheat		Club wheat		Total identified wheat		Total unidentified wheat		Total wheat		Total
	No.	%	No.	%	No.	%	No.	%	No.	%	No.	%	No.	%	No.	%	No.	%	No.	%	No.	%	
Early Roman (1st – 2nd century AD)																							
Cornwall	8	*57*	1	*7*	0	*0*	0	*0*	0	*0*	5	*100*	0	*0*	0	*0*	5	*0*	0	*0*	5	*36*	14
Devon	52	*19*	33	*12*	0	*0*	49	*31*	99	*62*	0	*0*	11	*7*	0	*0*	159	*82*	35	*18*	194	*70*	279
Somerset	24	*1*	34	*1*	0	*0*	0	*0*	2125	*95*	48	*2*	63	*3*	0	*0*	2236	*95*	119	*5*	2355	*98*	2413
Dorset chalkland							No data for this period																
Dorset heathland	36	*32*	20	*25*	0	*0*	0	*0*	0	*0*	10	*67*	5	*33*	0	*0*	15	*27*	40	*73*	55	*49*	113
TOTALS	**120**	***4***	**90**	***3***	**0**	***0***	**49**	***2***	**2224**	***92***	**63**	***3***	**79**	***3***	**0**	***0***	**2410**	***92***	**194**	***7***	**2609**	***93***	**2819**
Roman																							
Cornwall	2736	*25*	5491	*51*	0	*0*	8	*0*	615	*38*	691	*42*	316	*19*	0	*0*	1630	*72*	643	*28*	2273	*21*	10500
Devon	298	*27*	70	*6*	3	*0*	93	*35*	36	*14*	120	*45*	15	*6*	0	*0*	264	*35*	482	*65*	746	*67*	1117

(Continued)

Table 3.3 (Continued)

Site	*Oats*		*Barley*		*Rye*		*Emmer wheat*		*Spelt wheat*		*Emmer or spelt*		*Free-threshing wheat*		*Club wheat*		*Total identified wheat*		*Total unidentified wheat*		*Total wheat*		*Total*
	No.	*%*	*No.*	*%*	*No.*	*%*	*No.*	*%*	*No.*	*%*	*No.*	*%*	*No.*	*%*	*No.*	*%*	*No.*	*%*	*No.*	*%*	*No.*	*%*	
Somerset	99	*14*	53	*7*	0	*0*	31	*13*	89	*38*	92	*39*	22	*9*	0	*0*	234	*42*	339	*60*	573	*77*	725
Dorset chalkland	78	*11*	392	*56*	0	*0*	3	*7*	25	*54*	11	*24*	7	*15*	0	*0*	46	*18*	209	*82*	255	*36*	725
Dorset heathland	6	*17*	11	*31*	0	*0*	0	*0*	0	*0*	0	*0*	11	*100*	0	*0*	11	*157*	3	*9*	14	*20*	31
TOTALS	**3217**	***24***	**6017**	***45***	**3**	***0***	**135**	***6***	**765**	***35***	**914**	***42***	**371**	***17***	**0**	***0***	**2185**	***57***	**1676**	***44***	**3861**	***29***	**13098**
Late Roman (3rd – 4th century AD)																							
Cornwall	165	*25*	66	*10*	0	*0*	0	*0*	9	*3*	344	*96*	5	*1*	0	*0*	358	*85*	62	*15*	420	*65*	651
Devon	44	*14*	7	*2*	0	*0*	25	*16*	127	*81*	0	*0*	4	*3*	0	*0*	156	*61*	98	*39*	254	*83*	305
Somerset	22	*8*	36	*13*	0	*0*	2	*13*	14	*88*	0	*0*	0	*0*	0	*0*	16	*7*	208	*93*	224	*79*	282
Dorset chalkland	81	*3*	1712	*67*	0	*0*	26	*18*	94	*64*	19	*13*	9	*6*	0	*0*	148	*19*	622	*81*	770	*30*	2563
Dorset heathland	181	*3*	3727	*64*	0	*0*	59	*7*	303	*36*	257	*31*	53	*6*	0	*0*	672	*34*	1301	*66*	1973	*34*	5881
TOTALS	**493**	***5***	**5548**	***58***	**0**	***0***	**112**	***7***	**547**	***36***	**620**	***41***	**71**	***5***	**0**	***0***	**1350**	***37***	**2291**	***63***	**3641**	***38***	**9582**
All Roman combined																							
Cornwall	2909	*26*	5558	*50*	0	*0*	8	*0.4*	624	*31*	1040	*52*	321	*16*	0	*0*	1993	*74*	705	*26*	2698	*24*	11165
Devon	394	*23*	110	*6*	3	*0.2*	167	*29*	262	*45*	120	*21*	30	*5*	0	*0*	579	*48*	615	*52*	1194	*70*	1701
Somerset	145	*4*	123	*4*	0	*0*	33	*1*	2228	*90*	140	*6*	85	*3*	0	*0*	2486	*79*	666	*21*	3152	*92*	3420
Dorset chalkland	159	*5*	2104	*64*	0	*0*	29	*15*	119	*61*	30	*15*	16	*8*	0	*0*	194	*19*	831	*81*	1025	*31*	3288
Dorset heathland	223	*4*	3758	*62*	0	*0*	59	*8*	303	*43*	267	*38*	69	*10*	0	*0*	698	*34*	1344	*66*	2042	*34*	6025
TOTALS	**3830**	***15***	**11653**	***46***	**3**	***<0.1***	**296**	***5***	**3536**	***59***	**1597**	***27***	**521**	***9***	**0**	***0***	**5950**	***59***	**4161**	***41***	**10111**	***39***	**25599**

very few assemblages from rural sites. Where possible the Roman material has been divided between early and late, although many assemblages are simply dated as 'Roman'. The faunal remains from Exeter are discussed by Mark Maltby in Chapters 5–8 below, but note that he combined data from the Early and Late Roman periods, and his percentages are of all animal bones as opposed to just cattle, sheep/goat and pig, so his figures differ from those presented here.

Iron Age faunal remains (Table 3.4; online Appendix 3.3)

Although there is very little Early Iron Age material from across the wider South-West, there are significant assemblages dated as Middle Iron Age, Middle–Late Iron Age, and Late Iron Age. The proportions of the three main domesticates on non-hillfort sites in each of these three periods are fairly consistent with cattle at 33%, sheep/goat at 58%, and pig at 8%. This suggests little significant change over the course of the Middle and Late Iron Age, and so these assemblages have been combined in the following discussion. There is some evidence for local variation in animal husbandry with cattle less significant on the chalk downland and limestone (29%) than clayland *pays* (50%) – a trend that is well known (*e.g.* Hamledon 1999, 87–9) – and this is seen across the South-West in other periods too (see below, and Chapter 4). Hillforts present a rather mixed picture and this appears to reflect the character of their local environment: at Cadbury Congresbury, in Somerset – next to the rich pastures of the North Somerset Levels and the North Somerset Hills and Valleys – cattle were dominant (55%), in contrast to the limestone of Ham Hill in Somerset and chalkland of Maiden Castle in Dorset where sheep/goat dominated (*c.* 68%) and cattle were under-represented (*c.* 20%). The exceptionally high proportion of cattle at Hengistbury Head, in Dorset, is probably due to the very poor preservational conditions that favoured larger and more robust bones (Cunliffe 1987, 322), although it may also reflect the high status of this coastal trading settlement.

In the South-West Peninsula there are just two significant assemblages: the promontory hillfort at Trevealgue Head in Cornwall where cattle were 57%, and the coastal promontory and possible port-of-trade at Mount Batten beside Plymouth Sound, in Devon, where cattle were at 51%. The age-at-death data from Mount Batten, and indeed Cadbury Congresbury (Cunliffe 1988, 32; Rahtz *et al.* 1992, 186), are unusual for the Iron Age in that most of the animals were juveniles and young adults – prime beef age – with far fewer of the mature and elderly animals that dominate other Iron Age sites (including Maiden Castle and Trevelgue Head: Sharples 1991, 141; Nowakowski and Quinnell 2011, 302). This suggests that the community living at Mount Batten were consumers of food, rather than producers (the rich material culture assemblage suggests that it was a relatively high-status trading community: see above).

Romano-British faunal remains (Table 3.5; online Appendix 3.4)

It has long been known that the faunal assemblages from Romano-British sites of different social status vary significantly in their composition (*e.g.* King 1989; 1991; 1999), and this has been confirmed in more recent work (*e.g.* Rippon 2012; Rippon *et al.* 2015; Allen 2017). In this study sites have been classified as major towns (the two *civitas* capitals of Exeter and Dorchester), small towns and local centres (Bath, Crandon Bridge, Ilchester and Shepton Mallet, all in Somerset), villas, and farmsteads. These previous analyses of animal bones both nationally and from across the wider South-West have also shown that there were significant changes over the course of the Roman period, most notably a shift towards cattle, and although it was hoped to divide assemblages into Early (1st to 2nd centuries AD) and Late (3rd to 4th centuries AD) Roman, this was often not possible as so many reports lump all of the Roman-period bones together as one phase.

Across the wider South-West, and grouping all Roman-period assemblages together, on farmsteads cattle make up 27% of the cattle, sheep/goat and pig bones, and on sites where Early and Late Roman bones can be distinguished cattle increase from 23% to 40%. These figures are considerably lower than previous studies have suggested for Roman Britain as a whole, such as King's (1999, tab. 3) 47% for cattle, and Rippon *et al.*'s (2015, tab. 3.4) 49% in the Early Roman period and 53% in the Late Roman period. The relatively low figures for cattle within the wider South-West reflect, however, the dominance of chalkland sites where cattle were just 25%, in contrast to lowland *pays* with heavier soils such as the Vale of Taunton Deane (46%) and North Somerset Hills and Valleys (55%). There is very limited age-at-death data although at Shapwick and Yeovilton, in the Lowlands of Central Somerset, the majority of animals appear to have been kept into adulthood with just a small number dying very young (Gerrard with Aston 2007, 896; Lovell 2006). While it is possible that other animals were killed at prime beef age and then consumed elsewhere, the data from Ilchester and Shepton Mallet suggests that this was not a widespread practice as the majority of the individuals eaten there were adult or elderly (indicative of animals having been sent to market after they had performed a useful life in breeding, dairying or traction: Leach 1982a, 269; 1994, 175; 2001, 293; Birbeck 2002). A similar picture – of animals largely kept into adulthood – is also seen on the chalk downland of Dorset (*e.g.* Barton Field in Tarrant Hinton: Graham 2006, 164; Fordington Bottom near Dorchester: Smith *et al.* 1997, 272; Poundbury near Dorchester: Sparey Green 1987, 130) and in Dorchester (Smith 1993, 80; Woodward *et al.* 1993, 320). The small

Table 3.4 Iron Age animal bones from selected sites and pays *across the wider South-West (based on the sites listed in Appendix 3.3)*

Site	*Middle Iron Age*							*Middle to Late Iron Age*							*Late Iron Age*							*All Middle–Late Iron Age combined*						
	Cattle		*Sheep/goat*		*Pigs*		*Total*	*Cattle*		*Sheep/goat*		*Pigs*		*Total*	*Cattle*		*Sheep/goat*		*Pigs*		*Total*	*Cattle*		*Sheep/goat*		*Pigs*		*Total*
	No.	*%*	*No.*	*%*	*No.*	*%*		*No.*	*%*	*No.*	*%*	*No.*	*%*		*No.*	*%*	*No.*	*%*	*No.*	*%*		*No.*	*%*	*No.*	*%*	*No.*	*%*	
Cornwall																												
Trevelgue Head hillfort	197	*57*	101	*29*	48	*14*	346															197	*20*	101	*60*	48	*20*	346
Devon																												
Mount Batten								1423	*51*	741	*22*	781	*27*	2191								1423	*51*	741	*22*	781	*27*	2191
Somerset																												
hillforts	605	*55*	135	*12*	359	*33*	1099	245	*18*	904	*67*	194	*14*	1343								850	*35*	1039	*43*	553	*23*	2442
non-hillfort								25	*27*	63	*68*	5	*5*	93	456	*34*	715	*53*	167	*12*	1338	481	*34*	778	*54*	172	*12*	1431
Dorset																												
Maiden Castle hillfort	950	*22*	3012	*69*	405	*9*	4367								8	*18*	29	*64*	8	*18*	45	958	*22*	3041	*69*	423	*10*	4412
Dorset non-hillfort	143	*35*	233	*57*	30	*7*	406	1147	*33*	2112	*61*	228	*7*	3487	760	*33*	1304	*57*	205	*9*	2269	2050	*33*	3649	*59*	463	*8*	6162
chalk/ limestone								759	*30*	1610	*65*	126	*5*	2495	101	*21*	132	*28*	238	*51*	471	860	*29*	1742	*59*	364	*12*	2966
Clayland								1024	*51*	891	*44*	166	*8*	2017	60	*44*	62	*45*	15	*0*	137	1084	*50*	953	*44*	181	*8*	2154
marshand/ estuaryside															101	*21*	132	*28*	238	*51*	471	101	*21*	132	*28*	238	*51*	471
Hengistbury Head															255	*85*	17	*6*	28	*9*	300	255	*85*	17	*6*	28	*9*	300
All hillforts	1752	*30*	3248	*56*	812	*14*	5812	245	*18*	904	*67*	194	*14*	1343	8	*18*	29	*64*	8	*18*	45	2005	*28*	4181	*58*	1024	*14*	7200
All non-hillfort	143	*35*	233	*57*	30	*7*	406	1172	*33*	2175	*61*	233	*7*	3580	1216	*34*	2019	*56*	372	*10*	3607	2531	*33*	4427	*58*	635	*8*	7593
Iron Age total (including Hengistbury and Mount Batten)	1895	*30*	3481	*56*	842	*14*	6218	2840	*40*	3820	*54*	1208	*17*	7114	1479	*37*	2065	*52*	408	*10*	3952	6214	*36*	9366	*54*	2468	*14*	17284

Table 3.5 Romano-British animal bones from sites of different types across the wider South-West (based on the sites listed in Appendix 3.4). The data for selected pays *is given where there is a significant sample size*

Site	*Early Roman*							*Unphased Roman*							*Late Roman*							*All 'Roman' combined*						
	Cattle		*Sheep/ goat*		*Pigs*		*Total*	*Cattle*		*Sheep/ goat*		*Pigs*		*Total*	*Cattle*		*Sheep/ goat*		*Pigs*		*Total*	*Cattle*		*Sheep/ goat*		*Pigs*		*Total*
	No.	*%*	*No.*	*%*	*No.*	*%*		*No.*	*%*	*No.*	*%*	*No.*	*%*		*No.*	*%*	*No.*	*%*	*No.*	*%*		*No.*	*%*	*No.*	*%*	*No.*	*%*	
Cornwall																												
Farmsteads								**349**	***20***	**1259**	***73***	**113**	***7***	**1721**								**349**	***20***	**1259**	***73***	**113**	***7***	**1721**
Devon																												
Farmsteads								**58**	***34***	**95**	***55***	**20**	***12***	**173**								**58**	***34***	**95**	***55***	**20**	***12***	**173**
Somerset																												
Farmsteads (for selected *pays* with large samples sizes see below)	**144**	***24***	**420**	***69***	**45**	***7***	**609**	**1766**	***36***	**2592**	***52***	**588**	***12***	**4946**	**832**	***39***	**1172**	***54***	**151**	***7***	**2155**	**2434**	***35***	**3711**	***54***	**721**	***11***	**6866**
Vale of Taunton Deane								437	*46*	365	*39*	144	*15*	946	18	*49*	18	*49*	1	*3*	37	455	*46*	383	*39*	145	*15*	983
Central Somerset Lowlands	67	*16*	318	*77*	27	*7*	412	253	*34*	437	*59*	56	*8*	746	324	*34*	559	*58*	74	*8*	957	644	*30*	1314	*62*	157	*7*	2115
Jurassic Limestone Hills								590	*28*	1195	*57.2*	303	*14*	2088								590	*28*	1195	*57.2*	303	*14.5*	2088
North Somerset Hills & Vales								123	*55*	86	*38*	15	*7*	224								123	*55*	86	*38*	15	*7*	224
Jurassic Clay Vales	32	*39*	43	*52*	8	*10*	83																					
unreclaimed marshland															103	*27*	258	*67*	22	*6*	383	103	*27*	258	*67*	22	*6*	383
reclaimed marshland															146	*54*	108	*40*	16	*6*	270	146	*54*	108	*40*	16	*6*	270
Villas	**244**	***36***	**398**	***58***	**39**	***6***	**681**	**120**	***52***	**67**	***29***	**43**	***19***	**230**								**364**	***55***	**465**	***32***	**82**	***14***	**911**
Dorset																												
Farmsteads	**1025**	***23***	**3190**	***72***	**240**	***5***	**4455**	**4305**	***21***	**14091**	***69***	**1901**	***9***	**20297**	**903**	***42***	**1045**	***49***	**194**	***9***	**2142**	**5220**	***25***	**13859**	***67***	**1613**	***8***	**20692**
Dorset rural chalk	651	*22*	2140	*74*	117	*4*	2908	2999	*22*	9243	*69*	1148	*9*	13390	903	*42*	1045	*49*	194	*9*	2142	4548	*25*	12404	*67*	1454	*8*	18406
Dorset rural limestone								2244	*17*	9226	*71*	1428	*11*	12898								2244	*17*	9226	*71*	1428	*11*	12898

(Continued)

Table 3.5 (Continued)

Site	*Early Roman*							*Unphased Roman*							*Late Roman*							*All 'Roman' combined*						
	Cattle		*Sheep/ goat*		*Pigs*		*Total*	*Cattle*		*Sheep/ goat*		*Pigs*		*Total*	*Cattle*		*Sheep/ goat*		*Pigs*		*Total*	*Cattle*		*Sheep/ goat*		*Pigs*		*Total*
	No.	*%*	*No.*	*%*	*No.*	*%*		*No.*	*%*	*No.*	*%*	*No.*	*%*		*No.*	*%*	*No.*	*%*	*No.*	*%*		*No.*	*%*	*No.*	*%*	*No.*	*%*	
Dorset rural heathland	342	23	1007	69	115	8	1464	155	48	142	44	28	9	325								481	28	1133	66	110	6	1724
Villas								**2513**	**48**	**2227**	**43**	**443**	**9**	**5183**								**2513**	**48**	**2227**	**43**	**443**	**9**	**5183**
Towns	**6440**	**40**	**6100**	**38**	**3726**	**23**	**16266**	**4834**	**45**	**4852**	**45**	**1070**	**10**	**10756**	**5688**	**45**	**4057**	**32**	**2917**	**23**	**12662**	**16952**	**43**	**14981**	**38**	**7682**	**19**	**39615**
Exeter (excl. fortress)	3127	50	1741	28	1354	22	6222								1986	58	749	22	693	20	3428	5113	53	2490	26	2047	21	9650
Dorchester	3136	34	3925	43	2093	23	9154	1551	33	2438	52	723	15	4712	3540	40	3118	35	2132	24	8790	8227	36	9481	42	4948	22	22656
Both major towns (Exeter and Dorchester)	6263	41	5666	37	3447	22	15376	1551	33	2438	52	723	15	4712	5526	45	3867	32	2825	23	12218	13340	41	11971	37	6995	22	32306
Ilchester and Shepton Mallet								2923	57	1939	38	301	6	5163	54	65	24	29	5	6	83	2977	57	1963	37	306	6	5246
Bath	177	20	434	49	279	31	890	6	35	8	47	3	18	17	108	30	166	46	87	24	361	281	23	580	48	338	28	1199
All small towns and local centres	3304	46	2175	31	1633	23	7112	3283	54	2414	40	347	6	6044	2148	55	939	24	785	20	3872	8725	51	5500	32	2734	16	16959
Villas	**244**	**36**	**398**	**58**	**39**	**6**	**681**	**2633**	**49**	**2294**	**42**	**486**	**9**	**5413**								**2877**	**47**	**2692**	**44**	**525**	**9**	**6094**
Farmsteads	**1169**	**23**	**3610**	**71**	**285**	**6**	**5064**	**6478**	**24**	**18037**	**66**	**2622**	**10**	**27137**	**1735**	**40**	**2217**	**52**	**345**	**8**	**4297**	**8061**	**27**	**18924**	**64**	**2467**	**8**	**29452**

number of assemblages from Lowland Cornwall and South Devon are interesting in that they show a surprisingly low proportion of cattle bones (20% and 34% respectively) and this may reflect both the more limited arable and cultural change seen in this region. At Atlantic Road near Newquay, in Cornwall, the age-at-death data suggests that cattle were killed at a variety of ages including the prime age for beef (Ingrem forthcoming).

Urban settlements – whose occupants were not primarily engaged in food production – show slightly different patterns of food consumption with cattle providing a greater proportion of the food. There are, however, important differences between towns that reflect the character of the landscape around them. Within Exeter, for example, cattle were *c.* 52% in contrast to Dorchester – on the chalk downland – where they were just *c.* 35%. There is also marked variation in the patterns of food consumption within the three Somerset small towns for which we have large faunal assemblages. The proportions of cattle (*c.* 57%) and sheep/goat (*c.* 37%) within Ilchester and Shepton Mallet – both of which lay within the Lowlands of Central Somerset were very similar, and contrasts with Bath where cattle were just 23% and sheep/goat 48% reflecting the suitability of its local limestone hills for grazing sheep. The overall figure for pig (28%) in Bath is unusually high, and as this is seen in all three assemblage from the town it is probably a genuine phenomenon.

It is frustrating that there is so little Romano-British faunal material from the South-West Peninsula, but we can infer something about animal husbandry in the hinterland of Exeter. Table 3.6 shows that in almost all cases the percentage of cattle bones is higher in a town than in its rural hinterland, the exception being late Roman Dorchester (even where the data is not skewed by Poundbury). The average proportion of cattle bones on rural sites (excluding Late Roman Dorchester) compared to nearby urban centres ranges from 52% to 69%. In Exeter – where cattle bones were 50–53% – we would therefore expect a figure of *c.* 30–32% in Exeter's rural hinterland which is comparable to the very limited data we have from Lowlands of South Devon and Cornwall (where the site averages are 34% and 20%). Overall, it does appear that cattle were far less significant in the South-West Peninsula than elsewhere in lowland Roman Britain.

Exploring Exeter's hinterland-relationships through its meat supply: the isotope evidence in the Roman period

By Gundula Müldner and Delphine Frémondeau

Isotope analysis of faunal skeletal remains is an exciting new addition to the range of methods used by archaeologists to investigate urban-hinterland relationships. Rapid advances over the last two decades, especially in the application of strontium isotope analysis for the reconstruction of mobility, have now made the study of urban meat supply through direct data for the origins of animal remains a realistic undertaking. Although bone chemistry applications have an obvious potential to contribute to key questions about the urban economy, previous studies of urban assemblages have largely been limited to small sample sizes and single chronological periods (Gan *et al.* 2018; Madgwick *et al.* 2019; Trentacoste *et al.* 2020). The EAPIT project was the first to undertake such an investigation over the *longue durée* and with an ambitious sample size. In doing so, it had a very significant advantage: Exeter lies at the boundary between two major geological provinces – the Mesozoic lithologies of South-East England and the later Palaeozoic rocks of the South-West Peninsula (see Chapter 2 above) – which are well-distinguished by strontium isotope analysis. Unlike many other historic towns in Britain, which are situated in either isotopically very homogenous or, conversely, exceedingly diverse terrains, neither ideal for discerning meaningful patterns in faunal mobility data, Exeter is therefore extremely well-suited for this kind of analysis. The isotope analysis work package within the EAPIT project had two major aims:

1) To establish major trends in Exeter's meat supply through time by investigating from where livestock was being brought to the City between the Early Roman and later medieval periods.
2) To explore whether there was transhumant grazing between the fertile lowland hinterland of Exeter and uplands such as Dartmoor before this becomes a well-documented practice in the medieval period (Fox 2012).

Strontium isotope analysis was the method of choice, as it is best suited to the research questions, and formed the main focus of this work, although other isotopic systems (oxygen, carbon, nitrogen and sulphur) were employed in order to gain information about seasonality, aspects of animal husbandry and the landscapes animals were grazing in. The detailed results of this work will be published elsewhere in a series of papers including Müldner *et al.* (forthcoming), with the raw data available through the Archaeology Data Service (Müldner *et al.* 2020), but a summary is presented below.

The principles of isotope analysis for zooarchaeology

Isotopes are atoms of the same element, but with different atomic masses. The natural abundance of different isotopes varies systematically in the environment, and this variation is usually expressed in terms of differences between isotope ratios (*i.e.* the abundance of one isotope in relation to another of the same element). Animals, just as humans (see EAPIT 2, Chapter 19), assimilate the isotopic composition of the food and water they consume into their body tissues. Depending on the element analysed,

Table 3.6 The proportion of cattle bones within selected towns compared to their hinterlands

	Early Roman			*Late Roman*			*All Roman*		
	Town	*Hinterland*	*Hinterland as % of town*	*Town*	*Hinterland*	*Hinterland as % of town*	*Town*	*Hinterland*	*Hinterland as % of town*
Dorchester (chalk)	34%	22%	65%	36%	42%*	117%	36%	25%	69%
Dorchester (with hinterland excluding Poundbury)				36%	40%	111%	36%	23%	64%
Ilchester and Shepton Mallet (Central Somerset Lowlands)	no data	16%		65%	34%	52%	57%	30%	53%
Exeter	50%	*c.* 30% (estimated		53%	*c.* 34% (estimated)		53%	*c.* 31% (estimated)	

* The figure for the Late Roman hinterland of Dorchester is inflated by Poundbury

these compositions contain information not only about the types of food consumed, but also the environments they came from. The main aim of isotope analysis of animal skeletal remains is to trace these 'isotopic signatures' back to their respective sources and thereby gain information not only about the animal's diet, but also certain characteristics of the locations it was feeding in, thus allowing inferences about animal husbandry and 'provenance' (see Makarewicz and Sealy 2015).

Strontium isotope ratios ($^{87}Sr/^{86}Sr$) in faunal remains are mostly determined by the geological substrate of the animal's feeding range, depending on the age and type of the bedrock (Bentley 2006), while oxygen isotope ratios ($^{18}O/^{16}O$, most commonly reported compared to a standard, as $\delta^{18}O$ values) track the isotope composition of the water consumed. This composition is largely controlled by temperature and rainfall amounts and therefore varies significantly between seasons (Pederzani and Britton 2019). Carbon and nitrogen stable isotope ratios ($^{13}C/^{12}C$ and $^{15}N/^{14}N$, reported as $\delta^{13}C$ and $\delta^{15}N$) in faunal remains primarily give information on animal diet. The British Isles are dominated by plants of the C_3 photosynthetic pathway, meaning there are limited isotopic differences between vegetation types. $\delta^{13}C$ and $\delta^{15}N$ variation in herbivores therefore largely reflects environmental conditions, giving clues towards animal husbandry regimes and the environments animals are feeding in (*e.g.* Schulting *et al.* 2019; Scull *et al.* 2019). Sulphur isotopes ($^{34}S/^{32}S$ or $\delta^{34}S$) provide further information on diet, but they are also linked to geographical location. Best established are the relatively large differences between coastal and inland regions, because of the significant effect of the terrestrial deposition of marine sulphur (through sea-spray or precipitation) on coastal plants. The relationship between sulphur isotope variation in bedrock and soils and biosphere $\delta^{34}S$ values allows for further differentiation of sulphur isotope signals but is still less well understood (Nehlich 2015).

Strontium isotope variation in Exeter's hinterland

Understanding local isotope baselines is an essential prerequisite for all applications of isotope analysis in archaeology. Although the link between bedrock geology and strontium isotope variation is well-established, $^{87}Sr/^{86}Sr$ ranges expected for different geological formations cannot simply be inferred from geological maps. This is because the strontium that enters the food chain is only a specific, that is the 'bioavailable', fraction of the total strontium in the environment and its isotope composition can differ significantly from that of rock strontium due to differential weathering or additional environmental strontium inputs (*e.g.* sediment slip or marine strontium transferred by rainwater; see Bentley 2006). Although the mapping of bioavailable strontium in the British Isles is relatively advanced, the South-West Peninsula in general and key geological formations like Dartmoor in particular, were only poorly characterised at the start of the EAPIT project (see Evans *et al.* 2010). Work for EAPIT therefore had to include the analysis of modern plant samples as well as animals with known life-histories to improve baseline mapping for Exeter's hinterland in order to enable sound interpretations of the archaeological faunal data. The result, the first strontium biosphere map dedicated to South-West England, is a key output of the project (Müldner *et al.* forthcoming).

The mapping confirmed the expected good separation by strontium isotopes of Mesozoic (east of Exeter and South-East England more widely) and Palaeozoic (South-West Peninsula) lithologies. It was found that biosphere $^{87}Sr/^{86}Sr$ below 0.710 occur in the South-West Peninsula only in relatively small and discrete locales. The work also allowed refining $^{87}Sr/^{86}Sr$ baseline values for the Dartmoor granite, the Culm Measures, the Devonian of South-West England (including Exmoor), and the Permo-Triassic Exeter Group (part of the New Red Sandstone: see Chapter 2 above). The sizeable overlap between biosphere ranges of at least the latter three formations demonstrated that it may not be possible to confidently distinguish between these based on strontium isotopes alone (Figs 3.17–3.18), although meaningful interpretations are still possible. The most significant result of the mapping project was the identification of areas with very distinctive 'highly radiogenic' ($^{87}Sr/^{86}Sr$ >0.714) strontium biosphere values around the fringes of Dartmoor which, based on the mapping of soil properties, probably also exist on the other granite outcrops of the

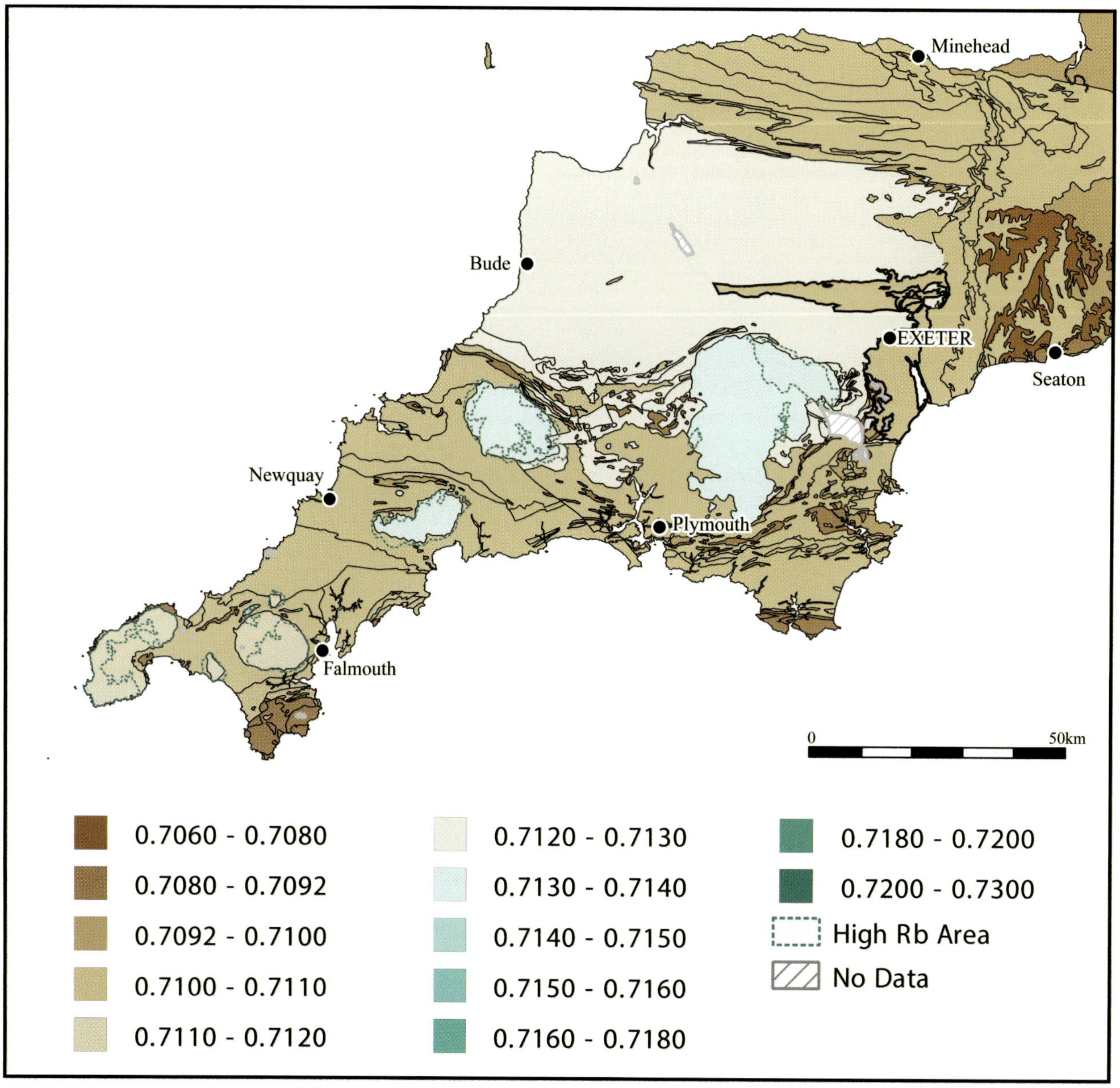

Fig. 3.17 Strontium isotope biosphere map showing median $^{87}Sr/^{86}Sr$ *for the major lithologies of the South-West Peninsula based on modern plant samples analysed for the EAPIT project and pre-existing data (see Müldner* et al. *forthcoming for details). High rubidium (Rb) areas indicate areas with distinctive 'highly radiogenic' strontium isotope values (>0.714)*

South-West Peninsula. Notably, these areas are at lower elevations (*e.g.* the valleys of north-eastern Dartmoor around Chagford, Moretonhampstead and Lustleigh) with landscapes and soils that are better suited to year-round agriculture than the high moors. The influence of the Dartmoor granite on biosphere strontium isotope values was also seen in elevated $^{87}Sr/^{86}Sr$ values in plants growing adjacent to the granite plateau, including on river meadows, which are still extensively used for livestock grazing (Müldner *et al.* forthcoming).

The archaeological animal samples

The archaeological dataset from Exeter comprises isotope data for 135 animals (70 cattle and 65 sheep), from seven chronological phases: (1) the Roman Legionary Fortress (*c.* AD 55/60–80/85), (2) the Early Roman Town (*c.* AD 160–200), (3) the Late Roman Town (late 3rd and 4th centuries AD), (4) *c.* late 10th to early 12th century (here: 'Medieval 1'), (5) *c.* AD 1150–1250 ('Medieval 2'), (6) *c.* AD 1250–1350 ('Medieval 3') and (7) *c.* AD 1350–1500 ('Medieval 4'). Unfortunately, there were too few suitable samples available from the early medieval (pre-10th century) period to produce meaningful results, so this period is not represented.

For all specimens a bulk sample of tooth enamel, representing an average $^{87}Sr/^{86}Sr$ signal over several months in the third year of each animal's life, was processed, in order to characterise the primary geological terrains that were used for livestock grazing (Minniti *et al.* 2014). Collagen carbon, nitrogen and sulphur isotope data were obtained from dentine or jaw bones of the same individuals whenever possible, for additional information. Finally, a few specimens from each time period were selected for sequential sampling of the tooth crown in order to address the question of possible transhumance. This method provides a time-resolved signal, in this case of *c.* 15–30 months of the animal's life. A combination of strontium, oxygen and carbon isotopes are used to track seasonal movement and diet (Balasse *et al.* 2002; Britton *et al.* 2009).

As expected, the strontium isotope results were the most important for addressing the main research objective of identifying major trends in Exeter's meat supply over time and will be the focus of this summary (Fig. 3.19).

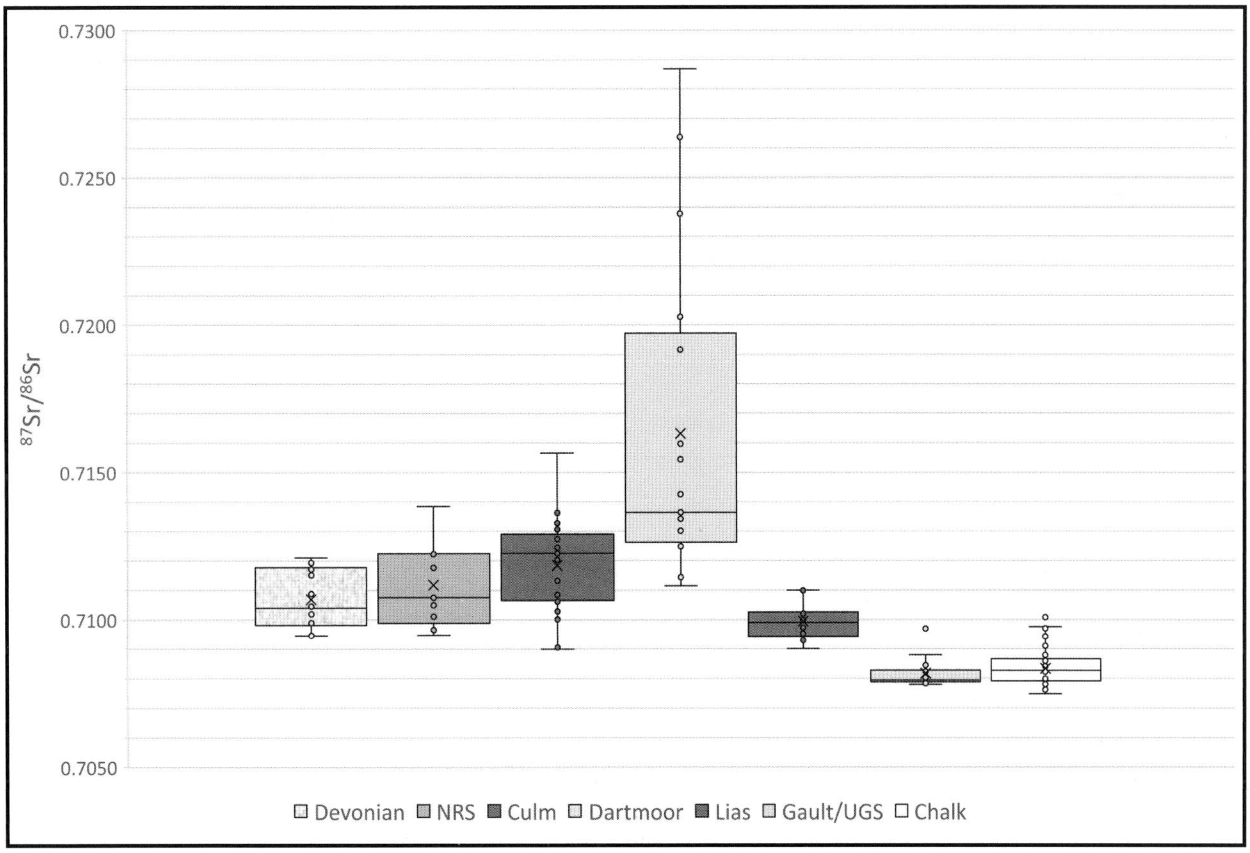

Fig. 3.18 Boxplots showing the range of biosphere strontium isotope values observed for key lithologies in Exeter's hinterland. Devonian, NRS (New Red Sandstone including Exeter Group), the Culm Measures and Dartmoor are the major Palaeozoic formations of the South-West Peninsula, while the Lias, Gault/Upper Greensand and Cretaceous Chalk the main Mesozoic formations to the east of Exeter. Simplified from Müldner et al. *(forthcoming) (drawn by Gundula Müldner)*

The legionary fortress phase (*c*. AD 55/60 to 80/85) is the only time period when a sizeable proportion of the animals evidently originated from terrains east of Exeter (8/23 samples (35%) with $^{87}Sr/^{86}Sr$ below 0.7100), and they were presumably brought to the site through the supply lines of the Roman army. Pottery studies have highlighted the special importance of two areas for the provisioning of the fortress at Exeter: South-East Dorset around Poole Harbour (the source of South-East Dorset BB1 pottery, and possibly salt), and the western side of the Blackdown Hills (the source of South-Western BB1 pottery: Holbrook and Bidwell 1991, 16–17; and see EAPIT 2, Chapter 12). The isotope values of the livestock would be consistent with either of these areas, although the data would also fit most of the South Coast or, indeed, much of South-East England (Evans *et al.* 2018). Few of the remains from the legionary fortress yielded sufficient collagen for sulphur isotope analysis, but at least one animal had a non-coastal origin.

Although, at least initially, the garrison at Exeter therefore relied in part on supplies from territories to the east that were already under Roman control, the isotope data also demonstrate the crucial importance of locally sourced foods: almost 40% (9/23) of the animals from the fortress phase have strontium isotope values above 0.7120, which are uncommon in southern Britain outside the South-West Peninsula, Wales and the Anglo-Welsh Border (Evans *et al.* 2018). Given that Wales was only just being brought under Roman control, these samples can therefore confidently be sourced to Exeter's western hinterland, although it should be noted that the method does not allow us to exclude Armorica (Brittany and Lower Normandy), which has a very similar geology to South-West England (Willmes *et al.* 2018). Imported pottery from Gaul suggest some links to Brittany and perhaps the use of Breton ports and given the amounts of pottery from northern France that reached Exeter in the military period and, on a smaller scale, through the 2nd century AD, it cannot be excluded that other cargos, such as livestock, were included in the shipments (see Chapter 5 below, and EAPIT 2, Chapter 12). A further 25% (6/23) of samples fall between 0.7100 and 0.7110, which is consistent with the lithologies of the South-West Peninsula, including Exeter's immediate surroundings, but such $^{87}Sr/^{86}Sr$ may also be found in South-East England and the aforementioned Blackdown

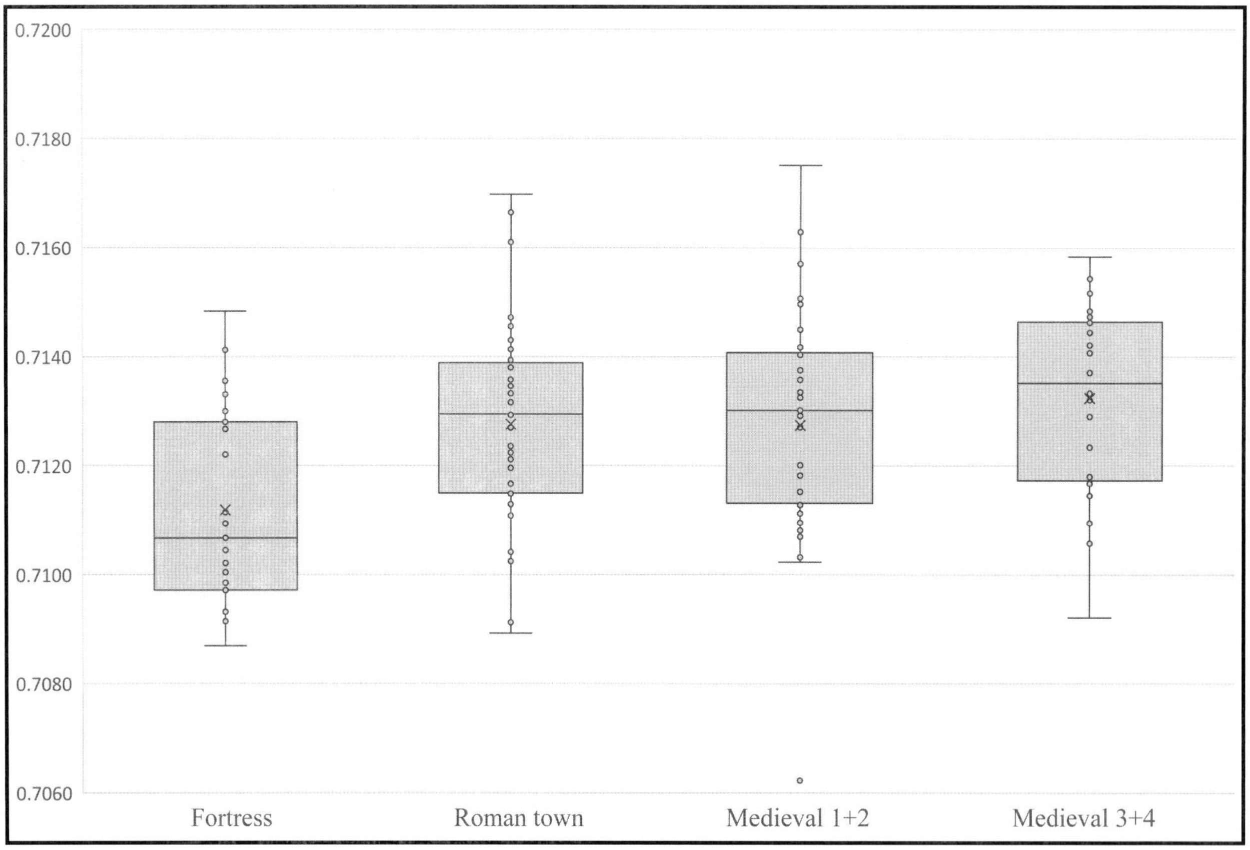

*Fig. 3.19 Box-plots representing bulk strontium isotope data for Exeter animals (cattle and sheep). For greater clarity, data from the seven chronological periods were collapsed into four: the Roman legionary fortress (*c. *AD 50/55 to 80/85; n=23), the Roman town (mid 2nd to 4th century AD; n=42), Medieval 1 and 2 (late 10th to mid 13th century; n=40) and Medieval 3 and 4 (*c. *AD 1250–1500); n=30). The line represents the median, the x the mean, and the box the 25th to 75th percentile. The whiskers indicate minimum and maximum values, excluding outliers; circles represent individual samples (drawn by Gundula Müldner)*

Hills in eastern Devon (Evans *et al.* 2018; Müldner *et al.* forthcoming). Although these and other percentages given in this chapter should not be taken as anything but broad indications as they are based on relatively small samples, the pattern that emerges, of relying as much as possible on local resources, is in keeping with the strategy of provisioning previously proposed for the Roman army shortly after the conquest (see Stallibrass and Thomas 2008).

If the results from the military phase suggest that it was not yet possible to supply Exeter's sizeable garrison through local resources alone, this had changed almost entirely in the period of civilian occupation, although it should be noted that even at its peak, the size of the civilian population at *Isca Dumnoniorum* (estimated to have grown from *c.* 1000 or less in the 2nd century AD to *c.* 2000–4000 by the 3rd–4th centuries AD) may still have been only one third that of the military base (see above, Chapter 1, Table 1.1). Only 2 of 43 (5%) samples from the Roman town have strontium isotope values below 0.7100 suggesting that they originated from areas east of Exeter. Instead, the majority (29/42, 69%) plot above 0.7120 and would therefore be hard to place outside the South-West Peninsula without suggesting long-distance transport of livestock from Wales or France. Within the South-West Peninsula such values are a good fit for rocks of the Culm Measures as well as Dartmoor and its adjacent areas where strontium biosphere values are influenced by the granite. $^{87}Sr/^{86}Sr$ between 0.7100 and 0.7120 (11/42, 26%) on the other hand are perhaps more indicative of Devonian and New Red Sandstone (Exeter Group) formations, although they are also commonly observed for the Culm Measures (Müldner *et al.* forthcoming; Evans *et al.* 2018). The emphasis on more radiogenic values (above 0.7120) in the faunal dataset from the Roman town, which continues through the medieval period (see Chapter 4), indicates the importance of these western areas for raising livestock: the heavy, wet soils of areas such as the Culm Measures and Dartmoor were not well-suited to arable (see above, Chapter 2 including Appendix 2.1) but historically were extensively grazed (*e.g.* see Chapter 2 above; Kowaleski 1995, 13f.; Allen and Lodwick 2017).

Strontium isotope values above 0.7140 proved to be of special significance for this study. Unlike most values which are consistent with a range of terrains across the South-West Peninsula, these 'highly radiogenic' $^{87}Sr/^{86}Sr$ can be traced to the Cornubian granite such as Dartmoor (Müldner *et al.* forthcoming). These 'highly radiogenic' values are therefore a useful proxy for Dartmoor's importance in the pastoral economy, although it must be emphasised that they are generally found in the valleys that fringe the upland as opposed to the very high moorland which many people associate with the term 'Dartmoor'. Probably because of peat cover and other pedological factors, the high moors usually host more 'muted' strontium biosphere values, which can be difficult to distinguish from the other Palaeozoic lithologies.

The Roman period on Dartmoor is archaeologically elusive (Newman 2011; Allen *et al.* 2015), although at least in part this may reflect the very limited archaeological

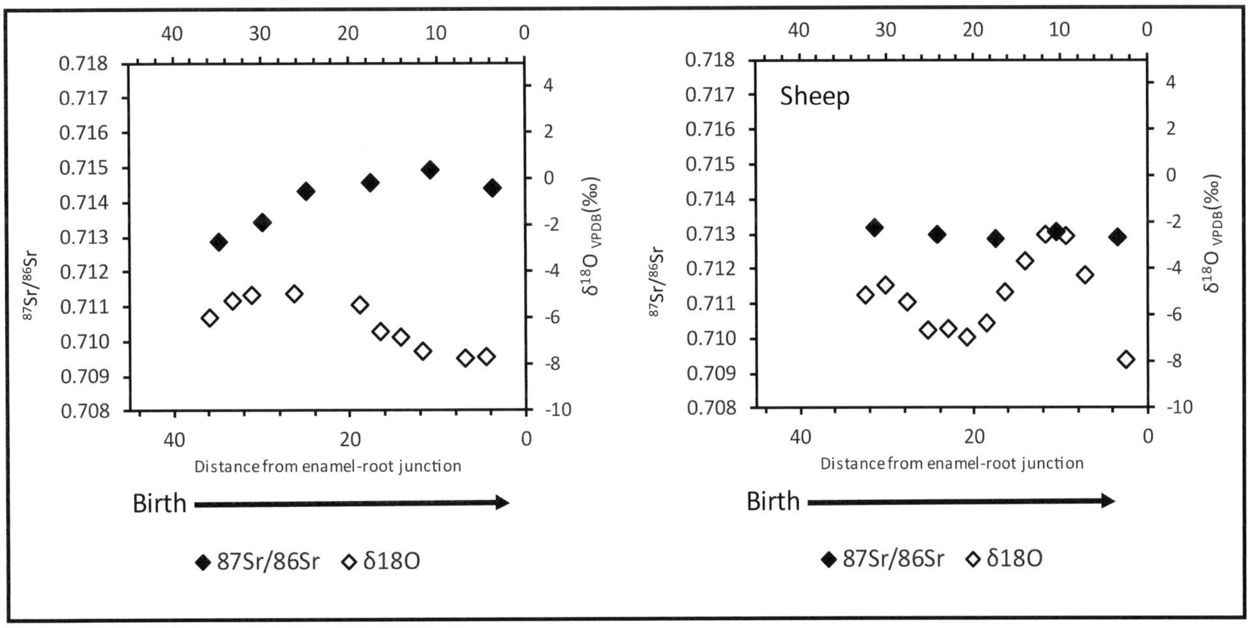

Fig. 3.20 Intra-tooth isotope profiles of a cattle tooth from the Roman legionary fortress and a sheep tooth from medieval Exeter. Oxygen isotope values reflect the seasonal amplitude (high δ-values = summer, low δ-values = winter) and strontium isotope values provide a proxy for animal movement. Whilst the cattle shows evidence for seasonal movement, the sheep does not (drawn by Gundula Müldner)

work that has been carried out both on the high moor and its fringes. There is, however, evidence for continued human presence in the pollen record, that shows a landscape that remained largely cleared of woodland, and geochemical evidence for continued tin extraction (see Straker *et al.* 2007; Meharg *et al.* 2012; Rippon and Fyfe 2018). The lack of extensive woodland on Dartmoor implies continued grazing of the moor which provides a context for the results of this study which show that $^{87}Sr/^{86}Sr$ above 0.7140 are present among the Roman faunal data from Exeter from as early as the military phase (2/23, 8%). They are relatively common in the Early Roman town (6/24, 25%) but much rarer again in the later period (2/18, 11%). This indicates the grazing of livestock on Dartmoor, at least in the more sheltered low-lying areas, such as around modern day Moretonhampstead, in the Roman period, and especially the 2nd century AD. Time-resolved isotope data from enamel serial sections suggests that this may have been in the form of year-round occupation at least occasionally, although data from the legionary fortress and later Roman town are more consistent with seasonal movement (see below).

Transhumance to Dartmoor and its importance for the pastoral economy of the South-West is well documented for the medieval period through the work of Fox (2012). The second aim of the isotope investigation was to obtain time-resolved isotope strontium and oxygen isotope data (reflecting geological signal and season, respectively) through sequential sampling of tooth-enamel, in order to explore the antiquity of this practice and investigate patterns of transhumance in the archaeological record. Sample sizes are small, as the method is very labour-intensive and mobility may be invisible, if the animal moved only for very short periods of time or between isotopically similar terrains (see Glassburn *et al.* 2018). Of six sequentially sampled teeth for Roman-period animals, three showed profiles that are consistent with seasonal mobility involving Dartmoor, while the other three may have stayed in one place or moved across isotopically similar terrain. Of the medieval animals, only two showed clear evidence of seasonal movement (Fig. 3.20). Whilst these results demonstrate the likely antiquity of seasonal livestock movement, they also demonstrate that this was not necessarily the norm for animal husbandry at the time. Nevertheless, because of the sizeable overlap in the strontium biosphere ranges of the different geological formations of the South-West, one must be mindful that not all animal mobility will be visible in the isotope record. The medieval isotopic data are discussed in Chapter 4.

Material culture and identity

An important manifestation of regional differences in landscape and society either side of the Blackdown and Quantock Hills, and potentially between what was to become Devon and Cornwall, are differences in the production and use of material culture. Whilst the Roman period saw a marked homogenisation across Britain, recent research is revealing the extent to which there were regional variations in the styles of objects such as belt fittings (Laycock 2008), brooches (*e.g.* Bayley and Butcher 2004; Plouviez 2008), finger rings (Daubney 2010), hairpins (Cool 1990; 2000) and toilet instruments (Eckardt and Crummy 2008; Eckardt 2014). Variations are also starting to appear in patterns of coin loss (Walton 2012; and see EAPIT 2, Chapter 16). Quinnell (1986; 1993) has already shown how the region west of the Tamar, for example, had a distinctive range of material culture (*e.g.* handmade pottery produced from gabbroic clays from the Lizard, as well as a range of stone mortars, bowls and weights), and a distinctive type of brooch with a cruciform-shaped bow and fantail foot can now be added to this growing list of distinctively Cornish objects (Hull type 31: Tyacke *et al.* 2011; Thomas 2018, 172–7, 295).

In Cornwall 34% of excavated rural settlements have produced brooches, a figure only just below those for the South and Central Belt regions of Britain (35 and 40%) but much higher than Devon (15%: Brindle 2018). In Cornwall brooches also form a higher proportion of items of personal adornment (31%) compared to Devon (20%) where beads, bracelets and hairpins are more common (Thomas 2018, tab. 6.2). An analysis of objects recorded on the PAS also shows that brooches (12%) form a greater proportion in Cornwall than Devon (4%) and this supports the assertion that there appears to have been 'different cultural expressions in the two areas' (Brindle 2016, 43, tab. 10.3). The more restricted range of dress accessories in Cornwall may be indicative of a community less enthusiastic about appearing 'Roman', although it must be acknowledged that the sample sizes of each artefact type are small. That there are more PAS finds of Romano-British date recorded in the PAS for Cornwall (693) compared to Devon (483) could reflect a variety of factors such as the number of active metal detectorists who are reporting finds there, although it may be a genuine trend as Devon also appears to have seen a lower level of pottery use (see below). The general sparsity of material culture on Roman-period sites across the South-West Peninsula is also reflected in the distributions of a wide range of objects including those associated with security, lighting, recreation and literacy (Smith 2018, figs 3.3, 3.5, 3.13, 3.19).

Thomas (2018, 163) concludes her recent study of Romano-British material culture from Devon and Cornwall by arguing that 'the river Tamar may have acted as a boundary, with only limited engagement by the elite with new ceramic forms and fabrics occurring to the west of the Tamar, while a deeper and more long-lived change took place to the east'. She goes on to argue that 'the only shared belief across all communities of the South-West related to hoarding practices', in that all of the examples from across the South-West Peninsula are from the edges of high ground, and that 'what we can see here is the river Tamar forming a discrete boundary of the Roman Empire, with the communities to the west being essentially beyond the Empire' (Thomas 2018, 301–2). While it does appear to be true that there are differences in cultural practice either side of the Tamar Valley – or more likely its western watershed marked by Bodmin Moor and Kit Hill – these differences should be seen in the context of even clearer differences to the east and west of the Blackdown and Quantock Hills (Rippon 2008a; 2012). It seems highly unlikely that this mineral-rich part of the South-West Peninsula was left outside the Roman empire, or was a separate *civitas* as there is no evidence for another *civitas* capital, and while Quinnell (2004, 215–17) has suggested that it may have had 'separate administrative arrangements', and Mattingly (2006, fig. 10) has argues that it was 'probably under long-term military, state and external control', another possibility is that we may be seeing two communities or districts (*pagi*) within a single administrative *civitas* that maintained their distinctive identities from the pre-Roman Iron Age through to the period of Roman control.

Pottery production and circulation

A detailed study of territorial arrangements across eastern England has recently argued that the distribution of locally produced coarse wares is one reflection of how spheres of socio-economic interaction survived from the later Iron Age through to the Roman period (Rippon 2018a). The extent to which the products of a pottery kiln are distributed across a landscape can shed light on how material culture circulated within and between separate socio-economic territories (*e.g.* Fig. 3.21; and see Hodder 1974; Hodder and Orton 1976; Rippon 2018a, chap. 6). In a simple distance decay model, vessels moved from a production centre in equal volumes in all directions with a steady decline in numbers with increasing distance from source. Such regular fall-off patterns will only occur where there are 'perfect' economic conditions including a completely uniform natural and cultural landscape, although in practice this did not exist as there will always have been distorting factors such as communication networks, with pottery vessels more likely to have travelled greater distances along well-made roads or navigable rivers as costs were lower. The command economy will also have distorted pottery distributions through attracting the products of some industries far greater distances than would have been the case through purely market-based trade (*e.g.* military procurement). Another distortion may have been where exchange was socially embedded leading to the products of a particular kiln/industry having been favoured, or shunned, by certain communities more than others.

Data collection and analysis

The problems associated with mapping the products of Romano-British pottery industries have long been recognised (*e.g.* Fulford and Huddlestone 1991; Fulford and Brindle 2016, 13–14; Rippon 2017; 2018a; Thomas 2018, 66), such as the wide range of different quantification methods used including sherd count, sherd weight, Estimated Vessel Equivalent (EVE, usually based on the rim sherds present) and Minimum Number of Vessels (MNV). Some older reports simply provide a catalogue of illustrated sherds. All of the quantification methods have advantages and disadvantages: the relatively high fragmentation rate of fine wares will lead to them being over-represented in simple sherd counts, whereas the far more robust coarse wares will be over-represented in quantifications carried out by sherd weight. Different specialists also use different ways of calculating MNV: at Trethurgy, for example, Quinnell (2004) identifies 550 vessels, whereas Thomas (2018, 68) just 309. Other methodological problems have been previously discussed (Rippon 2017), including the quality of some grey literature reports, although the *Standard for Pottery Studies in Archaeology* (Barclay *et al.* 2016) will hopefully improve the situation.

The methodology used in this study follows that adopted in the previous analysis of Romano-British coarse wares in eastern England (Rippon 2017; 2018a, 168–98). In addition, regression graphs have been prepared for selected fabrics in order to see whether there is significant deviation from the distance-decay model (for which only sites with 100 or more sherds are included). The dataset for the wider South-West includes 347,174 sherds from non-military sites excluding Exeter and Dorchester (Table 3.7 and online Appendix 3.5). It should be noted that some assemblages referenced in other studies (*e.g.* Leech 1977; Holbrook and Bidwell 1991; Thomas 2018) could not be used here as they were not fully quantified. The small number of assemblages quantified by weight have been converted to a predicted number of sherds using an average of 17.4 g per sherd – and 55 g for amphora – based on figures obtained from a series of reports that give both sherd counts and weight. Settlements were grouped into nucleated settlements (small towns and local centres: Bath, Charterhouse, Ilchester and Shepton Mallet, all in Somerset; and Dainton Elms Cross, in Ipplepen, and Pomeroy Wood, in Honiton, both in Devon), possible ports, villas and farmsteads. Kiln sites were excluded as those assemblages will clearly be dominated by the products of that particular kiln (*e.g.* Worgret near Wareham, where 99.3% of the 18,372 sherds were South-East Dorset BB1: Hearne and Smith 1992; and see Ladle 2012). Sherds were grouped by recognised fabrics listed in Tomber and Dore's (1998) *National Roman Fabric Reference Collection*, to which can be added the Cornish gabbroic ware (Quinnell 2004, 108–26), Somerset's Congresbury Ware (Timby 2000) and the Exeter

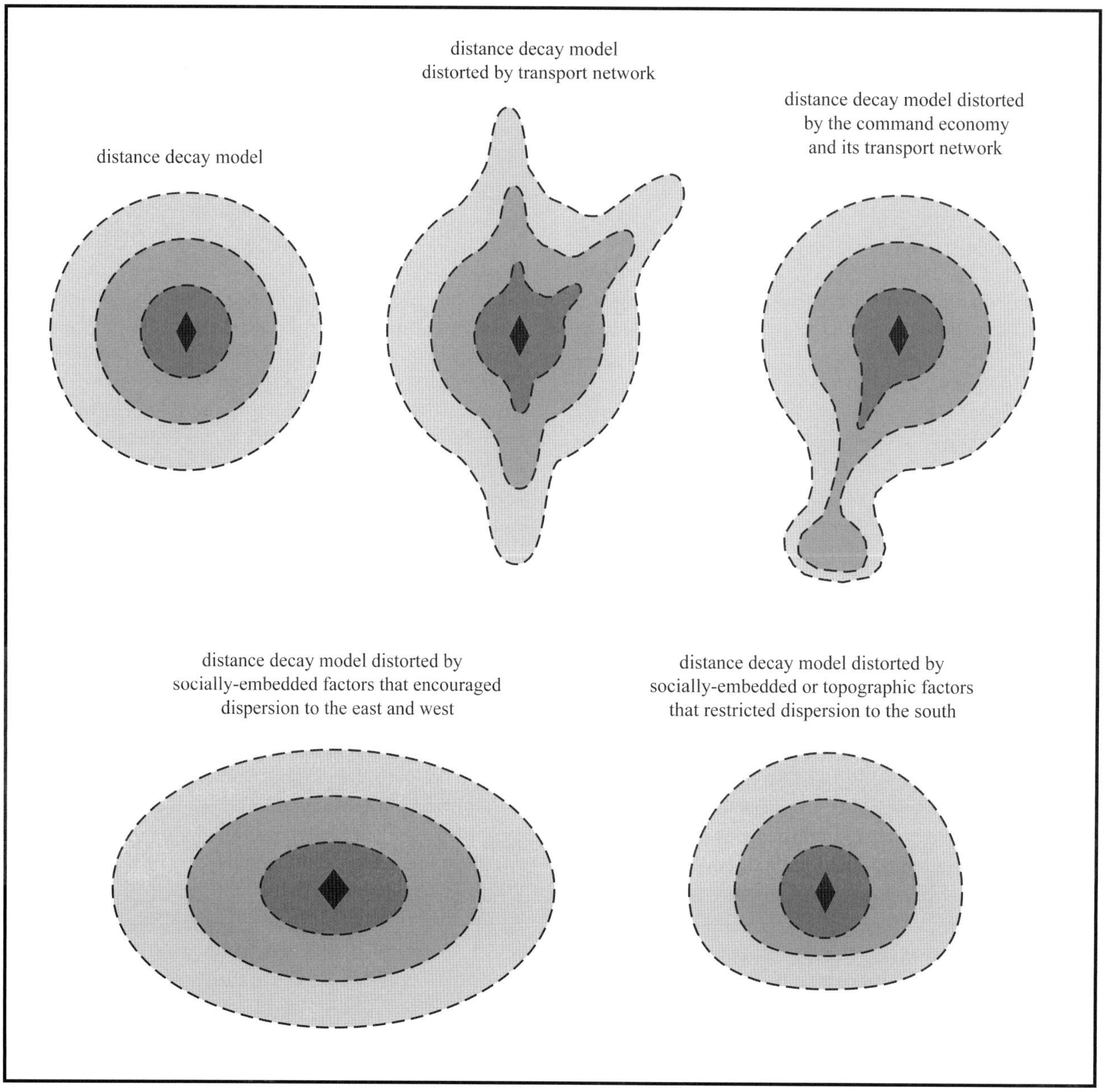

Fig. 3.21 Schematic models illustrating the different distributional mechanisms of Romano-British pottery. It is suggested that the distribution of certain fabrics across the wider South-West (such as gabbroic ware) show evidence for socially-embedded exchange in that their occurrence does not follow the simple distance decay model (drawn by Stephen Rippon)

Fabric Series (Holbrook and Bidwell 1991). EAPIT has also established the provenance of several important fabrics (EAPIT 2, Chapter 12): South-Western BB1 (Exeter fabrics 40 and 60) from the western side of the Blackdown Hills, South-Western Grey Ware storage jars (Holbrook and Bidwell 1991, 175) from the Ludwell Valley east of Exeter (previous work has shown that they were also produced elsewhere including Norton Fitzwarren in Somerset: Ellis 1989), and Fortress Wares from the Teign Valley (although this clay may have been transported to Exeter: EAPIT 2, Chapter 12). In Table 3.7 these fabrics are grouped by the county in which they were produced, with unsourced wares quantified in the final column.

The distribution maps below differ significantly from those published previously that either simply show the location of sites that have produced sherds of a particular fabric (*e.g.* Holbrook and Bidwell 1991a, figs 25 and 69), or show circles in proportion to the total number of sherds of that fabric irrespective of the scale of the excavation (*e.g.* Tompsett 2014, figs 67–73). The problem with the former is that they give equal weighting to sites whether a particular fabric forms 1% or 100% of the assemblage,

Table 3.7 Quantification of the Romano-British pottery assemblages from rural sites across the wider South-West

		Total	*Amphora*		*Samian*		*Mortaria*		*Other imports*		*All imports*		*Cornish wares*		*Devonian wares*		*Dorset wares*		*Somerset wares*		*All non-SW RB regional wares*		*New Forest wares*		*Oxfordshire wares*		*Unsourced wares*	
		Sherds	*Sherds*	*%*	*Sherds*	*%*	*Sherds*	*%*	*Sherds*	*%*	*Sherds*	*%*	*Sherds*	*%*	*Sherds*	*%*	*Sherds*	*%*	*Sherds*	*%*	*Sherds*	*%*	*Sherds*	*%*	*Sherds*	*%*	*Sherds*	*%*
Somerset	smaller nucleated settlements	59682	1239	*0*	1862	*13*	7	*0*	86	*0*	3194	*13*	0	*0*	70	*0*	23972	*30*	17488	*0*	3124	*6*	778	*0*	1169	*0*	11834	*50*
Devon	smaller nucleated settlements	17219	609	*4*	451	*3*	43	*0*	195	*1*	1298	*8*	1	*0*	4788	*28*	6524	*38*	18	*0*	349	*2*	205	*1*	134	*1*	4241	*25*
Devon	?port (Mount Batten)	278	0	*0*	5	*2*	1	*0*	0	*0*	6	*2*	33	*12*	221	*79*	10	*4*	0	*0*	2	*1*	0	*0*	2	*1*	6	*2*
Devon	Topsham	1524	41	*3*	245	*16*	8	*1*	31	*2*	325	*21*	0	*0*	767	*50*	169	*11*	16	*1*	6	*0*	3	*0*	3	*0*	241	*16*
Dorset	? Port (Weston Road, Weymouth)	14395	851	*6*	302	*2*	86	*1*	8	*0*	1247	*9*	0	*0*	0	*0*	12689	*88*	0	*0*	276	*2*	267	*2*	8	*0*	183	*1*
Somerset	villas	6312	46	*1*	99	*2*	2	*0*	11	*0*	158	*3*	0	*0*	38	*1*	2621	*42*	1207	*19*	113	*2*	25	*0*	64	*1*	2175	*34*
Dorset	villa	34367	116	*0*	286	*1*	10	*0*	59	*0*	471	*1*	0	*0*	0	*0*	32932	*96*	0	*0*	862	*3*	594	*2*	207	*1*	102	*0*
Devon	farmsteads	15753	161	*1*	331	*2*	50	*0*	83	*1*	625	*4*	148	*1*	9267	*59*	3247	*21*	56	*0*	94	*1*	36	*0*	39	*0*	2316	*15*
Cornwall	farmsteads	22514	120	*1*	132	*1*	8	*0*	47	*0*	307	*1*	19801	*88*	1696	*8*	501	*2*	0	*0*	54	*0*	0	*0*	46	*0*	155	*1*
Somerset	farmsteads	94246	527	*1*	1583	*2*	7	*0*	174	*0*	2291	*2*	0	*0*	3612	*4*	47859	*51*	14904	*16*	3960	*4*	916	*1*	2112	*2*	21620	*23*
Dorset	farmsteads	80884	537	*1*	658	*1*	98	*0*	288	*0*	1581	*2*	0	*0*	1191	*1*	73437	*91*	0	*0*	1025	*1*	869	*1*	125	*0*	3650	*5*
Total sherds		**347174**	**4247**	*1*	**5954**	*2*	**320**	*0*	**982**	*0*	**11503**	3	**19983**	6	**21650**	*6*	**203961**	*59*	**33689**	*10*	**9865**	*3*	**3693**	*1*	**3909**	*1*	**46523**	*13*
Total farmsteads		**213397**	**1345**	***1***	**2704**	***1***	**163**	***0***	**592**	***0.3***	**4804**	**2**	**19949**	***9***	**15766**	*7*	**125044**	***59***	**14960**	***7.0***	**5133**	**2**	**1821**	***1***	**2322**	***1***	**27741**	***13***
Total villas		**40679**	**162**	***0***	**385**	***1***	**12**	***0***	**70**	***0.2***	**629**	*2*	**0**	***0***	**38**	***0***	**35553**	***87***	**1207**	***3.0***	**975**	*2*	**619**	*2*	**271**	*1*	**2277**	*6*

while the latter approach is problematic as very extensive excavations generate large symbols for assemblages that were actually a very small proportion of the total pottery. Instead, the distribution maps presented here show the proportion of an excavated assemblage that is of a particular fabric in order to give a better impression of its significance. Excavated sites with quantified pottery assemblages that did not produce that particular fabric are also plotted (using white squares) in order to show whether gaps in the distribution are real or not.

When interpreting the significance of the proportions of different pottery fabrics within Romano-British assemblages, it should be borne in mind that the production and circulation of different industries varied over time. South Devon Ware, for example, was produced in the 1st and 2nd centuries AD, but only became widely distributed during the 3rd and especially the 4th centuries AD when it largely replaced South-Western BB1 in Exeter (Holbrook and Bidwell 1991, 178, fig. 5). Two sites near Exeter that were both occupied from the 1st to 4th centuries AD should, therefore, produce pottery assemblages with similar proportions of South Devon Ware, whereas if one was only occupied in the 1st to 2nd centuries AD it will have a lower proportion than a nearby site occupied in the 3rd to 4th century AD. In an ideal world, we would therefore be able to differentiate between Early and Late Roman assemblages but in practice this is rarely possible as most excavation reports simply quantify the pottery from the site as a whole. What is present below is, therefore, just a first attempt at seeing the 'big picture' and it is hoped that further work will add greater chronological definition.

The fabrics

Imports from outside Britain formed a significant proportion of the assemblages from small towns and local centres in Somerset (13%) and to a lesser extent the two roadside settlements in Devon (8%). They were far less significant on farmsteads, although it is curious that they were more significant in Devon (4%) than Dorset and Somerset (both 2%), which is discussed below. Imports from British regional industries outside of the wider South-West are only a small proportion of the assemblages, being highest for the small towns and local centres in Somerset. Rural assemblages are therefore dominated by locally produced pottery, but a major problem is the very variable amounts of unsourced coarse wares. In Cornwall, virtually all of the pottery on farmsteads (the only type of excavated settlement in that county) is from recognised industries, mostly the local gabbroic ware (88%), with just 1% of the pottery being unsourced. In contrast, 23% of the pottery from farmsteads in Somerset is unsourced, the problem being that there is no universally used fabric series equivalent to that developed for Exeter and which is used across Devon and Cornwall (Holbrook and Bidwell 1991). A fabric series was established in the 1970s for Ilchester (Leach 1982b; 1994), but while this is sometimes referenced (*e.g.* Brett and Mudd 2013) most of the specialists working in Somerset use their own fabric series with large amounts of the coarse ware being lumped together under descriptions such as 'Miscellaneous greywares: "catch-all" group for unoxidised fabrics' (*e.g.* Lovell 2006, Fabric Q100). Confusion abounds as, for example, Fabric 6 at Hillyfields in Taunton (Leach 2003) appears to be the same as Fabric 2 at Norton Fitzwarren (Ellis 1989) and Fabric 10 at Maidenbrook Farm (Ferris and Bevan 1993).

The gabbroic and South Devon industries

Pottery made from the gabbroic clays found on the Lizard in southern Cornwall dominates assemblages to the west of the Tamar from the 1st to the 4th centuries AD, but very little of it travelled further east during the Roman period (Figs 3.22 and 3.23): note that although the assemblage of 163 sherds from Tews Lane in Fremington, North Devon, comprised 45% gabbroic sherds this is essentially a Late Iron Age settlement that continued to be occupied into the mid 1st century AD (Rainbird and Quinnell 2018) and sites such as this are excluded from Fig. 3.22. It is possible that this restricted distribution of gabbroic ware reflects its socially embedded modes of production and distribution (as in Fig. 3.21) – being particularly valued by local communities in Cornwall and/or shunned by their neighbours east of the Tamar – although it is also possible that competition from South Devon Ware played a part.

South Devon Ware (Tomber and Dore 1998, SOD RE), which flourished during the 2nd to 4th centuries AD (Holbrook and Bidwell 1991, 177–81), is thought to have been produced from clays laid down in the valleys flowing south from Dartmoor (Holbrook and Bidwell 1991, 177–81). Figures 3.24 and 3.25 show that it dominated assemblages east of the Tamar, and that it travelled east to a far greater extent than it travelled west (most clearly evident in the 50–100 km from source zone). This asymmetrical pattern suggests that there were indeed social barriers disrupting normal market-based flows across the Tamar Valley as there were competing sources both to the east and to the west of South Devon Ware. It is also striking that while the Roman period saw new forms of vessel introduced into Cornwall via the importation of ceramics from outside the area – notably tablewares and drinking vessels – these were not replicated in the locally produced gabbroic ware (Thomas 2018, 95; although there is an imitation samian bowl at Carvossa: Carlyon 1987, fig. 3, No. 9).

The eastern Devon industries

Pottery production in the vicinity of Exeter is poorly understood. Early petrological analysis by Peacock (1969) suggested that one variant of Middle Iron Age 'Glastonbury Ware' – now called South-West Decorated Ware – was produced within the Exe catchment (due to

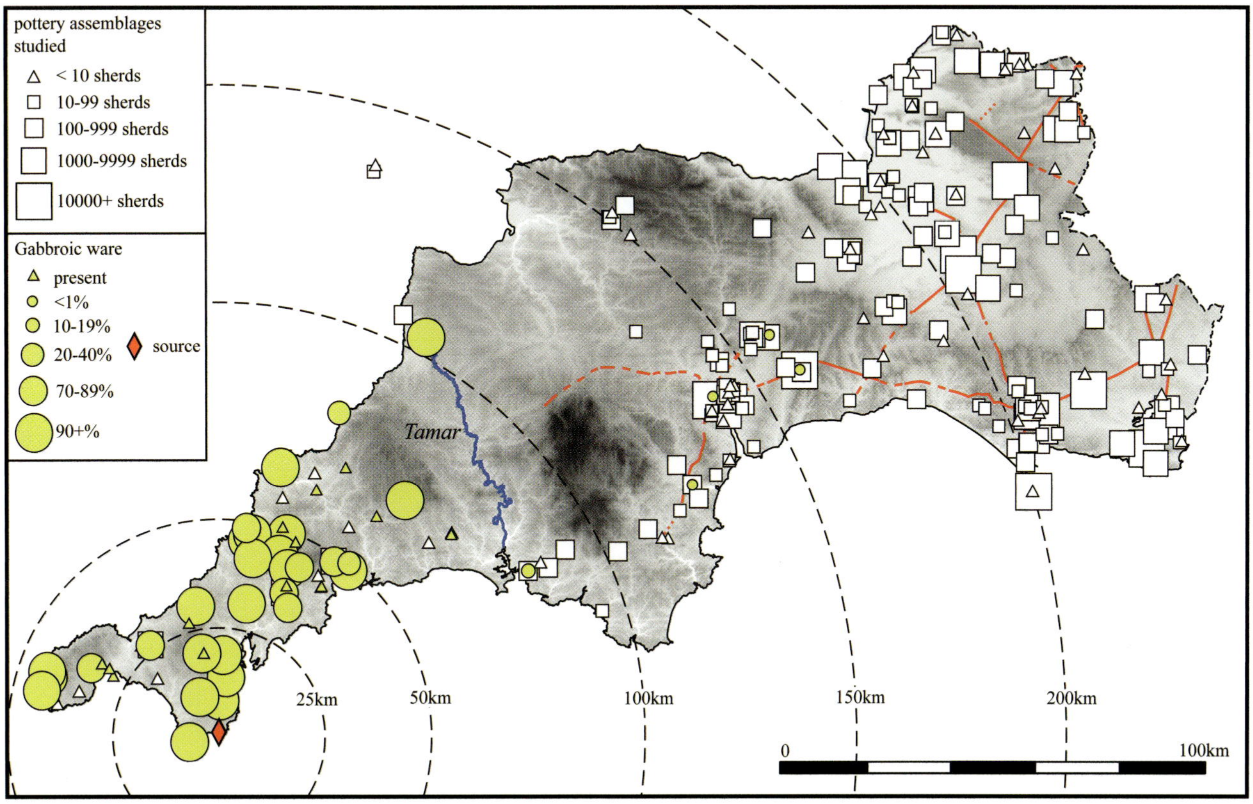

Fig. 3.22 The distribution of gabbroic wares in post-military period contexts, with the size of the circle reflecting the percentage of the total number of excavated sherds that were of that fabric (drawn by David Gould)

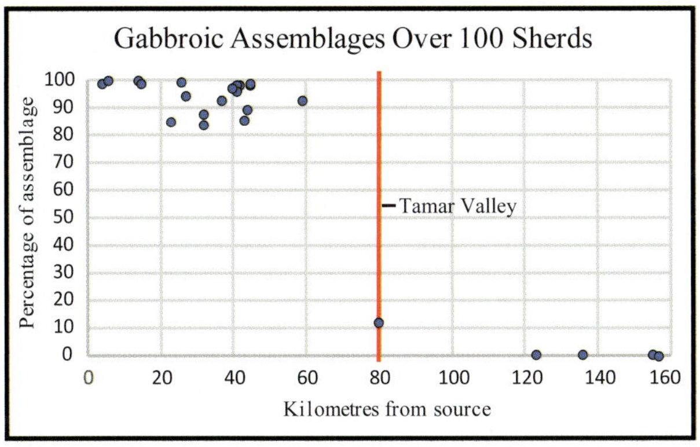

Fig. 3.23 The percentages of gabbroic wares in assemblages of over 100 sherds showing a very rapid fall-off at the Tamar valley (drawn by David Gould)

its Permian inclusions), and later work by Roger Taylor (2016; 2017) suggested the Ludwell Valley, 2.5 km east of Exeter, was the source. It appears that in the Roman military period the same clays were used for the production of tiles used at St Loye's College (Salvatore *et al.* forthcoming; Taylor forthcoming), as was the case with late 2nd to 4th century South-Western Grey Ware storage jars (Holbrook and Bidwell 1991, 175; EAPIT 2, Chapter 12). The published distribution map of these vessels (Holbrook and Bidwell 1991, fig. 69) shows that they are found in an area extending from the Exe Valley in the west, across to the Blackdown Hills in the east and up into the lowlands of central Somerset to the north, but this is likely to be misleading as production centres for very similar storage vessels have recently been identified in the Vale of Taunton Deane at Norton Fitzwarren (Ellis 1989) and Wellington (Welsh 1997). Wasters of grey ware storage jars found at Woodbury, near Axminster, may indicate another production centre on the Blackdown Hills (Weddell *et al.* 1993, 97). It is striking that the storage jars attributed to Exeter's South-Western Grey Ware storage jars are all found to the south and west of the Blackdown and Quantocks Hills (Fig. 3.26), whereas Norton Fitzwarren Ware has largely been identified to the north and east of its production site (Fig. 3.27). If these distributions are genuine then it suggests that the Blackdown/Quantock Hills marked another social barrier to pottery distribution, although it could simply be a reflection of pottery specialists attributing South-Western Grey Ware storage jars found in Devon to the Exeter (Ludwell Valley) source, and those found in Somerset to Norton Fitzwarren (and see discussion of South-Western BB1 below). A far wider range of forms were produced at Norton Fitzwarren, and its relatively high percentages in coastal and north-western parts of Somerset suggest that it was transported by boat from the Tone Valley and hence along the Parrett to the Severn Estuary.

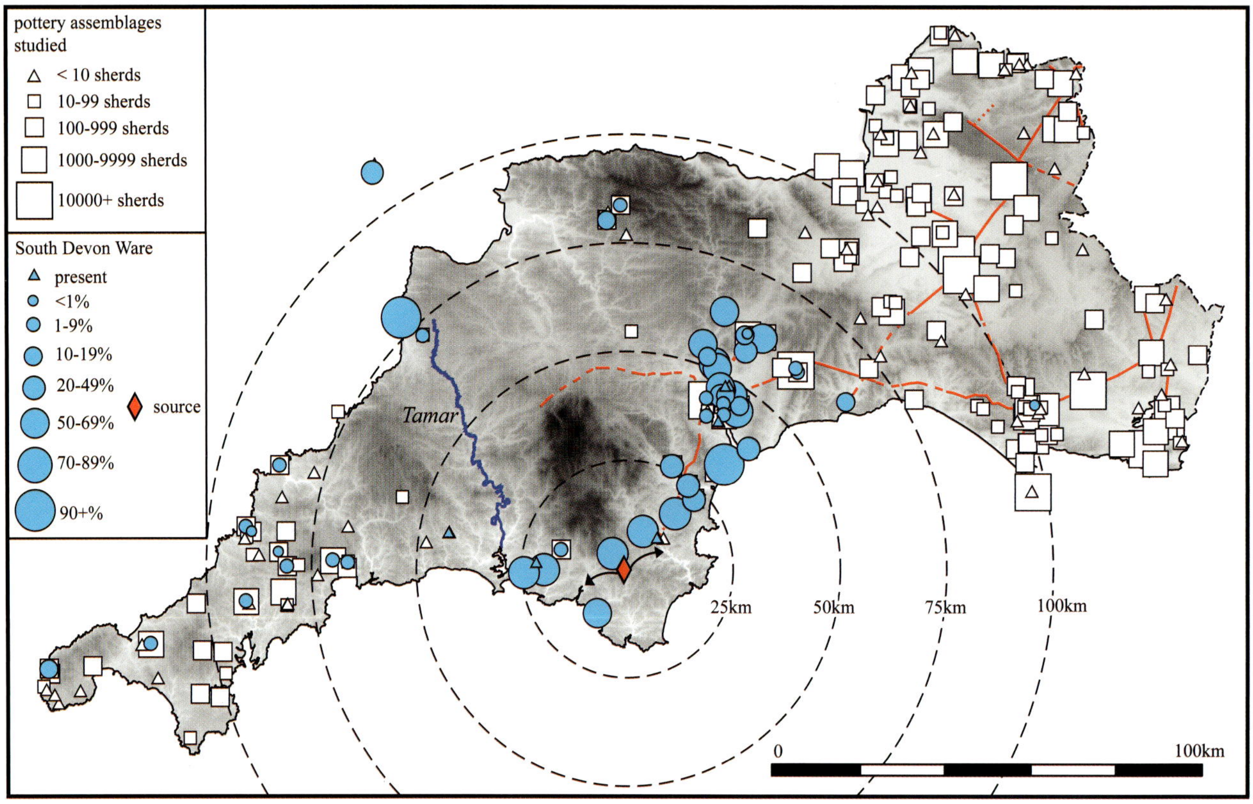

Fig. 3.24 The distribution of South Devon Ware (drawn by David Gould)

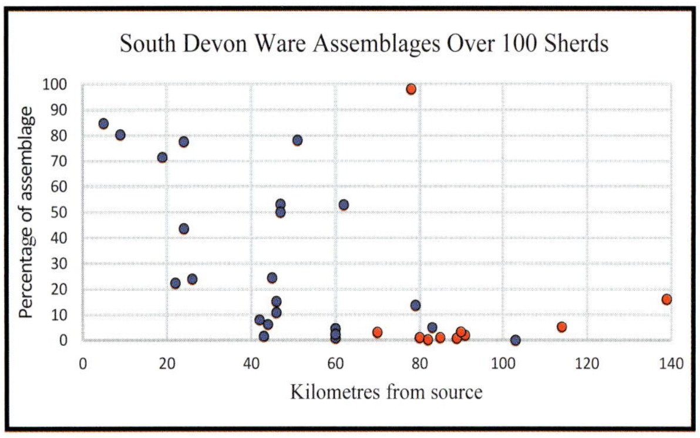

Fig. 3.25 The percentages of South Devon Ware in assemblages of over 100 sherds. The red dots are sites in Cornwall (drawn by David Gould)

The most important pottery industry within the South-West Peninsula was the South-Western BB1 (Tomber and Dore 1998, SOW BB1), whose origins appear to have been in the period of Roman military occupation and whose production ceased by the early 3rd century AD. Its source was, until recently, unclear. Roger Taylor's work as part of the *Exeter: A Place in Time* project has, however, suggested that it was produced somewhere in the western parts of the Blackdown Hills, an area that also had an important pottery industry in the late medieval period (Smart 2010; EAPIT 2, Chapters 12 and 17). South-Western BB1 clearly travelled very considerable distances, but the distribution map (Fig. 3.28) should be viewed with some caution. There were in fact two black-burnished wares produced in the wider South-West, the other being the larger-scale industry around Poole Harbour in South-East Dorset (Tomber and Dore 1998, DOR BB 1; *e.g.* Hearne and Smith 1992; Ladle 2012). The problems with mapping these industries are twofold. The first is that in some pottery reports South-Western BB1 and South-East Dorset BB1 are not distinguished, their being grouped together as 'BB1': these cases are excluded from Fig. 3.28, but assuming that some assemblages of 'BB1' include South-Western BB1 means that the latter's distribution is incomplete. The other potential problem is the possibility that some of what has been identified as South-Western BB1 is in fact South-East Dorset BB1 leading to it being over-represented on Fig. 3.28 (and vice versa).

Bearing these problems in mind, it does appear that South-Western BB1 travelled quite extensively across the South-West Peninsula, being found on the majority of Romano-British sites in Devon and some in Cornwall (Figs 3.28 and 3.29). It is, however, only found on some sites in Somerset which at face value suggests that either it was not as widely accepted to the east of the Blackdown and Quantocks Hills, or that its restricted distribution reflects competition from the South-East Dorset BB1

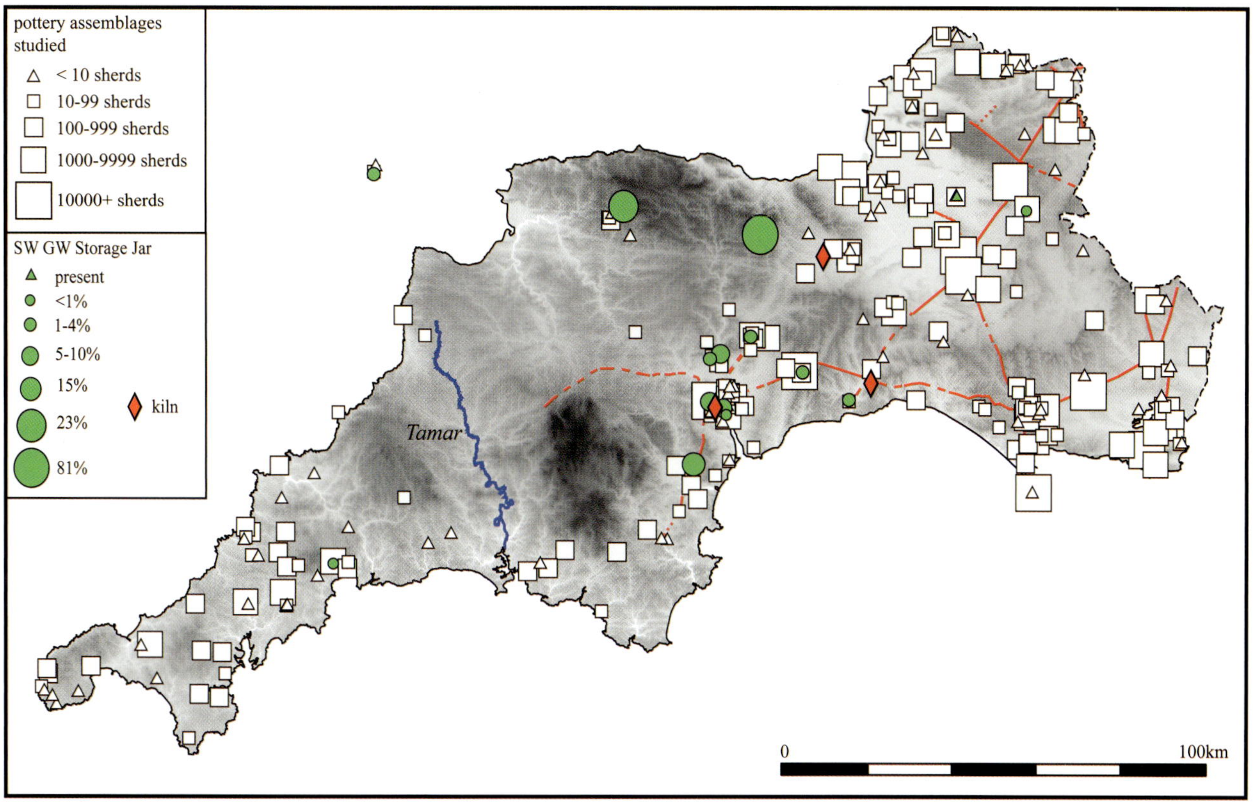

Fig. 3.26 The distribution of South-Western Grey Ware storage jars (drawn by David Gould)

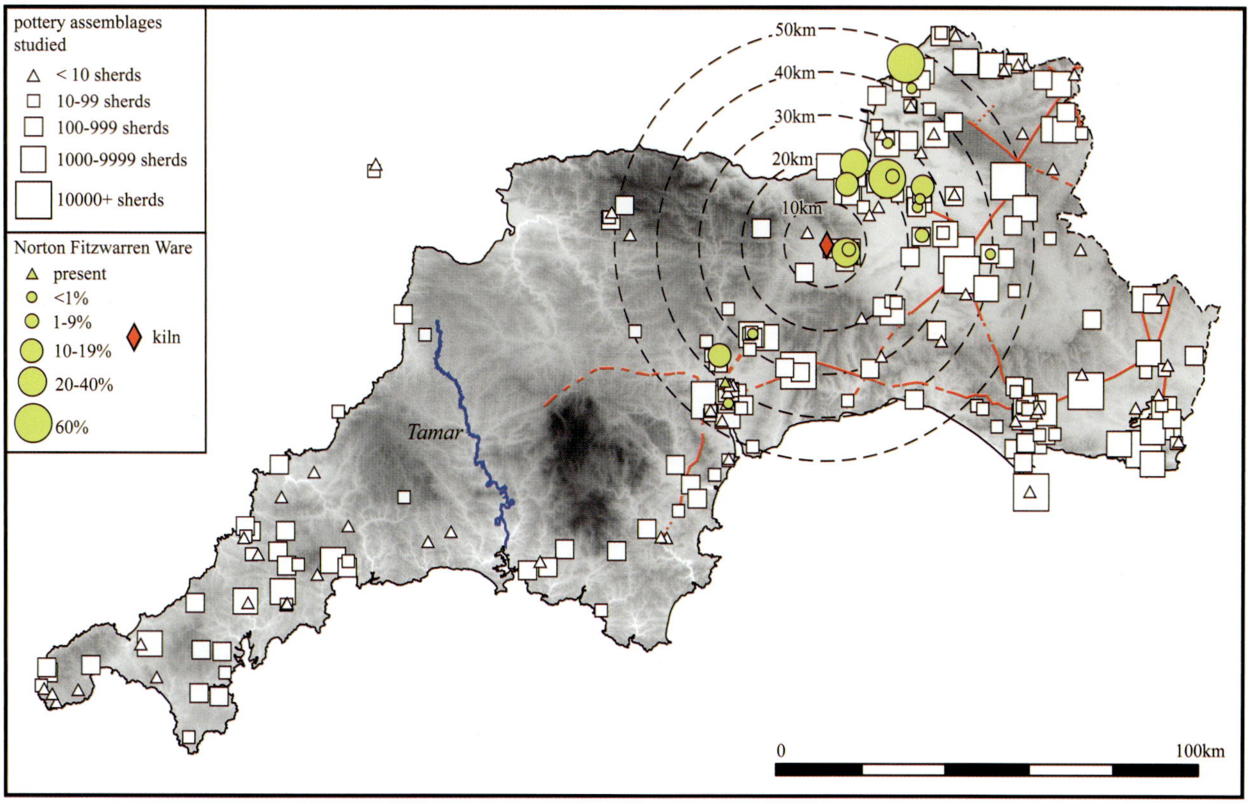

Fig. 3.27 The distribution of Norton Fitzwarren Ware (drawn by David Gould)

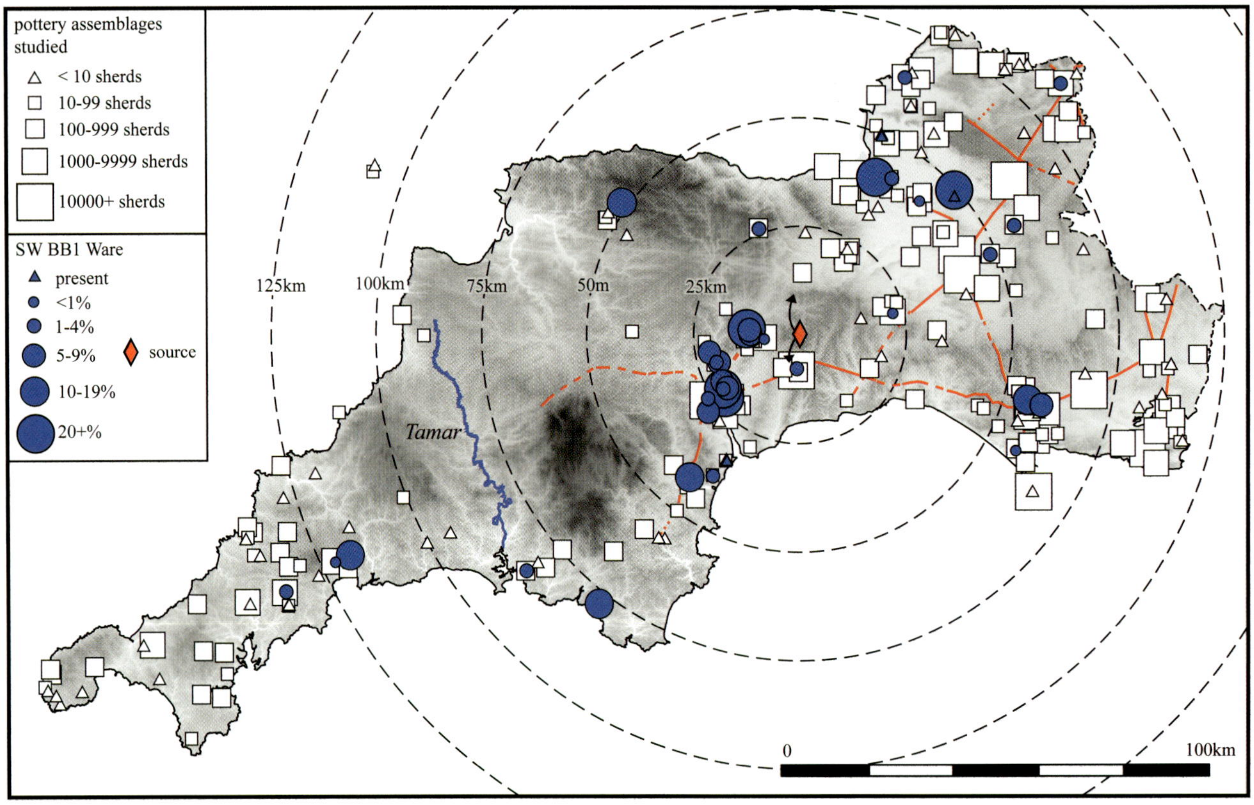

Fig. 3.28 The distribution of South-Western BB1 (drawn by David Gould)

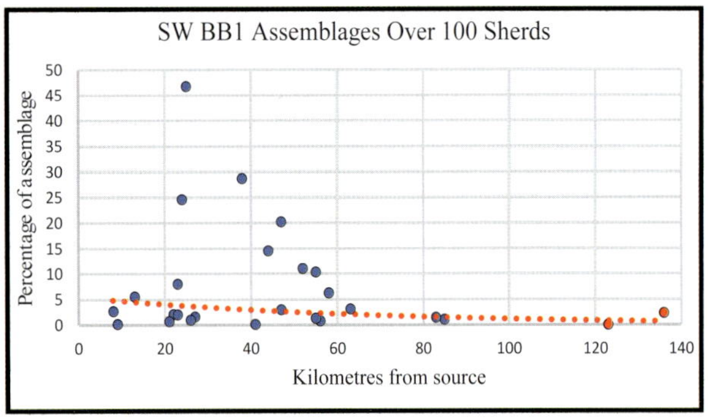

Fig. 3.29 The percentages of South-Western BB1 in assemblages of over 100 sherds. The red dots are sites in Cornwall (drawn by David Gould)

industry. As well as dominating coarse ware pottery supply in its immediate hinterland, South-East Dorset BB1 was an industry that was patronised by the Roman military establishment in Wales, with a supply route potentially heading from Poole Harbour to Dorchester, Ilchester and then a small transhipment port on the Parrett Estuary at Crandon Bridge where goods were transferred to vessels that could cross the Severn Estuary to the legionary fortress at Caerleon (Allen and Fulford 1996; Rippon 2008b). This supply route ran through the centre of Somerset and it may have been this competition from South-East Dorset BB1 that limited the spread of South-Western BB1. There is, however, another possible explanation for why there appears to be less South-Western BB1 to the north and east of the Blackdown Hills: that it has not been properly identified.

Regional imports

The distributions of locally produced coarse wares discussed above suggests that while market forces operated to a certain extent, some of the exchange was socially embedded which led to deviations in the patterns expected from a simple distance decay model. This can be explored further by looking at pottery from two of the major regional industries of Roman Britain: New Forest and Oxfordshire (Figs 3.30–3.33). Although the products of both industries did reach the South-West Peninsula, it is striking that New Forest Ware travelled less far, only rarely reaching Cornwall. It is also apparent that there is a sharp drop-off in the distribution of Oxfordshire Ware to the west of the Blackdown Hills (the vertical red line in Fig. 3.33, marking the distance to Honiton). It seems unlikely that this was caused by the natural topography – travelling across the Blackdowns will not have been that arduous – and it may instead reflect how there was less demand

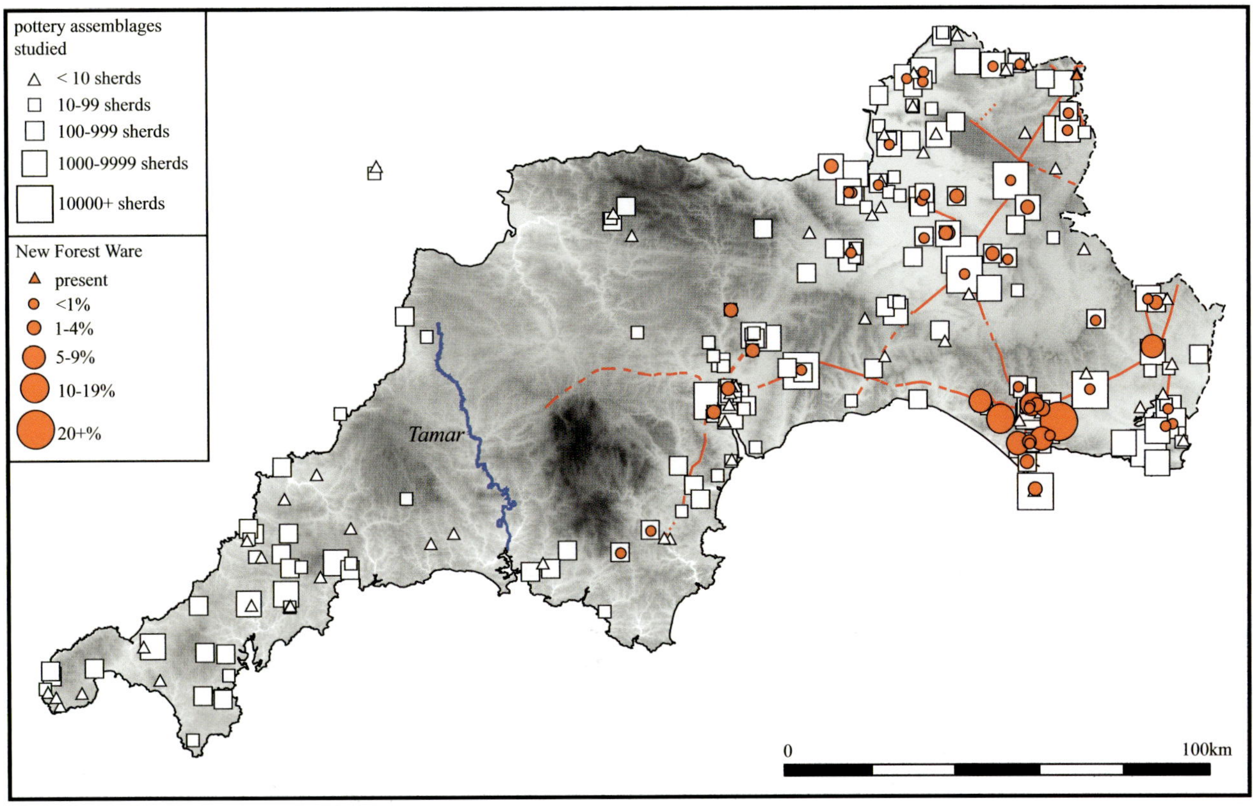

Fig. 3.30 The distribution of all New Forest Ware (drawn by David Gould)

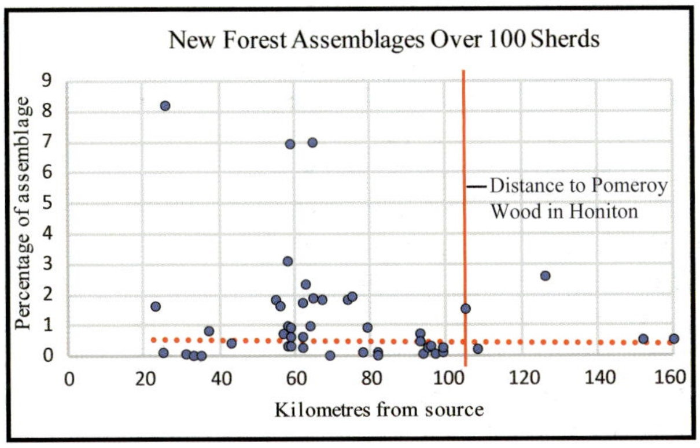

Fig. 3.31 The percentages of New Forest Ware in assemblages of over 100 sherds (drawn by David Gould)

within the South-West Peninsula for the products of these central-southern Romano-British industries.

Continental imports and sherd densities on excavated sites

Small amounts of material imported from continental sources are also found right across the region. It is striking that in Cornwall these continental imports form a smaller proportion (1%) of the total pottery assemblages than in Dorset and Somerset (2%), whereas in Devon they formed a slightly higher proportion (4%; Table 3.7). The figures for samian can be compared to Steve Willis's (2011) national overview which showed that it was 1.5% by weight on 39 rural sites, and 5.7% by Estimated Vessel Equivalent on 35 sites where that data was available (none of which were in the South-West Peninsula). That imports are less prevalent in Cornwall than in Dorset and Somerset is not surprising, but the figures for Devon are noteworthy as Holbrook and Bidwell (1991, 19, 81) have previously argued that following the departure of the Roman army there was a greatly reduced supply of imported fine ware to that area. The data in Table 3.7 are, however, based upon a far larger dataset than was available in 1991 due to the expansion in development-led archaeology, and there are also sites that could not be included in this analysis because they do not have a full quantification but which also have a slightly higher proportion of fine wares than might be expected (*e.g.* Kenn where there was 'an unusually large amount of colour-coated ware'; Bidwell 2016, section 2). One explanation for these figures is that there was a particular preference for exotic imports in Devon, although there is another distinct possibility: that the relatively high percentage of continental imports was due to less pottery being used in Devon overall (a trend also hinted at in other categories of material culture,

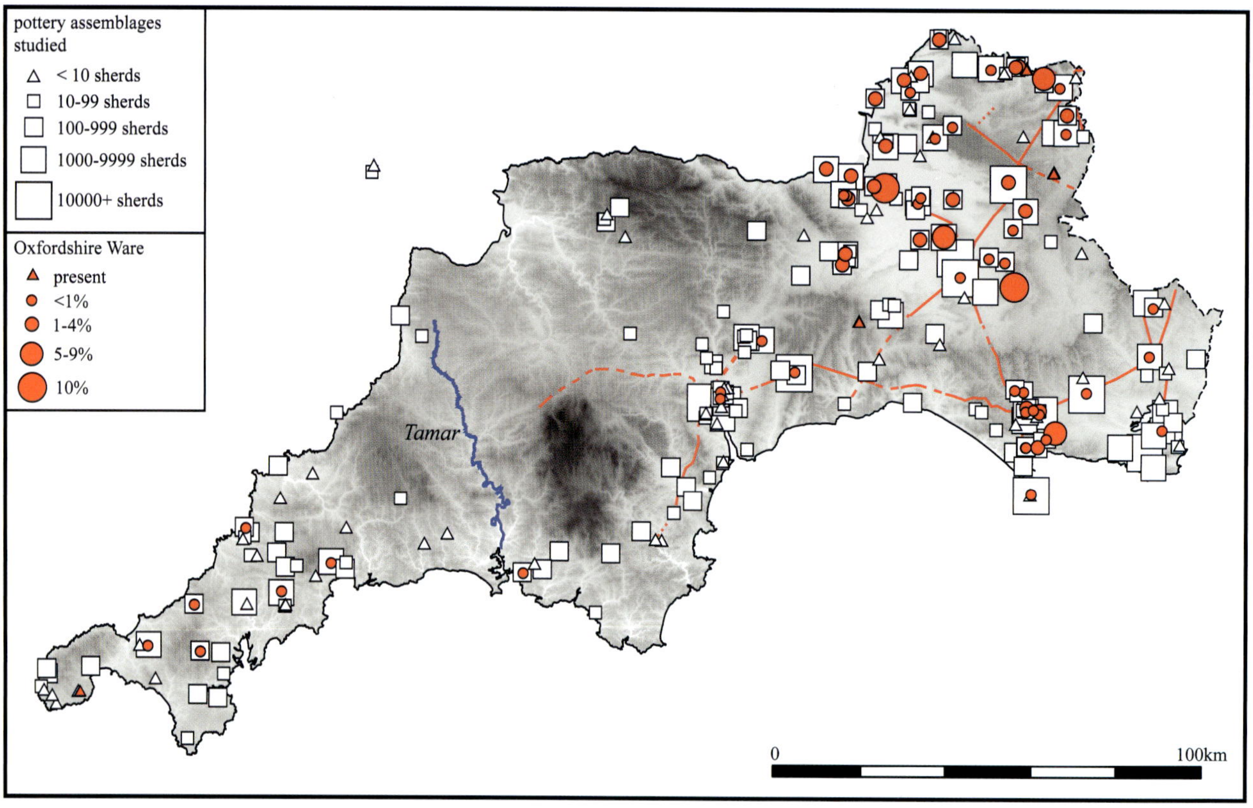

Fig. 3.32 The distribution of all Oxfordshire Ware (drawn by David Gould)

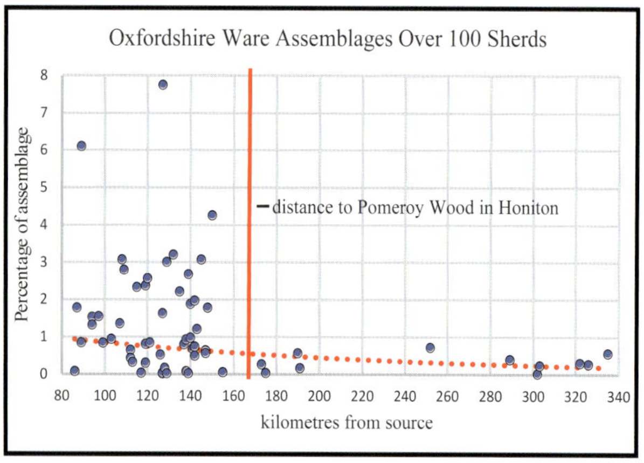

Fig. 3.33 The percentages of Oxfordshire Ware in assemblages of over 100 sherds (drawn by David Gould)

described above). Some cropmark enclosures that have been fieldwalked, for example, failed to produce any Romano-British material, such as Butland Farm, in Modbury (Horner 1993), Hayes Farm, in Clyst Honiton (Simpson *et al.* 1989), and Pond Farm, in Exminster (Jarvis 1976), and when these and other sites were subsequently excavated they typically produce very small amounts of pottery and other material culture. Two sites even appear to have been aceramic and were only dated through radiocarbon determinations (Parsonage Cross, in Littlehempston: Reed and Turton 2005; Dun Cross, in Dartington: Mudd and Joyce 2014, 94).

In order to try and establish whether the amount of pottery discarded on Romano-British settlements varied across the wider South-West an assessment was carried out of the density of sherds per area excavated. This proved to be a complex task, and the data presented in Table 3.8 must be treated with very great caution as artefact recovery rates will have varied enormously across different types of excavation (Fulford and Holbrook 2018; Rippon 2018a, 69–71; Smith and Fulford 2019). At Trethurgy, in Cornwall, for example, an entire settlement covering *c.* 2,000 m^2 was excavated and while the topsoil was removed by machine the whole area was cleaned by hand and found to contain a high density of stone buildings and other settlement-related features; the enclosure ditch was also extensively excavated (Quinnell 2004). Not surprisingly, this resulted in a large assemblage of finds, whereas modern development-led excavation will typically involve machining off the ploughsoil followed by only rudimentary cleaning of those areas where features are evident, and then sections cut across cut features with as little as <10% of the linears being excavated (depending on what is specified in the Written Scheme of Investigation agreed with the planning authority). As the careful and complete excavation of Trethurgy Round is anomalous

Table 3.8 The density of sherds per square metre of excavated area on Romano-British rural settlements

County	*Settlement type*	*Under 1000 m²*	*Over 1000 m²*
Cornwall	farmsteads (including Trethurgy, 3.5 sherds m²)	0.4	0.3
	farmsteads (excluding Trethurgy)	0.4	0.2
	higher status (Carvossa)	9.8	no data
Devon	farmsteads	0.3	0.1
	villas	1.4	0.6
Dorset	farmsteads	0.7	1.0
	villas	no data	10.0
Somerset	farmsteads	2.2	0.8
	villas	3.2	0.4

by modern standards, it is separated out from the other Cornish sites in Table 3.8. Villas are also distinguished from lower-status farmsteads.

Table 3.8 provides the data for each county, differentiating between small-scale excavations amounting to under 1000 square metres and larger scale work because small scale trenching – targeted on features surviving as earthworks or revealed through aerial photography and geophysical survey – will generally produce a higher density of sherds per excavated area than open area excavations (as the latter include large areas devoid of features). The data suggests that in Somerset and Dorset there was a higher sherd density than in the South-West Peninsula, and within the latter the sherd density in Cornwall is slightly higher than in Devon. Not surprisingly, sherd densities also appear to be greater on higher status sites. Overall, this analysis confirms a number of the trends evident in other aspects of the Romano-British material culture and landscape across the wider South-West: that areas to the east of the Blackdown and Quantock Hills made greater use of Roman-style material culture than areas to the west, and that within the South-West Peninsula Cornwall shows subtly different trends to Devon. It could indeed be this relatively low level of ceramic vessel use overall in Devon that explains why the proportion of imports is so high, as relatively fewer locally produced vessels were being used.

Case Study: the rural landscape east of Exeter

EAPIT was an investigation of not just Exeter itself but also its hinterland. The most extensively investigated Romano-British rural landscape in the South-West Peninsula is on the eastern fringes of modern Exeter, *c.* 5 km east of the Roman town, where extensive development along the M5 corridor, around Exeter Airport and the new town of Cranbrook has led to large-scale archaeological investigation, much of it carried out since the completion of data collection for the Rural Settlement of Roman Britain project (Brindle 2016). These development areas are shown on Figs 3.34 and 3.35 although in most cases the archaeological investigations were more limited in extent, consisting of geophysical survey, trial trenching and targeted open area excavations (*e.g.* Fig. 3.36). The vast majority of this fieldwork is as yet unpublished, and the sources used – mostly grey literature reports – are listed in online Appendix 3.6 (notes on the small-scale watching briefs can be found in the Exeter City Council HER). Some development areas have seen several phases of archaeological work that have referred to the site using different names, and just a single name has been used here. There is also some information from aerial photography (*e.g.* Hegarty *et al.* 2016), and where features on air photographic transcriptions – or indeed geophysical survey – can be dated through excavation they are shown on the illustrations below as a lighter tint (*e.g.* Fig. 3.36). Although the focus of this study was the Roman period, the antecedent landscape of later prehistoric field systems was also mapped as this is important in the discussion below of why there are so few Romano-British ditched field boundaries. The port at Topsham, on the north bank of the Exe Estuary is considered in Chapters 5 and 6 below.

An example of the complexity of the archaeology east of Exeter can be seen at Hill Barton, in Pinhoe, with Fig. 3.36 being based upon four separate phases of archaeological investigation by two archaeological units (Bennett 2010; Garland 2016a; Pears and Rainbird 2017; Farnell 2018a; Mudd *et al.* 2019). The area was covered by an extensive Middle Bronze Age field system oriented roughly east–west (various settlement features that have not been mapped in order to aid clarity), that during the Iron Age was replaced by a smaller number of field boundaries with a far more irregular layout. During the Late Iron Age/Early Roman period a farmstead was established comprising a roundhouse associated with a fence line and a group of pits containing large numbers of quern fragments (Garland 2016; 2017). This fence line was replaced by a ditched enclosure in the late 1st or early 2nd century AD, while in the mid 2nd century AD another

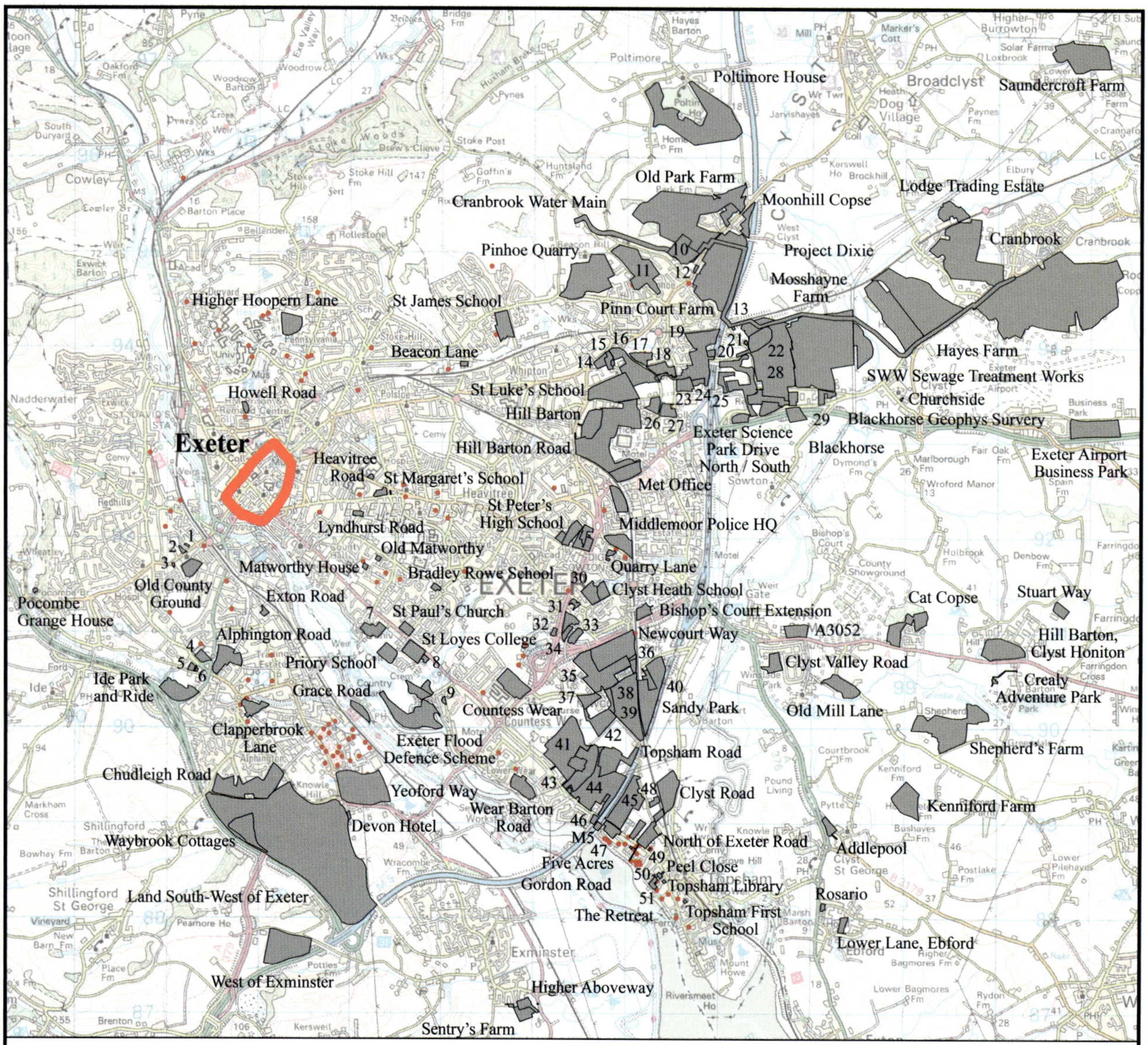

1. Fisher's Square
2. 137 Cowick Street
3. 63 Cowick Street
4. West Exe School
5. Oaklands
6. Villa Gardens
7. Earl Richards Road
8. Exeter Crematorium
9. Countess Wear Road
10. West Clyst School
11. Church Hill
12. Pinn Hill Road
13. Langaton House
14. Pilton Lane
15. Pinhoe Road
16. Cumberland Way
17. Pinn Brook Park
18. Harts Lane
18. Harts Lane
19. Tithe Barn Green, Monkerton
20. Tithe Barn Lane
21. Pinhoe Shooting Club
22. Tithebarn Green, Redhayes
23. Pinn Lane
24. The Vines
25. Exeter Science Park Geophysical Survey
26. Hollow Lane
27. South Field
28. Pinn Brook Enclosure
29. Honiton Road
30. Digby Drive
31. Rydon Lane Retail Park
32. Pynes Hill
33. Tesco Stores
34. Tesco Extension
35. Old Rydon Lane
36. Beech Cottage
37. Land off Newcourt House
38. Royal Navy Stores Depot Upper Site
39. Newcourt Drive
40. Bricknell's Bungalow
41. Royal Navy Stores Depot Lower Site
42. Exeter Golf Club
43. Seabrook Orchards Phase 2
44. Seabrook Orchards
45. Exeter Road
46. Aldi, Topsham Road
47. Wessex Close
48. Yeomans Gardens
49. Yarde's Field
50. The Mede
51. Nelson Close / Topsham First School

Fig. 3.34 Areas of archaeological investigation to the east of later Roman Exeter (modern OS basemap reproduced from the Ordnance Survey 1:50,000 map with permission of Ordnance Survey on behalf of The Controller of Her Majesty's Stationery Office; drawn by David Gould)

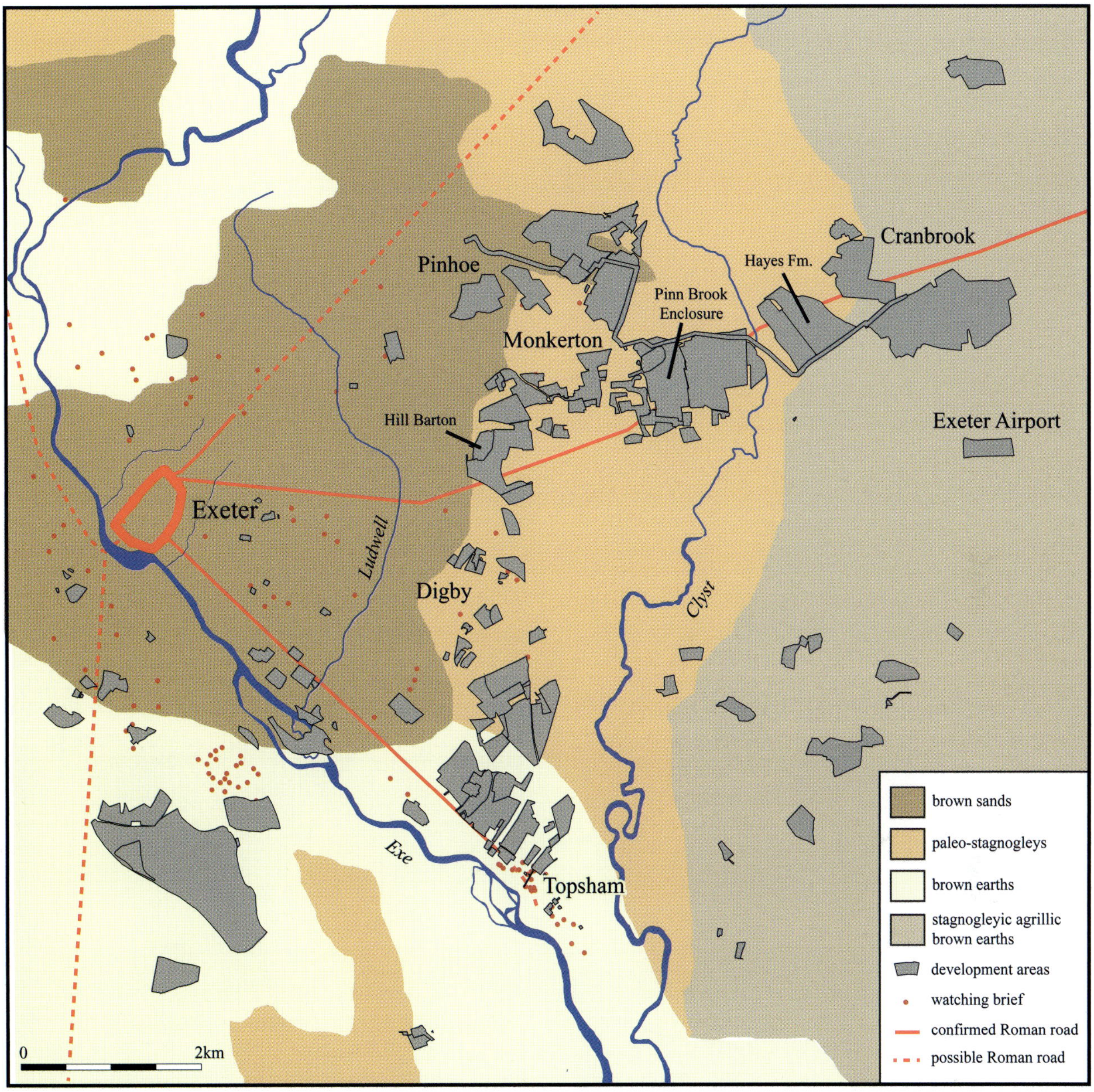

Fig. 3.35 Areas of archaeological investigation to the east of Exeter in relation to soils and later Roman Exeter. Small-scale watching briefs and evaluations are shown as red dots (after Mackney et al. *1983; drawn by David Gould)*

enclosure was constructed to the north: it is not clear whether this replaced the earlier enclosure – retaining the settlement's form as a single enclosed farmstead – or if the two enclosures were contemporary which would suggest the development of something approaching a complex farm. At nearby Tithe Barn Green it is similarly unclear whether the two adjacent enclosures were sequential or contemporary (Good 2016; Good and Massey 2017).

What is striking, however, is that these and other Romano-British farmsteads east of Exeter do not appear to have been associated with extensive ditched field systems. This cannot be the result of poor preservation as Bronze Age and Iron Age ditches survive across the entire area as well as to the south-east of Exeter (Fig. 3.37) where 16 separate excavations have revealed an extensive Middle Bronze Age field system and associated settlement, an open settlement of Iron Age date and occasional field boundaries, but just a single site with Romano-British activity at Bishop's Court. Another series of extensive excavations has been carried out at Hayes Farm and Cranbrook in the vicinity of Exeter Airport (Fig. 3.38). These similarly revealed extensive traces of Middle Bronze Age field systems but just a single square-shaped Romano-British enclosure, constructed around

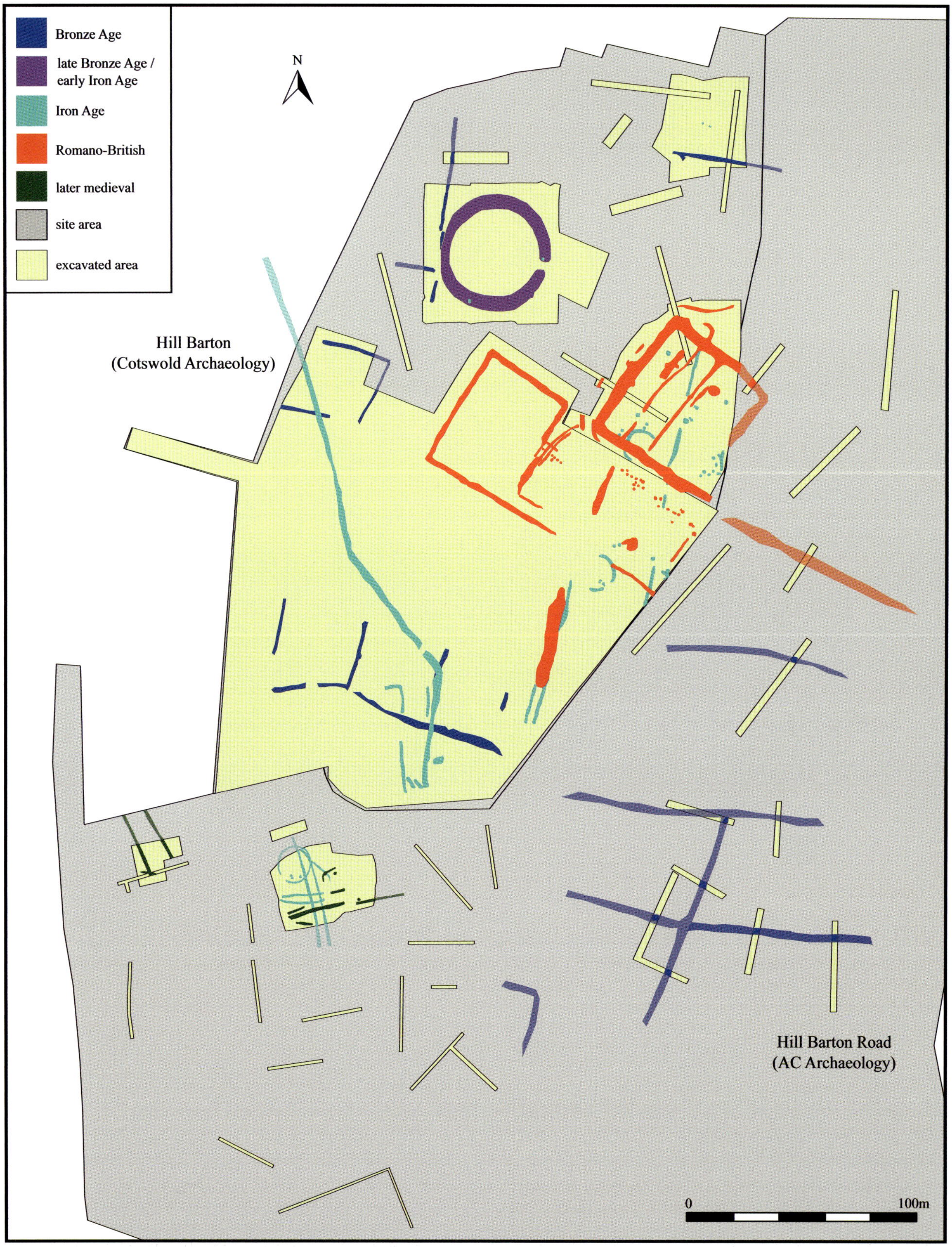

Fig. 3.36 The Bronze Age (only field systems are shown), Iron Age, Romano-British and later medieval features revealed through archaeological investigations at Hill Barton, in Pinhoe (drawn by David Gould)

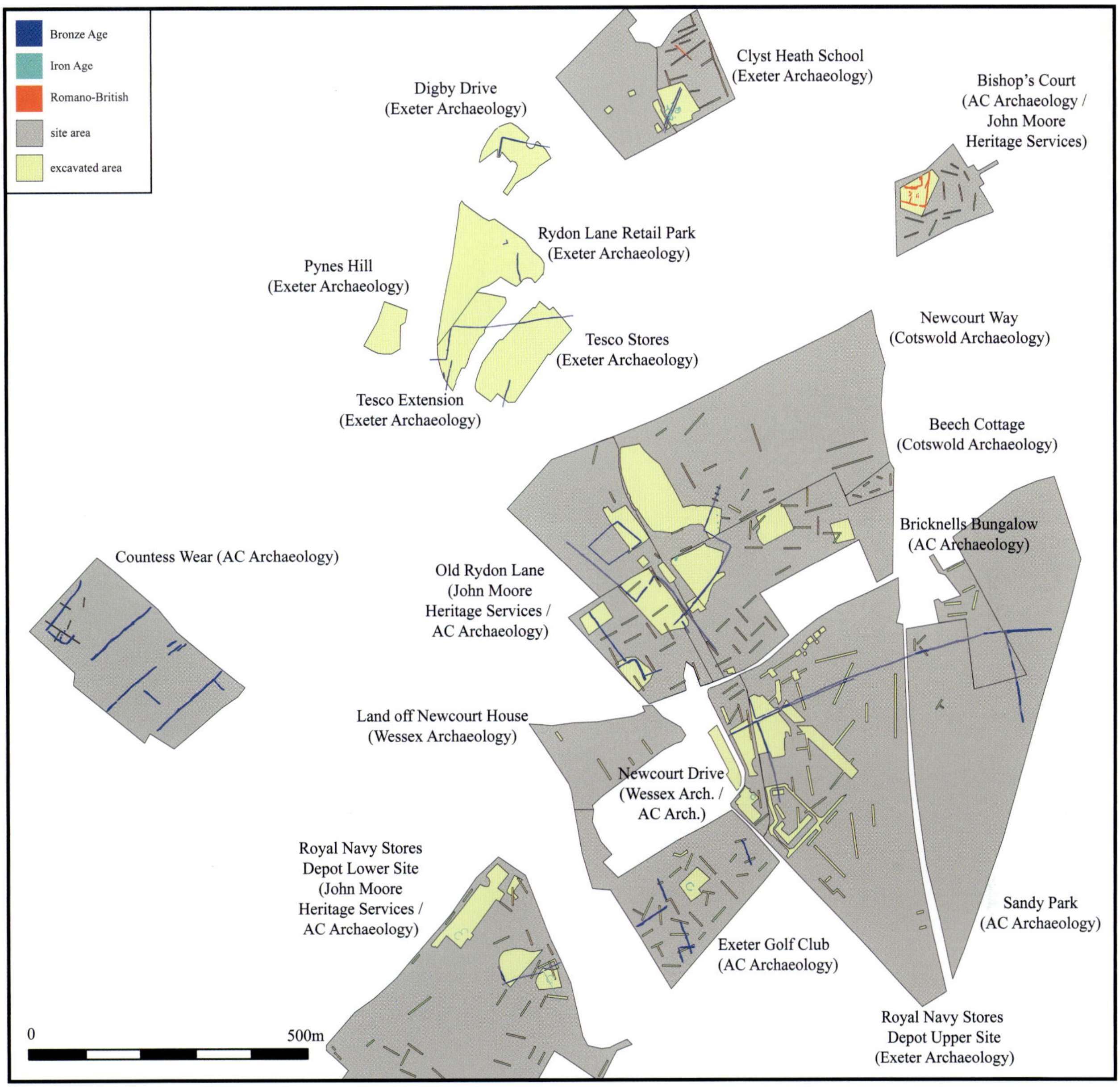

Fig. 3.37 The excavations south-east of Exeter between Digby Drive, Clyst Heath School, Sandy Park, the former Royal Navy Stores Depot and Countess Wear revealing an extensive Bronze Age field system but very little Romano-British activity. The key reports are Gilbert 2007a; 2007b; 2012; Pearce et al. *2011; Quinnell and Farnell 2016; other reports are Pink and Farnell 2014; Pears and Valentin 2015; Davis 2016; Govier 2017; Gillard* et al. *2018; Jones 2018; Orellana 2018; Rainbird 2020; Farnell and Fairclough forthcoming; Pears and Rainbird forthcoming (drawn by David Gould)*

the 2nd century AD and occupied through to the 3rd or 4th centuries AD, which does not appear to have been associated with a ditched field system.

The pattern that emerges from these and other excavations is therefore very clear: extensive Middle Bronze Age settlement and ditched field systems (although without the same regular co-axial layout as the Dartmoor 'reaves': Fleming 1988), some Iron Age settlements also with ditched field systems, and a series of Romano-British farmsteads that appear to have been in a largely open unenclosed landscape. Figure 3.39 is a schematic representation of the possible extent of ditched field systems east of Exeter during the Bronze Age, Iron Age and Roman periods. Areas with actual evidence for ditched field systems are cross-hatched, with their possible extent shown with a coloured shading (taking into account where archaeological work has shown an absence of ditched field systems of a particular date). This shows very clearly how extensive areas were covered in Bronze Age ditched field systems, followed by an apparent contraction in the

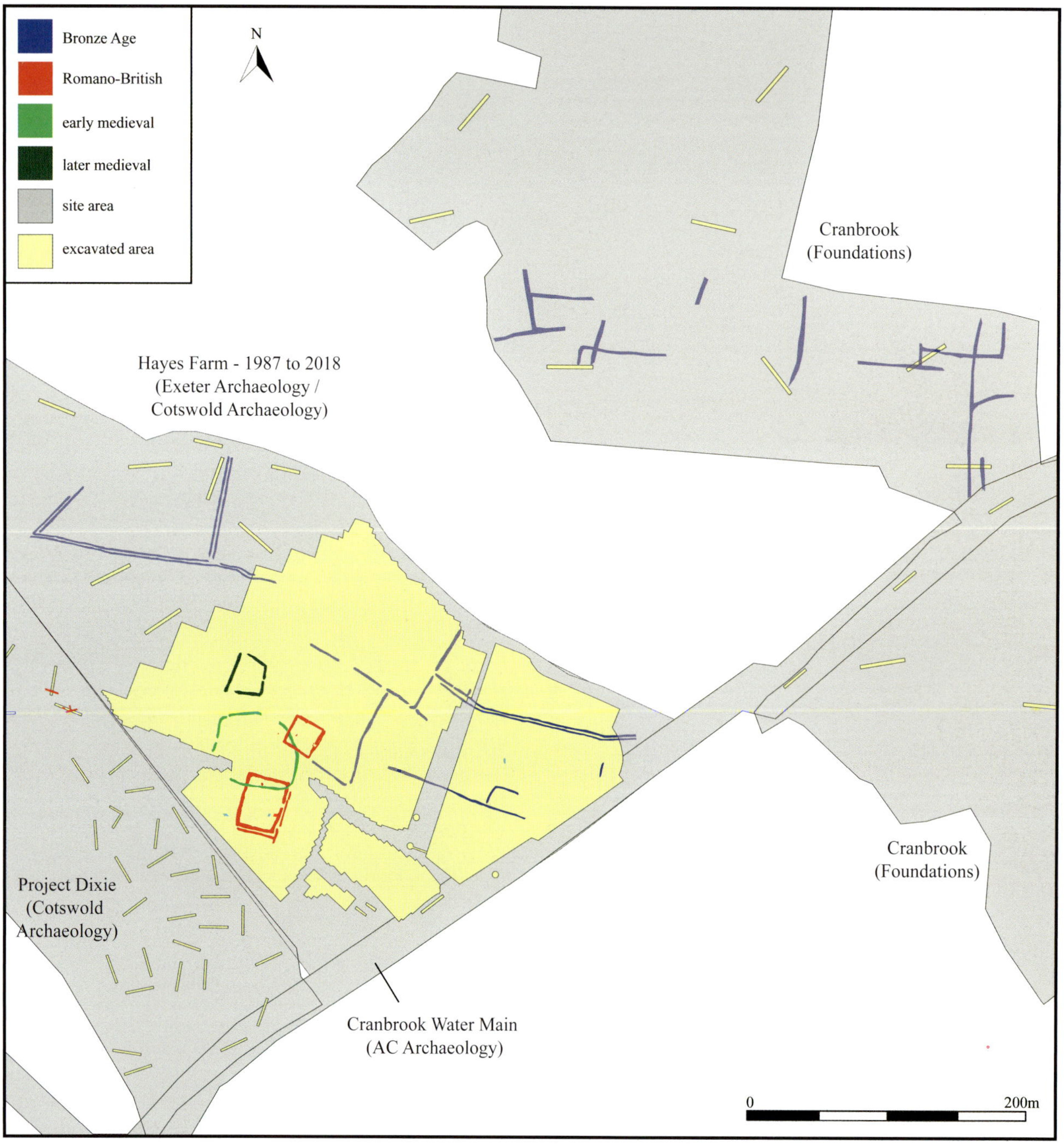

Fig. 3.38 Excavations at Hayes Farm and Cranbrook in the vicinity of Exeter Airport. The key reports are Brett 2011; Hughes and Rainbird 2016; King 2015; Simpson et al. *1989; Enright 1996; Barber 2000; Hart* et al. *2014; Gandham and Stubbings 2018 (drawn by David Gould)*

enclosed area during the Iron Age, and further reduction in the Roman period. This decline in ditched field systems was not due to an absence of settlement, but possible explanation for the absence of ditched field boundaries – that they have simply not been recognised – can be dismissed as the same excavations have revealed extensive Bronze Age and Iron Age field systems. It is possible that the absence of Romano-British field boundary ditches is due to fields having been defined in other ways such as hedges, fences or earthen banks. There are indeed some examples of Romano-British embanked fields on the limestone hills around Torbay (*e.g.* Lower Well Farm on Basely Common: Masson Phillips 1965; north of Ipplepen: Silvester 1980; Gallant *et al.* 1985; Quinn 1995), although this may have been influenced by the nature of the underlying geology: ditches would have been far more difficult to dig through hard limestone compared to the soft sandy soils east of Exeter.

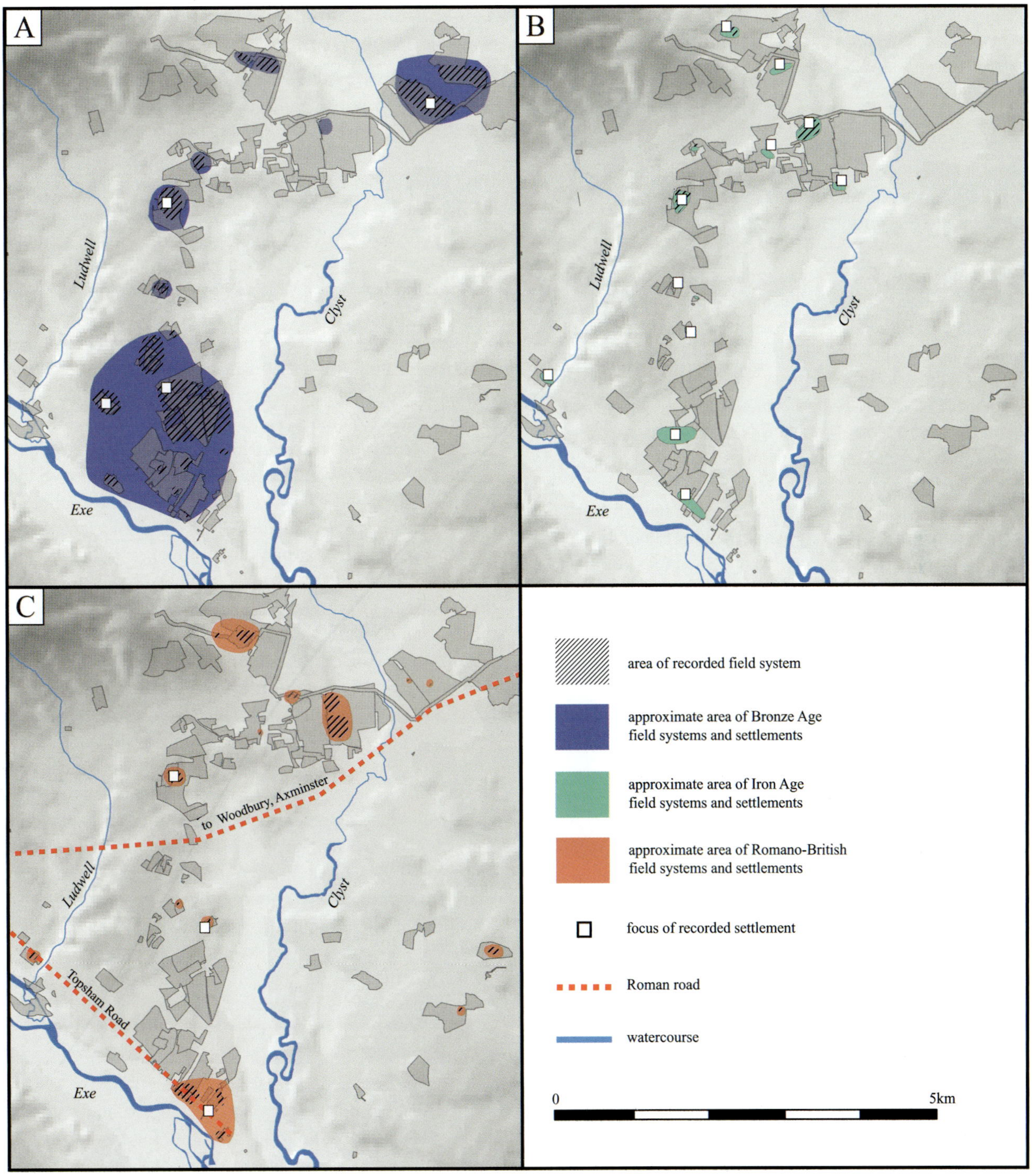

Fig. 3.39 Potential extent of the (A) Late Bronze Age, (B) Iron Age and (C) Romano-British field systems east of Exeter (drawn by David Gould)

Another possible explanation for the apparent scarcity of Romano-British ditched field systems is that the landscape was predominantly pasture. The area that has seen the most excavation to the east of Exeter corresponds to the light sandy 'paleo-stagnogley' soils of the Bridgnorth Association, derived from the underlying Permian Dawlish Sandstone (Fig. 3.35). These have given rise to what – in terms of modern farming – are regarded as amongst the best soils in the county, being Grade 1 in the former Ministry of Agriculture, Fisheries and Food's (1979) 'Agricultural Land Classification'. This classification reflects, however, modern farming requirements and it is possible that these relatively dry soils had become too dry and infertile by the Roman period to support extensive arable. There is other evidence to suggest that there was less arable in the South-West Peninsula as a whole compared to elsewhere in lowland Roman Britain. Across this region the aggregated pollen data suggests that just 1% of Total Land Pollen is from arable-indicative plants compared to 6% in South-East Britain and 3% in the 'Western Lowlands' (broadly the West Midlands; Rippon *et al.* 2015, fig. 2.11 and tab. 3.1). Although this figure includes some pollen sequences from relatively high ground, even in lowland areas such as at Mosshayne in the Clyst valley the pollen does suggest a predominantly pastoral landscape (Hawkins 2005). The South-West was not, however, a well-wooded region either: 27% of its pollen comes from trees, which is actually slightly lower than the 31% in South-East Britain and 33% in the Western Lowlands (Rippon *et al.* 2015, tab. 3.1), and so what we appear to be seeing is a landscape that was extensively cleared of woodland but where there was a higher proportion of the agricultural land put down to actively managed pasture in the lowlands and rough grazing and heathland on the more difficult topographies and soil.

There are other indications that arable was not particularly extensive in the South-West Peninsula such as the scarcity of Romano-British corn drying ovens on rural settlements. The most westerly rural example is at Membury on the Blackdown Hills, although they have been found in the roadside settlement at Pomeroy Wood near Honiton, and the small town at Topsham (Dyer 1999; Fitzpatrick *et al.* 1999b, 265; Tingle 2006; see below, Chapter 6, and EAPIT 2, Chapter 14). Possible rural corn driers have recently been excavated at Matford just south of Exeter (John Valentin pers. comm.) and Sherford, near Plymouth (Chaffey *et al.* 2016), but their interpretation as such is far from certain. A national analysis of the material culture on Romano-British rural settlements has also suggested that there are relatively few quern stones in Devon (Smith *et al.* 2016, 354–5), a phenomenon that is confirmed by Ruth Shaffrey (EAPIT 2, Chapter 14). Two were recovered from the farmstead at Tithe Barn Green, with larger numbers found at Hill Barton, and the charred cereal assemblages from both sites contained both grain and chaff suggesting that it was grown locally (Good 2016, 64–7; Garland 2016a, appendix 13; Mudd *et al.* 2019). At Hayes Farm – where the charred cereal remains also contained both grains and chaff – 'there is nothing in the weed flora to suggest that crops were not grown locally' (Simpson *et al.* 1989, 17–23). Overall, the artefactual and plant macrofossil evidence does suggest that the rural communities east of Exeter were engaged in some arable cultivation, but on a relatively small scale and this may account for the very limited evidence for ditched field systems.

Conclusion: Romano-British landscape and society in the South-West

Until recently, regional variation in landscape character and group identities within society have received less attention on the part of Romanists than amongst those studying the medieval period (Wallace and Mullen 2019, 75). It has, however, long been recognised that Romano-British landscape and society in the South-West Peninsula was significantly different to the rest of southern Britain, and the evidence for intra-regional variation is growing all the time (Quinnell 1986; 1993; Rippon 2008a; 2012; Smith *et al.* 2016).

Exeter was the only *civitas* capital and major town within the South-West Peninsula and – assuming that the reconstruction of the substantial basilica (complete with its *curia* [council chamber]) and forum are correct – then it will have been intended as an important administrative and economic centre. Whether its *civitas* extended across the whole of the South-West Peninsula is, however, unclear and there is increasing evidence for differences between its eastern and western parts that broadly conform to the historic counties of Devon and Cornwall. Today, these are divided by the River Tamar, although analogy with other territorial boundaries suggests that the sparsely settled high ground of Bodmin Moor and Kit Hill to the west are more likely to have formed the border zone: Millett (2017, 148, 153), for example, has suggested that there may have been valley-based communities in Kent, while in eastern England during the later prehistoric, Roman and early medieval periods this author has argued that territorial boundaries took the form of sparsely settled zones within the landscape, most commonly watersheds (Rippon 2018a). Overall, therefore, there appear to have been two separate *pagi* (communities) whose names – the Cornovii and the Dumnonii – were to become preserved by the later counties of Cornwall and Devon.

The distinctive character of Romano-British material culture in what is now Cornwall has already been highlighted by Quinnell (*e.g.* 1986; 1993; 2004), and Thomas (2018) has recently shown that this extends to the repertoires of locally produced pottery. While the Roman period sees the introduction of new vessel forms associated with food preparation (*e.g.* mortaria) and eating/drinking – with a shift away from communal practices such as passing around a jar towards individual portions using cups and beakers – in Devon this was achieved by local industries producing these new forms of vessel, whereas in Cornwall they had to be imported as the local gabbroic industry only produced its traditional range of vessel forms. It is also very striking how little gabbroic pottery travelled east of the Tamar Valley, suggesting that its production and circulation may in part have been socially embedded. The long-lived use of gabbroic clays found on the Lizard demonstrates the significance that some raw materials could assume, which may also have been the case with the highly micaceous clays used to produce South Devon Ware. We also now know that the Ludwell Valley and western side of the Blackdown Hills were areas associated with long-lived pottery industries. In part this could have been because of the inherent physical properties of these clays (that were particularly well-suited to making pots), although their popularity could also have resulted from a symbolic importance that formed part of a community's identity.

This same debate can be had about agricultural practices. The analysis of faunal remains and charred cereals has showed very marked differences in farming practices, some of which may have been linked to the inherent properties of particular soils and the requirements of individual animal species and cereal crops. But this alone may not account for the far more diverse arable cropping regimes in the South-West Peninsula; in the medieval period at least there appears to have been an element of cultural choice, and the same may well have been true during the Roman period.

There are also emerging differences in settlement patterns between the eastern and western parts of the South-West Peninsula. Exeter was the only settlement with urban characteristics, although there were nucleated roadside settlements to its east at Pomeroy Wood and south at Dainton Elms Cross, and possible examples to the west at North Tawton and north at Cullompton, and the presence of these nucleated roadside settlements suggests that the landscape and economy within a *c.* 20 km radius of Exeter was developing in a way that was similar to elsewhere in southern and eastern parts of Roman Britain. The South-West Peninsula also has very few villas and just a handful of possible complex farms, and once again these cluster within the immediate hinterland of Exeter.

There is, however, also evidence for a reluctance on the part of communities living in the South-West Peninsula to adopt Roman-style practices, reflected in the stubborn retention of circular (in Devon) and oval-shaped buildings (in Cornwall), alongside a predominantly pastoral economy and a far greater diversity of cereal crops compared to the wheat-dominated regimes seen in many of the regions further east. This was not, however, a particularly sparsely settled region – just as much of the landscape appears to have been cleared of woodland as in the South-East of Britain and its western lowlands – and recent development-led survey and excavation is revealing large numbers of farmsteads. The South-West Peninsula – while containing some upland areas – also possesses extensive areas of fertile lowland and rich mineral deposits and so should not be dismissed as a marginal area (see Chapter 2 above).

In the past these differences have been framed as the South-West Peninsula being less 'Romanised', but this a complex term has come in for very close scrutiny in recent years. Eckardt (2014, 127), for example, has noted how 'public and academic perception has perhaps had a tendency to focus on the homogenizing influence of Roman trade and, within the theoretical framework of Romanization, to look for uniformity rather than local diversity'. The connotations of top-down cultural change has also come in for much criticism (*e.g.* Mattingly 2006; 2011; Revell 2016), and instead what we appear to be seeing is far greater regional variation in material culture and landscape character. In the South-West Peninsula communities appear to have created distinctive identities for themselves by choosing to retain some aspect of their traditional lifestyles whilst being very selective about which aspects of Roman cultural influence they chose to adopt. The way that communities in Cornwall continued to patronise their traditional gabbroic industry, imported relatively small amounts of pottery from elsewhere, but were more enthusiastic than their neighbours to the east in using Roman-style dress accessories is a good example of 'creolisation' (the merging of elements from different cultures: Webster 2001; Pitts 2016, 724).

Other aspects of Romano-British material culture also reflect the South-West Peninsula's relative insularity. Ruth Shaffrey's study of quern stones in EAPIT 2, Chapter 14, for example, shows that there was a strong bias towards using local sources even where they were not of high quality for grinding, and that the stone sources used for querns across the rest of southern Roman Britain did not reach the South-West Peninsula. Brown and Moorhead (EAPIT 2, Chapter 16) have also shown how the patterns of coin circulation and loss in the South-West Peninsula were different to Dorset and Somerset, and that there were intra-regional differences: Devon has less coinage from the Flavian and Antonine periods, but more from the Late Roman period than Cornwall, although both counties have less Late Roman coinage overall compared to Dorset and Somerset.

So should the traditional view of 'Dumnonian poverty' be changed? Clearly it should. There is certainly far more evidence for Roman period settlement and material culture than when Fox (1952, 3) used that phrase, but the growing amount of archaeological survey and excavation is confirming that there was indeed a more limited uptake of new material culture and architectural styles, which is seen both in the countryside and Exeter itself (see Chapter 6 below, for example, where it is observed that there are very few mosaic pavements within the town and those that have been recorded are relatively poorly made). Visitors to the South-West Peninsula from South-East Britain will probably have noticed differences in the appearance of people, buildings, settlements and the wider landscape and may have interpreted it as reflecting cultural poverty, but this was only their perception. There are other ways of expressing wealth and identity, and the South-West was certainly rich in land, animals and minerals.

So was the South-West Peninsular less 'Romanised' (*e.g.* Fox 1969; Miles 1977a, 127)? While a few settlements are now being discovered that – in the context of the South-West Peninsula – will have been relatively high status (the small number of villas and possible complex farmsteads) – these are far from the well-appointed country houses seen clustering around small towns such as Bath and Ilchester. In the case of the immediate hinterland of Exeter it appears that landscape and society was moving in the same direction as the rest of Roman Britain in the 2nd and early 3rd centuries AD, but in a slower and more selective way, and that then appears to have faltered. Beyond the hinterland of Exeter, communities appear to have retained even more of their pre-Roman character reflected, for example, in the continued construction of circular and oval houses throughout the Roman period.

Finally, we must consider why the South-West Peninsula was so distinctive during the Roman period. Many archaeologists still portray the region as remote, dominated by sparsely settled uplands, and dissected by tidal river systems that made overland communication difficult (*e.g.* Mattingly 2006, 402–3). The tidal rivers were, however, actually a great asset as the foundation of Exeter at the head of the sheltered Exe Estuary and at the centre of a series of radiating roads, demonstrates. While Dartmoor, Exmoor and Bodmin Moor were visually prominent, these uplands actually form a small proportion of the South-West's landscape, and besides, what they lacked in arable potential they made up for in terms of the summer grazing and mineral wealth. For two parts of the medieval period – the 10th to 12th and late 15th to 17th centuries – Exeter was amongst the top ten wealthiest cities in England (see Chapter 1, Table 1.1 above) – and so its location and landscape cannot have been that bad.

Another explanation for the distinctive character of the South-West Peninsula in the Roman period is that it partly lay outside the system of civilian *civitates* and was 'probably under long-term military, state and external control', perhaps because of its particularly rich mineral wealth (*e.g.* Mattingly 2006, 402–8). There is, however, no direct evidence for *ager publicus* or an imperial estate, and the five 'milestones' that have been suggested as marking the boundary of imperial mining regions occur well down the Cornish peninsula not on the putative edge of the area under imperial control. Another possibility, therefore, is that what we are seeing in the South-West is not an impoverished community whose identity was stifled due to living within an imperial estate, but instead a physically discrete region – surrounded by water on three sides – that was rich in natural resources, in which societies developed and retained distinctive identities and practices that were well-suited to their surroundings and so slow to change.

4

'Richer in its bowels than in the face thereof': The Hinterland of Exeter during the Medieval Period

Stephen Rippon and David Gould

with a contribution by Gundula Müldner and Delphine Frémondeau

Introduction

Risdon's (*c.* 1630, 6) description of Dartmoor, in the middle of Devon, as 'richer in its bowels than in the face thereof' nicely encapsulates a common perception of Exeter's hinterland: that it was better endowed with buried mineral resources such as tin than in agricultural potential. The mining of tin was indeed crucial to the economic prosperity of Exeter during the early medieval period, but it was in fact the success of its farming – and in particular the production of woollen cloth – that resulted in its second era of great prosperity during the late medieval period.

Chapter 3 reviewed the development of the South-West's landscape during the Roman period, and the story will now be taken forward into the medieval period. There has been much debate over what happened as Britain ceased to be part of the Roman Empire, with some seeing it as a period of great political, social and economic upheaval and others arguing for far greater continuity (see Rippon *et al.* 2015 for an historiography). One reason why there are such divergent views of this period is that people at the time will have experienced it in very different ways: for those in society who were most closely engaged with the Roman way of life – supplying the military establishment, large-scale manufacturing industries reliant on the money-based market economy, and those living in urban centres – the late 4th and early 5th centuries will have been a period of very great change. For those less engaged with the Roman way of life, however, this period may well have seemed less traumatic and this was particularly the case with farming communities in the less urbanised parts of western and northern Britain. The South-West Peninsula also lay beyond the area that archaeological evidence suggests was subject to Anglo-Saxon folk migration with the most westerly find-spot of 5th-century artefacts being Hod Hill in eastern Dorset, and only a thin scatter of 6th-century sites as far west as central Dorset and eastern Somerset (Eagles 2018, 53, 63, 76). One reflection of a degree of socio-political continuity in the South-West Peninsula is that the Roman *civitas* of Dumnonia shares its name with a British kingdom of the 5th to 7th centuries (Pearce 2004; Higham 2008, 13–72), and for many within Dumnonian society it may have been the 7th and 8th centuries – when the region was assimilated into the West Saxon kingdom – that saw far greater change.

The early 5th to mid 7th centuries: a late antique period?

Local pottery production

Although the wider South-West is not rich in early medieval material culture, there are very significant differences within the region. Only Cornwall has a continuous ceramic sequence, with Roman-style gabbroic pottery from the Lizard continuing to be made into the 5th and 6th centuries (*e.g.* Trethurgy in Cornwall: Quinnell 2004, 108–27). A new ceramic tradition then emerged during the 6th to early 7th centuries in the form of 'Gwithian Style' wares that continued the Late Roman potting traditions seen in the gabbroic production and was contemporary with the importation of amphorae and tablewares from the Mediterranean (Thorpe 2011; Thorpe and Wood 2011; *e.g.* Boden Vean, in St Anthony-in-Meneage: Gossip 2013; Park En Venton, in Mullion: Brown *et al.* 2018). The distribution of gabbroic and 'Gwithian style' vessels is almost wholly restricted to Cornwall (Thorpe and Wood 2011, fig 10) and as such it continues the insularity seen within the Romano-British gabbroic ware: the only exception is a gabbroic vessel from the coastal port-of-trade at Bantham in South Devon (Reed *et al.* 2011, 108). From the 7th to 11th centuries 'Gwithian Style' wares were replaced by 'grass-marked' pottery that was produced in a far more restricted range of vessel types, and which before the 11th century is once again only found in Cornwall: from the 11th century onwards occasional sherds have been reported further east along the coast including Exmouth (Allan 1986, 132, No. 1) and Winkle Street in Southampton (Platt and Coleman-Smith 1975, 47).

The rural landscape

This continuous pottery sequence in Cornwall contrasts very sharply with Devon where there was little or no indigenous material culture that survives in the archaeological record from the 5th to 8th centuries. This is most clearly demonstrated by a series of wholly aceramic settlements across Devon that have been radiocarbon dated to this period (Table 4.1), while the wooden structures at Town Farm Quarry, in Burlescombe, have been dated to the 7th century by dendrochronology (Gent 2007). Aceramic settlements are similarly being radiocarbon dated to this period in Cornwall (*e.g.* Field 31, in Bossiney: Jones and Quinnell 2014, 12) and Somerset (*e.g.* South Petherton: Brett and Mudd 2013).

None of the early medieval settlements in Devon have seen extensive excavation, although some share certain characteristics: two lie within reoccupied Iron Age hillforts (High Peak and Raddon Hill) and another – Haldon Belvedere – lies on a hilltop. Hayes Farm is a small ditched enclosure, whose curvilinear form may represent a conscious departure from the rectiliniarity of the later Roman enclosure that it overlies. The curvilinear ditch at Pixie's Parlour, in Ottery St Mary, may also date to this period. It appears to have been part of an enclosure *c.* 50 m in diameter that post-dates a roundhouse gully associated with 2nd to 3rd-century AD pottery, and while the ditch itself contained two sherds of Roman pottery they could easily be residual; a pit within the enclosure contained a grain of barley radiocarbon dated to around the 7th or 8th centuries (Table 4.1).

It is striking that pollen sequences from across the South-West Peninsula show little evidence for a significant shift in the overall balance between arable, pasture and woodland suggesting that there was no widespread desertion of agricultural land in the 5th and 6th centuries (Fyfe *et al.* 2003; 2004; Rippon *et al.* 2006; Fyfe and Woodbridge 2012; Brown *et al.* 2014). An analysis of the orientation of excavated Late Roman field systems across the South-West found that a relatively low proportion (compared to central and south-eastern Britain) shared the same orientation as the overlying later medieval fieldscape, but rather than pointing to discontinuity in landscape use at the end of the Roman period, pollen sequences suggest that the discontinuity came around the 8th century (Rippon *et al.* 2006; Rippon *et al.* 2015; and see below).

Early medieval agriculture

While pollen sequences shed some light on the proportions of the major land-use types – woodland, pasture and arable – we must turn to excavated animal bone and charred cereal assemblages to tell us about specific farming regimes. Unfortunately there are very few faunal assemblages quantified by NISP from across the wider South-West, three of them coming from high status sites associated with pottery imported from the Mediterranean (the beach market at Bantham in South Devon, the coastal promontory at Tintagel in northern Cornwall, and Cadbury Congresbury hillfort in Somerset: Reed *et al.* 20011; Barrowman *et al.* 2007; Rahtz *et al.* 1992). Of the other two sites, Gwithian lay within sand dunes on the north Cornwall coast (Sturgess and Lawson-Jones 2006; Nowakowski 2007), and Poundbury on the chalk downland of Dorset (Sparey Green 1987). Tintagel has only a very small assemblage of 58 bones that is not statistically significant, but it is striking that the other four sites – including Poundbury – all have a relatively high proportion of cattle bones (*c.* 55%). The high status Bantham and Cadbury Congresbury have a high proportion of pig (20% and 36% respectively) compared to Gwithian and Poundbury – that appear to have been ordinary farming settlements – where pig was far less significant (*c.* 7%).

There are far more early medieval charred cereal assemblages, mostly dating to the 5th to 9th centuries, from which some very clear patterns emerge (Table 4.2). In Cornwall, sizable assemblages from two settlements are dominated by oats (69%) and barley (30%) with very little wheat (2%) (Penhale Round: Nowakowski and Johns 2015; Tintagel: Harry and Morris 1997; Barrowman *et al.* 2007). It is noteworthy that the assemblage from the oven at Black Cross near Newquay consisted entirely of oats (Nowakowski and Johns 2015). In Devon there was a more mixed pattern of arable cropping with sizable assemblages across seven sites containing a balance of oats (52%), rye (25%), barley (12%) and wheat (12%) (Aldi Site, in Topsham: Orellana and Garland 2016; Bantham Surf Club: Reed and Bidwell 2007; Hayes Farm, in Clyst Honiton: Hart *et al.* 2014; Langage, in Sparkwell: Salvatore and Quinnell 2011; Moore Farm, in Harberton: Mudd 2012; Tigley Site B, in Dartington: Mudd and Joyce 2014; Tiverton Road, in Cullompton: Morris and Rohan 2014). Two sites with large assemblages associated with drying ovens again show a very similar picture of mixed arable husbandry with oats 37%, barley 37%, wheat 25% and rye 1% (Cowick Lane, near Exeter: Caine and Valentin 2011; Pinn Brook Enclosure, in Pinhoe: Garland and Whelan

Table 4.1 Radiocarbon dates from 5th- to 7th-century rural settlements in Devon (excluding coastal trading sites)

Site	*Reference*	*Context*	*Lab. code*	*Uncalib. date(s)*	*Calib. date(s)*
Aldi Site, Topsham Road, in Topsham	Orellana 2016	settlement	SUERC-68426	1508+/–29 BP	cal. AD 430–631
Cranbrook, Clyst Honiton	Hood and King 2019	settlement	SUERC-57028	1551+/–29 BP	cal. AD 423–570
Dainton Elms Cross, in Ipplepen	Unpublished	cemetery	Beta-391541	1320+/–30 BP	cal. AD 655–765
			Beta-424799	1330+/–30 BP	cal. AD 610–670
			Beta-424800	1490+/–30 BP	cal. AD 540–640
			Beta-424801	1270+/–30 BP	cal. AD 670–775
			UBA-33489	1367+/–30 BP	cal. AD 610–757
			UBA-36416	1583+/–36 BP	cal. AD 400–553
			UBA-36417	1477+/–49 BP	cal. AD 430–655
			UBA-36418	1541+/–32 BP	cal. AD 425–588
			UBA-36419	1472+/–27 BP	cal. AD 549–642
			UBA-36420	1531+/– 41 BP	cal. AD 423–607
			UBA-36946	1631+/–28 BP	cal. AD 345–535
			UBA-39671	1480+/–30 BP	cal. AD 434–650
Haldon Belvedere, in Dunchideock	Gent and Quinnell 1999b	settlement	AA-34136	1390+/–45 BP	cal. AD 595–690
Hayes Farm, in Clyst Hydon (Chapter 3, Fig. 3.38)	Simpson *et al.* 1989	settlement	HAR-8676	1550+/–60 BP	cal. AD 390–630
Hazzard Farm, in Harberton	Pears and Rainbird 2014	settlement	SUERC-47025	1573+/–27 BP	cal. AD 420–550
			SUERC-47024	1512+/–29 BP	cal. AD 430–620
			SUERC-47026	1459+/–27 BP	cal. AD 560–650
Hill Barton, in Pinhoe		settlement	SUERC-77193	1511+/–27 BP	cal. AD 430–617
Kenn	Weddell 2000	cemetery	AA-19944	1520+/–65 BP	cal. AD 410–660
			AA-19943	1515+/–70 BP	cal. AD 420–660
			AA-19945	1405+/–65 BP	cal. AD 530–780
Langage, in Sparkwell	Salvatore and Quinnell 2011	settlement	SUERC-36234	1505+/–30 BP	cal. AD 430–640
Moore Farm, in Harberton	Mudd and Joyce 2014	settlement	NZA-36703	1619+/–20 BP	cal. AD 395–534
Oaklands, Cowick Lane, in Alphington	Caine and Valentin 2011	settlement	NZA-25991	1516+/–15 BP	cal. AD 460–610
Pinn Brook, in Pinhoe (Fig. 4.2)	Garland and Whelan 2016; Garland 2019	settlement	SUERC-67488	1492+/–29 BP	cal. AD 437–642
			SUERC-67490	1490+/–29 BP	cal. AD 437–644
			SUERC-67489	1357+/–29 BP	cal. AD 619–763
Pixie's Parlour, in Ottery St Mary	Mudd and Joyce 2014	settlement	NZA-36659	1351+/–25 BP	cal. AD 642–763
Raddon Hill, in Stockleigh Pomeroy	Gent and Quinnell 1999a	settlement	AA-29726	1405+/–55 BP	cal. AD 540–710
Sentry's Farm, in Exminster	Farnell and Salvatore 2010	settlement	SUERC-30753	1150+/–35 BP	cal. AD 770–980
Sherford	Wessex Archaeology 2018	settlement	UBA-35108	1526+/–28 BP	cal. AD 420–610
			UBA-35115	1492+/–39 BP	cal. AD 430–650
			UBA-35109	1398+/–27 BP	cal. AD 600–670
			UBA-35112	1408+/–27 BP	cal. AD 600–670
Tigley B, in Dartington	Mudd and Joyce 2014	settlement	NZA-36702	1462+/–20 BP	cal. AD 583–632

(Continued)

Table 4.1 Radiocarbon dates from 5th- to 7th-century rural settlements in Devon (excluding coastal trading sites) (Continued)

Site	*Reference*	*Context*	*Lab. code*	*Uncalib. date(s)*	*Calib. date(s)*
Tiverton Road, in Cullompton	Morris and Rohan 2014	settlement	SUERC-42997	1586+/–29	cal. AD 414–543
			Wk-13087	1635+/–53 BP	cal. AD 250–550
Wembury	Reed 2005	settlement	Wk-13086	1552+/–45 BP	cal. AD 410–620
			Wk-13088	1510+/–44 BP	cal. AD 430–640
Willand Road, in Cullompton	Hood 2010	settlement	SUERC-17958	1475+/–35 BP	cal. AD 530–660

2016; Garland 2019). The slightly greater significance of wheat in Devon compared to Cornwall repeats what was seen in the Iron Age and Roman periods, while the appearance of rye is also noteworthy: as it is found at three sites (Hayes Farm, Pinn Brook and Oaklands), all of which were on light soils in the immediate hinterland of Exeter, it was not an isolated phenomenon.

Although there are only two 5th- to 9th-century charred cereal assemblages in Somerset – both in the Central Lowlands – they are consistent in showing a very different picture to Devon in that wheat was dominant (87%) alongside only moderate amounts of barley (10%) and very low levels of oats (2%). This suggests that there was not a significant shift away from wheat after the Roman period, and that the high levels of oats across the South-West Peninsula is a genuine regionally distinctive pattern of arable farming. In Dorset there are single sites on the chalk downland (Poundbury: Sparey Green 1987) and sandy heathland (Bestwall Quarry: Carruthers 2006). At Poundbury the non-corn drier assemblage was dominated by wheat (73%), with moderate amounts of barley (22%) and some oats (5%): in contrast, the very large assemblage associated with the corn driers was associated with roughly equal amounts of wheat (33%), barley (36%) and oats (31%). At Bestwall, in contrast, another large assemblage was dominated by rye (57%) – again showing its significance on dry soils – followed by barley (26%), oats (17%) and wheat (13%). The shift from hulled (spelt and emmer) wheat to free-threshing wheat is seen across the wider South-West and indeed more widely, although the reasons for this remain poorly understood (McKerracher 2018, 96–106).

Overall, the early medieval charred cereal assemblages suggest significant regional variation in arable regimes, which in part reflect how local communities were selecting cereals that were suited to their local environments, whether they be some of the damp heavy soils of the South-West Peninsula or the light free-draining conditions on the chalk downland and heathlands in Dorset. There is, however, also an element of cultural choice as the physical landscape of lowland eastern Devon and lowland central Somerset were broadly similar yet cropping regimes were very different. The broad continuity in these patterns from the Roman through to the early medieval period suggest that the collapse of the market-based economy did not profoundly change arable regimes that had become firmly embedded in the ways that these different communities practiced farming.

Trade with the Mediterranean, and the social structures behind it

A number of settlements across the South-West Peninsula have produced examples of mid 5th- to mid 6th-century pottery imported from North Africa and the eastern Mediterranean (Fig. 4.1). In Devon, this pottery is virtually all restricted to four locations on the south coast: the three well-known sites at High Peak near Sidmouth (Pollard 1966; 1967), Bantham (Reed *et al.* 2011) and the nearby Mothecombe (Turner and Gerrard 2004; Agate *et al.* 2012), and as well as the recently discovered site at Challaborough (Hughes 2017b, 2). Cawsands lies just across the Cornish border, on the western side of Plymouth Sound (Duggan 2018). None of this material has been found in Exeter, and the only inland findspot is something of a curiosity: a single small, abraded sherd, apparently identified by John Hayes as 'African Red Slip Ware' found in a far later context at Lydford Castle on the western fringes of Dartmoor (Saunders 1980, 169; Thomas 1981b, 9; Duggan 2018, appendix K, No. 112). Alcock (1995, 145) suggests that 'minimal though this is, it cannot be explained away, and must be taken as evidence for a high-status sixth century presence', and he goes onto suggest that the timber-reinforced bank sealed beneath the Late Saxon rampart from which the sherd came was 6th century in date. There is, however, another possible explanation for this small, abraded sherd. John Allan (pers. comm.) recalls that Trevor Miles, who undertook the study of the pottery, said that there was some uncertainty about the identification, not reflected in the final report, and the sherd was lost soon after. Ewan Campbell (1991, 386) never saw the sherd.

Table 4.2 Medieval cereals from across the wider South-West, excluding wetland sites and material from corn driers, etc. (based upon the sites listed in online Appendix 4.1)

Site	Oats		Barley		Rye		Emmer wheat		Spelt wheat		Emmer or spelt		Free-threshing wheat		Club wheat		Total identified wheat		Total unidentified wheat		Total wheat		Total
	No.	%	No.	%	No.	%	No.	%	No.	%	No.	%	No.	%	No.	%	No.	%	No.	%	No.	%	
Early medieval (5th C – mid-9th C)																							
Cornwall	1736	69	750	30	3	0	0	0	1	33	0	0	2	67	0	0	3	7	41	93	44	2	2533
Devon	1402	52	315	12	667	25	2	1	3	0	85	30	196	69	0	0	286	90	33	10	319	12	2703
Somerset	39	2	163	10	0	0	3	1	38	1	48	8	478	84	0	0	567	41	811	59	1378	87	1580
Dorset chalkland	85	5	352	22	0	0	0	0	30	3	0	0	918	97	0	0	948	82	213	18	1161	73	1598
Dorset heathland	143	17	218	26	476	57	0	0	0	0	5	5	105	95	0	0	110	100	0	0	110	13	947
Totals	**3405**	**37**	**1798**	**19**	**1146**	**12**	**5**	**0**	**72**	**1**	**138**	7	**1699**	**89**	**0**	**0**	**1914**	**64**	**1098**	**36**	**3012**	**33**	**9361**
High medieval (1066–1348)																							
Cornwall																							
Devon	11222	52	201	1	7840	37	0	0	11	1	10	1	1261	98	0	0	1282	63	740	37	2022	10	21285
Somerset	317	5	430	6	100	1	5	0	0	0	15	0	5175	100	0	0	5195	87	810	13	6005	88	6852
Dorset chalkland												No data											
Dorset heathland	91	11	82	10	121	14	0	0	0	0	0	0	548	100	0	0	548	100	0	0	548	65	842
Totals	**11630**	**40**	**713**	**2**	**8061**	**28**	**5**	**0**	**11**	**0**	**25**	**0**	**6984**	**99**	**0**	**0**	**7025**	**82**	**1550**	**18**	**8575**	**30**	**28979**

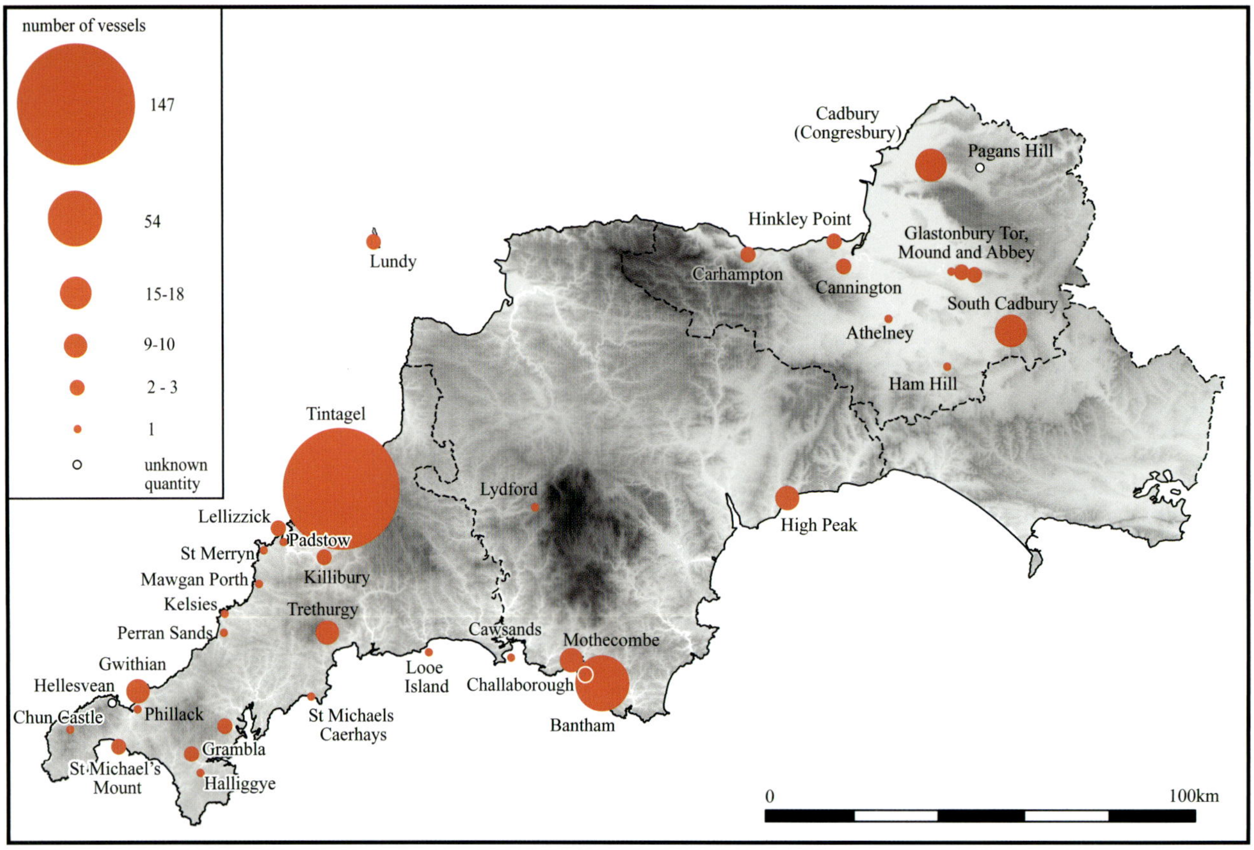

Fig. 4.1 Estimated numbers of 5th- to 6th-century Mediterranean vessels across the wider South-West (after Duggan 2018 and Hughes 2017b, 2; drawn by David Gould)

It is striking that none of these mid 5th- to mid 6th-century Mediterranean imports have been recovered from the growing number of radiocarbon-dated 5th- to 6th-century sites being identified across inland parts of Devon (see above), suggesting that their consumption was related to specific practices on coastal sites. The significance of this distribution of imported pottery becomes all the more significant in the light of the distribution of Byzantine coins. The antiquarian Shortt claimed to have found 15 such coins in and around Exeter, and while Boon (1991) dismissed all of the Exeter and Devon examples as recent losses there are a number of finds that could be genuine (Moorhead 2009; forthcoming; and pers. comm). One is a coin of Tiberius II (AD 581–2) found in a ditch 'near Princetown' on the western side of Dartmoor just 14 km south-east of Lydford: it is tempting to see this as being linked to the trade in tin. Another coin, of Anastasius (*c.* AD 498–515), from Exmouth is noteworthy as it came from the beach, and the PAS has recently recorded a metal detecting find, with good patina, from Otterton beach directly below High Peak (Tiberius II Constantine, AD 572–82; PAS DEV-AF8681). Added to this find are a group of ten coins – of which four have been reported to the PAS, again with good patina – found on the banks of the nearby River Otter that include examples of Justin I (AD 518–27) and Justin I or Justinian II (*c.* AD 518–37; PAS DEV-464726). The defended hilltop at High Peak lies on top of high, rocky, coastal cliffs and it is unlikely that the pottery was brought there from ships landing on the beach below, and instead they probably landed in the sheltered waters of the nearby Otter Estuary. Two of the three Cornish findspots of Byzantine coins – beside the Camel Estuary north of Padstow, and on the coast at Perranporth – were similarly found in coastal/estuarine locations (PAS CORN-72D1D7; PASCORN-1C01E3), while the third – from Chysauster – is from close to the coast on the West Penwith peninsula (Allen *et al.* 2004, 205, No. 44). Great care must be taken in interpreting finds of Byzantine coins, but if these are genuine early medieval losses then the coastal distribution is clear.

The scarcity of mid 5th- to mid 6th-century Mediterranean imported pottery from inland Devon is particularly surprising as in Cornwall to the west, and Somerset to the east, there have been numerous finds from inland sites (Fig. 4.1; Campbell 2007a; Duggan 2018). In part this may reflect the different histories of archaeological research in these three counties with Somerset, for example, having seen a series of excavations specifically targeting hilltop sites that were likely to have early medieval occupation such as Cadbury Congresbury

(Rahtz *et al.* 1992), Glastonbury Tor (Rahtz 1970) and South Cadbury (Alcock 1995). Cannington can probably be added to this list of high-status hill-top settlements: the hillfort has seen very limited excavation (although some Roman pottery was recovered: Rahtz 1969) yet it has a Roman villa (Hart and Mudd 2018) and post-Roman cemetery on its lower flanks (Rahtz *et al.* 2000), a configuration that is highly reminiscent of Cadbury Congresbury (Rippon 1997, 136). Cannington was a royal manor in Domesday and strong contender for the central place within an early medieval *regio* that extended from the Bristol Channel to the north, and across from the Parrett Estuary to the east and the Quantock Hills to the west (Rippon 2018b).

In Cornwall, small amounts of 5th- to 6th-century Mediterranean pottery are found on numerous sites both on the coast and inland, and whereas the assemblages from Devon are dominated by amphorae – that comprised 91% (Bantham), 100% (Mothecombe) and 100% (High Peak) of the vessels (Duggan 2018, 73, 80, 83) – in Cornwall and Somerset around a third to a half of the vessels are fine tablewares (*e.g.* Cadbury Congresbury: Rahtz *et al.* 1992; South Cadbury: Alcock 1995; Trethurgy: Quinnell 2004, tab. 5.3; Tintagel: Duggan 2018, 66–9). The way(s) in which these imports reached South-West Britain has seen much discussion (summarised in Duggan 2018), and it must be remembered that on the vast majority of sites the number of complete vessels represented by these sherds is very limited, with just *c.* 322 amphorae and *c.* 126 tableware vessels known from the whole of Britain and Ireland (Dugan 2018, 2). Some have argued for sustained trade led by the local secular elite in which the imported vessels were exchanged for metals such as tin (*e.g.* Campbell 2007a), while others have postulated smaller-scale and more episodic contact (*e.g.* Wooding 1996).

In Cornwall and Somerset it seems reasonable to see settlements such as Cadbury Congresbury, South Cadbury, Tintagel and Trethurgy as the residences of the communities who used the tablewares and consumed the products of the amphorae, although they presumably acquired these goods via coastal locations. In Devon the pattern is clearly different as the imports are largely amphorae and consumption appears to have been restricted to these coastal locations. Bantham has one of the largest number of vessels – still only 52 (Duggan 2018, tab. 6) – and has most recently been interpreted as a permanently occupied coastal port-of-trade (Reed *et al.* 2011). The problem with this concept is that it conjures up an image of the extensive and well-ordered Middle Saxon emporia of eastern England where large communities of merchants and craftsmen plied their trades all year round. The landscape context of Bantham was, however, very different to these eastern emporia as it lies stratified within an extensive area of shifting coastal sand dunes that would not have been a comfortable place to live all year round: the absence of a buried soil associated with the early medieval occupation shows that it was not associated with a period of dune stability (*e.g.* Silvester 1981b, 113). The various excavations at Bantham have, however, produced a large and relatively rich material culture assemblage alongside the Mediterranean pottery including imported glass, evidence for textile production, iron working and bone working, while the faunal assemblage suggests the large-scale consumption of meat (*e.g.* Fox 1955; Silvester 1981b; Griffith 1986; Griffith and Reed 1998; Reed *et al.* 2011). While a number of hearths, postholes and stakeholes have been recorded there is no evidence for substantial buildings and it is hard to see how this location in the dunes will have been chosen for a permanently occupied port-of-trade as opposed to a seasonal settlement (the stone-revetted rampart, forming the corner of a rectilinear enclosure *c.* 200 m inland, pre-dated a soil containing 38 sherds of 2nd to 4th-century AD pottery, but no 5th- to 6th-century imports were found: Griffith and Reed 1998). The same was presumably also the case at nearby Mothecombe (at the mouth of the River Erme) where another settlement has been found eroding out of coastal sand (Agate *et al.* 2012; Duggan 2018, 77). The view of this author is that Bantham and Mothecombe were seasonal settlements in liminal coastal locations where British communities undertook craft production and met traders from the Mediterranean, but were not themselves permanent settlements of the social elite. It is likely that one of the goods being exchanged for amphorae and their contents was tin, and it is noteworthy that a hoard of 40 albeit undated tin ingots has been found at the mouth of the Erme Estuary in Bigbury Bay (Fox 1995).

So where were the social elite living? Are we missing hilltop sites in Devon (equivalent to those in Somerset), or were the socio-economic means by which Mediterranean pottery reached the two areas different? The first of these questions is difficult to answer as relatively little excavation has been carried out inside Devon's hillforts, although a thorough review of the evidence by Grant (1995, 97) suggested that – unlike in Somerset – reoccupation was not a widespread phenomenon. This picture has changed slightly by recent work at Raddon Hill where aceramic early medieval occupation was found through radiocarbon dating (Gent and Quinnell 1999a), but small-scale work within the hillforts at Berry Ball, in Crediton Hamlets (Manning and Quinnell 2009), Hembury (Todd 2007a) and Cadbury Castle, near Thorverton (Wilkes *et al.* 2012) has not produced any post-Roman material. The only example of mid 5th- to mid 6th-century Mediterranean imports from a reused hillfort in Devon therefore remains High Peak which lies on the East Devon coast (Pollard 1966). In Somerset, the presence of late Romano-British material has been taken a possible indication of continued use of hilltops into the early medieval period, but it is striking that very little Roman material has been found in Devon's hillforts either (Grant 1995; Manning and Quinnell 2009), the dump of artefacts in a well or shaft at Cadbury Castle, near Thorverton, being a notable exception (Wilkes *et al.* 2012). The identification of the multivallate Posbury hillfort, near Crediton, with the battle of *Posentesburh* ('Posente's stronghold') that the *Anglo-Saxon Chronicle* records in 661 (Swanton 1996, 32) is intriguing, as is the place-name of Denbury hillfort – 'fortified place of the *Defnas*, the men of Devon' (Watts 2004, 183) – although it could simply reflect later perceptions that it was once a citadel, as opposed to reality (and see Higham 2008).

It appears, therefore, that the socio-economic means by which Mediterranean pottery reached Devon was different to elsewhere. In Cornwall and Somerset we see imported tablewares and the contents of amphorae being consumed by communities in their permanent residences, some of them presumably of relatively high social status. In contrast, the evidence in Devon – as it stands at the moment – suggests wine-fuelled feasting at seasonal beach markets. Although archaeologically one of the most visible aspects of the early medieval period in Devon, the numbers of vessels is actually very small and these may have been but fleeting episodes of trade and consumption.

Dumnonia and the 7th-century expansion of the West Saxon kingdom

In the late 5th or 6th century Gildas' *De Excidio Britanniae* ('The Ruin of Britain') recounts how King Constantine of Dumnonia brutally murdered two royal youths and their guardians (Winterbottom 1978, XXVIII.1; Higham 1994, 55, 111, 175–83), giving us a brief insight into the hierarchical society that appears to have prevailed in sub-Roman Britain. We hear nothing more of Dumnonia until the mid 7th century – around a hundred years after the trading links with the Mediterranean had ceased – when it was gradually absorbed by the West Saxon kingdom. Although it must be remembered that the *Anglo-Saxon Chronicle* was written from the perspective of the victorious Saxons, and as such will no doubt have glossed over any setbacks, the key dates appear to have been:

- 658 King Cenwalh [of the West Saxons, *c.* 642–72] defeated the British at *Peonnum* [probably Penselwood on the high ground of Selwood Forest that marks Somerset's eastern border] and drove them as far west as the River Parrett [*c.* 55 km NE of Exeter].
- 661 Cenwalh is said to have fought at *Posentes byrig* [*byrig* = OE *burh*, a stronghold; interpreted as Posbury on the Whitestone Hills 12 km WNW of Exeter and south of Crediton] (Yorke 1990, 137; Swanton 1996, 32–3; Pearce 2004, 249; Higham 2008, 88).
- 682 King Centwine [of the West Saxons, 676–85/6] is said to have 'put the Britons to flight as far as the sea' suggesting that they had taken the rest of Devon.
- *c.* 685 the Life of St Boniface – who was probably born about *c.* 675 of noble birth – implies that he received his education as a young boy during the 680s at a church in Exeter whose Abbot – Wulhard – had a Saxon name (Barlow 1980, 27; Holdsworth 1980, 52–4). This suggests that the church may have been founded by King Cenwalh who ruled the West Saxons from *c.* 642–72 (Yorke 1990, 137; Swanton 1996, 35; Pearce 2004, 249; Higham 2008, 88; Orme 2009, 2).
- 710 King Ine [of the West Saxons, 688–726] fought against Geraint, king of the [West] Welsh [*i.e.* Dumnonia] (Swanton 1996, 32, 39, 42; reginal dates from Yorke 1990, 133). It has been suggested that this battle was close to the Tamar Valley as Ine is said to have granted Glastonbury Abbey land at *Linig* – interpreted as between the Tamar and Lynher – soon after (710×722; Finberg 1954, No. 73). This is based upon Adam of Domerham's *De antiquitate*'s substitution of *Tan* in the original single-sheet charter of 705/6 (Sawyer 1968, S.248) with *Tamer*, but Abrams (1996, 231–2) notes that 'this identification is unquestionably mistaken as the single sheet shows clearly that the *Tan*, not Tamar, was intended'.

It would seem, therefore, that by the 660s the West Saxon kingdom had conquered eastern Devon, including Exeter, and that by the 680s they had pressed further west down the South-West Peninsula. There is, however, no evidence that this was anything other than a military and political conquest, and while the language of the landscape – its place-names – eventually changed, there is no reason why this should have been associated with a mass folk migration and displacement of the native British population.

The 'long 8th century': transformations in the countryside?

There is growing evidence from across southern Britain that the late 7th to early 9th centuries – a period that historians have referred to as the 'long 8th century' – was one of great change within society and the landscape (*e.g.* Hansen and Wickham 2000; Rippon 2010). This was the period when early folk-based territories had coalesced into large kingdoms (Rippon 2012, chapter 10), and trade between the South-East of Britain and the near continent was revived. In the countryside, palaeoenvironmental sequences show an increase in agricultural intensity, while archaeological excavations are revealing evidence for investment in infrastructure such as the construction of intertidal fish-traps and improvements in communications. The building of watermills and corn-drying ovens was often associated with the emergence of settlements whose character is that of estate centres where surplus agricultural produce was collected and processed. In South-East Britain the study of these developments has been made possible by the re-emergence of coinage and pottery production – themselves being indicators of an economic revival –

whereas in the wider South-West this key archaeological evidence is largely absent. Whilst there is a scatter of coins dating to this period across Dorset and Somerset, the PAS database records none to the west of the Blackdown and Quantock Hills (the most westerly find being a silver sceat of *c*. AD 715–730 from Milverton, just west of Taunton: SOM-3D9955). In Cornwall, however, there is a continuous ceramic sequence throughout this period (see above), and this lack of 7th- to 8th-century material culture across Devon is yet another indication of how communities living there clearly had a very distinct identity.

Radiocarbon dating, however, is starting to shed light on this period. A series of pollen sequences show some agricultural intensification during the 7th to 9th centuries including the clearance of valley-floor alder woodland at Aller Farm in Stockland, on the Blackdown Hills (Hatton and Caseldine 1991), the first appearance of cereals at Hellings Park in the eastern Devon lowlands (Hawkins 2005), and a marked increase in arable at Hares Down in Knowstone, Lobbs Bog and Windmill Rough, in Rackenford, and Middle North Combe, in Templeton, on the mid-Devon Culm Measures (Fyfe *et al*. 2004). It is also striking that a series of aceramic settlements and cemeteries radiocarbon dated to this period all appear to have been abandoned around the 7th to 8th centuries (Table 4.1), suggesting that settlement patterns were changing.

There are also several sites where there appears to have been investment in infrastructure at what could have been estate centres. At Pinn Brook, in Pinhoe, to the east of Exeter, the ditches of a large Iron Age oval-shaped enclosure were recut in the early medieval period and were silting up by the 7th to 8th centuries (based on radiocarbon dates). A pair of internal ditches divided off the western half of the enclosure – the terminus of one producing a radiocarbon date from wood charcoal in the

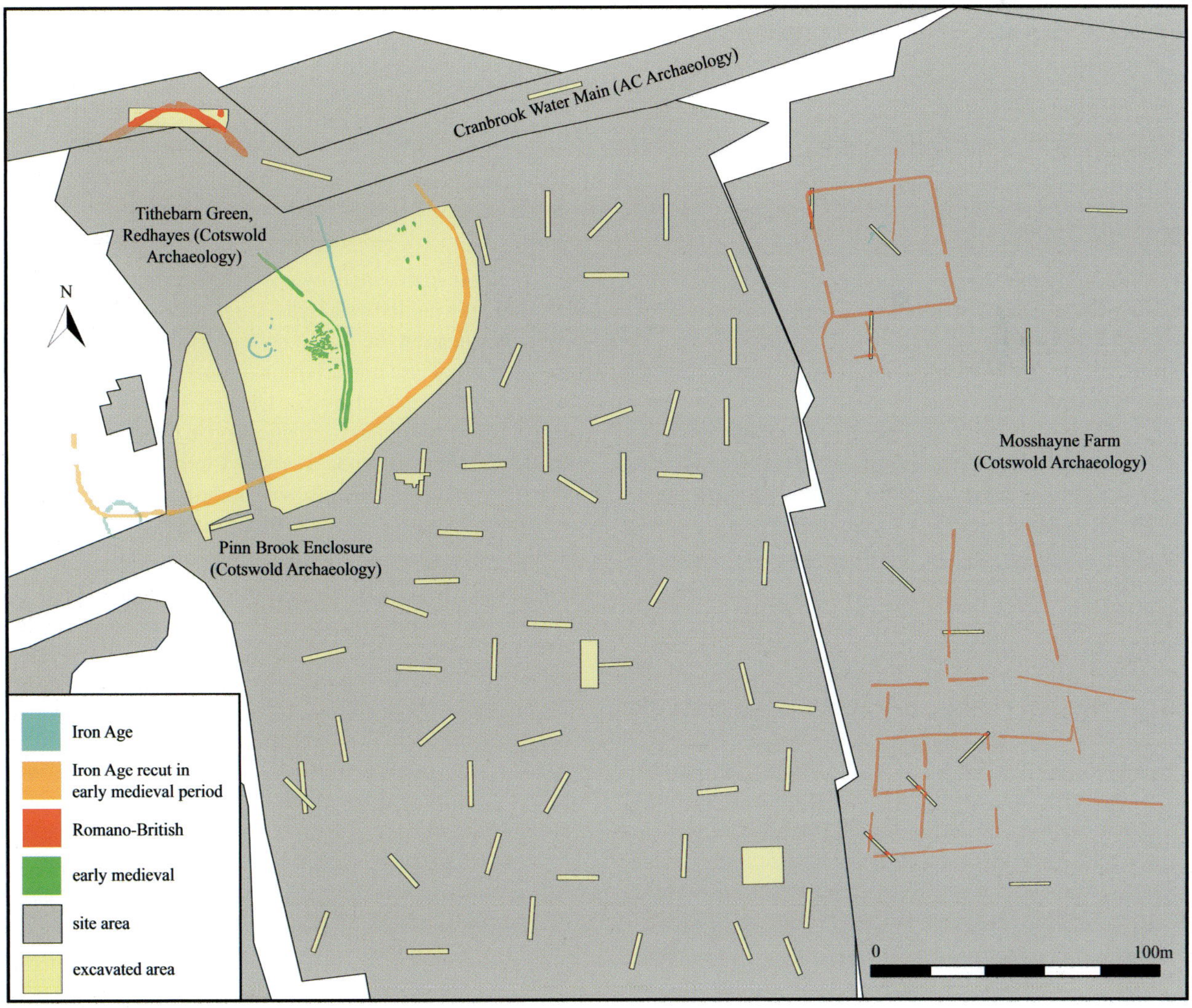

Fig. 4.2 The Iron Age, Romano-British and early medieval features revealed through archaeological investigations at Tithe Barn Green (Redhayes), Mosshayne Farm, Pinn Brook Enclosure and the Cranbrook Water Main (after Sheldon 2012; Ellis 2015b; Garland 2016b; Hughes and Rainbird 2016; Garland 2019; drawn by David Gould)

Fig. 4.3 Pinn Brook corn-drying oven 247 (see Garland 2019, 110–12; © Cotswold Archaeology)

lower fill of the mid 6th to mid 7th century (Garland and Whelan 2016; Garland 2019) – in a way that is reminiscent of Raddon Hill (Gent and Quinnell 1999a). A series of large corn-drying ovens inside the Pinn Brook Enclosure have produced dates of the mid 6th to mid 7th centuries (Figs 4.2 and 4.3), while furnace lining and iron smelting slag from the recut enclosure ditch indicates industrial production in the vicinity. An undated inhumation cemetery of east–west oriented graves surely dates to this period too, as its layout is so similar to securely dated 5th- to 8th-century cemeteries such as Ipplepen (the 13th-century buckle from grave 1007 is surely intrusive). Taken together they are suggestive of something more than a simple farmstead and may represent an estate centre similar to Higham Ferrers in Northamptonshire (Hardy *et al.* 2007). Another potential estate centre is at Berry Meadow, in Kingsteignton, where excavations within a large oval-shaped enclosure – in the south of which lies the parish church – revealed series of aceramic ditches containing charcoal radiocarbon dated to the 7th to 9th centuries (Weddell 1987). 'Teignton' was a royal manor and hundredal centre in Domesday, and its river + ton name is clearly indicative of an important place in the early medieval period.

It was during this period that we start to see the establishment of the church as a major land-owner. The first Anglo-Saxon charter recording the granting of land to the church that is likely to be genuine is King Æthelheard of Wessex's gift of 10 hides *in Torric* (*i.e.* the Torridge Valley, possibly Hatherleigh and Jacobstowe) to the church at Glastonbury in AD 729 (Finberg 1954, No. 1; Sawyer 1968, No. 1676; Hooke 1994, 83). Over time a series of 'minster' churches were established across the landscape, such as Axminster where a West Saxon *ætheling* [prince] was buried in the mid 8th century (Swanton 1996, 48–9; Orme 2011, 1–2, 8–9), and it was the fragmentation of these large minster territories that eventually led to the formation of the smaller parishes with which we are familiar today (Higham 2008, 86–100).

There is also evidence for an increase in the intensity of mineral working around the 8th century. The study of atmospheric tin dust from Dartmoor suggests an increase in mining from the 8th century (Meharg *et al.* 2012), while Optically-Stimulated Luminescence dating suggests the onset of tin streaming at Crownhill Down in Hemerdon, on the south-western fringes of Dartmoor, during the 8th to 11th centuries (Horner 2018, 10). An iron-smelting centre at Culmstock Road, in Hemyock, on the western side of the Blackdown Hills, has produced radiocarbon dates of cal. AD 663–775 and cal. AD 771–963 (Orellana and Evans 2018; Orellana and Massey 2019). At nearby Town Farm, in Burlescombe, another iron-smelting site dates to cal. AD 770–980 (Reed *et al.* 2006). Crucially, this increase in the intensity with which the rural landscape was being exploited post-dates the period of trade with the Mediterranean in the 5th and 6th centuries, and pre-dates the revival of urbanism within Exeter, the first signs of which are late 9th century (see Chapter 7 below). In eastern England a very similar intensification in the exploitation of the landscape was probably related to changes in society that also manifested themselves in the resumption of coin production and the creation of specialist coastal trading settlements such as *Hamwic* (modern Southampton), *Lundenwic* (London) and *Gipeswic* (Ipswich), but such emporia are not found around the South-West Peninsula: although Hodges (1982 33, 67) claims that there were imported sherds at Topsham they are not listed in any of the authoritative listings (*e.g.* Duggan 2018). Instead, we must assume that the surplus production – in the form of renders and tribute – was being creamed off by a rural elite who were perhaps emulating the higher echelons of society further east.

The lack of datable material culture makes it impossible to say when the settlement patterns and field systems of today's countryside came into being, but a strong case can be made for this also being from around the 'long 8th century' as well. It is during this period that the earliest Anglo-Saxon charters record grants of land from the King to the Church, and some of these contain descriptions of the boundaries of those estates: the earliest

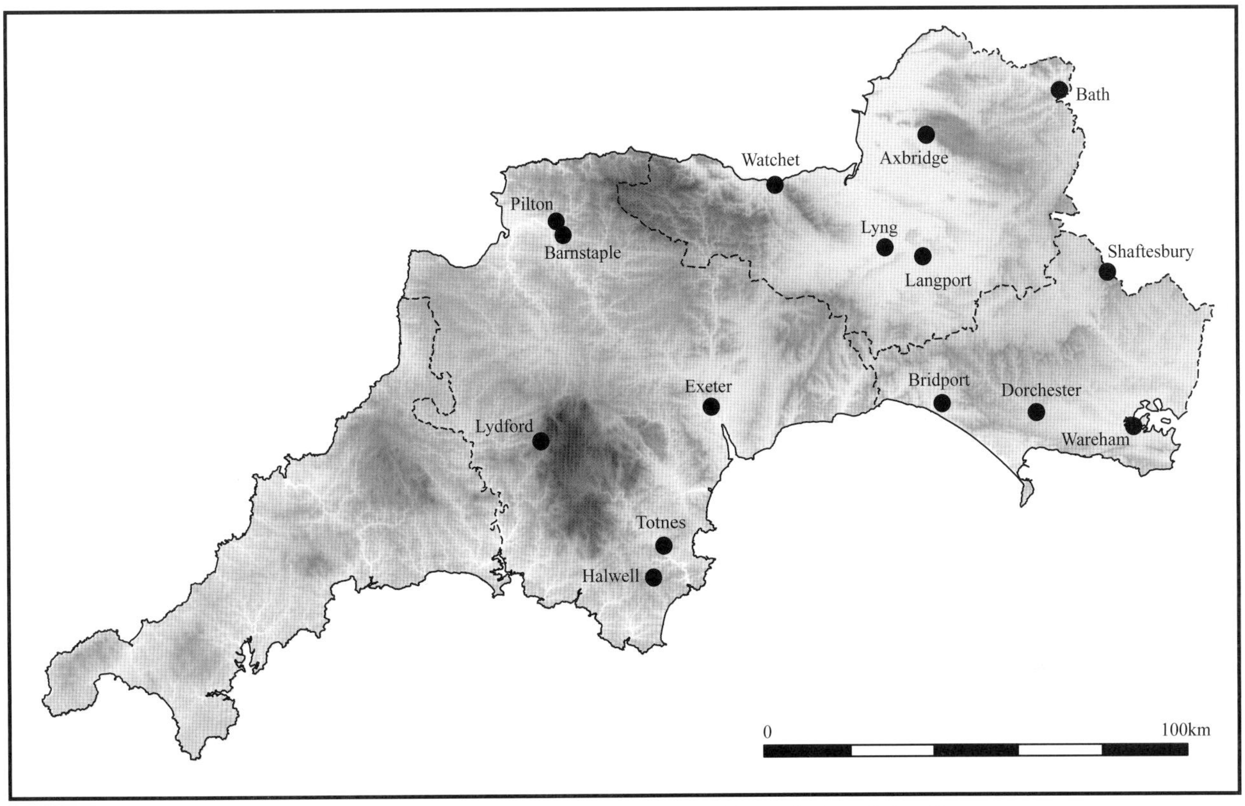

Fig. 4.4 Burhs *across the wider South-West (drawn by David Gould)*

of these – Crediton – is a genuine charter of 739 but whose boundary clause was created later (Sawyer 1968, No. 255; Hooke 1994, 86–99), but the grant of land in the South Hams between West Portlemouth and Kingston dated AD 847 appears to have a contemporary boundary clause that describes various features that still survive today (Sawyer 1968, No. 298; Hooke 1994, 105–12). The places referred to in other 8th- to 10th-century charters, as well Domesday in the 11th century, certainly give the impression that the basic structure of the medieval landscape was created well before the Norman Conquest.

The Late Saxon period

The revival of urbanism

The revival of urbanism across the wider South-West was built upon the foundations laid by the Alfredian *burhs* in the late 9th century and continued with the development of true towns in the 10th century (see Chapter 7, below). Figure 4.4 shows the locations of the documented *burhs* based upon the early 10th-century Burghal Hidage. Haslam (1984a, 267–76) has argued on topographical and geographical grounds for the existence of undocumented *burhs* at Kingsbridge, Kingsteignton and Plympton in Devon, and that a shortfall in total hidage values from Somerset requires there to have been a burghal territory of several hundred hides elsewhere in the county which he suggests was at Ilchester (Haslam 2013). These sites, for which there is no firm evidence, have not been mapped on Fig. 4.4.

The development of true urban centres across the wider South-West appears to have begun during the early 10th century, although agreeing on what constituted a town in such a poorly documented period is difficult (Palliser 2000c, 4–5). Biddle (1976a, 100) identified a bundle of 12 criteria indicative of a place having had urban status in the medieval period: defences, a planned street system, a market, a mint, legal autonomy, a role as a central place, a relatively large and dense population, a diverse economic base, urban-type house plots, social differentiation, a complex religious organisation, and a role as a judicial centre (although he noted that due to the dearth of evidence for the early medieval period only a small number of these criteria may be evident). Archaeologists have tended to focus on the physical characteristics of towns, such as their dense occupation and built-up street frontages, their large number of churches, their diverse economic base that included manufacturing, and the prominence of imports within pottery assemblages that is indicative of trade (Astill 2000, 41). In contrast, historians such as Reynolds (1977, ix) and Palliser (2000c, 5) have tended to identify broader criteria, one economic – namely that a town was a permanent and densely occupied settlement in which a significant proportion of the population was involved in non-agricultural activities (*i.e.* its residents lived off food produced elsewhere) – and the other social – in that a town formed a social unit more or less distinct from the surrounding countryside in that its inhabitants regarded themselves as different to communities living in the countryside. Keen (1984, 230) noted the importance of ecclesiastical sites and royal residences in the formation of early urban centres, although these are not in themselves evidence for a place having had urban status, while an added complication in the early medieval period is that 'central place functions' – administrative, judicial, ecclesiastical and market roles – were not necessarily all carried out in the same place (*e.g.* for Somerset see Aston 1986, 49–50, 63). Examples include the *burh* at Axbridge having been in a different location to the nearby royal vill at Cheddar in Somerset, and the towns at Langport in Somerset and Barnstaple and Totnes in Devon having developed in different locations to the nearby *burhs* at Lyng, Pilton and Halwell respectively. Overall, however, there is broad agreement that the key criteria for a place being regarded as urban are a mixture of physical, economic and social organisational traits:

- a permanent, densely occupied settlement (with a particularly high density of occupation along the major street frontages), that resulted in a large number of churches.
- major towns were enclosed (as well as being defensive, these walls were of symbolic value in confirming the population's special social status as well as controlling economic traffic).
- the majority of the population was not directly involved in agriculture but instead made their living through manufacturing, retailing, or other service provision.
- they provided a range of services both to the town's own inhabitants and the surrounding rural population, such as secular and ecclesiastical administration, and marketing (allowing people to buy and sell raw materials and manufactured goods).
- the urban population had a distinct social identity (usually confirmed with the legal status of being a borough that was conferred by the crown).
- a highly stratified society that resulted in a wide range of architecture.

We cannot expect all towns to look the same, and while major towns will have displayed all of these facets there will have been smaller towns that may have lacked some of them (such as defences), but what they all had in common was that they were central places within the landscapes providing goods and services to the surrounding rural communities, articulating a market-based economy, and which drew in food and raw materials from the countryside.

Those places that have evidence for urban characteristics in the early medieval period – status as a *burh*, the presence of a pre-Conquest mint, and burgesses and/or a market recorded in Domesday Book – are shown in Fig. 4.5. Some of the places that are referred to as *burhs* – notably Axbridge, Langport and Watchet in Somerset – appear to have been very slow to develop as urban centres, while Lyng in Somerset probably never progressed beyond being a defensive fort (Aston 1984, 170; Slater 2000, 590). A key characteristic of a town is the presence of a market, a significant number of which are recorded in Domesday Book. These are likely to have had pre-Conquest origins although in some cases, such as Okehampton in Devon, they were probably Norman creations associated with a castle. Several other places with markets in Domesday Book have no corroborative evidence of urban status before the Conquest, namely Ilminster in Somerset, Liskeard, Methleigh, St Germans and Trematon in Cornwall, and so their urban status before 1066 is open to question. It should also be borne in mind that the recording of burgesses in Domesday Book is notoriously incomplete.

Figure 4.5 also attempts to differentiate Late Saxon urban settlements by their size. Only sites with direct evidence for urban characteristics have been included (and so places that appear to have simply been defensive *burhs* such as South Cadbury, Lyng, Halwell and Pilton are excluded). Towns classified as 'small' generally have just a single indicator of urbanism, often a market recorded in Domesday Book, although Bodmin in Cornwall was recorded as having 68 burgesses but no market or mint and had not been a *burh*. Watchet in Somerset was a *burh* and also had a mint, but its coin output was extremely small, producing only 0.32% of the estimated national output of Long Cross coins and only 0.06% of Last Short Cross coins (Metcalf 1981, 72–78). Frome in Somerset had a market in Domesday Book and possibly a mint, although the latter is attested only by a small number of coins from the reign of Cnut minted by Britwhine at 'FRO' the identification of which as Frome remains conjectural (Dolley 1955). St Stephens (adjacent to the later Launceston) in Cornwall similarly had a Domesday market and a mint, although the latter was small and not active after Cnut's reign. Domesday records plots and houses in Yeovil in Somerset and Wimborne Minster in Dorset that may have been burgages, but as this interpretation is uncertain they have been classified only as small towns. Those sites regarded as 'medium-sized' towns have several strands of evidence including fewer than 100 burgesses, while places with over 100 burgesses have been classified as large towns. Axbridge and Langport in Somerset and Barnstaple and Lydford in Devon, for example, were all *burhs* and had mints, but with only 32, 34, 10 and 69 burgesses respectively they have been considered here as medium towns.

Another source of quantification is the production of coinage. The presence of a mint is generally a good

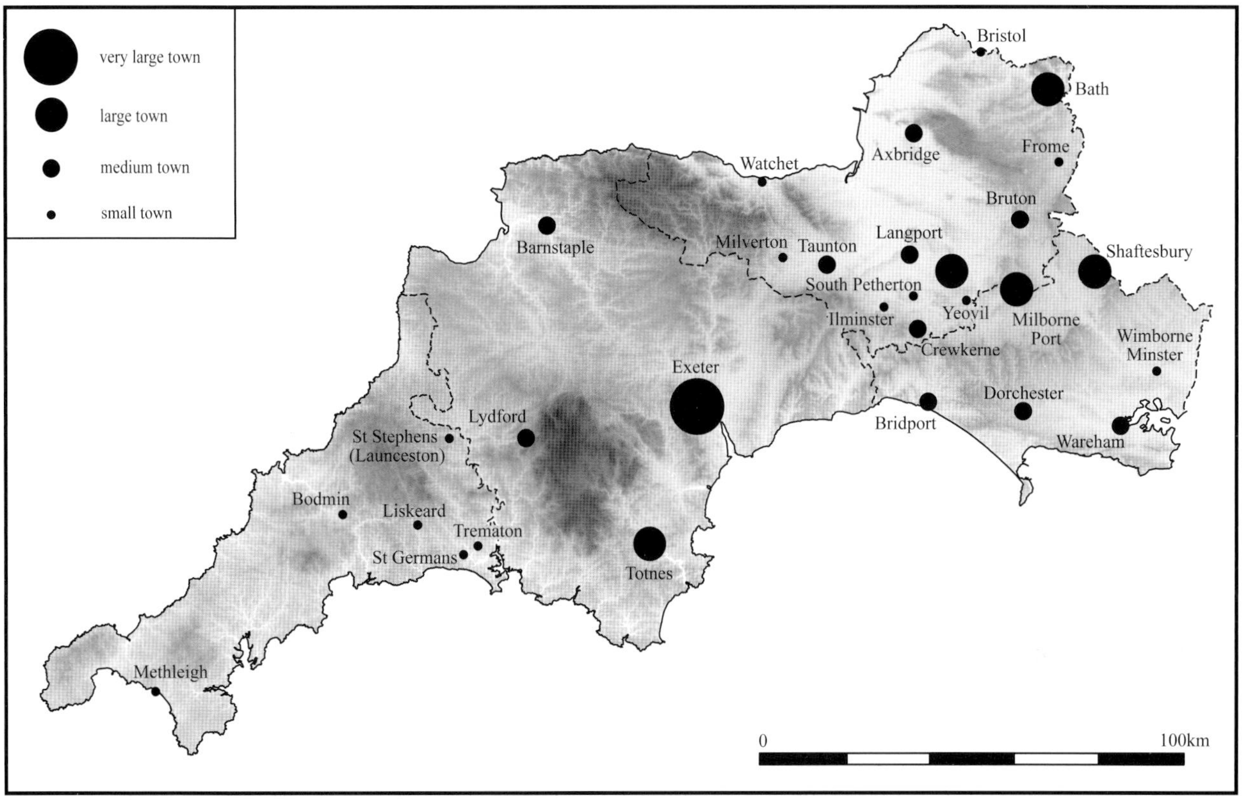

Fig. 4.5 Places with urban characteristics in the Late Saxon period across the wider South-West (drawn by David Gould)

indicator of urban status, although not in all cases: the reoccupied hillfort at South Cadbury in Somerset, for example appears to have temporarily housed a mint – probably relocated from Ilchester – as a defensive strategy in the face of the Danish threat rather than an attempt at urbanism (Astill 2000, 41). Metcalf (1981, 72–78) has produced estimates of the outputs of English pre-Conquest mints (Fig. 4.6) as proportions of the national total output for each coin type, and this helps to confirm the relative ranking of a town in Fig. 4.5. Taunton, for example, had only 64 burgesses recorded in Domesday, and Metcalf estimates that its mint accounted for only 0.16% of the national production of Short Cross coins and only 0.06% of the national output of Last Short Cross coins, figures that are considerably below those of several other South-West mints. Occasionally, the information from coin production can be used to compensate for the deficiencies of Domesday: Wareham, for example, has no burgesses recorded but Metcalf suggests that its mint produced 0.49% of the national output of Long Cross coins and 0.11% of the national output of Last Short Cross coins, demonstrating that it must have been a town. The output of Exeter's mint is important in classifying it as the region's sole very large town, as Metcalf estimates that it produced 3.74% of the national output of Long Cross coins and 3.55% of the national output of Last Short Cross coins, with the next nearest outputs in the South-West being Bath (1.71% of Long Cross coins) and Lydford (1.92% of Last Short Cross coins). The high output of Lydford's mint (*e.g.* Fig. 4.7) has yet to be fully explained, although it may reflect local production of silver in the nearby Tamar Valley (Claughton 1997). This high level of production was also short-lived and drastically declined during Cnut's reign (Allan 2002, 14, 18; and see Chapter 7 below).

The results of combining these various strands of evidence is the suggested urban hierarchy shown in Fig. 4.5. The development of medieval urbanism across the South-west has been reviewed by Slater (2000) and so a brief summary can suffice here. Exeter was by far the largest town in the wider South-West during the early medieval period: it was not simply an emerging county town, but the most important urban centre across the entire region. There is no firm evidence that Bristol was a significant settlement before the early 11th century. The hypothesis that Bristol started life as an 8th-century Mercian *burh*, associated with a minster at St Peter's church, has as yet no firm evidence to support it (Baker *et al.* 2018, 79–80). *Brycgstow* ('assembly place by the bridge' [across the Avon]: Watts 2004, 88) is first documented in 1051, although the earliest coins to be struck there date to 1009×1016 during the reign of King Æthelred II; the earliest pottery from Bristol is dated to the late 10th or early 11th centuries (Baker *et al.* 2018, 81–93).

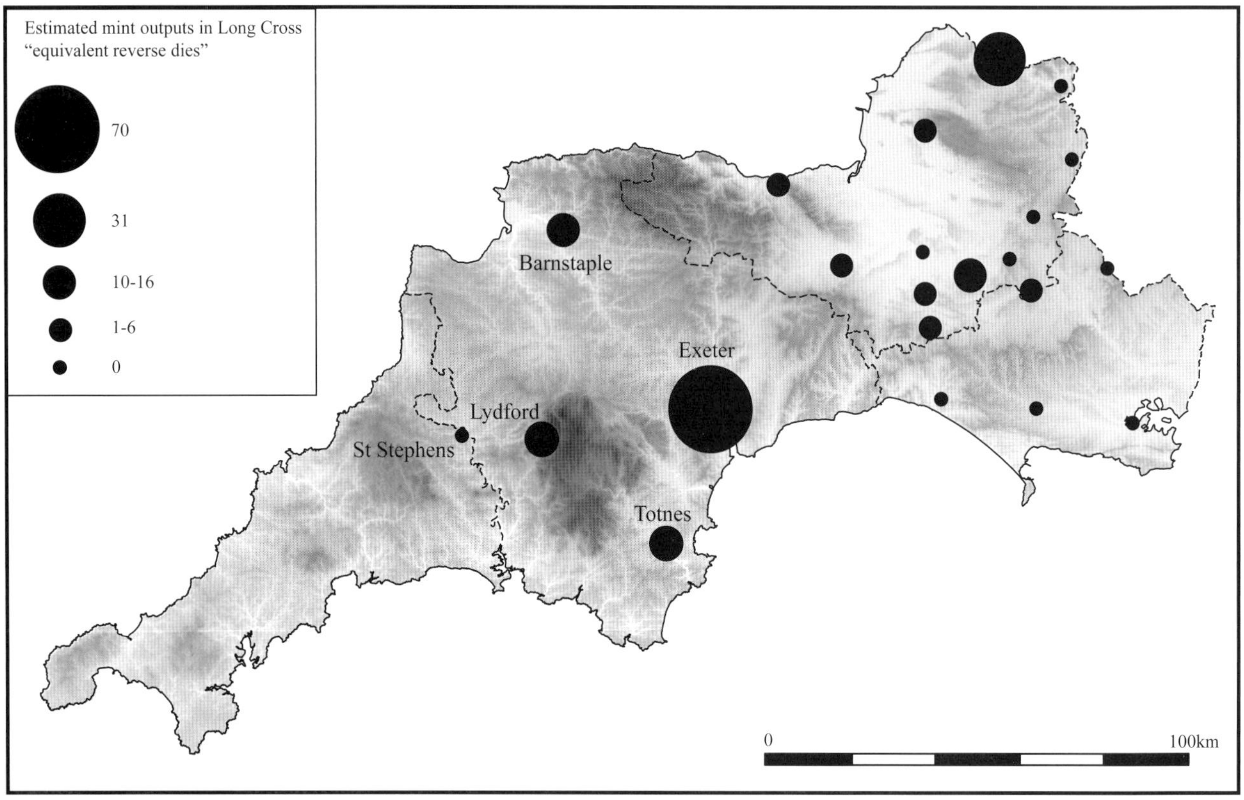

Fig. 4.6 Early medieval mints across the wider South-West showing numbers of 'equivalent reverse dies' of Long Cross coins dating to 997–1003 (after Metcalf 1981, appendix VI; drawn by David Gould)

Fig. 4.7 Silver long cross penny of Aethelred II (AD 978–1016) minted at Lydford by Godac. AD 997–1003 (PAS SF-73FDA4; © Portable Antiquities Scheme)

The Late Saxon rural landscape: agriculture and industry

While pollen evidence suggests that there was some agricultural intensification across the wider South-West from the 'long 8th century' onwards, there is unfortunately very little evidence for animal bone and charred cereal assemblages with which to reconstruct specific animal husbandry practices or arable regimes. There are just five sites with faunal assemblages dating to what is traditionally referred to as the 'Late Saxon' period: two urban (Bath and Exeter), one royal manor with an extremely high proportion of pig (Cheddar), and two rural settlements (Eckweek in Somerset, and Morgan Porth in Cornwall). The animals consumed in 9th- to 11th-century Exeter suggest a more mixed pattern of animal husbandry compared to the Late Roman period; cattle were 43% (down from 58%), with sheep/goat 41% (up from 22%), and pig 15% (falling from 20%) (and see Maltby in Chapter 7 below: note that the percentages given here are different to those in Table 7.1 as the analysis here is of the proportion of just cattle, sheep/goat and pig). It is striking that at Eckweek – on the Jurassic Limestone Hills – sheep/goat were dominant (66%) suggesting that geology/soils were affecting farmers' animal husbandry regimes. In contrast, at Morgan Porth in Cornwall, sheep/goat were 52%. There are no Late Saxon period charred cereal assemblages from the South-West Peninsula.

Domesday confirms that the immediate hinterland of Exeter contained large areas of fertile agricultural land that supported high densities of population and ploughteams (the Domesday figures for Cornwall seem very low, and there has to be a suspicion that resources were under-recorded: Figs 4.8 and 4.9). Domesday makes only passing reference to non-agricultural occupations, although four *ferrarii* (iron workers) are recorded at North Molton on the southern slopes of Exmoor in North Devon, and iron is mentioned in the customary dues owed by six places just east of the Blackdown Hills in Somerset. There was

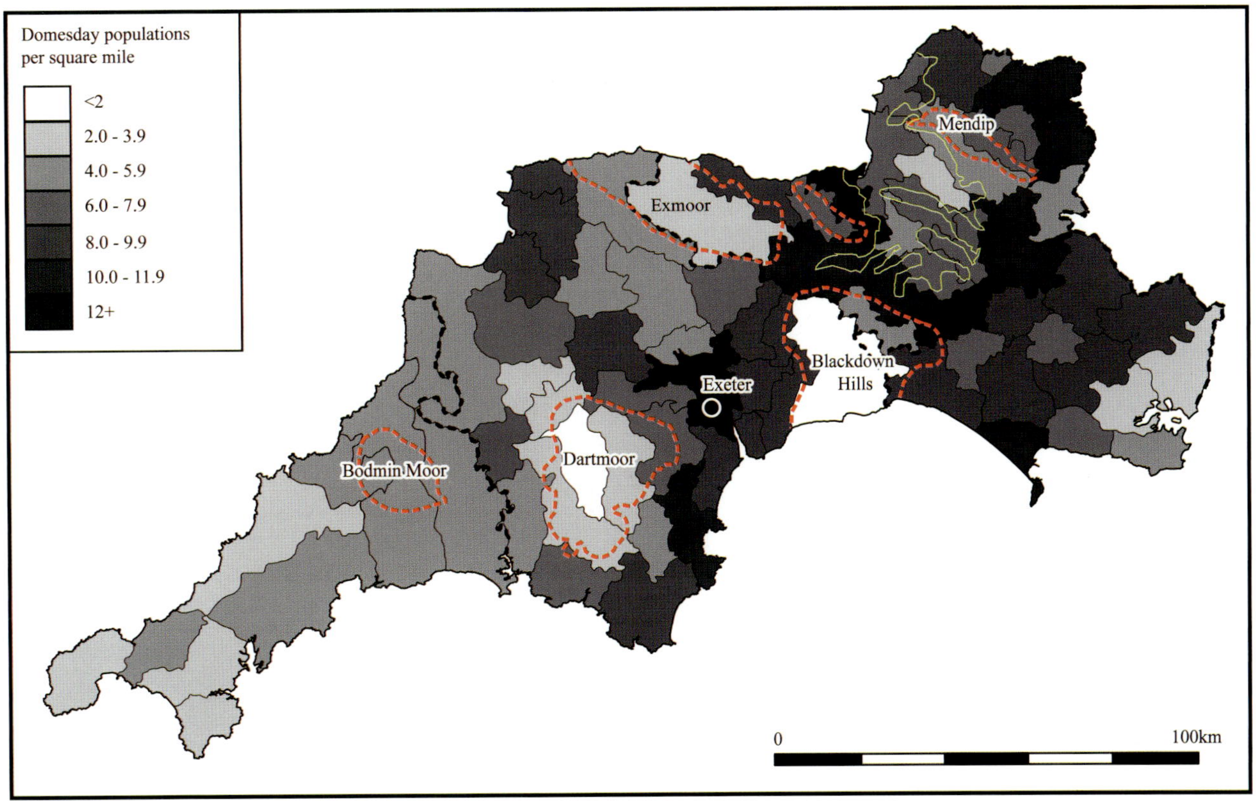

Fig. 4.8 The density of population per square mile in Domesday across the wider South-West (after Darby and Welldon Finn 1967; drawn by David Gould)

also clearly an important salt industry in coastal areas (Darby and Whelldon Finn 1967).

The High Middle Ages

There has been much debate over the impact that the Norman Conquest had on England (*e.g.* Hadley and Dyer 2017), and it is clear that across most of southern England it will have affected the higher echelons of society far more than those at the lower end of the social scale. It was traditionally thought that the imposition of castles on many major towns, and Domesday references to houses having been destroyed, is an example of how the new Norman overlords stamped their identity on their newly acquired territory. A reappraisal of the evidence from Exeter, however, suggests that their impact may not have been as great as previously thought, as the new castle at Rougemont may have been built on the site of an existing royal enclave (see Higham, in Chapter 7 below). Archaeological evidence suggests that life in Exeter (see Chapter 7 below), and across the South-West more generally, may not initially have changed very quickly although the 12th and 13th centuries saw continued economic expansion which is reflected in the proliferation of towns, foundation of new monasteries, the expansion of rural settlement, and intensification of agriculture. It is noticeable, however, that the growth across the South-West Peninsula was slower than in many other parts of southern England with Devon's annual population growth between 1086 and 1290 being just 0.21% compared to 0.37% in Dorset and 0.32% in Somerset (Broadberry *et al.* 2015, fig 1.03, tabs 1.07 and 1.09).

The proliferation of towns

Figure 4.10 is an attempt to reconstruct the urban hierarchy across the wider South-West during the first half of the 14th century. Following the Norman Conquest there were two major changes in the urban geography of this region: firstly, there were now two major towns – Exeter having been joined by Bristol – and secondly there was a dramatic increase in the number of places that had some urban characteristics (a change that was greatest in Cornwall and to a lesser extent Devon as these were less urbanised than Dorset and Somerset in the pre-Conquest period: cf. Figs 4.5 and 4.10). The identification and ranking of many of these later medieval towns is, however, far from straightforward. In this period a town could be regarded as somewhere having the legal status of a borough with its associated elements of self-governance granted by royal charter (Beresford and Finberg 1973, 26), although over the 12th to 15th centuries legal language and definitions changed and places regarded as boroughs in Domesday would not necessarily have had that status

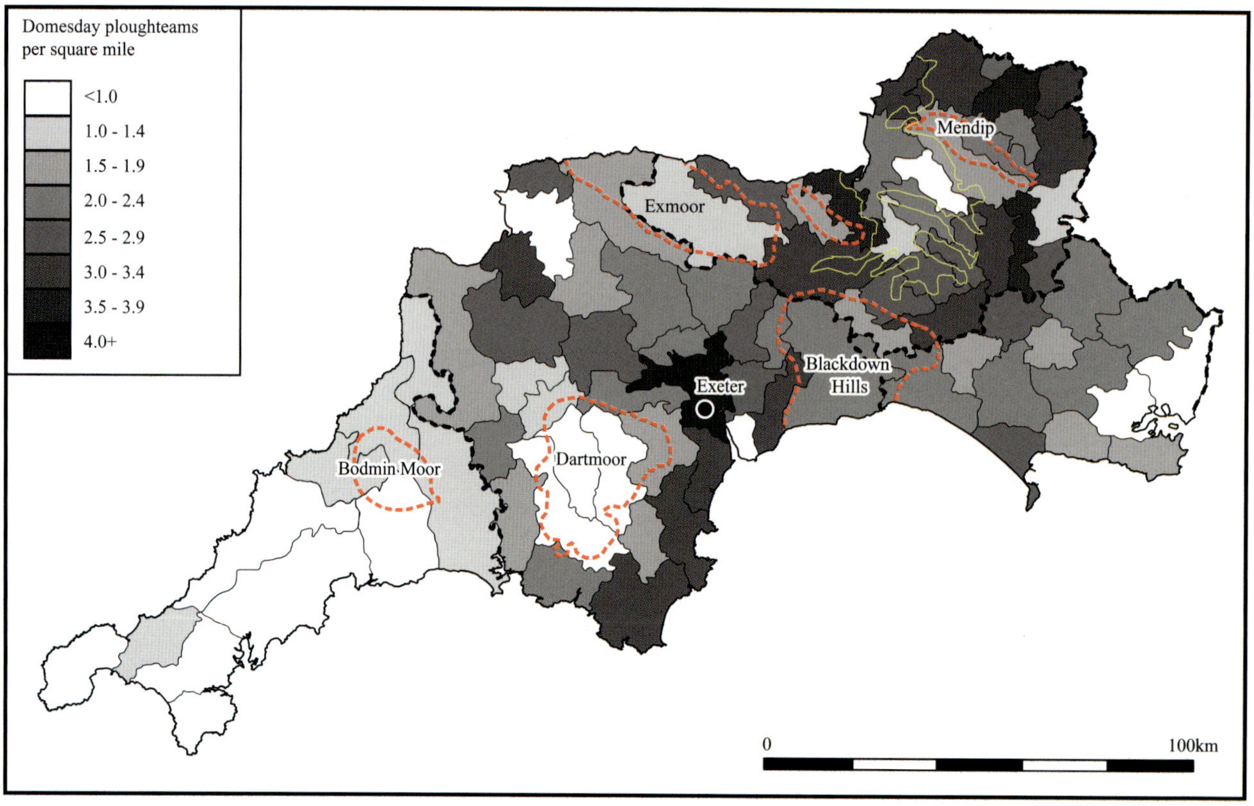

Fig. 4.9 The density of ploughteams per square mile in Domesday across the wider South-West (after Darby and Welldon Finn 1967; drawn by David Gould)

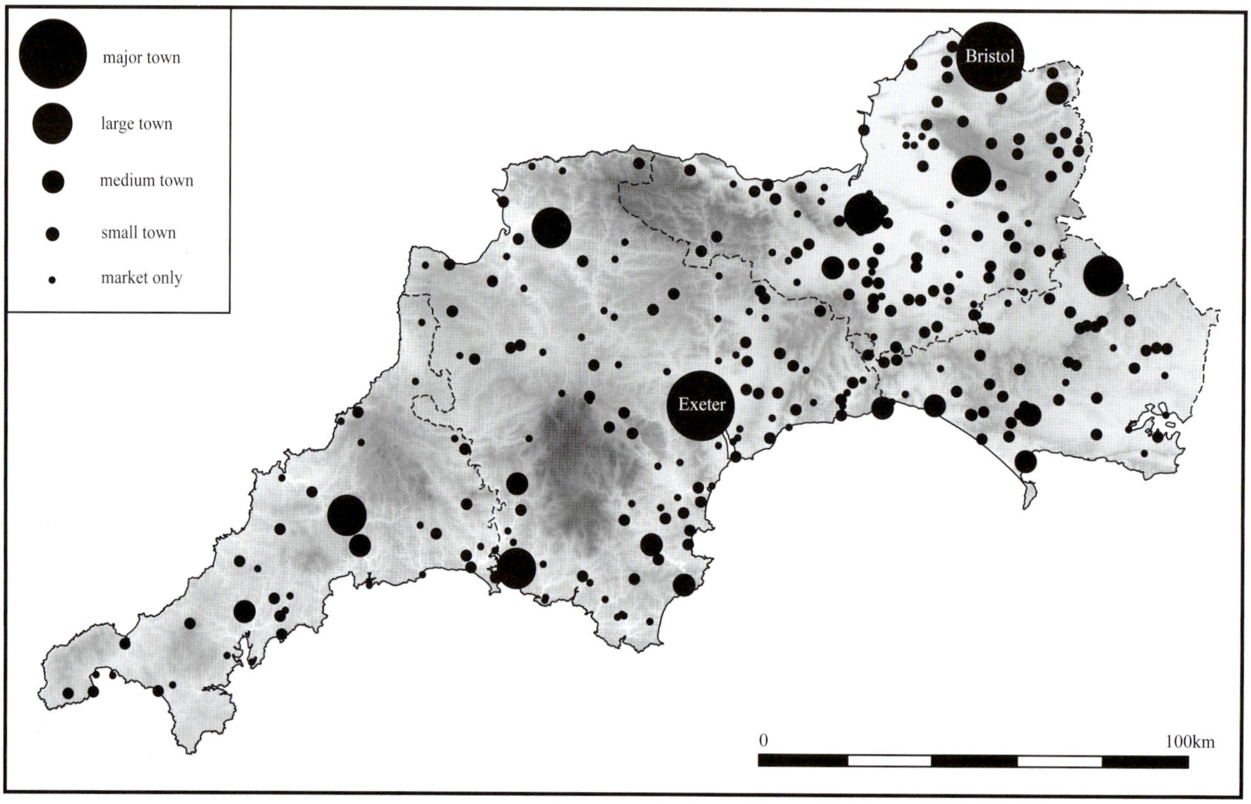

Fig. 4.10 Places with urban characteristics across the wider South-West in the first half of the 14th century (drawn by David Gould)

by the 15th century (Palliser 2000b, 131). Alongside these later medieval boroughs there were a large number of places that received royal charters permitting them to hold a market (Letters 2013), and these places – shown as 'market only' on Fig. 4.10 – were probably at the lowest end of the urban spectrum in later medieval England. It should also be noted that the urban hierarchy was constantly changing as some places prospered and other failed. Sheepstall, in Cornwall, for example, once had a market but went on to be deserted, while Poole, in Dorset, was a small town in the High Middle Ages but in the 15th century was the county's major port. There was a particularly high density of boroughs in Somerset, although a significant number of these were locations that received a borough charter but which failed to develop a major settlement with urban characteristics, being examples of Beresford's (1967, 297) 'abortive' new towns. Any reconstruction of the urban hierarchy can therefore only ever represent a snapshot in time, with Fig. 4.10 reflecting the situation in the first half of the 14th century (see Slater 2000 for a general discussion of medieval towns across the South-West).

At several locations across the South-West – but particularly in Devon and Cornwall – two or three places in close proximity all received borough charters such as Newport just outside Barnstaple, Bridgetown Pomeroy and North Ford outside Totnes, and Newton Bushel and Newton Abbot (two new towns that merged to become Newton Abbot), all in Devon. Previous studies have variously mapped these boroughs individually (which leads to a cluster of dots), or as single points that combine each of the individual boroughs (*e.g.* Fox 1999c, maps 51.1 and 51.2 respectively). The latter approach is followed here as these adjacent boroughs would have functioned as a single economic focus within the landscape, even if they were legally separate entities (Fox 1999c, 404).

There have been various previous attempts at differentiating later medieval boroughs and markets into an urban hierarchy, such as Dyer's (2000) rankings of the largest English towns based upon sources such as the 1334 Lay Subsidy and 1377 Poll Tax, although relatively few of the South-West's towns were large enough to have been included. Fox (1999c, map 51.2, 405) has attempted to reconstruct the sizes of Devon and Cornwall's towns in *c.* 1300, but there is no equivalent study for Dorset or Somerset. Another inconsistency across the wider South-West is that the key primary sources have not been published for all counties, such as the 1332 Lay Subsidy that is only available for Dorset (Mills 1977) and Devon (Erskine 1969). Beresford (1967) also provides some population indicators, although these are *ad hoc* examples and relate only to new foundations (*e.g.* noting how burgesses at Bow, in Devon, were recorded in a 1426 inquisition). The primary sources that do allow for the reconstruction of hierarchies across the whole of the South-West are therefore the 1334 Lay Subsidy (Glasscock 1975) and the 1377 Poll Tax (Fenwick 1998; 2001). The 1334 Lay Subsidy provides the value of taxable wealth across England, but there are some boroughs that were not assessed, such as Ilfracombe in Devon, hence the need to use the 1377 Poll Tax as well. All of these sources omit the urban poor and tax evaders, so it must be assumed that these were a consistent proportion of the population in all towns.

Bristol, assessed as £200 0s 0d in the 1334 Lay Subsidy, was clearly the region's most wealthy town, followed by Exeter, assessed at £36 12s 4d. A range of sources shed light on the extent of Exeter's economic hinterland at this time. A study of its newly admitted freemen from 1284 to 1349 suggests that Exeter's primary catchment was up to about 20 km (that accounts for 54% of the immigrants), but that there was significant immigration from 20 to 40 km (27%) and beyond (4% travelling 40 to 60 km): the remainder came from even greater distances. Whilst international trade was important – for example in the importation of wine – Exeter also served as the main export and marketing centre for the growing woollen industry in eastern Devon (Kowaleski 1995, 95). The distribution of traders who brought their goods to Exeter shows a strong bias towards central and eastern Devon, and western and southern Somerset (Kowaleski 1995, fig. 7.1). The evidence from pottery is discussed John Allan in EAPIT 2, Chapter 17.

The group of six second-tier large towns had assessed wealth between £18 (Barnstaple) and £26 (Bridgwater); a third group, of medium-sized towns, were assessed between £8 and £18; and the final grouping of small towns were assessed below £8 (Fig. 4.10). As the 1334 Lay Subsidy records wealth and not population it only provides a proxy for the likely size of each town, whereas a more accurate picture of urban population is included in the 1377 Poll Tax, although this occurred after the Black Death. While the Poll Tax does sometimes specify whether the taxation units were boroughs, vills, manors, hamlets, liberties, ancient demesnes, tithings or parishes, the status of many places is unfortunately not specified. This lack of specification has produced a small number of issues such as St Germans, in Cornwall, which is listed as having a taxable population of 766 and was subsequently included in Dyer's (2000, 759) English urban hierarchy, although it never received borough status and it is possible, if not probable, that the 1377 Poll Tax records also records the rural population of what was Cornwall's largest parish (similar issues affect other Cornish Poll Tax assessments, such as those of Lanteglos and St Keverne). In Dorset the returns are in a poor state of preservation (Fenwick 1998, 145) which may explain why the boroughs of Bridport, Dorchester, Melcombe Regis and Lyme Regis – all ranked as medium-sized towns based on the 1334 Lay Subsidy – are not recorded. The large Cornish town of Bodmin, and the medium towns of Truro and Lostwithiel, are not recorded in the 1377 Poll Tax returns either. Despite the various problems with the 1334 Lay Subsidy and the 1377 Poll Tax, the ranking of towns based upon the former's taxable wealth and the latter's taxable population align very closely.

The small towns and market centres close to Exeter – Crediton to the west, Cullompton to the north, and Honiton to the east – have only seen limited archaeological work, although documentary sources shed some light on their economy. In the 14th century Crediton –11 km west of Exeter – was around the 6th ranked town in Devon both in the 1327–34 Lay Subsidy valuations, and 1377 Poll Tax populations (Kowaleski 1995, tab. 2.1). It had markets on Tuesdays and Thursdays, and three fairs a year, and an indication that these posed significant competition to nearby Exeter is that when the mayor and councillors sent a messenger to Crediton to promote Exeter's Whitsuntide fair the Crediton authorities forcibly detained the messenger and took him to court (Kowaleski 1995, 65, appendix 2). Crediton was an important centre for the sale of livestock, as it lay at the point where routes from the important grazing lands on Dartmoor and the Culm Measures converged in the Creedy Valley, but retailers – selling relatively inexpensive items, as well as lending money – also operated there (Kowaleski 1995, 46, 49, 74, 127). Crediton was also a centre of manufacturing, as excavations at 35 East Street revealed evidence for a bronze foundry producing cauldrons (Allan *et al.* 2010). It was also home to merchants who imported goods such as wine and oil, as well as tinners, while by the late 14th century it ranked 12th in Devon for the production of woollen cloth (Kowaleski 1995, 23, 76, 266, 274). The inter-connectedness of the medieval economy is reflected in the way that Exeter traders travelled to the fairs in Crediton, Crediton merchants imported wine through Exeter, butchers resident in the parishes around Crediton sold their meat in Exeter, and how Crediton was supplied with pottery from North Devon and the Blackdown Hills as well as imports such as Saintonge ware, Raeren ware and South Netherlands Maiolica (Kowaleski 1995, 57, 259; Allan *et al.* 2010).

The expansion of agriculture

The South-West's agricultural productivity has received something of a bad press: the 12th-century chronicler William of Malmesbury thought that Devon's soils were so poor that they only produced oats, and along similar lines Richard of Devizes – writing in the late 12th century – said that Exeter's residents consumed the same food as their horses (Fox 1999a, 273). It does appear to be true that a smaller proportion of the landscape in Devon and Cornwall was arable (25%) compared to Dorset and Somerset (43%: Broadberry *et al.* 2015, tab. 2.07), but were the South-West's farmers really so bad at supplying their towns with food? The 11th to 13th centuries were certainly a period of expansion across the South-West – also seen in areas such as the Somerset Levels (*e.g.* Rippon 2000a) – although in a national context its assessed wealth was modest, with Devon ranking just 34th amongst English counties in 1334 (Kowaleski 1995, 10). Figures from a small number of manors across the wider South-West suggest that the population may have doubled between Domesday and the early 14th century, although this appears to have resulted in only a modest increase in the number of new settlements that are documented compared to other English counties (Hallam 1988b, 532; Hatcher 1988a, 235). This data could, however, be very misleading – particularly for Devon and Cornwall – as the region has very limited documentary sources compared to areas further east (Hatcher 1988a, 236), while another factor could be its highly dispersed settlement pattern: a large population increase could easily be accommodated by adding a farmstead or two to all the existing hamlets and farmsteads scattered across the landscape without the need to create new settlements (and hence new place-names).

There is, indeed, clear archaeological evidence for an expansion of settlement into some physically marginal environments, most notably the uplands such as Dartmoor where a re-examination of the pottery suggests that – contrary to the traditional view that settlements such as Houndtor had their origins in the Late Saxon period (Beresford 1979) – the main push into the upland fringe was during the 13th century, with local 11th- to 12th-century fabrics being absent (Allan 1994; Henderson and Weddell 1994). There is also documentary evidence for the clearance of woodland (*e.g.* the creation of a new settlement called Woodland, in Bishops Tawton) and the draining of marshland in order to increase the amount of agricultural land (*e.g.* Marsh Barton, in *Clistwick* (now Clyst St George): Hoskins and Finberg 1952, 105–17, 140, 319–21). Even within lowland parishes, place-names – and the first occasions when these places are referred to – suggest that patches of less-favourable soil were being colonised in the 13th century (*e.g.* Heathfield and Uppincott on the fringes of the Culm Measures, in Cadbury and Thorverton: Hatcher 1988a, 242).

The character of later medieval settlements and field systems across the South-West Peninsula were significantly different to those further east. To the east of the Blackdown and Quantock Hills landscapes were characterised by predominantly – but not exclusively – nucleated settlements (villages) associated with large open fields that embraced most of the improved agricultural land within the vill. These open fields were managed through a Midland-style 'common field' system of two, three, or four fields of which one in any year was fallow (*e.g.* Shapwick, in Somerset: Aston and Gerrard 2007). It has long been known that the South-West Peninsula lay beyond the region characterised by these Midland-style villages and open fields (*e.g.* Gray 1915; Rackham 1986; Roberts and Wrathmell 2000), and that settlement patterns were instead far more dispersed, typically with several small hamlets in each vill, open fields that were far smaller, and land use which rotated in a more complex way known as 'convertible husbandry' (Fox 1972; 1973; 1975; 1999a; Hatcher 1988b). The extent of these open fields has, however, seen much discussion, with the Historic Landscape Characterisation of Devon (Turner 2005; 2007) suggesting that they were far more extensive than previous attempts at mapping them (*e.g.* Shorter *et al.* 1969). A re-assessment of the Devon Historic Landscape Characterisation has, however, called into question whether all of the areas attributed to former open field did indeed have that origin (*e.g.* Rippon 2012, cf. figs 6.7 and 7.4, with 6.8 and 7.5), and indeed several decades ago Hatcher (1988c, 384) warned that:

> There appears to be little doubt that by far the greatest proportion of this land [agricultural land in Devon and Cornwall] lay in severalty by the end of the thirteenth century, and no doubt that the so-called 'open fields' of the south-west have received disproportionate amount of attention from historians. They would be better termed 'sub-divided fields'. Thus H.L. Gray's boundary of the two- and three-field system, which he placed just to the Somerset and Dorset side off the Devon border, has scarcely been altered by subsequent research.

The South-West's regionally distinctive way of structuring and managing the landscape was complemented by a range of strategies to improve the region's damp acidic soils including the stripping, drying and then burning of turf followed by the spreading of the ashes that added potash to the soil and so facilitated the release of nitrogen (known locally as 'beat-burning', 'Devonshiring' or 'denshiring': Hatcher 1988c, 387; Fox 1991b, 309–10; 1999a, 273–4). Other methods of soil improvement included the spreading of seaweed and calcium carbonate rich sand across fields in coastal areas and even some inland districts, while marling was widespread and liming is recorded from the 14th century (Hatcher 1988c, 387–8). Areas of particularly poor soil were cultivated only occasionally – through an infield-outfield system – while in the summer livestock were driven up to the moors in a system of small-scale transhumance (Fox 1996b; 2012; and see Müldner and Frémondeau below). Exeter was the final destination for some of the animals, and the examination of cattle bones from the city shows that the vast majority were adults with a high kill-off at prime beef age between three and six years; there are very few bones from calves suggesting that intensive milk production was not practised (Maltby 1979, 31–2; and see Maltby in Chapter 8 below).

Arable regimes: the evidence from charred cereals (Table 4.2 above)

The documentary evidence for arable regimes across the wider South-West during the High Middle Ages is summarised in Chapter 2 above. There is unfortunately no archaeological material from Cornwall in this period, although in Devon six large assemblages were dominated by oats (52%) and rye (37%), with small amounts of wheat (10%) and just 1% barley (although at Island Farm, in Ottery St Mary, barley was 26%: Mudd *et al.* 2018). This pattern of mixed cropping in Devon, and the relatively low levels of wheat, does suggest continuity with the early medieval period. There is also a single assemblage from the uplands of Exmoor – at Ley Hill in Luccombe (Richardson 2019) – where oats dominated (71%), with some rye (24%) and barley (5%) and virtually no wheat (1%). A very different picture is seen in lowland Somerset where six large assemblages are dominated by wheat (88%), with small amounts of barley (6%), oats (5%) and rye (1%); again, this reflects broad continuity with earlier periods. The only data from Dorset are from two sites on the heathlands where wheat was the main crop present (65%) alongside modest amounts of rye (14%), oats (11%) and barley (10%). Overall, data from the High Middle Ages once again shows marked variations in arable regimes on different soils, with features common to other periods being the greater diversity of crops and particular importance of oats across the South-West Peninsula, and the consistent dominance of wheat in lowland Somerset. There is insufficient late medieval data to make any meaningful discussion possible.

Animal husbandry: the evidence from animal bones

The documentary evidence, such as it is, for animal husbandry across the wider South-West during the High Middle Ages is summarised in Chapter 2 above and that can now be compared to the archaeological evidence (Table 4.3; note that attention here focussed on rural settlements excluding monasteries as the latter's food will probably have been drawn from their outlying manors that were scattered across many *pays*). While there are a larger number of faunal assemblages from the High Middle Ages compared to the early medieval period, they are spread very unevenly across the study area with very few in the South-West Peninsula (due to its acidic soils) or the Dorset chalkland due to a lack of excavated sites, making comparisons with the Roman period difficult. There is, however, clear evidence for variances in animal husbandry practices across different *pays* with geology/soils playing a very significant part in shaping animal husbandry regimes. In the Lowlands of Central Somerset, cattle dominated while sheep/goat were far more important on the Jurassic Limestone Hills.

Exploring Exeter's hinterland-relationships through its meat supply: the isotope evidence in the medieval period

By Gundula Müldner and Delphine Frémondeau

The methodology adopted for the isotopic study of medieval Exeter's cattle and sheep/goat bones was presented in Chapter 3 alongside a discussion of the Roman period results. The detailed results of this work will be published elsewhere in a series of papers including

Table 4.3 Later medieval animal bones from selected sites and pays *across the wider South-West (based upon the sites listed in online Appendix 4.2)*

Site	High medieval (1066-1348)							Late medieval (1348-1500)						
	Cattle		Sheep/goat		Pigs		Total	Cattle		Sheep/goat		Pigs		Total
	No.	%	No.	%	No.	%		No.	%	No.	%	No.	%	
Cornwall														
Restormel Castle	11	58	5	26	3	16	19							
Launceston Castle	558	32	612	35	596	34	1766	1208	41	950	32	767	26	2925
Devon														
Rural settlement	15	50	9	30	6	20	30							
Okehampton Castle	646	31	693	33	752	36	2091	489	36	674	50	185	14	1348
Somerset														
Rural settlements combined (for selected *pays* with large samples sizes see below)	1231	44	1335	47	259	9	2825							
Central Somerset Lowlands	1670	43	1617	42	585	15	3872							
Jurassic Limestone Hills	128	23	342	63	76	14	546							
North Somerset Hills and Vales	336	59	165	29	65	11	566							
Reclaimed Marshland	620	49	352	28	293	23	1265							
Unreclaimed Marshland	113	38	183	61	3	1	299							
Glastonbury (town)	314	32	354	36	307	31	975							
Ilchester	1737	45	1796	47	289	8	3822							
North Petherton	7	64	3	27	1	9	11	52	54	34	35	10	10	96
Shepton Mallet														
Taunton	2246	49	2123	46	259	6	4628	8	30	18	67	1	4	27
Bath	3406	36	4803	50	1306	14	9515	39	26	41	27	71	47	151
Dorset														
Dorset rural heathland	9	39	13	57	1	4	23							
Dorset rural clay	47	65	21	29	4	6	72							
Christchurch	157	61	67	26	33	13	257	256	55	167	36	42	9	465
Dorchester	1007	44	943	42	321	14	2271							
Shaftesbury	294	56	167	32	64	12	525							
Wimborne Minster	43	39	36	33	30	28	109							

Müldner *et al.* (forthcoming), with the raw data available through the Archaeology Data Service, but a summary is presented below.

The analysis of the strontium isotopes suggest that there was little overall change in where animals had been grazing between the Roman and the late 11th- to early 12th-century town, although the period of the earliest urban revival in the 10th century is unfortunately not represented in the dataset as there were too few suitable samples available. As previously, the focus of the meat production for medieval Exeter appears to have been squarely on the Palaeozoic terrains of the South-West Peninsula. Only one sample in the entire medieval dataset plots below 0.7100 and the number of samples with $^{87}Sr/^{86}Sr$ values >0.7120 is above 60% in all four medieval phases. The most notable trend in the medieval dataset is the increasing occurrence of animals with strontium isotope values above 0.7140 (indicating grazing on Cornubian granite, most likely Dartmoor). Their number rises from 15% (3/20) in Medieval 1 and around 40% (8/20 and 6/16) in Medieval 2 and 3 (*c.* 1150–1350) to 57% (8/14) in Medieval 4 (*c.* 1350–1500). This change most likely reflects the agricultural expansion on Dartmoor (see above; Newman 2011; Fox 2012) and other moorland areas (*e.g.* Bodmin Moor: Johnson and Rose 2008) in the 12th and 13th centuries. Whilst strontium isotopes cannot easily identify the most characteristic change in this period, the expansion of permanent settlement into the high moors, since these lack distinctive isotope signals (see Chapter 3 above), the data nevertheless suggest a shift in emphasis to the granite uplands for the supply of livestock to Exeter. Nevertheless, medieval Exeter cast the net for its food supply widely and among the documented shipments of agricultural produce that reached its ports in the later medieval period are live cattle from Brittany (Kowaleski 1995, 243). Based on current strontium biosphere mapping these would likely be indistinguishable from animals raised in South-West England and may well include 'highly radiogenic' $^{87}Sr/^{86}Sr$ values above 0.7140 (Willmes *et al.* 2018). Although the relative ease of sourcing animals locally makes it unlikely that these foreign cattle significantly skewed the distribution of Exeter's medieval faunal data, the possibility must nevertheless be raised. Time-resolved isotope strontium and oxygen isotope data (reflecting geological signal and season, respectively) through sequential sampling of tooth-enamel revealed two clear examples of seasonal movement of animals in the medieval period (see Chapter 3, Fig. 3.20 above).

To conclude, the faunal isotope dataset from Exeter is the largest so far produced from an urban site. The data successfully reflect major trends in the meat supply to the city, most notably the change in the Roman period between the Roman legionary fortress, which was partly supplied by non-local animals from South-East England to the civilian town which appeared to rely almost exclusively on its own hinterland, as well as the growing importance of the granitic uplands, probably Dartmoor in the medieval periods. Sequential sampling of tooth enamel demonstrates that seasonal transhumance involving Dartmoor was likely already practiced by the Roman period.

The expansion of mining

We know from a wide variety of sources that the South-West's rich mineral resources had been exploited since prehistory, but it is impossible to compare production over several millennia due to the different sources that are available for each period. The palaeoenvironmental record, notably the deposition of atmospheric lead – released through the mining of tin – within rain-fed peat bogs on Bodmin Moor and Dartmoor reveals sporadic peaks during the later prehistoric period, very marked increases during the Roman period and the late 1st millennium AD (from *c.* 700 to *c.* 1000), and then lower levels and just sporadic minor peaks during the High Middle Ages (Meharg *et al.* 2012). This is, however, contradicted by documentary sources that suggest tin production in the South-West grew rapidly during the 12th and 13th centuries, with Cornwall outstripping Dartmoor (Hatcher 1973, 18–26; Fox 1999b, map 40.1). The 15th century saw a gradual rise in production which peaked in the early 16th century (Fox 1999b, fig. 4).

Late medieval period

The late medieval period saw the South-West share in the nation's sharp decline in population following the Black Death and subsequent outbreaks of plague, although both urban and rural communities adapted to the new economic conditions remarkably well. Indeed, Devon's population growth was amongst the highest in the country (Broadberry *et al.* 2015, fig 1.03, tabs 1.07 and 1.09), and the assessed wealth of Devon rose from 34th in 1334 to 18th in 1515, making it the county that saw the fastest economic growth in this period (Kowaleski 1995, 10). This prosperity was due to a variety of factors including burgeoning cloth production – especially in the eastern Devon hinterland of Exeter – continued tin production, and international trade at ports including Exeter, Barnstaple, Dartmouth and Plymouth. It is to this period that some of the most distinctive features of the South-West's landscape belong, including the standing fabric of the vast majority of its churches (perhaps 95% of Devon's pre-Victorian churches date predominantly from the perpendicular period in the 15th and early 16th centuries: Cherry and Pevsner 1991, 42–3), as well as a particularly extensive rebuilding of its domestic houses (Beacham 1991) and the emergence of specialised coastal fishing villages (Fox 2001).

Documentary sources suggest that the late medieval period saw a small shift from arable to pasture that fell from around 67% of the improved agricultural land in the early 14th century to around 55% in the late 15th century (Fox 1991, tab. 2.16). Some of this decline was the result of a contraction of settlement and agriculture from physically more marginal areas such as the fringes of the uplands (*e.g.* Fox 1991a, tab. 2.17; Allan 1994a; Henderson and Weddell 1994), and while this has traditionally been seen as a result of climatic deterioration (*e.g.* Beresford 1979) a far wider range of socio-economic factors were actually responsible such as the lower population leading to falling grain prices and hence the need for less arable (*e.g.* Fox 1991a, 153). This was, however, a region whose agriculture was well-placed to adapt to the new economic conditions as the early enclosure of open fields meant that farmers were able reap the rewards of careful management practices and specialise in diverse pastoralism including dairying in the fertile lowlands, cattle rearing in the uplands, and sheep rearing for the burgeoning cloth industry.

While many settlements contracted, and within landscapes once characterised by small hamlets there were increasing numbers of isolated farms and the 'engrossment' (combining) of tenements to create far larger landholdings, there is little evidence for wholesale desertion of settlements (*e.g.* Fox 1991a, fig. 2.2; 1991c, 722–3). This appears to have been associated with enclosure by agreement of the open fields, although documentary sources suggest that arable regimes remained diverse with oats the dominant crop overall, followed by wheat, rye and barley, but with major variations across the region depending on the local conditions (unfortunately there are very few charred cereal assemblages from this period). Yields, however, were still very good being higher than the national average for oats, rye and wheat (Fox 1999b, 303–12) suggesting that despite the popular perception of the South-West as being an upland region with poor soils, it was actually more agriculturally productive that its neighbours due to its regionally distinctive practices such as beat-burning and convertible husbandry. Livestock densities were also relatively high, with a focus on cattle dairying in some regions – such as the hinterland of Plymouth – a greater emphasis on cattle rearing in western and north parts of the region, and a mixed pattern of both meat and dairy production in eastern Devon where Exeter provided a major market (Fox 1999b, 312–23). The uplands continued to provide summer pasture for livestock – the so-called 'stranger beasts' that were driven there during the warmer months – while there were also permanent movements of animals such as surplus calves being sent for fattening before slaughter and sale at market (Fox 1999b, 319).

Although Exeter went on to become a major producer of wool – in the late 15th century the number of cloths exported from Exeter was greater than all other ports apart from Bristol and Southampton – in the late 14th century the industry was extremely small (Fox 1991c, 740–1; Havinden 1999, 338–9). Indeed, the productivity of its sheep – in terms of fleece weight – in the late medieval period was low, and the coarse nature of the wool was noted by contemporary writers. The reasons for this poor quality of the fleeces is unclear but it cannot have been down to the pasture as some of the lowest figures for fleece weight come from the fertile soils of the Clyst Valley east of Exeter, and instead it seems to have resulted from the sheep having been inherently coarse and short wooled (Fox 1999b, 320–1). The growth of the South-West's woollen industry – that was therefore based upon the production of cheap cloths – appear to have lain in the mid 15th century and was initially focussed around the Cornish and Dartmoor stannary towns, with the shrinkage in tin production leading to its former workers seeking new forms of employment (Fox 1999c, 740–1). A period of more dramatic expansion happened in the 1480s and 90s when another focus for production emerged in the lowlands of eastern Devon which led to a rapid expansion of the cloth industry in Exeter as well as Tiverton which is reflected in the high density of fulling mills in the Exe Valley (Fox 1991, 741; Kowaleski 1995, 22–6; Havinden 1999, map 42.1). In addition to fulling, Exeter was also a centre for the finishing of cloth, and early maps and pictorial representations show large numbers of drying racks around the southern side of the city (as depicted on a series of 16th-century and later maps of Exeter (Oliver *et al.* 2019; and see EAPIT 2, Chapter 8 for the excavations at Rack Street in Exeter).

Discussion: the South West in the later medieval period

A major theme, explored in Chapter 3 above, was that during the Roman period there were significant regional variations in landscape character across the wider South-West, with far greater cultural change to the east of the Blackdown and Quantocks Hills compared to areas further west. There is also a growing body of evidence to suggest differences between the eastern and the western parts of the South-West Peninsula, in what were to become Devon and Cornwall. While the end of Roman Britain brought about significant changes right across the region, it is striking how the inter- and intra-regional differences continued.

The town of Exeter was virtually abandoned in the 5th century, and in its immediate hinterland there appears to have been a severe dislocation within the economy as the use of pottery largely ceased on all but a handful of coastal sites. This is in sharp contrast to Cornwall where there was a continuous ceramic sequence throughout the early medieval period, which suggests that its locally produced ceramics were seen as an integral part of that society's identity, in contrast to Devon where pottery was seen as something that people could do without. This rejection of *Romanitas* might also be seen in the shift from rectangular to curvilinear enclosures, although at present this hypothesis is based upon a very small number of sites. What is clear, however, is that the landscape of Devon was not abandoned as pollen sequences clearly show that there was no widespread woodland regeneration and there is a growing number of aceramic sites that are being radiocarbon dated to this period. Another difference between Devon and Cornwall is the location of pottery imported from the Mediterranean: in Cornwall – as in Somerset – it is found on numerous permanently occupied settlements spread right across the landscape, whereas in Devon it is largely found on a very small number of coastal sites (the exception being a single unstratified sherd from Lydford in the western edge of Dartmoor). A growing number of Byzantine coins – that may be genuine 5th- and 6th-century losses – add to this picture of coastal trade between communities living in the South-West Peninsula and the Mediterranean, the basis of which was presumably tin.

In the mid 7th century the South-West Peninsula started to be drawn into the West Saxon kingdom, and there appears to have been a church with a West Saxon abbot in Exeter by the 680s. During the 'long 8th century' that followed, the South-West appears to have shared in the intensification in landscape exploitation that was seen across southern Britain. Pollen sequences suggest an expansion of arable, and there are two sites close to Exeter that have large corn-drying ovens including the possible estate centre at Pinn Brook. There was also an intensification in the exploitation of minerals. The late 9th century saw the creation of a small number of defended *burhs* spread across the wider South-West, and by the early 10th century Exeter at least had started to develop urban characteristics. It became the largest town across the whole of the wider South-West until the emergence of Bristol in the 11th century. The landscape recorded by Domesday Book included a series of towns spread right across the South-West Peninsula, the first time that this had been the case as during the Roman period the only town was Exeter. Domesday also shows that large parts of lowland Devon had densities of population and ploughteams that were comparable to Somerset and Dorset.

The 12th and 13th centuries were a period of expansion across the South-West Peninsula, although the growth in population and agriculture appears to have been slower than elsewhere in lowland England. There developed a regionally distinctive way of structuring the landscape characterised by dispersed settlement patterns and only small-scale open fields, and there were also different patterns of crop husbandry compared to areas east of the Blackdown and Quantock Hills. The isotopic analysis of faunal remains from Exeter supports the documentary evidence for the movement of livestock between lowland and upland parts of the region. Exploitation of the South-West's rich mineral resources formed another distinctive part of its economy, and in the late medieval period the production of woollen cloth became a source of great prosperity for both Devon generally and Exeter specifically.

5

The Legionary Fortress and its Landscape Context

Paul Bidwell

with a contribution by Mark Maltby

Introduction

In recently conquered frontier provinces, legionary fortresses were linchpins in the systems of Roman control and administration. They were in a sense military cities, and their development reflected wider changes in Roman society. In the Augustan period, for example, the fashion for palatial architecture in the Mediterranean zone was rapidly translated from masonry to timber construction in the plans of residences for senior officers in the German fortresses (Förtsch 1996). The earliest bath-houses were of timber construction despite their large size, but when the use of stone began their plans followed metropolitan rather than provincial trends, as can be seen at Exeter (Bidwell 2002; and see below). Alongside such external influences, the internal arrangements of fortresses changed in the 1st century AD from loose groupings of buildings within an irregular defensive circuit to regular orthogonal layouts generally within a rectangular enclosure. As will be seen, the circumstances of these changes are uncertain, but many of the earliest examples of these more regular arrangements are to be seen in the Claudio-Neronian fortresses of Britain, including Exeter which now has the most complete plan. The Exeter fortress is thus of great importance in understanding one of the essential institutions that held the Roman world together. On a regional level it is the main source of information about the early stages in the absorption of the South-West Peninsula into the province of *Britannia*. Finally, the fortress plan provides the key to understanding the function of the surrounding complex of smaller military and dependent civilian sites.

Until 1964 nothing had emerged from excavations in the modern city of Exeter to indicate unequivocally that the *civitas* capital had been preceded by a period of military occupation. The discovery in that year of a defensive ditch at the South Gate of the later town (Site 36) was the first glimpse of a complex of military sites that is more extensive, as far as is known, than anywhere else in Britain during the mid to later 1st century AD. These sites were dominated by the legionary fortress which lies under the modern city centre; it had an area of 16.6 ha and was built in *c.* AD 55–60 to accommodate the 5,000 soldiers of *legio II Augusta.* It is argued below that at Princesshay, north-east of the fortress, there was a separate fort with another defended enclosure beyond it, and that to the south-east were the *canabae* (an extra-mural civilian settlement); north-west of the fortress, on the other side of the Longbrook Valley, was a palatial residence at Mount Dinham, presumably for a high official of the province, and to the south-west was a defended annexe of unknown purpose. It is also proposed below that at St Loye's College, some 2.2 km to the south-east, there was a small town, beyond which, at the head of the Exe Estuary, was a port.

Buildings of the fortress were first recognised in 1971–2 at a time when knowledge of the Roman army in Claudio-Neronian Britain was advancing dramatically. Foremost amongst many discoveries, in addition to those at Exeter, were the identification of a previously unknown fortress at Usk and the precise location of others at Colchester and Wroxeter, while at Gloucester and Lincoln there were extensive excavations inside fortresses long known but previously little explored. Apart from at Wroxeter, most of this new information resulted from work funded by central government and carried out in advance of building development. It transformed our understanding of the Roman conquest and consolidation of southern Britain, as can be seen by comparing the relevant chapters in the first and fourth editions of Frere's *Britannia* (1967, 61–95; 1999, 49–81). In 1975 von Petrikovits published an exhaustive study of the interior buildings in legionary fortresses across the whole empire (von Petrikovits 1975b). He included the very recent investigations of Claudio-Neronian fortresses in Britain, and their international significance is clear: collectively, their plans, though incomplete, provide the best picture of the transition from the irregularly-planned fortresses of the pre-Claudian age to the more standardised designs that are evident from the Flavian period and beyond.

At a local level the origins of some of the most historic English cities were seen more clearly, none more so than at Exeter. The excavations of timber military buildings are unspectacular, especially in urban contexts where often only parts of buildings can be explored, and their remains are usually riddled by later intrusions such as medieval rubbish pits. However, the fortress baths at Exeter, overlooked by the 14th-century west front of the cathedral, were an unforgettable sight (Fig. 5.1):

And here
Under the West Front Saints' crumbling features
The Roman Garrison bath-house is being unearthed
Out of the dried blood of the redland marl—
Splayed, bleeding in the rain, like an accident,
Gaped-at, photographed, commented-on, and
Coddled with waterproofs. Nobody knows what to think of it.
'Here is the Cathedral', by Ted Hughes in *Moortown*, 1979

The Exeter baths and the Temple of Claudius at Colchester are the earliest examples in Britain of Roman architecture on a grand scale. A scheme for the display of baths in an underground museum was drawn up in 1973 (Arup Associates 1973), but was abandoned because of funding problems, and two later projects have also failed. It is sad that the well-preserved remains of this magnificent building, a symbol of the irruption of the Roman world into the landscape of Britain, lie hidden under the lawns of the Cathedral Close and the prosaic paving of a modern processional way.

The discovery of the baths and the controversy surrounding their future at times overshadowed the other extensive excavations that eventually recovered the plan of the fortress, at some sites in great detail and elsewhere in outline. The archaeology of the fortress is better preserved than that of later periods: in the core of the later city the earliest levels are deep enough down to be untouched by the medieval and later cellars that line the frontages of the main streets, while in the peripheral areas it is often only these deposits which have survived terracing. Effective implementation of planning regulations and a spirited

Fig. 5.1 The fortress baths in 1972 from the south-west, with the West Front of the Cathedral to the right, showing the caldarium *and, to the left, part of the* tepidarium; *they are crossed by the walls of the later basilica. The 1971 excavations under the church of St Mary Major, centre of the picture, have been grassed over (author's collection)*

policy of intervention by the former Exeter Museums Archaeological Field Unit (EMAFU) led to the recovery of a fortress plan which is more extensive than any other of the Claudio-Neronian period in Britain. The background to all this work is discussed further in Chapter 1 above.

This chapter summarises the Exeter excavations and explores their wider significance. A detailed analysis of the fortress plan appears in EAPIT 2, Chapter 3.1. The extent and complexity of the extra-mural settlements emphasise the importance of the Exeter fortress. They are described in some detail below, together with a section on army supply which includes a specialist report on the animal bone by Mark Maltby. For basic information about most of the fortresses cited in this chapter, together with plans and bibliographies, see Bishop 2012; references to later or more detailed accounts are given where necessary.

The site of the fortress

The physical setting of the fortress and later town has been well described by Fox (1952, 1–2, fig. 1) and Henderson (1988, 92–4, fig. 5.1). Their sites occupied a spur overlooking the River Exe which was defined to the north-west by the steep-sided Longbrook Valley (Fig. 5.2). The fortress was built on fairly level ground to the south-east of the valley. Immediately beyond its northern corner was the volcanic outcrop extrusion of Rougemont, a hill which limited the extent of the fortress in that direction. To the south-west, the defences followed the top of a marked slope down to the River Exe and to the north-east the edge of the Coombe Valley. These topographical restrictions probably account for the small size of the fortress and its elongated proportions relative to other Claudio-Neronian and Flavian examples (Table 5.1; Henderson 1988, 95). The areas immediately outside the fortress, except for the Longbrook Valley, were enclosed by the later defences of the town, but were clearly considered too precipitous to accommodate the regular planning and large, tightly-packed buildings of the fortress. The natural subsoil on the site of the fortress is river terrace deposits overlying shillet and, towards the northern corner, volcanic rock.

The spur was selected for the site of the fortress almost certainly because it commanded the lowest convenient crossing point of the Exe, a short distance above the tidal limit of the river. To the north-west and south-east, there were cliffs along the riverside and farther downriver the land was marshy. In the earlier medieval period there was a ford across the river south-west of the town, and it remained fordable after a stone bridge was built in *c.* 1200 (Brown 2019, 6–7, 10, fig. 8). Construction of a timber bridge to serve the fortress is very likely, enabling passage across the river when it was in spate. It would have been a major project: the medieval bridge was *c.* 180 m in length between its abutments (Brown 2019, 14).

Exeter and *legio II Augusta*: previous research

According to the geographer Ptolemy, *Isca* (Exeter), supplied with its longitude and latitude, was one of the four *poleis* of the Dumnonii and the location of *legio II Augusta* (Rivet and Smith 1979, 144). The presence of the legion in Devon during the Claudian conquest was once thought to have been confirmed by the stamped tile from Seaton, now known to have been of much later date (Chapter 3 above, and EAPIT 2, Chapter 13.3). Indeed, it seemed likely to R.G. Collingwood (Collingwood and Myres 1937, 92, note 1) that Ptolemy had confused the River Axe, near the mouth of which Seaton is situated, with the Exe. However, finds of samian ware and coins of Claudian date, according to Davies Pryce (1938, 37–8), confirmed the identification of Exeter as a base for the legion. This idea was not supported by the excavations in the War-damaged areas of the city, where none of the earliest buildings seemed to indicate military occupation (Fox 1952, 15–17). Ptolemy's location of *legio II Augusta* at Exeter was now apparently explained by the remarkably confusing fact that from *c.* AD 75 the legion was at another *Isca*, Caerleon in South Wales. For much of the geography of southern Britain, Ptolemy, though writing in the early 2nd century AD, had relied on an earlier source of Claudio-Neronian or early Flavian date which would have included *Isca*-Exeter. If up-to-date information available to Ptolemy gave *Isca* as the location of *legio II Augusta*, he would naturally have assumed it was the place named in his earlier source (Rivet and Smith 1979, 115). Following the discovery of the fortress at Exeter, Ptolemy's error is even easier to understand, for in all likelihood the earlier source would have stated that *legio II Augusta* was at *Isca*-Exeter (Bidwell and Boon 1976).

At a conference in 1963, Webster (1966, 41, 45, n. 62) included Exeter amongst his 'civil sites where there is evidence suggesting a military origin', relying on the same sort of evidence that Davies Pryce had cited. At the same conference Lady Fox maintained the civil origins of Exeter, but in the subsequent publication noted the discovery in 1964 of a 'military post' at the South Gate of the later Roman town (Fox 1966, 51, n. 2; Site 36). It was represented by a ditch which in the full report was taken to have been part of the defences of a fort in what is now known to have been in the area of the extra-mural settlement south-east of the fortress (Fox 1968, fig. 3). Meanwhile, Frere (1967, 74) had suggested that a fortress had been established at Exeter by *legio II Augusta* shortly after the conquest. Its emergence in 1971–2 was thus not entirely a surprise, but its date, size and inclusion of very large baths were unexpected. There was understandably much debate about the status of the fortress and whether it had contained a full legion, but its existence was soon acknowledged in authoritative accounts of the earlier stages in the conquest of Britain (*e.g.* Webster 1978, 95; Todd 1981, 88).

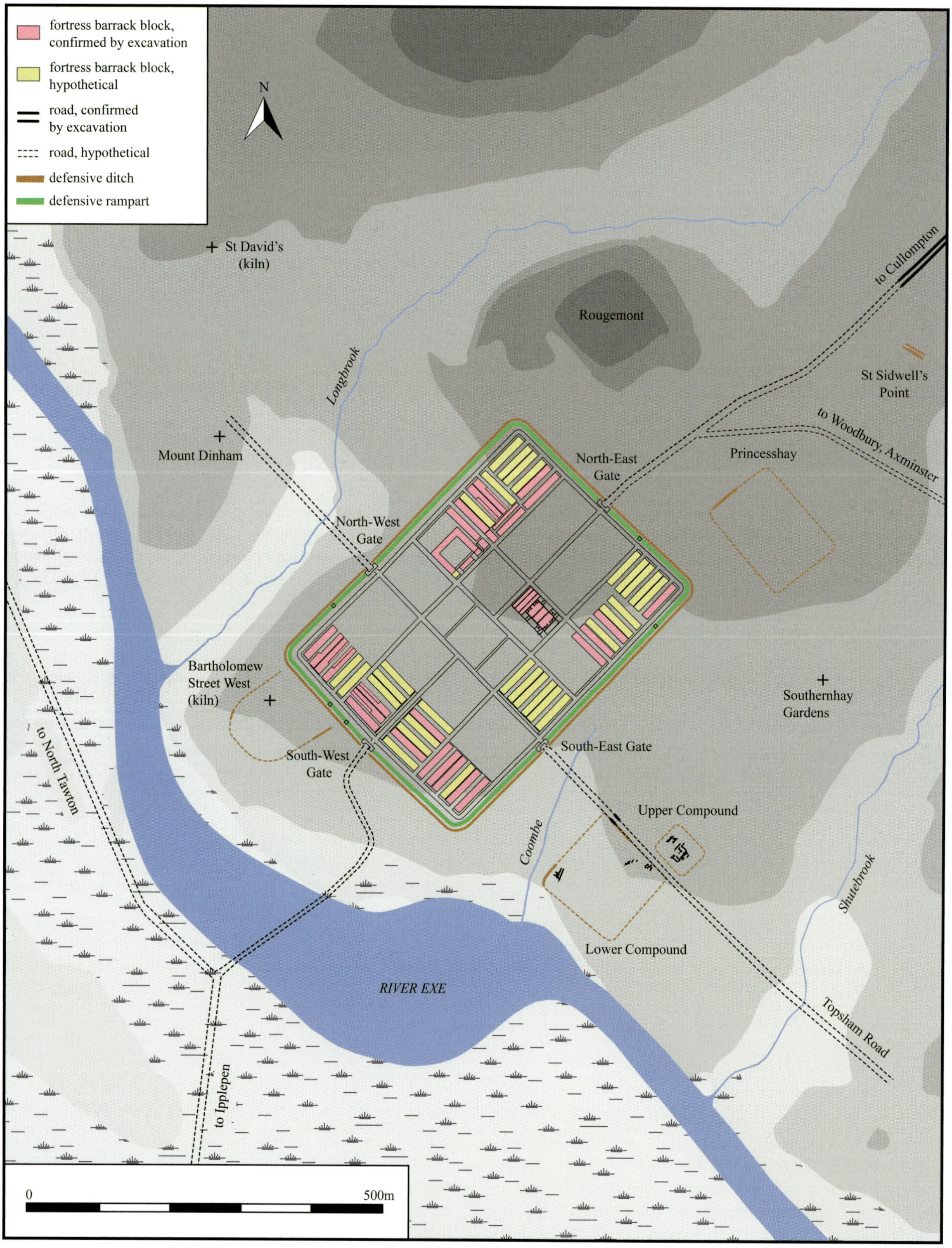

Fig. 5.2 The setting of the fortress (drawn by David Gould)

Fig. 5.3 Two fragments of the dolphin antefixes from Exeter with to the right an example from Caerleon which was made in the same mould (© RAMM)

Fig. 5.4 Fragment of mosaic from the demolition levels in the caldarium *of the fortress baths; width 15.5 cm. Above the plain band are parts of two hoofed creatures, probably capricorns, confronting what is perhaps a celestial globe (© RAMM)*

The only direct links between Exeter and Caerleon, the subsequent posting of *legio II Augusta*, are the dolphin antefixes found at both fortresses which were made in the same mould (Fig. 5.3); it must have travelled north with the legion (Bidwell and Boon 1976; EAPIT 2, Chapter 13.3). Other material evidence that would confirm the presence of *legio II Augusta* at Exeter is the likely identification of motifs on a fragment of mosaic from the fortress baths as capricorns, emblems of the legion, confronting a celestial globe (Fig. 5.4; Smith 1979; Cosh and Neal 2005, 57).

The fortress

The results of excavations in the fortress are reviewed at length in EAPIT 2, Chapter 3.1 (Fig. 5.5). In this chapter there are more general observations about some of the buildings and the history and function of the fortress in its wider setting. First, it must be emphasised that the more detailed review supports earlier arguments that accommodation was provided for the entire legion, consisting of about 5,000 men and perhaps a few hundred

Fig. 5.5 Plan of the fortress. For a detailed commentary, see EAPIT 2, Chapter 3.1 (drawn by David Gould)

Fig. 5.6 The north-east end of barrack G2 exposed in the back garden of an 18th-century house at Bartholomew Street East in 1980–81 (Site 73); for its position see Fig. 5.5 Site 73 (© RAMM)

more if the size of the first cohort had been increased. Henderson (1988, 103–5) argued that space was also allowed for one or more auxiliary units, but this now seems unlikely.

The defences and intervallum

The defences, their line established on all sides of the fortress (EAPIT 2, Chapter 3.1, Table 3.1), consisted of a single ditch 4–5 m wide and 2 m deep and a rampart with a width of 4.8–5.4 m and a clay core, revetted with cheeks of turf or clay blocks and laid on a corduroy of logs and branches (Henderson 1988, 107–8). Five interval towers have been examined, but none of the four gates has been seen. The *intervallum* was *c.* 6.5 m wide and at two sites accommodated a series of buildings. Excavations at Catherine Street in 1987–8 (Site 89) suggested to Henderson the existence of sleeper beams running along the front of the rampart, their purpose being to accommodate the timber uprights of a vertical facing (1991, 75–80). Citing a parallel to this type of construction at Wroxeter (see now Webster 2002, 22–3, 67–78), Henderson went further, proposing that the vertical face had been rendered, incised with lines in imitation of masonry and perhaps whitewashed (Henderson 1991, fig. 13.11). Against this is the absence of any record of plaster, mortar or lime fragments in any of the excavations on the rampart. Although no signs of sleeper beams along the front of the rampart were noted in the excavations preceding those at Catherine Street, the possibility of a vertical facing needs to be investigated further, even if the likelihood of a decorative rendering is remote.

The barracks

The ten cohorts of the legion would have required 60 barracks in addition to at least two for *immunes* and perhaps another four if the numbers in the first cohort had been augmented. The barracks were built using the post-in-trench method, where the main walls were formed by a series of vertical timbers set in continuous trenches and forming a framework filled with wattle and daub (Fig. 5.6). The technique was standard for the principal walls of military buildings in 1st-century AD Britain, though occasionally other forms of construction are found, as at Colchester where the main walls of the barracks were built of clay blocks on mortared stone plinths (Crummy 1997, 46–8). In some of the Exeter barracks internal partitions were supported by sleeper beams. There is no evidence that the roofs were tiled, and they were presumably covered by wooden shingles or thatch. Floors were of earth or clay.

A remarkable aspect of the Exeter barracks is their small size. None has been completely excavated, but the plans of a number can be confidently reconstructed, showing that their overall length was *c.* 60–64 m. Most of the barracks had 12 *contubernia*, though at least one example perhaps had rooms for under-officers at the end opposite the centurion's quarters. At Caerleon the barracks also had 12 *contubernia* but were *c.* 10 m longer than at Exeter. The Colchester and Inchtuthil barracks had 14 *contubernia*; the latter barracks were even longer than the Caerleon examples, but the greater length of the Colchester barracks when compared to those at Exeter are largely accounted for by their additional two *contubernia* (for comparative plans of these barracks, see Henderson 1991, fig. 13.12). No doubt the small size of the Exeter fortress dictated the modest dimensions of its barracks, but these restrictions were clearly acceptable when the specifications for fortresses were less standardised than in later times (Table 5.1).

The other buildings

Substantial parts of the fortress baths and a *fabrica* have been excavated, which are discussed in two of the following sections. Fragments of the *praetorium* and *principia* have been seen, as well as granaries, but many other buildings remain to be discovered. The baths were the only masonry building in the fortress. As in the barracks, construction in timber generally employed the post-in-trench method. The only exceptions were the *praetorium* and *principia* where the uprights were driven directly into the ground; they were also apparently the only timber buildings in the fortress which had tiled roofs.

The fortress baths

The Temple of Claudius at Colchester and the Exeter fortress baths were broadly of the same date and were the first masonry buildings ever to have been conceived and built on a grand scale in Britain (Figs 5.1 and 5.5). Some villas and the Neronian palace at Fishbourne were also of this period, but they were on a less ambitious scale. The buildings at Colchester and Exeter therefore mark the beginning of British architectural history.

The main excavations on the baths took place in 1971–2 (Fig. 5.7). Following their publication (Bidwell 1979), a series of Roman walls were found in 1994–5 on the north-west side of the plot occupied by the baths, in the basements of buildings between the Cathedral Close and High Street (Site 121, 2 Broadgate [Tinleys]). Henderson considered that the earlier walls, together with fragments nearby recorded in 1911 and 1977 (Site 62) were likely to have been part of an aisled hall which served as a changing room (*apodyterium*) and covered exercise area (Esmonde Cleary 1996, fig. 17: Henderson 1999b), also a feature of the Caerleon baths (Zienkiewicz 1986). There were strong architectural affinities between the baths in these two fortresses of *legio II Augusta*, but they were also shared by the Claudian baths at the fortress of *Vindonissa* in Switzerland where there were two *frigidaria*, probably also used as *apodyteria*, which flanked an open-air pool (Bidwell 1979, 43–6, fig. 10). A similar arrangement is certainly possible in the Exeter baths.

Table 5.1 Proportions and sizes of 1st-century AD legionary fortresses. Asterisks (*) denote examples where the dimensions have definitely been measured from the inner edge of an inner ditch or the front of a rampart. At Nijmegen the small triangular expansion on the dextral side of the praetentura *has not been taken into account.*

Fortress	*Dimensions (m)*	*Proportions width to length*	*Size (ha)*	*References*
Exeter	349 x 476*	1:1.36	16.6	Henderson 1988, 95
Colchester	422 x 515*	1:1.22	21.7	Bishop 2012, 64, fig. 36
Wroxeter	402 x 462	1:1.15	*c.* 19.0	Webster 1988, 123
Lincoln	390 x 480	1:1.23	*c.* 18.7	Jones 1988, 149, with addition of 15 m on each side for defences
Gloucester	375 x 475*	1:1.27	17.8	Holbrook 2010, 186
Usk	410 x 475*	1:1.16	19.5	Manning 2010, 189
Nijmegen	346 x 442*	1:1.27	15.3	Driessen 2009, fig. 2 (exc. irregularity)
Chester	412 x 593*	1:1.44	24.4	Mason 2010, 172
Caerleon	418 x 490*	1:1.17	20.5	Boon 1972, 13
Inchtuthil	460 x 475*	1:1.03	21.9	Pitts and St Joseph 1985, figs 83 and 85

There is no need to repeat in summary the description of the baths published in 1979, but subsequent research on baths relevant to Exeter needs to be reviewed. In the middle decades of the 1st century AD, the architecture of Roman baths was transformed by a demand for larger and more luxurious buildings which were well illuminated by natural light; the greatly increased size of their covered spaces required new techniques of construction and more efficient heating systems. The earlier stages of this architectural transformation are obscure, which is why the small group of baths to which *Vindonissa*, Exeter and Caerleon belong is particularly important. Together with another example at the Roman city of Avenches in Switzerland, they are earlier than the known examples of the Imperial Type, but share the strict axial symmetry of the type in a simplified form. The earliest, built late in the AD 40s, was at the legionary fortress of *Vindonissa* in Switzerland; Exeter came next and then the baths at Caerleon and at Avenches. In all the reports on the excavations of these buildings, the earliest published on *Vindonissa* in the 1930s (Laur-Belart 1935), the baths have been recognised as an early stage in the development of the Imperial Type which is not represented in the surviving architectural record of Rome or other Mediterranean cities. The argument is that the architects in these frontier provinces drew on lost Italian models for their bath-houses. There were no local traditions on which they could depend: at *Vindonissa* the earlier bath-houses at the fortress were built in timber, as at other pre-Claudian fortresses in Germany (Bidwell 2002). In his standard work on the architectural development of Roman baths, Yegül (1972, 75) contrasted the symmetrically arranged plans of the group in the north-west provinces with baths of much the same period at Pompeii and Herculaneum. He was nevertheless only willing to accept that the group was a stage in the development of the Imperial Type if it could be shown that the architects of imperial projects in Rome 'travelled with the legions'. Since Yegül's publication, the extent to which the architecture of buildings in early legionary fortresses reflected contemporary metropolitan developments has become clear (Förtsch 1996). It will perhaps never be possible to establish direct links between imperial architects and the group of baths in the north-western provinces, but there is no reason to doubt that there were sometimes close links between architecture at legionary fortresses and at Rome and other Mediterranean cities.

The hypocausts of the Exeter baths had features which are without parallels (Bidwell 1979, 30–4) (Figs 5.8–5.9). In the *tepidrium* and *caldarium* they were each divided into four segments by lengths of tile walling forming channels which were intended to circulate heat from the furnaces more effectively. The hypocausts were also reinforced with ironwork: in front of the furnaces, the floors of the baths were underpinned by iron frameworks, and elsewhere iron bars were laid over the tops of the tile supports (*pilae*) of the hypocausts to support the floors of the rooms above. These innovations seem to have been experimental responses, not apparently repeated elsewhere, to the challenge of heating much larger spaces than previously found in baths and perhaps also to the need to achieve higher temperatures.

The building materials for the baths would have been found by prospection in a landscape which had never before been exploited for such purposes. Clay for making brick and tile was available locally, and trap, the main building stone, could have been quarried from the volcanic deposits at Rougemont. Three other types of stone came from East Devon: Triassic sandstone, perhaps from the coast between Budleigh Salterton and Sidmouth, which was used

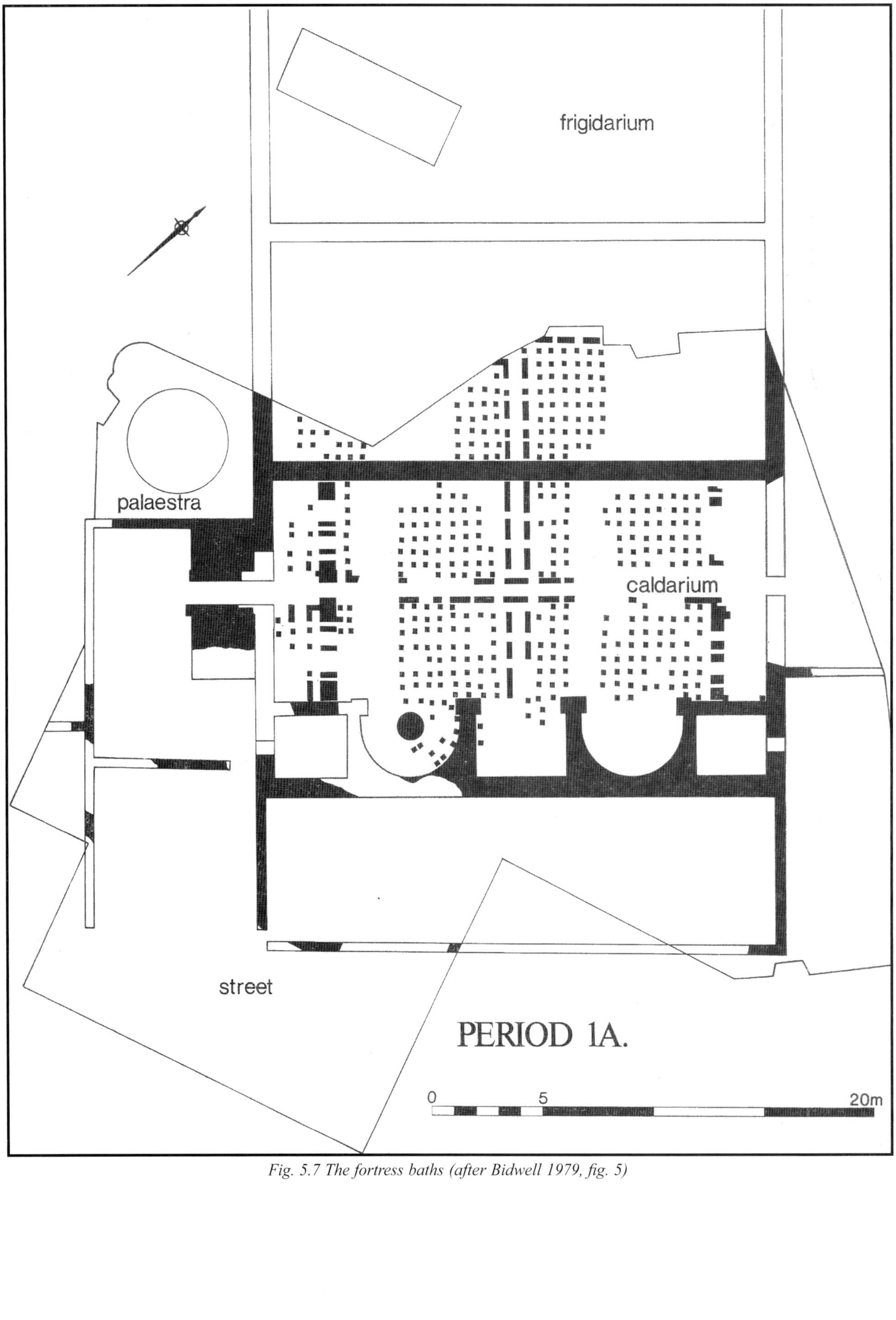

Fig. 5.7 The fortress baths (after Bidwell 1979, fig. 5)

Fig. 5.8 The caldarium *of the fortress baths looking south-east and showing the two apses flanking a rectangular recess. At centre, the north-east wall of the basilica nave and, beyond the back wall of the* caldarium, *the Period 2B/3A extension of the basilica (© RAMM)*

for architectural details, and a porcellanous White Lias probably from near Axminster and olive-grey mudstone local to Exeter, both used for floor-tiles (Scrivener 1979). Purbeck marble came from South-East Dorset, one of the outputs of the geomaterials industry in the Purbeck and Poole Harbour area which also supplied tesserae for the mosaics: blue-grey tesserae came from carbonate rock in the Kimmeridge Clay Formation, and white tesserae possibly from chalk in that area (Fig. 5.4; Allen and Fulford 2004; Allen *et al.* 2007). The use of Purbeck marble at Exeter is of great significance, because it possibly represents the first time that the quarry was exploited to supply a large building project. It is even conceivable that the quarry was discovered by masons prospecting for materials for the baths, unless the source had already been exploited for the building of the Neronian palace at Fishbourne (Fulford 1996, 14). Lead was used extensively in baths. The Mendip lead-ores were being worked by AD 49, probably with the direct engagement of *legio II Augusta* (Todd 2007b, 69–71). A likely source of iron was the Blackdown Hills where ores were being smelted in the Roman military period (see Chapter 3 above).

One of the reasons for the construction of the baths at Exeter has been expressed well by DeLaine. This provision of the usual facilities of Roman life 'cannot, however, wholly explain the exceptional degree of architectural elaboration found in the Exeter baths, or in the whole group of mid to late 1st-century AD examples from the legionary camps of *Vindonissa*, Caerleon and *Aventicum* to which these belong. These are rather show-pieces of Roman power in newly acquired territory, buildings which in scale, construction methods, and function would have been totally alien and awe-inspiring to the majority of the native population, while at the same time offering a taste of the magic of Rome itself to co-operative local élites' (DeLaine 1999, 161). A more immediate audience for the baths was the legion itself. The building might have been at least in part an act of munificence by the legate, the aristocratic commander of the legion, who perhaps paid for some of the costs to add lustre to his reputation.

The sites immediately outside the fortress and in its hinterland

In recent years remarkable progress has been made in revealing the wide range of installations and settlements which supported and serviced the legion at Exeter. Until the main excavations at Princesshay in 2005 (Site 156),

Fig. 5.9 The caldarium *of the fortress baths looking south-west towards one of the two furnaces which served it. Note channels dividing the hypocaust into four segments so as to distribute the heat more evenly. The wall crossing the room from left to right represents the front of the later basilica; part of the* tepidarium *to the right (© RAMM)*

knowledge of extra-mural occupation was mainly confined to the lower-lying area south-east of the fortress, on either side of the road to Topsham. Installations are now known also to the north-east and north-west of the fortress, and extensive settlements have been excavated at St Loye's College and Topsham (Fig. 5.10).

In common with Exeter, fortresses held for more than a few years were served by a series of satellite sites, some under direct military control and others with civilian populations which could be granted limited or complete autonomy. Looking across the whole sweep of the European frontiers, from Scotland to the Black Sea, Exeter is now known to have the largest series of such dependent sites amongst fortresses dating to between the Augustan and early Flavian periods. The entire series has been recovered by excavations in advance of development, which is one reason for doubting whether Exeter is entirely exceptional. What seems to have been the most important axis of supply and industry – the road between the fortress and its port at Topsham – survives as a modern route which has seen much building since the 1970s. A second reason is that settlements outside some fortresses established in the 1st century AD and held until the end of the Roman period grew into very large towns, and moreover, as for example at *Vindobona*, *Carnuntum*, *Aquincum* and *Apulum*, there might have been two such towns, one immediately outside the fortress and another 2–3 km distant. Earlier stages of their development, on a scale comparable with the extra-mural sites at Exeter, might be obscured by their later growth. One fortress in Britain which sits in a landscape largely free of recent buildings is Inchtuthil, and its extra-mural sites – the compounds and nearby fort at Cargill, possibly occupied at the same time as the fortress – are much less extensive than those at Exeter (Pitts and St Joseph 1985); Wroxeter, set in a more populated rural landscape, is surrounded by a number of military sites, none investigated in any detail (White 2010). Whether, in these respects, fortresses such as Usk, Gloucester and Colchester, their environs covered to varying degrees by modern developments, will eventually prove to resemble Exeter rather than Inchtuthil is a matter for speculation.

Settlement and installation types

Before describing the recent excavations on extra-mural sites and some earlier discoveries at Exeter, several things need to be said about the character of occupation outside fortresses. Common to all fortresses occupied for any length of time were the *canabae legionis*, literally the huts of the legion, which is the name acquired by the settlements of traders and artisans which grew up outside the defences. There was frequently a second civilian

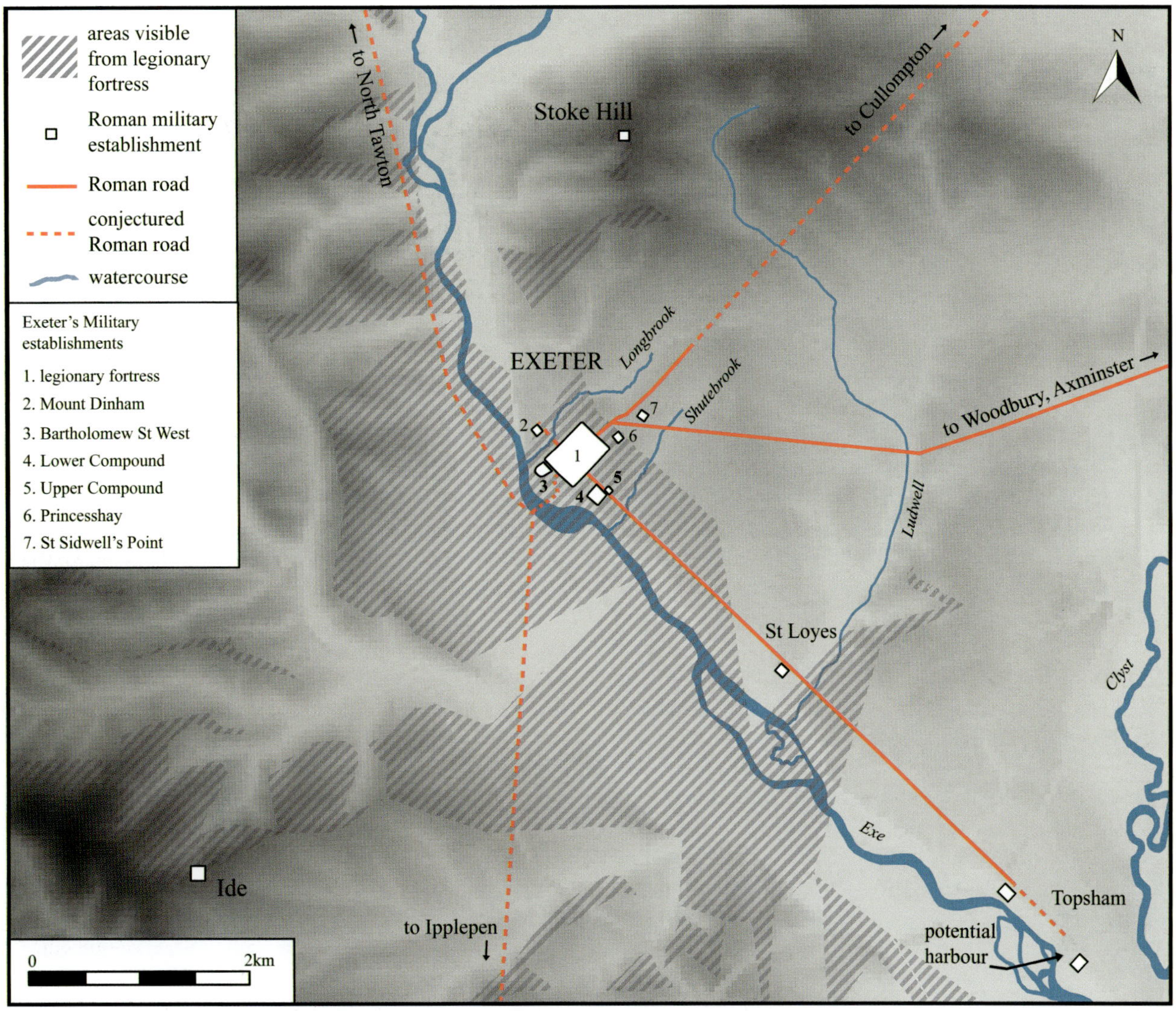

Fig. 5.10 The location of the fortress, its extra-mural sites, and a viewshed analysis showing areas visible from the fortress (drawn by David Gould)

settlement 2–3 km distant from a fortress. Another common occurrence was an auxiliary fort; in some instances they are known to have accommodated cavalry which would have compensated for the very small size of this element in the composition of the legion (Zienkiewicz 1993, 82). These various adjuncts to fortresses are known at least as early as the Claudio-Neronian period. Amphitheatres, large baths and various official buildings appeared in the next decade or so. Outside some fortresses of exceptional strategic and administrative importance, there were very large complexes that accommodated high officials of the province, comparable to the building at Mount Dinham (see below).

At Exeter enclosures containing buildings to the south-east of the fortress were thought shortly after their discovery to have been supply bases or works depots (Bidwell 1980, 41). Later descriptions have been neutral (for example, Salvatore 2001, 128, 'military compounds'), with some justification. Supply bases such as those at Augustan Rödgen, in Germany (Schönberger and Simon 1976), and 3rd-century AD South Shields (Bidwell and Speak 1994; Hodgson and Bidwell 2009), where accommodation for large numbers of soldiers was combined with buildings capable of storing thousands of tonnes of cereals, are not known in the immediate vicinity of fortresses. The Uferkastelle (Hofestatt), a series of riverside enclosures 200 m south of the Augustan fortress at Haltern, in Germany, contained in its final period what had been interpreted as a very large granary, and accordingly was thought to have had a supply function (von Schnurbein 1974, 25–34). The remains of the supposed granary are now regarded as those of a series of slipways for naval craft (Kühlborn 2006, 289). Likewise unknown immediately outside fortresses are works depots such as that at Holt, in Clwyd (Grimes 1930), 12 km upriver from the Chester fortress, with accommodation for soldier-craftsmen alongside the industrial areas.

It has been calculated that about 42% of the Exeter fortress was occupied by buildings other than living accommodation (EAPIT 2, Chapter 3.1). A glance at other more complete fortress plans will show that these other buildings, apart from the *principia*, consisted mainly of *fabricae* and granaries, and also of courtyard buildings, many of which, although conclusive evidence is lacking, are likely to have been store buildings. Comparisons with auxiliary forts are instructive. They also contained granaries which seem to have occupied relatively as much space as in the fortresses, if not more (detailed comparisons have still to be undertaken). Usually absent from forts are other types of store buildings and purpose-built *fabricae*, although metalworking sometimes took place in parts of their interiors. Forts seem to have relied more on their civilian settlements for the day-to-day supply of consumables other than cereals, while fortresses probably held large stocks of such consumables in their store buildings, supplemented by highly organised systems of manufacture in their *fabricae*. Moreover, immediately outside many fortresses there were very large courtyard buildings, presumably controlled directly by the legions, which could have had a considerable storage capacity; an example with an area of almost 2 ha was recently found next to the River Usk at Caerleon (Guest *et al.* 2012). Large-scale production of pottery and ceramic building materials would be located where the best natural resources were available, often some distance from the fortress as at Holt.

Sites around the periphery of the fortress

South-west side, beyond the porta praetoria: the land falls steeply southwards down to the river, but near the south-west corner of the fortress, where the land is more level, there appears to have been an annexe with an area of perhaps 1 ha, represented by ditches found near Friernhay Street in 1981 (Site 75) and at Paradise Place in 1994 (Site 104).

North-west side, beyond the porta principalis dextra: this side of the fortress overlooked the steep-sided Longbrook Valley. The most important discovery in this area emerged at Mount Dinham in 2007–9 and 2011 (Site 154), on the opposite side of the valley *c.* 150 m north-west of the fortress. A building complex measuring at least 55 m by 35 m had at its centre an aisled hall 15 m by 9 m. Its fragmentary plan had similarities to Augustan *praetoria* in the fortresses at Haltern and Marktbreit. The building appears to have been the residence of a high official. Though there was more than one episode in the history of the fortress when such an official might have been present (see the concluding paragraphs of this chapter), further discussion of its plan and context must await the publication of the final report (Passmore forthcoming). In trenches excavated *c.* 30 m to the north-east there were small pits and postholes, also of the military period. The orientation of the building was north–south, varying by about 45 degrees from that of the fortress. If the road leading to the *porta principalis dextra* had approached directly from the north-west, it would have crossed a site at Exe Street, excavated in 1985–6 (Site 69), but there was no sign of it. Perhaps the road took a diagonal line across the south-east slope of the valley and also ran up the opposite side diagonally, which might explain the alignment of the Mount Dinham building.

A ditch running at right angles to the line of the defences was seen at the North Gate site in 1978 (Site 69), *c.* 50 m north-east of the *porta principalis dextra*; it perhaps drained the fortress ditch at the lowest point in the course of the defences on their north-west side (Bidwell 1980, 23). At St David's Church, 260 m north-east of the fortress, a tile kiln was found in 2016 (Site 191). It was probably operating towards the end of the fortress period or perhaps a little later (EAPIT 2, Chapter 13.3; Steinmetzer forthcoming).

North-east side, beyond the porta decumana: the diagonal line of the street between *Insulae* X/XXI/XXVI and XXII/XXIII/XXIV/XXVII/XXVIII/XXIX of the later town was established during the fortress period. Structures on the site at Princesshay (Site 156), *c.* 110 m south-east of the road leading to the gate, served two successive and remarkably different purposes during the military period. A cremation burial containing two complete flagons and other pottery seemed to be associated with a large round-ended enclosure, 25 m across and at least 34 m in length, which was represented by post pits at intervals of *c.* 3 m. In the forthcoming report (Bidwell in Steinmetzer, Stead, Pearce, Bidwell and Allan forthcoming) the enclosure is tentatively identified as part of a funerary garden, and a curving feature cutting one of the post-pits might have been a bedding trench. Rectangles ending in hemicycles were ornamental features in the repertoire of military architects; they appear in what are probably garden courts in the *praetoria* of the double legionary fortress at *Vetera,* in Germany, and in a building apparently serving the same purpose at Caerleon (von Petrikovits 1975b, 67, Bild 13, 4–5, who calls these features 'Hippodromgärten' because of their resemblance to the outline of a circus).

These arrangements were swept away when defences were built across the site, running roughly parallel to the road leading to the *porta decumana* and not at a right angle to the north-eastern defences of the fortress. They included two interval towers *c.* 21 m apart, more closely spaced than those of the fortress which were 29.3 m apart, and at first a single ditch which was replaced by two larger ditches. Nothing remained of the rampart, but the filling of all three ditches included turves. The defences, which faced north-west, were *c.* 50 m from the eastern corner of the fortress, too close to have formed part of an annexe unless it had extended around the circuit of the fortress defences to join their south-east side, which seems improbable (Fig. 5.2). The Princesshay defences seem to have formed a separate enclosure, probably a fort which might have been built to accommodate a cavalry unit.

In September 2019 two parallel ditches running from north-west to south-east were found at St Sidwell's Point (Exeter Bus Station), 500 m west of the fortress (Site 189; Clarke 2019). The results of the excavations are still being assessed, but there is no reason to doubt that the ditches formed the north-east side of a military enclosure: the south-western ditch had a Punic profile with the near-vertical side to the north-east, a sure indication that the interior of the enclosure lay to the south-west. The filling of the ditches contained mostly 1st-century AD pottery, mixed with some later material. The excavators regarded the enclosure as broadly of the same date as the fortress. Because of its distance from Princesshay, any connection with the probable fort in that area can probably be ruled out. The enclosure seems to have been a separate establishment but was perhaps occupied for only a brief period. It could be another example of the apparently temporary bases which have been identified at Dalswinton, in South-West Scotland, and North Tawton, in Devon, which, as at Exeter, were defined by double ditches (see section below on '*legio II Augusta* and the annexation of the South-West').

South-east side, beyond the porta principalis sinistra: the Topsham road ran directly to the gate, crossing the Coombe Valley which was shallower and had more gently sloping sides than the Longbrook Valley north-west of the fortress. On the level ground to the south-east and on either side of the road, there was extensive occupation which has been explored in a long series of excavations, the first in 1964–5 (Site 36). The largest projects, at the Valiant Soldier site (1973–4, Site 44), Holloway Street (1974, Site 50) and Lower Coombe Street (1989–90, Site 97), will be published in the near future by Salvatore (forthcoming), with references to some of the smaller interventions (Sites 46, 65, 74, 94 and 96). The occupation on the main sites is characterised by small rectangular buildings set within compounds delineated by ditches, banks or fences, best seen at the Valiant Soldier and Lower Coombe Street sites (previously illustrated in Frere 1991a, fig. 27, and Salvatore 2001, fig. 2). There is no evidence for the *canabae* to the north-west and north-east of the fortress where instead there are official or military installations on the level ground. Much of the area to the south-west, excluding the area of the probable annexe, slopes down steeply to the flood plain of the Exe. That leaves only the area to the south-east as a likely site for the *canabae*, which could have extended across the coombe as far as the fortress defences. The building plans published so far seem to represent strip buildings, and the enclosures might represent a response to the same emergency that led to the provision of defences around the detached settlement at St Loye's College.

The occupation seems to have been very extensive. Rubbish pits of the military period were found at a second site south-west of Holloway Street in 1978, near the Roman road to Topsham and some 350 m from the fortress (Site 65). It is possible that the boundary of the occupied area was formed by the Shutebrook Valley (Fig. 5.2). At Southernhay Gardens (Site 49) *c.* 300 m north-east of the Topsham road, a rectangular building and a well were excavated in 1974; further finds of the military period were made nearby at Dean Clarke House in 2013 (Site 167).

The extent of the fortress and all the other sites listed above covers an area very approximately of 100 ha. Its limits are established not by a definite lack of evidence of activities in the adjacent zone but by the absence of investigation in the suburban areas of Exeter where there have been few major building developments in recent decades. Much of the housing was built in the second half of the 19th and the early 20th centuries, when there was no-one following in the footsteps of W.T.P Shortt, an assiduous antiquary who rewarded building labourers for information about archaeological discoveries and published them in newspaper articles, most of them collected in his *Sylva Antiqua Iscana* and *Collectanea Curiosa Antiqua Dumnonia*, both books appearing in 1841.

The main military cemeteries have yet to be found, but they probably lie under the Georgian and Regency suburbs or in areas developed after Shortt left Exeter in 1855.

The St Loye's College site

The settlement

Excavations in 2010, 2013 and 2015–16 explored an extensive series of buildings which was situated immediately south-west of the assumed line of the road between the fortress, 2.2 km to the north-west, and Topsham, 3 km to the south-east. The full report, though completed, has yet to appear (Salvatore *et al.* forthcoming); a detailed summary has been published by Salvatore and Steinmetzer (2018), and an interim report on the 2013 excavations is available online (Stead and Payne 2013).

The earliest structural remains were of an Iron Age round house set within an enclosure and of a second roundhouse to the south-east. The enclosed roundhouse was sealed beneath a complex of timber buildings apparently arranged around a courtyard, but there were large quantities of Roman pottery and other finds in the upper filling of the enclosure ditch, demonstrating that there was occupation of the earlier fortress period nearby before the complex was built. There were two other groups of buildings to the north-east and east which were divided by what appears to have been a street (Fig. 5.12). All were contained within a defensive circuit consisting of double ditches and enclosing an area measuring *c.* 200 m from north-west to south-east. There were no

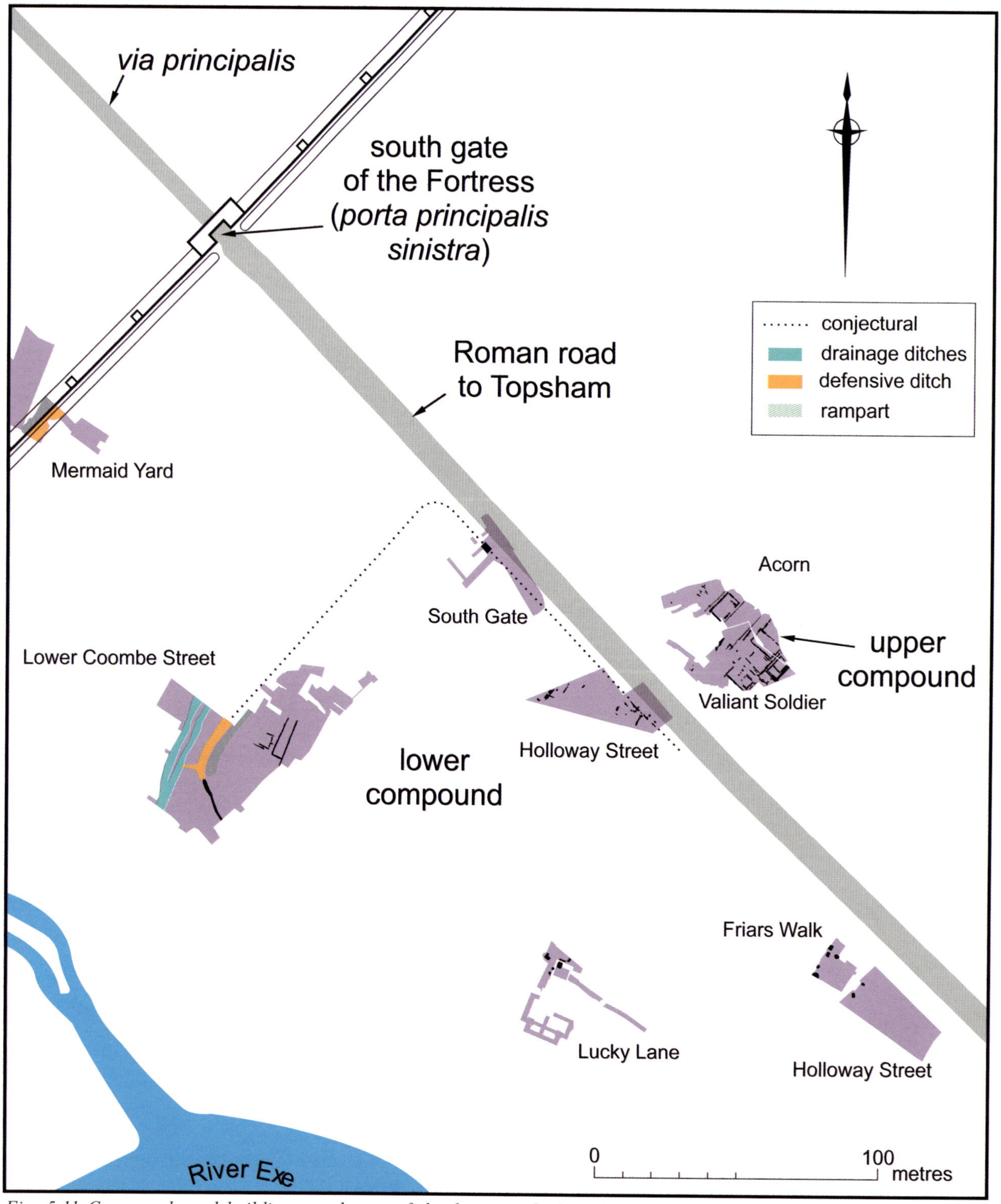

Fig. 5.11 Compounds and buildings south-east of the fortress which probably formed part of the canabae *(the civilian extra-mural settlement) (Salvatore forthcoming, fig. 15, drawing by Tony Ives, reproduced courtesy of John Salvatore; © Exeter City Council)*

interval towers and, on the south-west side, no gate; an associated bank or rampart would have been removed by later cultivation and development, as were almost all the Roman floor surfaces and occupation levels across the whole site (Stead and Payne 2013, 2). Salvatore and Steinmetzer (2018, 797) thought it likely that the defences were added some years after the settlement was established, possibly as an emergency measure during the Boudican rebellion. The defences might have enclosed only the core of the settlement: timber buildings were

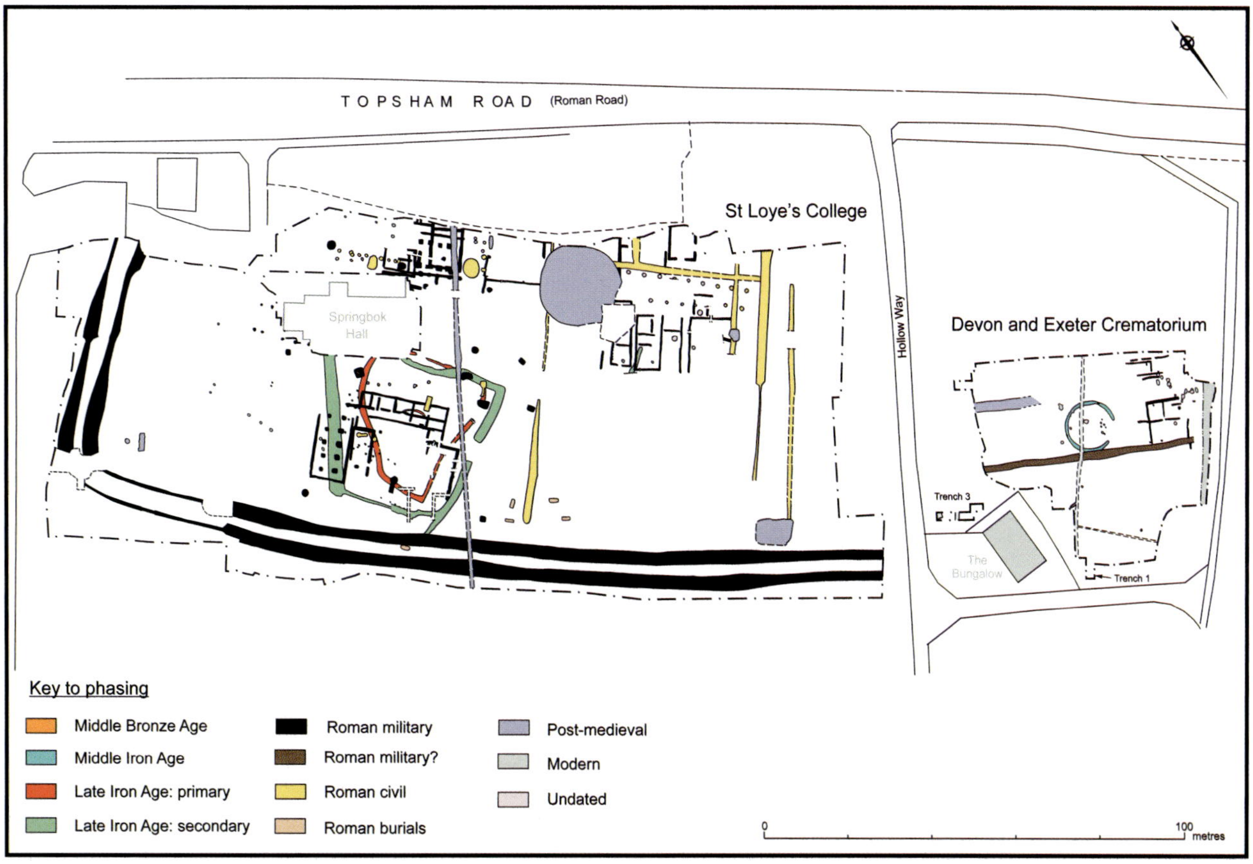

Fig. 5.12 The settlement at St Loye's College (after Salvatore and Steinmetzer 2018, fig. 2, with additions, drawing by Tony Ives, reproduced courtesy of John Salvatore and AC Archaeology; © Exeter City Council)

seen in 2015–16 south-east of the enclosure. Occupation continued into the early Flavian period, and there were small amounts of later pottery, mainly of late 1st to early 3rd-century AD date.

The buildings and their functions

Salvatore and Steinmetzer (2018, 798) regarded the St Loye's College site as probably 'a Roman military supply base where some metal-working also took place' though the presence of separate supply or stores bases in the vicinity of fortresses is doubtful (see above). Holbrook (2015, 97–8) preferred to see St Loye's College as a civilian settlement established by the army, pointing out that some of the building plans are types which occur in urban contexts. It is often difficult to distinguish the various types of sites which serviced fortresses when only fragments have been seen, but at St Loye's College there are two means of identifying the function of the settlement. One is its location, discussed below. The other is an analysis of the building plans, already undertaken by Salvatore and Steinmetzer but which can be developed further.

In the south-eastern part of the site was a row of rectangular buildings, their long axes at right angles to the line of the road between Exeter and Topsham, which Salvatore and Steinmetzer (2018, 795) identified as strip buildings. They were excavated in 2013 and are described in some detail in an interim report (Stead and Payne 2013). Two of the buildings were divided by a gap 1.1 m in width and measured 14.6 m by 4.5 m (Fig. 5.13, Building 154) and 12.2 m by 5.8 m (Building 108). In the interim report the area to the south-east of Building 108 was interpreted as an open space 4.6 m in width with a very narrow building (Building 237, 12.0 m by 1.9 m) beyond it, even though a post-trench ran across the space near its north-east end. It seems far more likely that the supposed open space was a third building sharing a party wall with that to its north-west (Building 108), both buildings being of the same length. The only difference is that the third building seems to have been open-ended, though as will be seen this is often the case in structures of this type. Building 237 will then have actually been a gap, with another building to its south-east which was represented by two post trenches meeting at a right angle, one representing a side wall of the same length as that on the other side of the gap. The other post trench, at least 6.5 m in length, shows that this fourth building was much wider than the other three. It was apparently open-ended unless a south-western wall

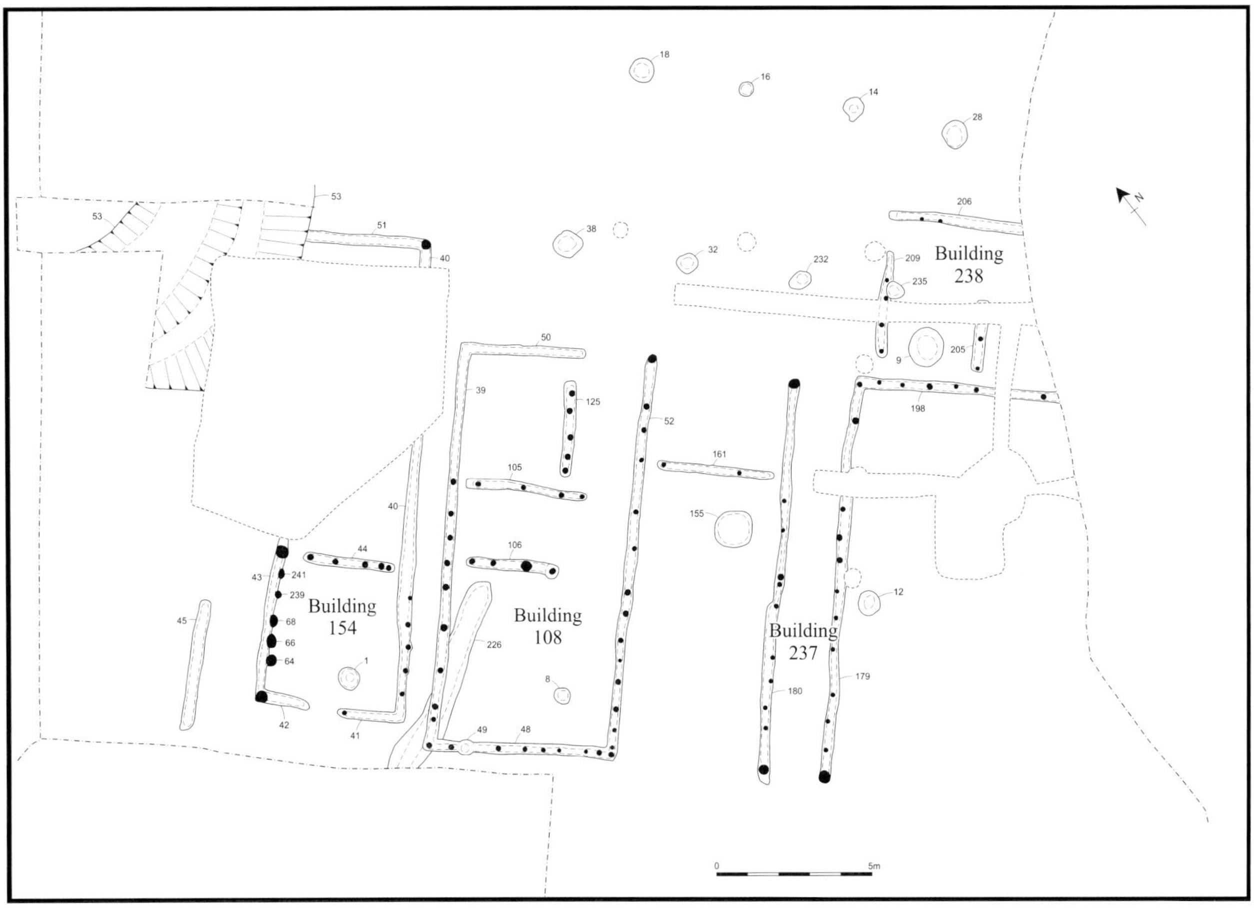

Fig. 5.13 The south-eastern group of strip buildings at St Loye's College. The feature in the top left-hand corner is a post-Roman feature; the two parallel rows of postholes at the top of the plan are apparently later than the military period (from Stead and Payne 2013, fig. 2; © AC Archaeology)

had been removed by later cultivation. The small structure adjoining it to the north-east (Building 238) might well have been a lean-to extension of the main building. An isolated post-trench (45) to the north-west of Building 154 could represent a fifth building, most of which had been destroyed by cultivation.

These four or five buildings were arranged with frontages to the south-west where their ends were more or less in line. Building 154 preserved an entry on that side, and a posthole (49) might have been for a door jamb in the front wall of Building 108, though there was also an entry in its rear wall. The north-east ends of the four buildings were irregular: Building 154 extended further back than the others, and there seems to have been an extension (Building 238) to the south-easternmost building, a feature also of at least one of the strip buildings at Topsham (Fig. 5.14) and of several at the newly-discovered military *vicus* at Okehampton (Anon. 2019). The area to the north-east was probably occupied by back lots, beyond which was the end of a building *c.* 5.5 m wide and at least 7.5 m in length, excavated in 2010 (Fig. 5.12). The illustration appears to show doors in its north-east and south-east sides, but as yet no detailed description of this building is available. It presumably had a frontage to the north-east, possibly on the main road from the fortress beyond the limits of the excavation.

To the north-west there were various post-trenches, none associated with intelligible building plans, and beyond the possible street a complex which clearly represents more than one period of buildings. They include the south-east ends of what might have been two strip buildings sharing the same frontage as the fragments to the south-east.

In Britain and other north-western frontier provinces, strip buildings were the standard form of accommodation in the military *vici* attached to forts and in urban and smaller roadside settlements. The building type, first appearing in Britain during the Claudian period, had emerged in northern Gaul and along the lower Rhine (Perring 2002, 55–6). Its uses were both commercial and domestic, with a shop or workshop at the front and living quarters at the back which were often divided into a number of small rooms. The Neronian to early Flavian strip buildings at Okehampton are the earliest examples known from military *vici* in Britain and closely resemble the buildings at St Loye's College, where their presence might lead naturally to the assumption that the occupation was civilian.

Salvatore and Steinmetzer (2018, 795), however, were reluctant to ascribe a particular function to them all, though they thought some perhaps were for storage. There is indeed a slight difficulty in automatically assuming they were civilian. Storage was also the function attributed to a series of strip buildings at Red House, in Corbridge, some if not all open-ended (Hanson *et al.* 1979, 77–80, figs 2–4), in common with at least one of the buildings at St Loye's College and all those at Topsham. The Red House strip buildings were originally thought to have been situated within the defences of an Agricolan supply base, but it now seems more likely that they were part of a civilian settlement outside a fort (Hodgson 2008, 48). Hanson cited other parallels for open-ended buildings in military contexts, the most compelling of which are those at Richborough, in Kent, associated with a series of very large granaries and part of a Claudio-Neronian to early Flavian supply base (Cunliffe 1968, 236–7, figs 27–8). Less persuasive is the comparison with *tabernae* in legionary fortresses referred to in EAPIT 2, Chapter 3.1: they are smaller than most strip buildings, built in continuous ranges rather than often being separated by alleys, and are without the irregular partitions as seen at St Loye's College, Topsham and Okehampton. Setting aside Richborough as an unexplained anomaly, strip buildings invariably signal the presence of civilians.

The south-western complex of buildings at St Loye's College was thought to have been arranged around a courtyard, with an aisled building measuring *c.* 8.0 m by at least 17.0 m on its north-west side and on its north-east side a range of six rooms fronted by a series of smaller rooms or possibly a corridor with two rooms at its south-east end. The courtyard, if it existed, seems to have been open to the south-west; on its south-east side was a building of which only two adjacent walls survived. Salvatore and Steinmetzer (2018, 795–7) compared the aisled building to the hall in the fortress *fabrica* at Exeter and the adjacent range of the *immunes* barracks (EAPIT 2, Chapter 3.1). At the same time they cited Holbrook's (2015, 96–8) observation that in a civilian context the complex might be seen as the replacement of the Iron Age roundhouse and enclosure by a villa, the north-east range resembling the type with a winged corridor. Another parallel for the north-east range, but from an urban context, might be the row-type house, as for example at *Verulamium* (*Insula* IV.2; Wheeler and Wheeler 1936, 98–9, pl. XXXI; cf. Perring 2002, 64–5, figs 16–17). Furthermore, Salvatore and Steinmetzer noted that the aisled building found a ready parallel at the villa site of Gorhambury, in Hertfordshire, in a hall apparently dating to the Late Iron Age which might have been a barn or living quarters. The building types possibly represented in the complex are thus ambiguous, typically neither military nor civilian.

One further uncertainty about the south-western complex is whether the buildings were indeed arranged around a courtyard. The south-east end of the aisled building could have been in line with that of the narrow building immediately to its south-east and also with the end of that taken to border the south-east side of the supposed courtyard. There would have been space between the last two for more strip buildings, their post trenches removed by cultivation as was much of the building to the south-east. The multi-roomed building to the north-east could have been of a different period; its relationship to the aisled building seems uncertain.

The plan of the settlement

The only metalling on the site that seems to have represented a street was a fragment running south-westwards from the north-eastern edge of the excavations. Its line was at right angles to the main road from Exeter to Topsham which seems to have lain north-east of the site. The position of the buildings suggest that two other streets ran parallel to the main road. The line of one is indicated by the frontages of the south-eastern group of strip buildings; the other would have run south-west of the aisled hall, if it is accepted that the fragmentary remains to the south-east of the hall represent strip buildings. The road between Exeter and Topsham cannot have followed either of these streets: there was no sign of an entry through the north-western defensive ditches, and later Roman boundary ditches ran across the lines of the streets. The settlement in its final state therefore seems to have been nucleated with two streets lined with buildings running parallel and to the south-west of the main road, to the north-east of which there might also have been further streets. The settlement might have begun as ribbon development along the main road, expanding to the south-west and perhaps also to the north-east before it was enclosed by a defensive circuit. That would explain the origin of the large amounts of pottery in the upper filling of the enclosure ditch which was sealed by the buildings of the south-western complex.

Duality of settlement

Another revealing aspect of the settlement is its location in relation to the fortress. It corresponds to a common pattern, recognised many years ago, which has been described as duality of settlement (Mason 1988, 176–8, with references to previous discussions). At fortresses on the Rhine and further east in Europe, in addition to the *canabae* there were separate settlements usually at a distance of 2–3 km. These settlements were civilian, and some grew to a great size in the late 1st and 2nd centuries AD, receiving the status of *colonia* or *municipium*. Others were less extensive. At Neuss (*Novaesium*), in north-western Germany, the civilian settlement was

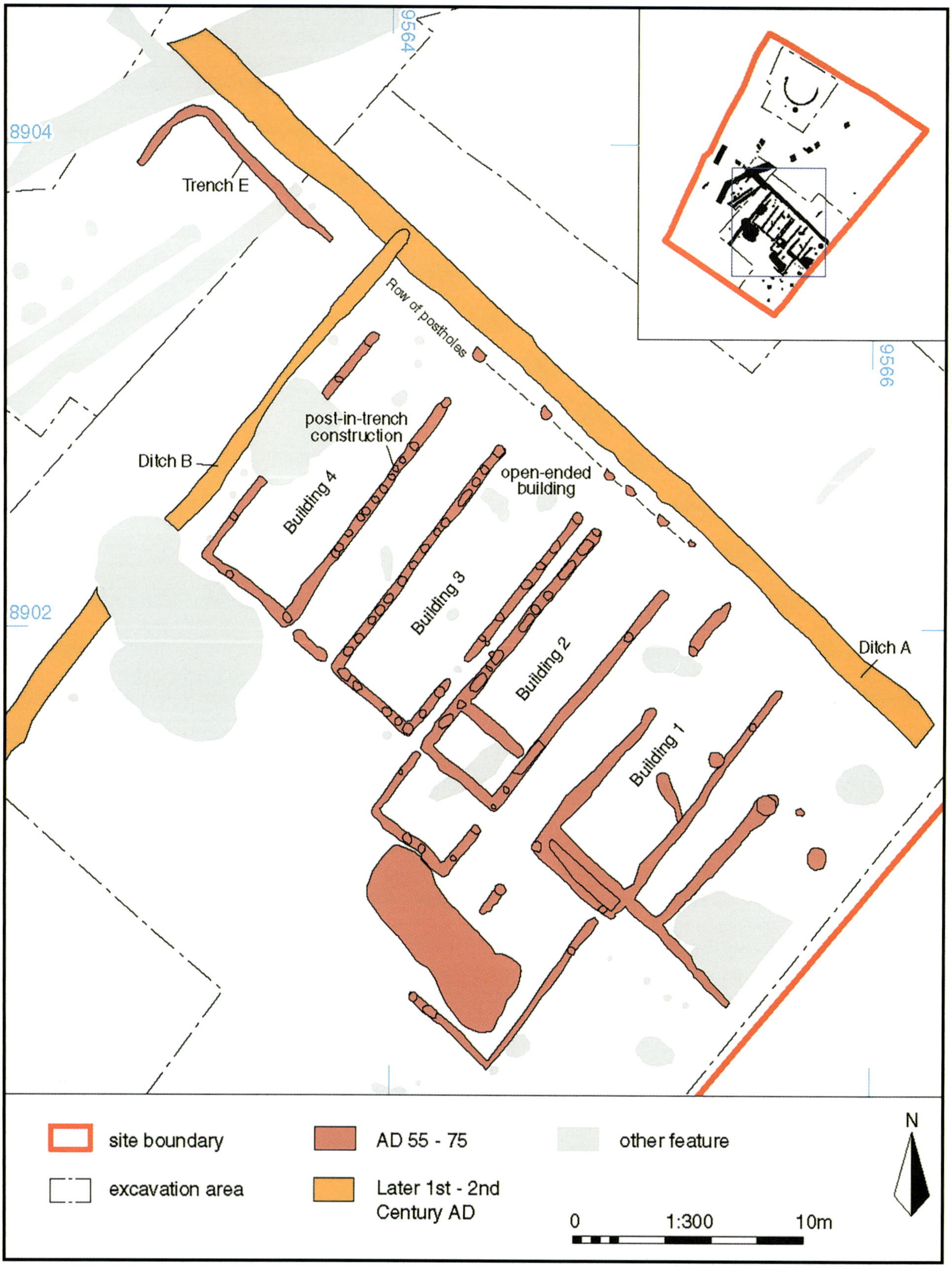

Fig. 5.14 Strip buildings at the Aldi site, in Topsham (Garland and Orellana 2018, fig. 4; © Cotswold Archaeology)

established during the occupation of a Tiberian fortress located 2 km to the south-east (von Petrikovits 1975a, 43–5, Abb. 5; Horn 1987, 580–9). The settlement survived the rebuilding of the fortress on a new site just to the south-east of its predecessor and the replacement of the fortress by a much smaller fort probably in the mid 2nd century AD. Little is known in detail about the plans of the settlement and its buildings, but it seems to have extended for a distance of *c.* 500 m along the road leading to the fortress. Mason (1988, 176–81) cited two likely examples of this duality of settlement in Britain. Roadside strip buildings or traces of occupation dating from the 1st century AD have been recorded at Heronbridge, beginning 2 km south of the fortress and its *canabae* at Chester and continuing for a distance of 1 km (Mason 2012, 127–30, 156–8, fig. 92). Similar remains have been found along a road at Bulmore at about the same distance from the fortress at Caerleon, where *legio II Augusta* moved from Exeter (Evans 2010).

St Loye's College can be classed amongst these settlements. It is earlier than most, but the Tiberian origins of the example at Neuss shows that they were features of fortress hinterlands at least a generation before Exeter. The explanation for their location some distance from the fortresses on which they depended seems to be to do with their legal status. The *canabae* immediately outside the fortresses were on land directly controlled by the legions and which was part of the *prata legionis* (literally, the meadows of the legion). In the Danubian regions the detached settlements were elevated to *municipia*, and Mócsy (1974, 137–9; cf. Mason 1988, 177–8) argued that they were originally established on land that belonged to the *civitates* rather than the legions. Their later designation as autonomous towns would not have affected control by the legions of their own adjacent territories. In Neronian and early Flavian Devon there was no *civitas*, and how the land not actually owned by the army was administered is uncertain. St Loye's College was probably classified as a *vicus*, which would have allowed or obliged its inhabitants to act as a corporate body without conferring on it the rights of a *colonia* or *municipium*. One liability would have been taxes, and the regime at St Loye's College might have differed from that prevailing in the *canabae*, with a system that, for example, might have been more attractive for merchants operating on a large scale.

The abandonment of the Early Roman settlement at St Loye's College and the later history of the site

The latest vessels in the 1st-century AD assemblage of samian ware from the site are two decorated bowls dating from *c.* AD 70 and 75, and there is nothing amongst the other wares from contexts associated with the early settlement that is necessarily later (Bidwell forthcoming). Intensive occupation of at least the excavated part of the settlement thus ended at about the same time that most of the legion left the fortress. Nevertheless, there were later activities on the site. The south-western of two rows of postholes cut Building 238; they are assumed to have been of Roman date. There was also a well, filled in the later 2nd or early 3rd century AD, as well as pits broadly of this period. The boundary ditches which have already been referred to contained pottery no earlier than the second half of the 3rd century AD. On the south-west side of the site were a scatter of graves presumably of Late Roman date.

There is no doubt that the later occupation was on a smaller scale than in the military period, from which there is more than ten times as much pottery as from the later contexts. However, survival of the part of the settlement along the road from Exeter to Topsham seems likely. The well, pits and graves represent activities that might typically be found around its periphery.

Topsham

Finds and structures of the military period

The settlement at Topsham was situated 5.5 km south-east of the fortress at the head of the Exe Estuary, above which navigation was probably very difficult in the Roman period (Henderson 1988, 92). First-century AD finds made in the 1930s, long before the discovery of the fortress at Exeter, led to the suggestion that occupation had begun when an early military harbour or supply base was established (Radford 1937, 10; Fox 1973, 160). Excavations since the 1970s have uncovered what was thought to have been a small fort (Sage and Allan 2004) and, *c.* 700 m to the north-west, strip buildings and another of row-type, all of Neronian to early Flavian date (Figs 1.2 and 5.14; Jarvis and Maxfield 1974; Garland and Orellana 2018). Much material of this date, including two mould-made glass beakers showing circus scenes, had previously turned up in building operations in the intervening fields (for a gazetteer, see Sage and Allan 2004, 32–6, fig. 21).

All that has been seen of the supposed fort are two parallel ditches which would have been on its south-east side and which turned towards the north at their north-east ends (Sage and Allan 2004, figs 5 and 15). These ditches, with V-profiles and depths for the outer of *c.* 2.4–2.6 m and for the inner of 1.3–1.5 m, were clearly defensive. The lower filling of the outer ditch contained the larger part of a flagon of 1st or 2nd-century AD date; in the upper filling was pottery probably no earlier than the 3rd century mixed with 1st-century AD sherds. In 2018 a continuation of the outer ditch was seen on a site *c.* 10 m to the north of the earlier excavations (Brown and Hughes 2018). Its alignment suggested that the turn of the ditches did not represent the eastern corner of a rectangular enclosure but something far less regular (Fig. 6.17). The identification of these features as part of a fort now seems less certain, and they might even represent part of a civilian defensive circuit of post-military date (see below, Chapter 6).

The buildings some 700 m to the north-east of these ditches lay between the river and the modern Exeter Road. On the Aldi site four open-ended strip buildings, each *c.* 12.0 m by 4.0 m, were excavated in 2015–16 (Fig. 5.14). No occupation levels survived within the buildings, but pottery from features apparently associated with them was of the military period. The group of buildings, in a line parallel to Exeter Road but *c.* 50.0 m to its south-west, fronted onto the Roman road to Exeter which lay immediately to their north-east, and not under the line of the modern road, as was previously thought.

Another building of this period was excavated in 1974 *c.* 40.0 m to the south-east of the Aldi site (Jarvis and Maxfield 1975). A rectangular house divided into three rooms, it seems to have had a veranda on its longer south-east side and was thus a row-type building presumably fronting onto a road running from the north-east down to the riverside. The large quantities of pottery from the site were of the military period. The house, although originally thought likely to have been an isolated farmstead, can now be regarded as part of the same settlement as the nearby strip buildings.

At Wessex Close, immediately to the south-east, possible traces of post-in-trench buildings were recorded in 2015–17 together with three cremations in pottery vessels, all apparently of the military period (Rainbird and Farnell 2019). North of the modern road various excavations have encountered boundary ditches and at least one enclosure succeeding later Iron Age occupation which included roundhouses. These later features have not produced much dating evidence, but some might have originated in the military period (see below, Chapter 6).

The character of the early occupation at Topsham

It is far from obvious how the defended enclosure, if it is of Neronian or early Flavian date, relates to the buildings 700 m to its north-west. South-east of these buildings, which are typical of military *vici*, there is a large area which has produced many chance finds of the military period. *Vici* outside forts rarely extend for much more than 200 m along the approach roads, and these findspots could represent the site of a fort, perhaps serving as one of the bases for the British fleet. The defensive ditches to the south-east, if they are of this period rather than later, might represent an irregularly-planned annexe to this fort.

The populations in the settlements dependent on the fortress

The settlements directly south-east of the fortress and at St Loye's College were of considerable extent and must have had large populations. Little about the origins of the people can be deduced directly from the archaeological remains, though the absence of roundhouses is significant. In the South-West Peninsula, as elsewhere in Britain, they were the standard pre-Roman house type, which continued after the conquest (see Chapter 3 above). When examples occur in contexts where Roman provincial building types predominate, as at London in the 1st century AD, they can be taken to indicate the presence of Britons (Hingley 2018, 36). Other Britons might have adopted styles of housing current in the north-western Roman provinces in the course of a single generation, and some, at least in South-East England, were already living in rectangular houses before the conquest (Perring 2002, 28–30). Whether Britons around Exeter would have absorbed such provincial influences within a few years of the conquest seems doubtful, and it may well be that the absence of roundhouses means that few local Britons lived in the extra-mural settlements. Once military operations ended, the foundation of any relationship between the local population and the army would have been the supply of food and other animal products such as hides. As much as possible would have been obtained from the region, and it would generally not have been in the army's interests to encourage drift from the land. Exceptions perhaps were craftsmen, especially metalworkers, but they would have been few in number; other artisans working in local traditions might well have stayed in their original settlements, which was certainly the case for the potters making gabbroic wares in Cornwall and BB1 in South-East Dorset (see Chapter 3 above; EAPIT 2, Chapter 12).

No matter what steps were taken to maintain agricultural production in the South-West Peninsula, output was unlikely to have met all the army's needs. Imports would not only have included wine, olive oil and fish products from the Mediterranean areas, essential to the military diet, but also cereals and meat products from other parts of Britain and the continent. In terms of volume, cereals, particularly wheat, were likely to have been the most important of these imports. The archaeobotanical record for the South-West Peninsula in the military period is thin, but a contemporary parallel for reliance on supplies of wheat from distant sources can be found amongst the military sites on the Lower Rhine (Reddé 2018). It is also worth noting that the military areas in northern Britain seem not to have achieved self-sufficiency in supply until well into the second half of the 3rd century AD, even though there were long periods in the preceding century or so when that part of the province was peaceful (Bidwell 2017). Civilians involved in the logistics of army supply – *negotiatores* (merchants) and their agents, freedmen and slaves, shippers and retailers – would have been one part, and perhaps collectively the wealthiest, of the population in the extra-mural settlements.

Some, perhaps only a few, of the artisans could have been of local origin, but others were probably veterans or from other parts of Britain and the continent. Many would have followed the legion to Exeter from its previous postings, along with the family dependents of the army, who were likely to have been the largest element in the civilian population. Legionaries and auxiliaries, unless they were the most senior officers, could not contract legally valid marriages while serving. Some naturally had relationships with women, free or slaves, and supported families, while parents or siblings might have followed the postings of other soldiers, practices which are known as early as the Augustan period (Haynes 2013, 49–50). The majority of these dependents presumably lived in the *canabae*, as close as possible to the fortress.

Evidence elsewhere for the identities of populations in settlements associated with fortresses is later, mostly of 2nd or 3rd-century date, and mainly concerns the most prominent inhabitants. In the Danube region, where epigraphic material is far more abundant than in Britain and on the Rhine, the elected officials of the *municipia* at *Carnuntum* and *Viminacium*, settlements detached from neighbouring fortresses, are known to have been 'foreigners' (Mócsy 1974, 141); circumstances were different at the *Aquincum municipium*, similarly situated but with officials who, though Roman citizens, were of local origin.

Most of the extra-mural populations at Exeter would have departed with the legion. Some veterans might have remained if the conversion of the fortress into a *colonia* seemed in prospect (see below), and other inhabitants might have developed commercial interests in the South-West Peninsula or acquired substantial land holdings which made it worth staying on. They probably made up a substantial part of the population in the early town.

The fortlets in the hinterland of Exeter

The fortlet at Stoke Hill, discovered in 1953 and situated *c.* 3 km north of the fortress, was originally described as a signal station and ascribed to the later Roman period, the only datable finds from the site being a chip of samian, a sherd from a colour-coated bowl, probably Oxford Ware of 4th-century AD date, and a coin of Carausius (Fox and Ravenhill 1959). Situated at a height of 158 m OD and commanding wide views all around, it was intervisible with Exeter and another fortlet at Ide, some 5 km south-west of the fortress (Fig. 5.10; Griffith 1984, 17, fig. 3, pl. 3). Both conform to the same type as Martinhoe and Old Burrow on the North Devon coast, where the fortlets, *c.* 25 m square internally, were set in much larger enclosures *c.* 90 m across; the remains of barracks at Martinhoe suggested that the fortlet accommodated about 40 men (Symonds 2018, 57). The two examples at Exeter are so similar to the North Devon examples that they must likewise be of Neronian or early Flavian date; the later finds from Stoke Hill, all of which were from surface deposits, presumably came from late 3rd and 4th-century occupation in the vicinity.

At Stoke Hill there were no signs of internal structures, but part of the rampart had been denuded to the level of bedrock and presumably there had been similar losses of the original ground surface in the interior. The absence of any 1st-century AD finds might nevertheless suggest a short occupation, as seems to have been indicated at Old Burrow (Fox and Ravenhill 1966, 22). Ide has not been excavated. Their sites, far from any known roads, were presumably chosen for their wide outlooks, bringing the farther hinterlands of the fortress under surveillance. Whether this was during the initial phase of occupation or was a result of some later emergency is impossible to determine.

It is also possible that they played some part in controlling the land allocated to the legion, the *prata legionis* or *territorium* of the fortress. Salvatore and Steinmetzer (2018, 798) followed Mason's (1988, 168) suggestion that the legion had appropriated part of the Exe Valley, extending as far south as Topsham, but perhaps its holdings were more extensive.

The history of the fortress

Legio II Augusta *and the annexation of the South-West*

Ptolemy's placing of the legion at Exeter and some supporting evidence were discussed at the beginning of this chapter. A plausible historical context for the establishment of the fortress at Exeter is the governorship of Didius Gallus in AD 52–7 (Bidwell 1980, 10). According to Tacitus (*Agricola* 14) '*mox Didius Gallus parta a prioribus continuit, paucis admodum castellis in ulteria promotis, per quae fama aucti officii quaereretur*' ('The next governor, Didius Gallus [following Ostorius Scapula], held on to what his predecessors had acquired. Some forts, but very few, were pushed into the outlying regions, so that he could get the credit of having expanded the task assigned to him', trans. Birley 1999, 12). The building of the fortress at Usk, almost certainly occupied by *legio XX*, also fell within this period, and Manning (1981, 34) considered that its establishment was part of a 'general reorganisation of the western frontiers of the new province', downplayed because of Tacitus's 'hardly veiled hostility' to Didius Gallus.

Before this reorganisation of the western frontiers occurred, parts of the South-West Peninsula were already within the orbit of Roman traders, and there might have been some exploratory expeditions, perhaps diplomatic as well as military (EAPIT 1, Chapter 3; EAPIT 2, Chapters 12 and 16). The building of the Exeter fortress would have been preceded by military campaigns which annexed its surrounding territories. In this initial phase, units operating in the Peninsula would have had their bases further east in territories that already had been secured (Maxfield 1991, 56–7). The lands of the

Durotriges had fallen to Vespasian, then legate of *legio II Augusta*, within a year or two of the Claudian conquest; their military occupation continued into the mid to late AD 50s, though the fort at Hod Hill had been given up earlier. To the north, in the territory of the Dobunni, the occupation of forts established in the later Claudian period can be shown to have continued at least to the late AD 60s at Charterhouse, Bath (the unpublished Walcot sites) and Cirencester, while at Kingsholm there was a vexillation fortress, if not a full legionary fortress (Fig. 5.15). The earliest campaigns in the Dumnonian lands were probably launched from these military sites to the east and must have secured eastern Devon and the area around Exeter. The operations seem to have extended at least as far west as North Tawton where there is a large enclosure defined by double ditches which has been identified as a vexillation fortress, accommodating either part of a legion, legionary and auxiliary cohorts, or a battle group of the latter (Table 5.2). No interior buildings are visible in the aerial photos, and the base was perhaps not held long enough for buildings to be erected. At Bankfoot, part of Dalswinton, a Flavian site in South-West Scotland, there is a comparable enclosure: not a temporary marching camp, which typically would have had only a single ditch, but nevertheless only intended for short-term use (Hanson *et al.* 2019, 296–7, 314, fig. 4). A large concentration of forces stationed only 26 km west of Exeter, even for a brief period, is unlikely

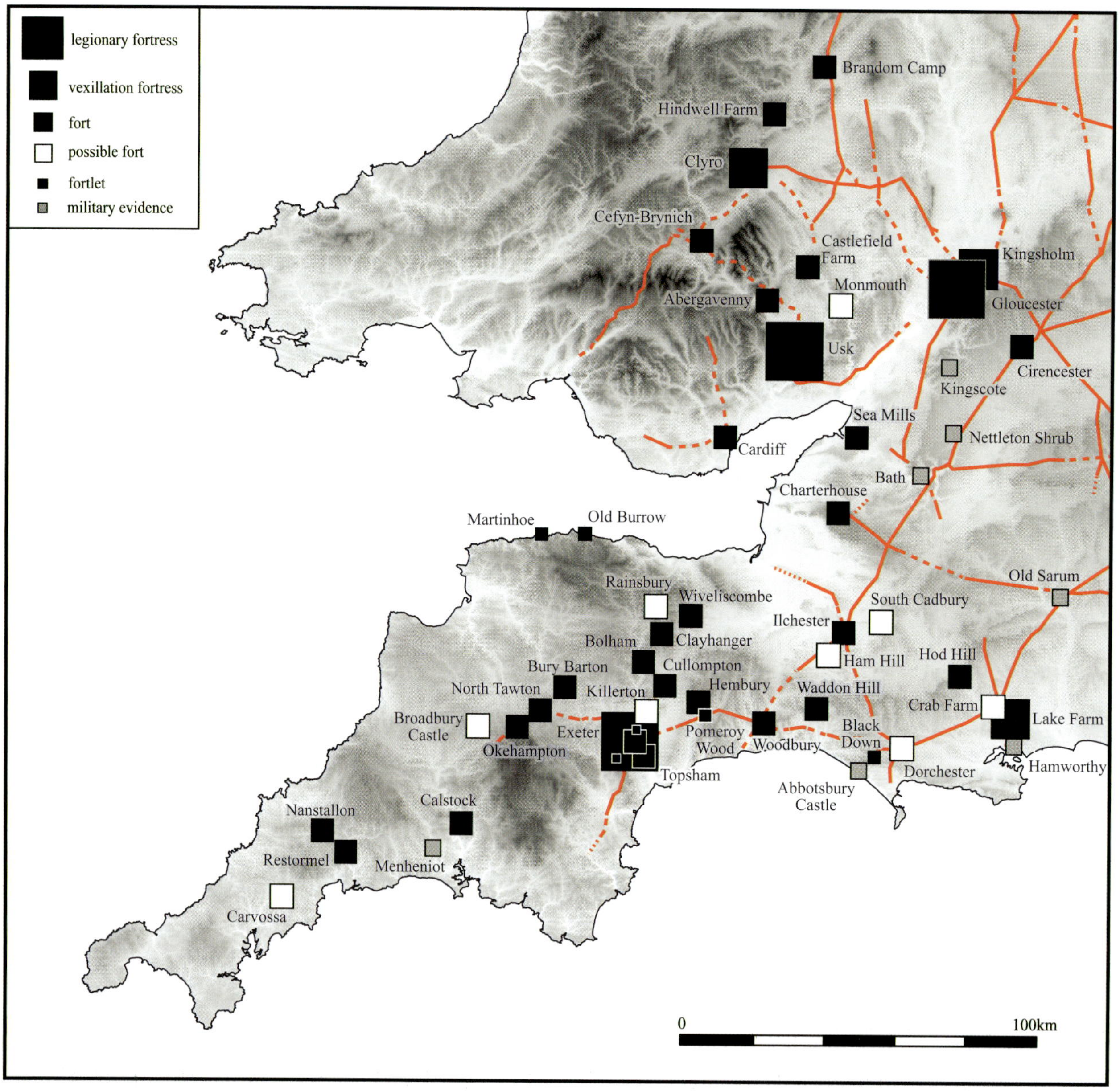

Fig. 5.15 Claudio-Neronian and early Flavian military sites in South-West England and South Wales (drawn by David Gould)

Table 5.2 The areas and dimensions of forts and larger fortlets or small forts in the South-West Peninsula and neighbouring areas, excluding those with areas of unknown extent. Carvossa, identified as a native site within an enclosure of c. *2 ha (Carlyon 1987), is excluded even though the 1st-century AD finds point to the existence of a military site nearby (Todd 1987, 202) or perhaps within the enclosure where it might be obscured by later occupation. Killerton, a triple-ditched enclosure* c. *90 m across internally, seems to have been five-sided, which by no means excludes a Roman military function, but it requires excavation to determine whether it is a fort (Griffith 1984, 25, fig. 6; Hegarty* et al. *2016, 83, fig. 56). References are to the main publications of these sites or to more recent commentaries which include significant new information.*

Site	*Area (ha)*	*Dimensions (m)*	*Ratio length to width*	*No. of ditches*	*Comments*	*References*
North Tawton 'vexillation fortress'	13.00?	?		2	More likely to have been a short-term base rather than a vexillation fortress	Welfare and Swan 1995, fig. 46
North Tawton fort	2.80	200 x 140	1:1.42	?	Annexe to W	Griffith 1984, 20; Welfare and Swan 1995, fig. 46
Calstock	2.56?	170 x 170?	1:1	2	External baths?	Smart 2014
Bury Barton, in Lapford	2.16	180 x 120	1:1.5	3		Todd 1985; 2002
Woodbury, in Axminster	2.13	160 x 133	1:1.20	2?		Weddell *et al.* 1993
Wiveliscombe	1.45	128 x 113	1:13	2		Webster 1958/9
Okehampton	1.40	140 x 100	1:1.40	2	Substantial military *vicus*. Adjacent fortlet?	Hegarty *et al.* 2016, fig. 52; information from AC Archaeology
Cullompton	1.33	148 x 90	1:1.64	3–4	Annexe to E? Cremation 400 m S of fort	Simpson and Griffith 1993; Hegarty *et al.* 2016
Bolham, in Tiverton	1.23	128 x 96	1:1.33	1		Maxfield 1991
Clayhanger	1.21	110 x 110	1:1	4	Annexe?	Griffith 1991
Rainsbury	1.00	110 x 90	1:1.22	1?		Riley and Wilson-North 2001
Nanstallon	0.82	100 x 82	1:1.22	1		Fox and Ravenhill 1972
Restormel	0.56	80 x 70	1:1.14	2		Nicholas and Hartgroves 2018
North Tawton fortlet 2	0.59			1		Griffith 1984, 20
Charterhouse on Mendip Site 2	0.51	72 x 71	1:1	1		Todd 2007b
North Tawton fortlet 1	0.46			1		Griffith 1984, 20
Pomeroy Wood	0.42	75 x 56	1:1.34	2	Outwork	Salvatore 2011
Hod Hill	4.12	230 x 179	1:1.29	3		Richmond 1968
Shapwick	3.99	210 x 190	1:1.11	2–3	Identification disputed	Field 1976; Papworth 1997

once the legionary fortress was fully established. There are also temporary marching camps at North Tawton, as well as at Alverdiscott (Welfare and Swan 1995, 53–6) and probably in South Devon at Twinyeo Quarry, in Chudleigh Knighton (Farnell 2015a, as reinterpreted in Chapter 3 above).

In what are generally regarded as the lands of the Dumnonii, comprising the whole of the South-West Peninsula west of the Rivers Axe and Parrett, there are 11 forts ranging from about 1 ha to almost 3 ha in size (Table 5.2), excluding Hembury and the possible or probable examples in the immediate vicinity of Exeter, the extents of which are uncertain (Chapter 3 and Fig. 5.15). Unlike the marching camps, they were intended for long-term occupation, though changes in policy might mean they had to be abandoned within a few years. There are also small forts or fortlets at North Tawton, Restormel and Pomeroy Wood, with smaller fortlets at Old Burrow, Martinhoe, Ide and Stoke Hill (see above). Not all need have been in occupation simultaneously, but considerable numbers certainly were. The larger forts can be divided into three groups, according to the likely progress of the conquest. Almost all the dating evidence has come from forts in Central Devon, including Bolham, in Tiverton, and in Cornwall, and this group needs to be considered first.

The Central Devon and Cornwall Group. The samian assemblages from Bolham, in Tiverton, Okehampton (but almost entirely from the military *vicus* rather than the fort), Calstock and Nanstallon indicate that occupation began in the AD 60s, some years after the Boudican rebellion; from the site at Carvossa, near a fort or perhaps actually its site, there are likewise far fewer Claudio-Neronian than Neronian and Flavian pieces (a geophysical survey of the site was inconclusive: Cripps 2007). Apart from the Dr. 29 discussed in EAPIT 2, Chapter 12, the few sherds of samian from Bury Barton, in Lapford, are Neronian (information from G. Dannell). From Restormel there is pottery of Neronian to early Flavian date (Nicholas and Hartgroves 2018). There is nothing from North Tawton to indicate the date of the various installations, though the probable vexillation fortress might have been very short-lived if it was connected with the campaigning that preceded the establishment of the Exeter fortress. A sample showing that four out of these seven forts were later rather than earlier Neronian, with no dating evidence from the others, is a reasonable basis for assuming that the full military occupation to the west of Exeter took place as much as a decade after the fortress was established at Exeter.

The East Devon Group. From Hembury and Woodbury, in Axminster, there are a few sherds of Claudio-Neronian and Neronian samian, but nothing to date the beginning of occupation more precisely; there is almost nothing from the fort at Cullompton. The exception is Pomeroy Wood, in Honiton, where the samian has been taken to show that occupation began in the later Neronian period. This dating does not necessarily apply to the other forts in this group, especially as Pomeroy Wood was a small fort or fortlet which could have been added later in the military occupation of East Devon to improve control of the road to Exeter. From a strategic point of view, if the fortress at Exeter was in a forward position until forts were established to its west in the later Neronian period, the East Devon forts would be needed to control the newly occupied territory in its hinterland. Cullompton, Hembury and Woodbury are unlikely to have been built later than the fortress and might even have been slightly earlier.

The North-East Devon and Western Somerset Group. Nothing is known about the occupation of Rainsbury, Clayhanger and Wiveliscombe. They could have originated in the same period as the East Devon group, but equally, if the main line of penetration in the earlier Neronian period was the Fosse Way, they might have controlled territory annexed in the later Neronian period. The fortlets at Martinhoe and Old Burrow were certainly occupied in the Neronian period, but they have not produced enough pottery to date them more closely (for their contemporaneity, see Symonds 2018, 59–60).

The fortress at Exeter was established in a forward position. Usk, where the fortress was built after difficult and costly campaigns against the Silures, serves as a parallel. It stood at the south-western limit of territory controlled by a series of forts (Fig. 5.15); beyond it was only Cardiff, sited on the coast. There was a comparable arrangement at Inchtuthil, where the fortress stood near the centre of a line of forts facing the highlands to the north-west.

If the establishment of the Exeter fortress was preceded by campaigning farther to the west, as suggested by the presence of the probable vexillation fortress at North Tawton, there seems then to have been a hiatus in establishing a system of control in those areas. Some of the initial gains might have been given up because there had been stronger resistance than expected, and for the time being it was necessary to concentrate on holding eastern Devon and the area around Exeter. The Boudican rebellion would have further delayed the final resolution of these military problems (the possible effects which the rebellion had in the South-West are being studied by Salvatore: Salvatore and Steinmetzer 2018, 799, n. 22).

Exeter and the location of legions in western Britain during the Neronian and early Flavian periods

A date of *c.* AD 55–60 for the building of the fortress at Exeter has been widely accepted since the 1980s, but its later history has been a matter for debate. Henderson (1988, 109) argued that in *c.* AD 66 the legion at Exeter moved to Gloucester where it built a new fortress. He suggested that Exeter continued in occupation, held in smaller numbers by auxiliary units as well as a legionary detachment of administrative staff and specialists, the presence of the latter established by occupation of the *fabrica* which continued into the Flavian period. It was at this stage, he argued, that the legionary baths were reduced in size, to be followed in AD 75 by a further reduction in the numbers holding Exeter, and then by the final withdrawal of the army from Exeter and the South-West in AD 80–5 by which time it had been decided to replace the fortress by a town.

The alterations to the baths, however, are not dated more closely than to the later Neronian or early Flavian periods (Appendix 5.1), and none of the structural alterations elsewhere in the fortress is necessarily associated with changes in the size or identity of the unit or units in occupation. Henderson's scheme was devised to fit the occupation of Exeter into an overall pattern of legionary dispositions elsewhere in Britain, but in the 1980s there was no consensus about those arrangements, disagreements which are still unresolved. Holbrook and Bidwell (1991, 3–8) restated the views set out earlier by Bidwell (1979, 13–19), though they were able to justify them on the basis of a much larger body of information, not only from Exeter but from the publication of other sites, particularly Usk. They argued that the fortress remained in full occupation until *c.* AD 75 and was then held by a reduced force.

There the matter rested, as far as detailed consideration of the Exeter fortress was concerned. More general accounts of the army in southern Britain during the Neronian and Flavian periods illustrate some of the wider difficulties. The contrary opinions about the movements of the legions pivot around the departure of the unit at Usk, almost certainly *legio XX*, and the establishment of the fortress at Gloucester, which both seem to have occurred in *c.* AD 66. Manning (1981, 50; 2000, 75) maintained that *legio II Augusta* had moved from Exeter to Gloucester and *legio XX* from Usk to Wroxeter in *c.* AD 66, while Hassall (2000, 62, tab. 6.10) and Todd (2004a, 51) regarded *legio XX* as the garrison of Gloucester, moving there from Usk, while *legio II Augusta* remained at Exeter. Maxfield (1987, 16–18) thought it possible that Gloucester was founded in the early AD 70s, rather than *c.* AD 66, and that *legio II Augusta* was there briefly before moving to Caerleon. Frere (1991b, 75) proposed that Gloucester was built by *legio II Augusta* in *c.* AD 66, with the legion moving back to Exeter when it was replaced in AD 69 by *legio XIV*; that legion was only in Britain for a year, and it is not clear what then would have happened at Gloucester.

Scepticism about the validity of such arguments was expressed by Hurst (1985, 121–2). The imprecision of archaeological evidence when used for dating sites and the possibility of mixed garrisons in fortresses, combining auxiliary units and legions or even vexillations of different legions, meant that 'the *detailed* study of the movement of individual legions is not worth pursuing' (Hurst's italics). The pursuit of Hurst's chimera nevertheless continued unabated and unabashed, not least because a great deal of new information was soon to appear. Studies such as Kenyon's (EAPIT 2, Chapter 15) demonstrate how excavated finds, when available in sufficient quantity, can be used to define periods of occupation in the mid 1st century AD quite closely. The question of auxiliaries is discussed elsewhere (EAPIT 2, Chapter 3.1), and the notion that some fortresses might have contained vexillations of different legions is a red herring. There are double legionary fortresses, as at Xanten-*Vetera I*, in Germany, with an area of 57.8 ha, but none of the fortresses in the range of sizes of Exeter, Gloucester and Colchester has produced evidence for the simultaneous presence of vexillations from two or more legions.

If the character and date of occupation in a fortress can be established within reasonable bounds, as at Exeter and Usk, the next stage will inevitably be an attempt to identify the legion present. That in turn will lead to a review of where the other legions in the province were stationed at the time. At the present stage in the study of this question, the data published from Exeter and Usk is far greater in scope and quantity than from any other fortress of the same period in Britain. The history of these two fortresses must be the starting points for looking at movements of the legions. It is not necessary, in the face of the evidence from Exeter, to accommodate a movement of *legio II Augusta* to Gloucester, where the construction date of the fortress has only a late Neronian *terminus post quem* and consolidated lists of finds have yet to be published. Problems in locating the other legions certainly remain, but they can only be solved by further research into the occupation of the fortresses at Gloucester and Wroxeter, knowledge of the latter being very sketchy.

The significance of the Exeter fortress

Difficulties in the South-West might have been underestimated, but even so there were probably none of the serious setbacks or hard-fought successes which Tacitus describes in Wales and the Marches. Strategically, the Peninsula was already sealed off by military occupation to the east when the Exeter fortress was established, and there were no neighbouring peoples not under Roman control to be unsettled by any turmoil amongst the Dumnonii. Their territory could be annexed when more urgent problems had been dealt with, and if circumstances elsewhere meant that campaigns had to be suspended, any resistance could be contained by the Roman forces established to the east.

If the military problems in the South-West Peninsula were never as pressing as in some other parts of Britain, why then was the fortress held for so long, and why was it surrounded by a series of military sites and dependent settlements which as far as we know were more extensive than at any other 1st-century AD fortress in Britain? Its longevity is partly explained by its vital position in the economic and political geography of Neronian and early Flavian Britain. Exeter seems to have been the first port of call for ships bringing imports from Spain in voyages along the Atlantic coasts; that at least is implied by finds of pre-Flavian Spanish colour-coated ware which are more prolific at Exeter than at other sites in Britain. Similarly, Exeter is the main find-spot for a type of mortarium which is likely to have come from Western Gaul, an early instance of a trading connection which was very evident in the later 3rd and 4th century AD (EAPIT 2, Chapter 12). Another important sea-route was from the east, along the Channel coast not only from the mouth of the Rhine but also from that of the Seine or from ports further along the coast to its north-east. The pattern of pottery supply from northern Gaul at Exeter and indeed in western Britain as a whole is quite distinct from that to London and the South-East.

During the period in question much of the south coast was occupied by Togidubnus's kingdoms. They were certainly not areas from which the army was excluded (Maxfield 1987, 13), but it would have been more straightforward to land supplies at Exeter where military control was immediate and complete and from where some of the consignments could then be taken inland along heavily supervised routes. Perhaps there were at first subsidiary military ports on the Dorset coast, but by the later Neronian period the army seems to have withdrawn from the territory of the Durotriges.

Exeter was primarily the base for the conquest of the South-West Peninsula. If it was intended in the early Neronian period that the province of *Britannia* was not to have expanded much beyond what was already in the process of occupation, there might also have been the expectation that a legion would remain at Exeter for the foreseeable future, controlling one of the major points of entry to the island and overseeing the western borders of Togidubnus's territories. For a while, the Boudican rebellion in AD 60–61 would have made Exeter of vital importance. Poenius Postumus, the *praefectus castrorum* of *legio II Augusta,* fell on his sword, having disobeyed an order from the governor, Suetonius Paulinus, to reinforce the army facing the rebels, thus depriving the legion of the honour of taking part in the eventual victory (Tacitus, *Annals* 14.37; Frere 1999, 76; Birley 2005, 73). The prefect was the third most senior officer in the legion; the other two officers had perhaps joined Paulinus with part of their legion for the assault on Anglesey which was in progress when the rebellion broke out (Webster 1978, 95). Postumus, left in Exeter with the rest of the legion, probably feared an outbreak in the South-West. That it never happened, at least to a significant extent, would have removed any justification for Postumus's conduct, and it was perhaps personal disgrace as much as discredit to the record of the legion that led to his suicide. With London and other towns in the South-East devastated and in the hands of the rebels, Exeter would have been the safest point for the landing of reinforcements and supplies. Following the defeat of the rebels, there would have been access by sea again to the South-East for troop transports and official traffic, but it would have taken longer to restore the infrastructure for the handling of supplies (though the recovery of London was swifter than once thought: Tomlin 2016, 55–6; Hingley 2018, 59–63). For several years some of the supply lines that had passed through London and Colchester might well have been diverted to Exeter.

Another effect of the Boudican rebellion was apparently to delay the planting of forts along the Peninsula to the west of Exeter. This stage in the annexation might have already been postponed if part of the legion had been involved in Paulinus's campaign in Wales. In the aftermath of the rebellion, resources were concentrated on pacifying the centres of resistance. The advance into central Devon and Cornwall was to be the only acquisition of territory in western Britain during the AD 60s. Resumption of Paulinus's campaigns in Wales would have demanded larger forces perhaps with less certainty of success. Indeed, in *c.* AD 66 *legio XX* was withdrawn from Usk, which was then held by a smaller force, and sent to Gloucester. At about the same time *legio XIV* left Britain. In the late AD 60s there were disputes between the legates of the three remaining legions and such animosity toward the governor, Trebellius Maximus, that he was expelled from the province. It was probably then that 8,000 men were sent from Britain to fight in the civil war which had started with a military revolt in Gaul and Spain early in AD 68, further depleting the strength of the army in Britain (Birley 2005, 55). This expeditionary force probably included a vexillation from *legio II Augusta*. Britain was then ruled by the legionary legates, with Roscius Coelius of *legio XX*, presumably at Gloucester, the dominant partner. In AD 69 Vitellius, briefly emperor until he was deposed and murdered by Vespasian's supporters, sent Vettius Bolanus as the new governor. *Legio II Augusta* came out for Vespasian, who had been its legate during the Claudian invasion, in the face of opposition from the other legions (Tacitus, *Hist.* 3.44). A decoration and promotion received by Antistius Rusticus, a *tribunus laticlavius* (second in command) of the legion, which are recorded on an inscription from Pisidian Antioch, in Turkey, were almost certainly awarded because of his support for Vespasian (Maxfield 1981, 111–2, 154: Birley 2005, 280).

For two brief periods, in the early and late AD 60s, Exeter had therefore been a pre-eminent centre of Roman power in Britain, a position it was never to achieve again. In December AD 69 Vespasian became emperor, but it was not until AD 71 that Bolanus was replaced as governor. He was followed in AD 73/4 by Julius Frontinus who resumed the campaigns against the Silures and soon ordered the transfer of *legio II Augusta* from Exeter to Caerleon. Any direct connection between Exeter and written history now ends until post-Roman times.

Fortress into town

Building of the fortress at Caerleon is thought to have begun in *c.* AD 75, but it might have been some time before it was ready to accommodate the whole legion. Timber from a later building phase, presumably reused, yielded a dendrochronological date of AD 72/3 ± 1, but Zienkiewicz (1993, 39, 48) dismissed it as evidence for the date at which building began at Caerleon because it might have been 'old stock'. Although Burnham and

Davies (2010, 43) accepted it, more dendrochronological dates are needed. In a general survey Zienkiewicz (1990) endorsed the foundation date of AD 74/75, long believed to have been at the initiative of Julius Frontinus early in his governorship. He envisaged completion of building early in AD 77/78 at the beginning of Agricola's governorship, but the work could easily have taken a few years more: at Inchtuthil, after about four or five years of building work, some of the major buildings, including the legate's *praetorium*, had not been started (Pitts and St Joseph, 1985, 273–9).

Stratified finds, especially from Friernhay Street (1981: Site 75), establish that the Exeter fortress remained in at least partial occupation for some years after *c.* AD 75 (see Appendix 5.1). The six ovens built after *c.* AD 75 in Exeter's south-west *intervallum*, if intended to serve six centuries, indicate that Cohort Block H was fully occupied. At Trichay Street (EAPIT 2, Chapter 5) at least part of the *fabrica* and Barrack 6 were probably still standing in the early AD 80s. Continuing occupation of course does not in itself mean that the legion was still present, but none of the barracks displayed the sorts of modifications that were made at Usk to accommodate auxiliary cavalry after the full legionary occupation of the fortress ended (Marvell 1996; Manning 2010, 190–1).

The reduction in size of the fortress baths was originally associated by Bidwell (1979, 65) with the first stage in the development of the town. Henderson (1988, 108) placed the alterations after the departure of part of the legion, remarking that the baths would still have been large enough to serve 'several thousand men'. To be more specific, the reduced area of the *caldarium*, excluding the apse, was *c.* 95 m^2, about three times larger than the equivalent rooms in baths at later 1st-century AD auxiliary forts and about double the size of such rooms in some urban baths of the same period (Bidwell 2009, 60–1). Another aspect of the early town which has become more apparent since Henderson's article is the sparsity of its population, at least within the defences, which again suggests that the baths were altered to serve a military presence, perhaps three legionary cohorts, that is about 1500 men, or other units with equivalent numbers.

Possible confirmation of a date after *c.* AD 75 for the reduction in the size of the baths comes from the renewal of the system of water supply, as seen at Trichay Street and, though less certainly of this period, at High Street, NatWest Bank (Site 62; Bidwell 1979, 60). The renewal or extension of the system at Friernhay Street (1981; Site 75) is also of this period (EAPIT 2, Chapter 3.1).

The final withdrawal from Exeter seems to have taken place in the late AD 70s or at the beginning of the AD 80s, when the fortress at Caerleon was probably complete. At about the same time, or in some cases perhaps a little earlier, the forts in the South-West Peninsula were given up. There is a connection with campaigns in northern Britain under Agricola, governor from AD 77 to 84.

Fig. 5.16 Aureus *of Vespasian, found in 1906 in the High Street area of Exeter (© Exeter City Council)*

Pottery made at or near Exeter (examples of Fortress Wares and a mortarium) has been found at York and at Flavian forts in Scotland, evidence either of the transfer of units, the pottery travelling in the baggage of soldiers, or, as now seems more likely, an attempt by Exeter potters to exploit the military market in the North to compensate for its disappearance in the South-West (EAPIT 2, Chapter 12).

Demolition of the fortress buildings might not have followed immediately, but they seemed to have been unoccupied. There were no structural alterations similar to those at Colchester and Gloucester which resulted from the conversion of the barracks into domestic housing (Crummy 1997, 64–5; Hurst 1988, 56–9). The rebuildings of the barracks at Exeter (EAPIT 2, Chapter 3.1, Table 3.2), though consistent with their longevity, conformed to their original plans. Colchester and Gloucester were adapted to serve as *coloniae* intended for retired legionaries and their families, but Exeter became a *civitas* capital. In one respect, however, the development of all three towns was similar: they all retained their fortress defences, as did Lincoln, the third of the 1st-century AD *coloniae* in Britain. At Wroxeter, the only other *civitas* capital in Britain which succeeded a fortress, the defences were demolished following the final departure of the army in *c.* AD 90 (Webster 2002, 56–60, 83). The new town at Exeter also reused much of the fabric of the fortress baths in its basilica and forum. The adaptation of parts of the fortress raises the possibility that they had survived because Exeter was at first intended to be a *colonia*. As we have seen, *legio II Augusta*, once commanded by Vespasian (Fig. 5.16), supported his accession against opposition from the other legions in Britain. A *colonia* with the benefits it could have conferred on the veterans might have been seen as a reward for the more recent loyalty of his former legion. Perhaps at the time of Vespasian's death in June AD 79, the formalities were still to be completed, and his successors were unwilling to confirm Exeter's status. Existing plans for the physical transformation of the fortress into a town might nevertheless have been followed, including the retention of the defences, even if it was not until *c*. AD 90 that resources were available for a start on the public buildings.

The economy of the fortress and its extra-mural settlements

The impact of the Roman army on society and its economy in the South-West Peninsula would have been enormous. Some of its likely effects are assessed in the section above on the populations in the extra-mural settlements. The pottery (EAPIT 2, Chapters 3 and 12) and the animal bones (see below) provide the main evidence for the organisation of supply to the fortress and its dependent settlements.

The exploitation of animals

by Mark Maltby

Although animal bones have been analysed from Roman military features from ten sites in Exeter, the assemblages are generally small. From all these sites, only 1,762 mammal and 126 bird bone fragments have been identified, with the largest samples obtained from Goldsmith Street, Cathedral Close and Friernhay Street (Table 5.3). However, this is one of the largest assemblages associated with the Early Roman military occupation of Britain and a very rare assemblage of late prehistoric or Roman date from Devon where soil conditions preclude the survival of bones from most sites (Hambleton 2008; Allen 2017; see also Chapter 3 above).

Although not always the most frequently identified on some sites, cattle were the best represented species overall, in terms of the number of individual specimens (NISP) counted, providing over 40% of the identified mammals. NISP counts favour large mammals and minimum number estimates have indicated that it is feasible that more pigs and sheep may have been slaughtered (Maltby 1979, 95). However, taking carcass weights into account, cattle would have comfortably been the main source of meat for the fortress. Bone assemblages from military sites in Britain have often been dominated by cattle (King 1984; Stallibrass 1999) but it should be noted that the percentage of cattle in Exeter is lower than in most Romano-British military assemblages, particularly those on Hadrian's Wall.

Ageing evidence has shown that most of the cattle found in Exeter throughout the Roman period, including the military phase, were adults (Maltby 1979, 155–158; EAPIT 2, Chapter 9, Fig. 9.4). Many of these would have calved and some perhaps served as plough animals prior to slaughter. One assumes that most of the cattle brought to the fortress were supplied from the local area, although the strontium isotope analysis showed that at least one of the animals was raised elsewhere (Müldner and Frémondeau in Chapter 3 above). All the measured bones came from cattle of very small stature (EAPIT 2, Chapter 9, Fig. 9.5), and presumably were from local indigenous stock.

Although we are handicapped by the lack of Iron Age evidence from Devon (see Chapter 3 above), it is likely that cattle slaughtered at the fortress were processed in a manner that was very different to traditional methods. Analyses from elsewhere in Roman Britain have contrasted Iron Age butchery methods, which relied heavily on the use of knives with those of the Roman period, which saw a much greater reliance on the use of heavy blades and cleavers, particularly in larger civilian settlements and on military sites (Wilson 1978; Seetah 2006; Maltby 2007; 2010a; 2016). Butchery evidence from Exeter was not recorded in depth by Maltby (1979) but this omission has been rectified by detailed analyses of material from more recent excavations (Lauritsen 2019; EAPIT 2, Chapter 9) and by examination of some of the Roman material by Nicolle Orgill (2014). Both studies have shown that systematic butchery using heavy blades and cleavers was taking place in the military phase in Exeter. These included the longitudinal splitting of some upper limb bones to access marrow. Orgill's study showed that some of the cattle upper limb bones, scapula, pelvis and mandibles from military deposits had distinctive 'scoop' marks that were created by running a heavy blade along the surface of the bones during filleting that removed slivers of bone. These types of marks have been observed frequently in larger Romano-British settlements, particularly in major towns and *vici* but they are either absent or found very infrequently in assemblages from smaller settlements (Maltby 2007). It has been suggested that specialist butchers operating systematically and quickly were the creators of these marks (Seetah 2006; Maltby 2007). Maltby (2019) has suggested that these methods may have military origins and the evidence from Exeter and from an Early Roman military assemblage from Cirencester (Thawley 1982) has provided strong support for this theory. The Friernhay Street assemblage also contained higher proportions of cattle mandibles, radii and metapodials compared with later Roman phases from that site (Lauritsen 2019) and some features from Goldsmith Street produced a high proportion of mandibles, teeth and cranial elements (Maltby 1979, 106). This suggests that these were areas where more deposition of primary butchery waste of cattle may have taken place at some stage.

Sheep/goat elements were the second most commonly recorded overall in the mammal NISP counts (30%), although they were much less well represented in the Friernhay Street assemblage than in those examined from earlier excavations (Table 5.3). Ageing evidence is fairly limited but the assemblage includes a higher

Table 5.3 Number of identified specimens (NISP) of mammals in military deposits

Site Code	*GS I-III*	*TS*	*CC*	*RS*	*PH*	*BSE*	*FH*	*MY*	*PS*	*QS*	
EAPIT Site	*37 and 39*	*42*	*40*	*52*	*156*	*73*	*75*	*63*	*76*	*68*	*Total*
Cattle	307	61	119	10	11	12	97	20	4	1	642
Sheep/Goat	194	66	125	3	6	9	43	26	2	2	476
Pig	127	40	109		3	9	66	12	2	3	371
Horse	4				6	1	8	1	1		21
Dog	2		6				16				24
Cat	2		1							1	4
Red Deer	2	9	1	1			13	1			27
Roe Deer		1									1
Hare	2										2
Otter			1								1
Wild Boar							3				3
Total Mammal	**640**	**177**	**362**	**14**	**26**	**31**	**246**	**60**	**9**	**7**	**1572**
% NISP											
Cattle	48.0	34.5	32.9				39.4				40.8
Sheep/Goat	30.3	37.3	34.5				17.5				30.3
Pig	19.8	22.6	30.1				26.8				23.6
Horse	0.6	0.0	0.0				3.3				1.3
Dog	0.3	0.0	1.7				6.5				1.5
Cat	0.3	0.0	0.3				0.0				0.3
Red Deer	0.3	5.1	0.3				5.3				1.7
Roe Deer	0.0	0.6	0.0				0.0				0.1
Hare	0.3	0.0	0.0				0.0				0.1
Otter	0.0	0.0	0.3				0.0				0.1
Wild Boar	0.0	0.0	0.0				1.2				0.2
Total Mammal	**640**	**177**	**362**	**14**	**26**	**31**	**246**	**60**	**9**	**7**	**1572**
Cattle	48.9	36.5	33.7				47.1				43.1
Sheep/Goat	30.9	39.5	35.4				20.9				32.0
Pig	20.2	24.0	30.9				32.0				24.9
Total C+S+P	**628**	**167**	**353**	**13**	**20**	**30**	**206**	**58**	**8**	**6**	**1489**
% S of S+P	60.4	62.3	53.4				39.4				56.2
% Horse of C+H	1.3	0.0	0.0				7.6				3.2
% Wild	0.6	5.6	0.6				6.5				2.2

Counts exclude bones of small mammals but do include bones from associated bone groups

GSI-III = Goldsmith Street
TS = Trichay Street
CC = Cathedral Close
RS = Rack Street
PH = Princesshay
BSE = Bartholomew Street East
FH = Friernhay Street
MY = Mermaid's Yard
PS = Paul Street
QS = Queen Street

% S of S+P – percentage of sheep/goat of total sheep/goat and pig
% Horse of C+H = percentage of horse of total cattle and horse
Data for GSI-III, TS, CC and RS adapted from Maltby (1979)
Data for PH adapted from Coles (forthcoming a)
Data for BSE, FH, MY, PS and QS adapted from Lauritsen (2019)

proportion of immature and sub-adult animals than in the case of cattle (Maltby 1979, 171–173; EAPIT 2 Chapter 9, Fig. 9.4), indicating a greater emphasis on meat production. The sheep were generally very small even by Iron Age standards (Maltby 1979, 182–183; EAPIT 2, Chapter 9, Fig. 9.6), which suggests they were mainly of local origin.

Pigs have tended to be better represented on military sites than in any other type of Romano-British settlement (King 1984; 1999). Combining results from all sites, pigs provided 24% of the mammal NISP counts, outnumbering sheep/goat in the Friernhay Street assemblage and they were also very well represented on the Cathedral Close site (Table 5.3). Compared to France, pigs are poorly represented in most British Iron Age and Roman assemblages (Hambleton 1999; King 1999; Allen *et al.* 2017), which has led to suggestions that continental dietary preferences could partly account for higher levels of pigs in forts and towns. Pigs would also have been valuable for legionary fortresses whose personnel needed access to plentiful supplies of meat. Whether sufficient numbers of pigs were available locally is unclear, as we have very few Iron Age assemblages to compare. It is worth noting that pigs outnumbered sheep/goat in the later Iron Age assemblage from Mount Batten, beside Plymouth Sound (Grant 1988), although the interpretation of that assemblage is complicated by evidence that suggests pigs may have been brought there for trading purposes (Maltby 2006b; and see Chapter 2 above). Most pigs, as expected, were killed immature, although most survived at least into their second year (Maltby 1979, 186, 189).

The importance of horses to the Roman military is not likely to be fully reflected in assemblages derived mainly from food production and consumption, as there is little evidence that their carcasses were processed for meat. The Friernhay Street assemblage was the only one where horses contributed more than 1% of the mammal NISP counts. Similarly dog bones were only recorded in small numbers on three of the sites (Table 5.3). Bones of cat were even rarer with only four specimens recorded from three sites. However, their presence is significant (provided the bones are not intrusive) in that they are the earliest records of cats from Devon and are probably a Roman introduction.

Although wild species have provided only 2% of the total NISP counts of mammals overall, they constituted over 5% of the assemblages from Trichay Street and Friernhay Street (Table 5.3). Red deer were the most prominent of these species being represented by both fragments of antler and bones. Roe deer has only been recorded at Trichay Street. Venison was a rare addition to the diet but, as Lauritsen (EAPIT 2, Chapter 9) points out, bones of red deer in particular have been found in many Roman military assemblages and they would have been a useful supplement to the diet. The mammal assemblages also include two bones of hare and the only otter bone recorded from any period from Exeter (Table 5.3).

Most of the 126 identified bird bones came from the pre-1976 excavations (Maltby 1979, 201–202). Overall they provided 2% of the total mammal and bird bones (Table 5.4). This should be regarded as a minimum figure, as smaller bird bones are more likely to be overlooked in hand-collected assemblages. The avian assemblage was dominated by chicken (domestic fowl), which occurred in most of the assemblages investigated. As in the case of cat, these are the earliest records of chickens from Devon and Cornwall. A few bird bones were found in Iron Age deposits at Mount Batten. These were not further identified, although it was assumed that most of them were from wild species (Grant 1988). Chickens were first brought to Britain during the Iron Age but their bones are absent from most Iron Age assemblages in southern England (Hambleton 2008). It is therefore possible that chickens were originally brought to Exeter by the Roman forces, to supplement their diet.

Chickens provided over 14% of the total sheep/goat and chicken NISP counts. Chicken bones have been recovered more commonly in military establishments than in most Romano-British rural settlements (Maltby *et al.* 2018).

Only four other species of bird have been recorded in military deposits (Table 5.4). The goose and duck bones came from birds the size of grey lag and mallard respectively but there is no certainty that these were from birds kept in captivity. Woodcock would have been captured during wildfowling expeditions. Twenty-six of the raven bones came from the skeleton of one individual. Maltby (1979, 73) suggested that ravens found in this and subsequent phases may have been kept as pets. More recent reviews have demonstrated that ravens may have played a significant role in Roman beliefs and ritual, which sometimes resulted in their bodies being deliberately buried in specific locations (Serjeantson and Morris 2011).

Fish bones were found in small numbers in military deposits from pre-1976 excavations but none have been recovered in subsequent excavations (Wilkinson 1979; Coles forthcoming a; Lauritsen 2019). The limited amounts of sieving have handicapped their recovery.

Overall, although limited in size, the faunal assemblage from military deposits in Exeter demonstrates that the Romans had a significant impact on animal exploitation in the region. Although they relied mainly on local stocks of cattle and sheep, they probably introduced new species (cat and chicken) and may also have brought in more pigs to bolster local supplies of pork and bacon. Specialist butchers introduced new methods of carcass processing, which continued to be practised in the *civitas* capital. The significant Roman presence would have disrupted traditional modes of exchange and redistribution of both livestock and food, and there is some evidence that young adult cattle and

Table 5.4 Number of identified specimens (NISP) of birds in military deposits

Site code	*Pre 1976*	*PH*	*BSE*	*FH*	*MY*	*PS*	*QS*				
EAPIT Site number	*52*	*156*	*73*	*75*	*63*	*76*	*68*	*Total*	*% Bird*	*% B+M*	*Ch:S*
Chicken	70	1	1	6	1			79	62.7	4.7	14.2
Goose	2							2	1.6	0.1	
Duck	2							2	1.6	0.1	
Woodcock	3				1			4	3.2	0.2	
Raven	39							39	31.0	2.3	
Total	**116**	**1**	**1**	**6**	**2**	**0**	**0**	**126**		**1677**	**555**

Counts include bones from associated bone groups
Pre 1976 = bones from GSI-III, TS, CC and RS combined. Data adapted from Maltby (1979)
See Table 5.3 for site codes and data sources for other sites
% B+M = percentage of total bird and mammal
Ch:Sh = percentage of chicken of total sheep/goat and chicken

sub-adult sheep and pigs were particularly targeted. The military diet was supplemented by some hunting, fishing and fowling with the main target being red deer.

The history of the Exeter fortress summarised

Coins and samian establish a date of *c.* AD 55–60 for the establishment of the fortress, which would have been preceded by campaigns in the South-West Peninsula. In all likelihood the decision to advance from the territories to the east had been taken by AD 57 during the governorship of Didius Gallus.

There was no perceptible diminution in the intensity of occupation at Exeter in the AD 60s. The Boudican rebellion, while making Exeter a vital point of entry to Britain, apparently delayed the deployment of the army into a number of forts west of Exeter until the mid AD 60s, and the legion would be needed to lead the building programme and to provide the overwhelming force needed during the final annexation of the South-West. Towards the end of the AD 60s the army in Britain was unsettled, and the empire lurched towards civil war. In the closing stages of the war, the legion at Exeter supported Vespasian.

In the AD 60s events in Britain and on a wider stage had made Exeter sometimes of vital importance, but once campaigns were resumed in Wales and the North in the early AD 70s the presence of the legion was no longer necessary. By *c.* AD 75 the move to Caerleon had begun, but the process was lengthy, and the final withdrawal of the army from Exeter and the South-West Peninsula was probably not completed until the early AD 80s.

A later military presence in Exeter and the South-West?

As a postscript to the history of the fortress, mention can be made of what appears to have been a timber granary at 228 High Street (Boots Cellar, 1975; Site 61; see EAPIT 2, Chapter 3.1). It had been built over the north-eastern *via sagularis*, indicating that it dates to the civilian period when the interior of the former fortress had been reorganised. The construction of the granary was on a substantial scale and hints at a military connection. Could there have been a small compound inside the town next to its north-east gate, perhaps the *statio* of a *beneficiarius consularis* who was an officer carrying out administrative duties on behalf of the governor? There are two 2nd or 3rd-century AD items of military equipment from Exeter (Bidwell 1979, fig. 73, no. 15, and fig. 74, no. 56), but they were from the basilica and forum and from the public baths.

According to Rivet and Smith (1979, 335–8, 424–5), there are three place-names in the Ravenna Cosmography, all probably in the South-West Peninsula, which include the *statio* element: **Derventio statio*, *Devionissum statio* and *Nemeto statio*? (probably North Tawton, though Todd (1985, 55) preferred Bury Barton). These names surely signify the existence of official posts, manned by a junior officer and a handful of soldiers; continental parallels, especially in Gaul, suggest that their posts would not necessarily have been in defended enclosures and perhaps consisted of a few buildings of modest size (see the papers collected in France and Nelis-Clément 2014 and Colleoni 2016). The main duties of these men were likely to have been local administration, especially tax collection, and the accommodation of visiting officials.

At Seaton there is a complex of buildings originally identified as a villa. Todd (1987, 221) wondered whether it was 'an official installation connected with a nearby harbour', while for Holbrook (1987, 71–2) the remains were an obvious candidate for a *mansio*. A military presence is indicated by the tile stamp of *legio II Augusta* (EAPIT 2, Chapter 13.3), and is now supported by the identification of a copper-alloy object as a harness mount of 3rd-century

AD military type (Silvester 1981a, fig. 14, no. 12, cf. Bishop and Coulston 2006, fig. 124, no. 14; information from Alex Croom). There is no clear distinction between a *statio* and a *mansio*, and Seaton probably served the same purpose as the South-Western sites named in the Ravenna Cosmography. At some stage there might have been a much more substantial military presence at Seaton. There are antiquarian accounts of a rectangular enclosure of *c*. 1.2 ha at Couchill, some 300 m south-east of the excavated sites; it apparently had stone walls, and, if a Roman fort, would thus have been of 2nd-century or later date (and see Chapter 3 above; Holbrook 1987, 65–8).

Appendix 5.1

Dating of the occupation of the fortress and its satellite sites

Introduction

In 1991 a detailed analysis of the evidence for the dates of the military occupation at Exeter was published. The authors considered that '*c.* 55 is likely to be the earliest possible date for the foundation of Exeter, and that the period *c.* 55–60 would cover most of the possibilities'; the legion remained at Exeter until *c.* AD 74 when it transferred directly to Caerleon (Holbrook and Bidwell 1991, 6, 8). The passage of three decades has seen the recovery of more coins and samian from Exeter, essential to the dating of early military sites in Britain, and many relevant publications, not least the corpus of samian stamps, *Names on Terra Sigillata* (*NoTS*) (Hartley and Dickinson 2008–12). This new material for the most part reinforces the conclusions reached in 1991 but allows some refinement of the final stages of the fortress occupation.

In the following paragraphs, page, group and sub-group references are to the EMAFU Reports online in the Exeter Archaeology Archive Project (2015) unless otherwise stated. The catalogue numbers for coins and samian (decorated ware and stamps) are as in Holbrook and Bidwell 1991 for sites excavated until 1979 (including antiquarian finds); samian from sites excavated from 1980 to 1990 is listed in Holbrook and Bidwell 1992, but the coins from the military levels in these excavations are only described in the EMAFU Reports (2015, identification by Norman Shiel).

The foundation date of the fortress

Coins have been vital to establishing when occupation began, and it has been thought that 'coin use reached the Exeter region with a military influx in the mid to late 50s' (Reece 1991a, 38). Further support for this narrow date range comes from Kenyon's analysis of Claudian copies (EAPIT 2, Chapter 15), arguing that at Exeter their character is consistent with occupation beginning in the early Neronian period. Table 5.5, though primarily intended to illustrate the strength of early Flavian occupation at Exeter, incidentally confirms the similarities with the quantities of earlier coins at Usk, where the fortress was founded at about the same time as Exeter. The percentages of pre-Neronian coins and copies are decreased at Exeter by the higher numbers of Neronian and especially Vespasianic issues, but at both sites the ratios of official Claudian and pre-Claudian issues and their copies are close. The coins from Wroxeter display a much larger proportion of the official issues, and this accords with Kenyon's observation that coin supply at Exeter began 'some time after' it was established at Wroxeter. Occupation at Wroxeter is currently thought to have begun in *c.* AD 56/7 (Webster 2002, 80), but perhaps Haverfield (1924a, 109) and some yet earlier writers were correct in dating it from *c.* AD 47 (cf. Hassall 2000, tables 6.2–4).

The samian ware recovered from excavations at Exeter until 1979 conforms with an early Neronian date for the foundation of the fortress (Holbrook and Bidwell 1991, 3–5); subsequent finds have the same character (Table 5.6; Dannell 1992; Dickinson 1992). *NoTS* has revised the dates of some potters' stamps, partly resolving an anomaly in the Exeter list. Comparative histograms had included stamps from a few potters who apparently began their careers before any attested at the Claudian base at Richborough and at Lake Farm where part of *legio II Augusta* had probably been accommodated from shortly after AD 43 (Holbrook and Bidwell 1991, fig. 2). One of these potters is now dated to a later period: Firmo ii, working *c.* AD 60–85, was formerly identified as Firmo i, working *c.* AD 35–55 (Dickinson 1991, nos 35 and 168; also Dickinson 1992, no. 27, not included in the histogram). Other stamps have now been identified as examples used towards the end of potters' working lives: die 11h of Paullus i, working *c.* AD 35–65 (Dickinson 1991, no. 68), and die 5q′ of Salvetus i, *c.* AD 30–55, the die now dated to the 'early 50s' (Dickinson 1991, no. 79).

The publication of *NoTS* now makes it easier to make direct and more detailed comparisons between sites. Of the 26 South Gaulish stamps from the vexillation fortress

Table 5.5 Numbers of pre- and early Flavian coins from Exeter and other military sites (including post-military contexts unless otherwise stated). Wroxeter baths site: Brickstock and Casey 2002; Usk: Boon 1982; Exeter 1971–9: Shiel 1991; Exeter fortress 1945–84 (stratified in military and demolition levels in the fortress): Fox 1952, Shiel and Reece 1979, Holbrook and Fox 1987, Shiel 1991, identifications by Shiel in EMAFU reports; Exeter to 1942: Fox 1952, tab. on p. 104; The Lunt: Reece 1975

	Wroxeter baths site	*Usk*	*Exeter 1971–9*	*Exeter fortress 1945–84*	*Exeter to 1942*	*The Lunt*
Pre-Claudian Ae	6%	1%	2%	2%	?	1%
Claudian (official)	21%	5%	2%	0%		5%
Claudian copies	58%	76%	53%	66%	(38%)	26%
Neronian	6%	14%	20%	18%	(32%)	41%
Vespasianic (to 72–3)	4%	2%	18%	12%		23%
Vespasianic (77– 9)	3%	1%	3%	0%	(30%)	3%
Vespasianic, not closely dated	3%	1%	2%	2%		1%
Total no. of coins	**129**	**242**	**105**	**56**	**(229)**	**73**

Table 5.6 Comparison of the dates of samian from military levels at Friernhay Street (1981, Site 75) and from earlier excavations

Date	*All sites 1971–9 (%)*	*Friernhay St 1981 (%)*
Pre-Claudian–Claudian	5	4
Claudio-Neronian	39	31
Neronian	12	15
Neronian–Flavian	13	14
Flavian	12	17
1st-century AD	19	18
Total no. of vessels	**293**	**97**

at Lake Farm, six represent dies of which there are one or more examples at Exeter, and a seventh stamp was an impression from an intact die which is also represented on a stamp from Exeter which had been made after the die was damaged:

- *Albinus iii, die 5b (*c. *AD 30–65)*: no. 3 (identification revised in *NoTS*), Trichay Street 1972–73 (Site 42), 206; also at Cirencester
- *Aquitanus, dies 2a and 12a (*c. *AD 40–65)*: no. 118, found at the Western Market in 1841; no. 6, Bartholomew Street East 1980–81 (Site 73), 58
- *Maccarus, die 13d (*c. *AD 30–65)*: no. 48 (but die 13d′, *i.e.* use of die continuing after minor damage), Mermaid Yard 1977–78 (Site 63), 1088
- *Marinus i, die 4a (*c. *AD 40–65)*: no. 34, Friernhay Street 1981 (Site 75), 1061; also on a Claudian Dr. 29 at St Loye's College (Dickinson forthcoming, no. 6)
- *Modestus i, die 2g (*c. *AD 40–65)*: Dickinson 1979, no. 9 (one of his later stamps, see *NoTS*), fortress baths, 22:2126; two examples from Usk and one from Cirencester, Ditch III group
- *Virthus, die 2a (*c. *AD 45–85)*: no. 94, Trichay Street 1972–73, 611.

These parallel occurrences make it probable that occupation at Lake Farm, and perhaps at Alchester (Sauer 2000) if *legio II Augusta* was split between these two bases, continued for a while after the fortress at Exeter was established. Only one of the Lake Farm dies occurs at Usk, where it is represented by two examples, further evidence of differences in the systems for supplying the fortresses at Usk and Exeter (Holbrook and Bidwell 1991, 5).

Later occupation and the withdrawal of the army from Exeter

Evidence for the early Flavian occupation of buildings in the fortress and the date of their eventual demolition was set out in detail in 1991 when it was argued that there was no reduction in the military presence until *c.* AD 74 (Holbrook and Bidwell 1991, 7–9). There is now a fuller picture because of subsequent finds and the fuller analysis of the stratigraphy at some of the older excavations.

The fortress baths

For the reduction in the size of the baths (Period 1B), there is now only a Neronian *terminus post quem* based on a very small assemblage (Holbrook and Bidwell 1991, 8). The partial demolition and incorporation of the remaining fabric into the new basilica and forum was dated to *c.* AD 80 (Period 1B demolition and Period 2 construction: Bidwell 1979, 86–7, but with the addition of Group 2 (p. 65)). Stamp no. 5 (Iolius 1a) has been re-dated to *c.* AD 40–65, a change of some importance because this rare stamp, for which originally a Flavian or Flavian-Trajanic date was suggested, has been used to argue that construction of the 'stone forum' might be as late as the AD 90s or *c.* AD 100 (Todd 1989a, 84). However, on other grounds Holbrook and Bidwell (1991, 9) subsequently argued for a start on the building in *c.* AD 90 (see below for comments on the relevant stratified coins).

Trichay Street 1972–73 (Site 42, see EAPIT 2, Chapter 5, and EMAFU Report 93.35)

There were few finds from Barrack C6, but in occupation layers in the room at the eastern corner of the *fabrica* (Sub-group 28.2) there was a samian stamp dated *c.* AD 65–85 (no. 76, 267) and a Dr. 29 of *c.* AD 70–85 (113). The filling of the trench for a wooden water-pipe, associated with its insertion rather than its removal, in the street south-east of the *fabrica* contained a well-circulated *as* of Vespasian issued in AD 72–3 (no. 74, 118; Sub-group 53.1; cf. possible Dr. 37 from the bedding layer in a water-pipe trench north-west of baths: Bidwell 1979, 60). A gully was dug along the south-east and north sides of the *fabrica*, apparently after the laying of the pipe (Group 54); in its filling was a large group of pottery which included sherds from 18 samian vessels, two of broadly 1st-century AD date, one Flavian and the remainder pre-Flavian (49). There is some doubt about a second context (71) which is listed with a question mark in Group 54, but which in the context descriptions is equated with context 49 without reservation (p. 39). The second context contained a very worn *sestertius* of Nero (64–8; no. 49); the original listing of the small group of pottery from this context, carried out in the 1970s, included a samian Dr. 37 which would have been no earlier *c.* AD 70, but this group was omitted from the 1993 report. From a possible drip trench (611, Sub-group 16.7) there was a mortarium from Gallia Belgica originally dated to *c.* AD 70–150 (Hartley 1991, fig. 82, TC32). In June 2010 Kay Hartley (*in litt.*) questioned when the type first appeared in Britain, preferring a date of *c.* AD 80, later stating that its dating 'leaves much to be desired' (Hartley and Tomber 2006, 24). These features respected the positions of fortress buildings; the finds from their fillings supply a date for the demolition of the buildings.

Finally, amongst the 23 samian vessels from the filling of Well 3, discussed in EAPIT 2, Chapter 5, there were seven Flavian Dr. 37s; the latest two, from layer 3, were of *c.* AD 80–100.

Goldsmith Street 1971–72 (Site 37, see EAPIT 2, Chapter 6 and EMAFU Report 93.34)

A well-circulated coin of Nero (no. 53) was found in a post-trench probably forming the party wall between the centurion's quarters and adjacent *contubernium* of Barrack C2 (689; Sub-Group 4.1). Post-trenches in the fortress generally had clean clayey fillings, but very often it was not possible to distinguish the post-tubes; when the buildings were demolished, the uprights were presumably pulled out, and the original material filling the trench then presumably collapsed into the holes. It was at this stage that most of the finds probably found their way into the trenches, amongst them this coin of Nero.

A gully along the front of the same barrack (652; Sub-Group 6.2) contained a Dr. 29 of Flavian (?) date. It was originally stated that a Flavian Dr. 29 came from another post trench in this barrack (410; Sub-Group 15.1), but this was a result of confusion with another context of civilian date, as later explained (Report, pp. 7–8; cf. Holbrook and Bidwell 1991, 7).

Preston Street 1976–77 and Mermaid Yard 1977–78 (Sites 60 and 63, EMAFU Report Nos 92.38–9)

Finds from Mermaid Yard were taken as evidence that occupation in this part of the fortress had continued into the Flavian period (Holbrook and Bidwell 1991, 7). They consisted of a coin of Vespasian (no. 445), issued in AD 71 and virtually uncirculated, and five samian vessels of *c.* AD 70 or later from a ditch on the south-east side of the *via sagularis* (Sub-group 4.6). There was more Flavian samian from pits north-east of Barrack J6 in an area apparently free of buildings (Sub-groups 6.1 and 6.3) and from the *intervallum* area (Group 5). However, because there has been no mention of an early civilian horizon on this site, the possibility that these deposits were post-military cannot be excluded. At Preston Street, two pits had been dug across the lines of the back walls of Barracks J4 and J5 (Group 3). One contained a mortarium from Gallia Belgica originally dated to *c.* AD 70–150 (508; Hartley 1991, fig. 81); it is of the same general type as the example from Trichay Street discussed above, for which a date no earlier than *c.* AD 80 is now preferred. The pits might well have been associated with the demolition of the barracks; the same might apply to the pits at Mermaid Yard.

Bartholomew Street East 1980–81 (Site 73, EMAFU Report No. 92.33)

From occupation following the second stage of refurbishment in the building north-east of Barrack G3 (142, Group 15), there was a stamped Dr. 29 for which a date in the AD 70s was suggested (no. 7, stamp no. 13). A well-circulated coin of Nero issued in AD 65 (Report, p. 47) was found in the top of a posthole (60) in the trench for the central wall of Barrack G3 (Group 2; Report, fig. 9); its position indicates that the coin was associated with the demolition of the barrack. Finally, the filling of a gully (125; Group 17) in the open area at the north-eastern extremity of the site contained a well-circulated coin of Vespasian (Report, p. 47; not slightly worn as stated in Holbrook and Bidwell 1991, 7). The gully was sealed by an overall demolition deposit (Group 20), which also covered the building to the south-west and the barracks); the latest samian from the deposit was of Neronian–Vespasianic date.

Friernhay Street 1981 (Site 75, EMAFU Report No. 92.35)

The south-west *intervallum*, which was 6.5 m in width, was examined in whole or in part over a length of 30 m. Two buildings (EAPIT 2, Chapter 3, Fig. 3.6) were sealed by a series of dumps or accumulations (Group 10) in which the latest objects were as follows: Dr. 27, Flavian? (928); *as*, Nero, 'Temple of Janus type, mid AD 60s', very worn (877); Dr. 15/17, Flavian (823); Dr. 30, *c.* AD 70–85 (no. 5, 822.2). The upper levels seem to have been laid down to form a platform for two new buildings, probably with open sides facing the *via sagularis* (EAPIT 2, Chapter 3, Fig. 3.11); each contained rows of three large ovens, *c.* 1.6–2.2 m in diameter. Each oven might have served one of the six centuries in Cohort Block H immediately to the north-east. Two layers of trample and raked-out ash from the ovens included samian exclusively of Flavian date: from Sub-Group 13.5 (838), Dr. 18R, and from Sub-group 18.3 (817), Dr. 18, 27 and 35/36, Dr. 29 (*c.* AD 70–85, no. 3) and Dr. 37 (*c.* AD 75–90, no. 4). The ovens in the south-east building were levelled, and from a pit (Sub-group 28.2, 1053) cut through a floor laid over their remains there was a Dr. 18 of Flavian (?) date. After a partial rebuilding, another oven was inserted in the building, sealing a Dr. 18 and a Dr. 27 both of Flavian (?) date. The later Building 6 was perhaps of the civilian period.

The trench for a water pipe was inserted after a resurfacing of the *via sagularis*; it also cut 'deposits that post-dated the life of one of the ovens' (Report, p. 37) and was therefore dug no earlier than *c.* AD 75. A further resurfacing of what had been *via sagularis* included 'much masonry rubble, hypocaust tile and concrete, possibly derived from the clearance of the legionary bath-house' (Report, p. 3) and must have been of the early civilian period.

The filling of the fortress ditch: dating evidence

When first encountered at Rack Street in 1975 (Site 52; EAPIT 2, Chapter 8), the fortress rampart seemed to have been fronted by two ditches. It emerged during further excavations at Rack Street in 1977–8 (Site 64) that the larger outer ditch was later and cut the inner ditch. The preliminary spot-dating of the finds suggested that the earlier ditch was filled during the fortress period (Bidwell 1980, 23; Henderson 1988, 107), but the full analysis placed the filling after *c.* AD 75 (Holbrook and Bidwell 1991, 7). This is crucial to our understanding of the transition from fortress to town, and the stratified sequence at Site 64 needs to be summarised here, together with the relevant finds. They were all from Sub-group 1.3, 'a series of layers dumped over the [very shallow] natural silt accumulation in the bottom of the ditch'. The lowest layer (1007) contained three Dr. 29s dated *c.* AD 50–65?, AD 65–80 and AD 75–90, the layer above (1005) a Dr. 29 of *c.* AD 60–65 and the highest layer another Dr. 29 of *c.* AD 65–80; all have been illustrated (nos 9–13). In addition, there were three plain wares, two pre-Flavian and one possibly Flavian, recorded from the ditch (1471) but not from a specific layer. From the earlier excavations at Rack Street there was a Dr. 37 of *c.* AD 75–90, but it was in a layer near the top of the ditch filling which might have been levelling after the original filling had subsided (240.4; Sub-group 1.3).

Excavations elsewhere on the circuit of the ditches have been less extensive. There were samian sherds from the inner ditch at Mermaid Yard (Site 63), Friernhay Street (Site 75) and Paul Street (Site 76), but they were all pre-Flavian.

The extra-mural sites

The building at Mount Dinham (Site 154) was presumably demolished when the fortress was abandoned, if not before: most of the pottery from the site was pre-Flavian. The defences of the probable fort at Princesshay (Site 156) were levelled no earlier than the early Flavian period. More can be said about the final phase of occupation south-east of the fortress. At Valiant Soldier (Site 44) a scattered hoard of 14 coins with a terminus of AD 73–5 had presumably been originally concealed in a building which had remained in occupation during the early Flavian period (Shiel 1991, 32). A cremation burial which cut an enclosure ditch included two samian Dr. 29s of *c.* AD 70–85 (Dannell 1991, fig. 10, no. 22; Salvatore 2001, 133–4). From the buildings at Lower Coombe Street (Site 97) there was no samian necessarily later than the pre-Flavian period; the filling of canalised streams included samian of *c.* AD 70 or later, including a Dr. 37 (Dannell 1992, fig. 2, nos 18–20, fig. 3, nos 28–90), but also coarse-ware types not found in fortress levels and which were later than *c.* AD 75 (Holbrook and Bidwell 1992, 37).

Occupation of the buildings at St Loye's College seems to have continued into the early Flavian period, though this date depends on two Dr. 29s of *c.* AD 70–85 and AD 75–90 from pits thought to have been associated with the settlement.

Coin supply and usage during the later occupation of the fortress

Reece (1991a, 38) demonstrated that coin supply at Exeter continued strongly until shortly after AD 73. There was then a hiatus until AD 77/8 reflecting the closure for four years of the mint at *Lugdunum*, but fewer of the later coins of Vespasian reached Exeter (Holbrook and Bidwell 1991, 7–8, fig. 3).

A straightforward comparison with three other military sites supports the contention that Exeter was held in strength until *c.* AD 75 (Table 5.5). Usk, a fortress established at about the same time as Exeter, has proportionately fewer coins of Nero than Exeter and scarcely any of Vespasian. This is entirely consistent with the legion having left Usk in AD 66/7 and its replacement by a cavalry unit until the fortress was finally demolished in *c.* AD 75 (Manning 2010, 191). The size of the garrison would have been reduced by 90% (the standard cavalry *ala* had a strength of 480), and even if the *ala* had been brigaded with a legionary detachment, as Manning thought possible, the reduction would still have been 80% if a single cohort was in question. The coin list from the fort at The Lunt, Baginton, provides a stark contrast to that at Usk, with Neronian issues dominant and far fewer earlier coins and their copies; early coins of Vespasian are plentiful, slightly more so than at Exeter, but his later issues are scarce. Reece (1975, 24–5) dated the occupation of the fort to *c.* AD 60–75, associating the two later Vespasianic issues with post-military occupation in the 2nd century AD. In comparison with the other sites, the quantities of Neronian and later coins at Wroxeter are very small, which is startling as the fortress is believed to have been held until the late AD 80s (Webster 2002, 80). Part of the explanation might be that the list is of coins from a restricted area rather than from a series of excavations as at the other sites. Nevertheless, in earlier excavations the numbers of Neronian issues are still small, though Vespasianic issues are better represented (Atkinson 1942, 306–7).

The Exeter coin lists certainly show that a drastic reduction in the intensity of occupation took place shortly after AD 73. Individual finds indicate a somewhat later date for the end of the fortress buildings or, as at the baths, their eventual conversion to another use. In the survey above, four coins of Nero and two of Vespasian were associated with the demolition of these buildings, excluding the baths. Two coins of Nero, from Trichay Street and Friernhay Street, were very worn, and two others, from Goldsmith Street and Bartholomew Street East, were well circulated, as were the two coins of Vespasian, from Trichay Street and Bartholomew Street East. In more general terms, it has been noted that most of the early coins of Vespasian from Exeter are well circulated or very worn, showing that 'military occupation continued for a few years after the date of their issue' (Holbrook and Bidwell 1991, 8).

In a recent study, Brickstock (2017) has tentatively set out a scheme for estimating when coins were lost after their dates of issue according to their states of wear (their 'revised dates'):

- unworn or unworn/slightly worn: add 0 years
- slightly worn/worn: 15 years
- worn: 25 years
- worn/very worn: 40 years
- very worn: 70 years
- very worn/extremely worn: add 100 years
- extremely worn: add 135 years or more.

The scheme was based on the states of wear displayed by the coins in the hoard of 470 *denarii* from Rudchester on Hadrian's Wall; the latest coins were minted in AD 167. According to Brickstock's 'revised dates', the two very worn coins of Nero in the Exeter assemblage would have been lost in the AD 130s and the well-circulated coins of Vespasian no earlier than the last year or so of the 1st century AD, if Shiel's description of the latter corresponds to Brickstock's 'worn'. There are of course many imponderables, not least subjectivity in assessing states of wear (Brickstock 2017, 335), but the date for the loss of the coins of Nero is not credible. Another approach is to compare the Exeter coins with those from 1st-century AD military sites where the states of wear are recorded, confining the comparisons to the *aes* coins. The most instructive site is the fort at Elginhaugh in southern Scotland which was established in *c.* AD 80 and given up by AD 88 at the latest (Hanson 2007, 647, 649). The eight *aes* coins of Domitian well enough preserved to assess their states of wear were unworn, very slightly worn or slightly worn (Bateson 2007). The states recorded for the 19 earlier *aes* coins were as follows (Bateson 2007):

- Nero: fairly worn (2)
- Vespasian (AD 71–3): slightly worn (1); fairly worn (4); worn (1)
- Vespasian (AD 77–8): slightly worn (5); fairly worn (4)
- Vespasian (not closely dated): fairly worn (1); worn (1).

In contradiction to Brickstock's scheme, the degrees of wear on the Elginhaugh coins represent much shorter periods of circulation in a much more irregular pattern. If for the purposes of illustration the median point in the occupation of the fort is dated to AD 84 and used as the hypothetical time at which the coins were lost, six of the coins that were minted about ten to 20 years earlier were already fairly worn, though another was only slightly worn and the eighth was worn, both after about ten years of circulation. Five of the nine later coins of Vespasian were only slightly worn seven to eight years after they were lost, but four were already fairly worn. Comparing the two coins of Vespasian in the Exeter group with the Elginhaugh patterns of wear (assuming that 'fairly worn' can be equated with Shiel's 'well circulated'), the chances are that they were not lost before the end of the AD 70s and probably in the AD 80s. The two well-circulated coins of Nero could have been lost earlier, but it seems unlikely that the other two coins of Nero, which were very worn, were lost any earlier than the coins of Vespasian; indeed, they might push the date of demolition towards the end of the AD 80s, for the two coins of Nero from Elginhaugh were only fairly worn.

There were also six coins of Nero and Vespasian from the demolition of the fortress baths and construction of the basilica and forum. The later structural history of the baths differed from that of the other fortress buildings, and the coins need to be considered separately (for their contexts, see Bidwell 1979, 86). Two coins of Nero were virtually fresh and a third well circulated; of the three coins of Vespasian (of AD 71 or 72–3), two were little worn and one well circulated. The lesser states of wear of this group, though from contexts of much the same date as those of the group from elsewhere in the fortress, can probably be explained by their recovery from furnace ash and levelling layers which contained much residual material.

Samian ware and the end of the fortress

In the excavations carried out up until 1979, Dr. 29s and Dr. 37s from the fortress and its extra-mural areas were present with a ratio of 55:7, similar to the ratios at forts in Germany which were abandoned under Vespasian (Holbrook and Bidwell 1991, 7). Histograms comparing the dates of samian stamps from Exeter with those from Usk, Lake Farm and Richborough showed that Exeter had proportionately larger numbers spanning the early Flavian period than Usk (Holbrook and Bidwell 1991, fig. 2), and the same difference is now evident in an analysis by Dickinson and Bird (2014, fig. 186) where Exeter and Usk are compared with Colchester, Lincoln and Wroxeter; in this analysis Exeter does not drop significantly below the latter three sites until 80–85.

The quantities and dates of samian ware recovered up to 1979 were therefore consistent with no diminution of the intensity of occupation until *c.* AD 75. The largest assemblage recovered subsequently inside the fortress was from Friernhay Street in 1981 (Site 75). Its date range was broadly similar to that recovered in 1971–9 (Table 5.6), though there were slightly largely percentages for the Neronian and Flavian vessels, as might be expected at this site where occupation continuing beyond *c.* AD 75 was strongly represented.

6

The *Civitas* Capital

Neil Holbrook

with contributions by Paul Bidwell and Mark Maltby

Introduction

Study of the Roman town of Exeter has an illustrious history, starting with Lady Fox's heroic rescue excavations from the 1940s to 60s followed by a step change in scale and resource in the 1970s and 80s as Exeter Museums Archaeological Field Unit (EMAFU) worked tirelessly in advance of urban redevelopment (see Chapter 1). But as with so many historic towns and cities in Britain it proved impossible for publication to keep pace with fieldwork and it is fair to say that the archaeology of the Roman town was considered something of a poor relation compared to spectacular discoveries associated with the Roman legionary fortress, although the medieval archaeology of Exeter has if anything received even less attention from scholars. Until the start of the EAPIT project, the comprehensive account of work on the basilica and forum was the only substantial excavation of Roman civilian deposits to have been fully published (Bidwell 1979; but now see EAPIT 2, Chapters 5–8). In the 1970s EMAFU recognised the potential danger that knowledge of the significant discoveries made in Exeter would be limited to a relatively small number of individuals working in the city and that was the motivation behind the publication of Paul Bidwell's *Roman Exeter: Fortress and Town* (Bidwell 1980). Although now 40 years old that book admirably collated the state of knowledge of *Isca Dumnoniorum* as it appeared in early 1980 and remains far and away the best general survey of the Roman town of Exeter. But new discoveries and new knowledge have continued to accumulate since then, and a programme of post-excavation analysis of sites excavated in the 1970s and 80s was undertaken in the early 1990s, although this focused almost exclusively on the period of Roman military occupation. Significant new knowledge of the later Roman and medieval city wall has also emerged since 1980 thanks to meticulous study by Stuart Blaylock (1995). His work has demonstrated that the wall, whilst much altered in later centuries, contains a hitherto unrealised survival of Roman fabric, and his excavations at Paul Street (Site 76) in particular have made an important contribution to knowledge of the development of the defences. The work at Paul Street also uncovered the timber supports for a bridge carrying an aqueduct pipe across the ditch of the early town defences. These timbers yielded the only dendrochronological date from Roman Exeter which we currently possess (EAPIT 2, Chapter 11), and this has important ramifications for the chronology of the public building programme, as is discussed below.

The primary focus of Bidwell's account was the presentation of the structural evidence for the Roman town and the interpretation of the stratigraphic sequence. The latter is still very much an issue of contemporary importance as certain critical elements of the sequence have still not been established beyond doubt. The principal areas for debate relate to the chronology of the transition from the legionary fortress to the *civitas* capital; whether the defences of the former fortress were actively maintained through the 2nd century AD and thus whether the town can be considered to have been defended at this time; and lastly the chronology of the very latest Roman and early post-Roman occupation in Exeter.

This chapter tries not to repeat too much of what was said in *Fortress and Town* when there is little new to add as that book is still widely available through the second-hand market. Instead it concentrates on new information that has come to light since then that either refines, or in a few cases refutes, what was said. For instance, the detailed post-excavation analysis of four sites excavated in the 1970s (Trichay Street, Goldsmith Street Area III, 196–7 High Street and Rack Street: Sites 42, 39, 43, 52/64) undertaken as part of this project, and published in EAPIT 2, Chapters 5–8, has provided greater detail than was available to Bidwell in 1980. The lack of detailed analysis and publication of other major excavations has undoubtedly hampered this review, although that is an issue which impedes knowledge of all periods of the archaeology of Exeter (and many other historic towns as well; Fulford and Holbrook 2015). Friernhay Street and Paul Street (Sites 75–6) were particularly significant investigations that warrant full analysis in the future, alongside more recent work at Princesshay and Quintana Gate (Sites 156 and 169; see Chapter 1 for a broader discussion).

The study of Roman Britain has of course moved on over the last four decades with new avenues of research supplanting more traditional agendas. In particular there is currently much more emphasis on the creation of a social archaeology of Roman Britain as opposed to the elucidation of urban geography or (pseudo) historical narratives of political events. I have tried to reflect some of these newer topics in this account although in many cases the quality of data retrieval and the lack of subsequent analysis impede progress. As will be seen, while the faunal assemblages recovered from excavations in the city have seen considerable research, the palaeobotanical record for Roman Exeter is pitifully weak as routine environmental sampling was not a commonplace component of the fieldwork methodologies adopted in rescue excavations in the 1970s and 80s. There are also very few examples of the application of geoarchaeological and geochemical techniques to excavated deposits (Macphail and Courty 1985 is the only published example, and that not overly instructive; Chapter 7). These should be priorities in the design of future excavations within the city as work conducted within a research context in *insula* IX at Silchester, in Hampshire, ably demonstrates the insights into past activities that can be retrieved by the application of these methods (Fulford *et al.* 2006; Fulford and Clarke 2011).

The archaeology of the Roman town remains a vibrant topic for future research. As one of 22 or so major towns of Roman Britain that had an overt administrative function (*coloniae, municipia* and *civitas* capitals) Exeter was manifestly an important place, and its location in the South-West Peninsula makes it a good test bed to examine the impact of the Roman state away from the core of the province further east. To Francis Haverfield, writing in 1924, Exeter was an 'outpost of Romanization in the far west' (Haverfield 1924a, 214). While this view would now be wrapped up in different, more nuanced, language, many people doubtless still essentially share this view of Exeter. The Rural Settlement of Roman Britain Project (RSRB) has clearly demonstrated at a national level how the countryside of Roman Britain was far from uniform, instead stressing the considerable regional variation evidenced in the archaeological record, and this builds on earlier studies which have long highlighted the distinctiveness of the South-West Peninsula at this time (Smith *et al.* 2016; this topic is explored fully in Chapter 3 above). In seeking to contextualise Roman Exeter comparison will be made primarily with other towns situated within regions away from the heartlands of Roman Britain where complex farms, as defined by RSRB, and villas are well represented. These towns predominately lie in western Britain, in particular the *civitas* capitals of Wroxeter (within the Central West region defined by the RSRB) and Caerwent (at the extreme south-western end of the Central Belt). The nearest towns to Exeter (Dorchester and Ilchester, the latter not a *civitas* capital beyond doubt; see Chapter 3 above) lay in very different *pays* but are instructive in seeking to provide a broader contextualisation of *Isca Dumnoniorum*.

In this chapter the nomenclature adopted for the streets and specific buildings relates to the gazetteer entries in EAPIT 2, Chapter 3, Sections 3.2 and 3.3, which provide full referencing. The orientation of the long axis of the Early Roman town is described (correctly) in this account as north-east to south-west, and thus the gates in each side of the defences are referred to as the South-East Gate, South-West Gate, etc. The orientation of the later Roman town followed the same alignment as the early town, but the medieval and post-medieval successors to the Roman gates in the expanded defences have been known for centuries by the cardinal points of the compass (thus South Gate, not South-East Gate). This nomenclature is so well established in the literature that it would be confusing to diverge from it now, so consequently the later Roman gates will be referred to in this chapter by their common, cardinal, names (see Chapter 1 and Fig. 1.11).

The early town

The process and chronology by which the abandoned legionary fortress was transformed into the new town of *Isca Dumnoniorum* has to some extent been elucidated by excavation, although a number of fundamental issues remain unresolved as the excavated evidence is open to interpretation in differing ways (Fig. 6.1). On current evidence all timber buildings within the fortress were demolished after the departure of the army as in many places dumped deposits sealed the post-trenches of the fortress buildings. At Goldsmith Street Area III (Site 39) for instance, these dumps were formed from yellow to red clays, some redeposited natural clays, but also with inclusions of organic refuse, charcoal lenses, daub and pottery (the daub presumably derived from the demolished walls of the fortress buildings spread over the site as levelling: EAPIT 2, Chapter 6). This process was conducted with care as the dumps have not been found overlying military streets that were retained to form the

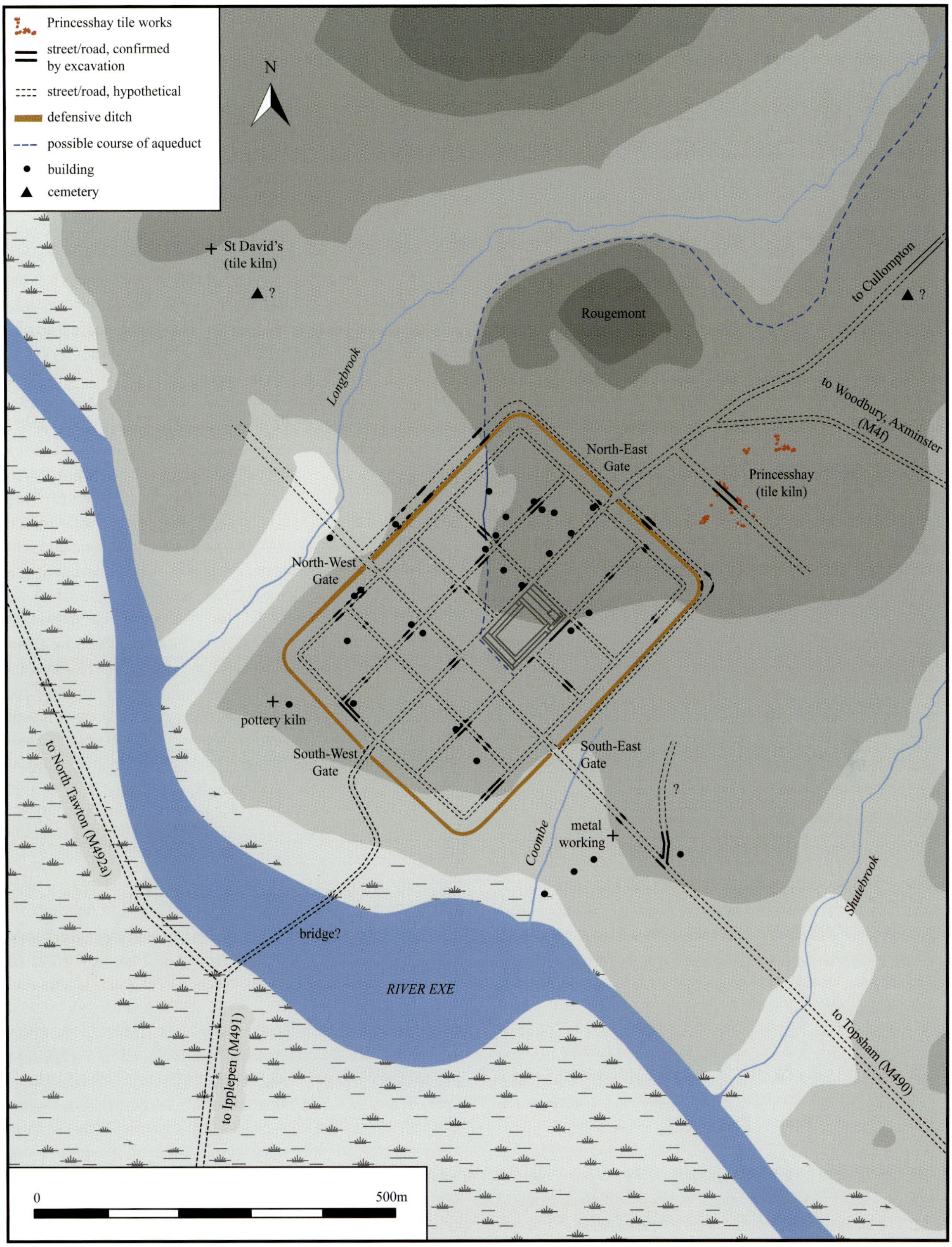

Fig. 6.1 The Early Roman town and its environs. The roads are numbered according to Margary's (1955) scheme (drawn by David Gould)

framework of the new town. At Friernhay Street (Site 75; Street observation B6i) the 5.5 m wide *via sagularis* of the legionary fortress was reduced in width to only 2.5 m, little more than a narrow lane. The first civilian resurfacing of the street was composed of a thick layer of demolition material which included much masonry rubble, hypocaust tile and concrete, doubtless derived from the demolition of the fortress baths. Unless we are to believe that this material was stockpiled, it would indicate that work on resurfacing the former streets of the fortress was underway while the basilica was being formed from the shell of the baths. This in turn suggests that the intended transformation of the fortress site was already envisaged at the time of demolition and the process was carried out with care.

The Roman State was surely heavily involved in the creation of the new town and was the principal funder of the public building programme given that there is little local evidence in the South-West Peninsula for a highly stratified social elite in the Late pre-Roman Iron Age, in contrast to some societies further east (see Chapter 3 above; Millett 1990, 17–35; Hanson 1988 reviews the evidence for state involvement in town creation). Indeed, we should not uncritically assume that the Dumnonii necessarily possessed a unified identity that stretched back into the pre-Roman Iron Age or extended over the whole of the Peninsula given that the Iron Age culture of Devon differed from that of Cornwall (see Chapter 3 above). Certain *civitates* were probably artificial creations of the new provincial government (or perhaps amalgamations of different social groups), created to facilitate the empire's chosen scheme of regional administration, as is often assumed to have been the case with the Belgae for instance (Moore 2011). Whatever their pre-conquest pedigree, the Dumnonii were identified as such by Ptolemy in the second quarter of the 2nd century AD, and he relied on a map of Britain produced by Marinus of Tyre around the turn of the 1st and 2nd centuries AD (Rivet and Smith 1979, 103–47, 342–3). The dedicators of a 1st-century AD tombstone of the sailor Aemilius in Cologne chose to record his Dumnonian origins rather than use the more commonly attested names Britannus, Britto, etc. (see Chapter 3 above, Fig. 3.1; Maxfield 1984; Ivleva 2014). A Dumnonian identity had therefore formed before the end of the 1st century AD, although it is possible that the name could have had a connotation like 'west-countryman' rather than referring to membership of a distinct tribal entity. This inscription is probably the earliest epigraphic evidence of the Dumnonii as it appears to pre-date the building stones from Hadrian's Wall which Hodgson thinks are associated with either Antonine or Severan rebuilding on the frontier (Hodgson 2017, 110). Aemilius, who was said to have been a Roman citizen by the time of his death, was quite plausibly recruited in Exeter (or even Topsham), an appropriate home for a sailor.

The majority of the initial population of the town was doubtless drawn from veterans, both legionary and auxiliary given the number of forts in Devon, and accompanied by their families and slaves. If veterans had acquired land holdings in the vicinity of Exeter during the period of military occupation that would have been a reason to remain. Legionary veterans in particular would have been wealthy by local standards although, as is explored below, as yet we have little indication of substantial or rapid investment in private housing in the town. The veterans would have been supplemented by traders who had either established businesses servicing the needs of soldiers but chose not to move on with the legion, or those newly attracted to Exeter by the commercial possibilities the new community might bring (cf. the discussion by Fulford of the origins of the founding populations of the 1st-century AD *coloniae* in Britain; Fulford 1999; and see Mann 1983). The continued production of Fortress Wares after the departure of the legion again testifies to the continued residence of some artisans in the Exeter region after *c*. AD 75/80 (see EAPIT 2, Chapter 12). Some civilians may have been actively encouraged to stay in Exeter, especially if they had been resident at the St Loye's College site during the period of military occupation (see Chapter 5 above for the argument that this was an essentially civilian rather than military settlement). Indeed it may not be overly simplistic to regard the new town of Exeter as a replacement for that settlement once the fortress site became available. Over time there would doubtless have been drift from the countryside into the town but it seems hard to conceive that native Devonians formed a significant proportion of the founding population of Exeter. If sufficient human skeletal remains which can be associated with the period of early civilian occupation one day become available for study, isotopic and other scientific techniques might help shed some light on the question of the origins of the urban population.

It is important to recognise at the outset of any consideration of the character of the Early Roman town the dramatic effect that the withdrawal of the legion must have had on the local economy of Exeter and its hinterland. In Chapter 1 and the previous chapter Bidwell suggests that the population of Exeter and its satellite settlements of St Loye's College and Topsham could have been in the order of 10,000, on the assumption that the civilian population would have been roughly equivalent to the military one. There is little sign to date of intensive domestic occupation within the early town and the population is unlikely to have been substantial. An estimate of no more than 1,000 has previously been suggested (Holbrook and Bidwell 1991, 18), to which we should add the continuing populations at the port of Topsham and, on a lesser scale, the roadside settlement at St Loye's College. The drop in population at the end of the 1st century AD could therefore have been in the order of at least three quarters, which would vastly have diminished the importance of Exeter and its region as a market for imported goods (a topic discussed at further length below).

The creation of urban infrastructure

The street plan for the town was in large measure inherited from the fortress, although streets were invariably re-surfaced with gravel or river cobbles and in some places their width differed from the military predecessor (thus, for instance, the civilian street metalling of Street C overlay the post-trenches of military buildings (Street observation C4i; Bidwell 1980, 49). Two longitudinal streets were retained from the fortress (Streets C and E), their course confirmed by sightings at a variety of locations (Fig. 6.2). The fate of the *via praetoria/via decumana* (Street D) is less clear. Adjacent to the forum excavation showed that the fortress-period street was abandoned and replaced by a new street 3 m to the north-west, presumably to increase the space available for the forum (Street observation D2i). This new street would have been the *cardo maximus*, the principal north–south thoroughfare which linked two of the town gates. A watching brief during the laying of gas pipes in High Street in 1994 seems to have demonstrated that the postulated extra width of this street where it separated *insulae* X and XIV did not in fact exist (Exeter City Council 1994, 8; cf. Bidwell 1980, 47). Lateral streets F and G had military origins, although the course of Street G was interrupted by the forum. Street I was a new creation to sub-divide this part of the town into two blocks of four *insulae*. It does not appear that the large *insulae* V/X/XIV and XIX were subdivided as a lateral street would have been expected to have lain with the areas examined in the Goldsmith Street excavation (Sites 37 and 39). The *via sagularis* to the rear of the legionary rampart (Street B) was also retained on at least three sides (evidence is lacking on the north-east side, although it was at least partly obscured on this side of the town by the construction of a military-style granary; EAPIT 2, Chapter 3, Street observation B1i).

The legionary bath-house, the only masonry building within the fortress, was not levelled as part of this activity, and the process by which it was transformed into the basilica for the new town has been fully published (Site 40: Cathedral Close; Bidwell 1979, 60–6). Not only did the baths provide a convenient shell and source of materials from which to form the basilica, the choice of their site for the forum rather than that of the former headquarters building (as occurred at Gloucester and Lincoln) permitted the new civic centre to be built adjacent to the *cardo maximus*, rather than interrupting the course of this major street as was the case at the two *coloniae* (Hurst 1988; 1999b; Jones 2011, 54–6). This was presumably the reason why the fortress baths were not modified to form the public baths of the new town, a transformation that has yet to be demonstrated in Britain although it did occur at *Vindonissa*, in Switzerland, for example. There, after a period of abandonment, much smaller baths were built reusing the walls of the legionary *frigidarium*, while a civilian *vicus* developed along the two main streets of the former fortress (Hartmann 1986, 110–15). The Exeter baths had been reduced in size at some point, an event Bidwell (1979, 65) originally associated with the creation of a smaller bath-house to serve the population of the incipient civilian town. He now prefers, following Henderson, to associate this modification with a reduced military garrison in Exeter for a few years after *c.* AD 75 (see Chapter 5). Even these reduced baths would have been too big for the demands of the much reduced population of the new town and perhaps prohibitively expensive to maintain. The work involved in modification to civilian baths might simply not have been worth the effort. The partial demolition of the bath-house therefore occurred as a prelude to the construction of a new civic centre for the town, the gutting of the bath-house and construction of the basilica seemingly two stages of a single building programme. The south-west furnace house of the baths was levelled and the main baths building reduced to a shell, the side and rear walls to be incorporated into the fabric of the new basilica. The front wall was not ultimately to be retained but was left standing (although perhaps reduced in height) during the construction period (it was eventually replaced by a new wall 5 m to its rear). In front of this free-standing wall, and thus within the area of the former *palaestra*, stood a substantial timber building in excess of 15.6 m long and 8 m wide. The postholes of this structure were subsequently sealed beneath the forum courtyard and thus the building was abandoned when the civic complex was completed.

Bidwell (1980, 56) considered that this timber building could have provided temporary accommodation for the commercial life of the town while the main forum was under construction. Fulford, however, suggested that a longer life should be attributed to it which would then push the date of the construction of the masonry basilica and forum back to the very end of the 1st, if not into the early 2nd, century AD (Fulford 1985, 58). While such a date cannot be entirely excluded, it is pertinent that coarse ware pottery types that appear in Exeter immediately after the end of the military period are absent from the construction levels of the masonry basilica and forum (Bidwell Period 2A), deposits that yielded a good quantity of pottery (a minimum of 609 vessels; 79 kg; Bidwell 1979, tab. 9). Even on the most elongated chronology the timber building, whether or not it is to be regarded as a temporary basilica, was quickly replaced, and we may note that while the existence of timber *basilicae* have been suggested at some other British towns, the evidence is not decisive outside of Silchester where a purpose-built structure lasted for at least half a century (ibid.; Fulford and Timby 2000, 569–73). Lincoln might be another pertinent example, although the association of a paved surface with a timber forum is only conjecture (Steane 2006, 139–43, 186–8, 269–70; Jones 2011, 65–7). On balance the date of *c.* AD 90 for the commencement of construction of the Exeter basilica proposed by Bidwell

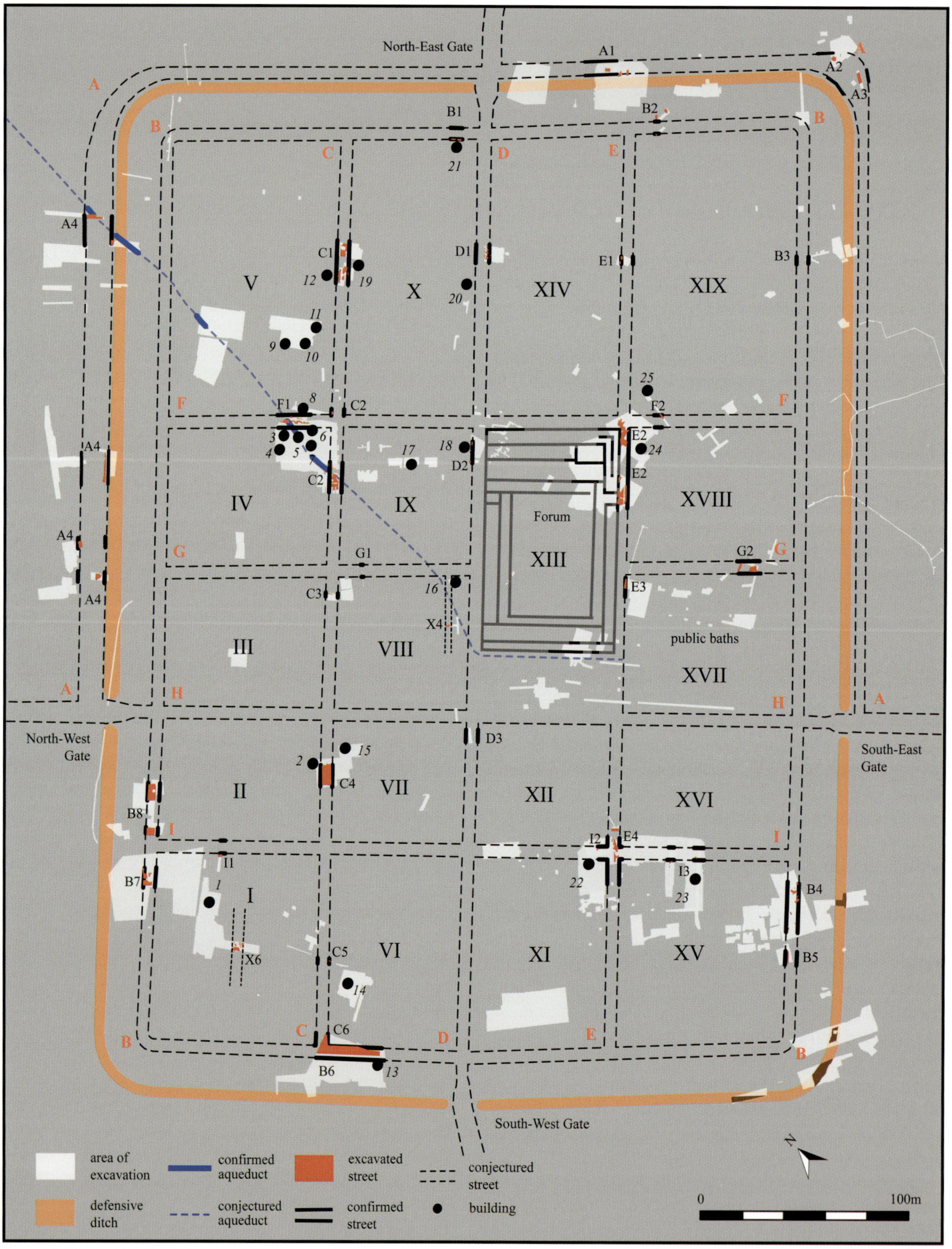

Fig. 6.2 Plan of the Early Roman town, c. *AD 100–160/80. The codes ascribed to the street observations and the numbers of individual buildings refer to the gazetteer entries in EAPIT 2, Chapter 3.2 and 3.3 (drawn by David Gould)*

and Holbrook in 1991 still seems appropriate (Holbrook and Bidwell 1991, 9; and see the Appendix to Chapter 5 above for the important re-dating of a samian stamp which has been used in some previous considerations of the date of this event).

The form of the masonry basilica and forum has been fully discussed elsewhere (Bidwell 1979, 78–86; Fig. 6.3). While excavation has inevitably only examined a small part of the overall complex there is no reason to doubt the interpretation of the public building as a basilica at the north-east end of a forum. Quite simply what else could it be? The main body of the basilica was 10.4 m wide, reducing to 9 m at the south-east end, with monumental steps leading up into the main hall (Figs 1.5 and 6.4). To the north-east of the hall there was a range of rooms, that at the south-east end plausibly identified as the *curia* or council chamber. At an early stage in the life of the basilica, and conceivably even during the course of construction, a 4 m-wide aisle or passage was added to the front of the hall. The only pertinent new evidence to come to light since the publication of the 1970s excavations pertains to small-scale work in 1995–6 which revealed the northern corner of the basilica at 2 Broadgate (Site 121). Here the north-west end wall of the rooms to the rear of the main hall was found and a second foundation 2.5 m further out could have been the rear wall of a portico or shops fronting onto Street D to the north-west. This discovery confirms that the range of rooms behind the hall was *c.* 50 m long (excluding porticos). The forum-courtyard was separated from the street to the south-east (Street E) by a portico and range of rooms. Reconstruction of the length of the forum rests upon the interpretation of a pair of parallel walls found in 1945–6 as an external portico on the south-west side of the courtyard. This is likely enough, but not certain. If correct the basilica and forum covered one and a half *insulae* (a total length of 106 m), with the remainder of the available space occupied by a gravelled market place. The forum was thus conceived and built on a reasonably large scale, noticeably so given the relatively small urban area enclosed within the defences, although it is not clear whether the walls found in 1945–6 were part of the original plan or a later modification. If the size and grandeur of a civic complex can be taken as a material manifestation of the aspirations of the founding city fathers, then the Exeter forum suggests a high degree of urban ambition.

The public baths were situated in the next *insula* (XVII) to the south-east of the forum, but they are very poorly understood (Bidwell 1979, 121–3; 1980, 52–3; Fig. 6.3). Several chance discoveries of walls and tessellated pavements have been recorded in this area since the 1830s; an excavation in 1932 (Site 6) revealed a stone-lined pool 16.75 m long and 1 m deep, surrounded by a free-standing colonnade (Fig. 6.5). Nothing is known of the main bathing suite and the date of construction is unclear.

Was the early town defended?

The fortress defences were not levelled when the army moved on. The rampart has been found in excavation preserved up to a height of 0.8–1.0 m at Friernhay Street, Mermaid Yard and Quintana Gate (Sites 75, 63 and 169). No evidence has been recovered for post-military refurbishment of the rampart, although such evidence would have been destroyed when it was substantially levelled in the later 2nd century AD. Two (in places three) ditches have been revealed by excavation outside the legionary rampart. It is argued in Chapter 5 by Bidwell that the inner ditch should be associated with the occupation of the fortress (it was not infilled before *c.* AD 70 at earliest) and the outer one with the period immediately following the establishment of the new town. Pottery from the dumps at the bottom of the outer ditch at Rack Street is commensurate with a date *c.* AD 100–20 for their deposition (Holbrook and Bidwell 1991, MF 1.61, feature RS 363.7; and see EAPIT 2, Chapter 8). In 1980 Bidwell further proposed that a new (third) ditch, 10 m wide and 2 m deep, was created in the mid 2nd century AD to replace the now infilled outer ditch, based upon an interpretation of sections recovered from Rack Street and Mermaid Yard (Bidwell 1980, 46–7, where he termed this feature the 'early civil ditch'). Henderson took a different view. He thought that Bidwell's 'early civil ditch' was not in fact a distinct defensive feature, the recorded sections at the two sites being a product of the digging of broad and extensive quarry scoops to extract clay from the ditch fills. He therefore maintained 'Although … the fortress defences were retained to mark the boundary of the new town, it seems unlikely that the rampart and ditch were maintained in a defensible condition, since there is no evidence that the ditch was ever cleaned out or recut' (Henderson 1988, 115). However, the similarity in the profiles of the ditch sections at the two sites (cf. Bidwell 1980, fig. 26 (Site 63: Mermaid Yard) and EAPIT 2, Chapter 8, Fig. 8.3 (Site 52: Rack Street)) is sufficiently marked to make it implausible that these were the fortuitous product of opportunistic clay quarrying, and thus a new mid 2nd-century AD ditch around at least part of the defensive circuit seems plausible. It may not have been considered necessary to go to this effort along the north-western and south-western sides of the town, however, where the ground naturally falls away beyond the limit of the defences, and this would explain why somewhat different sequences have been detected in investigations on these sides of the circuit. A 2nd-century AD recut is not immediately apparent at Friernhay Street (Site 75) on the south-west defences, although a full profile across the ditch system was not obtained here.

Preservation of biological remains at Friernhay Street demonstrated that the bottom of the outer ditch contained standing water in the late 1st/early 2nd century AD (Straker *et al.* 1984; a partial ditch section is published

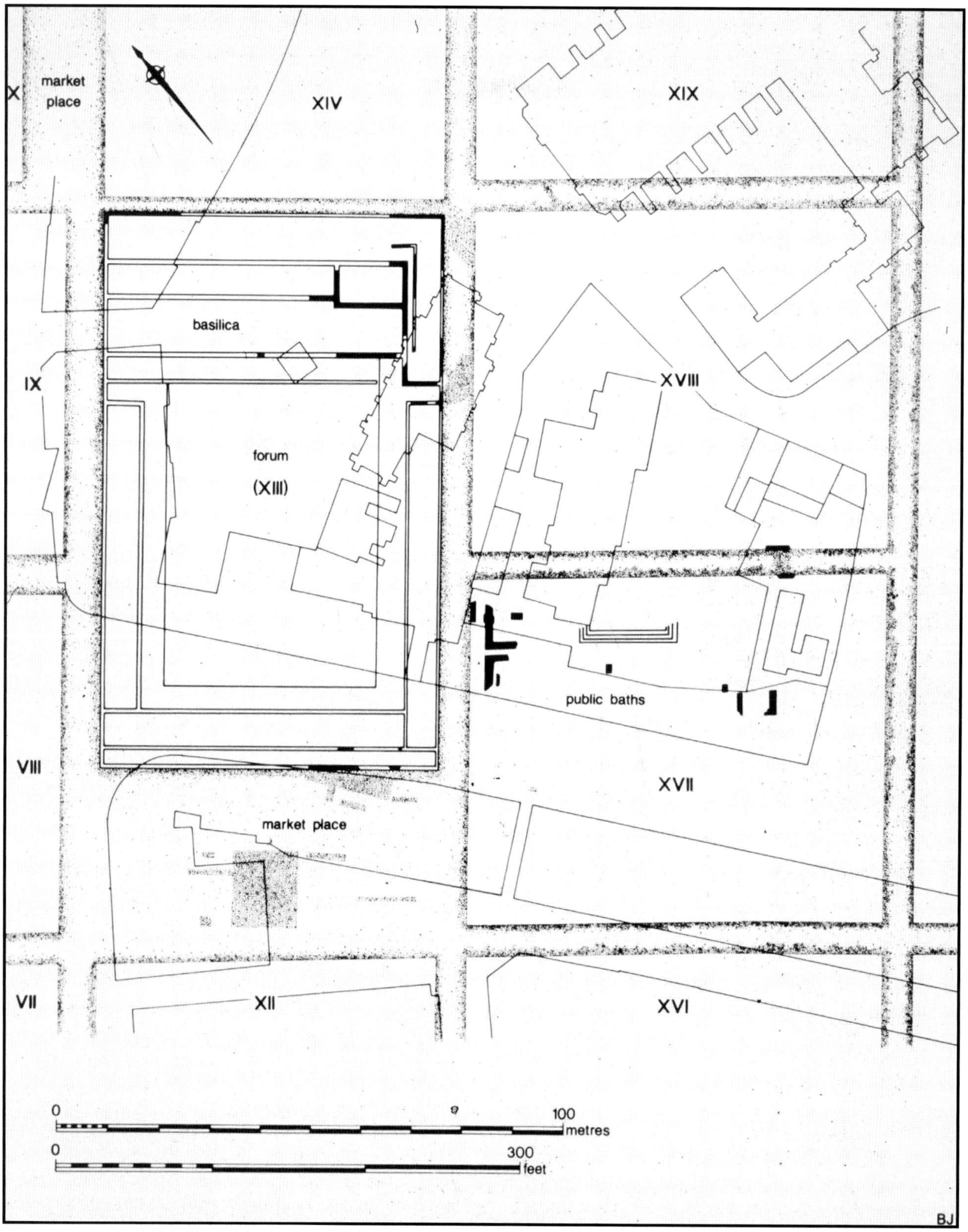

Fig. 6.3 Plan of the basilica, forum and public baths (Bidwell 1979, fig. 28; © Exeter City Council)

Fig. 6.4 The steps at the south-east end of the forum portico leading into the basilica, with column-base and gutter block to left. A near-white and dull pink sandstone were used for the steps, the contrasting colours being used for decorative effect. The lowest step rests on the hypocaust basement of the underlying fortress baths (© Exeter City Council)

there as fig. 1). The plant, insect and ostracod remains combine to reveal a picture of much rotting vegetation in the base and on the sides of the ditch. Plants included stinging nettle, dock, thistle and sedges. Dung from large herbivores such as horse and cattle was also present, although perhaps no more than might be found in proximity to pastureland. Cereals were predominately represented by chaff, presumably the waste fractions from the processing of wheat and barley which was fed to the animals. The types of seed and insect present imply that open habitats such as arable or pasture fields lay in close proximity to the ditch, but the urban environment is unsurprisingly also represented in the flora and fauna which included woodworm beetle and *Lyctus linearis* which tend to infest structural hardwood timbers, and grain weevils which only attack stored grain, not cereal fields. While the ditch waters were undoubtedly filthy and polluted, the conditions were not as foul as some Roman and medieval urban deposits in other parts of the country.

At Paul Street (Site 76) on the north-west side of the town the bottom of the outer ditch was filled with silt and slumped clay, including a substantial slippage from the steep outer face which partially blocked its course (Blaylock 1988, 4–5; Henderson 1988, fig. 5.10, 115–16). The lower parts of six wooden stakes were found at this location which were dated by dendrochronology to AD 100/101 (EAPIT 2, Chapter 11; see below for the interpretation of this bridge structure). The excavators considered that the stakes had been driven through 0.4–0.5 m of silt which had accumulated above the slippage of natural clay, although it seems just as possible that the silt could have accumulated around the stakes. If the ditch was no longer maintained, as Henderson believed, surely it would have been a simpler solution to construct a solid causeway across the ditch than create a timber bridge? That effort was expended on a timber structure more likely suggests a desire to retain the ditch as an open feature, albeit that it had been partially blocked by slippage in this one location at least. Following the disuse of the bridge, silts continued to accumulate in the ditch before they were sealed by dumps of refuse containing later 2nd-century AD pottery which were in turn sealed by clay from the levelled fortress rampart (see below for a consideration of the date of this event). Thus it can reasonably be argued that the early town was intended to be defended from the outset, although the ditch was not everywhere maintained. As we have seen at Paul Street the ditch became choked in places, while at Rack Street (Site 52) a large quantity of

Fig. 6.5 The sandstone slab pavement surrounding the open pool of the public baths, with shallow gutter in the centre, as exposed in excavations in the Old Deanery Garden in 1932 (Site 6) (© RAMM)

cattle butchery waste was dumped into the bottom of the ditch in the early 2nd century AD, presumably an example of opportunistic waste disposal (the deposit contained fragments from a minimum of 49 cattle, 15 sheep/goats, 5 pigs and 4 horses; Maltby 1979, 11 and below). So it is no surprise that a new ditch was recut with a different profile on the south-eastern side of the town at least. While no evidence survives for the refurbishment of the rampart, the eroded bank could easily have been supplemented by a new wooden palisade or breastwork, all trace of which was destroyed when the rampart was substantially levelled in the later 2nd century AD.

There is one other piece of fragmentary, yet tantalising, possible evidence which may be of relevance here. On the south-east defences at 15 Cathedral Close (Site 100) a very small excavation in 1991 revealed a posthole of one of the timber interval towers of the legionary fortress, and immediately in front of it, layers lapping up from the infilling the outer ditch. These dumps were abutted by a short length of stone wall, 0.65 m wide, aligned with the front of the rampart and built above the infilled inner ditch. The wall turned a corner to head back across the body of the rampart. These discoveries might be related to another length of stone wall found nearby in 1936 (Site 12: Cathedral outside of Speke Chapel) in which case they would have formed a structure *c.* 3.4 m wide. One possibility is that these wall fragments formed part of a stone interval tower sat astride the rampart, a so far unique discovery in Exeter and one that has not been replicated at any of the four other timber interval towers so far investigated. If correctly interpreted, there are two possible contexts for a stone interval tower. It could date to late in the period of military occupation, as in Britain the replacement of the earthwork defences of legionary fortresses in stone began in the Flavian period, as is so clearly demonstrated by the unfinished stone wall at Inchtuthil, in Scotland, abandoned *c.* AD 86 (Pitts and St Joseph 1985, 61–9). Alternatively, the tower could be associated with an attempt to refurbish the town defences at the very end of the 1st or first half of the 2nd century AD (masonry towers were associated with the earthen rampart of the urban defences of Cirencester; Wacher and Salvatore 1998, 79–81, 96–8). In either case the putative refurbishment must have been quickly aborted. It must be stressed, however, that the work in 1991 was of very limited extent and no plan of the findings is readily available. Further work will be required to verify the findings and the tentative interpretation proposed by the excavators.

If, as it now seems, the civilian town of Exeter was defended from the outset, then it bears certain similarities with the three *coloniae* established on abandoned fortress sites in Britain (Colchester, Gloucester and Lincoln), although they were characterised by the replacement of the old turf and timber legionary ramparts with stone walls by the earlier 2nd century AD (Wilson 2006a, 3–6). This was manifestly not the case in Exeter, unless the tentative evidence for a masonry tower at 15 Cathedral Close marks an aborted attempt at this process. Exeter does, however, contrast quite markedly with the sequence at Wroxeter, another Neronian/early Flavian fortress which developed into a *civitas* capital, and indeed the whole trajectory from abandoned fortress to civilian town was not inevitable. This is demonstrated at Usk, where the fortress was replaced by a reduced level of military occupation while a *civitas* capital was established on a fresh site at Caerwent, conveniently located on the main road to the new legionary fortress at Caerleon (Burnham and Davies 2010, 187–92). At Wroxeter, to extrapolate from small-scale excavations at a single point on the defensive circuit, the legionary rampart was levelled and the ditch carefully infilled in preparation for the construction of civilian buildings bordering Watling Street (Ellis 2000, 11; Webster 2002, 56–60; White *et al.* 2013, 174). The fortress plan dictated the skeleton of the central *insulae* at Wroxeter, but aerial and geophysical survey give no indication that the legionary defences were retained in the same manner as Exeter.

Exeter is not, however, unique in Britain in having earthwork defences before the widespread adoption of such circuits by urban communities in the second half of the 2nd century AD. Roger Wilson reviewed the evidence in 2006: late 1st or early 2nd-century AD defences can be demonstrated or reasonably inferred at Cirencester, *Verulamium* and Winchester (Wilson 2006a, 17–20). Wroxeter might be another example as there a rampart and ditch occupy a line distinct from that of the legionary fortifications, although it has been proposed that these defences enclosed an annexe to the legionary fortress and were thus unrelated to the early town (White *et al.* 2013, 167–8). In the absence of further work the evidence is insufficient either way for certainty. Wilson also speculated that London might be another example of early urban defences, but recent work does not lend any support to the notion that the landward walls there date earlier than *c.* AD 190–230 (Perring 2015, 33–4). Wilson wondered whether *Verulamium*, Cirencester and Winchester might have received their earthen defences as a symbol of their elevation to the rank of *municipium*, but this is unproven and not otherwise attested in the western provinces. It may not be too fanciful to conceive that Exeter was intended at the outset to function in the manner of a *colonia* (the scale of the public building complex supports the view that there was considerable State investment), although the absence of stone walls before the end of the 2nd century AD and the presence of a tribal suffix in three separate sources (Antonine Itinerary, Ravenna Cosmography and Peutinger Table) strongly suggest that it never obtained that status (Rivet and Smith 1979, 378).

Urban development

Attempts to refine the chronology of urban development in the decades immediately following the abandonment of the legionary fortress are hindered by the scarcity of sizeable assemblages of pottery and coins from deposits that can be securely related to the earliest urban activity in the town. Late Flavian and Trajanic samian is not that plentiful in Exeter compared to that produced in the preceding decades, a pattern that reflects both the considerably reduced population of Exeter at this time, but more so national trends in the supply of samian ware to Britain (Willis 2004, section 6.2; a graph showing the date range of the stamped samian ware from Exeter can be conveniently downloaded from the samian research website: https://www1.rgzm.de/samian/home/frames.htm). New types and forms of coarse ware pottery do appear in Exeter in the decades following the departure of the legion, but there is an inevitable imprecision in dating the appearance of many forms, although some appeared very soon after AD 75 given their presence in a deposit at the fort of Bolham, in Tiverton which, on the basis of the samian, is unlikely to date much after AD 85 (Maxfield 1991, 66).

The Appendix to Chapter 5 above summarises the salient dating evidence for the earliest post-military activity in Exeter. The date of the forum-basilica has been discussed earlier, but beyond this the evidence for late 1st-century AD domestic occupation is scarce and we cannot as yet conclusively date a single private building to this period. In this respect Exeter is by no means alone amongst western towns. At Caerwent and Wroxeter there has been little in the way of modern excavation of the relevant areas, whilst the techniques utilised in the older excavations were not always subtle enough to detect ephemeral timber buildings. Somewhat better evidence for 1st-century AD timber buildings has been recovered from the Greyhound Yard excavation in Dorchester, where in the Early Roman period one *insula* seems to have contained a low density of separate timber houses on the street frontages, with enclosures in the centre. The dating of these structures may not be as firm as is suggested in the excavation report and their pre-Flavian origin is not assured (Woodward *et al.* 1993, 359–64). Cirencester also has a current lack of securely-dated Flavian houses (Holbrook 2008, 312–13), but how much this reflects the true state of affairs is more difficult to determine. In many currently occupied historic towns opportunities to examine the earliest urban deposits on anything but the most limited scale have been very rare (London excepted), and so an absence of evidence rather than evidence of absence will be a significant factor in the national picture as we currently perceive it.

In Exeter we are heavily dependent upon a critical assessment of more general considerations and arguments for our understanding of the early history of the Roman town. Several strands of continuity between the military and subsequent civilian occupation point to there being no significant chronological break and thus a period when central Exeter lay largely unoccupied. Continuity can be discerned in the local pottery industries of Exeter, and the introduction of a new repertoire of forms in regional fabrics such as South-Western BB1 could have been a response to disrupted lines of supply immediately after the withdrawal of the legion (see EAPIT 2, Chapter 12). Tile production in the area to the north-east of the fortress/early town probably represents another strand of continuity from the period of military occupation, although fortress-period tile production did not occur within the bounds of the Princesshay excavation area itself (Site 156; see EAPIT 2, Chapter 13). Tile production hereabouts doubtless serviced the construction needs of the public building programme, the duration of which has been clarified by the significant discovery at Paul Street in 1982 (Site 76) already mentioned. There, the lower parts of six oak stakes forming a structure 1.2 m wide were found driven into the partial infilling of the outer ditch outside the old legionary rampart; two further postholes were found *c.* 17 m distant cutting the metalling of a street (Street A) that followed the outer edge of the ditch. Through an incisive piece of interpretation Henderson identified these timbers as the supports for a bridge crossing the ditch which supported an aqueduct that approached the town defences as a raised wooden launder founded on the timber posts dug into the street metalling (Frere 1983a, 320–3; Henderson 1984a, 2–3; 1988, 115; Blaylock 1988, 4). He thought that the aqueduct was fed by springs on the flank of Rougemont or the Longbrook Valley, the water transported in an open leat or timber-lined channel akin to that found outside Dorchester (Putnam 2007, 63–71). Four of the posts within the ditch were shown by dendrochronology to have been felled in the winter of AD 100/101 and would doubtless have been used very shortly thereafter (Hillam 1984; EAPIT 2, Chapter 11). This part of the aqueduct did not have a long life as the rotted stubs of the posts within the ditch were covered by further deposits, and within the town the water pipe was removed and its trench backfilled and built over by the Hadrianic/early Antonine period. The aqueduct may thus have only functioned for a couple of decades at most, after which it was replaced by a different system of water supply. The significance of this discovery is that it demonstrates that water was being brought into the town in AD 100/101, and it is reasonable to associate this event with the completion of the basilica and forum, if not the public baths as well. A decade-long building programme for the basilica and forum is entirely credible, especially if skilled labour (and/or finance) was scarce, as it may well have been in the late 1st century AD when major public construction projects were underway at various British towns.

Inside the town the water was transported in trench-laid wooden water pipes such as those discovered at Goldsmith Street Area I and Trichay Street in the early 1970s (Sites 37 and 42; EAPIT 2, Chapter 5). The water pipe trench crossed *insulae* IV and V on an oblique, sinuous, course, an unusual occurrence since water pipes normally ran along the main streets (conceivably the trench found in the excavations was a branch to a specific building or fountain, tapping off a principal water main). As we have seen the aqueduct was short-lived; perhaps it did not function very efficiently? It might have been replaced by a more permanent structure, of which no trace has yet been found, or the needs of the urban population could have been served henceforth by wells and cisterns. There are comparatively few wells currently recorded in Exeter (see below) but this may be a product of the emphasis of excavators on structures rather than their surrounding areas. At Dorchester the aqueduct was derelict by the middle of the 2nd century AD yet the public baths continued in use into the 4th century AD. They were presumably supplied with water from a bucket-well or similar after the aqueduct failed (Putnam 2007, 69–71).

The course adopted for the water pipe demonstrates that *insulae* IV and V were largely undeveloped at the start of the 2nd century AD and that they had not been parcelled up into discrete building plots which had passed into private ownership. It seems unlikely therefore that the newly established town was rapidly filled with houses and shops, such development perhaps being restricted in the early decades to the area immediately surrounding the forum and along the frontages of the principal streets. This observation supports a relatively small initial population for the town, although the Trichay Street excavation demonstrates that the frontages of Street F separating *insulae* IV and V were occupied by timber strip buildings by the time of a fire in the Hadrianic or early Antonine period. A variety of constructional techniques were utilised in the timber buildings of the early town, which would support piecemeal development over 80–100 years rather than a systematic, time-limited, and officially-controlled building programme. Sill beam construction, with the beams laid either in shallow trenches or directly upon the ground surface, was the most common technique. In these cases wall lines are frequently only detectable in excavation where floor levels are preserved. Other methods represented included post-in-trench, post-pits and shallow stone footings or sill walls (see, for instance Fig. 6.14, buildings 3i and 8i in *insula* V). Open spaces were a characteristic of the *insulae* of the early town, to judge from the layout recovered from *insula* IV/V (Sites 37, 39 and 42) and at *insulae* XII and XVI where a cultivation soil presumably testifies to horticulture preceding the construction of a later Roman town house (Site 115: Market Street). The uses that these undeveloped spaces were put to largely elude us at present, and so the application of scientific techniques to appropriate deposits should be a priority for future excavations.

In Chapter 5 Bidwell raised the possibility that there may have been a continuing military presence in Exeter after the withdrawal of the legion based upon the discovery of what appears to have been a substantial timber granary built across the line of the north-east *via sagularis* of the legionary fortress at 228 High Street (Site 61). He wondered whether there might have been a small military compound inside the North-East Gate of the early town, and in this context we may also note that an early date has been claimed for a substantial timber building in *insula* X (Building 19i) which was in excess of 17.5 m long. There is, however, too little dating evidence for certainty and there is no reason why the building could not date to well into the 2nd century AD (the suggestion of an early date may derive in part from the use of military-style post-in-trench construction, a relatively uncommon building technique in the early town). The dramatic reduction in the military garrison of the South-West Peninsula by the start of the 2nd century AD would make a continuing military presence in Exeter plausible, even though military compounds are currently unknown in the towns of southern Britain outside of London (Bishop 1991, 27 notes two finds of 2nd or 3rd-century AD military fittings from Exeter).

Suburban activity

The Roman road system in the immediate vicinity of Exeter is not well understood, although the course of the Fosse Way approaching from Woodbury, in Axminster, to the east through Heavitree can be reasonably inferred (Fig. 6.1, and see Chapter 3, Fig. 3.5; Margary 1955, route 4f). The road system, including the bridging point of the Exe, would have been inherited from the military arrangement although there was doubtless subsequent development and modification. It is reasonable to presume that the Roman river crossing was close to the site of the medieval one and slight evidence for a Roman road on the opposite (Cowick) bank has apparently been found at Guy's Allotments (Site 92; Brown 2019, 4–6). Once the river had been crossed, the road split into two, one route over Haldon Hill towards Ipplepen in South Devon (Margary route 491), the other along the north side of Dartmoor towards North Tawton and Okehampton (Margary route 492a; Salvatore *et al.* 2019).

A metalled road has been found immediately beyond the exterior lip of the outer ditch on two sides of the town: to the north-east at St Catherine's Almshouses and Princesshay (Street observations A1i and A2i), and on the north-west side at Paul Street and North Gate Court (observation A4i). The road was not continuous around the circuit to judge from its absence at Mermaid Yard, Rack Street and Friernhay Street on the other two sides (Sites 63, 52/64 and 75). The road has previously been considered to be of military date (Henderson 1988, 92), although now the outer ditch is thought to belong with the early town, so presumably does the road as well as it clearly respects the line of the ditch (while it might just be argued that the outer ditch filled a gap between the rampart and the road, this does not seem overly plausible). The road must in part date to the early years of the town as the street metalling at Paul Street was cut by postholes associated with the aqueduct bridge dated by dendrochronology to AD 100/101, although its distinctive composition of a pebble surface above a make-up of volcanic chippings set in clay might suggest that some parts of the road utilised waste from the construction of the town wall and thus relates to the enlargement of the street grid within the expanded circuit of town defences in the early 3rd century AD. This is supported by its variable width, even allowing for the fact that it had been eroded in places by the collapse of the outer face of the ditch, and orientation. In one trench at Paul Street the far edge of the road lay at 16 m from the outer edge of the ditch, which the excavators believed demonstrated that the road deviated northwards away from the line of the defences at this point. Until more is seen of this road such an interpretation must be considered speculative. A suburban road has also been recorded to the north-east of the town at Princesshay (where it is termed 'Road II'; Steinmetzer, Stead, Pearce, Bidwell and Allan forthcoming), 120 m beyond the outer face of the ditch. It was of insubstantial construction and may not have been in use for a protracted period.

Immediately outside the South-East Gate occupation has been found on either side of the road to Topsham. To the north-east of the road the land had been divided up into a series of small ditched plots (Site 44: Valiant Soldier). Sometime after the mid 2nd century AD the ditches were infilled and a roughly metalled track 6–8 m wide was constructed over them which met the road to Topsham at an oblique angle (Fig. 6.1). The track perhaps bypassed the town to join with the road to Woodbury, in Axminster. On the opposite, south-west side, of the Topsham road fragmentary post-trenches and pits testify to some manner of ribbon development (Sites 45, 50 and 65), while three fragmentary timber buildings of probable 2nd-century AD date were found at Lower Coombe Street (Site 97). They might have lined a lane that led from the Topsham road to the Exe foreshore.

Little other evidence has been found to date for domestic structures in the suburbs, save for occasional and seemingly isolated timber buildings at Bartholomew Street West, Exe Street and Paul Street (Sites 47, 83 and 76), and at least one extra-mural site which was occupied in the military period shows a marked absence of later civilian activity (Southernhay Gardens: Site 49). There is more evidence for industrial activity. At Bartholomew Street West (Site 47), 65 m to the south-east of the defences, there was a late 1st to early 2nd-century AD pottery kiln producing mortaria and flagons (Holbrook and Bidwell 1991, 285–6; 1992, 64–5). This is the sole pottery kiln for which we have structural evidence from Exeter although mortaria and flagon wasters from Lower Coombe Street (Site 97) testify to the presence of at least one other kiln in the near vicinity where production once again seems to have commenced at about the time the fortress was abandoned (Holbrook and Bidwell 1992, 62–7; EAPIT 2, Chapter 12). The Ludwell Valley between Exeter and Topsham has also been suggested as a source of pottery and tiles on the basis of petrological inspection (Taylor forthcoming; EAPIT 2, Chapters 12 and 13.3).

In the area beyond the North-East Gate of the early town extensive evidence for tile manufacture has been detected at several separate locations in the form of clay quarry pits (and indeed possibly the wholesale reduction of the contemporary ground surface for clay extraction) and dumps of tile wasters (Sites 9, 26 and 156). No kilns have so far been located. Pottery associated with these activities at the Princesshay site (156) is predominately of the 2nd century AD, and it is evident that tile production did not commence in this particular locality until after the end of military occupation given the absence of tile waste from the backfills of fortress-period features. Bidwell (1980, 40; Holbrook and Bidwell 1991, 281–2) has, however, suggested that tile production in the general area to the north-east of the fortress commenced in the military period as tile waste was incorporated into the make-up levels of the road leading to the North-East Gate of the fortress (Site 127: St John's School) and that this industry was the principal source of tiles used in the fortress baths, a chronology supported by Peter Warry's more recent analysis (EAPIT 2, Chapter 13.3). The 2nd-century AD expansion of the area used for tile production to include the Princesshay excavation site is best associated with servicing the requirements of the public building programme (tile production was certainly underway in this area before *c.* AD 160–80 as wasters were sealed beneath the rampart of the new town defences). Whilst the basilica and forum date to the very end of the 1st century AD, construction of the baths and possibly other public buildings such as a market or temple, which are as yet unknown, could easily have stretched throughout the first half of the 2nd century AD and thus be commensurate with the chronology of tile production at Princesshay. It is questionable whether there would have been sufficient demand for ceramic tiles for the tilery to have functioned continuously from the late 1st century AD until the Antonine period. Perhaps there was a revival in tile production associated with repairs to the forum and basilica which are dated to the period after *c.* AD 150 (see Appendix 6.1, Period 2B)? The siting of an extensive tile works immediately outside the bounds of the early town is worthy of comment as it shows there was no demand to utilise this space for suburban occupation, and nor were the civic authorities unduly concerned about the impact of the smoke and fumes generated by the kilns on the urban environment.

Princesshay was not the sole tile works in the vicinity of the early town as a second tilery is attested in the vicinity of St David's church (Site 191) from dumps of tile waste which include rare examples of ceramic pilaster tiles (Durrant forthcoming). The chronology of this industry is disputed. Bidwell and Wild (forthcoming) date production to the late military period on the evidence of the associated pottery, whereas Warry places the output of the kilns in the civil period on the basis of his chemical characterisation of their products, with production continuing well into the 2nd century AD (no Group C *tegulae* cutaways, which Warry dates to *c.* AD 160–260, are known in this fabric grouping). Curiously, Warry's analysis suggests that none of the products of this industry seem to occur within the town, but instead were marketed to other sites in Devon including St Loye's College (EAPIT 2, Chapter 13.3). Further work is required to confirm the date of the St David's industry, and whether it is the source of the two pilaster tiles so far recovered from sites within the defences of Exeter.

Tileries would have consumed a considerable amount of timber to fuel the kilns, and there must have been substantive tracts of woodland in the vicinity of Exeter to serve both the tile and pottery industries. In some places tileries were set up a few miles distant from a town, as for instance at Cirencester (Minety kilns), Lincoln (Heighington) and Silchester (Little London) where presumably there was plentiful woodland and no pressure on space (McWhirr 1979a; Warry 2006, 122–34; Fulford *et al.* n.d.). But Exeter is not unique in its peri-urban tilery and the Princesshay and St David's industries invite comparison with St Oswald's tilery a short distance outside the *colonia* defences at Gloucester (the tilery lay close to the bank of the Severn rather than on an island in the river as Hurst suggested; Hurst 1999b, 123–4; Rhodes 2006, 12, n. 27). Like Princesshay, St Oswald's was probably established to serve the legionary fortress but continued in production well into the 2nd century AD (Warry 2017, 79). In both cases proximity to the fortress for security and control might have been required initially, and thereafter the presence of the necessary infrastructure presumably militated against a move to a different location. More generally the location of industry on the urban fringe was common in Gaul and provided that there was an adequate source of raw material and available space, such locations provided a concentrated local market for the products, ready labour and excellent access to transport networks (Goodman 2007, 105–12).

Non-ferrous metalworking also took place in the suburbs of the early town in the mid 2nd century AD. Two hearths and a spread of metalworking debris were found adjacent to the road to Topsham near the site of the later South Gate of the expanded town (Site 36). Chemical analyses showed that there was 1% of lead in some animal bones within one of the hearths which suggests that it was used for cupellation to extract silver from lead and copper alloys (Fox 1968, 9). The metalworking presumably took place adjacent to buildings fronting on to the road.

To date there is very limited evidence for burial outside the early town. Antiquarian records of cremation urns beyond the North-East Gate demonstrate a cemetery here, although whether of military or civilian date (or both) is currently impossible to determine (Goodchild 1952, 103). A 'Roman family sepulchural vault' found in 1836 in High Street seems unlikely to be a Roman monument. Goodchild (ibid.) thought it more probably a mis-identified medieval pottery kiln, and while Collingwood and Richmond accepted it as a Roman '*columbarium*', this seems doubtful as such monuments are only found in the countryside of South-East England (Collingwood and Richmond 1969, 167; Bidwell 1980, 58, n. 26). A cremation urn from the St David's area also indicates early burial here, and a number of the finds of Early Roman coins and a bronze lamp recorded from hereabouts might also have accompanied burials, although once again the form and chronology of these interments currently eludes us (Goodchild 1952, 103).

The later town

The new urban defences

At a date currently estimated to lie in the range *c.* AD 160–80 the decision was taken by the town authorities (and undoubtedly with the sanction of the provincial government) to more than double the enclosed area of Exeter from 16.6 ha to 37.5 ha (92 acres) through the construction of a new circuit of earthwork defences 2.3 km long (Figs 6.6–6.7). In 1980 Paul Bidwell argued that it was most likely that this earthwork bank was merely the first stage in the construction of the masonry town wall, but the discovery of a timber gate beneath the masonry South Gate in 1989 disproved this idea and thus Exeter, like many other towns in Britain, possessed an initial phase of earthwork defences which were subsequently replaced in stone (Bidwell 1980, 62; Henderson 2001). The new defences adopted a superior strategic line compared to those of the former fortress, incorporating naturally defensive topographical features in the circuit: the volcanic knoll of Rougemont in the northern corner, the steep valley of the Longbrook stream on the north-western side, and high bluffs above the River Exe on the south. The expansion of the town does not seem to have been driven by an immediate or obvious pressure on space for further urban development. As we have seen there is currently little evidence for extensive suburban activity outside of the early town and within its bounds there is little impression that space was at a premium. While an increase in the defended area at this time is by no means unique, and indeed finds parallel at Winchester, such investment did not invariably occur (Ottaway 2017, 94). The *colonia* defences at Gloucester, for instance, were never enlarged to encompass a greater area, despite the extensive extra-mural suburbs there, even though Lincoln demonstrates that this could be accomplished (Hurst 1999b, 120–1; Jones 2011, 75–86).

The earthwork defences comprised a bank which has been found at every point where the defences have been examined archaeologically, now over 15 separate observations (Blaylock 1995, fig. 9 for the location of interventions up to 1994). The bank was formed from dumps of clean mixed clays, the composition of which matched the local subsoil extracted for the creation of one or more external ditches. At Paul Street (Site 76) the bank survived to a height of 1.5 m in one trench, but the tip lines showed no evidence for levelling out such as might indicate proximity to its original top. An attempt to project the full original height of the rampart here based upon constant gradients for the slope of the bank and underlying ground level yields a maximum height of between 2.1–2.5 m (Blaylock 1988, 5–8). In certain places where the ground falls steeply away outside the defences the bank was considerably lower, presumably a consequence of the absence of external ditches in these sectors (Henderson 2001, 63–4). The bank was of variable width, but in some places at least can be estimated to have been as much as 14 m which would make for a curiously wide, yet low, bank (ibid., fig. 10). The rampart probably had a timber or wattle front revetment (that in every place excavated so far has been destroyed by the insertion of a later masonry wall). Excavation at the South Gate (Site 96) demonstrates that the earthwork defences were equipped there with a timber gateway, set back by about 7 m from the estimated front of the rampart. There was thus an open court in front of the portal flanked by the curving sides of the rampart, as at Silchester (Fulford 1984, 50–8; Fulford *et al.* 1997, 96–7).

The amount of pottery recovered from the body of the rampart bank is quite meagre, but it is reasonable to suppose that the defences of the former legionary fortress were finally slighted when the expanded defensive circuit was created. In contrast to the bank, there are large and consistent pottery assemblages from the upper fills of the ditch surrounding the early town, and the potential for this material to date the creation of the earthwork defences has been carefully reviewed and a date in the range *c.* AD 160–80 proposed (Holbrook and Bidwell 1991, 10–11; 1992, 39–40). The date and motivation for the creation of Romano-British urban defences in earthwork have been discussed in detail by Hartley (1983) and Frere (1984), although the latter drew very different conclusions from

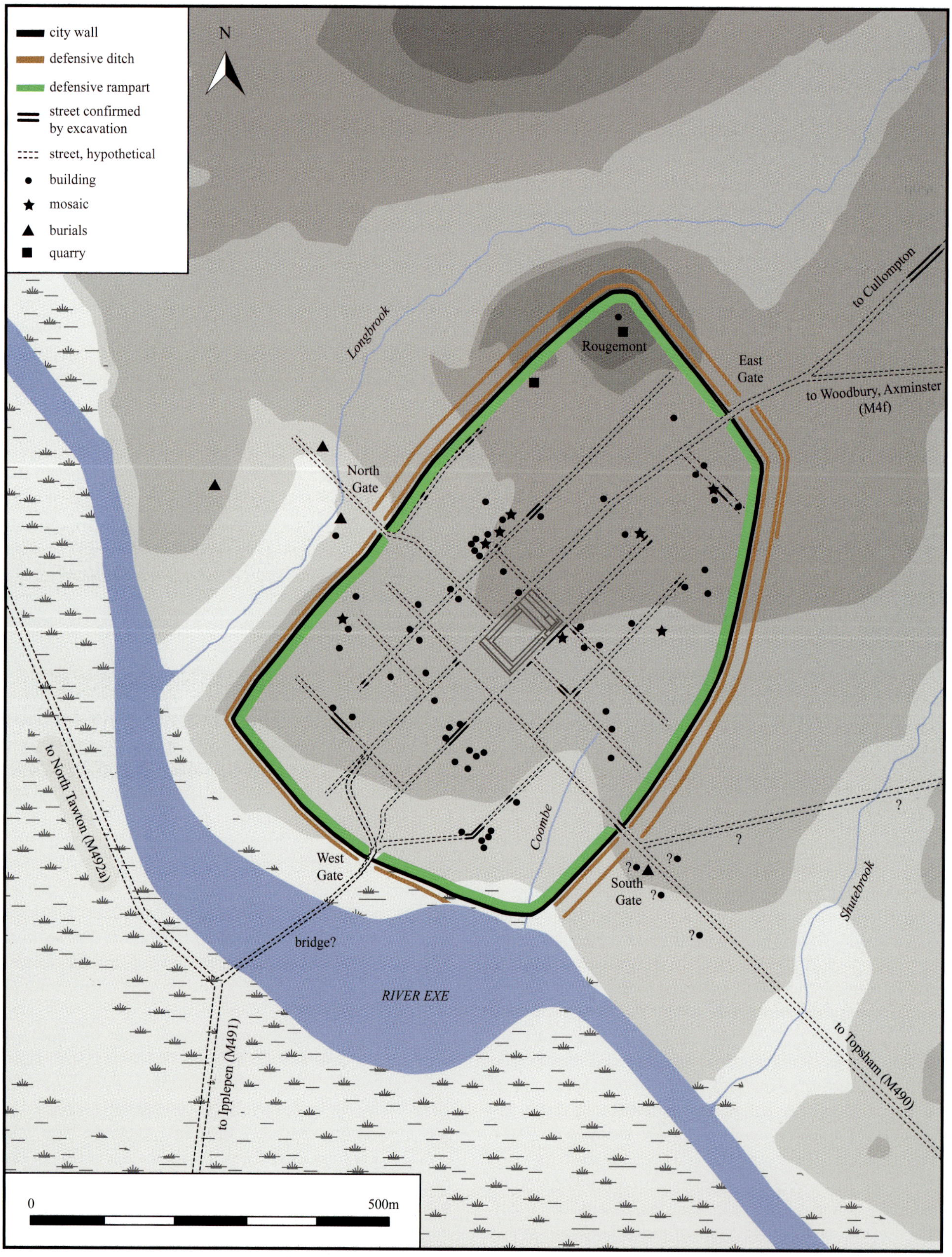

Fig. 6.6 The later Roman town and its environs (drawn by David Gould)

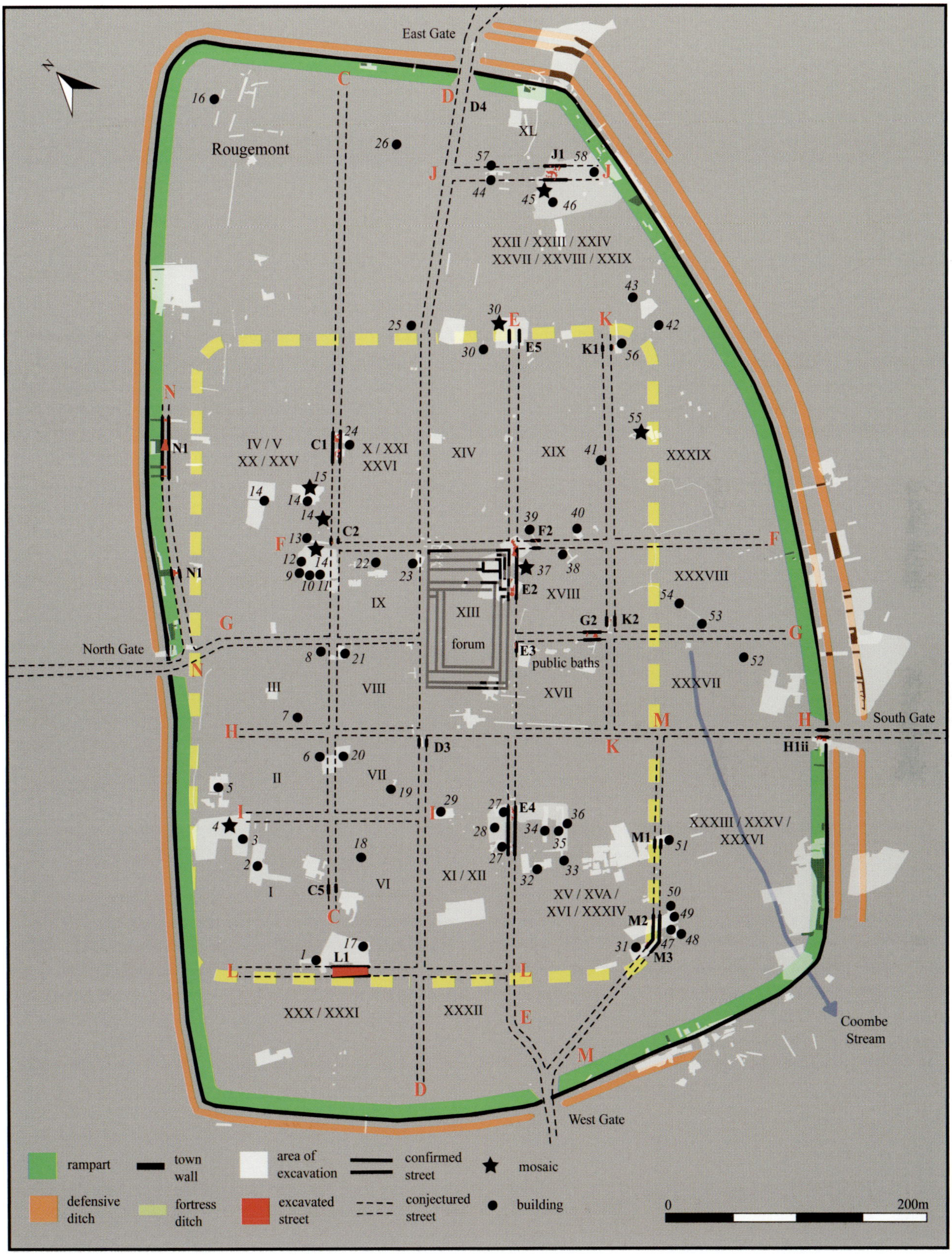

Fig. 6.7 Plan of the later Roman town, during the 3rd to 4th centuries AD. The codes ascribed to the street observations and the numbers to individual buildings refer to the gazetteer entries in EAPIT 2, Chapter 3.3 (drawn by David Gould)

the former. Of late, however, this topic has somewhat fallen out of academic fashion, a product perhaps of a lack of new information as conservation policies have discouraged development in the zones occupied by urban defences. Hartley (1983, 93) regarded these urban circuits as the product of separate 'purely civilian initiatives', but Frere argued forcibly that they were built at the same time and in response to a short-lived emergency in the AD 180s or 90s (and see Esmonde Cleary 2003 who places the British urban defences in their continental context). While the form of the Exeter defences would be consistent with a hastily constructed circuit around this time, self-evidently the refurbishment of the old legionary defences would have been a quicker and much less labour-intensive option.

Work at North Gate and to a lesser extent at Paul Street suggest that the top of the bank may have seen some exposure and use as a surface before it was covered with a heightening of the rampart associated with the construction of the masonry wall. At North Gate (Site 69) the bank was covered with a dark grey organic clay containing daub, charcoal, cess and pottery (perhaps material cleaned from the ditch and dumped here) which was in turn partially sealed by a rough surface of cobbles and volcanic stone. In one of the trenches at Paul Street the natural ground surface behind the tail of the first bank was marginally lower than that preserved beneath the bank, suggestive of a period of wear or erosion before it too was sealed off by construction deposits relating to the building of the wall (Blaylock 1988, 7–8). While not conclusive, this evidence provides some support for the notion that that the bank had an existence independent from the later masonry wall and heightened rampart, although the replacement in masonry does seem to have occurred within a few decades to judge from the, admittedly sparse, dating evidence. Henderson (2001, 67–8) remarked on the absence of a turf line above the early bank and took this to support only a relatively short interval between the erection and initial decay of the primary rampart and the addition of the masonry wall to its front. Pottery from the second bank contemporary with the construction of the wall contains no types which need be later than *c.* AD 200, but it would be unwise to place too much reliance on this upper date until more material is recovered (Holbrook and Bidwell 1991, 9–11; 1992, 39–40; Henderson 2001, 74). There is ample evidence from other Romano-British towns for a protracted period of construction and reconstruction of their stone circuits, and we should not necessarily assume that building the Exeter circuit was a quick event (Wacher 1998a). If a date at the start of the 3rd century AD for the Exeter wall proves to be correct, this would put it at the beginning of a date range for the masonry walls of other *civitas* capitals in Britain that spans much of that century (Millett 1990, 152–3). Covering an area of 37.5 ha, Exeter was the thirteenth-largest defended town in Britain.

Intensive research by Stuart Blaylock has refined our knowledge of the Roman wall as it was built (Blaylock 1995, fig. 10 maps the comparatively limited areas of surviving original facework; Northernhay, Southernhay and Quay Lane are the best surviving lengths: Fig. 7.6). The wall was built in three stages. First un-mortared clay-bonded footings were laid, partially or wholly, within a trench cutting the primary bank (these occasionally included sandstone river cobbles in addition to trap rubble); once fully above the top of that bank the rear of the wall was continued in un-faced mortared footings until properly faced work commenced. These three stages were approximately mirrored by stages in the deposition of the layers of the rampart heightening. At Paul Street (Site 76) it could be demonstrated that the building up of the rampart proceeded more or less simultaneously with that of the wall, thus providing easy access to the construction level (Blaylock 1988, 8). The wall was constructed from local volcanic trap, doubtless quarried from the Rougemont outcrop, although it was not until 2011 that excavations at Bradninch Place (Site 157) revealed two quarry pits infilled during the 3rd century AD, the first secure evidence for the quarrying of trap in Exeter in the Roman period (further evidence for Roman quarrying was also recovered from Site 193: Exeter Castle).

Typical Roman facework consists of coursed blocks, with a tendency for a lower section of deeper courses, followed by numerous courses of thinner blocks. There was a plinth at or near exterior ground level (Fig. 6.8). A break in build is sometimes observed 2.5–3.0 m above the plinth, represented by a change in colour and/or texture of the stone, and a repetition of two to three courses of deeper blocks at the base of the second build. Whether this represents a hiatus in construction or simply a change in the supply of materials, is unknown. Masonry coursed on a gradient (*i.e.* following the contour of the ground surface) seems to be another characteristic of Roman work, and sometimes enables its identification (Blaylock 2015b, 2). The wall had a mortared rubble core, often set in alternating diagonally-pitched (herringbone) courses, which in the sector between the South Gate and the river was formed from not only local trap but also numerous blocks of chert, the closest sources for which are the gravels of the Haldon Hills south of Exeter and the Blackdown Hills to the east (Blaylock 1993, 3; 1995, 109). A mortar-mixing pit was found dug into the surface of the tail of the early rampart bank at Cricklepit Street (Site 48; Bidwell 1980, fig. 33). Overall the wall was about 3 m wide at the base, narrowing to *c.* 2.0–2.25 m at the top. A wall-walk at least 4.5 m, and probably 5 m, above ground level is suggested by the combined evidence from Lower Coombe Street and Northernhay Gardens. The rear face was constructed in a series of steps by which the wall was narrowed (Fig. 6.9). There is no evidence for a regular system of masonry towers, although a rectangular tower, 6.5 m × 3.3 m internally, was added to the back of the wall at Paul Street

Fig. 6.8 Roman plinth and facework to full height of the City Wall in Quay Lane (photo by Gary Young; © Exeter City Council)

Fig. 6.9 Roman rear facework and footings of the inside face of the City Wall in South Street/Western Way (photo by Gary Young; © Exeter City Council)

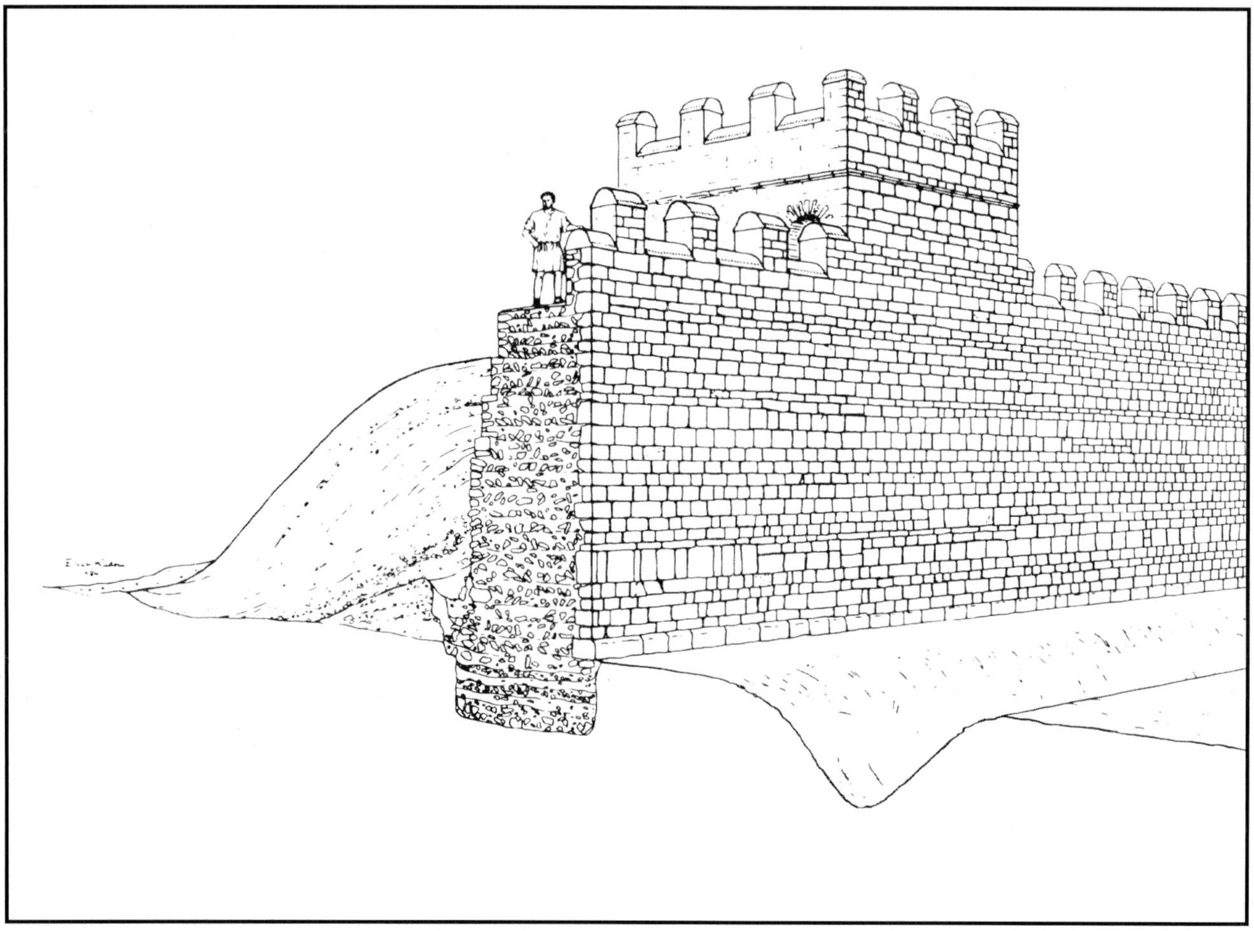

Fig. 6.10 Reconstruction of the City Wall and internal tower at Paul Street (Site 76) as envisaged by Christopher Henderson and drawn by Erich Kadow (© Exeter City Council)

(Site 76; Fig. 6.10). The surviving projecting semicircular towers on the wall all appear to be post-Roman additions (Blaylock 1995).

It is reasonably assumed that the Roman town was equipped with four principal gates on the sites later occupied by their medieval successors, although we should be mindful that Roman fabric has only been firmly identified at the South Gate in 1964–5 and 1989 (Sites 36 and 96). Here the Roman masonry gate was built flush with the face of the stone curtain wall, which abutted it, and thus lay about 7 m in advance of its timber predecessor (Fig. 6.11). It is unclear if the gate had a single or double portal and only one of the flanking towers has been seen, 5.1 m wide externally and 5.0–5.35 m deep (Fig. 6.12). Given that the gate is structurally earlier than the curtain wall it is conceivable that it replaced the timber one during the life of the earthwork defences, an association found at Cirencester, Silchester and *Verulamium*, although it is also possible that the gate could just represent the first stage in the construction sequence of the masonry defences (Frere 1983b, 34–5; Fulford 1984, 55; Wacher 1998b, 37–46, 96). The presence of other minor postern gates on the circuit cannot be discounted although there is no evidence for a Roman precursor to the Watergate built in 1564–5 at the southern corner of the town. Excavations at Exeter Quay (Site 112) below the Watergate showed that there was no suburban activity here before the Elizabethan period. Any Roman quays or jetties would have lain further upstream (Blaylock 1995, 2), but these would only have been for small vessels as sea-going craft unloaded at Topsham, 6 km further downstream, their cargoes reaching the town by either flat-bottomed barge or by road (Jackson 1972; Brown 2019, 2).

There has been only limited investigation of the Roman ditch system in front of the wall, due in large measure to the extensive remodelling of this area in the medieval and (especially) Civil War periods. The more naturally defensible sections of the defences may not have required ditches, but they certainly existed on the north-east and south-east sides where the approaches are level. The most instructive investigation occurred at Princesshay (Site 156), adjacent to the East Gate, where the lines of three, apparently contemporary, extra-mural Roman ditches were traced at distances of 13 m, 28 m and 39 m out from the face of the wall (Chapter 8 below, Fig. 8.3). The inner ditch was the least understood, as it was largely removed

Fig. 6.11 Reconstruction of the South Gate of the Roman town as envisaged by Christopher Henderson and drawn by Piran Bishop (© RAMM)

Fig. 6.12 The footings of the South-West tower of the Roman South Gate built at the start of the 3rd century AD, as exposed in excavations in 1989 (Site 96) (© Exeter City Council)

by later recutting; the middle ditch was 3 m deep and the outer ditch *c.* 4.5 m deep. The other notable investigation of the ditch system took place in the vicinity of the South Gate where a ditch was found at a distance of 25–28 m from the face of the wall which appears to have been infilled in the 3rd century AD (Sites 58 and 88). There would doubtless have been another ditch nearer the wall here, but all trace of it had been destroyed by later activity. Bidwell (1980, 64–5, fig. 36) raised the possibility that two 4th-century AD ditches might have been added in this area, but the one 44 m out from the wall might in fact be of Saxo-Norman date (unless it was a comprehensive recutting of the outer ditch found at Princesshay) while the other at 81 m from the wall is probably too distant to have formed part of the defences.

Deep shear cracks are visible in the core of the wall between Rougemont and Paul Street where parts of the wall have tilted forward. At Paul Street (Site 76) it was demonstrated that this movement took place during the course of construction, and the source of this instability is doubtless a consequence of building the wall on top of the first bank without deeper foundations beneath the rear face. A more drastic example of instability has been found at Cricklepit Street (Site 81), where excavations in 1988–9 showed that a length of the wall, here built on a steep slope, had collapsed and had been rebuilt 1.5 m further back, although it is not clear whether this occurred during the Late Roman period or subsequently (Simpson 1993b, 7). In this case the failure of the wall can be ascribed to the backing up behind it of water from the Coombe Stream, which rises in the grounds of the Bishop's Palace and flowed in a valley now submerged beneath the modern townscape (Fig. 6.6; investigations at 5–7 Palace Gate (Site 106) in the upper part of the valley found natural silts overlaid by deposits containing Early Roman pottery). Little else can be said about the fate of the defences in the Late Roman period due to subsequent remodelling. John Leland noted two Roman inscriptions built into the walls near Southernhay in 1542 but we cannot know whether this reuse of spolia took place in the Late Roman or post-Roman period (Leland Itineraries III. fo. 33; Toulmin Smith 1964, 228). The apparent absence of projecting towers, which in some other towns typically date to around the middle of the 4th century AD, occasions little surprise and need not imply any lack of importance or wealth in Exeter at this time.

Urban development

As far as we can tell the process by which urban fabric filled the newly-enclosed area was gradual rather than sudden. The new earthwork defences, initially at least, seem to have enclosed considerable tracts of undeveloped land, although the storage of agricultural produce or the shelter of livestock in these areas might leave little archaeological trace. Despite the infilling of the now abandoned defensive ditch around the early town, the zone occupied by the former defences remained largely undeveloped and there does not appear to have been a comprehensive and systematic attempt to level and consolidate this area ready for new construction. For instance at Mermaid Yard (Site 63) the legionary rampart still stood 0.9 m high after demolition and a section across the ditch at Rack Street (Site 52) showed that its late Antonine filling had subsided gradually over a period of about a century. A similar situation pertained at St Catherine's Almshouses where a corridor mosaic of late 3rd or early 4th-century AD town house 30ii had subsided by 0.4 m where it overlay the uncompacted fills of the old ditch (Fig 6.15).

The newly enclosed area may have been less rigorously divided into *insulae* than previously supposed (compare Fig. 6.7 with Bidwell 1980, fig. 37) and the extension of the street system seems have been a protracted process rather than a single event. Naturally the principal streets leading to the gates would have been established at the same time as the defences, and in most cases this would have involved little more than minor alterations to the alignment of existing extra-mural roads (as has been shown at the South Gate: Sites 58 and 88). The site adopted for the West Gate would have been determined by the course of the existing road leading down to the crossing of the Exe and in consequence there was no major street leading directly from the East Gate to the West Gate. Some of the streets of the early town were maintained in the later Roman period. In several places two or three resurfacings occurred during the life of the early town (as for instance at Street observations B3i, B4i, G2i and I1i), most usually formed from gravel or river cobbles. Later metallings were frequently formed from fragments of trap which could date to the time of the construction of the city wall when there would have been plenty of waste from the dressing of the facing stones. If that association holds true then the presence of trap fragments in a resurfacing of the *via sagularis* at observation B3i could suggest that this section of the street was maintained into the 3rd century AD rather than going out of use as soon as the town was enlarged. Volcanic chippings were also recovered from Street A which ran along the outer edge of the ditch at Paul Street (see above); perhaps part of this street was also somewhat later than has been previously supposed? In one location a timber building (18i) defined by four post-pits had encroached upon the line of Street D, which indicates a not particularly rigorous enforcement of the public realm hereabouts, a rare occurrence in Early Roman towns.

When the town was enlarged at the start of the 3rd century AD some remodelling of the street system inevitably occurred (for instance it is possible that it was at this time that the street separating *insulae* IV and V was removed to create a single large *insula*; EAPIT 2, Chapter 5). But other elements of urban fabric were introduced on a more piecemeal basis. At Princesshay the former extra-mural road was replaced by a new street which contained a large quantity of volcanic trap fragments in its make-up and so is more likely to be contemporary with the construction of the city wall rather than the earthwork defences (Street observation J1ii). But the street did not survive and in the late 3rd century AD masonry houses were built across its line. New Streets L and M were created a short distance beyond the infilled ditch, although Street M was not constructed before *c*. AD 275 (Street observation M3ii; EAPIT 2, Chapter 8), a century after the establishment of the earthwork defences. At Paul Street a track or street (Street N) was found immediately to the rear of the rampart bank of the town defences, but this is the only place it has been found and it may have been quite short lived (Street observation N1ii).

At Market Street the full sequence of four successive surfaces of Street E was revealed, 0.7 m thick in all (Street observation E4i/ii). The uppermost two surfaces dated to after the mid 2nd century AD. This must testify to a good degree of traffic and wear along the street, and equally to continued investment in maintenance and repair. Some streets clearly fell out of use during the later Roman period, however. The south-west end of Street C had been built over at Friernhay Street (Site 75) by the 4th century AD while the courses of Streets A, I and J had been obliterated at certain points at least by the construction of masonry houses 30ii, 27ii and 45ii/58ii respectively (the construction of the former building dates to the late 3rd or early 4th century AD; the others are not well dated).

We have little useful evidence for how long the street system was maintained in Exeter. Street E adjacent to the forum, and thus at the very heart of the town, was resurfaced on multiple occasions. The last surface before the rebuilding of the basilica in the second or third quarter of the 3rd century AD was deeply rutted and the mud which had accumulated on its surface had been piled against a boundary wall. Later surfaces were not rutted but were covered with silt or mud which was not cleared away before further resurfacings which may have been little more than footpaths along one side of the street (Bidwell 1979, 103). A similar sequence of thick deposits of soft brown silt capped with thin gravel surfaces was also apparent in a section across Street G at 45–6 North Street (observation G1i). Street E near the forum was finally at least partially blocked by a wall, although the date of this event is uncertain (Street observation E2ii; see Appendix 6.1). The reason for this restriction or total blocking of a major street in the centre of the town is hard to discern, although a not dissimilar action occurred in the street to the rear of the basilica in Cirencester in the later 4th century AD (Holbrook and Timby 1998a, 109–10).

Public buildings and infrastructure

Our best evidence for the later history of the public buildings of Exeter derives from the excavations of the basilica and forum. Paul Bidwell has reconsidered the evidence which underpinned the structural sequence proposed in his 1979 excavation report (Bidwell 1979), and he now suggests a modified, but in some respects simpler, sequence (Fig. 6.13). His detailed arguments are presented in Appendix 6.1. The range of rooms on the south-east side of the forum piazza was remodelled sometime after *c.* AD 150 (Bidwell Period 2B), but in his reappraisal he now suggests that his former Periods 2C and 3A can be amalgamated into a single, but substantial, episode of rebuilding which can be dated to the second or third quarter of the 3rd century AD. This involved the extension to the south-east of the basilican hall across the site of the demolished rooms which served to increase the length of the room identified as the council chamber. A structure which might have functioned as a tribunal was added next to it. A room equipped with a channelled hypocaust was inserted into the south-east forum range and the adjoining street was covered with a thick layer of ceramic tiles and wall plaster, doubtless stripped from the building prior to its re-roofing with stone rather than ceramic tiles. In Bidwell's original (1979) chronology the extension to the basilica was dated to after *c.* AD 340/50 (his Period 3A), and this reconstruction has been remarked upon by some commentators as a notably late incidence of the refurbishment of a basilica in Britain, and thus by inference the continued use of the building for civic functions (*e.g.* Esmonde Cleary 1989, 71).

The revised scheme, however, now potentially brings Exeter more into line with the evidence from other western towns where there is good evidence for either the total dereliction of the forum-basilica complex, or else use for very different functions, in the 4th century AD (Esmonde Cleary 1989, 71; Rogers 2011, 75–83, 130–4). At Caerwent, for example, around AD 340–50 some of the basilica floors were removed and the nave taken up by numerous metalworking hearths, perhaps for the production of nails. The building was systematically levelled 20–30 years later (Brewer 2006, 43). At Wroxeter the forum-basilica complex burnt down in the late 3rd or early 4th century AD. The basilica does not seem on face value to have been rebuilt although the forum courtyard was retained (Atkinson 1942, 105–7; White and Barker 1998, 112; White *et al.* 2013, 205). Unfortunately we know very little about the history of the Exeter complex in the second half of the 4th century AD. The hypocaust within one of the rooms flanking the piazza was demolished after *c.* AD 340, an event that seems to have occurred before the final demolition of the complex and the systematic removal of debris from the site, although for what purpose we cannot say. A new floor within the basilica appeared to seal a well-circulated coin minted between AD 365–78, but doubt attaches to the evidential weight that can be placed on this coin as it was recovered from the cleaning of the grave cut of a post-Roman burial dug through this floor level and could thus be intrusive (Bidwell 1979, 109). The clearance of the basilica site had been completed before a cemetery was established on the site at some point between the 5th and 7th centuries AD (see Chapter 7).

We have no knowledge of the date of construction of the public baths, but by inference the late 1st or first half of the 2nd century AD is plausible. Fragmentary evidence indicates rebuilding of some description around or after AD 200. Pottery and a coin from a major outfall drain and the infilling of the open-air swimming pool suggest the baths fell into disuse at some point from the late 3rd century AD onwards (Bidwell 1979, 121–3). Where our evidence is of sufficient quality, the public baths in the major towns of Roman Britain were mostly maintained in use well into the 4th century AD, as for instance at Dorchester and Wroxeter (White and Barker 1998, 112–15; Ellis 2000, 75–7; Putnam 2007, 70–1; Rogers 2011, 83–9). We lack evidence for other public buildings in Exeter, but that is not to say they did not exist. At Friernhay Street (Site 75) a substantial 4th-century AD boundary wall defined the corner of an enclosed space (at least 28 m long on the north-west/south-east axis, and 17 m on the other). The latter wall was also identified at St Nicholas Priory (Site 109) which would extend the length to in excess of *c.* 60 m on the north-east/south-west axis. This wall might have defined the *temenos* (sacred enclosure) around a temple, perhaps of the Romano-Celtic form found at some other towns in western Britain such as Caerwent, Carmarthen and Wroxeter, even though they lay outside the main distribution of these structures (Smith 2018a, fig. 5.10).

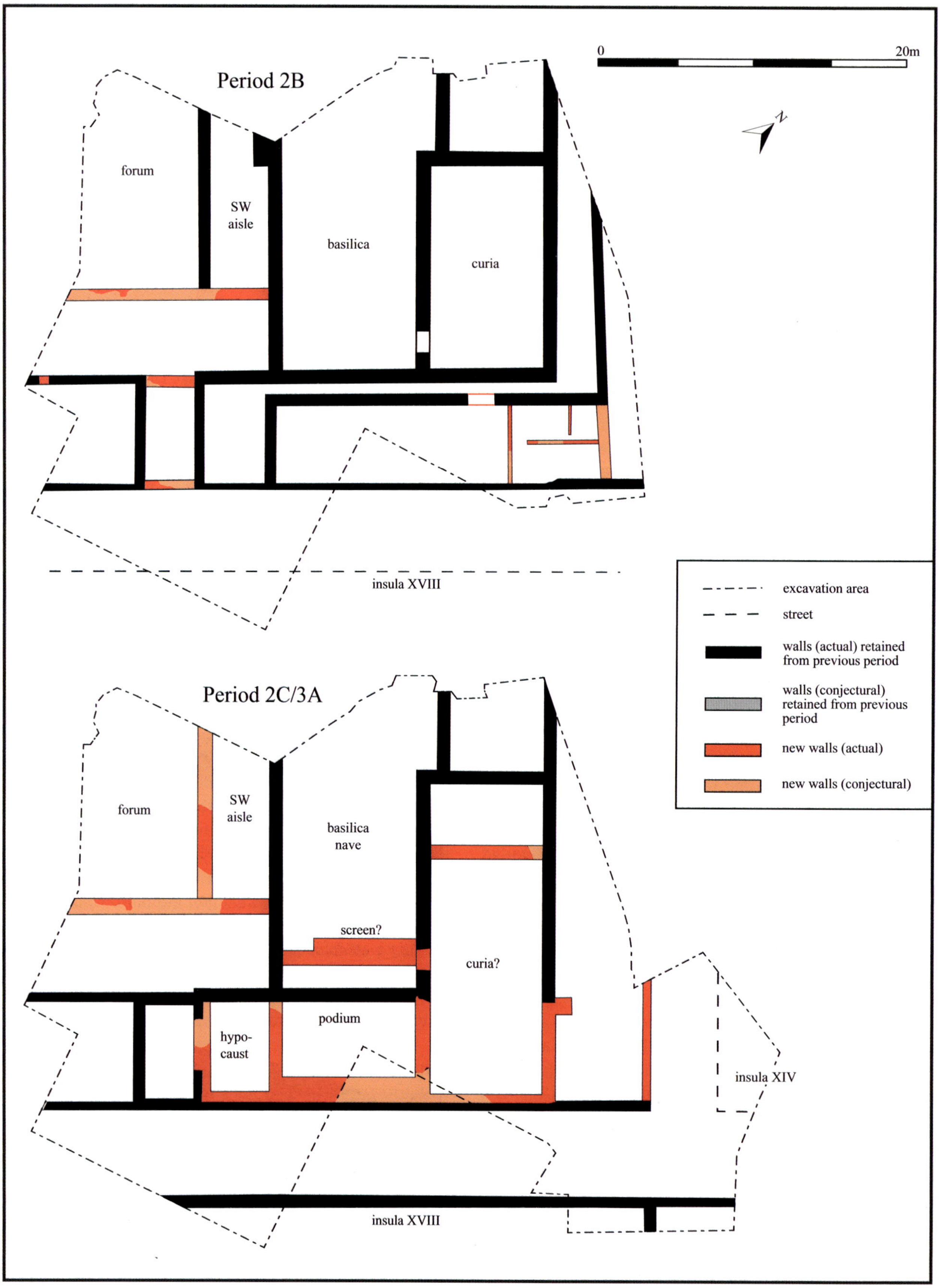

Fig. 6.13 A revised structural sequence for the basilica (drawn by David Gould)

Urban layout and private housing

Appreciation of the structural and spatial sequence of urban development can only be ascertained where investigation has taken place on a reasonable scale and in a modern city such opportunities are a rarity. Three excavations can, however, be selected to illustrate the processes of urban development in Exeter. The first, Trichay Street (Site 42; EAPIT 2, Chapter 5), lay within the bounds of the early town; the other two (Princesshay and Rack Street; Sites 156, 52/64; for the latter see EAPIT 2, Chapter 8) within the area enclosed by the expanded defences after *c.* AD 160–80. At Trichay Street, as we have seen, two *insulae* (IV and V) were merged into one by the suppression of a street in the second half of the 2nd century AD (the date of this event is imprecisely known and it might have been associated with the construction of the expanded circuit of earthwork defences).

Amalgamation of *insulae* is difficult to parallel in Roman Britain, even at towns unencumbered by later development where the disposition of streets and masonry buildings is tolerably well known from aerial photography and geophysical survey. That it occurred in Exeter does suggest a lack of pressure or desire to develop the street frontages, and perhaps the larger area in the middle of the newly formed *insula* lent itself more conveniently to functions such as horticulture or stock rearing. Two buildings were arranged on either side of a yard by the 3rd century AD. Building 11ii (Fig. 6.14) was of part-timber, part-stone construction with an apsidal masonry reception room at one end of the house and a small heated chamber at the other. The buildings did not face onto the street, and indeed Building 10ii was purposely separated from the public thoroughfare by a wooden fence. This deliberate partition of presumably private land from public streets has also been found elsewhere in Exeter (at Princesshay and Rack Street discussed below, and at Friernhay Street (Site 75) in *insula* VI where a wooden fence bordered the junction of two streets). Perhaps these fences and walls testify to the need to contain animals and prevent them from straying into the streets? The 3rd-century AD arrangement at Trichay Street was swept away at some date between the mid 3rd and mid 4th century AD to be replaced by a masonry courtyard house 14ii (Fig. 6.14) built on an appreciably grander scale than the earlier structures.

At Princesshay an extra-mural road was replaced around the same time as the town wall was built by a new street J which was flanked by a substantial wooden fence, but there were no buildings within the excavation area at this time. The street was abandoned in the late 3rd century AD when a short-lived timber building and then two masonry ones (Buildings 45ii and 58ii; Fig. 6.14) were built over its former course. At Rack Street fragmentary traces of possible timber buildings overlay the backfilled ditch of the early town defences, before a new street was laid out in the late 3rd or early 4th century AD flanked on one side by timber buildings of rectilinear plan. They were replaced by a row of three stone rectangular structures (Buildings 48ii, 49ii and 50ii) on one side of the street, with another building (31ii) on the opposite side, although a good length of that frontage was separated from the interior of the *insula* by a fence (later replaced by a stone wall). This separation of the interiors of certain *insulae* from their street frontages is not peculiar to Exeter. At Silchester Fulford (2011, 326) comments on the inward-looking character of *insula* IX in the 2nd century AD where a sturdy fence performed a similar function.

It is unfortunate that the frontage of the main street leading from the East Gate to the forum (Street D) has seen very little archaeological investigation, as where a major road passed through a town, as for instance the course of Watling Street through London and Wroxeter, Ermin Street through Silchester, or the road to Caerleon through Caerwent, there is plentiful evidence for rectangular *tabernae*-type structures (strip buildings presumed to have functioned as shops or workshops; MacMahon 2003), built end-on to the street to service the demands of passing trade. In Exeter later Roman *tabernae*-type structures have only been confidently identified at Rack Street, as just described. One of these buildings (49ii) contained several ovens, and the absence of slag suggests a function associated with food preparation.

The focus of attention in previous excavations has naturally enough been on structures, but the areas around buildings can provide valuable evidence on the functions that were being carried out in these spaces. The distribution of wells, for instance, can provide insights into how families or social groups inhabiting various parts of the town acquired their water. In Exeter wells have not to date been commonly encountered in excavations, perhaps a consequence of that lack of investigation of open areas between buildings. Three late 1st or earlier 2nd-century AD wells were found adjacent to Street F in *insula* IV at Trichay Street (Site 42; EAPIT 2, Chapter 5). They might have been dug before piped water was brought into the town *c.* AD 100/101. Beyond this the record is meagre with only four certainly Roman wells (Sites 3, 68, 105 and 156) and one possibly of this date (Site 115) so far revealed. That at the Cathedral Close (Site 105) was infilled in the mid 2nd century AD, Queen Street (Site 68) in the late 2nd century AD, and Princesshay (Site 156) in the 3rd century AD. Late Roman wells have to date only been found in the suburb outside the South Gate at Holloway Street and Friars Gate (Sites 45 and 65). Perhaps there were public wells serving the population living within the walls at this time, while the suburban dwellers drew water from wells located within their properties?

Another example of the value of examining the area around buildings comes from Trichay Street where the area to the rear of a wing of a masonry courtyard house was utilised as a stockyard: a layer of dirty trample, presumably from the hooves of animals, overlay a

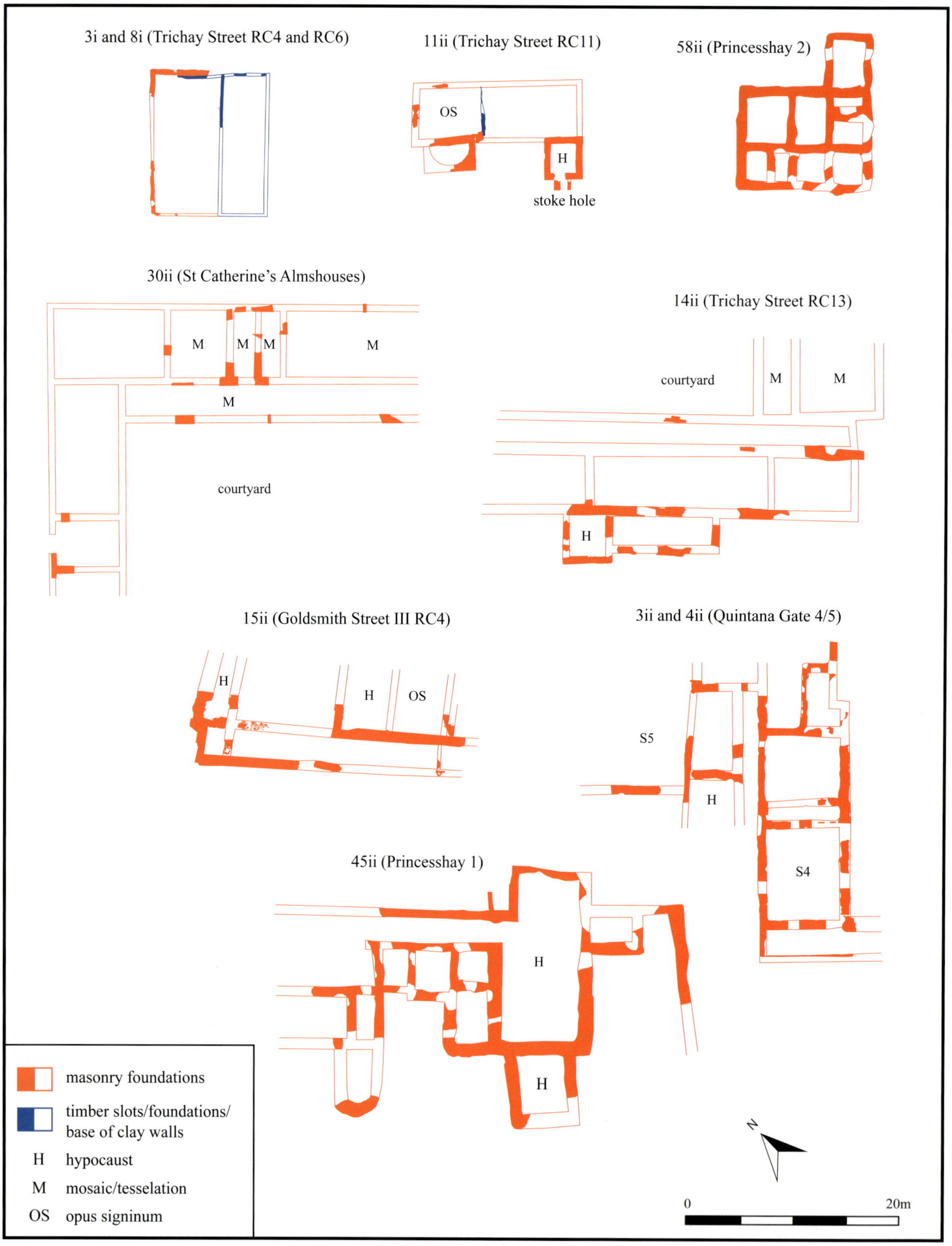

Fig. 6.14 Plans of private buildings in Roman Exeter: for Building Numbers see EAPIT 2, Chapter 3.3 (drawn by David Gould)

metalled surface which contained a water trough fed by a pipe (EAPIT 2, Chapter 5). An associated timber building (9ii) is of uncertain function but gives no indication that it was used as a house. The yard dates to the mid to late 4th century AD and provides valuable evidence for the keeping of stock in the heart of the town in the Late Roman period. Nearby a series of small ditched enclosures were also presumably used for the control of livestock. The backfill of two of these ditches contained discrete dumps of discarded butchery waste composed of fragmented cattle skulls and jaw bones (Site 52; Maltby 1979, 12, 30). Pigs were reared in the town to judge from neonate bones from Princesshay and piglets at Cathedral Close (Sites 156 and 40; Maltby below). At Princesshay a small building (58ii; Fig. 6.14) was built hard-up against the back of the rampart of the city wall in the later 3rd or 4th century AD. This peripheral location suggests that much of the land within the town was now under private ownership, even if not necessarily developed with buildings. That said, the great majority of excavations within the circuit of the Roman town have encountered one or more robber trenches for stone walls (either parts of buildings or boundaries) which points to a reasonably well-developed urban space. The valley of the Coombe Stream is, however, notable for its absence of building remains in the area immediately to the rear of the town defences (Site 97: Lower Coombe Street). Instead this area was occupied by a ditched enclosure, presumably for some manner of agricultural activity, and an accumulation of colluvium up to 1 m thick that covered the floor of the valley and spread up its sides. It must denote cultivation nearby and was covered by a Late Roman clay loam cultivation soil, up to 1.3 m thick, at the base of the valley.

The 3rd-century AD Building 11ii at Trichay Street mentioned above displays a level of architectural pretension beyond the functional timber strip and rectilinear buildings found in the town in the 2nd century AD. There are, however, only a very few complete or near complete plans of stone houses known from the whole town, although as far as we can tell they seem to fit into the normal provincial milieu for such structures: rectangular blocks with longitudinal and transverse corridors, often arranged in either an L-shaped or courtyard disposition (Fig. 6.14). The fullest house plans are those found in *insulae* IV/V (Building 14ii), XIV/XXII (Building 30ii) and XXVIII/XXIX (Buildings 45ii and 58ii). Given this fragmentary evidence little can usefully be said about the size of domestic buildings, although if the structures grouped as Building 14ii were indeed parts of a single house (which is by no means assured) then this indicates a sizeable courtyard house comparable with some of the larger houses at Caerwent for example (the reconstructed dimensions of the Exeter house of 60 m by 45 m compare with House 2s at Caerwent which covered an area of 76 m by 36 m; Ashby *et al.* 1902, 121–37; EAPIT 2, Chapter 5). The overall provincial urban trend for houses to become larger in the later Roman period compared to those of the 1st and 2nd centuries AD is probably represented at Exeter as well. At Princesshay two rooms of Building 45ii were equipped with channelled hypocausts and formed a single interconnected space as the party wall between them probably only supported rebates for a wide opening. The smaller room probably served as a winter dining-room with the framed opening providing diners with a view into the larger room which was furnished with painted wall plaster, almost certainly a mosaic floor and doubtless other movable fittings. As such this house fits into a tradition of later Roman bipartite dining-rooms (*triclinia*) and by Exeter standards was built on some scale (Cosh 2001, 233–6).

Later 2nd-century AD Building 37ii is the earliest example of a masonry house in Exeter for which we have reasonable dating evidence and stone became the dominant material for domestic structures in the later Roman period, although timber was still used (as for instance in the late 3rd or early 4th-century AD buildings 47ii at Rack Street; Site 64, EAPIT 2, Chapter 8). Whether the walls of the masonry houses were fully of stone construction or had part-timber superstructures is unknown. Another architectural development which began in the later 2nd century AD is the introduction of stone roofing tiles in preference to ceramic ones; by the 4th century AD stone was the predominant roofing material to judge from the evidence of roof falls at Buildings 14ii and 48–9ii. The stone tiles in Exeter came largely from the slate-beds of South Devon, although Somerset White Lias was also used (see below). This trend is recognised across much of Roman Britain and was a product of changing fashions as well as economic considerations (perhaps to do with the localised depletion of fuel sources to fire tile kilns; Warry 2006, 134). The Exeter ceramic tile industry declined considerably in the 3rd century AD and the Princesshay industry may have closed altogether following the incorporation of at least part of the brickworks within the area enclosed by the town defences. Warry dates the end of local tile production to around the mid 3rd century AD, the latest products found in the town falling within his Central Grouping of unknown source (EAPIT 2, Chapter 13.3). Some masonry houses were furnished with hypocausts of both the *pila* and channelled variety, although it is telling that the hypocaust within Building 4ii was made from reused tiles, and the *pilae* of a hypocaust in the 4th-century Building 14ii were formed from mortared cobbles rather than ceramic tiles, which further suggests that such tiles were not easily obtained locally at this time. No domestic bath suites are known in Exeter, although they presumably existed (the fragmentary apsidal rooms known from Buildings 41ii and 45ii (Fig. 6.14) could have been part of such suites).

The use of brick mortar (*opus signinum*) as a flooring material is reasonably well attested in the town from the 2nd century AD onwards (as for instance in 2nd-century AD timber Building 9i at Goldsmith Street Area III) but was more widely used in the later Roman period. Parts of eight *in situ* mosaics are known from Exeter, four of them from house 30ii at St Catherine's Almshouses, as well as quantities of loose tesserae which demonstrate the former existence of such pavements in other houses such as 45ii. This is a poor showing compared to some other towns, although the history of excavation and later history in different places means that valid comparisons can only be drawn at the most general level. For instance, while only 11 mosaics are known from Wroxeter, there are 41 from Gloucester, 59 from Caerwent and 63 from each of Cirencester and Dorchester (Cosh and Neal 2005; 2010). Bidwell (1980, 79, n. 3) related the paucity of mosaics from Exeter to the extent of disturbance of Late Roman levels by medieval and post-medieval activities. Whilst the detrimental impact of later activities undoubtedly impacts the coherence of later Roman levels, it is hard to escape the conclusion that mosaics were not as common in Exeter as at many other British towns. Cosh and Neal (2005, 55) concluded 'The paucity of mosaics in Exeter and their generally low standard of workmanship may indicate a lack of wealth' although cultural factors are a more likely explanation: the citizens of Exeter, like those of towns such as York (a later Roman provincial capital with only nine mosaics known; Neal and Cosh 2002) chose not to express their wealth through this medium (and see Chapter 3 above for a broader discussion of Dumnonian identity).

The earliest evidence for the mosaic craft in Exeter (beyond the fragments from the legionary bath-house) is a pile of unused black and white tesserae from 2nd-century AD timber Building 9i at Goldsmith Street Area III. They were probably destined for use in another building. All of the *in situ* Exeter mosaics were of geometric design and date to the Late Roman period (construction of Building 30ii at St Catherine's Almshouses dates to the late 3rd or early 4th century AD, although the corridor mosaic (Cosh and Neal 2005, cat. no. 157.7; Fig. 6.15) is clearly a later addition). None of the mosaics from the town fit comfortably into the established mosaic groupings (so-called schools) of south-western Britain, despite two of them being centred around Dorchester and Ilchester, and the corridor mosaic in Building 30ii has no very close parallel with any other Romano-British mosaic. Cosh and Neal do, however, consider that it is not inconceivable that the same craftsman may have been responsible both for a mosaic from Pancras Lane in Exeter (cat. no. 157.1; Fig. 6.16) and one from Dorchester (cat. no. 165.34).

Painted wall plaster provides another expression of domestic art. Whilst fragments of such plaster are common enough in later Roman levels, we can rarely say much about the design and schemes used. Plaster from Building

Fig. 6.15 The corridor mosaic within Building 30ii revealed in excavations at St Catherine's Almshouses in 1987–8 (Site 89; for a plan see Fig. 6.14). The centre of the mosaic has subsided markedly as it overlay the uncompacted fills of the defensive ditch surrounding the early town (© Exeter City Council)

45ii at Princesshay included a fragment with an image of a bird, the only faunal painted plaster image known from Exeter, while another scheme possibly included human figures. Otherwise a variety of geometric schemes and imitation marble dados are represented. The record of Romano-British sculpture from the town is also slight, but Exeter is far from alone in this. A small marble human head was doubtless an import into the province from the Mediterranean. It perhaps came from a memorial bust set up within a private house or tomb and was several centuries old when it was finally deposited into the ground (Holbrook and Bidwell 1991, 230–1; Henig 1993, pl. 61). We know very little about domestic fixtures and fittings, furniture or lighting.

Suburban activity

Extra-mural areas beyond the town defences have been relatively little explored, especially in the vicinity of the roads leading from the principal gates where activity is

Fig. 6.16 Drawing of the corridor mosaic discovered in Pancras Lane in 1887 which may have been part of Building 14ii (© The Trustees of the Devon and Exeter Institution)

most likely to be encountered. Best known is the area outside the South Gate along the road to Topsham where 4th-century AD pits and wells attest to continuing activity in the backlands, and by inference on the road frontage also (Site 50: Holloway Street; Site 45: Friars Gate; Site 46: Friars Walk; Site 44: Valiant Soldier). The 2nd-century AD road which branched off the Topsham road went out of use in the later Roman period and Henderson postulated the existence of another suburban road to replace it. This he considered to have spurred off the Topsham road immediately outside the South Gate to follow a course now represented in the modern streetscape by Magdalen Street to join the road to Woodbury, in Axminster, to the north-east of the town. There is little actual evidence for this road (it is inferred from a slight narrowing in the width of a defensive ditch near to the gate; Site 88) and its existence must for now be regarded as conjectural (Henderson 2001, 65, fig. 4, periods 4 and 5). Beyond the North Gate on the steep slope of the Longbrook Valley a small timber building at Exe Street (Site 83) dated to the later 2nd century AD. A solitary 2nd or 3rd-century AD inhumation was found on the lower slopes of the valley, and in the 3rd century AD layers of clay with occasional lenses of domestic rubbish were tipped down the hillside, accumulating to a depth of 2 m at one point. Perhaps these were a product of periodic cleaning out of the defensive ditch outside the wall?

We have no significant information for activities beyond the East and West Gates, but we can be reasonably confident that Exeter lacks the extensive later Roman inhumation cemeteries known at towns such as Dorchester, Ilchester, Gloucester and Cirencester. In this regard it invites comparison with the other towns of western and northern Britain such as Caerwent, Carmarthen and Wroxeter where these so-called managed cemeteries have not so far been encountered. While the acidic subsoil of Exeter is not conducive to the preservation of human or animal bone, except in places such as the Cathedral Close where the burial environment is largely a product of anthropogenic processes, grave cuts would surely have been recognised more frequently in excavations if extensive cemeteries had once existed. That said, a lack of surviving skeletal remains and a paucity of grave goods (including urned cremation burials) might account for the sparse records of such finds when the suburbs of Exeter were under construction in the 18th and 19th centuries (Goodchild 1952, 103–4). Burial is not entirely unknown, however, as grave cuts, some containing iron nails from wooden coffins, have been revealed in a couple of controlled excavations. Outside the South Gate only a scatter of graves is so far known (Bidwell 1980, fig. 36; Site 44: Valiant Soldier) while beyond the North Gate the isolated burial at Exe Street has already been noted (a further two graves were found further out in the base of the Longbrook Valley at 28/9 Lower North Street: Site 159). These burials sit comfortably within the pattern of rural dispersed inhumation burial found over large swathes of the province and locally at St Loye's College and Topsham (see below; Smith 2018b, 216–26).

As discussed above an Early Roman cemetery can be reasonably be inferred in St David's based on antiquarian finds, and recent work has demonstrated that the area was also utilised for burial in the later Roman period. A 6 m-square ditched enclosure at Mount Dinham (Site 154) contained a 1.8 m-long shallow depression at its centre which contained some charcoal and burnt bone (not certainly human) in the backfill. The ditch contained late 2nd or 3rd-century AD pottery, plaster and mortar, and its sloping profile demonstrates that it was indeed an open ditch rather than a robber trench for a masonry wall. This funerary enclosure invites comparison with similar Late Roman monuments known from Dorchester and Winchester for example, and more locally at Kenn, 7 km from Exeter, although there the cemetery dated to the 5th to 8th centuries AD (Weddell 2000; Pearce 2015, 159–60).

The latest Roman sequence

Bronze coins are not as plentiful as site finds in Exeter as at some other towns of Roman Britain, which combined with a low representation of Late Roman fine ware pottery hinders attempts to refine the chronology of late 4th-century and early 5th-century AD deposits (EAPIT 2, Chapter 16). To judge from coin finds, occupation was reasonably extensive within the walled area into the second half of the 4th century AD, although occupation outside of the South Gate either contracted or ceased altogether by *c.* AD 360 (Holbrook and Bidwell 1991, 11–14). The Exeter coin list is characterised by only a single issue of the House of Theodosius (minted AD 388–402; Reece period 21), the latest low denomination coins to reach Britain. This came from 196–7 High Street (Site 43) in the centre of the town, although unfortunately from a medieval deposit (Shiel 1991, coin cat. no. 402; EAPIT 2, Chapter 16). In 1991 Holbrook and Bidwell (1991, 11–13) showed that coins of the House of Valentinian (AD 364–78; Reece period 19) are abundant finds from within the walls and they considered that occupation was still widespread within the town in the third quarter of the 4th century AD. The relatively extensive excavations in the south-western half of the town, however, had failed to produce any artefacts that can be dated unequivocally to the last quarter of that century and they concluded that settlement had contracted towards the centre of the town by the closing decades of the 4th century AD and that while occupation continued here, other tracts within the walls were already in decline. Work subsequent to that discussed in 1991 has done little to amend the picture presented then. The extensive excavation at Princesshay (Site 156) on the periphery of the walled area produced 146 Roman coins, which included six issues of the House of Valentinian but none of the House of Theodosius. This also seems to have been the case at Quintana Gate (Site 169) in *insula* I where 51 coins were found including issues of the House of Valentinian but none of the House of Theodosius.

The pattern of some houses being abandoned during the second half of the 4th century AD, but not wholesale abandonment or depopulation, is one that finds reflection in some other British towns, although excavation needs to have been on a reasonable scale for reliable data to be gathered. At Winchester, for instance, abandonment of buildings is indicated at two major sites, although there was some continuing occupation and activity (Zant 1993; Ford and Teague 2011). At Chichester work in the north-west quadrant of the town also showed some houses to be in disrepair at this time (Down 1978, 81–3). But perceptions can change as more evidence accumulates. In London previous views of gradual decline from the late 3rd century AD onwards have been replaced by newer narratives that favour reasonably intense occupation until the early 5th century AD (Gerrard 2011; Hingley 2018, 221–9).

We are now in a position to better contextualise the scarcity of Theodosian bronze coins from Exeter as Moorhead and Walton (2014; and see EAPIT 2, Chapter 16) have shown that sites which have particular concentrations of these coins (whether hoards or site finds) frequently lie at nodal points in the road system in southern and eastern England and might be associated with an attempt by the Roman State to maintain links between Britain and the Rhineland. In the west the strong showing of these coins at towns such as Caerwent and Cirencester surely relates to the presence of State officials or soldiers. The paucity of Theodosian coins does therefore suggest that Exeter, along with certain other towns and villas in the west, became disassociated from the provincial monetary economy at the very end of the 4th century AD, but it is less easy to understand the causes behind this. Was it a product of a contraction of State control in Britain, or does it reflect more that by this time the population of Exeter was seriously diminished? Disassociation from the provincial economy might also be reinforced by the almost complete absence from the town and the South-West Peninsula of crossbow brooches and distinctive belt and buckle sets which denoted some manner of military or otherwise official status. Worrell and Pearce (2012, 383–93) recorded the known findspots up until 2011, and since then only two crossbow brooches have been recorded by the Portable Antiquities Scheme (PAS) for Devon: one from *c.* 300 m outside the South Gate of Exeter; ref: LEIC-EEE688) and one from South Brent, south of Dartmoor, a locality that has also produced Theodosian coinage (DEV-E1A6A8; Thomas 2018, 217, fig. 6.24; EAPIT 2, Chapter 16). We can also note the two buckle pins of 4th-century AD type recovered from excavations within Exeter (Allason-Jones 1991a, fig. 111, nos 44–5). These odd examples aside, if State officials or soldiers were present in Exeter at the end of the 4th or early 5th century AD in any numbers, their rank must have been denoted by some other means and they were not using bronze coinage.

While this lack of Theodosian coins makes dating of the latest Roman structures and deposits in Exeter especially difficult, the preservation of those deposits is in itself frequently poor given the detrimental effects of medieval pit digging and post-medieval terracing. At Goldsmith Street Area III (Site 39) for instance the vestiges of a Late Roman town house were found immediately below modern tarmac. Intact deposits associated with the demolition or decay of the latest Roman structures are a rarity in the town. The basilica and forum were systematically demolished and the building materials removed from the site, for reasons for which are as yet unknown, prior to the establishment of a cemetery at some point between the 5th and 7th century AD (Site 40). In a domestic context deposits of stone roofing tiles derived from the collapse or dismantlement of a roof are known from Trichay Street, Rack Street and St Catherine's Almshouses (Sites 42, 52/64 and 89). At Trichay Street (EAPIT 2, Chapter 5) a trample deposit in a yard adjacent to masonry house 14ii yielded one very worn issue of AD 363–7 and five others of the House of Constantine. Demolition deposits within the yard produced another coin of AD 364–7 while those within house 14ii seem to have been cut by a pit which yielded a quantity of cattle and sheep bones. A localised spread of oyster shells overlay the demolition materials. These deposits testify to some, seemingly low-intensity, activity on the site after the demolition of house 14ii, but before the accumulation of dark earth which yielded a coin of AD 387–8 as well as some clearly intrusive medieval pottery.

Demolition deposits from three *tabernae*-type structures at Rack Street (Buildings 48–50ii) yielded a latest coin of AD 350–60, while well-circulated coins of AD 364–7 and 367–75 and were retrieved from the overlying dark earth (EAPIT 2, Chapter 8). At St Catherine's Almshouses an occupation layer above a mosaic within Building 30ii yielded a latest coin of AD 350–60. This occupation was covered by a demolition deposit of stone roofing tiles which was in turn sealed by dark earth which also produced Falling Horseman copies of AD 350–60. The latest coin from the site was an issue of the House of Valentinian (AD 364–78). These coins only provide the earliest dates when these events could occur, but the lack of stratified issues of the Houses of Valentinian and Theodosius does contrast with certain other towns such as Cirencester and Gloucester where such coins are found sealed beneath the floors of Roman buildings (Holbrook and Timby 1998b, 244–5). For a later date to be accepted for these events in Exeter we would need to assume that there was a greater degree of residuality amongst the bronze coinage than at some other settlements, perhaps a consequence of an earlier cessation of coin supply linked to a declining integration with the provincial monetary economy.

Pottery provides little assistance in dating the final Roman activity as the latest South-East Dorset BB1 forms yet identified in Exeter seem to have appeared no later than the last quarter of the 4th century AD (squat bowl and cooking-pot types 21 and 47). Bidwell (2016) concludes that the importation of Dorset BB1 into Exeter probably did not cease before the end of the first quarter of the 5th century AD, and possibly somewhat later, given continued production of the fabric in Dorset into the 5th century. No distinctly 5th-century AD types can be identified in any type of pottery in Exeter, however, although production of outwardly 4th-century AD types may have continued beyond AD 400. This might have been the case with South Devon Ware, for instance, although the absence of this fabric from the mid–late 5th-century AD site at Bantham shows that production had ceased sometime before then (Reed *et al.* 2011). Eastern Mediterranean pottery, and to a lesser extent certain types of North African amphorae, were imported into other parts of the South-West Peninsula from *c.* AD 475–550 (Fig. 4.1 in Chapter 4), and Bidwell attributes their absence from Exeter not to chronology (*i.e.* there was no one living here at that time) but rather to the status of the settlement associated with the Cathedral Close burials (Chapter 7). This community need not necessarily have been integrated with the trade networks that led to the presence of these pottery imports at other sites in the Peninsula. Radiocarbon dating has yet to be applied in any systematic way to organic remains stratified in 'latest' Roman deposits, beyond the small number of dates retrieved from the post-Roman burials dug into the site of the abandoned basilica (EAPIT 2, Chapter 19). Whilst the radiocarbon calibration curve for the 5th and 6th centuries AD is far from helpful for the fine-grained chronological questions we want to ask, such an exercise is surely worth attempting on suitable organic samples (either on fresh deposits revealed in future investigations, or on animal bones retained from previous sites such as Trichay Street). While dates with calibrated ranges commencing in the mid 4th century AD will not tell us overly much, dates with ranges that lie fully in the 5th or 6th centuries AD would be instructive. In the current state of knowledge there is little more that can be usefully said about when a distinctly Romano-British urban culture came to an end in Exeter. Indeed just how 'urban' was Exeter in the second half of the 4th century?

Topsham and St Loye's College

The military origin of the Roman settlement at Topsham has been discussed in Chapter 5 with fortress-period timber strip buildings detected in excavations adjacent to the road to Exeter at the Aldi and Wessex Close sites. Topsham was the port of military and civilian Exeter, with imported goods transported to *Isca Dumnoniorum* 6 km upstream by either road or flat-bottomed barges. That Roman occupation continued in Topsham during the 2nd and 3rd centuries AD at least is not in question, although the form and nature of this activity is less clear. The consolidated Roman-period evidence of various archaeological investigations in and around Topsham is presented in Fig. 6.17 which builds upon an earlier collation of the evidence published in 2004 (Sage and Allan 2004, 32–6). The previous identification of a small fortlet defended by two parallel ditches has been made less convincing by a more recent sighting of one of the ditches which indicates a less regular defended circuit than would have been the norm with a fort or fortlet (Chapter 5). The ditches are not well dated and need not necessarily be contemporary with the period of 1st-century AD military occupation. Instead the ditches could relate to a civilian defensive system, either in a 1st-century AD context akin to those found at St Loye's College (and indeed conceivably part of a co-ordinated response to the same emergency) or alternatively date to the later 2nd-century AD when a number of roadside settlements were furnished with earthwork defences (Smith and Fulford 2019). We have little idea of the area protected by the defences. Sage and Allan (2004, 17) suggested that a narrow cut on the line occupied by modern Ashford Road might have defined the north-western limit of the defences, but Andrew Pye (pers. comm.) thinks that a more naturally defendable line would be along the crest above a coombe now marked by Hamilton Road, which would allow for a larger area than Allan and Sage suggested.

It is reasonably assumed that the Roman road from Exeter to Topsham is followed for much of its course by the modern road, although the Roman line diverged to the south as it approached the settlement itself, presumably to head down to harbour installations on the bank of the Exe. The excavators at Wessex Close thought the road lay to the north-east of the aisled building found there and that it was defined by a pair of ditches 8–9 m apart and a thin spread of gravel (Rainbird and Farnell 2019, 389). However the road may actually have lain to the south-west of that building which has the advantage of placing the 1st-century AD strip buildings found at the Aldi site on the road frontage rather than 65 m behind it. This would allow a 2nd-century AD ditch that cut across the frontages of those buildings and then extended into the M5 excavation area and Wessex Close to have defined the southern side of the road (Fig. 5.14).

To judge from the distribution of recorded finds it would seem the principal area of Roman settlement at Topsham lay between the Exe foreshore and the line of modern Exeter road, and thus on both sides of the Roman road. To date traces of Roman activity have been recorded in a zone *c.* 850 m long from north-west to south-east, and *c.* 300 m wide. The recovery of Roman building materials from multiple locations suggests that the settlement contained numerous structures. Topsham can therefore be considered to have been an agglomerated settlement focused around a harbour on the Exe foreshore capable of receiving ocean-going craft. A developed area in the order of 20–25 ha can be compared with the suggested 10 ha extent of the port settlement at Sea Mills on the north bank of the Bristol Avon (Ellis 1987, 103, 99–104).

Two excavations provide insights into the type of buildings present in Topsham. At Wessex Close, adjacent to the line of the road, Early Roman, possibly military period, field boundaries were superseded in the 2nd century AD by a masonry aisled building, 32 m long by 18 m wide (Fig. 6.18). Two successive ovens in the front aisle were used for the processing of spelt wheat and oats, and for the preparation of salted fish sauce (*allec*). A projecting entrance was subsequently added to the building, flanked by a pair of small square rooms, which faced towards to the estuary. A small part of a second building was examined to the south of the aisled building; it is suggested by the excavators to have been a detached bath-house, although the basis for this interpretation is not made clear in the report. The buildings sat within ditched enclosures and there is no evidence for the further development of the road frontage within the excavation site. Demolition levels from the building yielded a coin of AD 268–70 and activity on the site had largely ceased by the end of the first quarter of the 4th century AD (Rainbird and Farnell 2019). Aisled buildings which combined domestic accommodation with a variety of other functions (which here included ironworking, crop processing and fish sauce production) are a well-known feature of the countryside of Roman Britain at villas, farmsteads and nucleated settlements (for example in the latter category in western Britain at settlements such of Cheddar and Gatcombe, both in Somerset, and Cowbridge in the Vale of Glamorgan (Smith 2016a, 67–9; Allen *et al.* 2018, records 21014, 21032, 43007).

A Late Roman masonry building 15.8 m long by 7.2 m wide containing at least two drying ovens and six fragments of quern stone was excavated in 1938 at Yarde's Field on the north side of the Roman road and described at the time of discovery as a bakehouse (Fig. 6.18). A

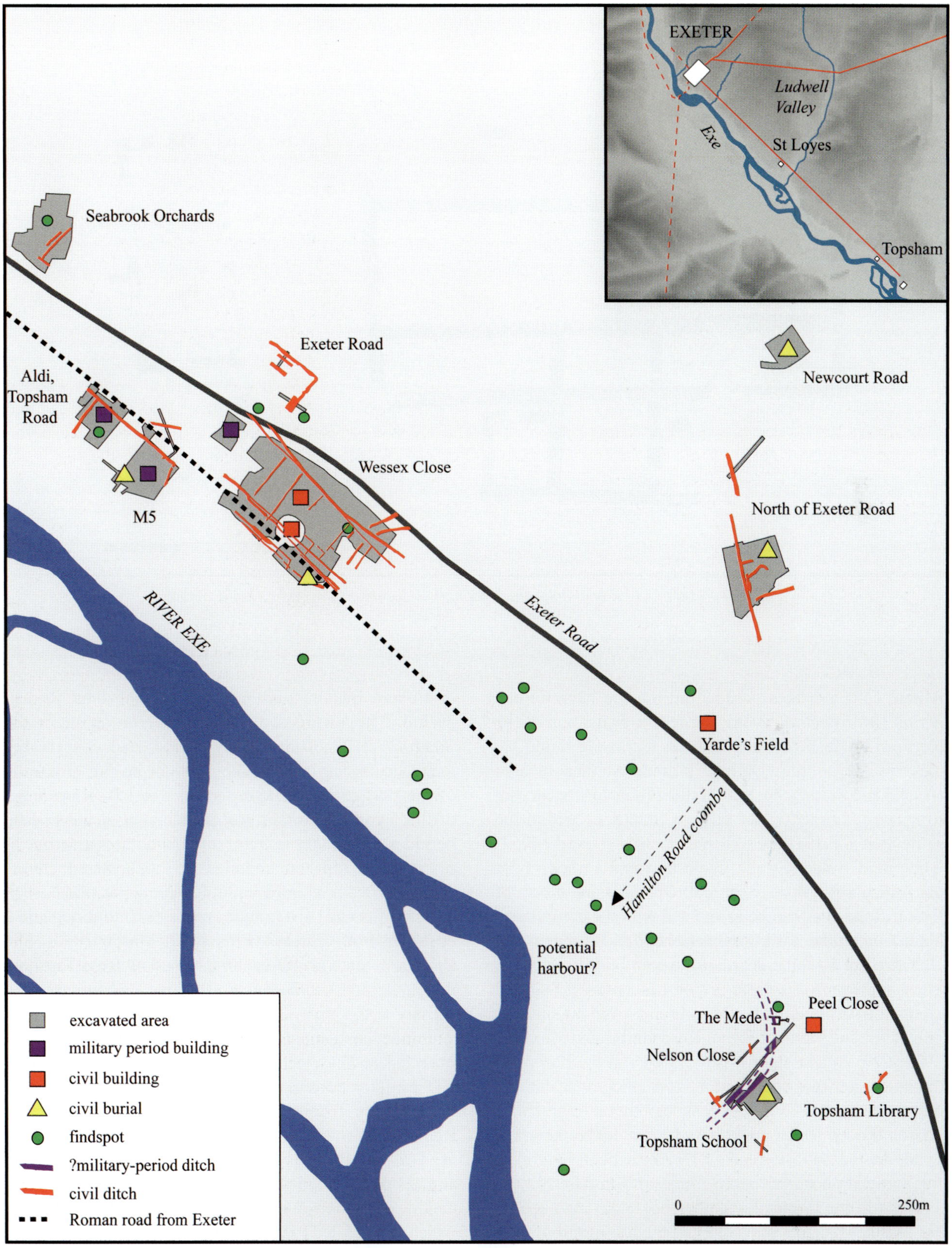

Fig. 6.17 Plan of Roman activity at Topsham (drawn by David Gould)

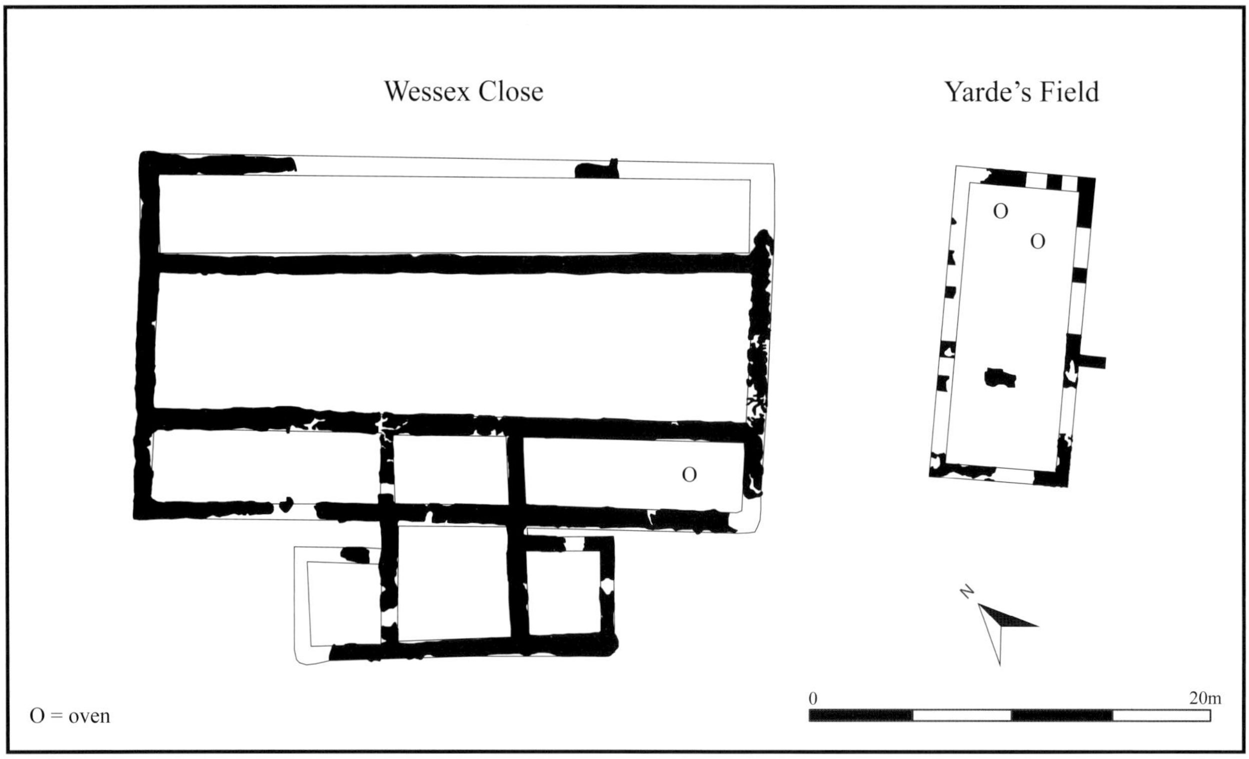

Fig. 6.18 Plans of two Roman masonry buildings in Topsham (drawn by David Gould)

radiate coin indicates occupation into the later Roman period (Morris *et al.* 1938) and recent evaluation at the North of Exeter Road site indicates that the building lay close to the northern periphery of the settlement area (Austin and Massey 2018). Another probable crop-drying oven was recorded under salvage conditions within the settlement at Peel Close (Allen *et al.* 2018, record 19052) while field systems, wells, enclosures and a trackway at the Aldi, Exeter Road, Seabrook Orchards and North of Exeter Road sites can be associated with the agricultural hinterland on the north-west periphery of Topsham.

There are various records of human burials from the Topsham area. An isolated 3rd or 4th-century AD urned cremation was found at the M5 site and seven inhumation graves at Land North of Exeter Road (Jarvis and Maxfield 1974, 227; Austin and Massey 2018). All the burials at the latter site were contained in wooden coffins, and one burial had hobnailed footwear and another a fragment of an iron brooch which might have been a deliberate grave good. At the opposite end of the settlement 13 graves for inhumation burials were found at Topsham School adjacent to the former ?urban defences discussed above. No skeletal remains survived, although a group of iron hobnails in one grave testifies to burial with footwear (other nails were derived from wooden coffins). There is no relevant dating for these graves (Sage and Allan 2004, 11–15, 20–2). Scattered inhumation burials were a common aspect of certain regions of the countryside of Roman Britain, particularly so in the later Roman period. They were, however, never common in the South-West Peninsula at any period, and conceivably their occurrence in Topsham was due to the proximity of the port (Smith 2018b, figs 6.13–6.15). Knowledge of the layout of British port settlements in the Roman period is weak in the extreme, although it is reasonable to suppose that Topsham included the shops, manufactories and storehouses akin to buildings known at places such as Sea Mills and (in a military context) Heronbridge, just upstream from Chester (Ellis 1987; Mason 2010). The absence to date of 4th-century AD coins from Topsham is notable and could denote a decline or contraction in activity at this time.

Further settlement along the road to Exeter is to be expected, and has been found on the site of the 1st-century AD military-period settlement at St Loye's College, 3.5 km from Topsham and close to the point where the Roman road crossed the Northbrook stream at the base of the Ludwell valley (Fig. 6.17 inset; Chapter 5). Ditches aligned on the road defined a series of small fields and paddocks, which contained scattered pits and a well which was infilled in the later 2nd or 3rd century AD. No buildings of this date have yet been found, but that is not surprising as they would have lain along the road frontage beyond the limits of the area available for excavation. Such structures could well have been the source of some of the ceramic tiles recovered from the site. There was a scatter of five graves at the back of the site. They are not closely dated and no skeletal remains survived, but such inhumation burials are a regular occurrence in the backlands of roadside settlements (Stead and Payne 2013; Salvatore *et al.* forthcoming).

Religion, superstition and structured deposition

No structural evidence for a temple has yet been found in Exeter, unless the walls found at Friernhay Street and St Nicholas Priory discussed above do indeed define the boundary of a religious *temenos*. Our knowledge of formalised religion and superstitious practices in Exeter is therefore derived from artefacts with an intrinsically religious connotation, as well as the evidence for the structured deposition of artefacts or biological remains. No altars or monumental religious sculpture are known from the town, although some figurines may have had a religious purpose. These include pipe clay figurines (Allason-Jones 1991b, figs 127–8, nos. 1–3; Bidwell 1980, 81, fig. 46) and a cache of six copper-alloy figurines found in 1778 at 63 High Street (on the south-east side of *insula* IX) depicting Fortuna, Mercury (x 2), a cockerel, Mars and Apollo (Milles 1782; Bidwell 1980, 81, fig. 47; Durham 2012, cat. nos. 586–91). Single examples of Diana and a human figure are also recorded (Durham 2012, cat. nos. 736, 999). We know nothing of the context of the High Street hoard, although the figurines might have been associated with a temple or shrine. Metal figurines of this type are most commonly found in Britain on urban sites, with London producing by far the largest collection (the High Street hoard somewhat skews Exeter's showing in Durham's statistics). Two carved stone phalluses, perhaps originally set into walls, doubtless also had superstitious or apotropaic associations (Bidwell 1979, fig. 49, no. 9; Ling 1991, fig. 99; Henig 1993, Devon and Cornwall nos. 7 and 9). The best-known evidence for religious adherence in Exeter is the sherd of South-East Dorset BB1 inscribed after firing with a chi-rho Christian monogram recovered from the post-Roman dark earth to the south-west of the forum (Site 16; Fox 1952, 92; RIB ii, 2503.134). The use of this monogram in Roman Britain has been extensively discussed, but it is not always easy to move from the identification of a symbol with Christian associations to the identification of an object as connected to Christian belief or practice (Thomas 1981a, 86–91; Mawer 1995, 34, 37–8).

Awareness of the prevalence of structured deposition in Roman Britain as evidence for pervasive ritual behaviour was heightened considerably by the publication of an important paper by Fulford in 2001 where he reviewed the evidence from Silchester and selected other settlements (Fulford 2001). Since then excavators have been much more aware of the potentially ritual associations of deliberately placed complete artefacts and articulated animal remains. There is a danger, however, that this trend might have gone too far through the exclusion of consideration of more prosaic explanations for some of these finds (Smith 2016b, 651–3). In the 1970s and 80s excavators devoted much less attention to the factors behind structured deposition and it is possible that some examples of this behaviour went unrecorded in contemporary site records. Table 6.1 presents a (far from comprehensive) selection of plausible examples of structured deposition in the Roman town, excluding coin hoards (for which see EAPIT 2, Chapter 16). The deposition of whole or partially articulated animal skeletons is widely attested in Roman Britain, although to date it is hardly evidenced in Exeter (Maltby notes only two examples of partially complete dog skeletons; see below). This is likely to be a true state of affairs as it is difficult to believe that the absence can be entirely attributed to a lack of recognition or recording during excavation. Exeter was thus somewhat different from certain other towns in its lack of adoption of this practice. The association of ritual practice with watery places is well known and the springs and watercourses in and around Exeter would have been potential locations for such activity. In particular the spring that fed the Coombe Stream rose to the surface south-east of the forum and this location might repay future investigation (small-scale investigations at 5–7 Palace Gate (Site 106) near the source of the stream retrieved Early Roman pottery above natural silts).

The economy of the Roman town

Food supply: the exploitation of animals

By Mark Maltby

The data available for animal exploitation in the *civitas* capital is substantially greater than for the earlier military occupation. Thirteen sites have produced 10,482 identified mammal and 847 bird bones. Although the various faunal analyses have subdivided the Roman assemblages, the chronological divisions have been inconsistent and therefore the assemblages will be treated largely as a single entity. However, variations between different phases within sites will be noted.

Cattle continued to be the most important species exploited. They provided 50% of the identified specimens (NISP) of mammals overall (Table 6.2). There is, however, a lot of variability. Cattle percentages range between 32% (Cathedral Close) and 75% (Holloway Street). There are also chronological variations. Cattle were outnumbered by sheep/goat in Early Roman deposits at Goldsmith Street and Princesshay and by both pig and sheep/goat in contemporary deposits from Cathedral Close. The percentages of cattle increased in later Roman deposits from Goldsmith Street, Trichay Street, Cathedral Close and Princesshay but decreased from their very high levels in earlier Roman deposits at Rack Street (Maltby 1979, 96–9; Coles forthcoming a). Cattle percentages in

Table 6.1 Selected examples of possible structured deposition from the Roman town, excluding coin hoards. Abbreviations: EAR1 = Bidwell 1979; EAR4 = Holbrook and Bidwell 1991

Deposition	*Context*	*Date*	*Site*	*Comments*
Two complete copper-alloy *paterae* (saucepans)	In backfill of stone-lined cesspit	mid 2nd century AD	Site 75: Friernhay Street	The *paterae* were made on the continent in the 1st century AD and perhaps curated before burial. An infant burial was found near the pit. RAMM accession loan no. 119/2000/2
A number of near-complete coarse ware vessels, including a cooking pot (EAR4, fig. 38, no. 20.1c) and carinated bowl (EAR4, fig. 64, no. 28.1); a fragment of a ceramic lamp (EAR4, p. 76), the torso of a sculptured Purbeck marble eagle (EAR1, 130-2; Henig 1993, 83-4, pl. 61, no. 3); an iron spearhead (EAR4, fig. 120, no. 2); a bone hilt-guard from a sword (EAR4, fig. 122, no. 1) and an incomplete bone latch key (EAR4, fig. 124, no. 24).	In backfill of a well (TS 3)	*c.* AD 80–100	Site 42: Trichay Street	If the eagle came from a major sculptural group representing Jupiter, the only plausible context for it would be in the *aedes* (shrine) of the fortress headquarters building (*principia*) where it would have been the focus of the official rites of the legion (Toynbee 1979; Henig 1993, pl. 61, no. 3; EAPIT 2, Chapter 5). Such an important piece would hardly be broken up, leaving fragments scattered around for a decade or so. It seems much more credible that the fragments would be distributed in appropriate places, watery or otherwise, when the *principia* was demolished. It is possible that the upper fills of the well might have been deposited at a slightly later date after the primary fills had compacted, in which case the lower fills might date to the time when the fortress was finally abandoned, and the upper fills to a decade or so later. Toynbee (1979) also speculated that the sculpture could have come from a group showing Nero in the guise of Jupiter, accompanied by an eagle. She believed that the eagle was deliberately decapitated and the occasion may have been when the memory of Nero was officially damned following his death in AD 68.
A small greyware beaker (TS 576; EAR4, fig. 63, type 5.1) which contained a single 1st-century AD coin and an enamelled copper-alloy military strap end (EAR4, fig. 111, no. 48)	Buried underneath the floor of building RC2	late 1st or early 2nd century AD	Site 42: Trichay Street	Foundation deposit associated with the construction of the building (EAPIT 2, Chapter 5)
Hoard of six bronze religious figurines	Unknown	?	High Street. Found in 1782	Associated with a temple or shrine? Milles 1782; Bidwell 1980, fig. 47; Durham 2012, cat. nos. 586–91
Decapitated pipeclay figurine of Venus	Pit TS 1520	late 2nd or early 3rd century AD	Site 51: 45–6 North Street	
Child burial, probably a neonate	Beneath the floor of room 2 of building RC13	mid 3rd to mid 4th century AD	Site 42: Trichay Street	Foundation deposit (EAPIT 2, Chapter 5)

(Continued)

Table 6.1 Selected examples of possible structured deposition from the Roman town, excluding coin hoards. Abbreviations: EAR1 = Bidwell 1979; EAR4 = Holbrook and Bidwell 1991 (Continued)

Deposition	*Context*	*Date*	*Site*	*Comments*
22 bones from an adult dog skeleton	Pit 2	Not closely dated	Site 40: Cathedral Close	Maltby 1979, 62
30 bones from an adult dog skeleton	Well 2787	3rd century AD	Site 156: Princesshay	Dogs are regularly found in the backfills of wells in some parts of Britain and may have been ritual depositions (although other prosaic explanations are possible). Coles forthcoming a
70 bones from the partial skeletons of three juvenile pigs	Context 1140, one of the levelling deposits in the service area south-east of the baths associated with the Period 2A construction of the basilica	*c.* AD 90–100	Site 40: Cathedral Close	Maltby, below
Adult badger skeleton	Context 1083, a Period 2B dump in the passage that runs immediately outside the south-east end of the basilica	second half of the 2nd century AD	Site 40: Cathedral Close	Maltby below; EAR1, 95

Table 6.2 Number of identified specimens (NISP) of mammals in deposits associated with the civitas *capital*

Site Code	*GS I-III*	*TS*	*CC*	*RS*	*HL*	*HS*	*BS*	*PH*	*BSW*	*FH*	*MY*	*PS*	*QS*	
EAPIT Site	*37, 39*	*42*	*40*	*52*	*50*	*43*	*47*	*156*	*116*	*75*	*63*	*76*	*68*	*Total*
Cattle	1129	770	572	928	72	55	94	521	20	422	554	73	52	5262
Sheep/Goat	775	245	491	237	14	20	14	283	10	146	232	22	27	2516
Pig	601	263	570	91	10	11	4	218	2	108	147	14	38	2077
Horse	22	17	22	57			1	48	1	19	11	8	5	211
Dog	21	5	44			1		58		26	9	2	15	181
Cat	11	1						12		1				25
Red Deer	8	5	15	2						5	4	1	1	41
Roe Deer	8	5	7	5						3				28
Hare	23	20	17	1				21		1		1		84
Badger			42								1			43
Fox	12		2											14
Total Mammal	**2610**	**1331**	**1782**	**1321**	**96**	**87**	**113**	**1161**	**33**	**731**	**958**	**121**	**138**	**10482**
% NISP														
Cattle	43.3	57.9	32.1	70.2	75.0	63.2	83.2	44.9		57.7	57.8	60.3	37.7	50.2
Sheep/Goat	29.7	18.4	27.6	17.9	14.6	23.0	12.4	24.4		20.0	24.2	18.2	19.6	24.0
Pig	23.0	19.8	32.0	6.9	10.4	12.6	3.5	18.8		14.8	15.3	11.6	27.5	19.8
Horse	0.8	1.3	1.2	4.3	0.0	0.0	0.9	4.1		2.6	1.1	6.6	3.6	2.0
Dog	0.8	0.4	2.5	0.0	0.0	1.1	0.0	5.0		3.6	0.9	1.7	10.9	1.7
Cat	0.4	0.1	0.0	0.0	0.0	0.0	0.0	1.0		0.1	0.0	0.0	0.0	0.2
Red Deer	0.3	0.4	0.8	0.2	0.0	0.0	0.0	0.0		0.7	0.4	0.8	0.7	0.4
Roe Deer	0.3	0.4	0.4	0.4	0.0	0.0	0.0	0.0		0.4	0.0	0.0	0.0	0.3
Hare	0.9	1.5	1.0	0.1	0.0	0.0	0.0	1.8		0.1	0.0	0.8	0.0	0.8
Badger	0.0	0.0	2.4	0.0	0.0	0.0	0.0	0.0		0.0	0.1	0.0	0.0	0.4
Fox	0.5	0.0	0.1	0.0	0.0	0.0	0.0	0.0		0.0	0.0	0.0	0.0	0.1
Total Mammal	**2610**	**1331**	**1782**	**1321**	**96**	**87**	**113**	**1161**	**33**	**731**	**958**	**121**	**138**	**10482**

(Continued)

Table 6.2 (Continued)

Site Code	*GS I-III*	*TS*	*CC*	*RS*	*HL*	*HS*	*BS*	*PH*	*BSW*	*FH*	*MY*	*PS*	*QS*	
EAPIT Site	*37, 39*	*42*	*40*	*52*	*50*	*43*	*47*	*156*	*116*	*75*	*63*	*76*	*68*	*Total*
Cattle	45.1	60.3	35.0	73.9	75.0	64.0	83.9	51.0		62.4	59.4	67.0	44.4	53.4
Sheep/Goat	30.9	19.2	30.1	18.9	14.6	23.3	12.5	27.7		21.6	24.9	20.2	23.1	25.5
Pig	24.0	20.6	34.9	7.2	10.4	12.8	3.6	21.3		16.0	15.8	12.8	32.5	21.1
Total C+S+P	**2505**	**1278**	**1633**	**1256**	**96**	**86**	**112**	**1022**	**32**	**676**	**933**	**109**	**117**	**9855**
% S of S+P	56.3	48.2	46.3	72.3	58.3	64.5	77.8	56.5		57.5	61.2	61.1	41.5	54.8
% Horse of C+H	1.9	2.2	3.7	5.8	0.0	0.0	1.1	8.4		4.3	1.9	9.9	8.8	3.9
% Wild	2.0	2.3	4.7	0.6	0.0	0.0	0.0	1.8		1.2	0.5	1.7	0.7	2.0

GSI-III = Goldsmith Street
TS = Trichay Street
CC = Cathedral Close
RS = Rack Street
HL = Holloway Street
HS = 196-7 High Street
PH = Princesshay
BSW = Bartholomew Street West
FH = Friernhay Street
MY = Mermaid Yard
PS = Paul Street
QS = Queen Street
% S of S+P = percentage of sheep/goat of total sheep/goat and pig
% Horse of C+H = percentage of horse of total cattle and horse
Data for GSI-III, TS, CC, RS and BS adapted from Maltby (1979)
Data for PH adapted from Coles (forthcoming a)
Data for BSW, FH, MY, PS and QS adapted from Lauritsen (2019)

Roman civil urban assemblages were greater than those from military features in the sites studied by Lauritsen (EAPIT 2, Chapter 9, Fig. 9.2). Cattle percentages tend to increase on all types of settlement in the later Romano-British period (King 1984; Allen *et al.* 2017) and they increased overall from 48% in early features to 55% in later Roman deposits in Exeter. This could indicate that there was greater reliance on beef, following the national trend. However, cattle percentages vary dramatically within Roman towns because specialist butchers deposited large numbers of cattle bones in some areas after various stages of carcass processing (Maltby 2017). The classic example from Exeter came from Rack Street (RS 363.7) where head and foot bones from at least 49 cattle were deposited within a short period of time in the bottom of the ditch of the town defences, a deposit dated to *c.* AD 100–120 (EAPIT 2, Chapter 8). These were discarded after primary butchery and resulted in cattle forming over 78% of the mammal assemblage in that deposit (Maltby 1979, 11). Two later Roman ditches from Goldsmith Street (F47, infilled no earlier than the mid 4th century AD and F160/F618, infilled in the late 3rd or 4th century AD; the ditches were probably open at the same time) also contained accumulations of cattle butchery waste (Maltby 1979, 10–15). The Mermaid Yard assemblage was also dominated by cattle mandibles and metapodials (Lauritsen 2019).

Similar accumulations have been recorded in many Romano-British towns (Maltby 2010a, 283–7; 2015, 181; Hesse 2011, 223). They are often largely comprised of head and foot bones but other assemblages are dominated by split upper limb bones, scapulae or horn cores (Maltby 2010a, 286). These accumulations have been found in all areas of towns, but are more common in peripheral and extra-mural sites. Consequently cattle percentages tend to be higher in those areas (Maltby 2017, 192–194). The results from Exeter largely fit this pattern (Table 6.2). However, the accumulations of cattle head and foot bones in the Goldsmith Street ditches discussed above may indicate that more dumping episodes took place in areas where intensive occupation declined in the Late Roman period.

The techniques of cattle carcass processing that originated in the military phase in Exeter continued during the civilian occupation. There was a great deal of consistency in butchery marks and bone breakage patterns (EAPIT 2, Chapter 9, Fig. 9.3). Butchery was carried out principally with heavy blades and many upper limb bones bear characteristic filleting scoops and/or longitudinal fractures associated with marrow extraction (Orgill 2014). Scapulae from Friernhay Street and Mermaid Yard were butchered systematically during preparation for smoking (Lauritsen 2019). Horns were routinely removed from the skulls for working (Maltby 1979, 38–9; Lauritsen 2019). This consistency strongly suggests that specialist butchers did most of the processing. Specialist butchers, employing the same methods as those in Exeter, were operating in every major Romano-British town and their presence has also been attested in some smaller nucleated settlements (Maltby 2007; 2010a, 283–7).

Most cattle brought for slaughter in Exeter were adults (Maltby 1979, 155–8; EAPIT 2, Chapter 9, Fig. 9.4; Coles forthcoming a). Metrical analysis of the metacarpals has indicated that the vast majority of adult cattle were females (Maltby 1979, 32–4; Coles forthcoming a). This is a pattern commonly encountered in other towns, where cows aged between four and eight years old were the most commonly acquired (Maltby 2010a, 287–9). Most of these cows had probably produced several calves prior to slaughter. They could also have been exploited for milk, although few remains of young calves have been found in Exeter. Veal is often a by-product of intensive dairy production.

Cattle continued to be of small stature (Maltby 1979, 164–7; EAPIT 2, Chapter 9, Fig. 9.5) and there is little evidence for the presence of larger cattle that have been found in some other areas of the province (Maltby 1981; 2010a, 292–3; Rizzetto *et al.* 2017).

Sheep/goat contributed 24% of the total mammal NISP counts, with percentages ranging between 12% and 30% (Table 6.2). They were better represented overall in the earlier deposits (26%) than in later features (21%). Both sheep and goat were identified but the great majority of bones belonged to sheep. Goats were best represented by horn cores, some of which were probably from horns imported for working (Maltby 1979, 41). Ageing analysis has shown a focus on procuring immature, sub-adult and young adult sheep, indicating that the main priority was meat production, although some older sheep were also present (Maltby 1979, 42–3; Lauritsen 2019; Coles forthcoming a). The slaughter pattern is typical of many Roman towns (Maltby 2010a, 289–90). The sheep were horned and generally small and slender. They were on average slightly smaller than sheep found in most other areas of Roman Britain (EAPIT 2, Chapter 9, Table 9.6; Maltby 1981; 2010a, 294–5; 2017, 196–9).

The overall percentage of pig elements (20%) was lower than in the military assemblages (24%). The decline was particularly marked at Friernhay Street (Tables 5.3 and 6.2; EAPIT 2, Chapter 9, Fig. 9.2). The highest percentage (32%) was from Cathedral Close, where counts were bolstered by 70 bones from the partial skeletons of three juvenile pigs (from context 1140, one of the levelling deposits in the service area south-east of the baths associated with the Period 2A construction of the basilica; Maltby 1979, 95). Excluding these, the percentage from that site decreased to 29%. Romano-British towns tend to produce higher pig percentages than rural settlements (King 1984; 1999), indicating contrasts in availability, cultural preferences and economic status. There are, however, regional variations. The percentage of pigs in Exeter is greater than in many towns but lower than most assemblages from London, for example (Maltby 2010a, 266–7). High pig percentages have been encountered more commonly in sites located near the centres of towns compared to peripheral and extra-mural areas and in deposits associated with high status residents (Maltby 2015, 184). In Exeter the highest pig percentages were found at Cathedral Close, Goldsmith Street, Trichay Street and Queen Street, all located in central areas. All but one of the peripheral sites produced lower percentages of pigs (Table 6.2). The exception is Princesshay where the high percentage of pigs is largely the result of their abundance in an unusually rich 3rd-century AD pit (4880), which contained much pottery and animal bone interpreted by the excavators as debris from feasting (Steinmetzer, Stead, Pearce, Bidwell and Allan forthcoming). Bones of neonatal pigs were found in this pit, which suggests that pigs were being reared in this area (Coles forthcoming a). The piglet skeletons from Cathedral Close also suggest that some pigs were being bred within the Roman town, as there is no evidence that these were butchered. These may have been ritual depositions. Bones of slightly older piglets have been found in Exeter and several other Roman towns (Maltby 1979, 186; 2010a, 291), which indicates the consumption of suckling pigs, which may have been regarded as luxury food. However, more pigs in Roman Exeter were slaughtered in their second and third years when they had grown nearer to full size (Maltby 1979, 55–6; Lauritsen 2019; Coles forthcoming a), which is also typical of Romano-British urban assemblages (Maltby 2010a, 291).

Horses were poorly represented forming only 2% of identified mammal counts and 4% of the cattle and horse elements (Table 6.2), and so clearly played a very insignificant part in the meat diet. The low percentage of horse is again typical of Roman towns (Maltby 2010a, 269–70). Nearly all the bones came from adults confirming they were kept as working animals.

Dog bones (2% overall) were also found only in small numbers (Table 6.2). Counts include several partial skeletons. Twenty-two bones of an adult were found in Cathedral Close (Pit 2) and the 3rd-century AD infill of well 2787 from Princesshay produced 30 bones of another adult (Coles forthcoming a). Dog skeletons have been found in deep pits and wells in other towns including Dorchester and Winchester. Some of these may have been ritual depositions although more prosaic reasons have also been postulated (Woodward and Woodward 2004; Maltby 2010b). Whatever the explanation these associated bone groups infer that dog carcasses were rarely processed, although their skeletons often become scattered after deposition and subsequent disturbance and decay. Dog sizes varied greatly and included small lap dogs (Maltby 1979, 63), which were brought to Britain during the Roman period (Clark 1995). Cats were other companion animals occasionally found in Exeter (0.2% NISP overall).

Wild species formed only 2% of mammal NISP counts (Table 6.2). These included an adult badger skeleton from Cathedral Close (context 1083, a Period 2B dump in the passage that runs immediately outside the south-east end of the basilica), eight bones of an immature fox from Goldsmith Street, and 15 bones of a hare from Cathedral Close. Excluding all Associated Bone Groups (ABGs), wild species provided 1% of the mammal NISP counts. Hare, red deer and roe deer were occasional supplements to a few people's diet but there was a sharp drop in the percentage of red deer compared with military deposits at Trichay Street and Friernhay Street in particular. None of these species form more than 1% of the mammal bones in most Roman urban assemblages. The rare exceptions are usually associated with high status sites (Maltby 2010a, 271).

Birds provided 8% of the total mammal and bird bones (Table 6.3), a significant increase from Early Roman military deposits (Table 5.4). This is largely due to the 353 bones recovered from the rich Princesshay pit 4880, in which birds comfortably outnumbered the 211 mammal bones (Coles forthcoming a).

Chickens (76%) dominated the bird assemblages from all sites. They provided 20% of the total sheep/goat and chicken NISP counts and a remarkable 47% in the Princesshay assemblage. Chicken bones have consistently been recovered much more frequently in towns than in other settlement types (Maltby *et al.* 2018). Chickens were more common in settlements where Roman and other continental influences were prominent, reflecting the greater cultural diversity of the inhabitants. Around 10–15% of the bones came from young birds and, although most of the birds from Princesshay were hens, there was no evidence for medullary bone indicative of hens in lay (Coles forthcoming a) suggesting that meat rather than egg production may have been the focus of their exploitation.

Goose bones have been recorded on several sites but only in very small numbers (Table 6.3). They were all the size of wild greylag but could have been captive birds. Geese have been found less commonly in towns in the west of the province than in the east (Maltby 2010a, 273–5). Several duck species have been recorded providing 4% of the Exeter bird assemblage. Most were the size of mallard/domestic duck but other species, including eider and teal, were captured.

Woodcock provided over 12% of the avian assemblage. They were particularly abundant (53 bones) in Princesshay pit 4880 (Coles forthcoming a). Woodcock have been the most common wader recovered from Roman towns (Maltby 2010, 273) but the percentage from Exeter is currently the highest recorded suggesting that they were available in greater numbers in this estuarine region. Several other species of gamebirds have been recorded but only in very small numbers (Table 6.3). Several corvid species were also identified providing 3% of the bird bones with ravens the most common. There is no evidence that corvids were eaten. Most of the passerine bones were found in Princesshay pit 4880. Most of these

Table 6.3 Number of identified specimens (NISP) of birds in deposits associated with the civitas *capital*

Site code		*PH*	*FH*	*MY*	*QS*	
EAPIT Site Number	*Pre 1976*	*156*	*75*	*63*	*68*	*Total*
Chicken	332	251	18	28	12	641
Goose	9	1	1	1		12
Mallard-sized duck	13	12		2		27
Eider				1		1
Medium-sized duck		7				7
Teal	2			1		3
Gull		2				2
Woodcock	39	62		4		105
Crane	2					2
Curlew	1					1
Rail		1				1
Partridge	1					1
Pigeons	7	4				11
Raven	15		1		3	19
Rook/Crow	2	1				3
Jackdaw	7					7
Cuckoo	1					1
Passerine	4	15				19
Total Bird	**435**	**340**	**20**	**37**	**15**	**847**
% NISP						
Chicken	76.3	73.8				75.7
Goose	2.1	0.3				1.4
Duck	3.0	3.5				3.2
Eider	0.0	0.0				0.1
Medium-sized Duck	0.0	2.1				0.8
Teal	0.5	0.0				0.4
Gull	0.0	0.6				0.2
Woodcock	9.0	18.2				12.4
Crane	0.5	0.0				0.2
Curlew	0.2	0.0				0.1
Rail	0.0	0.3				0.1
Partridge	0.2	0.0				0.1
Pigeons	1.6	1.2				1.3
Raven	3.4	0.0				2.2
Rook/Crow	0.5	0.3				0.4
Jackdaw	1.6	0.0				0.8
Cuckoo	0.2	0.0				0.1
Passerine	0.9	4.4				2.2
Total Bird	**435**	**340**	**20**	**37**	**15**	**847**
% B+M	5.6	22.7	2.7	3.7	9.8	7.5
Ch:Sh	15.6	47.0	11.0	10.8	30.8	20.3

% B+M = percentage of total bird and mammal

Ch:Sh = percentage of chicken of total sheep/goat and chicken probably belonged to the thrush family but smaller finches were also represented (Coles forthcoming a). Given the richness of their context, these were probably birds that were eaten as luxury items.

Although fish bones have been recovered from most sites, they have not received detailed analysis. Limited sieving in some excavations has also restricted their recovery. Wilkinson (1979) identified at least 11 species from Roman features with hake being the most common. Seven percent of the Princesshay assemblage consists of fish bones (Cole forthcoming a). There has as yet been no evidence for fish sauce production or consumption in Exeter, although evidence for this has been found in several other Romano-British towns (Locker 2007; Hamilton-Dyer 2008) and locally in an aisled building at Topsham (Armitage 2017; Rainbird and Farnell 2019).

The faunal analyses from Exeter have shown the importance of examining bones from different parts of Roman towns. Variations in assemblages were created by the disposal of large quantities of butchery waste and the presence of inhabitants of different socioeconomic status in different sectors of the town. In many ways Exeter was typical of other Romano-British towns, for example, in acquiring and processing beef mainly through the agency of specialist butchers. Mortality patterns for the major species were similar to those encountered in many other towns. Pigs and chickens, some of which probably reared in Exeter itself, were exploited more frequently than in many rural settlements. However, unlike some other areas of the province, there was little improvement in the sizes of domestic stock during the Roman period.

Food supply: plants and other resources

By Neil Holbrook

Our knowledge of the plants grown and consumed in Exeter is woefully poor in comparison to the environmental record from several of the other principal towns of Roman Britain (cf. van der Veen 2016). In part this is due to the lack of attention devoted to environmental archaeology in the major excavations conducted in the city in the 1970s and 80s, a state of affairs by no means restricted to Exeter. Less understandable has been the low level of environmental sampling, processing and analysis from investigations undertaken in the developer-funded era from 1990 onwards. For instance, when the Princesshay excavations of 1997–2006 (Site 156) were being planned, a substantial programme of environmental sampling and analysis was intended to be an important component of the project. The site sampling was carried out and the samples assessed, but the results were rather disappointing and financial constraints led to the decision not to proceed to full analysis. Hopefully this prominent gap in the archaeological record for Exeter will be rectified when more recent excavations such as those at Quintana Gate (Site 169) and City Arcade (Site 204) are brought to publication. It is beyond doubt that deposits with high potential for the preservation of biological remains exist within central Exeter where the weathered Permian clay provides impermeable conditions. For instance, Bidwell (1980, 81) records that hazelnuts and plum stones were easily recognisable within the contents of a 2nd-century AD well at Queen Street (Site 68), but this material does not appear to have been otherwise analysed. The sole detailed description of plant remains published from the town comprises the late 1st/early 2nd-century AD waterlogged deposits from the base of the defensive ditch at Friernhay Street (Site 75) discussed above. Cereals were primarily represented here by chaff with emmer or spelt wheat and oat represented (Straker *et al.* 1984). The presence of a grain weevil in the ditch has been interpreted by van der Veen as evidence for the importation of grain into Exeter in the military period, the pest then becoming established amongst locally grown cereals in the early civil period (van der Veen 2016, 820). It is less clear whether the wild strawberries and elderberries in the ditch were growing locally or deliberately collected for food. At Princesshay (Site 156) the assessment of the plant macrofossils noted that a burnt layer associated with tile production included abundant wheat grains including spelt wheat alongside barley and oat grains. Later Roman deposits were mostly unproductive, but one deposit included frequent hulled wheat grains and glume bases with occasional weed seeds. This is a meagre showing therefore, especially when compared with the evidence from rural sites associated with agricultural production outlined in Chapter 3 which demonstrated considerable variations in the proportions of the principal crops being processed in different parts of South-West England, with Devon assemblages dominated by emmer and spelt wheat, although oats were also reasonably well represented.

Oyster shells are commonly recovered from Roman deposits within the town but to date no further analysis has occurred of this material. A localised dump of oyster shells from above the demolition deposits of Building 14ii indicates the continued exploitation of marine resources into the early 5th century AD.

Manufacturing

The population of Exeter would have included artisans involved in a variety of craft activities, although direct archaeological evidence is often lacking. Wood working and carpentry must have been common occupations although the frequently poor preservation of organic remains means we have little surviving trace of their products. Of the ten or so Roman wells known from Exeter there is only a single timber-lined example from Trichay Street (Site 42, well TS 348). It was of comparatively simple construction and did not display the sophisticated carpentry employed for certain wells in London for instance (EAPIT 2, Chapter 5; cf. Willmott 1982). It is reasonable to suppose that most of the small assemblage of wooden artefacts recovered from the town was locally made rather than imported, as is probably also the case with fragments of leather shoe from Friernhay Street (Site 75) (Earwood 1991). Bone and horn working are also evidenced (Allason-Jones 1991c, fig. 124, nos. 23–4). A Roman limekiln has been recently examined at City Arcade (Site 204), a notable find in an urban environment (there is another example from Dorchester, although more kilns are known in rural contexts; Durham and Fulford 2014, 40–2; Smith 2017, 208–9; for an example south of Exeter near Newton Abbot see Chapter 3 above).

Evidence for the exploitation of the mineral resources of the South-West Peninsula in the Roman period has been explored in Chapter 2. In seeking to determine the role that Exeter played in the processing and distribution of metals we are fortunate that specialists from the former Ancient Monuments Laboratory studied the metalworking debris from the city in the 1980s and produced technical reports. As part of the EAPIT project Carlotta Gardner re-analysed several metalworking crucibles which has added new insights into the activity being carried out here in the Roman period (EAPIT 2, Chapter 10).

There is important evidence from Exeter for the processing of precious metals. Seven sherds from parting vessels were recovered from the 2nd-century AD infill of a street-side ditch at Friernhay Street (Site 75), presumably dumped waste from a nearby workshop (Bayley 2001). Parting vessels were used to separate gold from silver, and the presence of copper in the vessels suggests that they were used to recycle artefacts made in the indigenous Iron Age tradition from mixed precious metals to create pure bullion for use in the imperial economy. Copper would not be expected if the vessels were used in the processing of freshly-mined Cornish gold as native gold does not normally contain that metal. This is rare British evidence for gold processing, with similar vessels also recognised from London, Chichester and Lincoln, all towns sited well away from the sources of gold in western Britain (cf. Dungworth 2016, 532–5). This suggests that these urban smiths were all primarily concerned with the recycling of existing artefacts in the Early Roman period. The processing of pure silver is also attested in Exeter by the evidence for secondary cupellation, a process to extract silver from silver-copper alloys. Once again, we are presumably dealing here with the recycling of artefacts, or even an unofficial response to the progressive debasement of silver coinage in the 3rd century AD through the melting down of older issues. Late 4th-century AD deposits at Rack Street (Sites 52/64) yielded a fragment of dense, lead- and copper-rich slag that could be from lithage (lead oxide), a by-product of the cupellation of silver, and silver has also been detected within a fragment of copper-lead alloy. A spread of mid 2nd-century AD metalworking debris adjacent to the road to Topsham and outside the bounds of the early town has already been mentioned. It is presumably debris from nearby workshops involved in silver cupellation. The evidence for the working of precious metals in Exeter matches that from several other major towns in Britain and indicates that this activity was officially sanctioned and conducted under some level of state supervision. As we have seen the Exeter smiths appear to have been primarily concerned with recycling rather than the processing of newly won gold from Cornwall and lead-silver from the Mendips. That activity doubtless occurred near the mines.

Looking beyond precious metals, a piece of slag derived from the production of gunmetal (leaded bronze) was recovered from a late 2nd-century AD deposit at Rack Street. Ferrous slag has been examined from ten sites in Exeter and Wilthew (1986) concluded that there was no evidence for iron smelting at these localities, and as the quantities of slag were small, there is no suggestion that any of these sites was involved in iron smithing on any scale. Fragments of hearth-lining with preserved tuyère (air) holes are recorded from Rack Street (Site 52) and James Street (Site 135). This conclusion occasions little surprise as while ironworking was a near ubiquitous activity in many parts of Roman Britain, this seems to have been largely at the workshop level in the major towns of Roman Britain, in contrast to certain small towns where the evidence is much more prominent and production on an industrial scale seems to be represented. The source of the iron worked in Exeter is undetermined, although as iron was extracted from Exmoor and the Blackdown Hills these are the most plausible candidates (see above, Chapter 2).

Interactions with the hinterland

It is material culture which gives the best insight into the wider connections of Exeter, principally through the evidence that can be gleaned from the distribution of pottery, ceramic tiles and stone artefacts. Much of this interaction occurred with other communities in South-West England, although the prime location of Exeter on a major navigable estuary on the Channel coast made it well placed to participate in sea-borne inter-provincial trade. Artefacts are also testament to occasional links with more distant parts of Britain, although not seemingly on any great scale. For instance, Late Roman fine wares such as those from the Oxfordshire and New Forest kilns are poorly represented in Exeter and its hinterland compared to sites in Somerset (see Chapter 3 above), a product of both the greater distance of Exeter from the kilns and to a lesser extent the local availability of an alternative fine ware, *céramique à l'éponge*, imported from Aquitaine (Fig. 6.19; see EAPIT 2, Chapter 12; Holbrook and Bidwell 1991, 21–3, 81–3). Shaffrey also remarks upon the regional stone sources exploited for querns and the absence from Exeter of products of the major quern industries of southern Britain (EAPIT 2, Chapter 14).

It is always tempting to use artefacts as a proxy to illuminate more substantial trade networks in commodities

Fig. 6.19 Sherds of céramique à l'éponge *from Exeter, a late Roman fineware produced in Aquitaine. Exeter is one of the sites in Britain where this fabric is best represented (© RAMM)*

which leave little trace in the archaeological record, principally foodstuffs and raw materials such as tin and iron. The isotope analysis of cattle and sheep from Roman Exeter also provides a new means of examining regional interactions, and in Chapter 3 above Müldner and Frémondeau have demonstrated, unsurprisingly, that the Roman town relied more heavily for its food supply on animals reared in its Devon hinterland than was the case during the period of military occupation. The settlement pattern and broader economy of South-West England has already been sketched in Chapter 3 above. This account is accordingly concerned primarily with the identification of the broad direction of regional trade into Exeter either side of the earlier 3rd century AD when a major dislocation in the supply network can be discerned. The pottery and ceramic tile evidence are discussed in detail in EAPIT 2, Chapters 12 and 13 by Bidwell, Machin and Warry. This section does not duplicate what is said there, but rather places that evidence within the context of trade between Exeter and its hinterland.

The withdrawal of the legion from Exeter, and within a decade or so the great bulk of other military forces stationed in the Peninsula, inevitably had a major impact on the supply networks as producers and merchants reacted to a markedly reduced market for their products. The initial civilian population of Exeter would not have been substantial, perhaps less than 1,000, although to this should be added the continuing resident population at Topsham and, to a lesser extent, at the St Loye's College site. Despite the reduction in population of the Exeter area by three quarters or more over the course of a decade or so in the late 1st century AD, investment in new urban fabric would have generated economic activity. The materials used in the construction of the new town were predominately drawn from local sources. Volcanic trap stone from Rougemont was the predominant building stone used in the basilica and forum, and presumably the public baths as well, but it was not well suited to finer architectural details such as column bases, capitals and mouldings (although that it was occasionally used for these purposes is shown by a trap column base from the Princesshay excavations; Site 156). In the basilica a grey-pink sandstone extracted from the extensive outcrops along the East Devon coast was employed for these details. Red sandstone, perhaps from South Somerset, and Purbeck marble were also employed (Bidwell 1979, 135, 146–8). Chert, imported from either the Haldon Hills in South Devon or the Upper Greensand of the Blackdown Hills, was also utilised in the core of the town wall. Water-rolled sandstone river cobbles were used occasionally in the footings of the town wall and in other structures such as the foundation for the tower added to the back of the wall at Paul Street (Site 76), and in the reconstruction of the south-west aisle wall of the basilica in the second or third quarter of the 3rd century AD (Bidwell 1979, 107).

Beyond the public buildings there is to date no evidence for domestic stone buildings in Exeter before the late 2nd century AD, and it was around this time or shortly thereafter that the town wall was also constructed. Trap was used to the virtual exclusion of other stone sources for 3rd or 4th-century AD masonry town houses in Exeter, although Purbeck marble was also used for decorative effect in at least a couple of domestic buildings (for instance Buildings 4ii and 24ii). Nor should we underestimate the demands for less visible construction materials in both timber and masonry buildings, principally wood but also thatch, gravel and clay. The sources of the ceramic tiles found in Exeter are extensively discussed in EAPIT 2, Chapter 13 by Sara Machin and Peter Warry who have adopted differing methods to research this material. To date no tile kilns have been found in the environs of the town, although dumps of wasters indicate manufacture in two areas: beyond the north-east defences of the early town (the area now known as Princesshay) and in the vicinity of St David's Church. A military origin for production to the north-east of Exeter is plausible and might also have been the case at St David's (although this is disputed). Production of tiles in the vicinity of the Princesshay excavation site on the north-east side of the town had ceased by *c.* AD 160–80 when the expanded town defences were constructed. It is possible that other kilns in the suburbs supplied the town with tiles in the late 2nd and 3rd centuries AD, although we know little of them as yet. Warry's Central Group might have been manufactured near to Exeter and he dates these products to the late 2nd–3rd century AD. The Central Group is found not only in Exeter but also at sites along the Exe Estuary. Not all the tile used in Exeter was made locally, however. Tiles in a distinctive buff fabric (Machin's fabric 4, which can be equated with Warry's Topsham Import Group) were clearly imported from further afield. The lower cutaways on the *tegulae* in this fabric suggest a 2nd-century AD date, but so far stratified examples have only been recovered from late 3rd- or 4th-century AD contexts in Exeter (although there are few sizeable assemblages from the town that can be firmly dated to the first half of the 3rd century AD). Machin and Warry both conclude that these tiles were imported into Topsham and Exeter by sea, perhaps from the Solent area (although that origin has not been established beyond doubt and a cross-Channel origin cannot be excluded). Tiles produced in the vicinity of Exeter were also exported to a variety of sites in Devon, although the chronology of this trade needs further work before it can be fully understood (compare for instance the distribution of tiles in Machin's CBM fabric 1/2/3 and that of Warry's St David's Group; EAPIT 2, Figs 13.2.50 and 13.3.29). Stone roofing tiles from the South Devon slate beds were increasingly utilised as a roofing material in Exeter in the 3rd century AD (the basilica was re-roofed in slate during this time) and it supplanted ceramic tile as the roofing material of choice in the 4th century AD. The Kate Brook formation seems to have been most favoured slate source, but other beds were used, as was White Lias that probably came from Somerset (Holbrook and Bidwell 1991, 282–4; Allan 1984a, fig. 169, maps the extent of the South Devon slate-beds).

The ceramic evidence is unsurprisingly to the fore in any consideration of the supply of the everyday essentials of urban life. From the late 1st/early 2nd century AD the proportion of South-East Dorset BB1 compared to South-Western BB1, which we can now reasonably infer was produced on the western flank of the Blackdown Hills, decreased markedly in domestic assemblages in Exeter (South-Western BB1 and its finer variant was in excess of five times more prevalent by weight than the South-East Dorset variety in mid to late 2nd-century AD groups from Exeter; Holbrook and Bidwell 1991, MF 1.19, tab. 19, groups 7–9; EAPIT 2, Chapter 12). This could be the result of the reduced market in Exeter leading to a decline in maritime trade from Purbeck, or a decision by the South-East Dorset industry to focus on export to the more lucrative military markets of Wales and northern Britain (either through free market considerations or the command economy). Exeter was always the principal market for South-Western BB1 and it does not occur in anything like the same quantity at other settlements. In 2nd-century AD groups South-Western BB1 comprises a good half of the total ceramic assemblage and was the predominant coarseware used by the inhabitants of Exeter. It would have reached Exeter by road and might have been accompanied by other products of the Blackdown Hills such as blooms of smelted iron, Upper Greensand quernstones, and perhaps ceramic tiles (although Machin's CBM fabric 5 has yet to be conclusively identified in the town itself) (see Chapter 3 above, and EAPIT 2, Chapters 13.2 and 14).

South-Western BB1 was supplemented by a variety of other greywares, some probably manufactured very close to Exeter. The Fortress Wares continued to be produced after the departure of the army, although the industry had closed by the early 2nd century AD (EAPIT 2, Chapter 12 provides a full discussion of the clay source used for some of these wares). Production of a new fabric, Exeter Gritty Grey Ware, began around the same time which was probably a local product. There was also production in Exeter of mortaria and flagons in the late 1st century AD in response to a decline in the availability of imported types following the end of the military occupation (Holbrook and Bidwell 1992, 62–7). There was little demand for these vessel types in the broader hinterland of the town. The predominant direction of regional trade in the 2nd century AD was therefore to the east, with trade beyond the Blackdown Hills accomplished primarily by sea. Westward links are not well represented in the archaeological record at this time. South Devon Ware first appears in Exeter in the 1st century AD, but only in very small quantities, and it is not until the late 2nd or early 3rd century AD that it begins to play a more significant role in the pottery supply to the town. Gabbroic pottery from Cornwall was never of any importance to the pottery supply of Exeter and its importation was restricted to the 1st and 2nd centuries AD (and see Chapter 3).

It is in the first half of the 3rd century AD that we find in the pottery a reflection of what was surely a major disruption to the established patterns of regional trade. It was at this time that the South-Western BB1 industry closed, as well as the much less significant production of Exeter Micaceous Grey Ware. The importation of Gaulish samian into Britain also ceased early in the 3rd century AD, provincial fine ware industries predominating thereafter. The factors that led to the closure of the South-Western BB1 industry in the Blackdown Hills are unclear, unless it was in some way tied to disruption of the iron industry there as well (we know virtually nothing of the chronology of ironmaking in the Blackdown Hills other than that production commenced in the 1st century AD; Griffith and Weddell 1996). From this time onwards Exeter was almost entirely supplied with coarse pottery by the South-East Dorset BB1 and South Devon Ware industries, supplemented by South-Western Grey Ware storage jars. The latter were produced at various locations in East Devon and South Somerset, including near Exeter (Chapter 3 above; EAPIT 2, Chapter 12). While storage jars were made in a number of places, their distribution is sufficiently marked to indicate the extent of a ceramic tradition that extended south-westwards from the Mendip Hills, although one that largely excluded the local heartland market for South-East Dorset BB1 (which produced its own storage jars, as indeed did the New Forest industry, and these reached Dorchester). The heightened use of South Devon Ware in Exeter at this time might also reflect increased contacts with this region associated with the exploitation of the slate beds for roofing material ('Devonian' slate has also been noted at a number of sites in South Somerset; Williams 1971, 107–8). Artefacts as yet provide little indication that Exeter played any significant role in the distribution of Cornish tin in the later Roman period. Gabbroic pottery was not used in the town at this time and Cornish stone mortars and quernstones made from granite, elvan and greisen are only occasional finds (Bidwell 1979, 242, no. 83; Holbrook and Bidwell 1991, fig. 133, no. 7; Shaffrey notes that elvan also outcrops around Roborough in the Tamar Valley as well as further west in Cornwall; EAPIT 2, Chapter 14). Nor is the production of pewter vessels attested in Exeter. While the manufacture of pewter vessels occurred at rural sites in Cornwall and South Devon (Chapter 2), the main focus of the industry was the Mendip Hills and Cornish/Dartmoor tin seems to have reached there by routes that largely avoided Exeter. While urban manufacture of pewter vessels is recorded at Gloucester and Silchester, the tin there was presumably acquired through the recycling of artefacts rather than being directly imported from the South-West Peninsula (Lee 2009).

Use and prevalence of artefacts

In 1991 the low number of coins retrieved from excavations in Exeter between 1971–9 was remarked upon and contrasted with towns such as Colchester where a programme of rescue excavation, also between 1971–9, yielded a considerably greater number (Holbrook and Bidwell 1991, 13). In recent years greater attention has been devoted to the vastly differing quantities of artefacts retrieved in excavations of rural settlements in different parts of Britain (Smith and Fulford 2016, 396–8, fig. 12.10). Further analysis is however seriously impeded by the considerable methodological problems inherent in determining the relative abundance of different types of artefact at different types of site and in different regions of Britain. The detailed mapping of these data is currently beyond us (but see Chapter 3 above for some analysis of the pottery), although the database created by the RSRB project forms a basis from which we can go forward. A broadly similar picture is also provided by the distribution of Roman artefacts reported to the PAS, although the complex biases in that dataset are now beginning to be more fully understood (Smith and Fulford 2016, fig. 12.4). The dichotomy between the artefact-rich zones of the Central Belt, South and East regions (as defined by RSRB) and the rest of the province is, however, clear enough, at an overview level at least. But what about the towns? There are considerable difficulties in making valid comparisons between different towns, such as accurate and accessible information on the volume of stratigraphy present, the types of deposit encountered, and the excavation methods adopted. This is exacerbated by the incomplete publication of quantified data on all major categories of artefact (Fulford 2015). It is therefore still the case that methodological issues hinder any meaningful comparison between different settlements, which is unfortunate as Exeter lay within a region where artefacts are poorly represented, both in the excavated record from rural settlements and the dataset produced by finds reported to the PAS (see Chapter 3 for the relative scarcity of pottery).

It would be instructive if we could determine whether that regional scarcity of artefacts is also reflected in the major town of the South-West Peninsula, or whether Exeter displays a similar level of artefact usage (or more precisely pattern of artefact loss) to towns further east (a similar state of affairs pertains with Carmarthen and Wroxeter as Roman material culture is likewise very poorly represented on many rural sites in their hinterlands; James 2003, 24–7; Gaffney *et al.* 2007, 280). Some readily accessible data concerning pottery, coins and metal brooches are presented in Tables 6.4–6.6 for Exeter and certain other major towns in western Britain, as well as Colchester for the purpose of contrast. While on face value the disparities in the quantities of artefacts recovered from Exeter and Colchester are stark, it may well be the case that larger areas were examined at Colchester than Exeter, and that the preservation of stratigraphy there was better. The extent of disturbance in Exeter to deposits associated with the Roman town should not be underestimated. For instance, the best preservation of later Roman levels so far found in the town was investigated at Trichay Street (Site 42), but even there about a quarter of those deposits had been destroyed by later cellars (EAPIT 2, Chapter 5).

The data recovered from the neighbouring *civitas* capitals are equally difficult to interpret. A single major excavation in Dorchester at Greyhound Yard looks to have produced as much pottery as all the Exeter sites put together, excluding the Cathedral Close. But Greyhound Yard only produced 233 identifiable coins, much less than Exeter. Indeed, the overall figures for Dorchester in Tables 6.4–6.6 are heavily skewed by the assemblages recovered from the 1937–8 excavation at Colliton Park (Durham and Fulford 2014). That site produced 1,395 coins and 41 brooches which must be directly related to the depth of Roman stratigraphy preserved there and lack of later disturbance. There might be some value in looking at the relative ratio of coins to pottery at different sites (x coins per y kg of pottery) but to be useful this would need to be a fine-grained analysis given

Table 6.4 Comparison of the quantity of Roman pottery recovered from excavations in Exeter compared to its nearest civitas *capitals, and for the purposes of contrast, Colchester*

Town	*Period of Excavations*	*Wt of Roman pottery (tonnes)*	*Comments*	*Reference*
Exeter	1971–9	0.9	0.15 tonnes reported in Bidwell 1979 (Cathedral Close); 0.75 tonnes in Holbrook and Bidwell 1991 (other sites)	
Ilchester	1974–5	0.4	Excavation on a considerably smaller scale than Exeter	Leach 1982b
Dorchester	1981–4	0.6	Greyhound Yard site only, and this just the weight of BB1 which constitutes *c.* 84% of the assemblage by sherd no.	Seager Smith and Davies 1993
Colchester	1971–86	15		Symonds and Wade 1999

Table 6.5 Comparison of the number of Roman coins from Exeter compared to its nearest civitas *capitals, and for the purposes of contrast, Colchester. The chronological phases are those of Reece. Phase A: up to AD 260; Phase B: AD 260–96; Phase C: AD 296–348 and Phase D: AD 348–402*

Town	*No. of coins*	*Excluding museum collection*	*Total Phase A*	*Total Phase B*	*Total Phase C*	*Total Phase D*	*Reference*
Exeter	1,625	572	623	360	448	194	Reece 1991a
Dorchester (intra-mural only)	1,915	1,915	121	817	618	359	Reece 1993
Caerwent	1,127	459	205	271	463	188	Besly 2003, table 8.3
Carmarthen	124	106	97	16	8	3	Besly 2003
Colchester	10,890	2,740	3,744	2,897	2,541	1,708	Reece 1987b

Table 6.6 Comparison of the number of Roman brooches from Exeter compared to its nearest civitas *capitals, and for the purposes of contrast, Colchester*

Town	*No.*	*Comment*	*Reference*
Exeter	44	1971–9 excavations	Mackreth 1991
Dorchester	76	Greyhound Yard (35) & Colliton Park (41) only	Crummy 2014
Ilchester	32	1974–5 excavations	Mackreth 1982
Carmarthen	41	1978–93 excavations	Webster 2003
Colchester	103	1971–9 excavations	Crummy 1983

the marked chronological variations in the frequency of coins recovered as site finds. Thirty years on from the publication of *Roman Finds From Exeter* we are therefore little further forward in our ability to determine whether the quantities of material culture used in the Roman town were comparable with, or less than at, towns further east. This could profitably be a research priority for future work in the town, but to be achieved it will require considerable planning prior to the commencement of fieldwork, and coordination during post-excavation analysis.

Conclusions

While interest in the Roman town has to some degree been over shadowed by the attention directed to the spectacular, but short-lived, period of military occupation, there is no doubt that Exeter has the potential to provide valuable insights into the process of urbanisation in a landscape far removed from the economic heartlands of Roman Britain. The legionary presence undoubtedly influenced the subsequent history of Roman Exeter although the sudden drop in population by three quarters or more towards the end of the 1st century AD would have had a profound impact locally, and more widely on the importance of Exeter as a destination for imported goods. As has been argued in the previous chapter, it now seems that there was already a civilian settlement at St Loye's College, 2.2 km south-east of the fortress and distinct from the civilian occupation immediately beyond its defences, as well as the port settlement at Topsham 3 km beyond St Loye's. When the legion was finally withdrawn from Exeter the decision was taken to turn the vacant fortress site into the administrative capital for the newly created *civitas Dumnoniorum*, and the State through the medium of the army was surely the primary driver in enacting this policy. Work in Exeter began on some scale, to judge from the size of the forum which is the 7th-largest such complex in Britain for which we have adequate information (Bidwell 1979, 80, tab. 6). This is a clear physical manifestation of the urban aspirations of the town authorities at the close of the 1st century AD. Indeed, Exeter was conceivably intended to function in the manner of a *colonia*, even though it never actually attained that legal status, and Bidwell has suggested in Chapter 5 that there may have been some continuing small-scale military presence in Exeter into the 2nd century AD, perhaps accommodated in a compound just inside the North-East gate of the early town.

While Exeter was undoubtedly the administrative centre, it was not a port-town itself despite its location at the lowest bridging point of one of the major estuaries on the Channel coast. That distinction lay with Topsham, 6 km further downstream, and it is important to recognise the importance of Topsham in its own right. Occupation looks to have extended over 20–25 ha and so Topsham must have had a reasonable resident population. What impact might the proximity of the port-town have had on the development of the new administrative centre at Exeter? With the exception of Southwark, on the south bank of the Thames opposite London, there are no other examples in Britain of a settlement the size of Topsham in such close proximity to a major town (there was roadside settlement at Barnwood, 3 km from Gloucester, but this was of no particular extent and might in fact just be part of the extensive extra-mural occupation around the *colonia*: Hurst 1999b; Holbrook 2018, 172–3). In addition, there was also continuing 2nd-century AD and later occupation at St Loye's College, although perhaps not on any great scale. As we have seen there is as yet little evidence for the rapid and intensive residential or mercantile development of Exeter in the decades either side of AD 100. Perhaps the existing population at Topsham inhibited the early development in Exeter, beyond the State-encouraged public building programme? But Exeter did develop over time, and some vitality is demonstrated by the sequence of timber buildings at Trichay Street (Site 42) where three successive structures predated a fire in the Hadrianic or early Antonine period, and two successive buildings were built after that event but prior to a re-planning which occurred no later than the early 3rd century AD (EAPIT 2, Chapter 5, Buildings RC5–9). Organised butchery was taking place in Exeter by *c.* AD 120 at latest to judge from the dump of waste cattle bones in a ditch at Rack Street (Sites 52/64), and Müldner and Frémondeau's analysis in Chapter 3 of stable isotopes derived from the teeth of cattle and sheep/goat demonstrates that the residents of Exeter were reliant in the 2nd century AD for their food on livestock reared in the Devonian hinterlands of the town, rather than imported from elsewhere as seems to have been occurred to some degree during the period of military occupation.

There is little evidence for pressure on urban space during the 2nd century AD, and it is some surprise that the defended area was more than doubled *c.* AD 160–80 by the construction of a new set of earthwork defences. Christopher Henderson was firmly of the opinion that these works were erected very rapidly (over just a few weeks or months) as an emergency measure and he thought the expanded area might have been used as a temporary refuge for the surrounding rural population, their animals and agricultural produce (Henderson 1999, 483–4; 2001, 65–6; for a discussion of the possible historical context for the urban earthwork defences in Britain see Frere 1984). The broad, yet low, form of the earthwork bank is, however, curious if it was intended as an emergency defence and it is not uncommon for Roman towns to enclose tracts of open land that were never developed (as at Cirencester amongst other places for example; Wacher 1995, 78–81; Wacher and Salvatore 1998, 96–8).

In its adoption of earthwork defences, subsequently enhanced in stone, Exeter falls within the British provincial urban norm, as it does in the appearance from the 3rd century AD of domestic houses built (at least partly) from dressed masonry and on a larger scale than previously. It would be wrong, however, to view Exeter as some kind of 'garden city', for where excavation has been extensive enough it shows that smaller timber and masonry buildings existed side by side with the town houses, with the central spaces of the *insulae* probably used for activities such as horticulture and stock-rearing. Exeter seems to have been a dirty and smelly place with muddy streets and open spaces. One of the discoveries that generated much interest at the time of excavation in 1972–3 was the recognition of a Late Roman stockyard, complete with water trough, in the heart of the town at Trichay Street, and nearby small stock-rearing pens which had their ditches infilled in a couple of places with dumps of primary butchery waste (Sites 42 and 37; EAPIT 2, Chapter 5). The role of some Late Roman towns in agricultural storage has since then become increasingly recognised, although it is surprising that to date Exeter has not produced any examples of the barns or tower granaries known from some other towns (perhaps this reflects a local emphasis on pastoral rather than arable agriculture?; Rogers 2011, 122–5; Fulford 2015, 199–201; and see Chapter 3 above). Buildings in some parts of Exeter were being abandoned in the second half of the 4th century AD, with occupation ceasing in the South Gate suburb by *c*. AD 360 and in the last quarter of that century we can plot a contraction in occupation towards the core of the town. Exeter is by no means alone in this trajectory, but sadly we have little or no evidence for how long a recognisably urban way of life persisted here after *c*. AD 400.

What kind of place was *Isca Dumnoniorum*? In some aspects of its history and layout it conforms quite closely with broad provincial urban trends. But its location 'out on a limb', and with no single place of any great significance beyond it to the west, must have impacted on the culture and identity of its citizens. Whether it was just the residence of bureaucrats, apparatchiks and those who made a living from the presence of these State-paid officials, or it did indeed function successfully as a market centre for its hinterland, is discussed in Chapter 9. The neighbouring *civitas* capitals to the east of Dorchester and (probably) Ilchester were not that far away in distance but lay in altogether different cultural regions. Mosaics, for example, are poorly attested in Exeter compared to those two places, and those that are recorded possess a somewhat idiosyncratic character distinct from the mainstream outputs of the workshops centred around the two towns. While we can debate the detrimental impact of later activity in Exeter on the potential preservation of mosaic pavements, the poor showing here compared to some other towns should not be taken as a simple reflection of impoverishment but rather as an indicator of differing cultural attitudes that attributed less significance to the possession of such floors. Cultural attitudes can be reflected in a variety of ways, however. For instance the contents of a late 3rd or early 4th-century AD pit dug just outside the winter dining room of Building 45ii at Princesshay (Site 156, pit 4880) contained feasting debris including the remnants of piglets and small birds; a grand meal very much in the Roman tradition it would seem (Maltby above).

In some respects there is a disparity apparent at Exeter. On the one hand its location on the Exe Estuary, with a port at Topsham, made it an important node in the inter-provincial Atlantic trade network, a practice that may have operated on quite a considerable scale (the ceramic markers available to us tell us something of the direction of this trade, but little of its intensity). We might reasonably envisage therefore quite a connected, cosmopolitan, population in Exeter and Topsham, yet at the provincial level Exeter – and its hinterland – displays a marked insularity. The ceramic networks which supplied the town were heavily regionally focussed, and distinct from those that supplied rural settlements in South Somerset, West Dorset and Cornwall (Chapter 3). Long-distance imports from South-East England never formed a significant part of the ceramic repertoire used in Exeter, in large measure a simple product of distance from these kilns. Insularity is also apparent in some other types of artefact such as the querns which were strongly reliant on local stone sources as opposed to the import of products of the major industries operating in other parts of the province (EAPIT 2, Chapter 14). The small size of the domestic stock consumed in Exeter also contrasts with some other parts of the province where animal sizes increased during the Roman period (Maltby above).

Haverfield may not have been too wide of the mark on the initial aspiration for *Isca Dumnoniorum* to serve as an 'outpost of Romanization in the far west', and indeed the founding fathers may have realistically hoped to see the elevation of Exeter to a *colonia* at some point. But that never happened, and we detect in the archaeological record a somewhat local take on the Romano-Gaulish idea of a town which seems to have been the inspiration behind the major urban centres of Britain. If Exeter does represent unfulfilled ambition, that does not make it any the less interesting for the study of the dynamics of Romano-British urbanism.

Appendix 6.1

A reappraisal of the basilica structural sequence

Paul Bidwell

According to the excavation report published in 1979 (Bidwell 1979; all the page, figure and plate references that follow in this appendix are to this publication unless otherwise indicated) the basilica and forum at Exeter underwent three periods of reconstruction: first in the late Antonine period, about a century after the buildings were converted from the remains of the fortress baths, then in the last quarter of the 3rd century AD and finally at a date no earlier than *c.* AD 340/350. The last was the most radical, involving a lengthening of the basilica at its south-east end and the rebuilding of its front aisle. One detail of these works seemed to confirm that the basilica was still the seat of local government. Originally there had been a room in the range behind the nave of the basilica at its south-east end which was likely to have served as the *curia* (p. 84–6). When the basilica was extended, this room was reinstated, preserving more or less the original proportions of its plan (p. 109). Perhaps also connected with a governmental function, and certainly ceremonial, was the insertion of a podium at the south-east end of the extended nave.

Civic buildings in the towns of the later Roman period in Britain had varying fortunes. That was already plain enough before 1979 when the Exeter report was published. Frere (1967, 244), for example, had contrasted the continued use and maintenance of the basilica and forum at Cirencester with the failure to rebuild such buildings at Wroxeter after a fire in the late 3rd century AD. Later surveys, the most recent of which is by Rogers (2011, 75–83), confirm this picture, while adding much more detail. It is against the background of this detail, particularly the question of what the continued use and alteration of these buildings represented, that Exeter seems to stand out as exceptional. The most extensive rebuilding in the 4th century AD elsewhere was at Cirencester where it might have been connected with adaptations for the government of *Britannia Prima*, a province established in the early 4th century AD (Holbrook and Timby 1998a, 121). Exeter is the only example where the rebuilding would point to a continuation of the original function of the basilica as the centre of local government in its traditional form.

There is no reason to doubt the significance of the rebuilding at Exeter, but, some forty years after the original publication, its date now seems less certain. When the basilica was built in the late 1st century AD, it incorporated the south-east and north-east walls of the Neronian fortress baths. The south-east wall, which formed the end wall of the basilica, had been part of the *caldarium*. On this side of the room there had been two apses flanking a rectangular recess, all three elements set between two small rooms in the corner of the building. There were thus four short lengths of walling which extended north-west of the main wall. When the baths were partly demolished, these lengths were largely removed, leaving only a few of their lower courses. Their junctions with the main south-east wall were cut back and faced across with rough mortared masonry. Higher up, in the fabric of the south-east wall that no longer survives, there must have been much more extensive rebuilding. Because the floor of the basilica was *c.* 0.70–80 m higher than that of the *caldarium*, the windows probably had to be repositioned. A gable would also have been added to the wall to support the roof of the basilica; the main rooms in the baths had been each covered with barrel vaults, their roof lines running at a right angle to that of the basilica.

Eventual failure of this much altered fabric might have been the occasion for rebuilding the end of the basilica. Following its demolition, the nave and the range at its rear were extended for a distance of 6.8 m to the south-east (Period 3A), which involved the demolition of a passage and range of rooms between the original end of the basilica and an adjacent street. Much of this extension had been destroyed by the medieval church of St Mary Major and, more extensively, by its Victorian successor. Its plan was clear enough, but not much was left of the surrounding stratigraphy. The crucial structural relationship was with a hypocaust that in the previous period (2C, dated in the original report to the last quarter of the 3rd century AD) had apparently been built in a room south-east of the basilica and which was then, it seems, demolished to make way for the front aisle of the basilica extension. The remains of this room were severely damaged by post-medieval graves, but sufficient survived to show that the hypocaust consisted of channels combined with a central area where the floor was supported by tile *pilae* (pp. 100–1, figs 30 and 36, section 1). In the filling of the hypocaust following its demolition, there was a large fragment of an Oxfordshire colour-coated bowl decorated with rosette stamps (p. 108, fig. 67, no. 207) of Young (1977), Type C78, dated *c.* AD 340–400. It was taken to provide a *terminus post quem* for the extension of the basilica.

The main reason for attributing the hypocaust to the earlier period was that its basement floor lay at a lower level than the top of the foundations in the extension. More generally, the insertion of the hypocaust was thought to have been part of the renovations at the beginning of Period 2C, the second extensive reconstruction of the basilica and forum. There is, however, another possible interpretation, overlooked in the original report, which, by combining the construction of the hypocaust with the extension of the basilica, has the advantage of simplifying the structural sequence (Fig. 6.13). That would allow the extension to have been part of the wider renovations in Period 2C instead of a separate and much later event, its date apparently established by the *terminus post quem* of *c.* AD 340 supplied by the pottery sherd from the demolition of the hypocaust.

The 1979 report made too much of the disparity in the levels of the hypocaust basement and the south-west foundation of the extension. The floor of the basement only survived at the north-western end of the room (fig. 36, section 1, 21A; the number is partly obscured, but the layer is the thin deposit that abuts the lowest course of the channel wall (p. 17) and the lowest tile of the *pila*). It was only a few centimetres below the surviving top of the rubble foundation (fig. 36, section 3, F91) at a point *c.* 3.0 m south of the surviving basement floor. In the absence of any direct relationship between the hypocaust and the extension, the possibility that the two went together cannot be excluded. In this case the hypocaust would have been inserted after the walls were built, and in forming its basement some of the foundation rafts might have been partly cut away. The walls of the extension were set on rubble foundations in very wide trenches (fig. 32, pl. XI), and a slight trimming of their edges when the hypocaust basement was dug out was unlikely to have threatened the stability of the structure.

If the hypocaust was part of the extension of the basilica, there would be implications for the history of its surrounding structures. There were two crucial relationships: one was with the rooms and narrow passage between the basilica and the street to the south-east which were demolished to make way for the extension, and the other was between the rooms and passage and the forum area where there was a structural sequence with some useful dating evidence. When the forum was built, a covered stone-lined drain was connected with a gutter that ran along the front of the south-eastern portico; it ran across the width of the portico and down the middle of a passage which opened into the street on the south-east side of the basilica and forum. The drain also had a branch that collected water from the apparently open passage immediately south-east of the basilica (fig. 19). The length serving the gutter along the south-east edge of the forum became redundant when the portico was replaced by a large room, and both sections of the drain had been filled in by the time the extension was built (p. 94).

At the beginning of Period 2B, after the drains went out of use, the level in the passage was raised and mortar floors were inserted in the rooms between the passage and the street to the south-east (pp. 94–5, fig. 26). After the level of these rooms was raised by a dump of clay mixed with mortar debris, another mortar floor was laid down (p. 101). The subsequent deposits were only preserved in a narrow pinnacle between grave cuts which survived to a height of 39.20 m OD, that is, to about the same height as the floor in the nave of the basilica. Unfortunately, it is impossible to know whether the deposits in this chance survival of stratigraphy relate to the extension or the room that preceded it. All that can be said is that the extension was later than the beginning of Period 2B and at least one phase of alteration when the floor was raised in the rooms south-east of the basilica.

The date of Period 2B needs clarification. The construction of the large room that replaced the south-east forum portico was tied into sequences of deposits in the forum and south-west aisle of the basilica. From the foundation trench of the north-west wall of this room, there was a mortarium (fig. 66, no. 173), which can now be confidently identified as a Rhineland product dating to *c.* AD 150–250 (Hartley 1991, Type C56), and a samian stamp dated to *c.* AD 115–145 (no. 3). Finds from levelling in the forum that preceded the building of the wall included a samian Dr. 37 of *c.* AD 140–60, and from the filling of gully 1 there came the base of a plain-rimmed dish in BB1 (DOR BB1; fig. 65, no. 161), a type not known from contexts earlier than the Antonine period (Holbrook and Bidwell 1991, 99). Deposits of Period 2B construction in the forum area were thus no earlier than *c.* AD 150. The late Antonine date proposed in the 1979 report for this period as a whole depended on samian of this date (pp. 95–6) from the courtyard behind the basilica; they were in a sequence of deposits isolated from the rest of the site and in retrospect can be seen to have no bearing on the date of the activities of Period 2B in the forum area and south-east of the basilica.

The next period of construction (2C) is a plausible context for the extension if it was earlier than the mid 4th century AD. The front wall of the south-west aisle of the basilica was rebuilt and the floor of the aisle was raised to the same level as that in the basilica; the level of the forum courtyard was also raised. In the 1979 report, the rebuilding of the north-west wall of the large room on the south-east side of the forum was allocated to this period (p. 100, fig. 29), despite the fact that it displayed the same construction techniques employed in the extension. Where the new work was on the same lines as pre-existing walls, the earlier fabric was taken down to ground level; trenches were then dug along the faces of the wall stumps and packed with rubble, producing the very wide foundations characteristic of the extension (pp. 104–7, fig. 32). It is a reasonable assumption that all the walls of this type were of the same period. Regrettably, robbing of the wall in the large room had destroyed the relationship between its foundations and the level from which they were inserted. Its renewal, however, may have been necessary because of the rebuilding of the aisle wall which abutted its north-west side, and that would carry with it the extension of the basilica because of the similarities of their building techniques.

The deposits which provide a date for Period 2C included Antonine samian mixed with earlier material. The latest sherds were from black-burnished ware cooking pots from South-East Dorset (DOR BB1), found in the south-west aisle and forum courtyard (p. 102; the flanged bowl, fig. 67, no. 200, is from the isolated area north-east of the basilica and is not relevant to the date of Period 2C). They were decorated with obtuse-angled lattice, a style which in 1979 was thought to date to no earlier than the mid 3rd century AD, but which was subsequently shown to have been current by *c*. AD 220 (Holbrook and Bidwell 1991, 96).

In Period 2B the rebuilding had been mainly limited to the replacement of the south-east forum portico by a room and a rearrangement of the rooms south-east of the basilica. Even if the extension of the basilica is excluded, the alterations in Period 2C were much more radical. Raising the level of the south-west aisle was an architectural transformation which brought the basilica closer to the usual form of its building type, with the floors of its main areas all at one level (the floor of the basilica nave had originally been 0.80–0.90 m above the level of the forum, and when the south-west aisle was added shortly after the basilica was built, its floor was at the level of the forum and the steps leading up to the higher floor of the nave were retained). Replacement of the probably defective end wall of the basilica by an extension to the south-east and not by a new wall on the original line would have been part of this transformation. The structural links of the extension with Period 2C may be tenuous, but in terms of the overall redesign the association is persuasive.

The *terminus post quem* for Period 2C and thus, as it has been argued, for the building of the extension, is *c*. AD 220. The upper limit of the possible date range is set by the absence from the relevant deposits of flanged bowls in South-East Dorset BB1, South Devon Ware and South-Western Grey Ware storage jars which are common in later 3rd-century AD deposits. A broad dating for the beginning of Period 2C to the second and third quarters of the 3rd century AD is indicated.

Later levels were truncated by burials beginning around the 6th century AD and continuing for more than a thousand years, or as late as Victorian times in the church of St Mary Major. In the south-west aisle there was a pit probably lined with planks, the filling of which produced a sherd of 4th-century AD pottery, and there were scraps of mortar floors in the aisle and nave that seemed to be later than the beginning of Period 2C (pp. 106–8). There were also fragments of two successive floors in the range north-east of the basilica (p. 108); they sealed debris from a fire that took place in the later 3rd century AD (p. 97, 101). The hypocaust in the room now regarded as part of the extension at the beginning of Period 2C was demolished after *c*. AD 340, as we have seen. The implication is that this part of the building was standing at that date: the hypocaust would hardly have survived the demolition of the room above it. It is of course possible that the hypocaust was demolished long before this part of the basilica and forum was levelled, which had taken place by the time burial commenced on the site sometime in the 5th to 7th centuries AD (see Chapter 7).

7

The Early Medieval Period *c.* 410–900 and Urban Revival *c.* 900–1200

John Allan

with contributions by Robert Higham, Mark Maltby and Stephen Rippon

Early medieval Exeter

By Stephen Rippon

Between the 5th and mid 9th centuries neither archaeology nor historical sources shed much light on the fate of *Isca Dumnoniorum*, before the town was revived first as a late 9th century *burh* and soon after a town. Although pottery imported from North Africa and the eastern Mediterranean during the mid 5th to mid 6th centuries has been found on a number of coastal sites in eastern and southern Devon – notably High Peak, Bantham and Mothecombe (see above, Chapter 4) – none has been recovered from Exeter. It is, however, one of only two Romano-British towns in southern Britain (the other being Dorchester) that have produced sherds of 4th-century North African amphora types that continued to be produced into the 5th century: a rim of Keay Type XXVB, produced from the early to mid 4th century through to the first half of the 5th century, was found in a 4th-century or early 5th-century context at Trichay Street (Site 42), while an unstratified basal spike, probably from the same type, was found at Queen Street (Site 68). It is impossible to say whether these vessels are 4th or 5th century, but tantalisingly sherds that may be from Palestinian amphorae dating to the 5th and 6th centuries have been found on three sites near the centre of the town where the latest Roman occupation appears to have been concentrated (Sites 40, 42, 89: Bidwell 1979, tab. 10; Holbrook and Bidwell 1991, tab. 14; 1992, 60, tab. 5). There are also a handful of unidentified sherds that might include some late Mediterranean imports (Reed *et al.* 2011, 113–14; Bidwell 2016).

The latest Roman coin from Exeter is a 'very worn' issue of Theodosius minted in AD 388–92 (Holbrook and Bidwell 1991, 31), and although numerous Byzantine coins are said to have been found in Exeter – more than in any other Roman town – none of them are thought to be genuine 5th or 6th-century losses. They lack the corrosion products typical of coins that have lain in the soil of Exeter for many centuries, but instead have the thin buff-coloured coating of coins from the Levant, or have been polished and scraped by collectors (Shortt 1841, 79–108; Haverfield and Macdonald 1907; Goodchild and Milne 1937; Allan *et al.* 1984, 257; Boon 1991, 40; Moorhead 2009).

Across most of Exeter the stratigraphic evidence points to widespread abandonment. The Roman street grid virtually disappeared, the exceptions being short stretches of road leading from the East and West Gates that will have survived because these were two of only four ways in and out of the city and so these roads will inevitably have been reused when urban life returned in the late 9th/early 10th centuries (Fig. 7.1). On many sites (where it has not been removed by later truncation) the latest Roman occupation is sealed by a so-called 'dark earth'. Deposits of post-Roman dark earth containing solely Roman artefacts are relatively rare, as in many cases later medieval pottery has been introduced through subsequent cultivation, and unfortunately this was the case with the only dark earth in Exeter – at Paul Street (Site 76) – to have been subject to micromorphological analysis (Macphail and Courty 1985). This sequence of dark earth accumulated to the rear of the rampart bank behind the town wall, where even the lowest levels (context 1205) contained both Late Roman pottery and later medieval (13th-century) material. The sampled deposits displayed considerable similarity, appearing to be uniform clay loams with few anthropogenic inclusions and

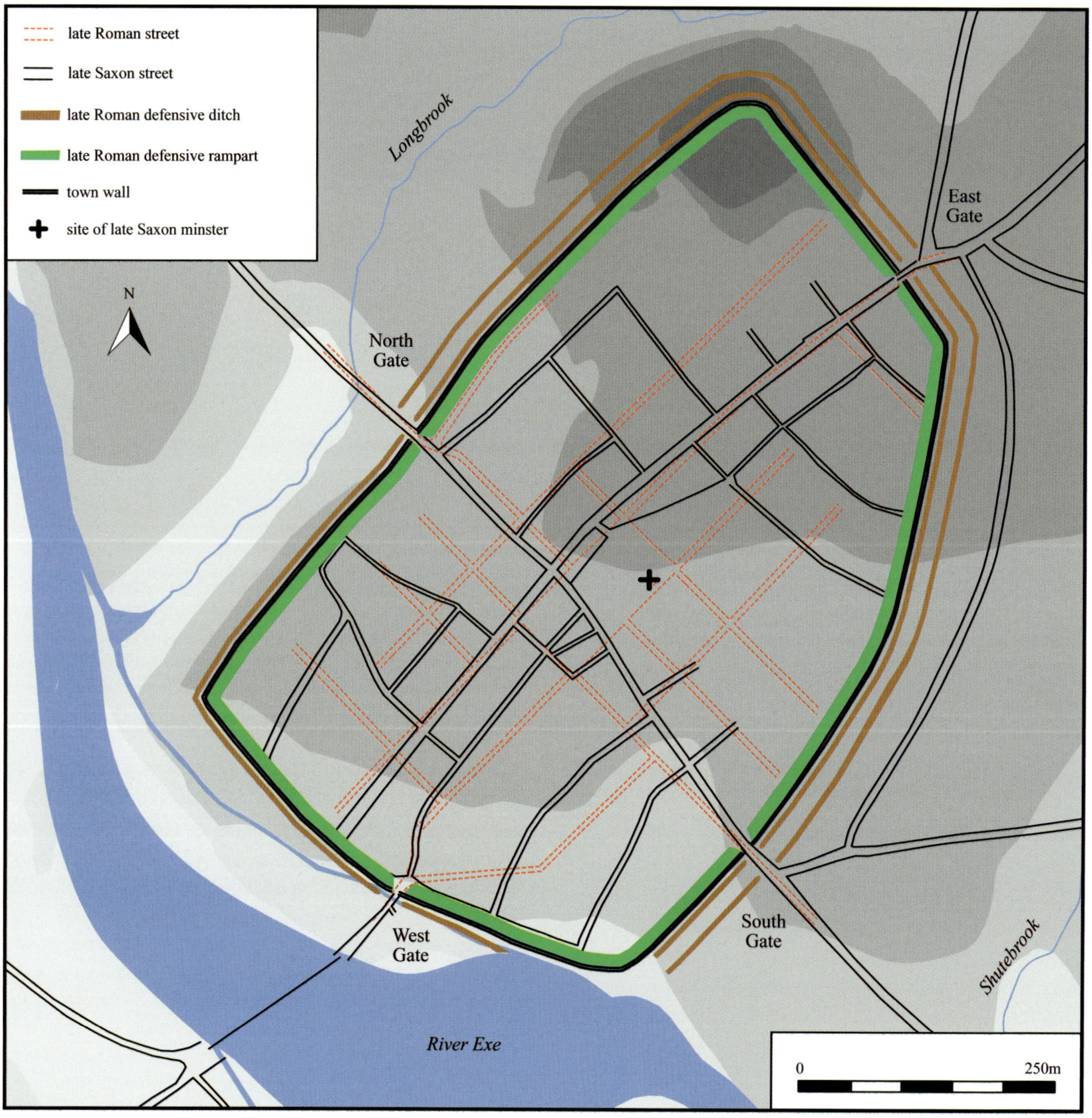

Fig. 7.1 The later Roman and Late Saxon street layouts, showing almost no relationship between the two (drawn by David Gould)

relatively little charcoal. Further work on the dark earths of Exeter is clearly required, for as yet the town has little to contribute to national debates about the processes which generated them. Dark earths are not the same in every town and can be the product of different land uses, with some indicative of activity (such as cattle rearing), and others of abandonment (dumping on disused plots). The dark earths in each town, and indeed each locality within a town, therefore need to be analysed on a case-by-case basis, and this should be a priority in future excavations in Exeter.

Astill (2000, 31) has argued that 'religion reclaimed Roman towns', when they were used as the location for Augustinian and later churches 'as a conscious and symbolic use of the Roman past' (and see Blair *et al.* 2020), and although that appears to have been the case in Exeter the origins of the church there may have been somewhat earlier. To date, the only evidence for activity within the walled city during the 5th and 6th centuries consists of the post-Roman burials excavated in 1971–2 following the demolition of the Victorian church of St Mary Major that stood on the site of the Late Saxon minster in Cathedral Close (Figs 7.2–7.3; Bidwell 1979, 111; Henderson and Bidwell 1982; Allan *et al.* 1984; Site 40). The determinations from the two burials that were

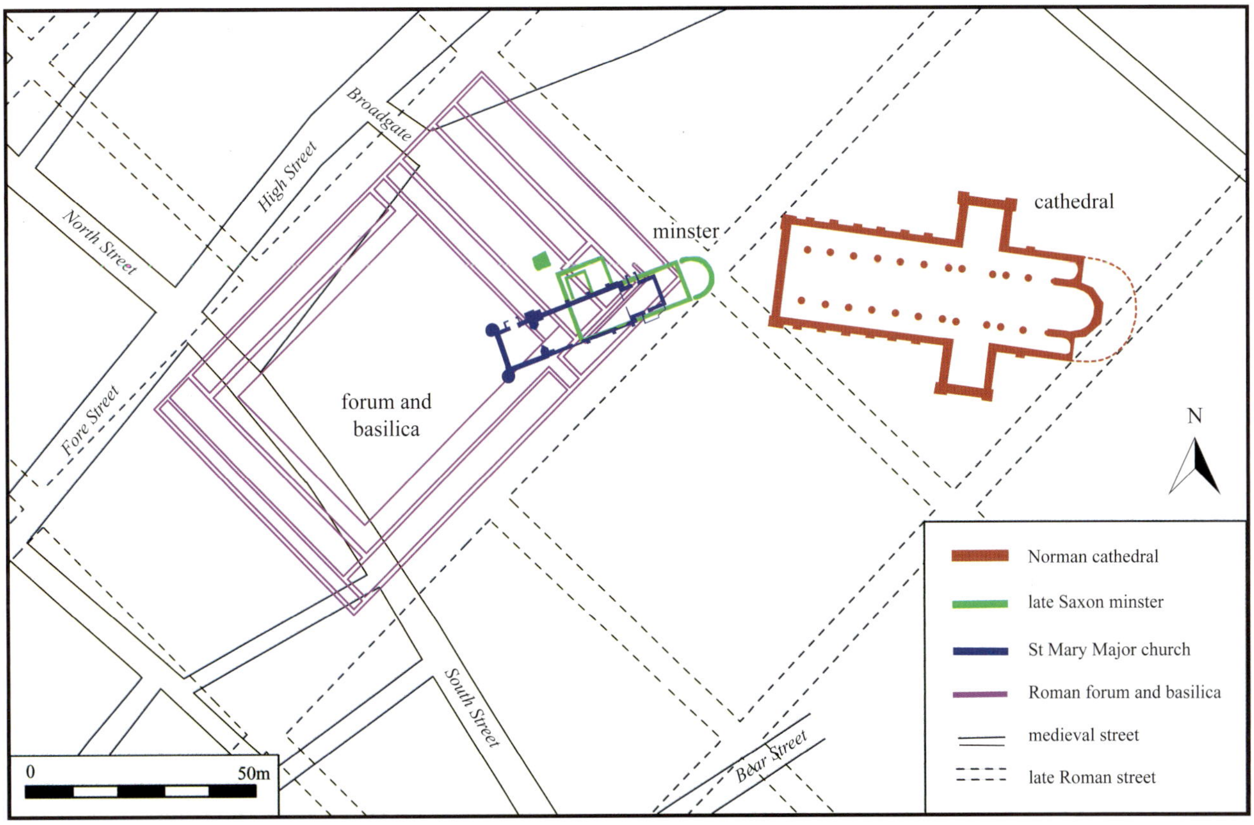

Fig. 7.2 The relative positions of the Roman basilica and forum, the Late Saxon minster which later became the church of St Mary Major, and the Norman cathedral (drawn by David Gould)

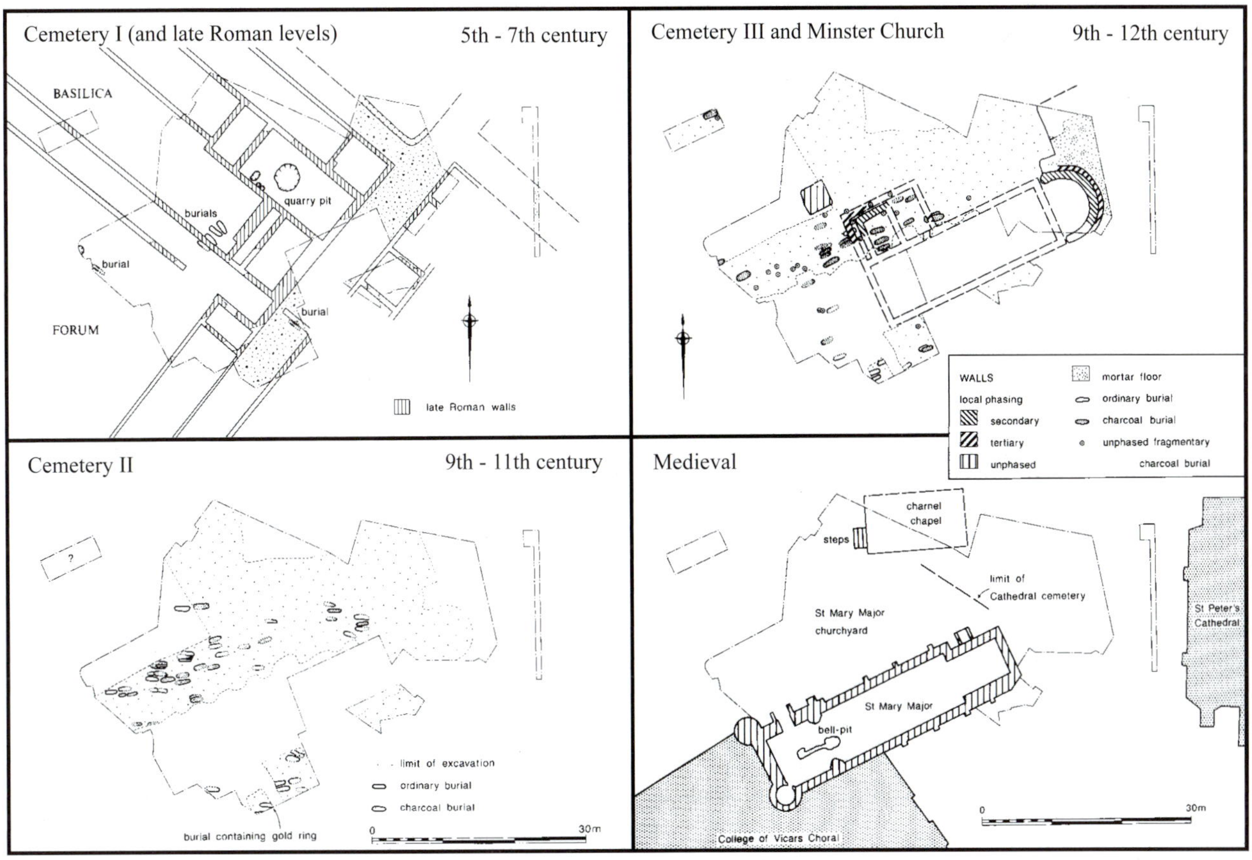

Fig. 7.3 The cemeteries and churches in the Cathedral Close excavations 1971–6 (Site 40), as published in Allan et al. *1984. Note that Cemeteries II and III are now regarded as broadly contemporary (Exeter Archaeology Archive; © Exeter City Council)*

radiocarbon-dated in the 1970s have now been recalibrated as cal. AD 390–650 and cal. AD 530–660 (OB278: HAR-1614 at 100% probability; OB486: HAR-1613 at 93% probability; EAPIT 2, Chapter 19). A second sample from the latter burial, submitted for dating in 2012, has given a date of cal. AD 428–619 (SUERC 57530 at 93% confidence). Rather than indicating a date in the 5th century as appeared to be the case in the 1980s, therefore, the radiocarbon dates from the post-Roman cemetery now indicate a general 5th to early 7th-century date.

These burials were oriented north-west to south-east, parallel to the walls and streets associated with the Roman forum-basilica, presumably indicating that their orientation was determined by elements surviving from the Late Roman town, but no evidence was recovered to indicate whether these were standing buildings, ruins or other features (Bidwell 1979, fig. 32). They lay beneath numerous burials of the medieval cemetery, and it was argued that the surviving graves were part of a more extensive 5th to 6th-century Christian cemetery, possibly associated with a church built in or around the ruins of the Roman basilica and forum (*e.g.* Bidwell 1979, 112–13; Allan *et al.* 1984, 386–9).

The burials overlying these early graves were interpreted in the 1980s as the remains of two successive cemeteries, the first with graves roughly on an east–west alignment (Fig. 7.3, Cemetery II), the second with burials aligned with the minster church, which is orientated almost 20 degrees to the north (Fig. 7.3, Cemetery III). It was tentatively suggested that the two different alignments reflected a change in orientation of the graves following the refoundation of the minster under Æthelstan in 932 (Henderson and Bidwell 1982). Cemetery II would then date from the 7th to early 10th century, and Cemetery III from the early 10th to early 12th century. The results of radiocarbon dating now indicate that the burials on the two alignments are in fact broadly contemporary, and they are now regarded as a single cemetery (see Allan below). The earliest burials in Cemeteries II and III for which we have radiocarbon dates belong to the late 8th or 9th century – very probably prior to the foundation of the *burh* in the 890s (OB 205 from Cemetery II: cal. AD 766–899 at 88% probability; CB 66 from Cemetery III: cal. AD 768–899 at 90% probability; Kingdom 2019, tab. 3.3). It should also be noted that the only stratified find from the cemetery which was thought to be of Middle Saxon date – the gold finger ring recovered from an inhumation to the south of the church (Graham Campbell 1982) – now appears to be rather later in date than was first suggested, or it was an heirloom, since the skeleton it accompanied has been radiocarbon-dated to cal. AD 949–1036 at 90% confidence (Kingdom, EAPIT 2, Chapter 19, burial OB 2).

Although no direct evidence for an early church was found, and no burials of the late 7th or 8th centuries have so far been identified, it still seems reasonable to associate the origins of the cemetery with the monastery first mentioned in the late 7th century where St Boniface is said to have received his early education (Willibald's Life of St Boniface; Barlow 1980, 27; Holdsworth 1980, 52–4; Orme 2009, 2). The saint was probably born about *c.* 675, and his education at Exeter would have been in the 680s. It is possible that the church was a West Saxon foundation as its Abbot – Wulfhard – had a Saxon name (see Chapter 4 above for a discussion of the West Saxon expansion into Dumnonia). The presence of a minster in Exeter may also be implied by Asser's Life of Alfred, written in 893, where it is stated that the King had granted the author 'Exeter with all the *parochia* belonging to it', although the meaning of this is somewhat unclear (Orme 2009, 5–6). The excavated fragments of church are presumably of later date, representing the minster refounded by Æthelstan in 932 and elevated to cathedral status when Bishop Leofric transferred his seat from Crediton in 1050 (Orme 2009, 7–10). It served as Exeter's cathedral until the consecration of the new Norman building in 1133 (Henderson and Bidwell 1982; Allan *et al.* 1984, 391).

The establishment of early churches within the ruins of abandoned Roman settlements – both forts and towns – was common practice following the Augustinian mission. It is first seen in the establishment of his own church in Canterbury, and followed soon after by the installation of Mellitus as Bishop of the East Saxons in London, and Justus as Bishop in Rochester in 604 (*Bede* II.3). In eastern England the trend continued in the mid 7th century, for example when in 664 Cedd founded a new church in the East Saxon kingdom at *Ythancaestir* (the ruins of the Roman fort at Bradwell-on-Sea; *Bede* III.22). In south-western Britain old Roman sites were similarly reused as the locations for Anglo-Saxon minsters, as seen at Bath when King Osric of the Hwicce founded the church there in 675 (Sawyer 1968, No. 51). Another example may be St Andrew's church in Northover, just outside Ilchester, as in Domesday it had a relatively large estate of 3 hides of land suggesting that it was an early minster (Dunning 1975; Costen 2011, 148–9).

As Devon was aceramic in this period (excepting the rare finds of E ware), and lay outside the zone within which coinage circulated, it is not surprising that there is no other evidence for activity during the 7th and 8th centuries, although there is remarkably little material from the 9th century either. In addition to the gold finger ring mentioned above, there have been two other 9th-century finds from the Cathedral Close (*i.e.* close to the presumed Saxon minster): a strap-end from the robbing of the Late Saxon minster (Graham-Campbell 1983), and a penny of Archbishop Ceolnoth of Canterbury (833–70; Montgomerie-Neilson and Montague 1934, 107), although it should be noted that coins of Ceolnoth remained in circulation until the early 10th century (*e.g.* in the Cuerdale hoard of *c.* 905; John Naylor pers. comm.). Another probably mid 9th-century coin – a forgery of a

Frisian derivative of a *solidus* of Louis the Pious (814–40) – was found on the banks of the River Exe at the Exe Bridge (Site 56) (Archibald 1984, 250; Brown 2019, 124), although these coins also remained in circulation until at least the late 9th century (*e.g.* at Torksey; John Naylor pers. comm.). The final piece of metalwork from this period is a copper-alloy strap-end from Princesshay datable only broadly to the 9th century (Steinmetzer, Pearce and Allan forthcoming). This is a very meagre haul, but it is unclear whether this reflects a genuine absence of occupation within Exeter, or simply the scarcity of durable material culture across the South-West Peninsula generally as sites that have been radiocarbon-dated to this period appear to have been aceramic (*e.g.* Berry Meadow, in Kingsteignton: Weddell 1987; Pinn Brook Enclosure: Garland and Whelan 2016). In contrast, Dorchester has produced more 7th to 9th-century finds including six sceattas, a gold finger ring, a dress hook, and a few sherds of Middle Saxon pottery (Keen 1984, 707; Woodward *et al.* 1993, 378).

Overall, the absence of datable material culture from Exeter in the 5th to 8th centuries is very difficult to interpret. While no mid 5th to mid 6th-century pottery imported from the Mediterranean has been recorded in Exeter, only one possible sherd has been found at any inland site in Devon (Lydford, discussed in Chapter 4). Indeed, there is so little datable material culture in the county before the 10th century that the small number of 9th-century finds – mostly from the vicinity of the minster – is particularly significant. The 5th to early 7th-century radiocarbon-dated burials may have been part of a larger cemetery, but we can only speculate that they were associated with a church. It can, however, reasonably be assumed that the overlying cemetery relates to the church at which the young Boniface studied in the late 7th century, and which in the early 10th century was rebuilt by Æthelstan before being promoted to a cathedral in 1050. In being an ecclesiastical centre from the later 7th century, Exeter is typical of many old Roman towns, but as yet there is no evidence for any other settlement until the late 9th century.

Urban revival

By John Allan

The Norman chroniclers spoke highly of Exeter. To Orderic Vitalis, writing about the siege of William I in 1068, it appeared 'a wealthy and ancient city, strongly fortified'; William of Malmesbury commented on the 'magnificence of the city and the wealth of its inhabitants', and the author of the *Gesta Stephani* called it 'a large city… the fourth place, they say, in England' (Whitelock 1955, 281; Chibnall 1969, 211; Potter 1976, 33). They were describing a city which had suffered some decline in national standing since the late 10th century (below), but while Exeter probably was not quite the fourth English city in the early 12th century, its relative status among English towns was far higher than that of the later medieval city, when it fell out of the listings of England's 20 leading urban places (Chapter 1, Table 1.1; Biddle 1976, 500–2; Dyer 2000).

Exeter must have undergone a dramatic rise in fortunes in the 10th century. Prior to Alfred's reign (871–99) there were no signs of urban life in the city or anywhere else in Devon, and indices of economic activity such as the usage of coins show how peripheral Devon was to economic developments further east in Wessex (see above, Chapter 4). For example, the distribution of coinage in west and central Wessex in the 7th and 8th centuries shows a near-complete absence of finds in Devon, contrasting not just with the situation in Wiltshire and east Dorset with their numerous examples but also Somerset and west Dorset, where numbers begin to tail off (Costen and Costen 2016, 5–23). Twenty Frisian coins, important indicators of continental trade in the 7th to 9th centuries, are now known from Dorset, but only one from Devon (the mid 9th-century find from the Exe Bridge site described by Rippon above, pp. 226–7; Brown 2019, 124). Exeter was still not, it seems, an urban place in the late 9th century, and when a Danish army occupied Exeter early in Alfred's reign in 877, the Anglo-Saxon Chronicle described it as a *faesten* – a fortress or refuge rather than a town (Earle 1865, 78–9, 92–3; Whitelock 1955, 179; Bately 1986). It was later in Alfred's reign, in 893, that Exeter was first described as a *burh,* and at the end of his reign, in *c.* 895–9, it issued pennies bearing the city's signature EXA (Whitelock 1955, 186; Dolley and Blunt 1961, 81, 87; Swanton 1996, 86). These are clear signs of Exeter's new urban status, and by the 970s it had risen to become the 5th most productive mint in England (see below).

In assessing the excavated archaeological evidence for the Late Saxon and Norman town, it should be noted that the resource surviving from this period is appreciably less well preserved than that of the underlying Roman fortress and town. The erosion or removal of deposits which arises from the sloping topography of the city, coupled with the digging of cellars on street frontages, has resulted in the loss of stratified Saxo-Norman deposits on almost all the sites investigated, often leaving the deeper deposits of the fortress and sometimes preserving stratification from the later Roman town. The archaeological evidence therefore arises from two main sources: the contents of pits dug in the back gardens of tenements, and the human remains from the city's cemeteries, although other forms of physical evidence, notably topography, numismatics and standing buildings, add greatly to an understanding of the city.

Late Saxon Exeter was the subject of a review in 1984 which followed more than a decade of large-scale excavation in parts of the city which were of great importance in the study of the Late Saxon town and Norman city – in Cathedral Close, on urban tenements at

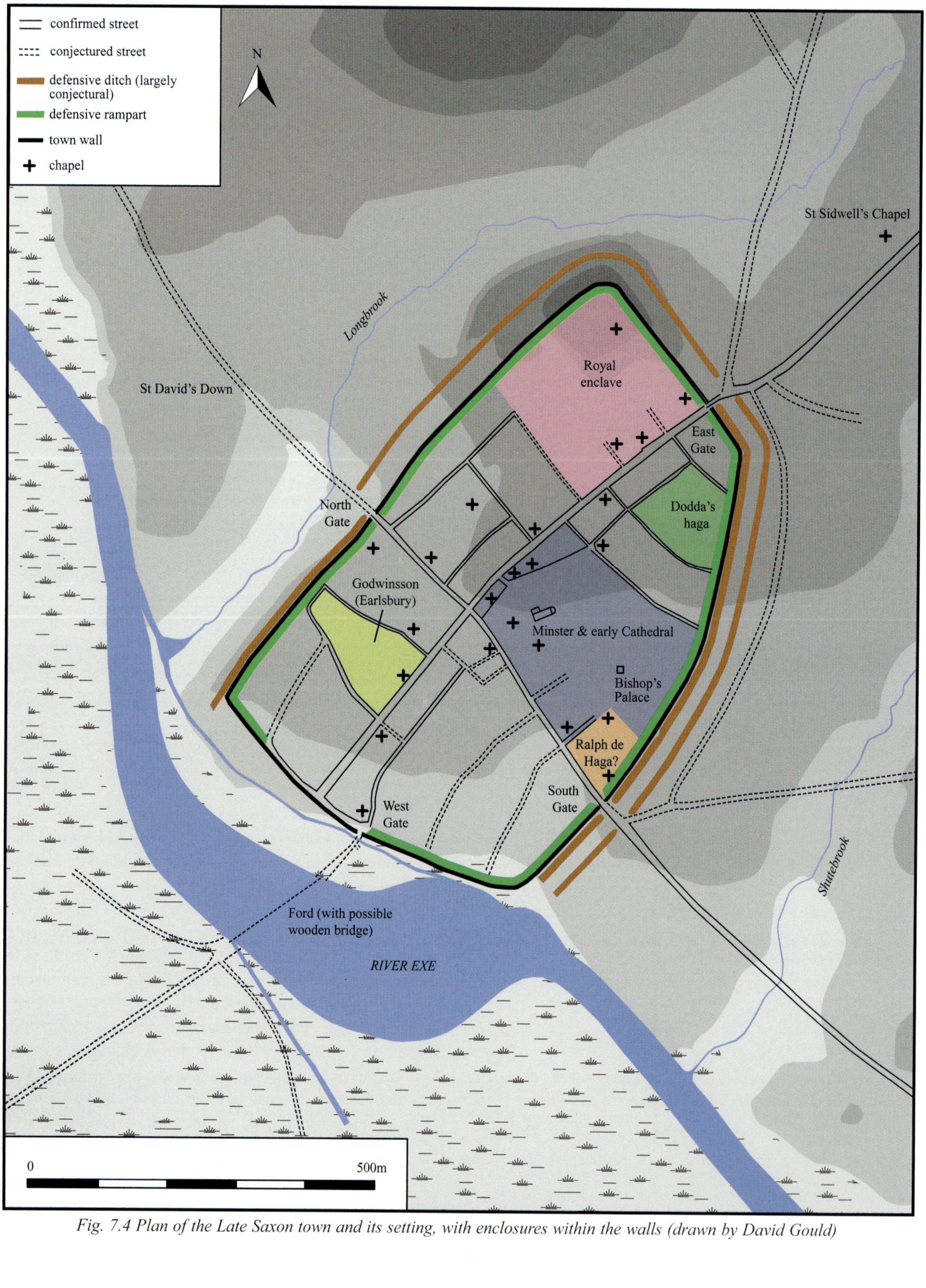

Fig. 7.4 Plan of the Late Saxon town and its setting, with enclosures within the walls (drawn by David Gould)

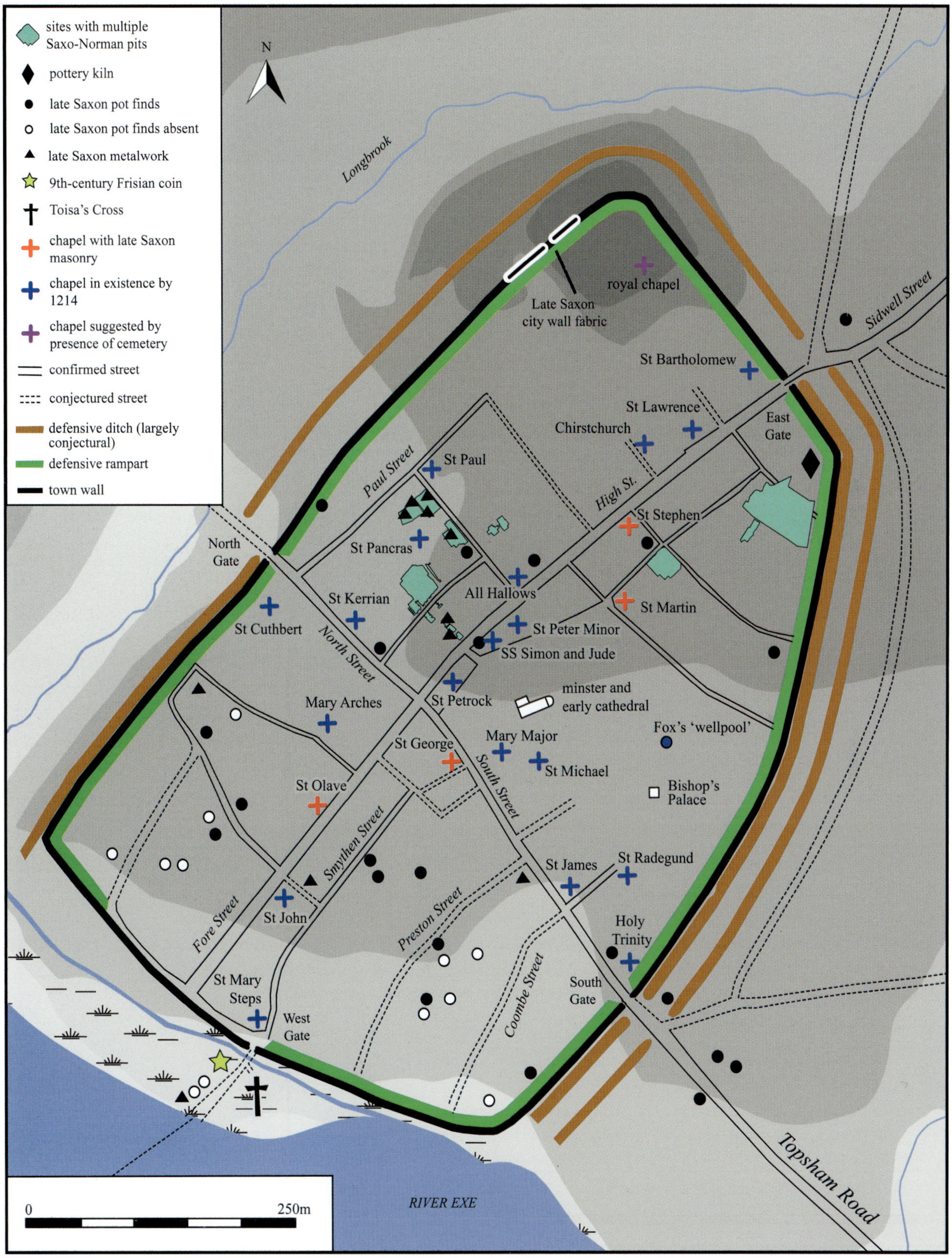

Fig. 7.5A Plan of the Late Saxon walled area (drawn by David Gould)

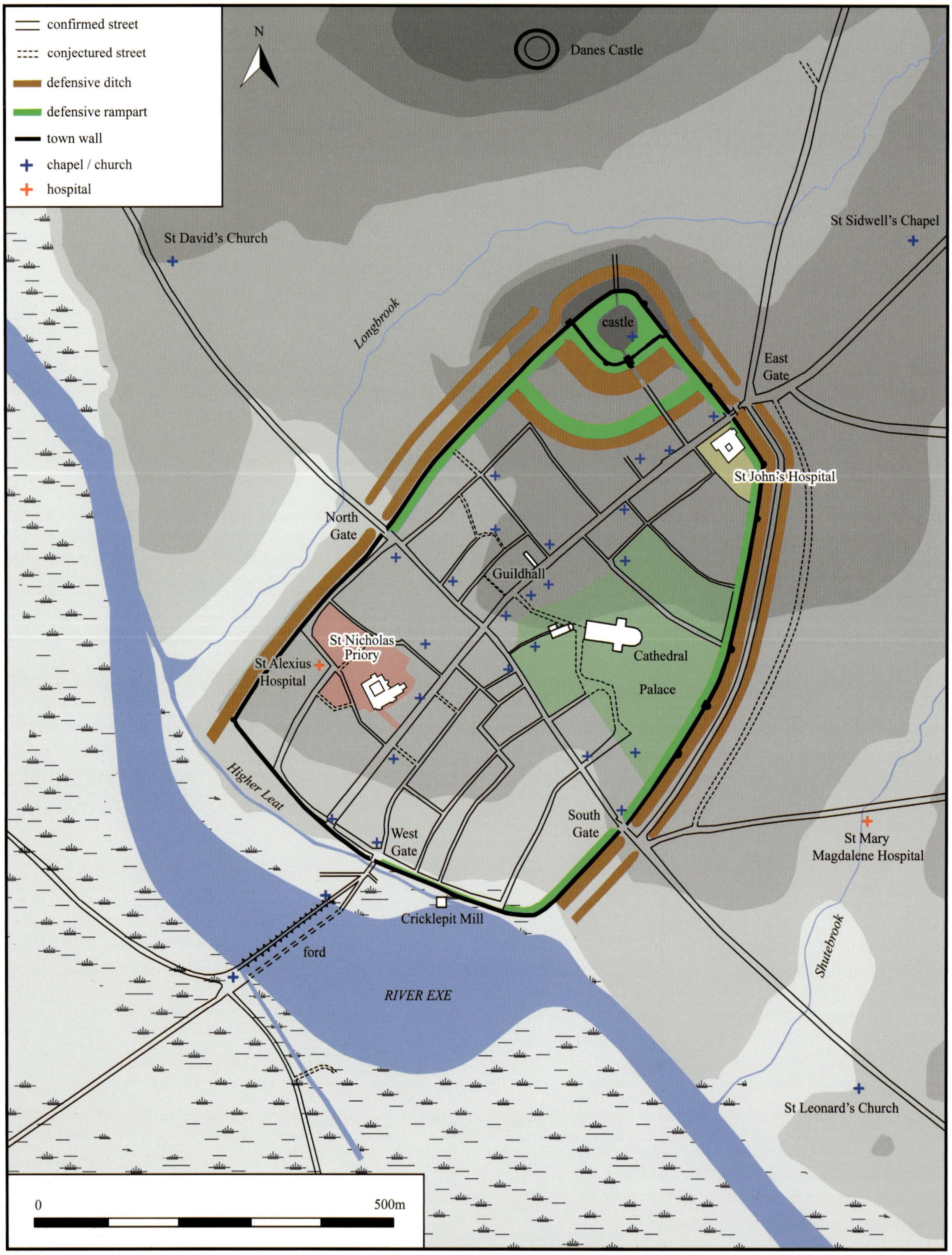

Fig. 7.5B Plan of the Norman city (drawn by David Gould)

the centre of the medieval city (notably Goldsmith Street, Trichay Street and High Street (all published in EAPIT 2, Chapters 5–7), and on a number of sites towards the periphery of the walled area and outside the South Gate (Allan *et al.* 1984). In subsequent years opportunities for excavation within the walled area became much less frequent, and the Exeter Museums Archaeological Field Unit's (EMAFU's) work moved largely to sites outside the walls which were not occupied in the Late Saxon or Norman periods. The material evidence for the character of the Late Saxon town, therefore, has not changed greatly since the 1980s. Discussion of the subject, however, has advanced significantly since that time – first with a remarkable paper by Maddicott (1989), and in the recent past with important accounts by Higham (2008; 2013; 2018) and Orme (2014; 2015a). Whilst some published information will inevitably be repeated here in order to achieve a continuous narrative, this account will not attempt to review every aspect of the city but will try to give prominence to those areas where the interpretation of the archaeological evidence has changed, or where new information can be offered.

The form of the Late Saxon *burh*

The defences

The review of Late Saxon Exeter published a generation ago followed a survey of 1978 in which it was realised that long stretches of the city wall which had previously been regarded as definitely or probably Roman were in fact of medieval date (Allan *et al.* 1984, 396–7). It concluded that 'only two or three short stretches of possible Roman work' survived in the entire circuit (*ibid.*, 396). Exeter Archaeology subsequently undertook detailed fabric recording of stretches of the wall (1988–91), leading on to a fuller survey in 1993–5 (Blaylock 1995). This has modified our understanding of the dating of some stretches and brought about some exciting discoveries; three conclusions are particularly relevant to an understanding of the Late Saxon town.

First, whilst it remains true that only a few lengths of the wall visible today are Roman, appreciably more of the standing facework is in fact of that date than was thought in the 1980s. One of the three principal stretches of probable Roman wall – at Rougemont – can now be demonstrated to be of that date (Fig. 7.6; see below), and more detailed examination of the wall fabric in Southernhay and between the Inner Bypass and the Quay has shown that they can be regarded as Roman with much greater confidence (Figs 6.8–6.9). The survey of 1993–5 identified further areas of Roman masonry, albeit sometimes small or poorly preserved, at Bradninch Place, Paul Street, Post Office Street and James Street (Blaylock 1995, 32). The 1993–5 survey also showed that substantial lengths of the city wall standing today represent rebuilding in the Civil War of the mid 17th century or subsequently – the latter sometimes made necessary by the excavation of the very deep Civil War ditch immediately in front of the wall, which undermined the foundations and probably accounts for the loss of much early masonry (*ibid.*, 3–4, 14–19). These considerations encourage the belief that long stretches of Roman wall on all sides of the city were probably standing in the Late Saxon period.

Second, the length of Late Saxon stone defence, first noted by Burrow (1977, 20–22), has been recorded more fully and reinterpreted by Parker and Blaylock (Fig. 7.6; Blaylock 1995). This masonry lies in the stretch of city wall in Northernhay Gardens which was later incorporated in Rougemont Castle. A classic succession of building periods is represented here. At the foot of the sequence is Roman masonry consisting of volcanic trap ashlar in regular courses. Although only about 0–2 m of Roman work is visible above the modern ground level, this is merely the top of the Roman wall, which stands in this area to a height of about 5 m, most of it being buried by the bank heaped up against the outer face of the city wall when the ringwork of Rougemont Castle was constructed in the late 11th century. The Roman masonry is overlain by about 2 m of completely different stonework: rather larger, roughly coursed white Triassic sandstone blocks, above which survives a series of merlons, each about 1.5 m wide, separated by embrasures of about the same width (Fig. 7.6). This is clearly a wall top, later than the Roman wall but preceding the Norman castle, and thus of Anglo-Saxon date. Above it stand two periods of Norman castle fabric, both attributed in the Exeter Archaeology survey to the late 11th century, with later medieval stonework rising to a height of 4 m or more above the Late Saxon wall. Almost 30 m of Late Saxon masonry is visible in the best-preserved stretch of walling which now forms part of the defence of the castle's inner bailey, and the same style of masonry can be traced further to the south-west, on the lower side of the 12th-century 'Athelstan's Tower', where the Roman city wall forms part of the defences of the outer bailey; the total length of Saxon stone defences is thus about 75 m.

The implications of this discovery will be discussed in detail in a report which brings together the results of various interventions around the castle (Blaylock and Higham in preparation), while the question of whether this may represent the *burh* defence or the provision of a Late Saxon stone defence around a royal enclave at Rougemont is discussed more briefly by Higham (below). This may indeed be the 'wall of squared stones' with which William of Malmesbury tells us Æthelstan (924–39) surrounded the city (Whitelock 1955, 281), although it is unlikely that it actually belongs to the early 10th century; the years around 1000 offer a more probable context (Baker and Brookes 2013, 77–83). It remains a unique example of Late Saxon stone defences standing in England, the crenellated parapet being a particularly remarkable survival, although excavations on the sites of

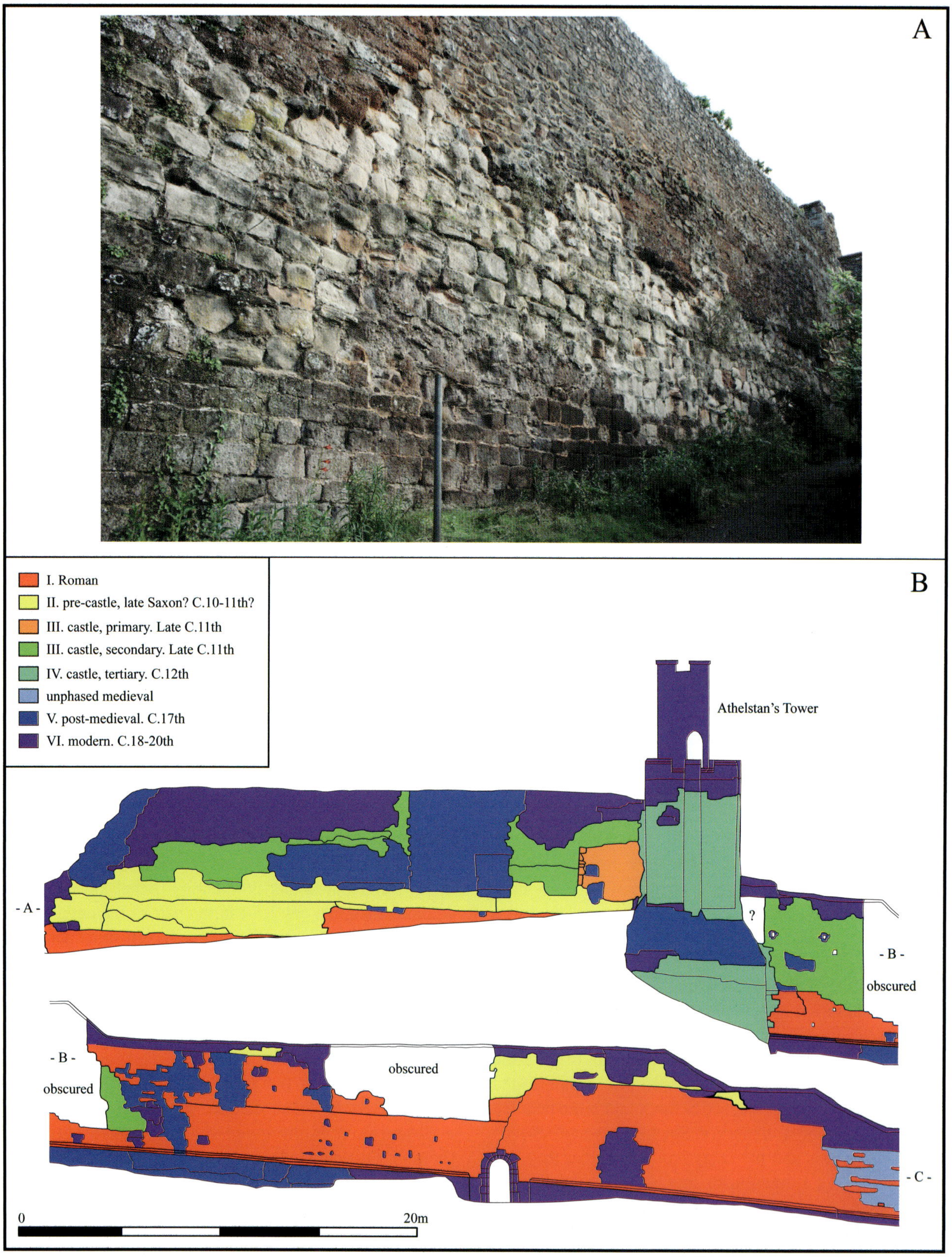

Fig. 7.6 The city wall in Northernhay Gardens. (A) View showing Roman, Late Saxon, Norman and later masonry. The Late Saxon crenellations in white sandstone are infilled with later masonry (photo: © Stephen Rippon). (B) Interpretation of the phasing (after Blaylock 1995, fig. 47; drawn by David Gould)

the castles at Oxford, Hereford, Taunton and elsewhere have offered some points in common with the sequence here, including evidence at Oxford for Late Saxon stone defences on a site with a church (Munby *et al.* 2019).

Third, the evidence for Late Saxon and Norman defensive ditches outside the city walls may be summarised, and here a small correction to the dating of the outer ditch may be noted. On every excavation which has examined the city's ditches, all evidence for a presumed inner ditch of early medieval date, close to the foot of the city wall, has been removed by later medieval ditches and especially by the very substantial circuits of defensive ditches dug in the Civil War. The presence of an outer ditch of early medieval date has been firmly established in only one area: between Southernhay and the South Gate, where it was examined in the Trinity Street/Magdalene Street excavations of 1976 and 1986–8, with a further possible observation in 2009 (Sites 58, 88, 163). Considering that it lay some distance outside the city walls (its outer edge was 33 m from the front face of the wall), it was a surprisingly substantial feature, *c.* 10 m wide and 3 m deep. The date of the infilling of the feature has been published as early 13th century (*e.g.* Allan *et al.* 1984, 397). Reconsideration of the pottery suggests that it could equally be of mid/late 12th century date. A large ditch preceding the Underground Passages, seen on the site of the ABC Cinema outside the East Gate, may also have been of this period, but no dating evidence was recovered (Site 90). These observations form the sole evidence for the lines of defensive ditches shown on Figs 7.4–7.5.

What did the early defensive circuit enclose? The length of manned defences which can be calculated from the entry in the Burghal Hidage (1009 yards [923 m]) amounts to rather less than half the circuit of the Roman wall of *c.* 2300 m (Hill 1969, 48–52). This discrepancy has been much discussed, some favouring the explanation that the entry records a lost circuit within the city around Rougemont (tentatively outlined in Hill 1974, 117; discussed by Higham in Appendix 7.1 below), others the manning of only the more vulnerable lengths of the Roman circuit (Burrow 1977, 33; Allan *et al.* 1984, 396). Whilst this problem remains unresolved, three pointers suggest – at least to this writer – that the second conclusion is the more probable. First, it has been shown that the total number of hides recorded for the four Devon *burhs* in the Burghal Hidage exceeds the total county hidage in Domesday Book, but corresponds quite closely to the total for Devon and Cornwall together (Brooks 1996). This appears to imply that there was not sufficient manpower to defend the entire circuit at Exeter. Second, although there has been limited excavation in the area of the castle, some of the observations which have been made in that area would probably have located an early defence, had one existed. For example, no ditch was seen in the long Post Office cable trench examined in 1974 between the City Library and Queen Street. The field records of this work are, however, poor and thus it does not appear on the list of excavations (Table 1.2). Further opportunities arose in the excavations at the rear of the Royal Albert Memorial Museum and on the slope between Gandy Street and the Arts Centre (Sites 132 and 157). In these investigations the bank and ditch of the outer bailey of the Norman castle were recorded, but there was no suggestion of an earlier enclosure. Third, there was clearly substantial occupation at the centre of town at an early stage in the life of the *burh,* some of it – as at 196–8 High Street and at Queen Street (Sites 55 and 68) – probably belonging to the early 10th century. This occupation, like the minster precinct, would lie outside a putative enclosure around Rougemont.

The street system

It is now well known that Exeter's medieval street system bears little relation to the underlying Roman street grid (Fig. 7.1) and displays some features in common with Late Saxon towns elsewhere: four main spinal streets (High Street and Fore Street, North and South Street); burgage plots of regular length (*c.* 40 m) on each side of them; secondary streets at right angles to the main streets (Goldsmith Street, Palace Gate, Bear Street), and back lanes parallel to the main streets (Waterbeer Street, Catherine Street, Smythen Street), some of them stretching back to the Roman rampart, uniting the streets and defences (Doddehay Street, Stryke Street, Cathedral Close) (cf. Biddle and Hill 1971; Allan *et al.* 1984, 400–4; Higham 2008, 170–3). It must be admitted, however, that dating evidence is lacking for any of the streets before the early to mid 11th century, when the placing of the churches of St Stephen, St Olave, St Martin and St George indicates the existence of the street frontages still used today on High Street, Fore Street, South Street, Cathedral Close and Catherine Street. The positions of some of these churches indicate the existence of subsidiary lanes at right angles to the main streets, such as St Stephen Street at the east end of St Stephen's church, or the former George's Lane beside St George's. The earliest examples of individual tenements which can be located on specific sites on the modern map also belong to the same mid 11th-century period; the instance of Ralph de Haga, whose property on the corner of South Street and Palace Gate passed later to Clareball, then was given in 1133 to Plympton Priory, is the earliest of these (Fig. 7.4; Lega-Weekes 1915, 114). The question of how much of the system was laid out in Alfred's reign or even at an early stage in the development of the Late Saxon *burh* is therefore unresolved. Occasions for recovering information about the street system by excavation below the streets have rarely arisen, and where this has been possible (for example in Cathedral Close in 1992–4 or in Princesshay in 2007–8), no street surfaces firmly datable before the late 12th century have been found (Sites 105 and 156; Bedford and Hall 1994; Steinmetzer, Pearce and Allan forthcoming).

Two previous versions of the Late Saxon street system have been published: one showing the later medieval street plan with one or two modifications where there is evidence for changes in the later middle ages (Allan *et al.* 1984, 403), the other a more ambitious reconstruction which incorporates further projected and conjectural components, providing a more developed plan with further back streets at the rear of tenements on the main streets and a continuous intra-mural street at the rear of the rampart in the style of Winchester (Henderson 1999a, 486). The additional elements of the street grid shown in the latter plan, such as those under the outer bailey of the castle, or between Paul Street and the city wall, are possible but no evidence for them has yet been found. Had there been a continuous intra-mural street at the rear of the rampart of the city wall, it should have been found both at Paul Street and at Princesshay, since substantial lengths of the tail of the bank were excavated in both instances. It seems unlikely that the evidence has been lost entirely, especially at Paul Street, where a well-preserved sequence of medieval deposits accumulated at the tail of the Roman rampart. A third version of the Late Saxon town plan, based on the same evidence as the previous two, is offered here (Figs 7.4–7.5A). It removes the more speculative elements of the plan of 1999 and distinguishes those streets which can be shown to have existed by the mid 11th century from those which are not attested until the 13th or 14th centuries, even when the latter may have existed at an earlier date. Similarly, it distinguishes those churches which contain Late Saxon fabric, although it is likely that many more of the city's churches existed by the Norman Conquest (see below).

Cathedral Close and the early minster

In this more cautious version of the street plan, one fundamental point seems secure: the layout of the main streets in the medieval town plan reflects the pre-existence of the minster precinct at its centre, and the central portion of High Street is bent around this early feature. The evidence for the cemetery and minster before the refoundation of Exeter in Alfred's reign has been summarised by Rippon above. Although no full site report of the post-Roman archaeology of the site has been published, the evidence for the Late Saxon minster and its associated cemetery was presented in some detail in the early 1980s (Henderson and Bidwell 1982; Allan *et al.* 1983, summarised in Fig. 7.3 above). The post-Roman cemetery (Cemetery I) was followed by Cemetery II with burials orientated roughly east–west, dating from the 7th to the ?early 10th century, that was thought to have been followed in turn by Cemetery III, with burials laid parallel to the Late Saxon minster and later church of St Mary Major, spanning the early 10th to 12th centuries.

Since that time there have been a number of developments. First, we now have 22 radiocarbon determinations from the burials excavated in 1971–2 around Mary Major church: ten from Cemetery II and 12 from Cemetery III (full results tabulated by Mandy Kingdom in EAPIT 2 Chapter 19, Appendix 19.1; all those quoted here are from human bone). In this sample there is a longer gap than previously envisaged between the few post-Roman burials of Cemetery I and the later cemeteries. Most of the orientated burials belong to the Late Saxon and Norman town, and several, both in Cemetery II and Cemetery III, probably fall in the late 10th and early 11th centuries (Cemetery II, OB 2: cal. AD 949–1036 at 90% confidence; Cemetery III: CB 40: cal. AD 942–1045 at 84% confidence and CB 52: cal. AD 978–1047 at 86% confidence. Burial on both alignments, however, probably began before the foundation of the *burh* in Alfred's reign, since one inhumation in Cemetery II and one in Cemetery III have yielded probable late 8th/9th-century dates (Cemetery II: OB 205, cal. AD 766–899 at 88% probability; Cemetery III: CB 66, cal. AD 768–899 at 90%, probability). And burial on both alignments certainly continued into the late 13th century or beyond: OB 448 in Cemetery II was dated to cal. AD 1286–1400, and OB 323 and 577 in Cemetery III to cal. 1449–1635 and 1410–1630 (at 95% probability). These results indicate that, rather than representing two successive cemeteries on different alignments spanning the Mid and Late Saxon periods, there was considerable overlap between the two; the variations in the alignments of burials therefore have little chronological significance. Some of the variations in orientation may simply reflect local topographical factors; most burials immediately beside the church of Mary Major conform to its alignment, but those further away are mainly aligned east–west, probably following the cathedral (Fig. 7.7).

Second, although there has been general acceptance that the fragmentary remains of the church preceding St Mary Major represent parts of the Late Saxon minster, it has been proposed that the excavated walls indicate a structure which was simply too small to have been the sole minster church, and that a second church awaits discovery; this might also explain the evidence for the joint dedication of the minster to SS Mary and Peter (Blair and Orme 1995; Orme 2014, 7–9). Here a simple problem is the very poor survival of the remains. The Victorian replacement of the medieval church of St Mary Major was built with massive foundations which removed almost every trace of the older church, which may well have retained standing portions of the Saxon minster. The interior of both nave and chancel were densely packed with post-medieval burials, destroying all earlier floors and most earlier features. The south aisle accommodated a sunken boiler house, destroying all but the deepest remains on that side.

It was only on the north side and east end of the church, outside the footprint of the medieval and Victorian building, that any remains survived. The foundation at the

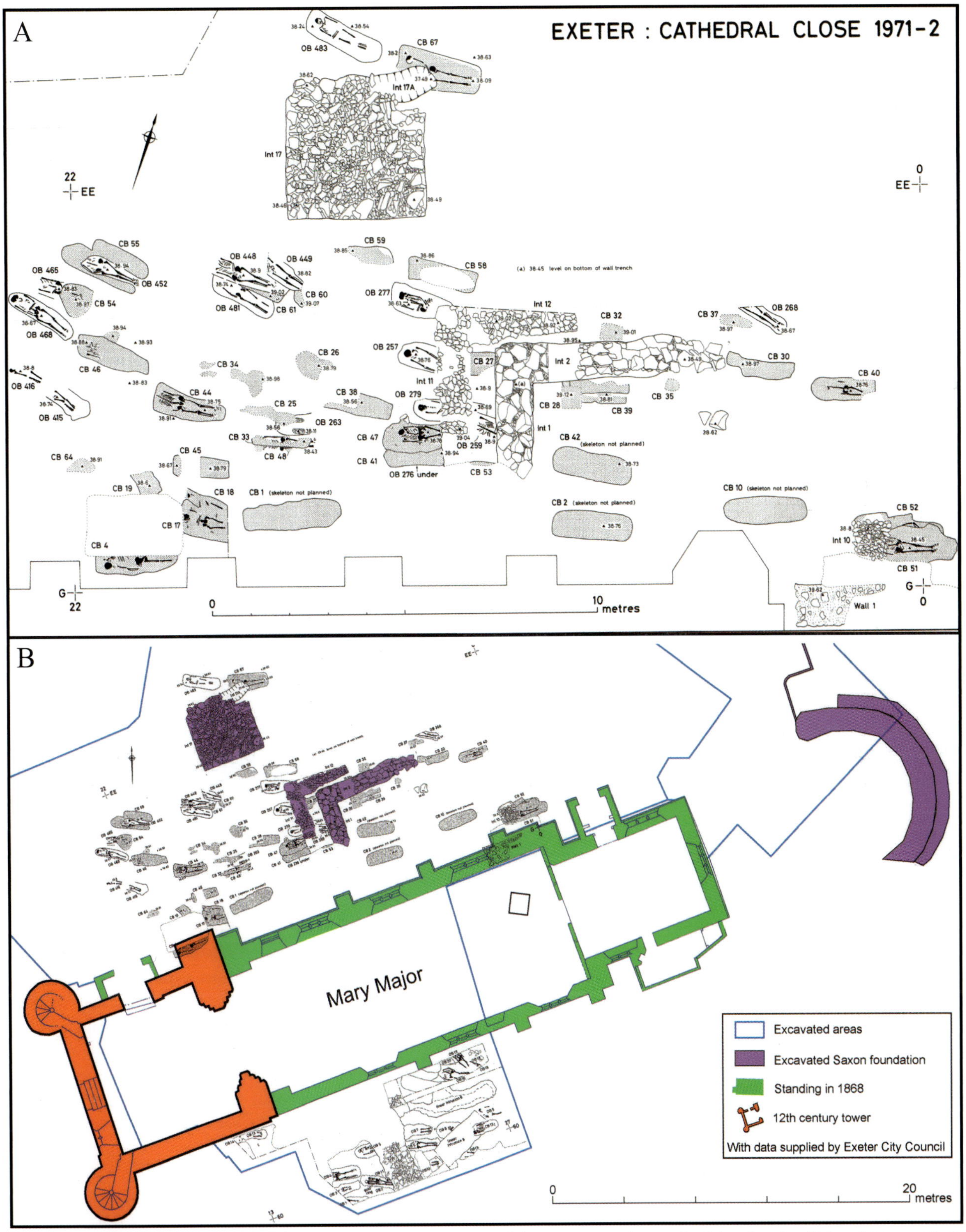

Fig. 7.7 (A) The burials of Cemeteries II and III, and the remains of the minster, to the north of the church of Mary Major with the buttressed north wall of the Victorian church at the foot of the drawing. Note that the drawing is laid out parallel to the church (Exeter Archaeology archive; © Exeter City Council). (B) The Saxo-Norman burials and fragments of the minster shown in relation to the later medieval church of Mary Major (John Allan and Tony Ives, from Exeter Archaeology archive; © Exeter City Council)

eastern end was a deeply founded apse 10 m wide, which must have been an addition to a preceding eastern end of which no trace survived (Fig. 7.7). Its terminations aligned on both sides with the wall-lines of the medieval parish church; it clearly represented a stage in the development of Mary Major when it had been a longer building. The excavated wall fragments in the graveyard represent two phases of addition on the north side of the nave. Presuming that their western end was also the west of the nave, these foundations indicate that the main vessel of the church was 35 m long, and this was the favoured interpretation in the 1980s (Henderson and Bidwell 1982; Allan *et al.* 1984, 389–91). If the square foundation found further to the north was also part of the minster, however, the church would have been 38 m long. If (as seems likely) the tower added at the west end of the parish church in the 12th century abutted the minster's west end, the church would have been 42 m long. At the east end, a sunken gravelled area beyond the eastern apse was seen as a further component of the plan, but observations further to the east in 2017 have thrown doubt on this, showing that this surface is more than 11.5 m wide – probably too wide for an 11th-century addition to the minster (Allan 2017).

Putting all these elements together, Christopher Henderson offered a reconstruction of a fully aisled church with western porticus on each side, a symmetrical westwork about 35 m wide with flanking towers and a large eastern crypt (Orme and Henderson 1999, 499–500). All these features are based on some form of evidence, but there are many uncertainties and the result is a very ambitious reconstruction based on limited evidence. If accepted, they would create a church rather smaller than Sherborne Abbey, the best-understood of the large churches of western Wessex (Sherborne was *c.* 60 m long in the early 11th century: Keen and Ellis 2005, 137–9).

The extent of the early minster cemetery

The discovery of burials below houses in Cathedral Yard and in South Street, indicating that the cemetery formerly extended closer to these streets, has been described in detail in an earlier paper (Allan *et al.* 1984, 394–6). Some more recent observations provide further evidence about the extent of the cemetery, and radiocarbon dates from this new material help understanding of the chronology of the burials (Fig. 7.8). They support the conclusion that by the 11th century the graveyard extended from its core around the minster church to Kalendarhay and the Deanery garden to the south, almost to South Street to the south-west and to the Cathedral Yard frontage to the north.

Medieval documents and observations made in the 19th century showed that the graveyard formerly extended as far as South Street, and that the properties on the Cathedral Yard frontage around Broadgate overlie numerous burials, but their date is unknown. A small excavation in 2006 encountered burials below the modern entrance to South Street (Site 202); two were dated to cal. AD 1010–1160 and cal. AD 1410–1530 (at 95% and 84% confidence: EAPIT 2, Chapter 19). The later burial shows that this area was built on only in the later Middle Ages or subsequently.

Ten new radiocarbon dates have been determined from human remains (mainly disarticulated) recovered from further small-scale excavations carried out between 2005 and 2018 on the part of the cemetery which lay to the south of the minster, in Kalendarhay and below the Deanery garden (Sites 170, 194 and 206), illustrating the value of such minor recording exercises. The results conform closely to the pattern in the graveyard around St Mary Major: one pre-*burh* date (SUERC-40322, cal. AD 766–899 at 89% confidence), the remainder belonging to or centring on the 10th and 11th centuries (details in EAPIT 2, Chapter 19 Appendix 19.1).

Whether burials formerly extended to the High Street frontage has been less clear, however; Jenkins' record of 'great numbers of human bones having been discovered for the foundations of houses' around St Petrock's church does not indicate precisely where they were found (Jenkins 1806, 366), and no modern archaeological work has recovered evidence on this point. Here, however, one significant historic record may be added. The discovery of Roman finds including pipeclay and copper-alloy figurines during the excavation of a cellar at 63 High Street in 1778 was published long ago (see Chapter 6 above; Milles 1782). Todd Gray has recently found further information about this find among the unpublished notes of the 18th-century Devon antiquary William Chapple (DHC 2610M/F/3), stating that burials were also found when the cellar was excavated. This is the first firm evidence that the cemetery formerly extended beyond the medieval bounds of Cathedral Close into the neighbouring properties on High Street (Fig. 7.8).

A strand of evidence which has not been discussed in previous considerations of the cemetery is the pattern of property ownership around the Close and on High Street. The extent of the Dean and Chapter's properties in this area can be reconstructed from various post-medieval sources (D&C 4536/2/2; D&C 4536, 7370; Lega-Weekes 1915, 180, 186–7). Their ownership of the strips of land along the northern and western boundaries of Cathedral Close is highlighted in green in Fig. 7.8. There is clear documentary evidence that some of these areas were first built on in the later Middle Ages or early modern period; all these properties were probably encroachments on the cathedral cemetery.

Fox's 'wellpool'

At the eastern end of the Close, fresh evidence has also emerged about the early 'wellpool' which Sir Cyril Fox investigated on the south side of the cathedral presbytery, which he regarded as an important factor in the siting of the Saxon minster (Fig. 7.5A; Fox 1956). Fox believed that the lowest excavated walls surrounding the pool

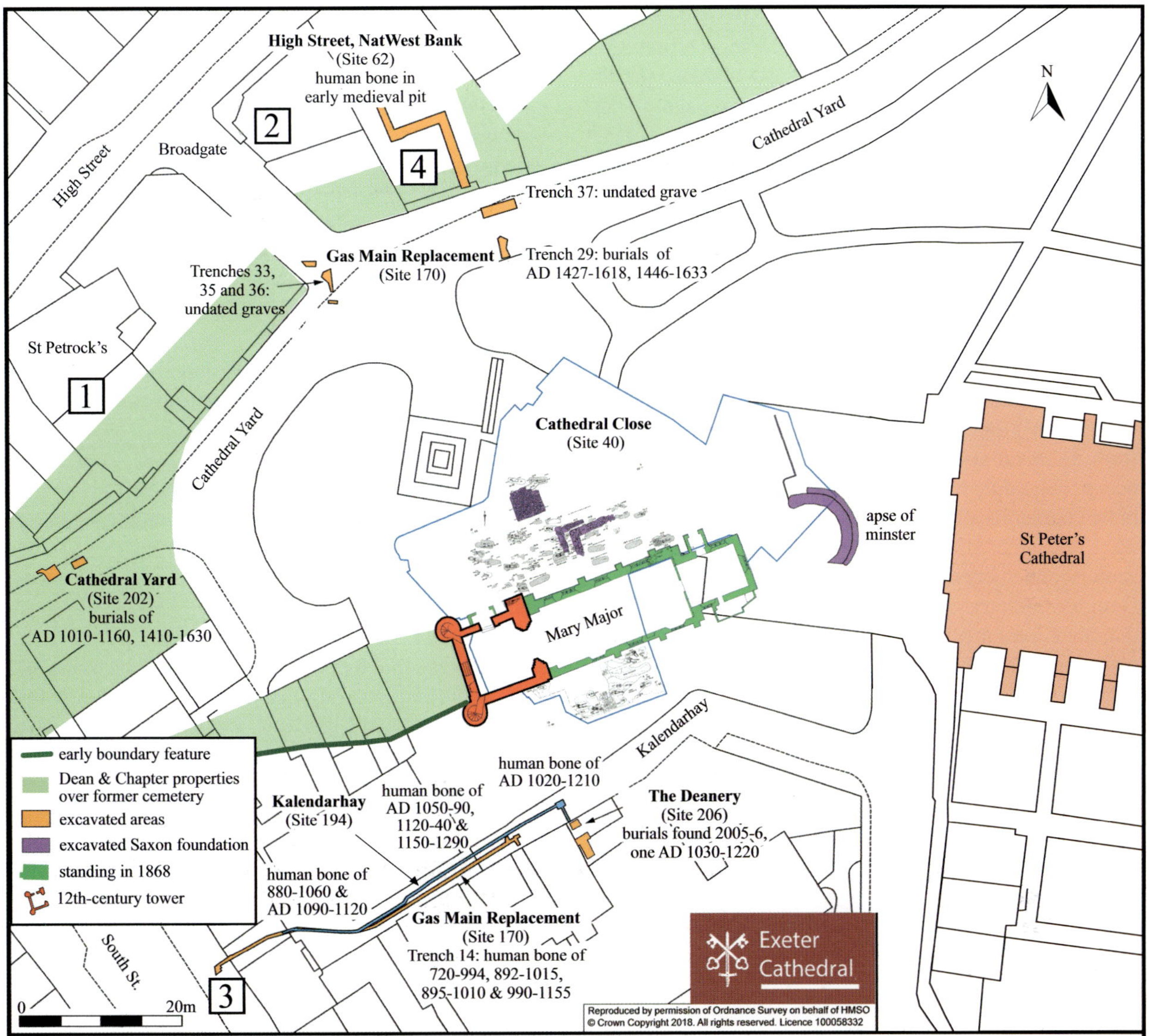

Other burials located in the vicinity of the Cathedral cemetery:

1. St Petrock's. 'The whole ground aound this church (now crowded with houses) appears to have been a cemetery; great numbers of human bones having been discovered for the foundations of houses' (Jenkins 1806, 366).
2. the cellar beside Broadgate where burials were found in 1778.
3. approximate site of the 'immense number of human bones' recovered during street widening in 1835 (Shortt 1841, 41).
4. part of a skeleton found during rebuilding in 1911 (Lega-Weeks 1915, 485).

Fig. 7.8 Evidence for the former extent of the early cemetery in Cathedral Close (drawing: John Allan/Tony Ives; © the Dean & Chapter of Exeter Cathedral)

could probably be attributed to the Roman period, with overlying masonry dating from the late 7th, 12th and early 13th centuries. In the 1980s it was pointed out that the early dating was unlikely, but the spring was nevertheless seen as a potentially significant feature of the Saxon topography of the Close (Allan *et al.* 1984, 394). The site was re-examined and subjected to detailed building recording by Stewart Brown in 2005. There is indeed a complicated succession of building phases here, but only the first two precede the building of the presbytery of the Gothic cathedral in the 1290s, and the foundation which forms the earliest element of the sequence is part of a large buttressed stone building of Norman date, with Caen stone in the foundation, which is part of the Bishop's Palace (Brown 2005). The realisation that the defensive ditches of the legionary fortress lie unexcavated below the site supports the conclusion that water could never have issued from it.

The extent of Late Saxon occupation

Bedford Garage Ware is a class of Late Saxon wheel-thrown pottery, made within the walled area of Exeter

(EAPIT 2, Chapter 17). Since it seems to have gone out of use around the time of the Norman Conquest, its presence or absence offers the best archaeological evidence for the extent of Late Saxon occupation in the town. Figure 7.5A shows its distribution within Exeter ('kiln site' and 'Late Saxon pot finds'), with dense occupation in the centre of High Street, extending back to the streets to its rear, notably Waterbeer Street and Goldsmith Street. There is a lighter scatter of findspots in the more peripheral areas of the walled area, as at Rack Street (Site 52) and Mermaid Yard (Site 63), with just a few sherds on sites within the walls at Paul Street and Lower Coombe Street (Sites 76 and 97). The most substantial new piece of evidence comes from Princesshay (Site 156), where a large (*c.* 1800 m^2) area lying behind the city wall and distant from the main streets was excavated. Little Late Saxon occupation might have been expected in this location, but in fact numerous pits of Late Saxon and 12th-century date were encountered, tailing off markedly in the late 12th century and succeeded in the 13th century by the city's Dominican friary. The implication of this excavation is that there were areas of the Late Saxon town where urban occupation shrank in the 12th and early 13th centuries, corresponding to a decline in the city's rankings in national league tables, but it is the only Exeter site where this pattern has been seen. Elsewhere – for example Rack Street, Mermaid Yard, Exe Bridge, Exe Island and Bartholomew Street (Sites 47, 56, 60, 63 and 175) – the picture is of expanding occupation in the late 12th and early 13th centuries.

Some fresh evidence for Late Saxon occupation in the suburbs has also been found. One of the very earliest pit groups known from the city was recovered from the Valiant Soldier (Site 44) 90 m outside the South Gate, and a second site a similar distance outside the South Gate (Friars Walk, Site 54) also produced a few features containing Bedford Garage Ware. The evidence for activity around the river crossing at Exe Bridge (a mid 9th-century coin, a timber with a tree-ring date after 951, as well as a Late Saxon cross shaft) has now been published by Brown (2019, 6–9, 124–5). Only very limited excavation has been possible outside the East Gate, but at 1–11 Sidwell Street (the John Lewis development, Site 185) the recovery of a pit containing a single find of Bedford Garage Ware hints at occupation immediately outside the East Gate in the suburb of St Sidwell's.

Tenements

The excavations at 196–7 High Street (Site 43) sampled the last surviving blocks of upstanding medieval deposits in the tenements at the centre of the city, and thus provide the only substantial archaeological information about the development of property divisions in the early medieval town (EAPIT 2, Chapter 7). Documentary evidence shows that the four long narrow properties which survived until the recent past had been created by the mid 14th century (EAPIT 2, Chapter 7; Fig. 7.9C). The form of the parish boundaries here, with two of the tenements (197–8 High Street) forming part of the parish of St Martin, intruding into the parish of St Pancras, indicates an earlier stage in development, where there were two wider properties, one of which was assigned to St Martin's parish (Fig. 7.9B). The excavations showed an earlier state of the evolution of this site in the Late Saxon

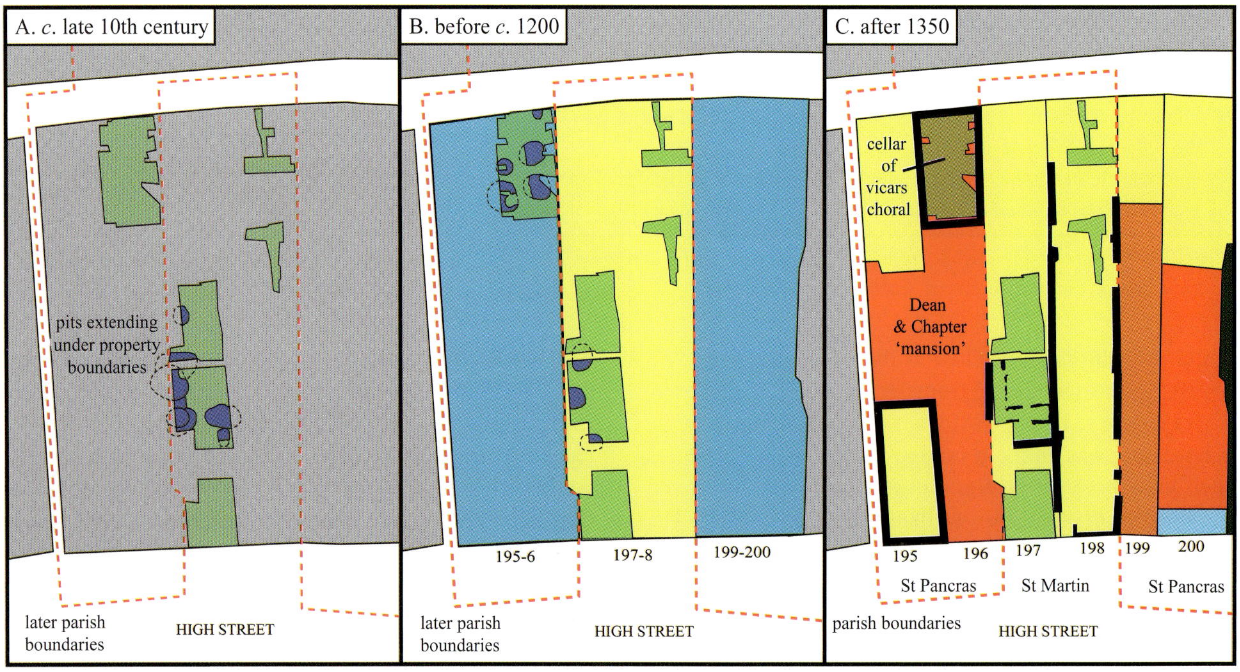

Fig. 7.9 Proposed evolution of tenements at 195–9 High Street (research by John Allan, and drawn by David Gould)

period; rubbish pits underlying the parish boundaries between 196 and 197 High Street, and between 198 and 199, show that these boundaries were not in place at that time (Fig. 7.9A): note that the pits between 198–9 High Street were recorded in a watching brief rather than a controlled excavation so are not shown on Fig. 7.9A: see EAPIT 2, Chapter 7). These four tenements, along with their neighbour at 199 High Street, seem therefore to have formed a single property with a frontage of at least 120 ft (36.6 m), which had been subdivided into properties with frontages about 40 ft (12 m) wide by the time that parish boundaries were set in the early 13th century, each of which was subdivided into tenements about 20 ft (6 m) wide before the Black Death.

On the opposite side of High Street the former presence of wide early properties, subsequently subdivided into pairs of narrow later medieval tenements, is evident in the pattern of property ownership (Fig. 8.19 below); for example, 41–2, 44–5, and 46–7 High Street are pairs of late medieval and 16th-century houses, formerly under the ownership of the Cathedral Chapter and Vicars Choral. Paired historic houses, or groups of three, were once very common in the city's main streets, and architectural evidence shows that they were sometimes successors to single houses extending along the street frontage. In a recent paper this phenomenon was seen as a characteristic of the late medieval city (Parker and Allan 2015, 56–63); the evidence from 195–9 High Street shows that process was also underway before the early 13th century.

Late Saxon churches

When Taylor and Taylor (1965) published their comprehensive catalogue of the Anglo-Saxon churches of England they included only one Devon site: the truncated remains of the crypt at Sidbury. Since that time our understanding of churches in rural Devon has changed little, although the recent discovery of a probable Saxon church below the parish church of Jacobstowe is a reminder of how much may await discovery in unexpected places (Lane and Blaylock 2017). The picture in Exeter, however, has changed greatly: five Anglo-Saxon churches (the minster and four parish churches, formerly chapels) are now known in the city (Fig. 7.10). The Taylors might themselves have included the remains of St George's, a two-cell church with a small side chapel exposed by wartime damage in 1942 and demolished in post-war redevelopment (Fox 1952, 25–9, pl. XV). This building also offers an interesting example of the way in which underlying Roman remains could affect the form of a church. As Richard Morris has pointed out, its irregular ground plan seems to 'reflect a compromise between the influence exerted by relict Roman topography and the constraints of street lines and standing properties that existed by the time the church was built' (Morris 1989, 195).

Late Saxon fabric was identified in St Martin's church in the 1980s, offering a second example of a small two-cell parish church with long-and-short work (Blaylock and Westcott 1989). Subsequent unpublished observations by Exeter Archaeology demonstrated that the west and north walls of the nave, and probably the north wall of the chancel, are also of Late Saxon date (EA projects 2128, 3027, 3097; Richard Parker pers. comm. 2019). Although heavily repaired, this is therefore an example of a Late Saxon two-cell church whose ground plan survives little altered (the east end alone seems to have been rebuilt), standing to its full height, its tall narrow proportions still reflecting its early origins. This is presumably the church whose dedication in 1065 is recorded in notes from an 'old missal' of the church, copied in the later middle ages into the St John's Cartulary (Orme 2014, 130; Higham, Appendix 7.1 below).

Further discoveries have followed at St Olave's. It has been known for many years that one of its nave quoins appears to be of long-and-short work, but the identification was not beyond doubt. Close examination of stonework and mortars by Exeter Archaeology confirmed that this is indeed of Anglo-Saxon date, and showed that the entire west wall of the church, excepting some repairs, is also of the same period (Parker 1999). The eastern end of the church appears to belong to the same building phase, so although the street front has been rebuilt and the northern side replaced by aisles, this too can be regarded as being in origin a small two-cell church of Late Saxon date. Its probable connection to the house of Godwin is described by Higham (2018; Appendix 7.1 below).

The final Exeter church which has proved to contain Late Saxon fabric is St Stephen's – clearly an important early church, donated by Henry I to the church in Exeter and with a vaulted Norman crypt whose damaged remains were first seen in the 1820s (Lega-Weekes 1915, 183; Hamlin 1976; Orme 2015, 167). Examination by Stewart Brown (2012, fig. 18) has shown that this crypt, which underlay the chancel and was probably of the early 12th century, was preceded by an earlier crypt without a vault, which was presumably of Late Saxon date. The fact that it had a crypt may show that it possessed a relic or relics.

Further examples of early two-cell Saxo-Norman churches probably await discovery. Possible cases include St Mary Steps, where the north nave wall is of early rubble construction and Parker has offered a likely reconstruction of a two-cell plan, and St John's on Fore Street, where the west wall, still standing despite the demolition of the rest of the church, is of volcanic rubble construction (unpublished). Allhallows Goldsmith Street and St Kerrian's are demolished churches of this plan, and Holy Trinity another possible example with an added aisle. Although it should be remembered that these simple two-cell plans were still being built in the late 12th or

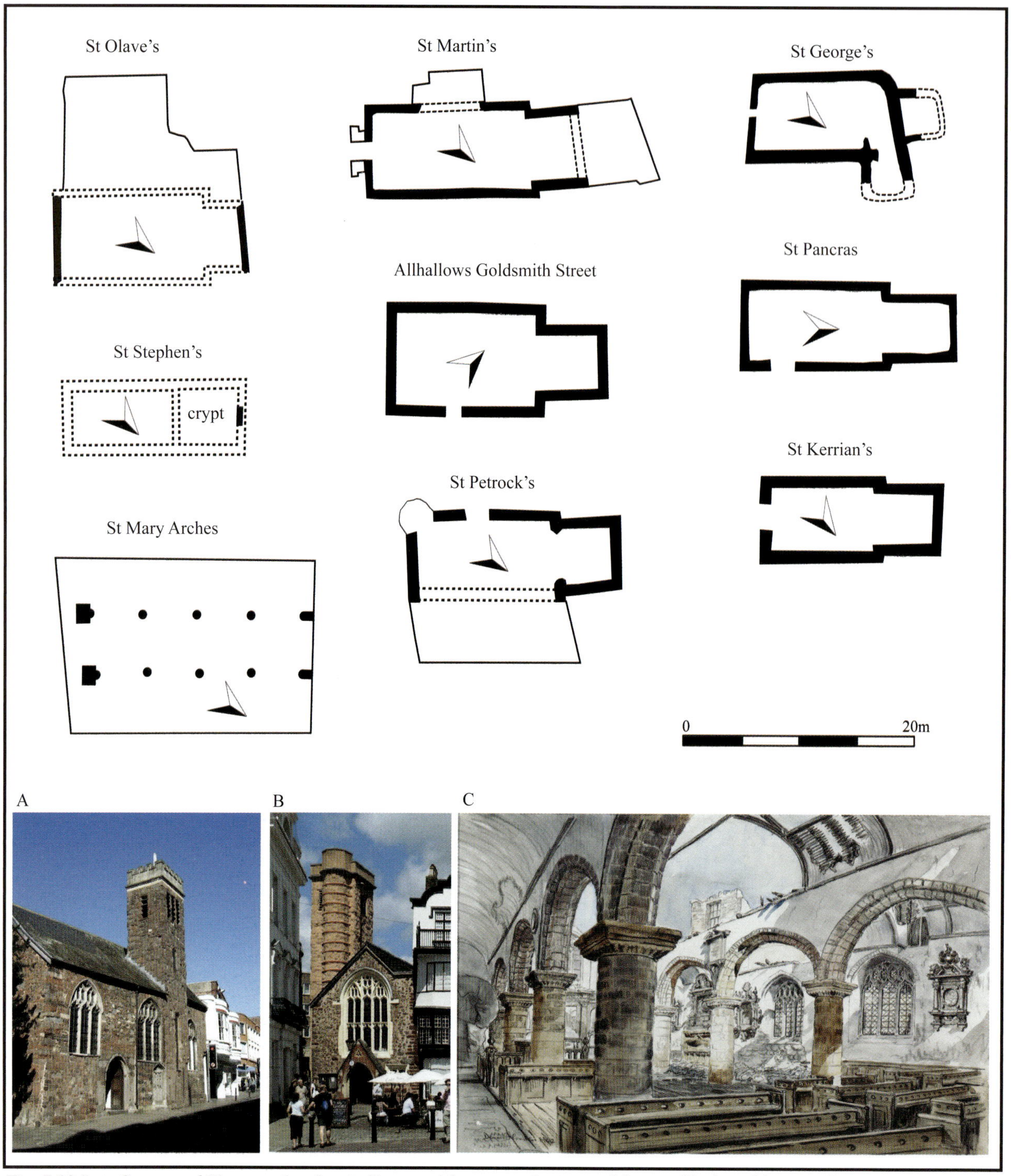

Fig. 7.10 Late Saxon and Norman churches in Exeter, with presumed primary fabric in black and later walls in outline (drawn by David Gould). (A) St Olave's; (B) St Martin's; (C) St Mary Arches (all © RAMM)

early 13th century, as St Pancras church illustrates, these instances show that many of the city's churches retained elements of Late Saxon or Norman fabric into the 18th and 19th centuries, and the five verified examples of Late Saxon stone churches are probably only a sample of those built before the Conquest. We may recall the later medieval tradition that 'King William' (I or II) had given 29 Exeter chaplains 1d from the collection of the market dues known as the *stepgable* (Orme 2014, 18–19, where reservations about the reliability of the source are expressed). By 1214 there were about 34 churches and chapels in and around Exeter (*ibid.*).

The new works of the Norman city

Rougemont Castle

Rougemont Castle is a ringwork, built in the northern corner of the Roman and Late Saxon walled area on a site chosen by the Conqueror himself, following his siege of Exeter in 1068/9 (Higham 2013, where the same writer's earlier discussions of the castle and its context are listed). In its primary form it consisted of an inner and outer bailey, enclosing in total an area of *c.* 4 ha (9.9 acres). Figure 7.11A–B show the site in its post-medieval state, when housing had spread over some of the outer bailey.

The principal surviving components are the formidable bank and ditch of the inner bailey, which was entered through the 11th-century gatehouse, and stretches of the Roman and later city wall which served as the north-western and north-eastern sides of the castle. Athelstan's Tower, the massive square tower with pilaster buttresses on the western side of the inner bailey, is an addition of 12th-century (early 12th-century?) date. Three D-shaped towers around the inner bailey and a fourth at the junction of the outer bailey and city wall were added later, probably in the early 13th century. The most detailed study of the castle is its Conservation Management Plan (Alan Baxter 2004 with contributions by Higham and Blaylock), although this is not widely available. A new assessment of the entire site is currently being prepared (Blaylock and Higham in prep.).

The primary form of the inner bailey evidently consisted of a stone gatehouse set in an earth bank with a timber breastwork (Blaylock and Higham in prep.). Figure 7.11C shows the elevations of the front face of the Early Norman gatehouse, taken from EMAFU's drawn survey of 1985. It shows the triangular-headed windows and long-and-short quoins in the Anglo-Saxon tradition, but also the archway of two orders with simple cushion capitals in Norman style. Since Anglo-Saxon building practice seems generally to have disappeared soon after the Conquest in major works, it seems very probable that this structure was built in 1068/9 or soon afterwards. A stone wall on top of the bank had been added by the time that King Stephen besieged the castle in 1136. The Pipe Rolls record royal expenditure on the castle amounting to more than £250 in the years 1169–81 (Brown *et al.* 1963, 648–9), and mention the king's chamber, but no trace of this or of other medieval domestic buildings survives within the inner ward.

The former presence of an outer bailey is evident from early depictions, parish boundaries and the pattern of land ownership; the position of its defences has been confirmed by three modern excavations and earlier observations (Fig. 7.5A Sites 82, 87, 157; Blaylock and Higham in prep.). The ditch was at least 4 m deep and 12 m wide. Judging by the small quantity of pottery retrieved in Site 82, it was infilled in the late 12th or early 13th century.

Danes Castle

Danes Castle is a small ringwork lying about 300 m to the north of Rougemont Castle, separated from it by the deep Longbrook Valley (Figs 7.5B and 7.12). The site was excavated by Exeter Archaeology in 1992–3 (Site 101), and a full report was published more recently (Higham and Henderson 2011). The earthwork proved to be a single-phase structure, built over a ploughed field with ridge and furrow. The diminutive central enclosure, which measured little more than 15 m across, was entered through a gatehouse with earth-fast posts, but no other structural evidence survived in the interior. No artefactual evidence relating to the castle was found, excepting a few sherds of Saxo-Norman pottery in the underlying ploughsoil. Although various possible contexts arise, much the most probable is King Stephen's siege of Exeter Castle in 1136 (Higham and Henderson 2011).

The Norman cathedral

The Norman cathedral was laid out on a new and more spacious site to the east of the old minster (Figs 7.2 and 7.5B). Work started in 1114, and the consecration of the building in 1133 may have marked the completion of the eastern limb and choir rather than the whole structure including the nave. The principal surviving elements are the two transeptal towers (Fig. 7.13), their positioning unique in England and without obvious parallel in France, but the aisle walls also survive up to the level of the window sills, both in the nave and the choir. The form of the east end is uncertain; a polygonal foundation seen below the later medieval choir may have been either the termination of the eastern limb or a sleeper wall for the arcade of an ambulatory around the high altar. The best discussion of the church is that by Thurlby (1991), which has a full bibliography of previous literature, but some features of that account have since been challenged (Allan 2014a).

In comparing the scale of the cathedral with that of other Romanesque churches, the overall length is the sole dimension which can readily be used. Exeter was *c.* 73 m long, placing it well below the giants of English Romanesque church building such as Winchester, Bury St Edmund's, Norwich, Canterbury, Ely and Durham (respectively 157 m, 149 m, 134 m, 132 m, 128 m and 123 m long (figures in Heywood 1996, 11; Fernie 1979, 2–30; Thurlby 1994, 163). Similarly, the seven bays of its nave may be compared with 11 at Peterborough, and 12 at Westminster Abbey, St Augustine's Canterbury and St Paul's London (Gem 1990, 57–8). These comparisons however are with some of the largest buildings constructed in northern Europe since Antiquity. In a regional context, Exeter was, unsurprisingly, smaller than Salisbury (Old Sarum: *c.* 100 m) and Glastonbury, the richest of the monastic houses of South-West England (*c.* 96 m long: Gilchrist and Green 2015, 399–400). It was closer in size

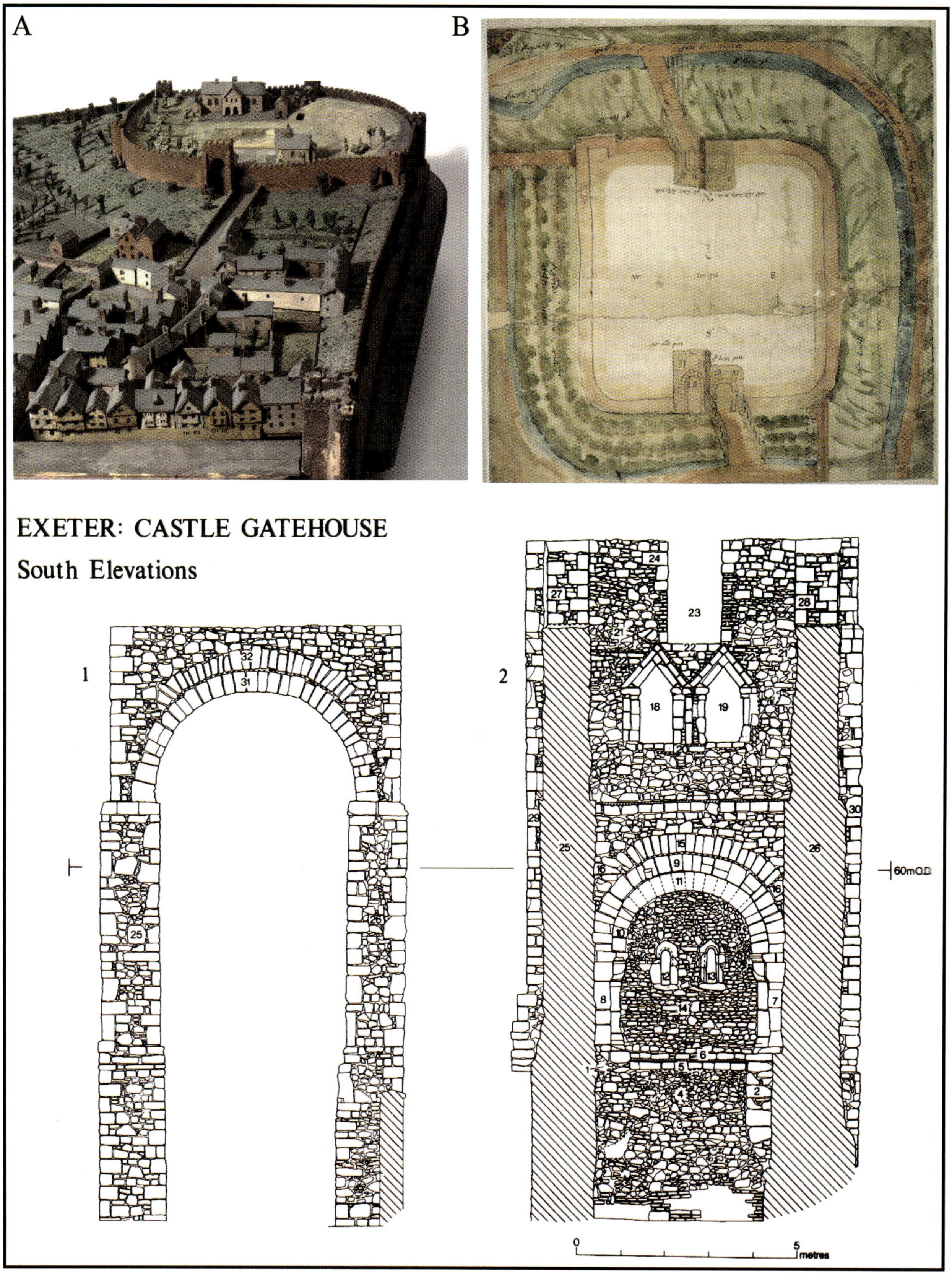

Fig. 7.11 Rougemont Castle. (A) As shown in the Hedgeland model of 1820, when housing had spread over much of the outer bailey (©RAMM). (B) As shown in a drawing of c. 1600 (BL Add MS 5027, art 70; © British Library). Bottom: Fabric survey of the front faces of the gatehouse (Exeter Archaeology archive; © Exeter City Council)

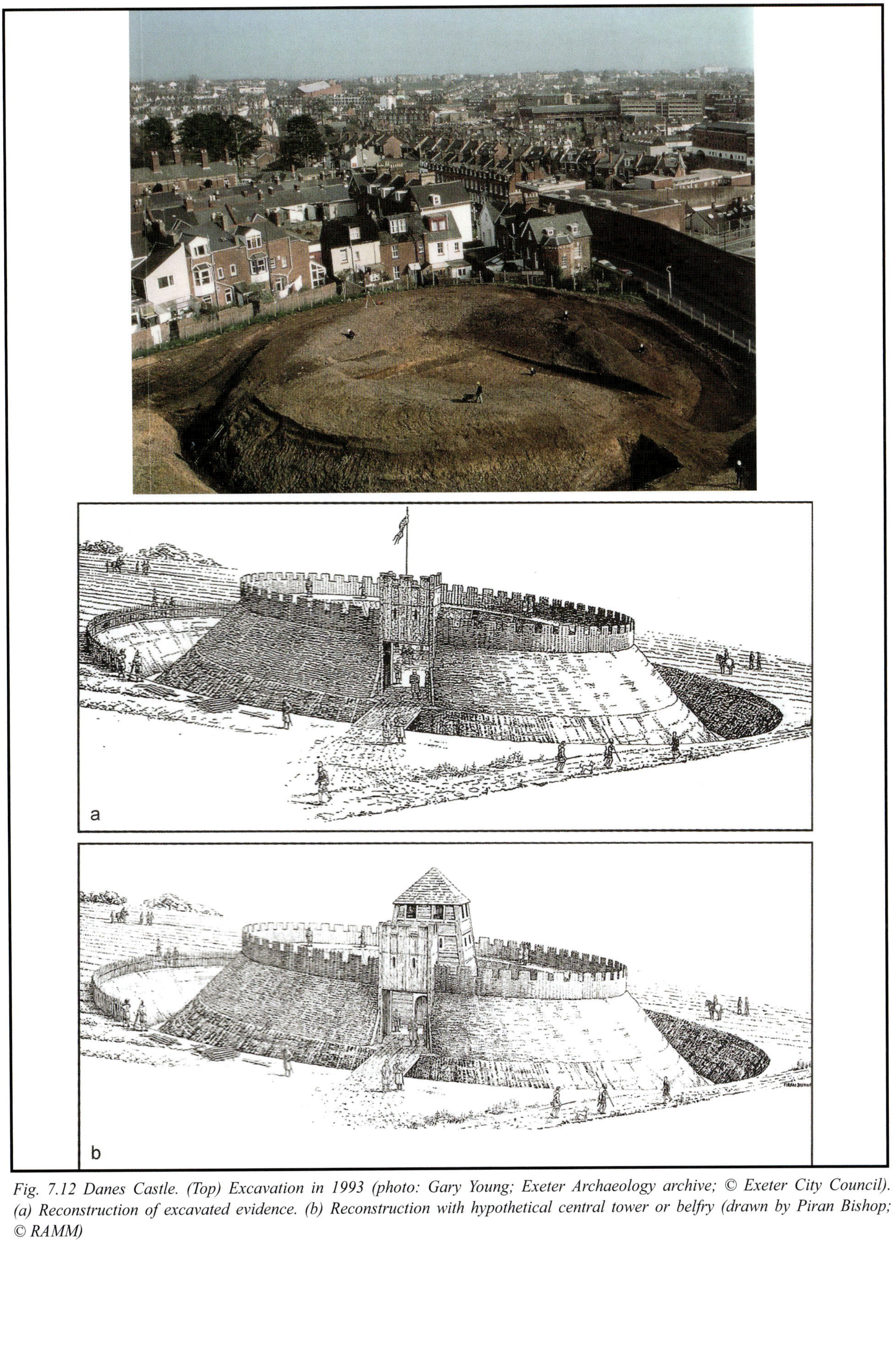

Fig. 7.12 Danes Castle. (Top) Excavation in 1993 (photo: Gary Young; Exeter Archaeology archive; © Exeter City Council). (a) Reconstruction of excavated evidence. (b) Reconstruction with hypothetical central tower or belfry (drawn by Piran Bishop; © RAMM)

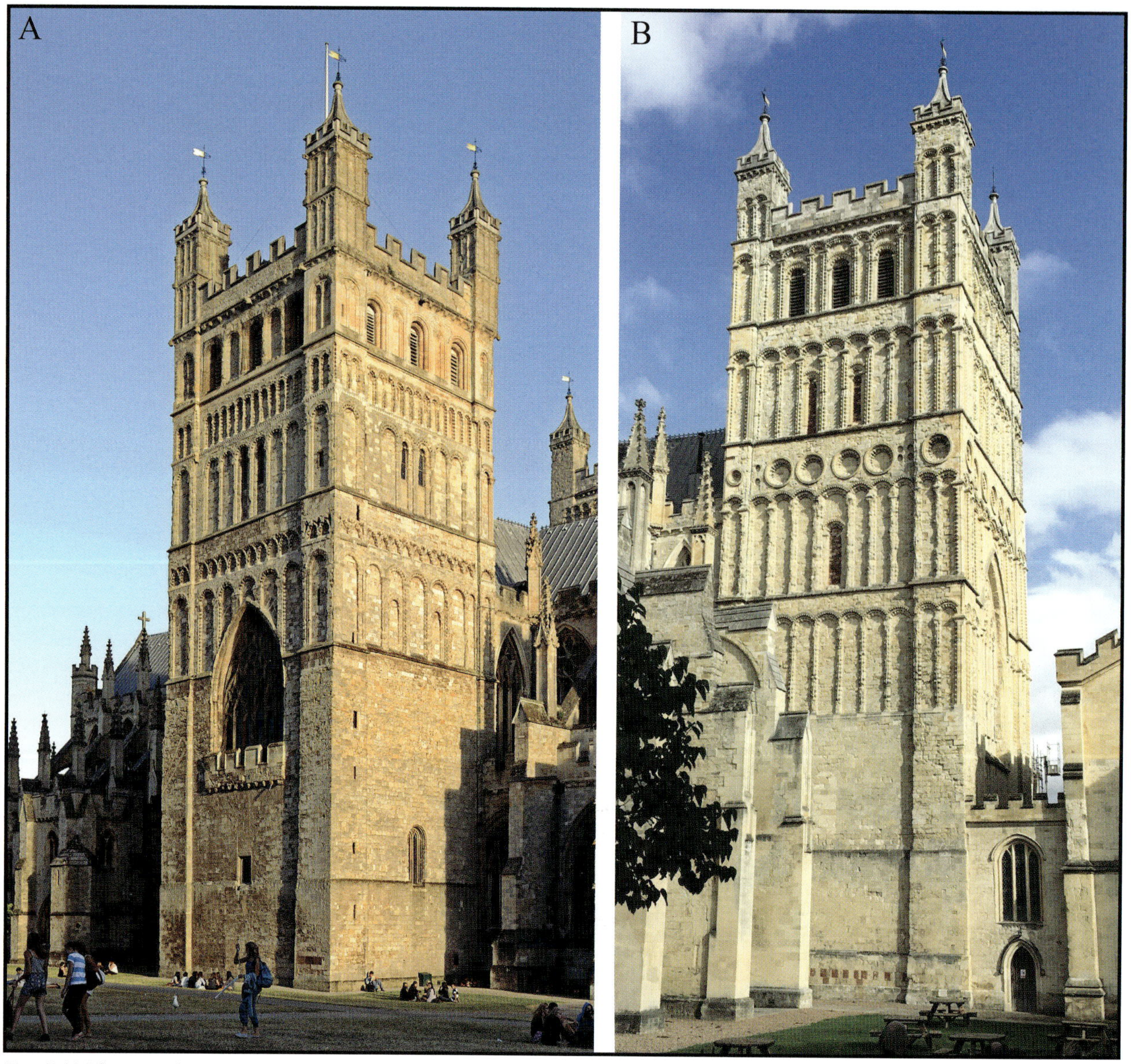

Fig. 7.13 The pair of Romanesque towers flanking the crossing of Exeter Cathedral. (A) North; (B) South (© John Thorp, John Allan)

to Sherborne Abbey (*c.* 50 m from the west end to the springing of the apse: Keen and Ellis 2005, 137) and not much bigger than the larger monastic houses of Devon such as Buckfast Abbey (*c.* 67 m excluding the Galilee: Robinson 2017, 40–1) or Tavistock (*c.* 64 m, measuring the later medieval church without the Lady Chapel: Stead 1999, 181–4). This relatively modest showing should not surprise us; in 1291 the Exeter diocese ranked among the five poorest in England (Alexander and Binski 1987, 227).

Hospitals

Three hospitals were founded in the city in the late 12th century: those of St John and St Alexius, and the extra-mural leper hospital of Mary Magdalene (Orme and Webster 1995, 226–39; Orme 2014). Little is known of the last two, but the layout of the buildings of St John's may be discerned in post-medieval maps (for location see Fig. 8.2). The rooms were laid out around a square courtyard, enclosed on the High Street frontage to the north by the chapel and a large buttressed room (?dining hall); the east range incorporated a Norman arcade with drum piers and scalloped capitals, presumably separating the two aisles of the infirmary (Fig. 7.14).

Houses

Timber buildings

The slight evidence for timber building in Late Saxon and Norman Exeter is presented in detail in EAPIT 2, Chapters 5–8. The lengths of excavated wall foundation

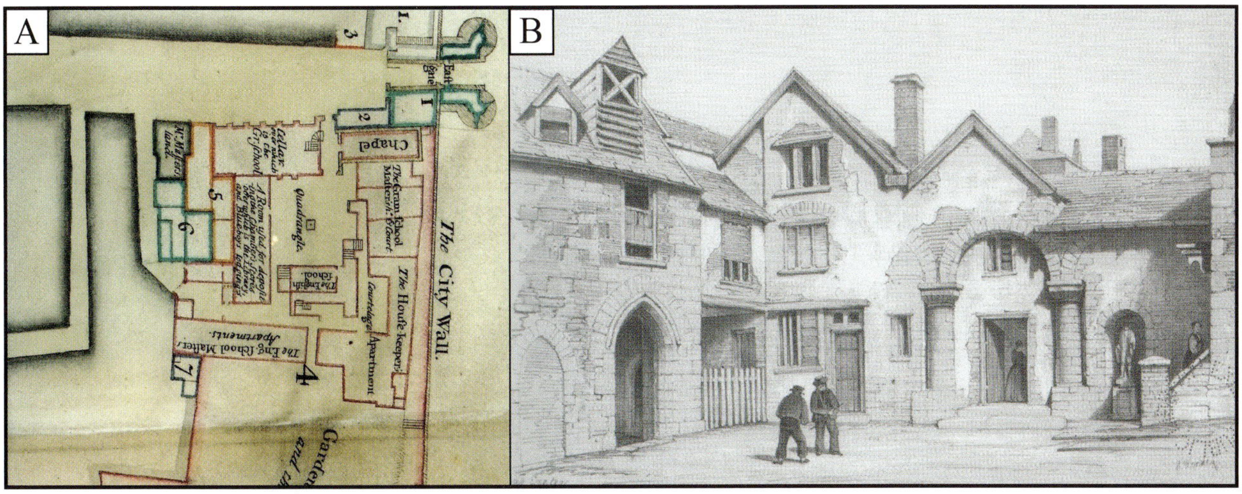

Fig. 7.14 St John's Hospital. (A) The plan in the mid-18th-century Map Book of the Chamber of the City, showing its buildings ranged around a central courtyard, with the chapel in the north range on the High Street frontage (© Devon Heritage Centre). (B) Spreat's engraving showing the Norman arcade in the east range (© Devon Heritage Centre)

found at High Street are the only known examples (EAPIT 2, Chapter 7), although slotted baulks of oak found at Trichay Street which are probably structural timbers are discussed by Gould (EAPIT 2, Chapter 5).

Norman stone town houses?

A house formerly standing on the corner of Preston Street and King Street was claimed in the early 20th century as an example of a Norman stone town house, and became known to a wider readership through its inclusion (with qualifications) in Margaret Wood's paper 'Norman Domestic Architecture' (1935, reissued 1974). Portman, however, was doubtful (Portman 1966, 83–4, with references to the earlier discussions), and consideration of its building stones, alongside detailed examination of the fragments of the very elaborate Caen stone doorway and string-course which survive in the RAMM collections, leaves little doubt that this was in fact a 16th-century house incorporating reused Norman architectural material, probably derived from St Nicholas Priory (the walls were mainly of Heavitree stone; for the fragments see Allan 1999, 10, fig. c, and 15).

Two other cases of possible early stone houses may be mentioned. Jenkins (1806, 82) published a crude engraving of an ancient stone building which stood in Waterbeer Street until its demolition in 1803; it was then known (wrongly) as the 'Old Guildhall' (Fig. 7.15). His description of its gable end on the street frontage, with three round arches on the ground floor and a window above – also with rounded arches – leading to a spacious hall within, suggests that this was a more convincing example of a Norman stone house. Still less well documented is an old stone house formerly in Paul Street known in the 18th century as King Athelstan's Palace. This too might have been a 12th-century town house.

Fig. 7.15 The 'Old Guildhall', Waterbeer Street, a possible example of a Norman town house of stone (Jenkins 1806)

No standing houses in the city are likely to be older than the hall of the Bishop's Palace, with its doorway of *c.* 1180–1220 (Blaylock 2017), or the former hall of the Old Deanery, whose shell may belong to the years soon after the establishment of a Dean at Exeter in 1225 (Keystone 2000). The recovery of roofing slates in pits in the city – for example in several 12th-century pits in Goldsmith Street and Trichay Street, and in early 13th-century deposits at Mermaid Yard and again at Trichay Street (Allan 1984a, 300) – may however reflect the spread of stone town housing in the Norman city, since slate roofs are traditionally associated with the building of stone-walled structures.

The economy of Exeter, 900–1200

The economic performance and ranking of the city

Coinage provides the fullest picture of the economic performance of Late Saxon Exeter, since the output of the English mints was broadly proportional to their economic activity (*e.g.* Metcalf 1981; Petersson 1990, 213–14). Pennies bearing the city's signature EXA were first struck at the end of Alfred's reign in the years *c.* 895–9 (Dolley and Blunt 1961, 81, 87) but the activity of the mint before the reform of the coinage under Edgar in *c.* 973 is poorly known, since so few pre-Reform coins bear a mint signature. The uniform recording of both moneyer and mint on the reverse of each English penny, which was an important component of Edgar's Reform, allows detailed comparisons to be made between the output of each mint, whilst the institution of the process of *renovatio monetae* – the regular renewal of the money supply in which the coinage was replaced with pennies of a new design and weight (the introduction of a new 'substantive type') after a fixed period of years, first of six years, later of three – allows the fluctuations in output at the different mints to be observed over the following two centuries (*e.g.* Metcalf 1998). Figure 7.16 shows a selection of the issues of the mint.

Throughout the Late Saxon period the four principal mints were those of London, Winchester, York and Lincoln, which together accounted for more than half the Late Saxon coinage (*e.g.* Petersson 1990, 213–18). Exeter reached its highest position, in fifth place behind these four, early in the reign of Æthelred II, but it declined later and its overall standing in the lists of mints for the entire period 973–1066 is 8th, behind Stamford, Chester and Thetford (Petersson 1990, 213). Its performance can be examined in more detail in various ways. A simple crude measure is by counting the number of moneyers at each place in successive issues, as shown, for example by David Hill (1984, 130) in his *Atlas of Anglo-Saxon England.* The results for the four Late Saxon mints of Devon are tabulated in Fig. 7.17A. The number of moneyers at Exeter rose from four in the 970s to 15 in the *Crux* issue of Æthelred (991–7), then declined a little before reaching a second peak of either 15 or 16 moneyers in the period *c.* 1017–29, then declining to eight or nine in the early 1030s and to just four by the mid 1050s. Devon's three other mints show a very similar pattern to that of Exeter; a joint total for the four Devon mints of 26 moneyers is known both in the *Crux* issue of the 990s and in the *Quatrefoil* issue of Cnut's reign, but overall numbers had fallen to ten by the 1030s and to fewer in subsequent issues.

Although the basic shape of the graph – expansion to a high level in the period 990–1025, then a sharp decline – is undeniable, this index fails to distinguish between prolific moneyers and those who struck just a few coins, and thus it tends to underplay sharp changes in the levels of production. Michael Metcalf's (1981) work, in contrast, presents a much more sophisticated measure of the output of the mints, both absolute and relative to the other centres, based on careful study of the dies and the use of statistical techniques to postulate the overall number of dies at each mint and in each issue. Figure 7.17B shows his calculation of the number of dies used in each Devon mint in successive issues from 973 until 1050. It shows that their highest levels of output were in the *Crux* issue of Æthelred, when over 280 reverse dies would have been used. Later medieval evidence shows that at least 10,000 pennies would regularly be struck from a reverse die, and on this basis the output of the Devon mints struck over a six-year period (991–7) can be estimated as more than 2.8 million coins. Metcalf's figures show just how dramatic the decline in output was in Cnut's reign; by the 1020s production in Devon had sunk below about 400,000 coins, and after 1030 the issues of Barnstaple, Lydford and Totnes become extremely rare. In reading the figures after 1035 we should note that each issue was current for only three rather than six years, and when this is taken into consideration the level of output in the city can be seen to have been maintained into the early 1040s, but thereafter Exeter's output too declined to less than 10 per cent of its former level.

These figures alone do not tell us about the prosperity of Exeter or the other Devon towns relative to that of other mints, since they reflect the overall national levels of output as well as local variation. The *Crux, Long Cross* and *Last Small Cross* issues of Æthelred were minted on a huge scale, unequalled in later generations. Here Metcalf's figures showing the percentages of each issue struck at each mint are especially revealing. In the major issues of the period 991–1016 the Devon mints struck about 6% of the national coinage, and this proportion did indeed decline to about 2–3% in the period 1017–42, before descending below 2% thereafter (Fig. 7.17C). The unexpected aspect of Metcalf's figures, however, is the remarkably high showing of Exeter and the other Devon mints in the *First Hand* and *Second Hand* issues in the early years of Æthelred's reign (979–91); in the latter Exeter struck almost 10% of the national coinage, and the combined total for Devon was 14%. Later in Æthelred's reign we may also note the remarkably high figure for Lydford in *Last Small Cross*, when it rose to rank briefly among the country's top dozen mints, with an estimated output in excess of half a million coins, even though the issue followed just 12 years after the Viking raid on south Devon in 997, in which nearby Tavistock Abbey was sacked (Metcalf 1981, 63–80; Allan 2002, 14–18).

Others have noted these notable signs of vigorous economic activity. Arguing from the numismatic evidence which demonstrates connections between Ireland and

A B C D E F

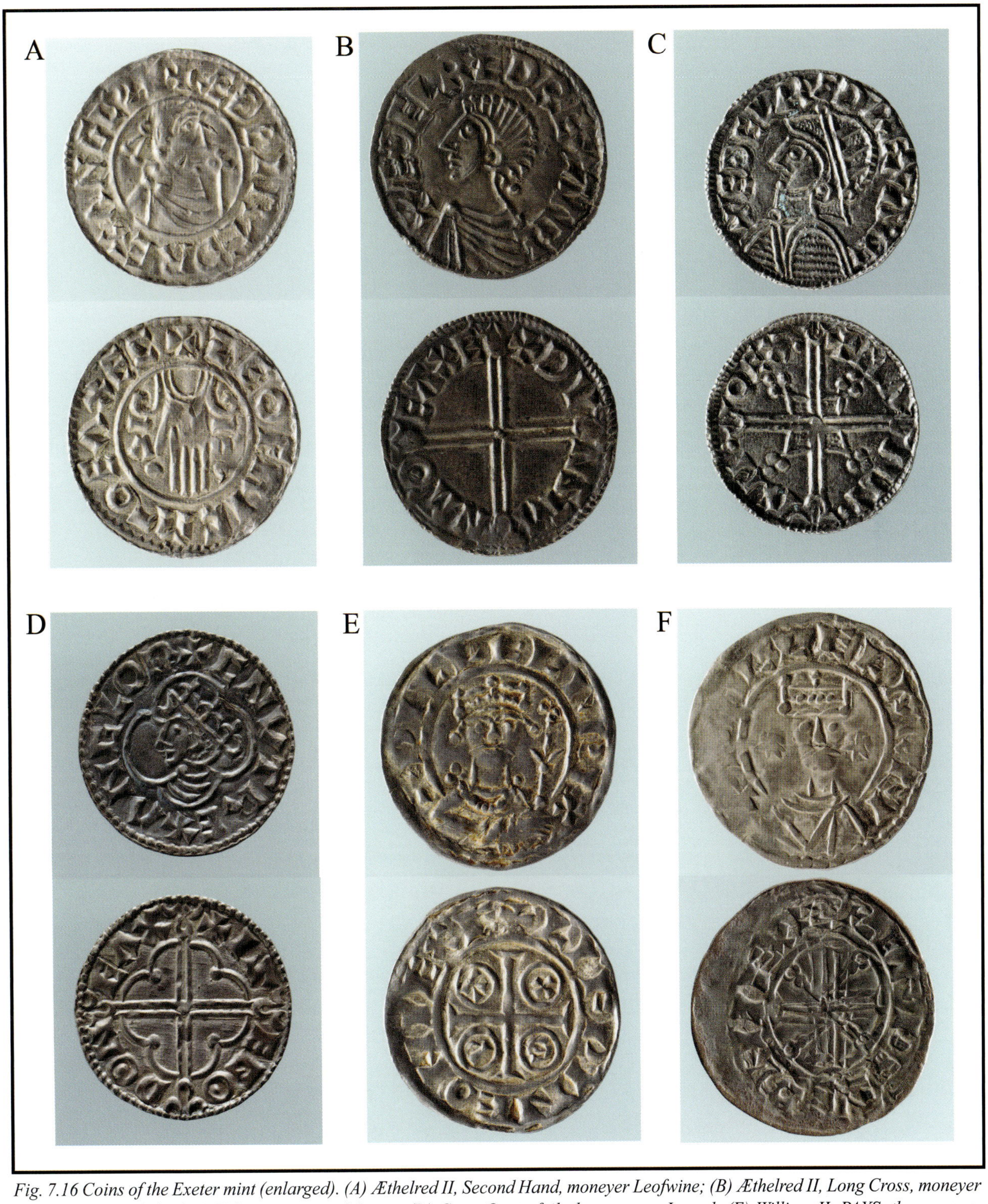

Fig. 7.16 Coins of the Exeter mint (enlarged). (A) Æthelred II, Second Hand, moneyer Leofwine; (B) Æthelred II, Long Cross, moneyer Dunstan; (C) Æthelred II, Helmet, moneyer Manna; (D) Cnut, Quatrefoil, the moneyer Isegod; (E) William II, PAXS, the moneyer Lifwine; (F) William II, Two Stars, the moneyer Leofwine (© RAMM)

South-West England early in Æthelred's reign (described below), Michael Dolley (1966, 36) suggested that the South-West benefited from the disruption of Chester's trade with Ireland which followed the Viking descent on the Wirral in 979–80, but, he argued, this prosperity was short-lived because Chester recovered later in Æthelred's reign and Bristol came to dominate this trade. Irish trade should certainly be considered as a significant factor in

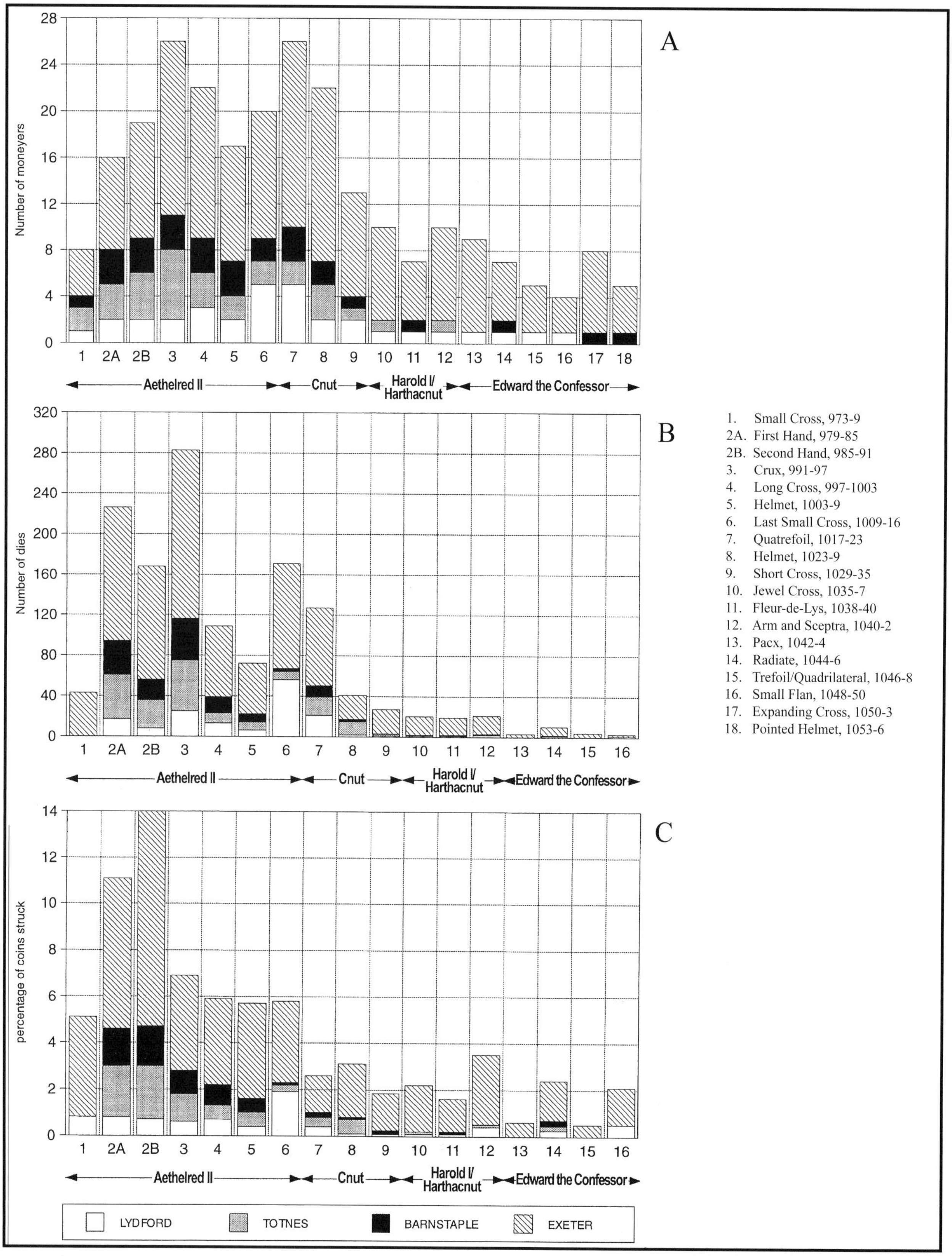

Fig. 7.17 The output of the Devon mints, c. *973–1056. (A) The number of moneyers in each type,* c. *973–1056; (B) Metcalf's estimate of the total number of reverse dies used in the Devon mints,* c. *973–1050; (C) Metcalf's estimate of the percentage of the English coinage struck by the Devon mints,* c. *973–1050 (Allan 2002, figs 6–8)*

the trade of Late Saxon Devon (see below), and it may be especially relevant at Barnstaple and Watchet, but it is difficult to see how it would have benefited Lydford, for example.

In a paper in *Past and Present*, J.R. Maddicott (1999) made a powerful case for linking this prosperity with mineral extraction, especially with tin. As he points out, Lydford lies in an area of poor agricultural land; its wealth can hardly have been generated by farming. The *burh*'s association with mining is probably reflected in the form of its huge parish, which encompasses the high moorland of Dartmoor including many sites of later medieval and post-medieval mining. The importance of Dartmoor as a mining area at the time of the earliest surviving documents in the period 1169–1214 was evident in Hatcher's classic study, but this gave no indication of levels of production at earlier periods (Hatcher 1973, 162). When Maddicott wrote, there was no archaeological evidence from Dartmoor to support his argument, but there are now firm indications of mining in this period. First, analysis of peat deposits in a bog at Tor Royal near Princetown shows peaks of chemical residues indicating tin-working in the periods AD 100–400 and 700–1100; this is thought to reflect tin-smelting on a substantial scale to the south-west of the site (Meharg *et al.* 2012). Second, the ongoing investigations at Crownhill Down, on the south side of the moor, are producing similar evidence of mining over a long period from prehistory until the mid 16th century, with activity in the 8th to 11th centuries recognised by OSL (Optically Stimulated Luminescence) dating (Horner 2018, 10; see also Quinnell 2017).

The possibility that silver was also mined at this time has also been raised (Metcalf 1998, 245), but archaeological evidence for such mining at this date has not yet been found. There were, however, important lead-silver deposits to the west of Dartmoor in the Tamar Valley which were worked extensively in the later medieval period (Rippon *et al.* 2009).

Much more substantial archaeological evidence has emerged in the last 30 years for a large and widely dispersed Roman and early medieval ironworking industry in the Blackdown Hills (Griffith and Weddell 1996; Reed *et al.* 2006; Cox and Gilmore 2013; Smart 2018). Over 100 ironworking sites are now known in Devon alone, spread over 13 parishes in a zone measuring about 25 km from west to east (Smart 2018, 216–17). The early medieval industry, including its technology and chronology, has been reviewed very helpfully in recent years in the report excavation at Churchills Farm, Hemyock (*ibid.*). Nine furnaces and more than one tonne of ironworking waste were recovered from that site alone; they have been described as 'the largest group of radiocarbon-dated furnaces of the late 9th to early 10th centuries currently known in Britain' (*ibid*). Churchills Farm is also the best-dated site currently known, since the post-excavation programme entailed the modelling of 27 radiocarbon dates. It was quite short-lived, starting in the date range cal AD 850–935 (870–910 at 68% probability) and continuing for a period of 1–70 years (*ibid.*, 49).

Other remarkable discoveries include the excavation of three large iron-smelting furnaces at Town Farm, Burlescombe, where probable anvil bases and more than two tonnes of iron slag were also found. In contrast with Churchills Farm, this also produced evidence for the smithing of iron blooms and the production of finished iron products. The site was radiocarbon-dated to cal AD 780–990 at 95% probability (Reed *et al.* 2006, modified slightly in Smart 2018, 40). The industry was evidently well established before the refoundation of the *burh* at Exeter at the end of the 10th century, as the evidence from Culmstock Road, in Hemyock, and Bywood Farm and North Hill, in Dunkeswell, illustrates. At the first site the group of furnaces and ironworking features was dated to cal AD 689–877 at 95% confidence (Rainbird and Young 2015; cal AD 720–945 for the last dated event as recalculated in Smart 2018, 40). Iron-smelting at the second site was dated to cal. AD 664–889 at 95% confidence, at the third AD 680–880 (Griffith and Weddell 1996, 33–4; Webster 2007, 175; remodelled dating in Smart 2018, 40, 61).

This major and widespread industry was potentially of high significance to the economy of Exeter. If the sites for which we have dating evidence are typical, the Mid–Late Saxon period represented the heyday of the industry. We may also note Tim Young's suggestion that the ironworking industries of Wessex may have been developed as an aspect of royal policy, since furnaces elsewhere in the kingdom lay on royal estates (Young 2018, 212). In the case of Churchills Farm there is a 68% probability that the earliest dated event from the excavation fell in the range AD 870–910 – the reigns of Alfred (871–99) or Edward the Elder (899–924). None of the sites currently known is likely to date after AD 1000, and this may be related to the relative decline of the economy of the West Saxon burhs after that date.

After the Norman Conquest Exeter's national standing declined somewhat but it remained among England's leading dozen cities into the early 13th century (Chapter 1, Table 1.1). Judged by the aids and tallages, it was in 5th, 6th or 7th place in the period 1130–70, and somewhere between 6th and 12th place in the period 1170–1215 (Biddle 1976, 500–2).

The food supply: the exploitation of animals

By Mark Maltby

The faunal data from this period is drawn from 11 sites. The zooarchaeologists who have studied these assemblages have used slightly different chronological divisions and terminology. The Goldsmith Street, Trichay Street and High Street assemblages are from Maltby's (1979) phases Md1–Md3 (950–1150). The Princesshay data comes from its Group 4 (Saxo-Norman 10th to 12th century) assemblage (Coles forthcoming b). The other five assemblages studied by Lauritsen (2019; EAPIT 2, Chapter 9) are from Phase 5 (Saxo-Norman 1, 900–1050) and Phase 6 (Saxo-Norman 2, 1050–1150) features. Altogether, these sites have produced 14,241 identified mammal bones (Table 7.1). The largest assemblages have been obtained from the Goldsmith Street sites in the north quarter of Exeter (as defined by Lauritsen (EAPIT 2, Chapter 9, fig. 9.1) and from Princesshay in the east quarter.

Cattle have provided the highest number of identified specimens (NISP) of mammals overall (41%), although this was only marginally greater than sheep/goat (40%) and cattle ranked behind sheep/goat in minimum number of individual (MNI) estimates (Maltby 1979, 109–17; Coles forthcoming b) or minimum animal unit counts (EAPIT 2, Chapter 9, Fig. 9.2). Although there are some variations in the relative abundance of elements from different parts of the body, there have been no very large accumulations of cattle butchery waste that were so characteristic of the Roman assemblages. Although butchery marks (mainly inflicted with heavy blades) and fracture patterns provided abundant evidence for carcass division, filleting, pot-boiling and marrow extraction, there was much less consistency in these patterns and there were some variations between assemblages from different areas of the town (Lauritsen 2019; EAPIT 2, Chapter 9). The mixing of bones of both high and low meat quality in most features suggests that a lot of the processing of the carcasses took place within properties.

Ageing analysis of cattle from all these Saxo-Norman assemblages has shown that the majority of cattle brought to Exeter were adults (Maltby 1979, 31–2, EAPIT 2, Chapter 9, Fig. 9.4; Coles forthcoming b). The focus on the culling of cattle between three and eight years old is fairly typical of cattle mortality patterns in Early Norman sites in England (Sykes 2006a, 59). Metrical analysis of the metacarpals from the northern quarter indicated that adult males and females were fairly equally represented (Maltby 1979, 33–5), although a heavy bias towards females was reported from the Princesshay site. However, pathological conditions often associated with traction animals were also observed in the Princesshay assemblage (Coles forthcoming b). This suggests that many of the cattle had served in ploughteams before been brought for slaughter. The very low numbers of bones from young calves suggests that dairy production was not of great importance.

Cattle continued to be mainly of small stature (Maltby 1979, 164–7). There were more cattle bones in the later Saxo-Norman levels that lay in the higher end of the size range than in the Roman assemblages (EAPIT 2, Chapter 9, Fig. 9.5), perhaps reflecting an increase in the proportion of males represented rather than a general increase in stature.

With the exception of horn cores, the great majority of the diagnostic sheep/goat bones from medieval features belonged to sheep (Maltby 1979, 41). As noted above, sheep/goat elements were generally more abundant than in the Roman assemblages providing nearly 40% of the mammal NISP counts. They were best represented in the Goldsmith Street features, where they outnumbered cattle elements (Table 7.1). Although there was some variation between sites and phases, the general slaughter pattern indicated that most sheep were culled in their second, third and fourth years, which represents a focus on meat production (Maltby 1979, 174–7; EAPIT 2, Chapter 9, Fig. 9.4; Coles forthcoming b). Small concentrations of horn-working waste were found in some features, for example in Trichay Street F227 (Maltby 1979, 17). Sheep generally were no larger than the small, slender types found in the Roman period (Maltby 1979, 181–5; EAPIT 2, Chapter 9, Fig. 9.6).

Overall, pigs were less abundant than in the Roman period, providing 14.7% of the NISP counts. They were best represented in the High Street and Queen Street assemblages (*c.* 20%), particularly in the early Saxo-Norman phases (Maltby 1979, 109–114; Lauritsen 2019; EAPIT 2, Chapter 9, Fig. 9.2). As in most archaeological samples, mandibles and other cranial elements featured prominently in the pig assemblages, but bones from all parts of the body were frequently encountered in the same features, suggesting that much of the carcass processing was carried out within properties. Most of the pigs were slaughtered in their second and third years (Maltby 1979, 57; Coles forthcoming b; Lauritsen 2019). A piglet skeleton found in a pit from Princesshay (Coles forthcoming b) could signify that some pigs were being kept in the town.

Horses were poorly represented forming only 1% of the total mammal NISP counts and never more than 2% in any of the assemblages (Table 7.1). Although, horsemeat was generally rarely consumed in the Saxo-Norman period, Coles (forthcoming b) observed butchery marks on 12 of the 78 horse elements from this phase at Princesshay, which shows that some of their carcasses were processed. Most of the horse bones came from adult animals.

Dogs were found in only six of the assemblages and provided less than 1% of the overall mammal NISP counts (Table 7.1). These included 16 bones from an adult from a Princesshay pit (Coles forthcoming b) and seven from another partial skeleton from Goldsmith Street (Maltby 1979, 115). None of the bones bore butchery marks. Cats accounted for 2% of the NISP counts, being particularly common in the assemblages from the northern quarter (Table 7.1). These counts were inflated by the inclusion of 88 bones from three partial skeletons from the Goldsmith Street and Trichay Street sites (Maltby 1979, 112–15). The bodies of companion animals and possibly stray cats and dogs were therefore often buried amongst household and butchery waste usually without any processing, although

Table 7.1 Number of identified specimens (NISP) of mammals in early medieval features

	North Quarter						*East Quarter*	*South Quarter*	*West Quarter*		*Extra-mural*	
Site Code	*GS I-II*	*GS III*	*TS*	*HS*	*PS*	*QS*	*PH*	*MY*	*BSE*	*FH*	*AC*	
EAPIT Site	*37–38*	*39*	*42*	*43*	*76*	*68*	*156*	*63*	*47*	*75*	*94*	*Total*
Cattle	1233	1535	821	105	11	129	1769	3	217	29	8	5860
Sheep/Goat	1549	1605	683	57	27	111	1418	7	169	19	1	5646
Pig	443	637	295	42		63	543	3	67			2093
Horse	12	36	9	4		1	78		4			144
Dog	5	17	13			1	84		1			121
Cat	66	135	50	1	1	11	20		1			285
Red Deer	5	9	1	2		1	2		2			22
Roe Deer	2		2	2		1	2		1			10
Fallow Deer	2	5		1								8
Hare	22	8	9			1	5					45
Rabbit		6		1								7
Total Mammal	**3339**	**3993**	**1883**	**215**	**39**	**319**	**3921**	**13**	**462**	**48**	**9**	**14241**
% NISP												
Cattle	36.9	38.4	43.6	48.8		40.4	45.1		47.0			41.1
Sheep/Goat	46.4	40.2	36.3	26.5		34.8	36.2		36.6			39.6
Pig	13.3	16.0	15.7	19.5		19.7	13.8		14.5			14.7
Horse	0.4	0.9	0.5	1.9		0.3	2.0		0.9			1.0
Dog	0.1	0.4	0.7	0.0		0.3	2.1		0.2			0.8
Cat	2.0	3.4	2.7	0.5		3.4	0.5		0.2			2.0
Red Deer	0.1	0.2	0.1	0.9		0.3	0.1		0.4			0.2
Roe Deer	0.1	0.0	0.1	0.9		0.3	0.1		0.2			0.1
Fallow Deer	0.1	0.1	0.0	0.5		0.0	0.0		0.0			0.1
Hare	0.7	0.2	0.5	0.0		0.3	0.1		0.0			0.3
Rabbit	0.0	0.2	0.0	0.5		0.0	0.0		0.0			0.0
Total Mammal	**3339**	**3993**	**1883**	**215**	**39**	**319**	**3921**	**13**	**462**	**48**	**9**	**14221**
Cattle	38.2	40.6	45.6	51.5		42.6	47.4		47.9			43.1
Sheep/Goat	48.0	42.5	38.0	27.9		36.6	38.0		37.3			41.5
Pig	13.7	16.9	16.4	20.6		20.8	14.6		14.8			15.4
Total C+S+P	**3225**	**3777**	**1799**	**204**	**38**	**303**	**3730**	**13**	**453**	**48**	**9**	**13599**
% S of S+P	77.8	71.6	69.8	57.6		63.8	72.3		71.6			73.0
% Horse of C+H	1.0	2.3	1.1	3.7		0.8	4.2		1.8			2.4
% Wild	0.9	0.6	0.6	2.3		0.9	0.2		0.6			0.6

Counts exclude bones of small mammals but do include bones from associated bone groups
% S of S+P = percentage of sheep/goat of total sheep/goat and pig
% Horse of C+H = percentage of horse of total cattle and horse
Data for GS, TS and HS adapted from Maltby (1979)
Data for PH adapted from Coles (forthcoming b)
Data for BSE, FH, MY, PS, QS and AC adapted from Lauritsen (2019)
GS = Goldsmith Street
TS = Trichay Street
HS = High Street
PS = Paul Street
QS = Queen Street
PH = Princesshay
MY = Mermaid Yard
BSE = Bartholomew Street East
FH = Friernhay Street
AC = Acorn Roundabout

one cat skull from Princesshay bore skinning marks (Coles forthcoming b).

Bones of other mammals (excluding rodent and other small species) accounted for only 0.7% of the mammal NISP counts (Table 7.1). Hares were the most commonly identified followed by red deer and roe deer. The red deer counts include a few fragments of antler. Several bones of fallow deer and rabbit were also recovered. The low percentage of deer, hare and rabbit is typical of Saxo-Norman urban sites (Sykes 2006b, 164). Although the fur of rabbits and hares may have been utilised, the presence of butchery marks indicates that the ones brought to the town were eaten. The presence of rabbit bones is notable that the earliest substantiated reference to a rabbit warren in the Isles of Scilly dates to 1176 and the earliest reference on the mainland dates to 1235. Earliest archaeological examples from elsewhere in England date from the late 11th century at the earliest (Gould 2016). It is possible that the Exeter rabbit bones are later intrusions but currently they are amongst the earliest finds of this species in medieval England.

Most of the bird bones belonged to poultry, with chickens being the dominant species, providing 69% of the bird bones from sites in the northern quarter and also forming the majority of bird bones from Princesshay (Table 7.2). Around a quarter of the chicken bones from the pre-1976 excavations were from immature birds (Maltby 1979, 209), indicating a focus on meat production. In contrast, only 7% of the chicken bones from the Saxo-Norman levels at Princesshay were from immature birds (Coles forthcoming b), which was similar to levels from contemporary sites in the Winchester suburbs (Serjeantson 2009). Most of the chickens were of small stature and generally no larger than those found in the Roman period (Maltby 1979, 67–70).

Bones of large geese were more common than in the Roman deposits forming 20% of the identified bird bones from the northern quarter sites (Table 7.2). It is likely that most, if not all, of these bones were from geese kept in captivity. Bones of duck were much rarer and included bones of teal as well as mallard/domestic duck. Woodcock continued to be the most common game bird, forming 6% of the identified bird bones from the northern quarter sites, probably indicating that they were locally available in good numbers. A few bones of other waders were also recovered (Table 7.2). A partial skeleton of a

Table 7.2 Number of identified specimens (NISP) of birds in early medieval features

		North Quarter		*East Quarter*	*South Quarter*	*West Quarter*		*Extra-mural*	
Site Code	*Pre 1976*	*PS*	*QS*	*PH**	*MY*	*BSE*	*FH*	*AC*	
EAPIT Site Number		*76*	*68*	*156*	*63*	*47*	*75*	*94*	*Total*
Chicken	664	5	34	177	1	4		1	886
Goose	199		5						204
Mallard-sized duck	6								6
Teal	2								2
Woodcock	60		2						62
Oyster Catcher	1								1
Curlew	3								3
Small wader	1								1
Pigeons	7								7
Raven	15		1						16
Rook/Crow	1								1
Sparrowhawk	10								10
Passerine	2								2
Total Bird	**971**	**5**	**42**	**177**	**1**	**4**	**0**	**1**	**1201**
% B+M	9.3	11.4	11.6			0.9			
% Chicken	68.4		80.9						
Ch:Sh	14.6	15.6	23.4	11.1		2.3			13.6

Counts include bones from associated bone groups

* only chicken bones counted. 276 other bird bones from all medieval phases not further identified

% B+M = percentage of total bird and mammal

Ch:Sh = percentage of chicken of total sheep/goat and chicken female sparrowhawk probably belonged to a captive bird trained for falconry. Bones of ravens and crows were also found in small numbers.

Although fish bones appear to be more abundant and from a wider range of species than encountered in the Roman period (Wilkinson 1979; Lauritsen 2019; Coles forthcoming b), none of the Saxo-Norman fish bones from post-1976 excavations have as yet been further identified and the medieval assemblage from earlier excavations was not subdivided into early and later medieval phases. Fishing will be discussed in more detail in Chapter 8.

Irrespective of their status, the residents of Saxo-Norman Exeter relied heavily on domestic animals for their meat supplies. The majority of the meat came from cattle, although sheep were probably slaughtered in greater numbers. Pigs began to decline in relative abundance. Fish and geese were slightly more important than they were in the Roman period. Cattle and horses were valued as working animals but dairy and wool production were not very prominent in animal husbandry practices.

Manufacturing

Metalworking

When, in the early 13th century, Henry of Huntingdon spoke of the renowned features of the English towns – the fish of Canterbury, the wine of Winchester, the chase of Salisbury, for example – he said that 'Exeter boasts its rich metallic ores' (Greenway 2002). Little archaeological evidence from the city itself which might support this striking statement has been found, but the evidence for a major Late Saxon ironworking industry in the Blackdown Hills, and the first indications of tin-working on Dartmoor, have been described above.

Bell-founding

A notable feature of the archaeology of Exeter has been the recovery of evidence for bell-founding and for the casting of bronze vessels on a series of sites ranging in date from the 12th to the 18th century. An account of the evidence from the city was presented some years ago (Blaylock 1995) and was reviewed more recently alongside comparable material from other sites in South-West England (Blaylock 2015a).

The earliest example of bell-casting in the city was discovered between the foundations of the Norman tower of Mary Major church in 1971 (Site 40; Blaylock 1995, 74–5; Scott *et al.* 2007, 42–3). It consisted of a narrow trench whose central part had been consolidated with rubble and burnt clay (Fig. 7.18B–C). On the ground surface to one side of the trench, an area of baked clay was found; its outer edge formed the arc of a circle centred on the trench. This was interpreted as the bottom of the core (the inner mould around which the bell was cast). Many thick but featureless fragments of fired clay were found in the trench, together with fragments of heavily burnt clay. The former were almost certainly remnants of the core and cope (the outer mould); the latter were perhaps fragments of furnace lining. Many sherds of large unglazed and handmade jars in Upper Greensand-Derived fabric were recovered, broadly datable to the late 10th, 11th or 12th century. Since the tower had architectural features of the mid or late 12th century (Fig. 7.18A), that seems the most probable date of the find. Blaylock has pointed out the similarity of the bell-pit to four examples excavated in the Old Minster and Cathedral Green at Winchester, and to others at the St Oswald's Priory in Gloucester, Gilberd School in Colchester, and in Chichester (Blaylock 1995, 74; forthcoming).

The processes entailed in casting this bell can be reconstructed by reference to the account of Theophilus' 12th-century treatise *On Divers Arts* (Hawthorne and Smith 1979, 167–76); Fig. 7.18D illustrates the procedures. A clay core was first built up around a horizontal spindle which was rotated in a frame (Fig. 7.18D, 1). A beeswax model of the bell was then added, and this too was rotated to achieve a circular shape (Fig. 7.18D, 2). It was then coated with layers of clay loam which formed the cope (Fig. 7.18D, 3). The entire fragile assembly of core, wax model and cope was then lowered over the trench, where a fire was lit, baking the clay, melting the wax model, and leaving a cavity in which the bell was cast (Fig. 7.18D, 4–5). The procedure used here may be contrasted with that employed in Exeter's early modern foundries at Cowick Street and Paul Street, in which the cope was built up around a vertical post and shaped by a paddle or strickle, then fired *in situ* (see below, Chapter 8). All these Exeter finds richly deserve further analytical work.

Metalworking: other evidence

The other signs of metalworking in the city are more limited. A total of over 50 small sand-tempered crucibles has been recorded from Saxo-Norman contexts on six excavations around the centre of the city; the latest examples from stratified contexts belong in the early 13th century. It has been suspected that these might be connected with the production of small metal objects, or with enamelling, or the working of precious metals but a recent assessment could shed no further light on their function (EAPIT 2, Chapter 10). The recovery of a probable touchstone (a stone used in assaying [compositional analysis] of precious metals) from a late 12th/early 13th-century pit at Trichay Street (Allan 1984a, 299–30, S.31) is the sole evidence for the activity of a goldsmith in the Norman city.

Textiles

The earliest evidence for textile production dates from the 10th and 11th centuries. The most common finds are spindlewhorls sawn from the ends of cow long-bones, which are known from High Street, Preston Street, Trichay Street and Goldsmith Street (Fig. 7.19; Allan 1984a,

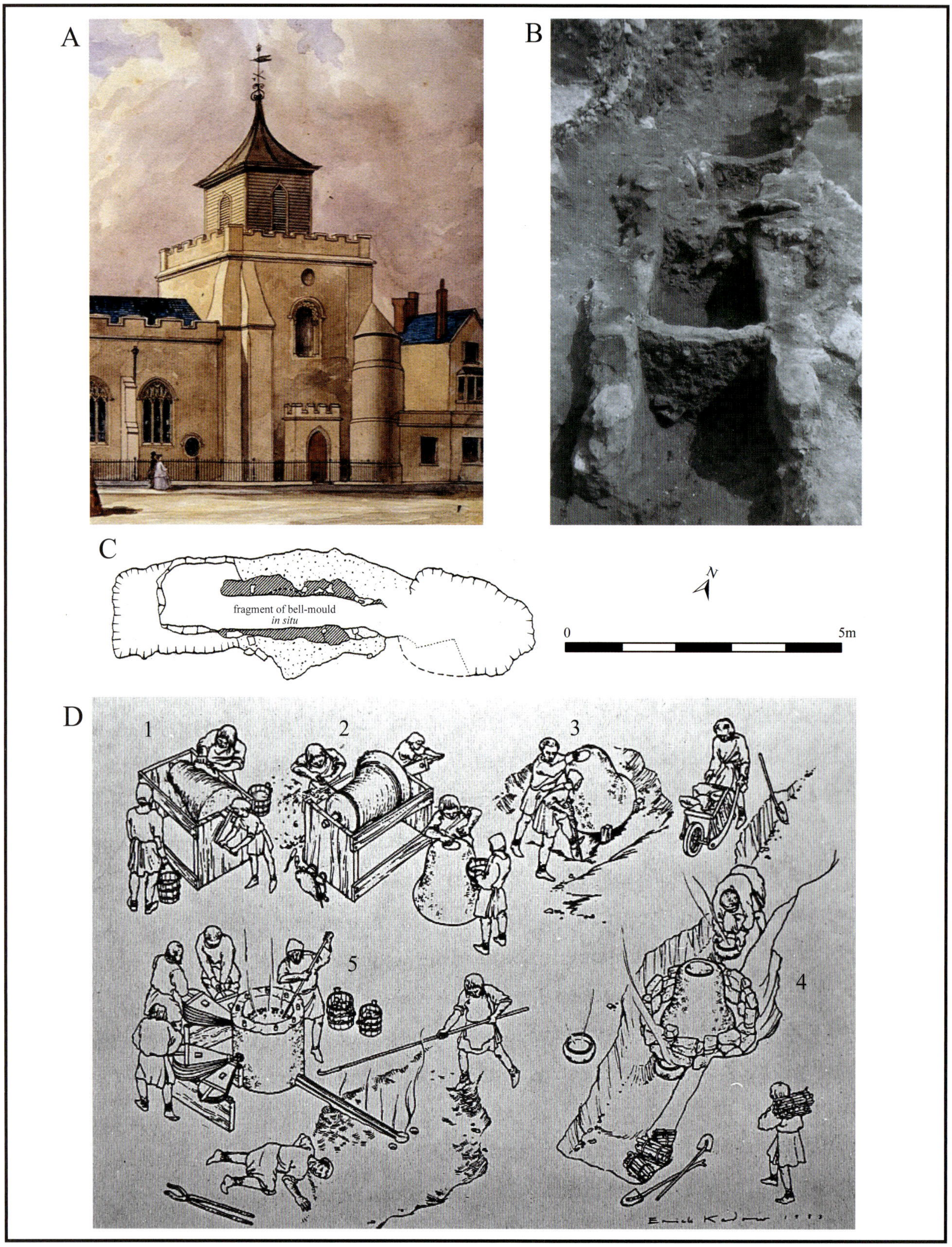

Fig. 7.18 The bell-casting pit in Mary Major church. (A) The tower in which the pit was found (© Devon and Exeter Institution). (B) View of the pit from the south-west. (C) Plan. (D) Reconstruction of the bell-founding process. Upper: forming the core; forming the wax model; lowering the assembled moulds into the pit. Lower right: baking the moulds. Lower left: casting the bell. The bell-founder listens to the ground as metal runs from the furnace into the casting pit and labourers work the bellows (B–D Exeter Archaeology archive; © Exeter City Council; (D) drawn by Erich Kadow, based on interpretation of Theophilus by C.G. Henderson)

350–1; Sites 39, 42, 43, 60). Examples of pin-beaters, used in weaving, have been found at Goldsmith Street and Rack Street, the former in a 12th-century context (*ibid.*, nos 21–2, Sites 39, 64). A variety of bone pins and needles, some of them with shafts polished by use, may also have been used in textile production.

Other trades

The preservation of organic finds in waterlogged pits at Goldsmith Street and Trichay Street allowed the recovery of Late Saxon and Norman objects of wood, leather and even textile which are unique in a regional context and uncommon finds elsewhere. Most of the leather objects are from vegetable-tanned cattle skin. The most common finds at Exeter are footwear, including a complete turnshoe and laces, but the collection includes fragmentary leather belts and straps, a high-quality object with whipped edges and engraved lines, and remains of kid leather and goatskin – the last a purse or pouch (Friendship-Taylor 1984, 323–7). Although their place of manufacture is unknown, it is likely that many or most were made locally, and the shoes were certainly repaired in the tenements where they were found; cobblers' waste was a common find in these contexts.

The carpentry trade is represented not only by the components of timber house walls (discussed in EAPIT 2, Chapter 5) but by a range of domestic objects – fragments of casks, stave-built tubs, buckets and barrels, two garderobe seats, and numerous riven oak boards, some nailed, which might have come from chests or other furniture. The emergence of the stone building trade is discussed below in the context of regional trade. The Bedford Garage kiln is discussed in EAPIT 2, Chapter 17; it is currently the sole known instance of the production of pottery within a Late Saxon *burh*. Finally, the plentiful evidence for the activities of horners may be noted. Their products have not been found but the characteristic waste of horn-cores has been seen repeatedly on sites of this period (Maltby, above).

Foreign trade

In his description of Exeter in the 12th century, William of Malmesbury drew a telling contrast between the wealth of the inhabitants and the magnificence of the city and the 'barren and unfruitful soil which can scarcely produce poor oats', and stated that a great concourse of strangers was to be seen in Exeter, bringing an abundance of every sort of merchandise (Whitelock 1955, 277–83; but see Chapter 2 above for a more balanced assessment of the South-West's agricultural potential). We learn of the city's foreign merchants at the time of the Norman Conquest as Orderic Vitalis' account of the siege of 1068 mentions that they were drafted in by the citizens to supplement their fighting force (Chibnall 1969, 211).

The recovery of a major collection of Late Saxon and Norman pottery provides valuable archaeological evidence for the vigour and direction of Exeter's foreign trade throughout the period 900–1200; the finds form one of the three large collections of Saxo-Norman imported pottery in southern England, the others being from Southampton and London. The initial publication of this material undertaken in the 1980s concluded that a high proportion of the imports were northern French, although the quantity of reference material for much of the Exeter pottery was then limited (Hodges and Mainman 1984). The chemical analyses undertaken by Michael Hughes in the present project (EAPIT 2, Chapter 17, Appendix 17.2) have drawn the important conclusion that many of the sherds which were broadly attributed to northern France in fact share a chemical signature closely comparable to that of wares from the lower Seine Valley around Rouen. This implies that the bulk of the material represented at Exeter was shipped from Rouen. A few other sources are represented: the fragments from Huy, in Belgium, identified by Giertz (discussed in EAPIT 2, Chapter 17, Fig. 17.6), and some highly distinctive micaceous wares which must come from further west in northern France, either from western Normandy or Brittany.

The contrasting sources of imported pottery in a series of samples from London, Southampton and Exeter have been tabulated in EAPIT 2, Chapter 17, Table 17.1. Although the figures from the three ports are not strictly comparable, since the date-ranges of the samples and the methods of quantification are not consistent, the differences between them are so pronounced that they must surely represent not just different patterns of pottery consumption but also of commerce. There are clear differences in the frequency of imports in these collections; when expressed as a percentage of all wares, they are about six times or more plentiful at Southampton than at Exeter or London. Their origins are also fundamentally different. London's imports came principally from the Low Countries and the Rhineland. By contrast, the central feature of the finds from Southampton and Exeter is the marked dominance of wares from northern France, principally from Normandy. In both these ports the most common types of imported pottery are unglazed Normandy Gritty wares and white wares, followed by northern French red-painted and glazed wares. The Exeter finds include vessels from the earliest contexts known from the *burh* which probably date from the 10th century, showing that foreign commerce developed at a very early stage in the town's revival.

In a regional context these finds are unique. In Devon and Cornwall the only other place where more than one or two examples of Late Saxon or Norman imported pottery are known is the *burh* and river port of Totnes, where about ten vessels have been recorded. With their predominance of French wares, including red-painted sherds, Normandy Gritty wares and yellow-glazed white wares, these finds are very similar in overall character to

Fig. 7.19 (A) Evidence of Late Saxon textile manufacture: spindle whorls, pin-beaters and needles. (B) An 11th to early 12th-century crucible from Goldsmith Street (Site 39). (C) Imported Saxo-Norman pottery (© RAMM)

the Exeter pieces. A recent find at Lympstone on the Exe Estuary by AC Archaeology in 2018 (unpublished) adds a third site on the southern coast of Devon, with a fourth possible example at Exmouth (Allan 1986, 133, no. 2); they serve to show that the creeks of the estuary may have been engaged in foreign trade, or at least were part of the network of redistribution. Finds of this sort may also be expected at Topsham, the outport of Exeter on the Exe Estuary which was already the place where wine was unloaded in the 12th century (Jackson 1972), but hardly any medieval deposits have been excavated there. Elsewhere, only about three further finds of the period have been recorded from the entire region, including a single find of Hamwic fabric 127 from Barnstaple and – extraordinarily – another from Padstow, in north Cornwall (Allan and Langman 2002–3). The virtual absence of continental imported ceramics of this period is particularly striking in Somerset, where there are major pottery collections of this date.

In his account of the siege of Exeter by William I, Orderic Vitalis tells us that Exeter lay beside the closest routes to Ireland and Brittany (Chibnall 1969, 211). Numismatic evidence supports the conclusion that trade with Ireland was a significant factor in the city's economy. Dolley noted that a disproportionately large number of the English pennies found in excavations in Dublin were minted in Devon; four of the ten single finds of English pennies of the reigns of Æthelred II and Cnut were struck in Exeter and Barnstaple (two each: Wallace 1986, 210–11). Similarly, coins of the Devon mints are unusually numerous in the Kildare hoard found in 1923. Among its 36 pence, all of the *First Hand* and *Second Hand* issues of Æthelred (979–91), six came from Devon: four from Exeter and two from Lydford (Wells 1923–4; additions and corrections in Thompson 1956, 51–2; Dolley 1966, 33–6). The evidence for a strong link with Dublin is supported by the fact that one of the earliest coins struck at Dublin is a copy of a Lydford penny (Dolley 1961a; 1966; Blackburn 1990, 11–20). And a new strand in the archaeological evidence for links between South-East Ireland and South-West England emerged in the 1990s with the publication of large quantities (at least 83 vessels) of grass-marked and bar lug pottery in the Cornish tradition from a sequence of structures in Waterford which yielded tree-ring dates in the late 11th to mid 12th century (Gahan and McCutcheon 1997, 288–90). Further finds of this type are also recorded from Wexford (McCutcheon pers. comm.;

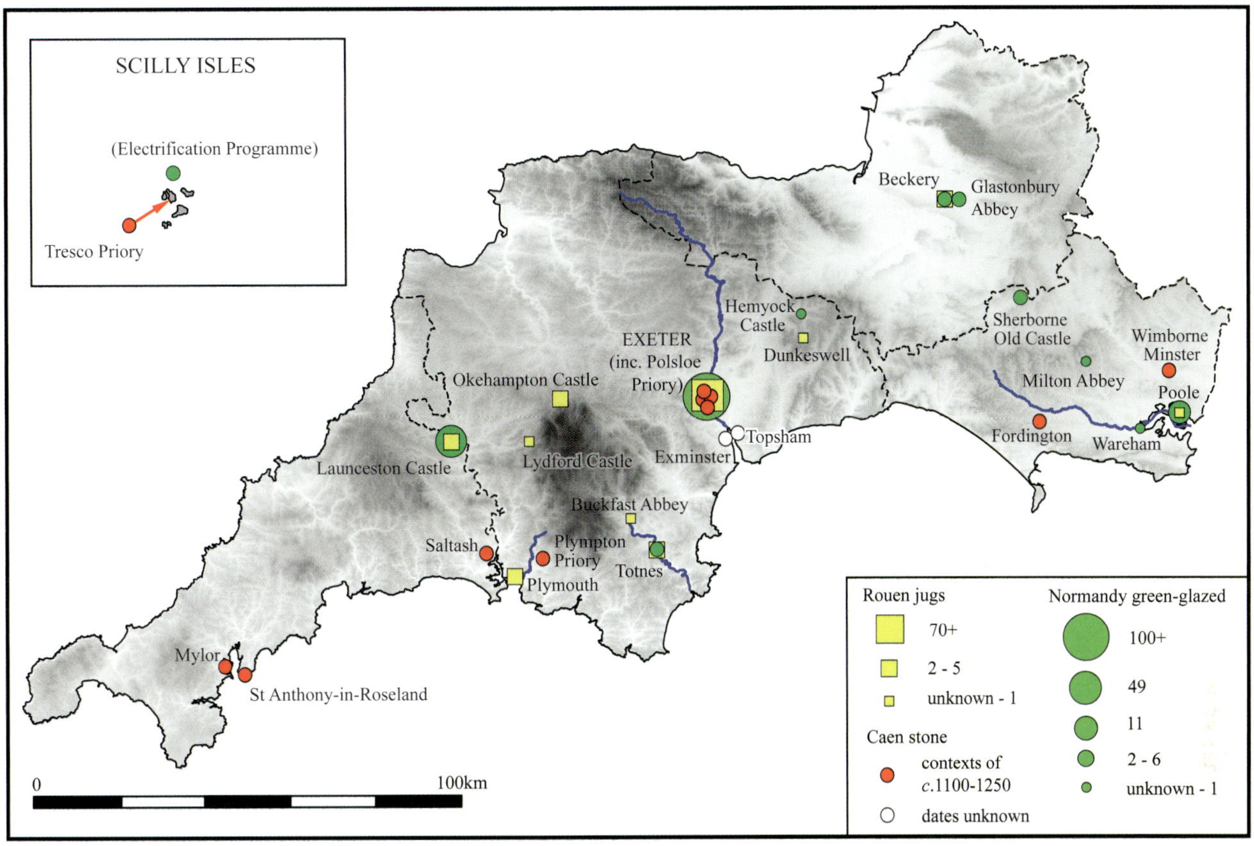

Fig. 7.20 Imported North French pottery, c. *1150–1250, and Caen building stone,* c. *1000–1250, in South-West England (research by John Allan, drawn by David Gould)*

Wood 2014, 228–9). Although further petrological work remains to be carried out on the fabrics of these sherds to determine their precise place of manufacture, this provides dramatic evidence for links between South-West Ireland and the South-West Peninsula in the 11th and 12th centuries.

Here the current work of Julia Crick on Norman trade with the West Country is highly relevant. She has argued (pers. comm.) that that South-West England acted as an intermediary in the trade between northern France (especially Normandy) and Ireland. She has emphasised the significance of the charter granted by the future Henry II in *c.* 1150 to the port of Rouen giving it monopoly rights over this trade, which evidently entailed regular and lucrative shipments of goods, including furs, from Ireland to Normandy. She points out that it is unlikely that such shipping would have been undertaken in direct voyages between Ireland and France, and probable that it would have entailed landfalls in Devon and Cornwall.

The trade in Caen stone

Apart from imported pottery, the trade in building stone from Caen (Normandy) offers the most extensive physical evidence for the region's trade with northern France in the post-Conquest period. This subject has not received the attention it deserves. Tatton-Brown's 'provisional survey' of stone in England (1997), much the best national study currently available, emphasises its export to the major centres of South-East England – Canterbury, London, Norwich, Rochester, Winchester and St Alban's – and its use in parish churches in Kent, Sussex and East Anglia. The present chapter offers a preliminary attempt to map the distribution of Caen stone in the four south-western counties in the period *c.* 1000–1250. Figure 7.20 shows the results, alongside the distribution pattern of North French pottery. The limitations of this exercise should be emphasised. First, there is the question of correct identification. Published identifications of Caen stone have often proved mistaken, even in otherwise reliable sources. In Somerset, the Caen stone identified at Glastonbury Abbey and elsewhere is now known to be from Dundry, south of Bristol, and there are at present no verified examples of Caen stone in the county (I am grateful to Jerry Sampson for confirmation of this point). In Dorset, the Royal Commission's identifications are surprisingly unreliable; their statement that the Romanesque tympanum at Fordington (Dorset) is Caen stone, for example, repeated in a number of other sources, has proved to be a mistake (RCHM 1970 xxxv–xlii; Peter Bath, pers. comm.). Caen stone is sometimes claimed in Cornish churches but most of the examples examined by this writer have proved to be of Beer stone. Figure 7.20 is based on visual examination by the writer, although some identifications have been verified onsite by geologists. The second limitation of Fig. 7.20 is that the coverage is uneven – fairly comprehensive in Devon (where all *c*. 500 medieval churches have been examined, for example), less complete in Cornwall and patchy in Dorset and Somerset, where I have kept notes but have also relied extensively on advice from others, notably Peter Bath, Jerry Sampson and Brian and Moira Gittos.

With these provisos, a number of points may be noted. First, Caen stone is not common in the south-western counties, and its distribution is largely coastal. In Dorset, it was used at Wimborne Minster on a large scale (Bath *et al.* 2019), and this is probably the most extensive use of the material in the region. The largest group of sites, however, is at Exeter, where it is present in at least five structures (the cathedral, St Nicholas Priory, St James Priory, Exe Bridge and the city wall; the Cedars Road fragments perhaps from a different site), some of them works of very high quality. It is also seen in parish churches in the Exe Estuary (Topsham and Exminster). The other finds in Devon and Cornwall are mainly in parish churches beside the estuaries of the Teign (Bishopsteignton), Dart (Totnes), Tamar (Saltash, Cornwall) and Fal (Mylor; St Anthony-in-Roseland), with one outlier on Tresco on the Isles of Scilly.

Regional trade: the evidence from pottery

Pottery of course provides the most abundant archaeological evidence for the operation of Saxo-Norman regional trade. The products of Exeter's Late Saxon Bedford Garage kiln provide some information about the distribution of goods from the city, although the evidence is surprisingly limited (EAPIT 2, Chapter 17). While hundreds of vessels of this type have been recovered from Exeter, it has proved very rare elsewhere in Devon, being known from just three places: the *burhs* of Totnes and Lydford to the west, and Stockland in east Devon. At Totnes there are several vessels, at the other two sites just a single find (unpublished finds from Fore Street, in Totnes and King's Thatch, in Stockland, all in the RAMM; for Lydford: Allan 1981, 133, no. 1).

The bulk of the ceramics used in the city was supplied by rural craftsmen working around the fringes of the Blackdown Hills of Devon and southern Somerset, about 15–20 km to the north-east of the city, whose products were tempered with inclusions derived from the Upper Greensand ('Upper Greensand-Derived' or UGSD wares). This area had been a major regional centre of pottery production since the Neolithic. The city formed part of a very wide market for their wares, since the potters of this area sent their products in great quantities and surprising distances. In the 12th century they were almost the only source of ceramics used in eastern Cornwall, most of Devon, the southern half of Somerset and in west Dorset, and a few have even been identified further afield – for example in Southampton and on the coast of South Wales (EAPIT 2, Chapter 17). The complete dominance of the UGSD makers over the Devon ceramics market was to be eroded in the late 12th and 13th centuries with the emergence of new potteries in the Exeter area, the South Hams and north Devon, but the industry retained a large regional market into the 19th century.

Before the late 12th century, the exceptions to this picture are the few limestone-tempered jars from Dorset or Hampshire, found in some of the earliest excavated deposits in Late Saxon Exeter (early to mid 10th century?), and rare sherds of scratch-marked pottery, exported from the same area in the 12th century. This last type is more common at Totnes, perhaps reflecting that town's easier access to products carried in the coastal trade (Allan 2014c). With the emergence of a new demand for high-quality jugs in towns and on the wealthier rural sites in the late 12th century, new trades in these wares developed along the south coast. They grew in importance in the early 13th century and will be described in Chapter 8 below.

Late Saxon moneyers and coin dies

A second class of artefact which provides valuable information about the operation of Exeter as a regional centre is coinage. The evidence for the distribution of the coins of the Exeter mint has yet to be assembled, but detailed analysis of the designs of English coins has shown that some distinctive styles of royal portrait are specific to particular areas of the country, demonstrating the operation of regional die-cutting centres, from which dies were sent out to local mints. Exeter was one of the centres making these dies in the latter part of the reign of Æthelred II and in the *Quatrefoil* issue of Cnut. The complex pattern of die-cutting in the latter issue has been studied in great detail, identifying no fewer than 42 different styles and sub-styles, among which the Exeter style is one of the most distinctive (Blackburn and Lyon 1986). The design of Exeter dies in Cnut's *Quatrefoil* pennies is characterised by the parallel hoops of the drapery and a distinctive form of crown in the king's portrait on the obverse (Fig. 7.16D). Dies in this style make up most of those used in the city and all of those at Barnstaple, Totnes and the lost site of **Geothaburh*. In the early years of the issue, Exeter also supplied most of the dies used in the Somerset mints, and even some of those used at Salisbury, but later in the *Quatrefoil* issue there arose a new style of die, probably made in Taunton, which supplanted the Exeter products (Fig. 7.21).

The trades in building stone in Late Saxon and Norman Exeter

The identification of Late Saxon fabric in the city wall and in five city churches allows some light to be thrown on the emergence of the market in building stone. Naturally, the predominant material in these churches is local volcanic

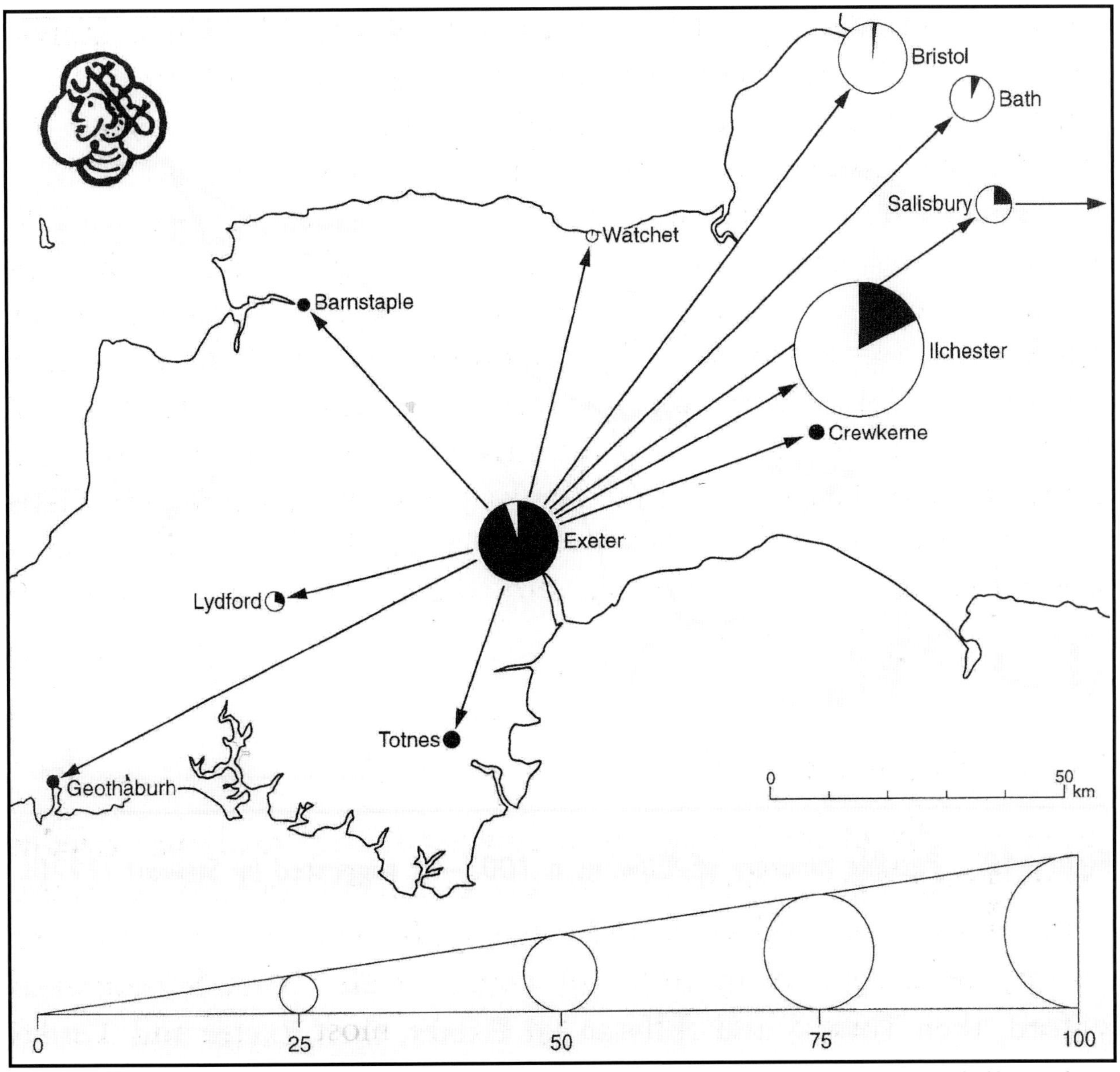

Fig. 7.21 The distribution of coin dies cut in Exeter in the Quatrefoil *issue of Cnut (Allan 2002, fig. 11, from data in Blackburn and Lyon 1986). The mint of* *Geothaburh *is placed at one proposed but improbable site – Castle Gotha, Cornwall – for want of an alternative*

rubble, as it had been in the Late Roman city. A common feature of the excavation of urban tenements within the walled city is the robbing of the foundations of Late Roman town houses in the 11th and 12th centuries, and these were no doubt the source of some of the materials employed. The Roman column base and fragments of Roman tile in the Late Saxon doorway of St George's church are the clearest instance of the reuse of Roman materials in Late Saxon buildings (Fox 1952, 25), but this practice was certainly common.

By the time of the Conquest, at least three other building stones were used in the city, reviving their exploitation in the Roman period. First, the presence of much Triassic sandstone in the Late Saxon town wall at Rougemont Castle has been illustrated above. This material is also seen in the long-and-short quoins of St George's (identifications by H. Dewey in Fox 1952, 27; one block in the re-erected fragment of the church now in the hall of the Vicars Choral, South Street), and in the same element of the church at St Olave's (Parker 1999). It could have been quarried from cliffs in the Exe Estuary and the adjacent coast (Fig. 2.2), or in quarries in the area of Woodbury, about 15 km to the south-east of the city, where it remained a popular local building stone in the later middle ages. Second, Salcombe stone, a yellow calcareous sandstone (within the Cretaceous Greensand formation) which outcrops in a restricted area on the south-eastern coast of Devon, about 30 km from the

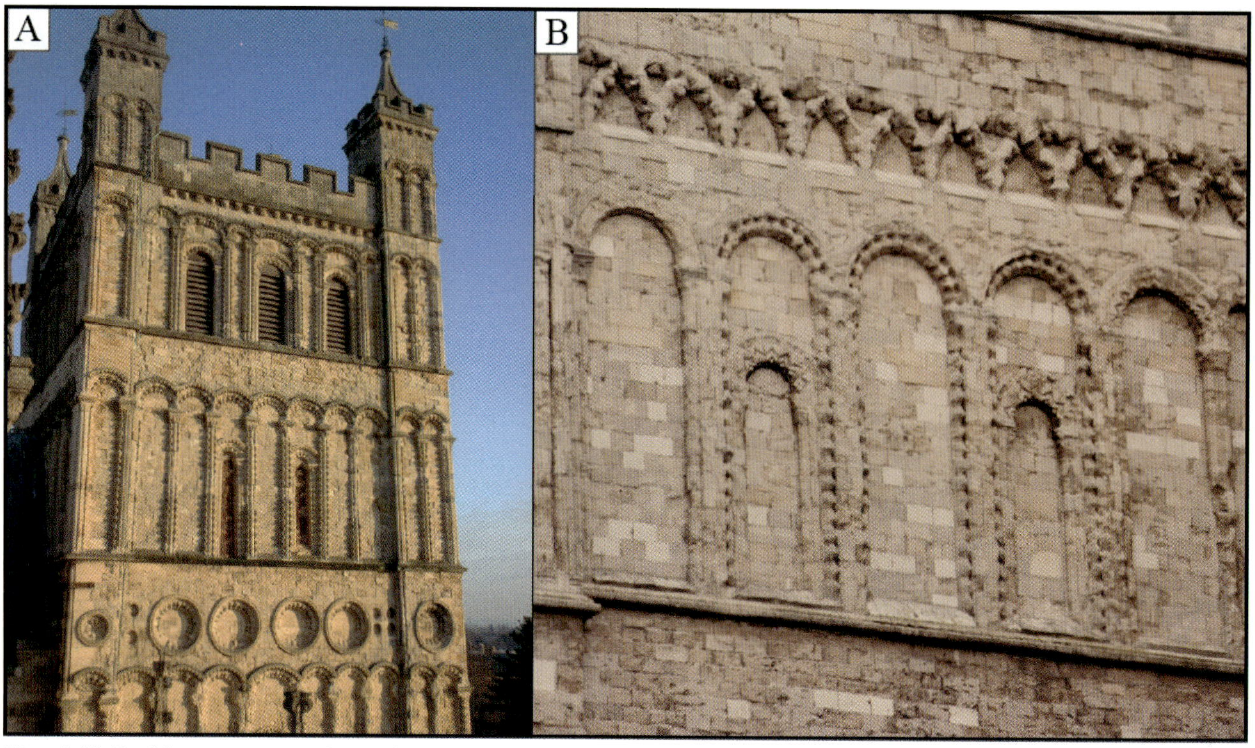

Fig. 7.22 Building stones at the cathedral. (A) The south tower: Salcombe stone with later repairs. (B) The north tower: yellow Salcombe stone intermixed with white Portland stone and bright cream Caen stone (© John Allan)

city (Fig. 2.2), was used for most of the long-and-short quoins from St George's which can be inspected today. It may have been transported overland or carried along the coast, as much of Salcombe stone carried to the city was transported in the later middle ages. Third, Beer stone, a chalk which outcrops a little further to the east on the Devon coast, about 35 km from the city (Fig. 2.2), was certainly quarried before the Norman Conquest; it was used in the long-and-short quoins of the crypt at Sidbury, as Martyn Jope noted more than 50 years ago (Jope 1964, 103). This building stone was probably used in Late Saxon Exeter (identification by H. Dewey in Fox 1952, 27) and was certainly used shortly after the Conquest in the quoins and capitals of Rougemont Castle gatehouse. Freestone, therefore, was already being transported 30 km or more, which was not unusual in southern England before 1066 (Jope 1964).

A fourth example of the transportation of stone in Late Saxon Exeter is represented by the granite cross shaft which formerly stood outside the city's West Gate and is now displayed in the RAMM (for the context: Brown 2019, 7–8). This has been identified as an example of the 'contaminated' granite worked around Sweltor, near Princetown in central Dartmoor – a surprisingly distant part of the high moor (Cramp 2006, 86, identification by R.C. Scrivener). Close examination of the 10th-century cross at Copplestone, 19 km north-west of Exeter, produced an equally unexpected identification: this too was quarried in the central part of the high moor, possibly near Merrivale (*ibid*., 82). Other Late Saxon cross fragments in Devon show that ambitious journeys were undertaken from the early 9th century, when (probable) Osmington Oolite from the Abbotsbury, west of Weymouth, was transported as far as Dolton in north Devon, a distance of 150 km (Jope 1964, 103; Cramp 2006, 81, 83, 89). The Bath stone used for the 9th or 10th-century fragment at Sidbury will have travelled about 130 km, and the Jurassic oolite used in the early 10th-century fragment at Braunton, North Devon, may have come from Doulting, in Somerset, also a distance of about 150 km.

This late Saxon evidence provides examples of the long-distance movement of heavy objects, but the quantities of stone being transported were small. Following the Norman Conquest, there was a great increase in the scale of transportation. This is most obvious in the case of the new cathedral, begun in 1114 and mainly completed by *c*. 1150, with work of *c*. 1150–80 in the upper parts of its towers. From the start of the Norman building campaign, Salcombe stone was the principal building stone for the cathedral's facework which entailed the carriage and dressing of many thousands of blocks (Fig. 7.22). This was not the only instance of the use of this material; 12th-century ashlar facework with the same geology was also employed in the superior churches of Otterton, Sidbury and Salcombe Regis (Allan 2017a, fig. 2; the first possibly monastic), and it was the favoured material for arcades in the Norman monastic houses of south Devon, notably Torre, Buckfast and Plympton. In Exeter it was the most popular freestone

Fig 7.23 The market in building stone in 12th-century Exeter. (A) Triassic Red Rock Sandstone at the cathedral. (B) Salcombe stone at St James Priory. (C) Beer stone at Mary Steps church. (D) Grey Lias at the cathedral (tomb slab attributed to John the Chanter). (E) Volcanic Trap, St James Priory; (F) Triassic sandstone, St Nicholas Priory. (G) Purbeck marble, St Nicholas Priory (photos: B, E–G: David Garner; A and D: John Allan; C: © Alex Woodcock)

for Norman monastic buildings (St James and St Nicholas), parish churches (St Mary Arches), early domestic buildings in The Close, and on Exe Bridge, where it was employed to decorative effect. Outside the city, its distribution in the twenty or so 12th- or early 13th-century century buildings extended from Plympton in the west to the Dorset border, but rarely far from the coast (Allan 2017a, fig. 2). This indicates that it travelled mainly by sea.

With the more plentiful evidence of stone building after the Conquest, the range of building stones represented in the city also increased. The presence of Beer stone in the castle gatehouse has been mentioned above. This material is not common in the county's buildings in the 11th and 12th centuries; this writer has recorded instances in the fabric of only four parish churches in the county, although it was used in twenty of Devon's Norman fonts including those of two parish churches in the city (SS Pancras and Mary Steps; Allan 2017a, fig. 1). It is therefore surprising that a batch of Beer stone has recently been identified in the White Tower of the Tower of London (Roland Harris *in litt.* to the writer 2011). In the early stages of the cathedral building programme (1114–33) Red Rock Sandstone from the lower reaches of the Dart valley was employed to decorative effect at the cathedral, extending the range of quarry sources into the Torbay area (Allan 2017a).

By the late 12th century, quite a sophisticated market had developed in building stones (Fig. 7.23). The practice of using freestones of contrasting colours to achieve polychromatic effects is evident from the early 12th century, when Red Rock Sandstone from the Dart Estuary was used at the cathedral and St James Priory with yellow Salcombe stone (Fig. 7.23A). At the end of the century pretty chequered effects were achieved at Exe Bridge by using contrasting dark volcanic stone with yellow Salcombe blocks. From the mid 12th century the range of limestones multiplied, introducing Caen and Portland stone, both of which are seen in the middle stages of the north tower of Exeter Cathedral (Allan 1991, 12). These are notable in a wider context, since such early examples of the movement of Portland stone are rare. With the development of a market for polished stonework from the mid 12th century, Purbeck marble found an early market here, as is evident from the use of this material in bishops' tombs at the cathedral, the earliest of which (the 'retrospective Leofric') dates from *c.* 1170. Towards the end of the century Grey Lias, probably from central Somerset, was introduced as an alternative polished stone at the cathedral. A mason working in Late Norman Exeter could therefore choose between ten different building stones, each with different properties. The buildings of St Nicholas Priory illustrate a progression from coarse local materials to the selection of more refined materials by the city's wealthier institutions. The priory used rough local volcanic stones for carved work in its earliest Norman buildings, switching to Salcombe stone and Triassic sandstone in the early 12th century, moving to the employment of fashionable Caen stone and polished Purbeck marble in the mid and late 12th century. The range of materials employed was clearly related to the status of the client: nine of the ten stone types can be seen at the cathedral, and five at St Nicholas, but only one, two or three in other buildings.

Ethnicity

Documentary evidence shows that Exeter was a cosmopolitan place with a merchant community, both before and after the Norman Conquest (above). As Crick has put it, someone walking in the streets of the Norman city might hear not just English and French, but Irish, German, Swedish and even Italian tongues (Crick 2014, 10). The numismatic evidence adds to this picture, with Scandinavian names 'unexpectedly well represented' among the city's moneyers of South-West England in the reigns of Æthelred II and Cnut (Smart 1986, 180; discussed in Higham 2018). There were three such men at Exeter late in Æthelred II's reign (Cytel, Thurgod and Carla), joined by Scula in the time of Cnut. Thurgod (presumably the same) also struck coins at Totnes; Wicing at Lydford may be another Scandinavian name. In the 1030s Farman, a second Totnes moneyer with a Scandinavian name, issued coins for Harthacnut. This evidence probably indicates a Scandinavian community in Exeter and perhaps also in Totnes, although Smart has pointed out that names of this sort did gain some currency in English communities (Smart 1986, 180). Analysis of skeletal material may one day add archaeological evidence to this.

One piece of excavated evidence fits into this picture: the Bedford Garage kiln. The potter who operated here clearly did so in a completely different tradition from that of the other potteries of South-West England, producing kiln-fired wheel-thrown vessels, sometimes glazed, at a time when his competitors were making only rough, handmade and unglazed products. Whilst there are other traditions of wheel-thrown pottery elsewhere in Late Saxon England, the close correspondence of the form of the Exeter products to the wheel-thrown jars made in the lower Seine Valley in the Late Saxon period (notably the striking similarity to the jars made here to Hamwic fabric 127) strongly suggests that that is the most likely origin of the Exeter potter (*contra* Allan 1984, 30). We may note the similar evidence for an immigrant Norman potter at Canterbury (Cotter 1997).

Conclusion

In the Late Saxon and Norman periods Exeter was a much more important place, relative to other English towns, than either the Roman town which preceded it or its later medieval successor. The excavated archaeological resource surviving from this period, however, is appreciably less well preserved: the loss of stratified deposits has been much more severe than in the Roman fortress and more extensive than in the later Roman town. For the later medieval period we have the compensation of a large body of standing buildings and monuments, but this kind of evidence is much more limited for the years before 1200. Archaeological evidence alone, therefore, gives us only a few indicators of the thriving city. Nevertheless, even without the documentary record, we would conclude from the pottery that this was a significant international port with a major trading connection to Normandy, and specifically to the area around Rouen, with links to Brittany and the Low Countries. The dense occupation of tenements in the city centre, with its evidence for a range of domestic objects and urban crafts, would show that this was a significant urban place.

So why was the city so successful? When Exeter returned to a high standing among English towns in the early modern period, the foundation of the city's wealth was Devon's cloth industry, whose early stages were conducted in the countryside. For the Late Saxon and Norman periods this seems an unlikely economic driver; crucially, the faunal evidence shows that most sheep eaten in Exeter were slaughtered young for their meat, rather than being kept into old age for their wool, as they were in the early modern period (Maltby 1979, 42–54; and above). Alongside the evidence for highly active foreign trade, William of Malmesbury's remark about the contrast between the poverty of the countryside and the wealth of the city (above) may be noted here, and so too may Henry of Huntingdon's comment about the city's renown for its 'rich metallic ores'. The exciting new archaeological evidence for the activity of tin mines on Dartmoor in this period surely supports the case made by Maddicott for the development of mining as a fundamental driver of the economy of western Wessex in the Late Saxon period. The new archaeological evidence for an extensive ironworking industry in the Blackdown Hills and on Exmoor, just starting to emerge when Maddicott wrote his paper, provides a new strand of evidence here. This industry clearly operated on a large scale in the Late Saxon period, and may well have been a major economic driver of the economy of Devon at that time. The numismatic evidence shows very clearly the prosperity of Late Saxon Devon, evident in the strong performance of all the county's mints in the period *c.* 973–1020. This kind of evidence is not available to us before the reign of Edgar, but the archaeological evidence for iron mining shows that this industry was active well before the time of Alfred. Evidence of tin-mining of Late Saxon date has until very recently proved more elusive, but the recent radiocarbon and OSL dates from Dartmoor have shown that there was an active mining industry on Dartmoor at this time. Further excavations of rural ironworking sites in east Devon, or analysis of the peat bogs of Dartmoor may tell us as much about the economy of Late Saxon Exeter as evidence from the city itself.

Appendix 7.1

High-status enclaves in Exeter's 11th-century topography

Robert Higham

Introduction

Published studies of Exeter just before and after the Norman Conquest have highlighted the city's importance as Devon's military, ecclesiastical and administrative centre and its role as the biggest commercial and defended place in the South-West region. The coinage, the testimony of Domesday Book and chroniclers, artefactual evidence indicating the production of objects of stone, leather, bone, wood and pottery, and the evidence for a stone building industry reflect a thriving community of merchants, craftsmen, manufacturers and clerics (as well as, presumably, many poor), led by an urban elite who occasionally appear in the documentary record.

The walled city did not, however, consist only of streets with houses. There were also some distinctive high-status enclaves which consumed much of the walled area, showing that medieval towns were not filled wall-to-wall with houses: they also contained open spaces – gardens, for example – and more specialised places. In the Exeter map and pictorial record, which starts in the late 16th century, some of these specialised areas are visible, notably the castle area (Rougemont), the precincts of St Nicholas Priory and of the Dominican friary, Cathedral Close, and the gardens of the Bishop's Palace. These enclaves were not new products at that time: they often had antecedents. This brief essay explores the origins and development of three areas in the Late Saxon and Early Norman periods:

a) that which became Rougemont Castle after the Norman Conquest. New thinking arises from a project on the castle assessing work conducted there from the late 19th to early 21st century (Blaylock and Higham in preparation).
b) the area around St Nicholas Priory. New thinking arises from a study of the Exeter interests of the Godwins, earls of Wessex, and identification of a comital enclave here. A full account has been published elsewhere (Higham 2018).
c) the area which became the Cathedral Close of the Romanesque and Gothic cathedral. New thinking arises from work (by the present author and John Allan) on the early episcopal enclave: the precinct of the minster church which became the cathedral in 1050. A full study will hopefully appear in a future study of the history and buildings of Cathedral Close.

Because the studies summarised here have been or will be fully published elsewhere, full details of data are not given and only a few references are provided. The author is grateful for discussion of some aspects of what follows with AC Archaeology, John Allan, Stuart Blaylock, Oliver Creighton and Mandy Kingdom and, in some cases, for use of their research in advance of its publication.

A. Rougemont Castle and its antecedent: a royal enclave and church *(Fig. 7.24)*

Up until 2006, received wisdom of the castle area was that:

a) before 1066 it contained citizens' housing, which tailed off towards the highest point in the north-east angle of the city wall;
b) following the siege of Exeter by William the Conqueror early in 1068, a castle was built here, whose construction involved the demolition of many houses belonging to the citizens;
c) this castle marked the imposition of a heavier level of royal authority in the city than previously;
d) Anglo-Saxon style in the gatehouse (long/short quoins, triangular windows) together with Early Norman features (entrance arch shape, cushion capitals) showed the employment or pressed labour of Englishmen under Norman direction.

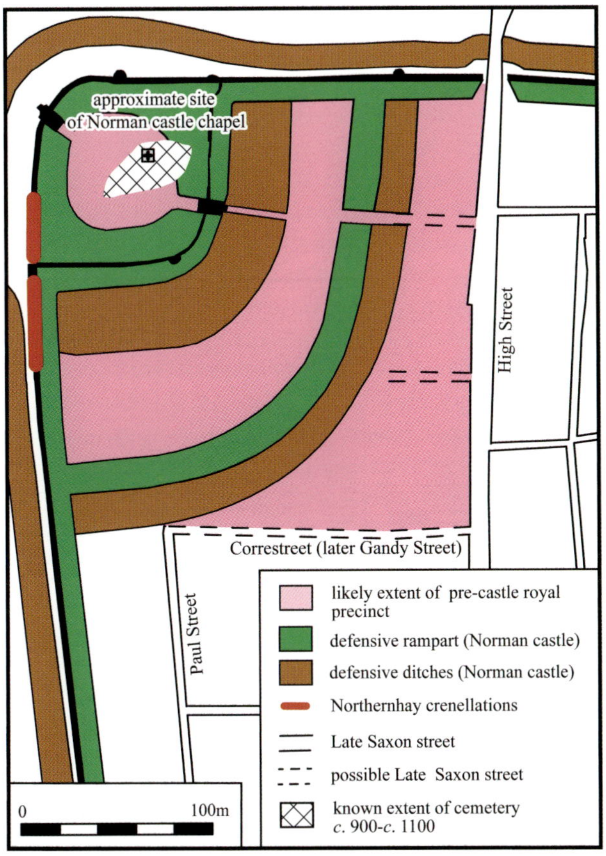

Fig. 7.24 Possible royal enclave predating Rougemont Castle (drawn by David Gould)

This interpretation (see Higham 2013 for background) was based on the narrative of the siege and of the castle's foundation (by Orderic Vitalis, following William of Poitiers), the tone of the narrative of the Conqueror's suppression of urban revolts in 1068–70 (Orderic/William and the *Anglo-Saxon Chronicle*), and on Domesday Book (which describes some house plots as 'wasted' – though no cause was specified for this).

A new interpretation of this corner of Exeter has arisen from excavation (by Stuart Blaylock and Andrew Passmore for Exeter Archaeology) in the castle inner bailey in 2006 (Site 193). Though limited in extent (some 5% of interior), as well as revealing details of the castle's later occupation, it produced important new evidence:

a) the 'hill' character of the inner corner is largely a product of the castle period; earlier there had been both accumulation and terracing, gentler slopes and occupation going back to Roman times.
b) in the Late Saxon period, a cemetery occupied part of the area, with a minimum of eight graves. Radiocarbon dating of the bones ranged from the 9th to 11th centuries. As well as having been used over a long period of time, it was a mixed cemetery (it included a child), and three graves contained charcoal burials – a burial practice associated normally with high-status people. This discovery was presumably part of the larger cemetery as the 18 graves (many on the same orientation as those excavated in 2006) were found in the 1890s when the castle lodge was built, suggesting that here is a sizeable cemetery here with at least 26 individuals and probably many more. The cemetery was cut by the foundations of the Norman castle chapel (see below), a further indication of its early date.

This was a remarkable discovery because during the middle ages the minster (and later the cathedral) held a monopoly on and control of burial rights within the city walls, which was a major source of income (Lepine and Orme 2003; Orme 2014). Clear evidence that this was upheld when the castle was newly-founded comes from a documented dispute about burial rights between bishop Osbern and St Nicholas Priory in the 1090s (sorted out only by the Pope and Archbishop intervening in the early 1100s): at this time, the cathedral was still the Saxon minster from whom this right must have been inherited. The minster was probably a royal foundation (perhaps late 7th century, re-endowed in the 10th century) and its enhancement to cathedral status in 1050 was also achieved with royal assent. The burial monopoly lasted until the 17th century and was broken only for the city's monastic houses.

This cemetery needs explanation. Given the long timespan, it was clearly a community cemetery, not a war cemetery. In this period cemeteries were associated with churches, but which church would have had sufficient status to be exempt from the minster's monopoly of burials within the city? The other city churches – strictly chapels – did not have early burial rights. So, one answer may be that the church which is presumed to have accompanied the cemetery was built by, or closely associated with, kings. Though there is no documentary evidence for such a church in or near this location, this does seem to be the most likely explanation. Canons of a church dedicated to St Mary are referred to in Domesday Book (Thorn and Thorn 1985, 16.89, 16.90, 16.91 and 16.92, and notes in volume 2; Orme 2014, 73–80), and it is deduced from later sources that this was the chapel in the castle founded by the castellan, Baldwin de Meules; perhaps its dedication was drawn from our putative Late Saxon church. If there was a church of royal status here, it is unlikely to have stood alone and was presumably part of a larger royal property. Here we may now make better sense of the Domesday evidence about the destruction of houses (48 out of 285 royal houses). The text actually puts these within its account of houses owned by the king, and so their destruction may not have been – as traditionally viewed – an act of violence against the citizens. It may have simply been part of a reorganisation of a city zone that had already belonged to kings, with houses for royal tenants and a church for their use, and quite probably a residence for occasional royal use.

To take this argument to one possible – though currently unprovable – conclusion, we may wonder whether the castle area – traditionally seen as 'Norman and new' – succeeded an earlier royal enclave. Exeter antiquarians, from Hooker in the 16th century onwards, have assumed that there must have been a Late Saxon royal palace here, although this was dismissed by historians a century ago, when it was customary to contrast the nature of (communal) Saxon urban defence with (private) Norman castle defence. They may, however, have been correct in their assumptions, as it is suggested here that this northern corner of Exeter may have been organised as a royal enclave by Alfred or by Æthelstan, who issued a charter in 928 from his 'royal citadel' of Exeter.

This might also solve another curiosity in Exeter's history: the length of the city wall circuit and Burghal Hidage calculation do not fit, the latter being far shorter than the former (see p. 231 above). But a perimeter which encompasses the eventual castle site (including its outer bailey), drawn along High Street and Gandy Street and the city wall, is close in length to that derived from the Burghal Hidage (about 1000 yards). So the royal enclave hypothesis may illuminate this long-standing problem: the *burh* whose defences were catered for in the Burghal Hidage may have been only part of the city, a part, which, in turn, became a royal property. If so, the Norman castle was slightly smaller (but more defensible) than this putative Late Saxon enclave. Northernhay Gardens' infilled crenellations in the city wall (described above) may thus have been 'royal' rather than 'urban' (that is, local to this high-status area rather than a feature of the whole city wall circuit). Hypothetical though this interpretation is, it has the merit of accounting for the key strands of (mainly unusual) evidence: a Late Saxon cemetery within a city where burial rights were monopolised by the minster/cathedral; Late Saxon crenellations in the adjacent city wall; the links between the Burghal Hidage allocation and the city's topography; demolition of royal houses and the creation of a new Norman castle; and the blended Saxon and Norman style of the castle gatehouse. It should, however, be emphasised that the idea of a pre-Norman royal enclave is not dependent on its location having been a primary defensive *burh.* Such an enclave may have been significant – with church and secular buildings – but not have been defended.

B. St Nicholas Priory precinct and its predecessor: a comital enclave and church *(Fig. 7.25)*

From the late 11th to 16th centuries, St Nicholas Priory and its precinct was – like Rougemont Castle – one of Exeter's most distinctive neighbourhoods. It was walled and secluded, with church, cloister, outbuildings and gardens. Its main features, like those of the castle, are shown on later map and pictorial records (Allan 1999, 17; Orme 2015a, 326; Higham 2018, 160). It occupied a sizeable zone behind the houses on the north side of Fore Street, running northwards between St Mary Arches Street and Friernhay Street. As with the Norman castle, however, there is reason to believe that this apparently 'Norman' creation (it started in the 1080s as a cell of Battle Abbey, who held the adjacent church of St Olave) was formed out of an earlier enclave – in this case a comital property.

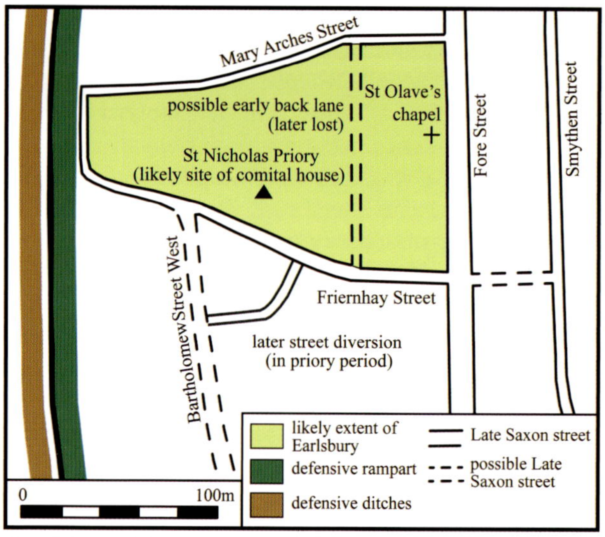

Fig. 7.25 Earlsbury, with postulated lane parallel to Fore Street (drawn by David Gould)

The detailed case for this Late Saxon comital enclave has recently been published; it rests on documentary evidence, on a surviving church and on analysis of the historic street pattern from maps and the existing topography (Higham 2018, where full supporting data for what follows will be found). The idea that the Late Saxon earls had a property in Exeter is not new: it was noted almost a century ago in Little and Easterling's (1927) study of the Franciscans in Exeter. On the basis of a more extensive examination of the documentary evidence, however, together with consideration of the historic street pattern, suggestions – albeit cautious – may now be made as to how the outline of the comital property may be reconstructed. The existence of the property rests on five references, all in sources with late 12th-century and later origins, to a former 'Earlsbury' (*Irlesbery* and other spellings) that is, in Old English, an *eorl's bur* or *burh* (an earl's house or enclosure). That this name survived for centuries in local memory and was used as a point of reference in the description of other property boundaries suggests that its original application – and thus the person or people after whom it was named – had been significant in Exeter's history.

St Olave's church was unusual in that it had two endowments of land in rural Devon (surviving in much abbreviated form in the early 14th-century cartulary of St Nicholas priory), presumably for the support of two priests. One was made by Gytha, widow of Earl Godwin of Wessex, the other by King Edward the Confessor (Orme 2014, 150–3). Since Gytha herself was Danish, and the cult of St Olaf (king of Norway, who died in 1031) was quickly espoused by the Danes, it is likely that the family founded the Exeter church. Since, however, it was also said to be dedicated to St Mary and St Thomas, its earlier existence is possible and Gytha may have been enriching it. Within the present late medieval structure of St Olave's, an early outline of nave and chancel can be reconstructed, with long-and-short quoins surviving at the west end: this outline is not later than late 11th century.

The earliest reference to Earlsbury is in a grant of land made by the abbot of Battle to William son of Ralph, a citizen, so he could found a hospital (St Alexius) *c.* 1170 (the surviving manuscript is much later). It was said that this land was at the corner of Earlsbury. Other sources describe the hospital being behind St Nicholas priory. Its functions were moved to St John's Hospital at East Gate by 1240.

That this part of Exeter was the Conqueror's to donate to Battle Abbey shows it was his by right of conquest: it had belonged to King Edward or the Godwins. When the first monks came from Battle, they used St Olave's as their church while developing their priory church, and probably also used existing domestic buildings as their residence while creating the cloister. The inference is that just as they first used the Godwins' church, they also lived in the Godwins' house until it was destroyed as the priory was built. The priory's jurisdiction known as St Nicholas Fee or Harold's Fee (possibly in memory of Harold Godwinson) was probably an inheritance of a Late Saxon arrangement.

There are several possible reconstructions of Earlsbury. Earlier writers favoured the south-west corner of the city, which was defensible and which became the sites of St Alexius hospital, the early Franciscan friary and St Bartholomew's cemetery. But a location closer to the priory and St Olave's seems more likely. One option is St Olave's parish (because parishes could be created from earlier secular estates), which straddles Fore Street and runs to the city wall, but this seems perhaps too large. Another option focuses on the plot of land between (the original course of) Friernhay Street and Mary Arches Street. The 'bottle' shape of this large plot – first, parallel to its two flanking streets but then narrowing northwards – is unique in the Late Saxon city and therefore in need of some explanation. It is possible that an original back lane behind Fore Street – joining the southern stretches of the two flanking streets – disappeared during the life of either Earlsbury or the priory (Fig. 7.25). All the possible interpretations of Earlsbury's extent cannot be explored in this brief commentary, but the simplest explanation is perhaps the most attractive: Earlsbury's house became the priory site, St Olave's church was preserved and Earlsbury's outer limits became (more or less) the priory precincts. An excavation in 2017 by AC Archaeology at the north end of Mary Arches Street (Site 169) produced Roman and later priory period features, but almost nothing in between. This lack of Saxo-Norman pits in the postulated northern part of Earlsbury is consistent with the area having been private land in the Late Saxon period rather than occupied by houses. Its open nature continued when it was the priory garden.

Domesday tells us that Battle Abbey had received eight houses with St Olave's church (and Earl/King Harold also had five houses attached to his manor of Tawstock, but their location not known). So, just as we can see the pre-Rougemont enclave, with church, tenants' houses and – presumably – a royal hall, being the base of royal administration in the city, we can see the enclave fronting onto Fore Street, with its church, tenants' houses and – presumably – a comital hall, being not only a residence but also the base in which the earl carried out his official function of presiding over the shire court (and perhaps that of adjacent shires, for convenience). One such shire court record, with Earl Godwin presiding, survives for 1045–6 and the court was held in Exeter, though the record does not indicate where.

The Godwin family had major financial interests in Exeter. King Edward gave two-thirds of its royal revenues to his queen, Edith (Godwin's daughter); the successive earls of Wessex (Godwin and Harold) had the other third (the national pattern). Domesday records that members of the family held the manors of Wonford (Edith), Pinhoe (Leofwine) and Topsham (Harold; the latter, according to bishop Leofric, stole it from the cathedral). As well as Gytha's Danish connections, a church dedicated to St Olaf may have appealed to any Scandinavian-related people amongst the tenants in Earlsbury. Six out of 20 Exeter moneyers working for King Cnut and his successors had Scandinavian names (see above).

The Godwins' development of an Exeter power – and property – base may have been encouraged by Bishop Leofric's move of the see from Crediton to Exeter in 1050. Previously, the only significant outside influence in Exeter (both city and minster) was royal; now it was also episcopal. So perhaps the family of the earls of Wessex now felt they must not be excluded from the region's principal city. There was a 12th-century tradition that Gytha was in Exeter (and escaped) during the Conqueror's siege of 1068. If true, she was presumably living in Earlsbury. When a scribe added a note in the Cathedral's 12th-century martyrology on the year 1066, it was about King Harold, his brother Tostig and the Norwegian King Harold Hardrada; the Godwins were long remembered here.

Discussion of Rougemont and St Nicholas Priory raises clear contrasts. In the former, the royal presence was intensified by the building of a more oppressive and defensible castle. In the latter, property that came into royal hands was granted to Battle Abbey so that monks could be introduced to Exeter (the first since King Edgar's short experiment at the minster, a century earlier). Both changes illustrate the sorts of physical and institutional transformation to which towns were subject after the Norman Conquest. At the national level, the Exeter evidence is important in giving topographical form – which is rare in the archaeological record – to subjects (Late Saxon royal and comital urban interests) whose importance is clear in the historical record.

C. The Cathedral Close and its antecedents: the episcopal enclave and the minster *(Fig. 7.26)*

Whereas Rougemont Castle and St Nicholas Priory overlie their putative predecessors but preserve something of their footprints, the situation may have been more complex in the city centre. From 1114, the building of a new cathedral to the east of the Late Saxon minster/cathedral, shifted the centre of gravity of the whole site eastwards. We know the Cathedral Close was walled and gated in the 1280s, by which time it had reached its current extent (Lega-Weekes 1915, 19–26). At the time of writing, work is still in progress on the earlier evolution of the Cathedral Close, but, cautiously, we can approach its predecessor(s) through five ideas.

First is the question of the minster's overall precinct. Most street and property alignments in this area (or known from maps if obliterated by later developments) relate either to the street plan of the post-900 *burh*, or to the late medieval Cathedral precinct. These include Vicars Choral/Kalendarhay, Bear Lane and Palace Gate, all running perpendicular to South Street and very likely originating as side streets of the *burh*. But two features are anomalies and, with due caution, may we wonder whether these are relics of an early minster precinct pre-dating the loosely-gridded plan of the *burh*.

a) a curvilinear feature, north of the west end of the later cathedral, identified by Oliver Creighton (pers. comm.) in a recent geophysical survey, whose course fits with no surviving part of the Close topography.
b) the northern boundary of the Vicars College, identified from maps and deeds by Allan (2005b, 31–3) (Fig. 7.26, 'likely early precinct/cemetery boundary'), which lay *obliquely* to the usual pattern and ran from South Street to the minster in a part-curving line. If newly-created (with the Vicars Choral) in the 1380s it would have been straight: that it was not, strongly suggests it followed an earlier and important line or boundary.

Second is the matter of precinct entrances. The western entrance was Little Stile, where a 'broad gate' was turned into a narrow postern when the Close wall and gates were created in the 1280s (Lega-Weekes 1915, 20–1). On the opposite side of South Street, an extension of Smythen Street (then the principal street from the city's West Gate) would have led to the gate, but the connection (not illustrated) was lost in the later medieval plan. Little Stile and Smythen Street are probably pre-*burh* features, given the importance of West Gate and the minster. The early boundary inherited by the Vicars Choral (above) started at Little Stile. Little Stile continued as a route leading to the minster (and later to St Mary Major church), eventually creating the 'street-like' line of buildings now known as Three Gables. Relevant here is the course of the (present-day) street called Cathedral Yard. Its eastern end is straight and parallel to High Street. But it then curves northwards to Broad Gate. As a curving lesser street behind a main one, it is unique in the city's plan. This anomaly probably arises from the early northward growth of the minster cemetery (see above), without which High Street here would presumably have been given a back lane (like Waterbeer Street, to its north) when the Alfredian *burh* was laid out. Indeed, a line connecting Little Stile and Catherine Street would have created such a back lane, defining plots of the same length as known elsewhere on High Street in this period. Perhaps the cathedral's own building encroachment on the cemetery, behind High Street, was deeper (that is, further south) to the east because the cemetery was less developed there and the start of a back lane had been laid out. To the west, nearer the early minster site and where burials were denser, early building encroachment southward from High Street was more limited, resulting in the curved line of Cathedral Yard.

Third is the question of where the other early entrances to the minster precinct may have been. Whether Broad Gate was a wholly new creation of the 1280s or had a predecessor is unknown. Given the origins of Martin's Lane and Catherine Street in the *burh* lay-out, the later (known) access from them to the cathedral area could well have had a Late Saxon predecessor, an equivalent of Little Stile. But a problem remains in that whereas Smythen Street led to the West Gate, Catherine Street did not lead to East Gate but continues as a back street to High Street.

Since earlier use of the later Bishop's Palace site is highly probable, an early entrance into the minster area from South Street, in the Palace Gate or Bear Lane location, is also likely. Although the early documentary and archaeological evidence for the Bishop's palace is late 12th-century, there must have been a principal residence for earlier bishops (and, before them, abbots) and continuity of location seems most likely. Also relevant here is the possibility (discussed above) that the excavated minster church was not the only one. If another church stood to its east (as did the Norman cathedral) then it was nearer to the Bishop's Palace site.

Late Saxon fabric (described above), and reference to 'St Martin's Street' in late 11th-century legal material in the Exeter Book of Poetry, are consistent with the (later recorded) 1065 date of St Martin's dedication by bishop Leofric. It occurs as a chapel of the cathedral in a list of

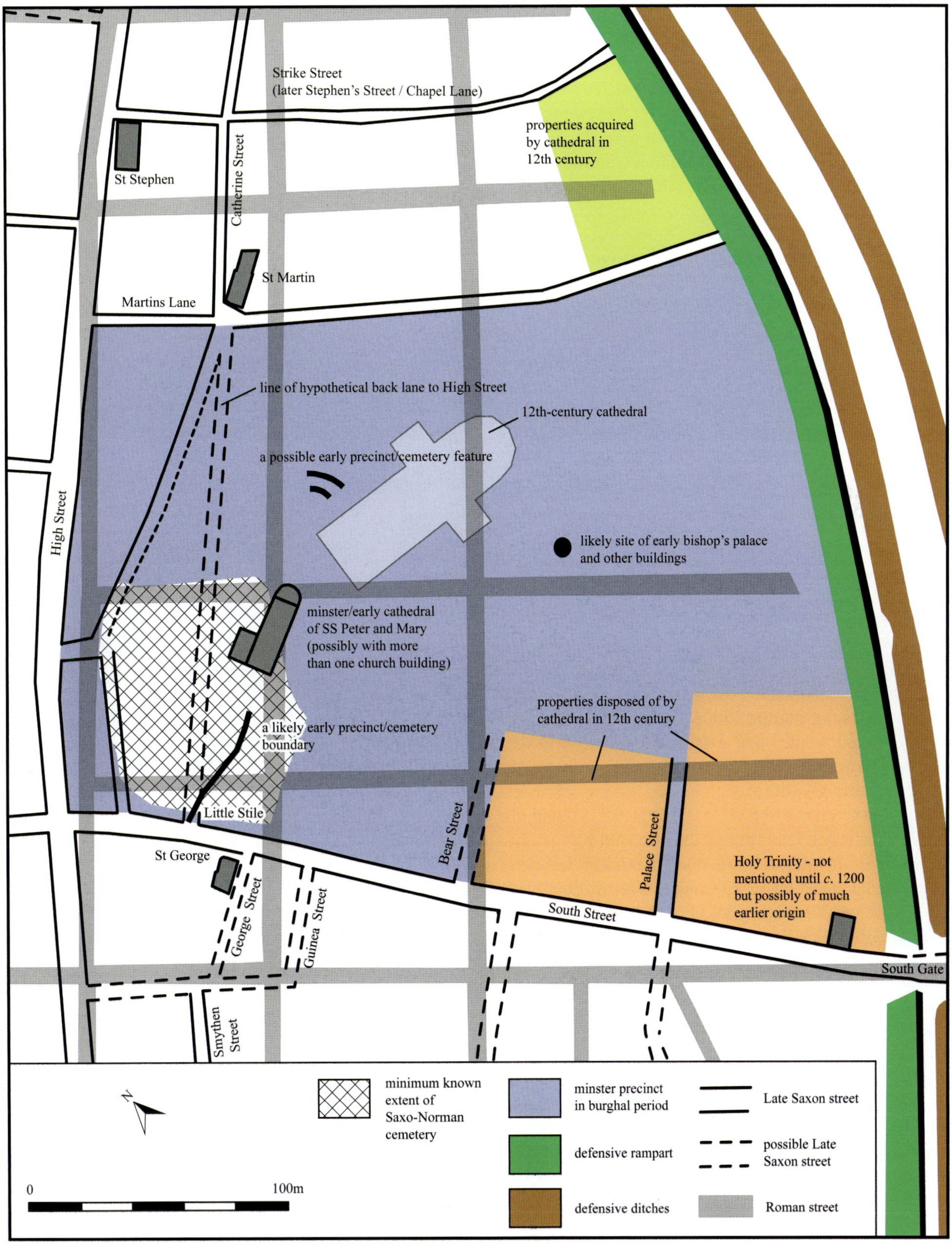

Fig 7.26 The precinct of the Late Saxon minster and Norman cathedral (drawn by David Gould)

c. 1200, when Bishop Henry Marshal enforced cathedral control of all city chapels (Orme 2014, 17–19). If St Martin's was an episcopal chapel at its foundation, then the cathedral's land extended by 1065 as far east as the corner of the later Cathedral Close. Another early church (St George's) stood near the western precinct entrance, opposite Little Stile on the west of South Street; perhaps these two churches were mirror foundations at major approaches to the minster precinct.

Fourth is the question of where the 48 bishop's houses (plus the two wasted by fire) noted in Domesday Book were located: around the perimeter of the (then) precinct or scattered in the city's streets? Addressing this issue involves plotting all the cathedral's later properties, and looking for clues as to where these 50 early houses were. For example, from the early 12th century, from Bishop Warelwast's time onwards, some existing cathedral property in South Street was gifted away and some new property was acquired on the east side of Martin's Lane, perhaps reflecting an eastward shift in the focus of property resulting from the more easterly position of the new cathedral.

Fifth, a crucial question is how the cathedral acquired all the land in its eventual Close. Was it a primary endowment of the late 7th century? Or an enlargement when Asser was perhaps a bishop in Exeter under Alfred, or when the minster was re-endowed by Æthelstan, or when the minster became a cathedral in 1050? Two main possibilities merit further exploration. First, the precinct is the result of growth in stages, starting with a (?) curvilinear enclosure near the early church and extended long before a new cathedral was started in 1114, and extended further in the late 12th century – with canons' houses and a new bishop's palace – when that cathedral was completed. Second, the whole area which later became the cathedral precinct had always been the Anglo-Saxon one – a primary feature of Cenwalh's foundation, or a secondary one of Æthelstan's re-foundation. This big block of land lay between High Street, St Martin's Lane, the city wall and South Street. This idea has the merit of simplicity. It explains why eastward growth (new cathedral and canons houses) and southward growth (new bishop's palace and garden) were easily achieved in the 12th century: all were on lands of the minster/early cathedral. But other issues about the streets bounding the area remain: a very early medieval endowment would presumably be bounded by the Roman streets, whereas the streets of the *burh* would define any later Saxon endowments.

Other enclaves?

In the late 12th and 13th centuries, other enclaves also appeared in the city: the hospital of St John, the Franciscan friary and the Dominican friary, adding to the complexity in variety and sizes of urban spaces (Fig. 8.2). In furtherance of the idea of Late Saxon antecedent, we may ask whether any of these later additions also had precursors in terms of organised space, if not of function. And, while the evidence is currently limited, we may cautiously make a positive response in the case of the St John's Hospital and Dominican (Blackfriars) sites.

The street running south from High Street which separated these two institutions was known by the 13th century as Doddehay or Doddeshay Street, that is Dodda's *haga* street. The name derived from a Late Saxon citizen called Dodda who was of such status for his name to be given to a property – a *haga*, in contemporary terms – and eventually to adjoining streets. The Doddeshay street name was also given to another adjacent lane (subsequently known as Catherine Street). There was certainly a prominent man (or men) named Dodda in Exeter: a moneyer (or moneyers) in the reigns of Æthelred II, Cnut and Harthacnut. Perhaps he was the citizen who gave his name to this *haga*. Whoever it was named after, it occupied much of the south-eastern corner of the city, between the city wall, East Gate and High Street. Excavation has shown this to have been fully occupied in the Late Saxon and Early Norman periods but it had declined by the late 12th century and was soon available for the building of the Dominican friary (Site 156).

Another possible early *haga* lay just inside the city's South Gate. Property records relating to cathedral canons in the early 12th century relate to an originally large plot here (Lega-Weekes 1915, 35; for the location: Fig 7.4; it was sub-divided in later times), include reference to its former owner Ralph de Haga. This name might preserve a pre-Norman designation of this property, presumably belonging to a prominent English family. It is possible, however, that canon Ralph took his name from Hayes, just across the River Exe (now Okehampton Street), which had recently been added to the prebendal estates supporting the chapel in Exeter castle (Orme 2014, 73–80). Even so, there seems to have been a large plot, just inside South Gate, of a sort that may have characterised parts of the Late Saxon and Early Norman city.

Conclusion

A variety of data reveal that three high-status enclaves, normally seen as products of the Norman period, had Late Saxon antecedents. These three areas were crucial to the character of Exeter in the 11th and 12th centuries. Their large, open nature contrasted with many streets occupied by the houses of merchants and artisans.

8

The Medieval City, 1200–1550

John Allan

with a contribution by Mark Maltby

Introduction

Over the period 1200–1550 Exeter experienced sharp changes in fortune. The city's marked decline in relation to the other English towns was already apparent well before 1200 (see above, Table 1.1 and Chapter 7), and continued into the early 14th century, when Exeter sank to about 27th position in the rankings of urban places in England (Kowaleski 1995, 9, 83, 326; Dyer 2000). The same pattern of relative economic stagnation is visible in rural Devon, whose population grew more slowly than that of any other English county between Domesday and 1334 – by merely 26% – and other indices of economic progress also indicate slow growth in the Devon countryside over the same period (Darby *et al.* 1979; but see Kowaleski 1995, 9, where the point is made that the traditional picture of stagnation is perhaps overstated and that Exeter's decline was relative rather than absolute). By 1377 Exeter had a population of about 3100 people (Darby *et al.* 1979, 371–5). In the late 15th and early 16th centuries, however, it experienced a rapid rise in fortune, first described by Carus-Wilson (1963); by the 1520s its population had doubled to about 7000, rising further in the following generations (MacCaffrey 1958, 11–12; Stephens 1958, 145). The surrounding countryside saw corresponding rapid growth, and Devon was the fastest-growing county in population between 1377 and 1525 (Darby *et al.* 1979, 258–9). This period of prosperity is very evident in the historic fabric of Devon and Cornwall today, reflected, for example, in the very high proportion of parish churches showing building work of this period.

The poor survival of buried archaeological evidence of medieval date on many sites in the city has been described above (Chapter 7). It is of course disappointing that structural evidence on street frontages rarely survives. The fragmentary house plans from 196–7 High Street and Rack Street, presented in detail in EAPIT 2, Chapters 7 and 8, some building remains from Friernhay (Site 75) and Bartholomew Street (Site 73), and the more complete published house plans from excavations on the floodplain of the Exe beside Exe Bridge and in Cowick Street (Sites 56 and 143: Blaylock 2000, 17; Brown 2019), are the only examples from Exeter. Elsewhere, the medieval archaeology of the city most commonly takes the form of groups of pits dug in back gardens. These features are sometimes rich in artefacts and faunal evidence, with well-preserved organic remains in some parts of the city, resulting in Exeter having the region's largest assemblages of medieval ceramics and faunal remains. A further important aspect of the city's archaeological resource is the major collections of medieval human remains, discussed separately by Mandy Kingdom in EAPIT 2, Chapter 19.

In approaching the archaeology of the medieval city, the Exeter Museums Archaeological Field Unit (hereafter EMAFU) took a broad approach, combining excavation with a strong emphasis on the investigation of standing buildings, accompanied by topographical and documentary study, and much influenced by Martin Biddle's work at Winchester and Alan Carter's in Norwich. In the early 1970s some of the EMAFU's work was innovative in a national context, but its impact was limited because it was not published. The examination of No. 38 North Street in 1971–2, for example, must have been one of the first occasions on which an urban archaeological unit stripped down and made detailed records of a large town house with a complex structural history, but the project was brought to publication fully 40 years after the building was demolished (Thorp 2012). In retrospect it is obvious that aspirations often exceeded resources, and the arrival of commercial tendering after 1990 made it much more difficult to sustain research exercises funded by local authorities. As a result, many pieces of valuable work remain unpublished in the EMAFU's archive. It is also unfortunate that the most remarkable organic remains were encountered in the period 1970–3, when environmental studies were in their infancy, the EMAFU had no fixed premises, and there were at first no conservation facilities in the city. Exeter has not therefore made the contribution it might have done to the study of the medieval environment.

In offering an overview of Exeter's late medieval archaeology, this chapter will seek to reflect the wide range of work in the city, drawing not just on excavations and records of historic buildings but on some of the documentary sources made accessible by the Unit's researchers and others. It will also use other forms of material evidence surviving above ground, including textiles, woodwork, stained glass, monumental brasses and bells, which throw light on the city's manufactures and on the operation of the regional economy. Where projects have been published fully elsewhere, or are in the course of publication, only brief summaries will be offered, with reference to the published or forthcoming report.

The form of the city, 1200–1550

The city's institutions and public works

The defences

From the late 1970s, EMAFU carried out a long-running programme surveying the standing fabric of the city wall (Figs 8.1–8.2). The results of the first 20 years of fieldwork were brought together in the 1990s (Blaylock 1995), and further recording exercises undertaken since that time have added detail rather than changing the overall picture presented there. In the 1980s the Unit also undertook quite large-scale excavation of the defensive ditches at Southernhay, followed in 2006–7 by further work at Princesshay, but both projects are currently unpublished. Henderson's (2001) paper on the excavations at South Gate (Sites 36 and 96) is the most recent contribution to the published literature and provides much additional information, not just about that site but about other aspects of the defences.

Alongside recording of the monument, the archaeological unit also undertook a parallel exercise gathering documentary evidence relating to the city's late medieval and later defences, especially those in Receivers' accounts – the city's records of income and expenditure – which survive in an almost unbroken series from 1339. The medieval references were assembled in two unpublished reports (Juddery *et al.* 1989a; 1989b), and Stoyle's acclaimed study of the city defences in the period 1485–1660 made very effective use of these sources (Stoyle 2003).

The circuit of Exeter's city defences is about 2.35 km (1.65 miles) long; about 72% of the wall (some 1.7 km) stands today (Blaylock 1995, 1). It is composed of many short lengths of masonry of different character, often separated by vertical joints, readily distinguishable from each other by abrupt changes in building materials and styles. A key factor in the process of interpreting the monument's many phases of medieval and later work has been the study of its building stones, whose use can be related to the changing pattern of stone quarrying evident in datable buildings elsewhere in the Exeter area.

We have seen that the Roman wall face is built solely of a vesicular volcanic rock known locally as 'trap', and the Saxon work at Rougemont is of Triassic sandstone (Chapter 7). The emergence of Heavitree stone (a local Permian breccia) as the most popular building stone of the late medieval and early modern city is a key to distinguishing parts of the city wall dating to after *c.* 1350. For the period prior to that, Blaylock drew an important distinction between the stretches of wall employing Triassic sandstone, which he saw as mainly or entirely pre-1300, and later masonry. This sandstone is seen most commonly in the lengths of wall between the defences around the East Gate, Rougemont and Southernhay, whereas the stretches overlooking the river and the Longbrook Valley are predominantly of neat volcanic blocks or in Heavitree stone. The earlier stretches are defended at intervals by D-shaped or polygonal towers for which a date in the 12th or 13th centuries is probable. As a crude generalisation, then, it appears that building work in the 12th and 13th centuries concentrated on the stretches of defence at Southernhay and around Rougemont and East Gate.

For the period after the 1330s it had been hoped that it might prove possible to use the references from the Receivers' accounts to relate individual stretches of standing fabric to specific medieval documentary references. Unfortunately this has rarely proved possible. Blaylock (1995) concluded that much of the medieval wall fabric had been built before the period of the earliest surviving accounts, and the later medieval documents rarely state the portion of wall being tackled. In fact the earliest instance where such a connection can be made is in 1530–1, when Richard Tuke was paid £30 1s 4d for making 82 ft (25 m) of wall at Friernhay (*ibid.*).

The documentation does, however, give a very full picture of the overall pattern of the money spent in defending the city. It shows that long periods of little or no expenditure on the walls were punctuated at intervals by sudden flurries of activity in times of crisis, followed quickly by a return to low expenditure. Two episodes of exceptional expenditure are evident: first in 1402–5, when over £170 was spent, and second in 1539/40, when the figure was about £200 (*ibid.*).

Although no post-excavation analysis has been carried out on the excavation records relating to the city ditches,

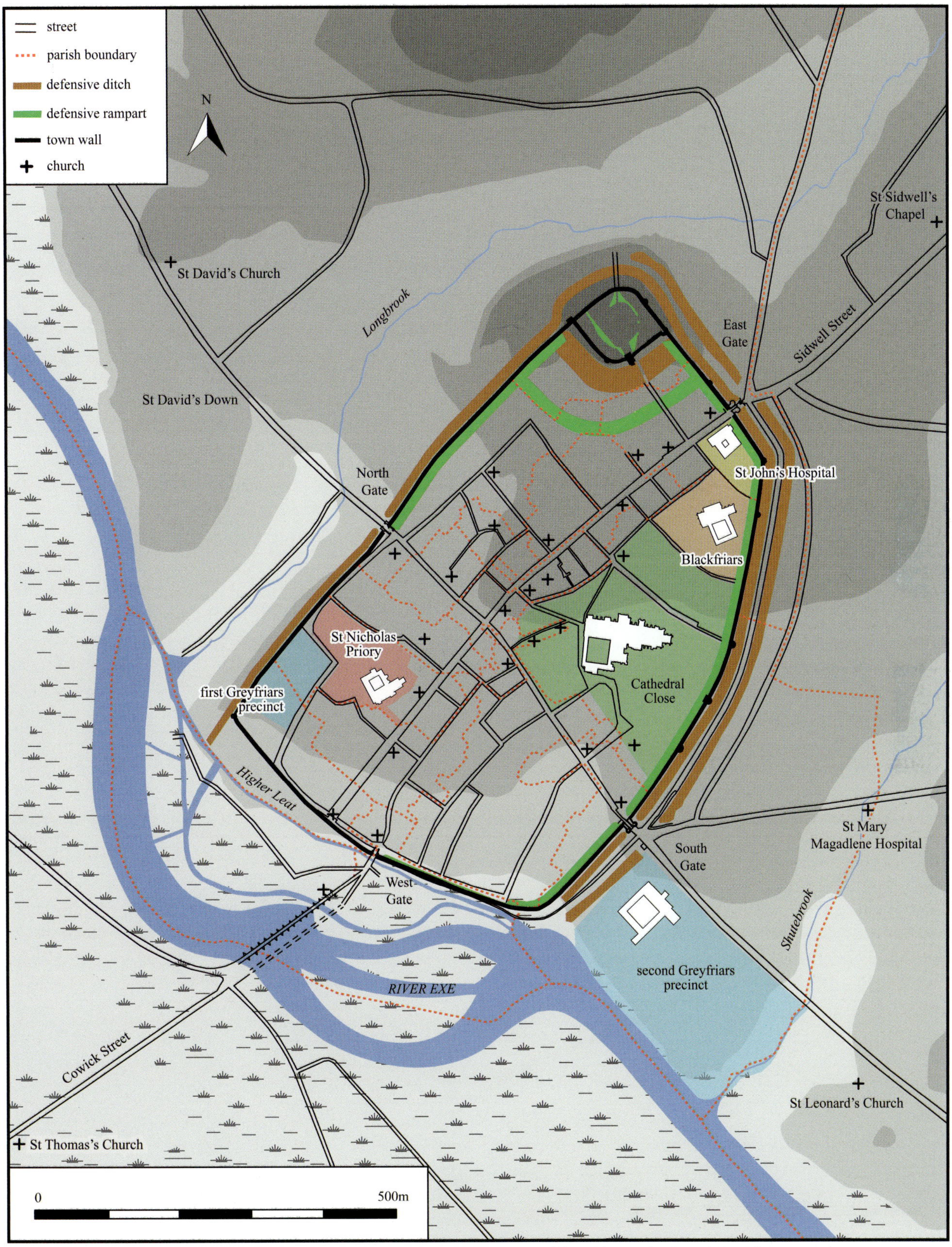

Fig. 8.1 The setting of Exeter in the period 1200–1550 (drawn by David Gould)

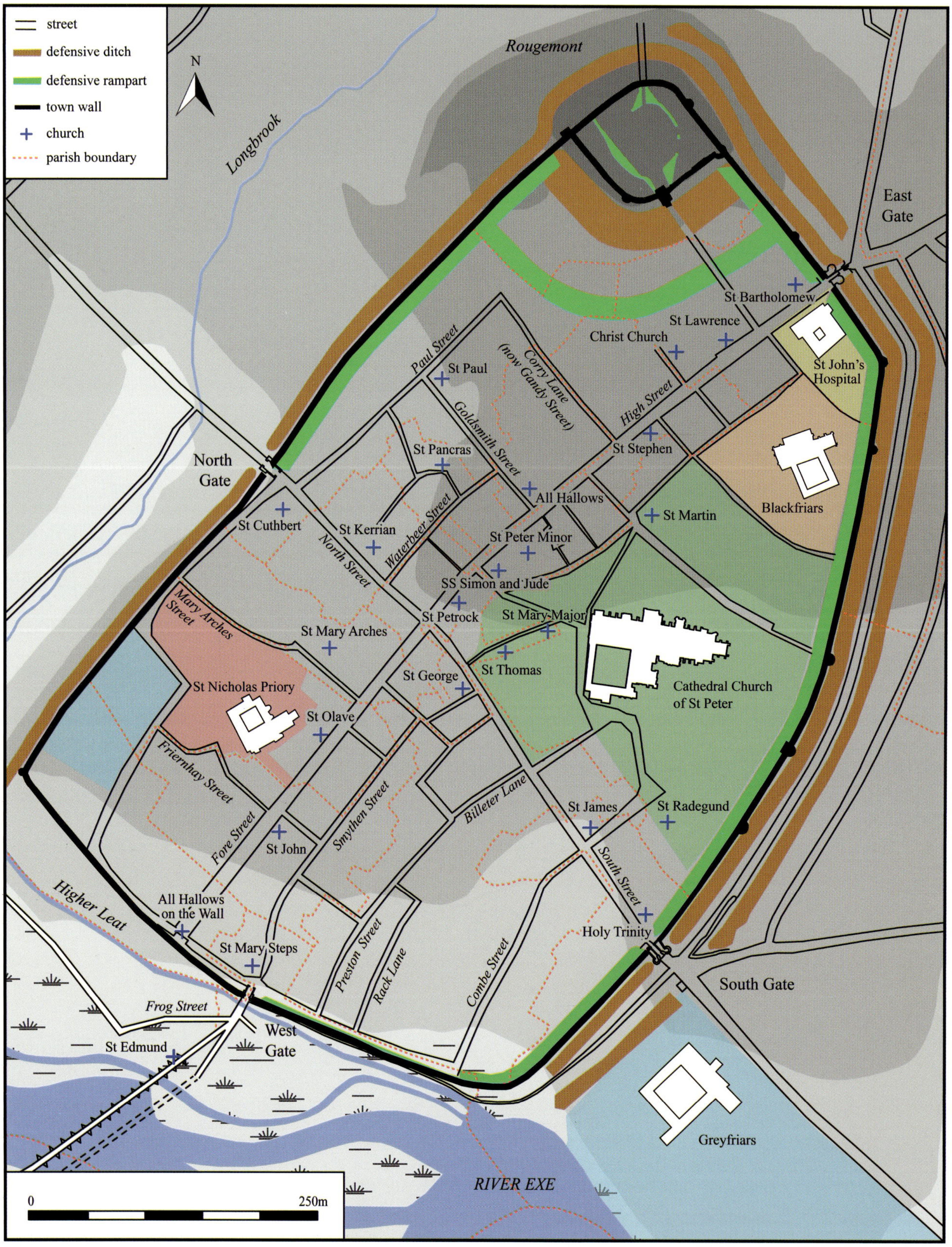

Fig. 8.2 The walled area of Exeter in the period 1200–1550 (drawn by David Gould)

Fig. 8.3 The city defences under excavation at Princesshay (Site 156) in 2005–6. (A) Section showing the different phases of ditches (from Stoyle 2014, 24, drawn by Tony Ives). (B–C) View of the inner ditch looking south, with a detail of the water pipe trench at the foot of the wall. (D) View with the Eastern Angle Tower to right (photos by Gary Young; © Exeter City Council)

some initial observations about their form and sequence may be suggested. The medieval inner ditch has been seen on three occasions – first in Magdalen Street in 1986 (Site 88), where it was sampled over a length of *c.* 150 m and was on average *c.* 15 m wide and 4 m deep (Blaylock 1995, fig. 11); second at East Gate, where its width was *c.* 14 m but its bottom was not found (Site 90: Blaylock 1995), and thirdly at Princesshay in 2006–7, where its depth was 4.2 m but its inner side had been destroyed in the Civil War (Site 156; Fig. 8.3). At Princesshay a second and slightly shallower ditch was found outside the first, its bottom about 20 m outside the city wall, with a third ditch 29 m from the wall face. Whether the two outer ditches were contemporary or successive is unknown, their relationship being destroyed by Civil War defences; the one furthest from the wall had been recut once. Further evidence for an outer ditch in a comparable position was seen at Southernhay (Blaylock 1995, fig. 11). A simple point may be made here: nowadays most stretches of the city wall look rather unimpressive, often because the wall top has been truncated or the bottom 1 m or more is buried below modern ground level. When viewed from the bottom of a 4 m-deep ditch, however, they look very much more imposing.

Much remains to be done in the study of Exeter's defences. Blaylock's report of 1995 should be updated and published, and his recommendation that fabric recording should be undertaken, not just on those parts of the wall which happen to need repair, but on areas which could tell us more, should be taken up (Blaylock 1995, 125–6). The site archives and finds relating to the excavations of the defensive ditches need to be re-examined, and the unpublished documentary records should be made available in some form.

Rougemont Castle

From the time of its construction in the winter of 1068/9 until 1348, Rougemont was a royal castle (Fig. 8.4). The medieval documentary evidence relating to the site before the mid 14th century was brought together in the *History of the King's Works* (Brown *et al.* 1963, 647–9). Regarding the physical evidence, the fullest account is not widely accessible (Alan Baxter Associates 2004); the best published guides are that of Blaylock and Higham (1990) and the briefer entry in Cherry and Pevsner (1989, 399–400). A report bringing together the architectural and archaeological evidence for the castle is currently being prepared (Blaylock and Higham in preparation). The subject will therefore be described quite briefly here.

By 1200, the castle consisted of a small inner bailey with stone defences, and an outer bailey, formerly with an earth bank and ditch, which had ceased, or was soon to cease, having any military use. A small excavation at Bradninch Place in 1986 showed that the ditch of the outer bailey was infilled in the late 12th or early 13th centuries (Site 132), but the line of the former outer defences remained the boundary of the lands of the Duchy of Cornwall, and of the adjacent parishes, into the post-medieval period.

Documentary evidence records that the late 12th-century building activity at the castle (described above, Chapter 7) was followed by further works strengthening the defences, carried out at intervals in the period 1207–51 (Brown *et al.* 1963, 647–9). They included the construction of a new tower in 1228 and the repair of another in 1250–1 (*ibid.*, 648). The former was probably one of the two D-shaped towers shown by Norden, one of which survives (Fig. 8.4B).

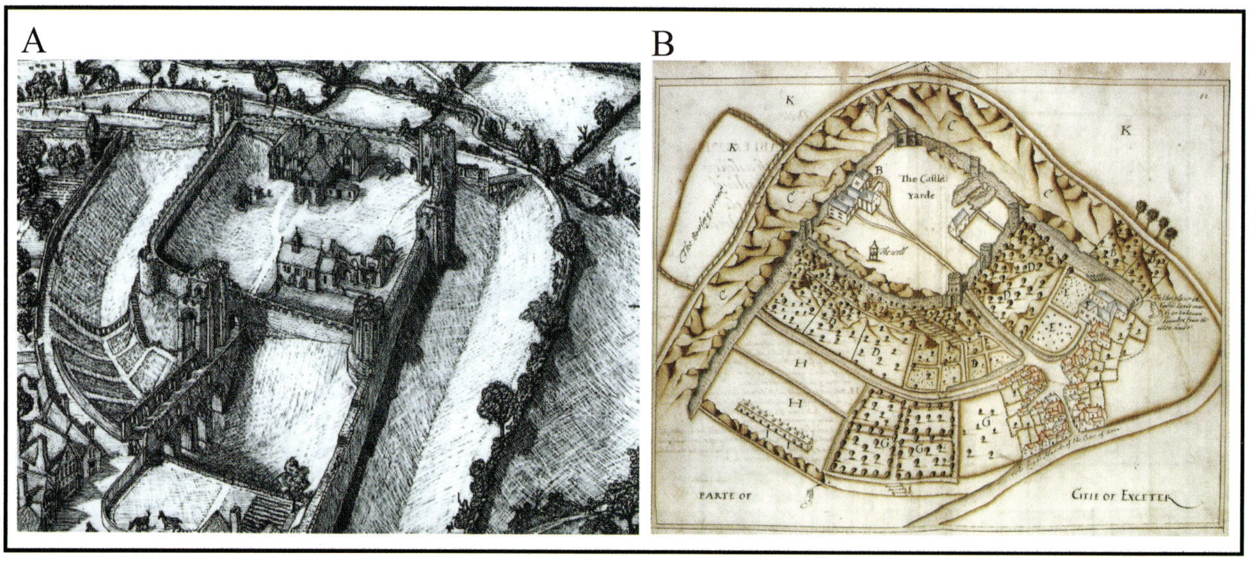

Fig. 8.4 Rougemont Castle in the later Middle Ages. (A) Richard Parker's reconstruction (© Exeter City Council); (B) Norden's bird's eye view of 1617 (© British Library, BL Add MS 6027, f81)

Records after the 1250s, however, describe the decay of the curtain wall and towers, and the collapse of the kitchen, stables and king's chamber. In the period 1321–5 the substantial sum of £224 was spent on the castle, seen by Allen Brown *et al.* as an attempt to 'save the castle from complete destruction' (*ibid.,* 648–9), but it seems clear that the military importance of the castle dwindled in the later Middle Ages. In 1348 the site was given to the Prince of Wales for life, and thereafter it became part of the Duchy of Cornwall. After that date the only records of building works are to its Shire Hall and Gaol.

Parker's reconstruction drawing offers a summary of current understanding of the site in the later Middle Ages, combining the evidence of documentation with standing remains and 16th and 17th-century depictions, the most informative of which is that by Norden (Figs 8.4A–B).

The Cathedral

Naturally, the remodelling and extension of the Norman cathedral and its ancillary buildings formed the city's largest building programme of the period 1200–1550, employing generations of city craftsmen and many itinerants. The years after 1200 saw first the construction of a new Chapter House (*c.* 1225–30), followed by the long-running programme in which almost the entire body of the church was rebuilt between *c.* 1270 and *c.* 1350. This work, with its elaborate tierceron vaults, complex window tracery, rich sculpture and costly liturgical furnishings, is regarded as the most complete example of the Decorated style in Britain. After a brief interlude following the Black Death, work resumed on the cloisters (1377–1414), followed by the rebuilding of the Chapter House (1412–*c.* 1470), the provision of new sculptures at the west front (*c.* 1460–80) and new chantries at the eastern end (*c.* 1510–20). The architectural history of the cathedral falls outside the scope of the present chapter.

A huge body of literature relating to the cathedral has accumulated over the last 250 years. The fullest overall survey of the fabric is the Exeter Cathedral Gazetteer (Keystone 2016), which provides an extensive bibliography. This is not currently available online but may be consulted at the Cathedral Library and Archive. The British Archaeological Association's *Medieval Art and Architecture at Exeter Cathedral* (Kelly 1991) contains a series of highly important papers, many reworked in more accessible form in Swanton (1991). Allan's most recent (2018) Quinquennial survey lists more than 50 grey literature reports, some very substantial, on archaeological projects undertaken over the last 40 years at the cathedral, including detailed recording of masonry and timbers, dendrochronological studies and excavation. Orme's (2009) *Exeter Cathedral: The First Thousand Years* gives a wonderful insight into the operation of the cathedral over this period.

Cathedral Close

In the later Middle Ages Exeter Cathedral had a staff of about 85–95 clergy (Orme 2009, 100–1). Since it was a secular establishment, it was served by a body of canons living in separate households, in contrast with a monastic house in which monks lived in common. They lived within the Cathedral Close, alongside the clergy who administered the diocese (the bishop and archdeacons), and the town houses of some of the monastic houses of the diocese. Their accommodation reflected their status: the 24 canons lived in large houses (canonries), the largest of which were held by the four Dignitaries – the Dean, Treasurer, Chancellor and Precentor. From the late 14th century the 24 vicars choral were obliged to live in a newly built college backing on to South Street, and from the 1520s a further college was provided for the annuellars (Exeter Archaeology 1997; Allan 2005b; Orme 2009, 89–105).

Figure 8.5 shows a reconstruction of the layout of Cathedral Close in the 1530s, bringing together standing buildings dating before *c.* 1550 with the earliest surviving plans of demolished buildings (many of them Georgian lease plans) and evidence of ownership. The wide range of housing types will be evident, from the great houses of the bishop and dean, designed for hospitality on a large scale, to the single-room house plans of the junior clergy.

A bibliography of the wide range of projects relating to the standing buildings and buried archaeology of the cathedral and Close, together with further period maps, will be found in Allan 2018. The same document lists the many episodes of archaeological recording on the standing fabric of the cathedral, which however lie outside the scope of the present chapter.

Monastic houses

In his study of Exeter's churches, Nicholas Orme documented ten later medieval religious houses within the area of modern Exeter (including three hospitals), in addition to the cathedral (Orme 2014, 34–5). Excavation has taken place at four of these: St Nicholas Priory, the Greyfriars, the Blackfriars and Polsloe Priory. The most complete picture of the layout of an Exeter monastery has been recovered from the last site, a house of Benedictine nuns of modest size, founded *c.* 1160 and dissolved in 1538 (Orme 2015b). The excavation examined all four ranges around the cloister and a sizeable area to the south (Fig. 8.6D). It recovered evidence of early temporary buildings, their replacement by late 12th-century stone ranges, and the many phases of later medieval building work. A summary with phase plans appeared in *Medieval Archaeology* (Webster and Cherry 1979, 250–1), and Orme (2015b) used some material from the excavation to good effect, but it remains otherwise unpublished.

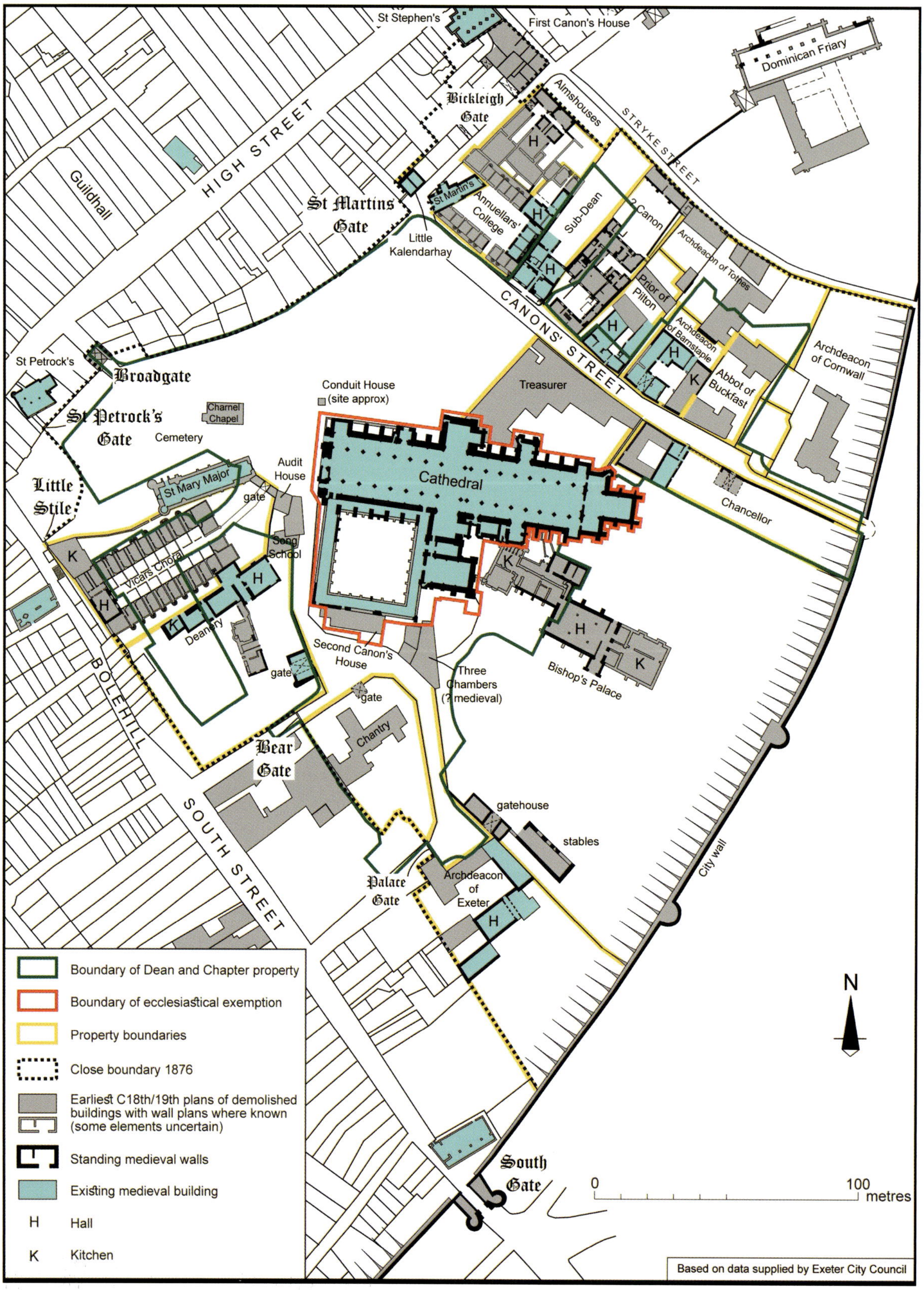

Fig. 8.5 Reconstruction of the plan of Cathedral Close c. *1530 (from Allan 2018)*

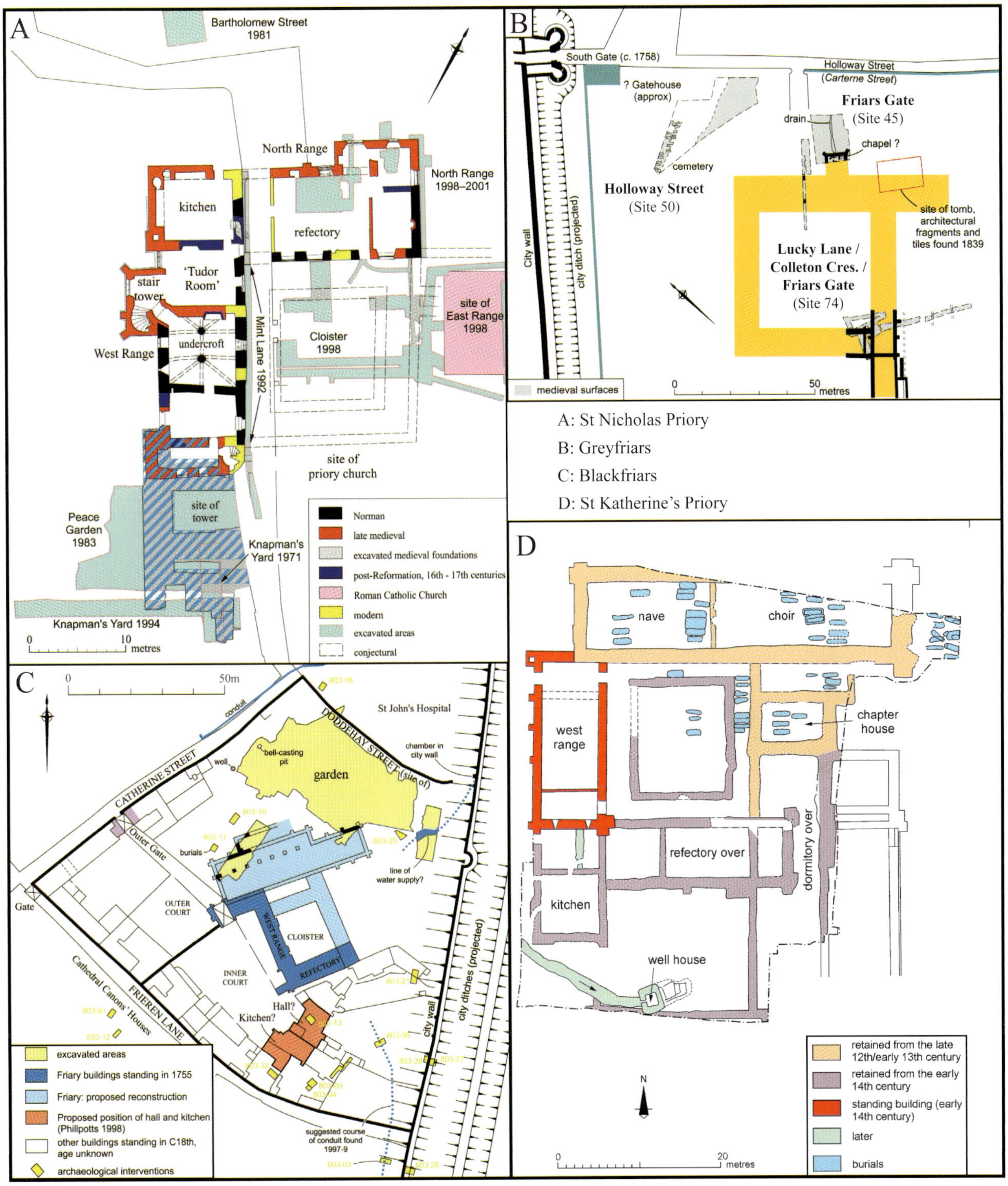

Fig. 8.6 Exeter monastic houses: comparative plans. (A) St Nicholas Priory. (B) Greyfriars. (C) Blackfriars. (D) St Katherine's, Polsloe in 1500 (from Allan 2019; Allan et al. *2016; Steinmetzer, Pearce and Allan forthcoming; Orme 2015). Note that the scales differ*

A detailed survey of the standing western range of *c.* 1300 was undertaken by Blaylock (1991; reconstruction drawing in Orme 2015b, 199).

Of the Dominican friary (the Blackfriars), founded *c.* 1232, nothing survives above ground. Excavations in 1997–2006 (Site 156) exposed fragments of the plan: one side of the choir, parts of the north nave aisle with a northern chapel, a small part of the cemetery and a large area of garden (Fig. 8.6C). Much of the context of these remains can be reconstructed from a plan of 1755 showing the buildings and precinct boundaries which survived the Reformation. A full report awaits publication (Steinmetzer, Pearce and Allan forthcoming, including a historical survey by Orme).

The Franciscan order (the Greyfriars) founded a house within the city walls of Exeter *c.* 1240 but moved to a new site outside South Gate at the start of the 14th century, where they remained until their dissolution in 1538. A substantial historical account of the house has recently been published, including a summary of the excavations (Allan *et al.* 2016; Orme 2016). Only a small northern chapel of the church has been excavated, alongside the south-eastern corner of the claustral ranges and part of an external cemetery (Fig. 8.6B).

For St Nicholas Priory (Fig. 8.6A), we also have the advantage of a fresh historical account by Orme which makes good use of the architectural and archaeological evidence (Orme 2015a). A fuller account of the excavations has recently been prepared (Allan 2019). Richard Parker's fine reconstruction of the priory at the Dissolution (Fig. 8.7) combines the evidence of the standing buildings, documents and excavation.

Parish churches

It has often been noted that the parish churches of Exeter are surprisingly small, and show limited evidence of the late medieval expenditure on church building seen in rural Devon and elsewhere in South-West England. Their subordinate status – mere chapels without burial rights – and meagre incomes no doubt explain this (Orme 2014, 47–50). Nevertheless, it is surprising to realise, for example, that a major figure of Exeter's history like John Gist, the six-times mayor of Exeter who lived in St Pancras parish in the late 14th century (EAPIT 2, Chapter 4), would have gone to church in a small two-cell building no grander than the poorest of rural Devon's parish churches. The late medieval merchant community of the parish did not even pay for a new window in their church.

Orme's study of the city's medieval churches now provides an authoritative guide to their history and context (Orme 2014). The fullest picture of the architectural development of a medieval city church is Stewart Brown's study of St Stephen's, one of the most ambitious in the city (Brown 2012). Parker has undertaken valuable building recording at St Olave's, St John's, St Mary Arches and St Petrock's (Parker 1999).

Guild halls

Two guild halls survive in the city, both of which have been subject to fabric surveys. A full study of the Guildhall in the centre of High Street, the centre of the

Fig. 8.7 Reconstruction of St Nicholas Priory c. *1530 (drawn by Richard Parker; © RAMM)*

administrative life of the city throughout the Middle Ages and beyond, was published in 1990 (Blaylock 1990); tree-ring analysis of the hall roof was carried out subsequently, showing that it dates from 1463–98 – a conclusion consistent with the historical record stating that the hall was rebuilt from 1466 (Blaylock 1990, 129; Howard *et al.* 2004). Tuckers Hall, the home of the Incorporation of Weavers, Fullers and Shearmen, was surveyed in 2008 (Allan 2008); reconstruction drawings showing its primary use as a guild chapel and its reconstruction in the early 17th century are shown in Fig. 8.8.

Almshouses

The fullest study of an Exeter almshouse is that of St Catherine's Almshouses, a house for 12 or 13 poor men, founded shortly before 1450, much altered subsequently, burnt in the Exeter Blitz of 1942 and now a ruin (Parker and Collings 2002; for its history see Orme and Webster 1995, 244–5; Orme 2014, 121). The accommodation was entered through a passage in the two-storeyed front range in Catherine Street (Fig. 8.9, on left), which led into a diminutive court surrounded by cells, also on two floors, behind which was a second court, largely occupied by a two-storey chapel, its upper room probably the common dining room, with surrounding cells in single-storeyed ranges. The whole layout was extremely crowded, and the cells were unheated. Parker and Collings (2002, 125–30) have drawn together pictorial evidence relating to the other almshouses, with comparative plans of their chapels.

Exe Bridge

Exe Bridge is a structure of wide interest, since the nine arches now standing on the floodplain of the Exe amount to the most substantial fragment of one of the major urban bridges of the 12th and early13th centuries surviving in Britain. A detailed fabric survey of the monument has recently been published, together with medieval building remains excavated on the adjacent riverside tenements (Brown 2019). Figure 8.10 shows the monument, with extracts from Parker's reconstruction drawings which summarise our understanding of the area shortly after the completion of the bridge (Fig. 8.10B) and in the mid 15th century (Fig. 8.10C). Many medieval buildings stood in this part of Exeter until the mid 19th century.

The water supply

A full study of the development of the medieval system of water supply to the city, combining abundant archaeological, pictorial and documentary evidence, has been published by Stoyle (2014). He has shown that the origins of the system lay in the late 12th century, when Exeter Cathedral, like other large ecclesiastical foundations elsewhere in England, invested in a water supply. Subsequently St Nicholas Priory, the Blackfriars and the Greyfriars each developed separate systems, and in the early 15th century the city provided its own independent system. The layout of Exeter's medieval aqueducts when they reached their greatest extent in the early 16th century is shown in Fig. 8.11.

Both the cathedral aqueduct and that of the city were ambitious engineering works requiring considerable maintenance. At the springs, the water was gathered in a vaulted stone well-house, where it was fed into a lead pipe buried in a trench which ran into the centre of the city, a distance of about 1.5 km. Outside the city walls, both supplies employed a siphon system which descended the Longbrook Valley and rose up towards the East Gate. In the area around the East Gate, both the city and the Dean and Chapter invested in stone-vaulted passages to facilitate maintenance – the 'Underground Passages' – now a visited Scheduled Monument.

Housing

About 25 houses dating before *c.* 1550 (including substantial fragments as well as complete buildings) survive in the walled area of Exeter and its medieval suburbs. They form a far from representative sample of the hundreds of pre-Georgian buildings still standing in the city a century ago, and a small fraction of the still larger stock of historic buildings known from late 18th and early 19th-century topographical drawings (Parker and Allan 2015, 35–43).

Survival has been greatest in Cathedral Close, where about 14 houses dating before 1550 may be seen. Even here, however, losses have been selective; all but four of the *c.* 40 small houses for the minor clergy (the annuellars and Vicars Choral) have disappeared, whilst more than half the grand mansions of the bishop, archdeacons, cathedral canons and other great officeholders have survived (Allan 2018 the most recent survey). Elsewhere in the city, only about six pre-1550 houses are known in the city's four principal streets (five of them in High Street), and four in the West Quarter.

The late medieval and early modern houses of Exeter were the subject of one of the first studies of housing of this date in a provincial English town (Portman 1966). Since that time, many of the buildings Portman described have been re-examined in more depth, often during alterations, producing fuller records and (inevitably) more complex structural histories. A significant number of historic buildings have also been discovered since Portman's day, often disguised behind flat Georgian facades. Accounts of individual building studies have been published for about half the surviving houses (Thorp 1990; 2012; Parker and Collings 2002; 2006; Matthews *et al.* 2011; Parker *et al.* 2013), and some of the information arising from this work has been used to good effect in general accounts of Devon buildings (Laithwaite 1989; 1990; Cherry and Pevsner 1989), but some key houses remain unpublished.

Fig. 8.8 Reconstructions of Tuckers Hall, Fore Street. (A) Pre-Reformation. (B) In the early 17th century (drawn by Richard Parker; © Exeter City Council)

Fig. 8.9 Reconstruction of the primary form of St Catherine's Almshouses (drawn by Piran Bishop; © RAMM)

In Cathedral Close, the earliest of these houses are the grandest – the Bishop's Palace and Deanery – which are in origin structures of the late 12th and early 13th centuries, albeit much altered. Elsewhere in The Close, a discovery of recent years has been the gradual recognition that portions of stone houses of the 13th or early 14th century (often just footings or lengths of boundary walls) survive in other Close properties whose main historic fabric belongs to the 15th century and later. Only one medieval smoke-blackened roof is known: a base cruck roof in the front range of 10 The Close (Thorp 1990, 48). Most of the medieval houses for which the Close is famous, including for example the other ten of its eleven surviving medieval roofs, belong to the 15th and early 16th centuries. It is clear that the clergy undertook wholesale rebuilding of their properties, sometimes with magnificent fireplaces, roofs and other architectural features, towards the close of the Middle Ages.

Elsewhere in the city, there is still considerable uncertainty about the date of the oldest houses. Prior to the last 20 years, it had been suspected that hardly any town houses dating before *c.* 1500 survived (*e.g.* Laithwaite 1989, 78; 1990). The use of radiocarbon dating at The Ship Inn showed that this row of houses probably dates from *c.* 1400, and this is currently the earliest attested group of town houses outside The Close (Hamilton and Dunbar 2011). Dendrochronological analysis confirmed the suspected date of the next firmly attested groups of houses – 36–8 North Street (now demolished) – in the late 15th or the start of the 16th century, and established the date of 46–7 High Street as 1495 × 1515 (Arnold and Howard 2009; Tyres 2012, 228).

Building materials

Building in stone

In standing Devon buildings there is a fundamental distinction between buildings of cob and thatch in the countryside and those of stone and timber-framing in towns (Cox and Thorp 2001, 11–14). In Exeter, as in the other towns of Devon and Cornwall, building practice conformed to the tradition of 'mixed construction' in which the tenement boundaries were normally of stone but the fronts, backs and internal partitions were of timber (Laithwaite 1989; 1990). The stone provided firebreaks and accommodated garderobes, fireplaces and other features; the timber fronts and rears were the main source of light. The changing pattern of use of building stone will be discussed further below (see 'Regional trade' below).

Cob

Even in the recent past, houses of cob and thatch could be seen immediately outside the city but not within the walls. A mid 16th-century example of such structures was excavated in Cowick Street in 1984: a single-cell house arranged along the street frontage, 10 m long and 6 m deep externally, its two rooms within separated by a

Fig. 8.10 (A) Exe Bridge (Site 56) in flood. (B) Extract from a reconstruction drawing by Richard Parker showing the bridge with its two chapels and almshouse shortly after completion, c. *1250. (C) Extract from a reconstruction drawing by Richard Parker showing the eastern end of the bridge* c. *1450 ((A) Exeter Archaeology archive; (B–C) from Brown 2019, figs 82–3; © Richard Parker)*

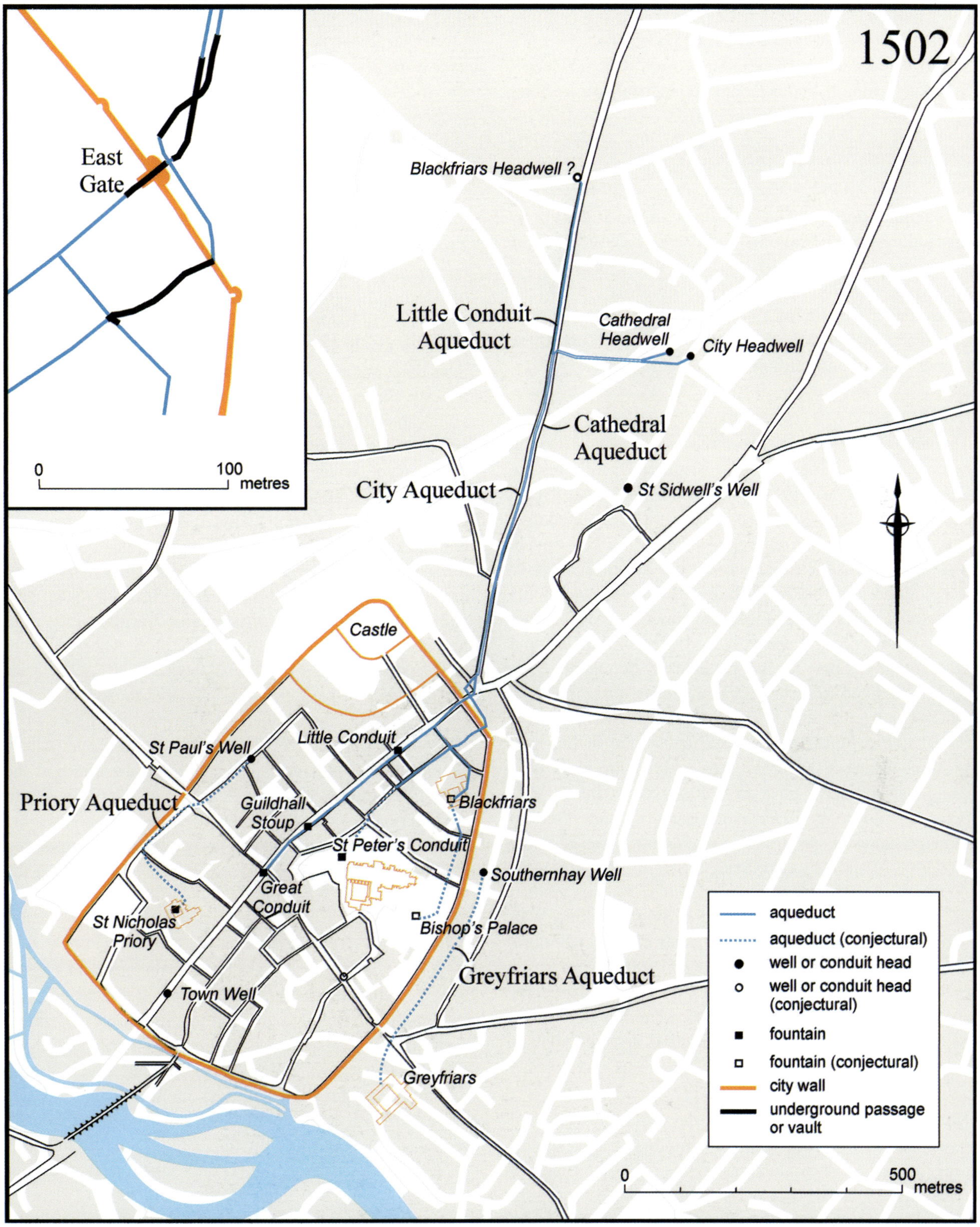

Fig. 8.11 The water supply to the city in the early 16th century (Stoyle 2014, 56)

light timber screen (Egan 1985, 182–3; Blaylock 2000, 15–17). Perhaps its most interesting feature was its construction technique: the cob walls, which were about 1 m wide, sat directly on the ground surface, without the stone wall footings which are normal in the post-medieval vernacular tradition. This method of construction has been recognised in only one standing Devon building: Cross-Town Cottage, in Whimple, east Devon (Parker and Allan 2015, 65; Nat Alcock pers. comm.). It is likely, however, that it was once commonplace, since the same practice has been recorded both at Fore Street and Chapel Street at Exmouth, and is mentioned in local 16th-century documents (Weddell 1986, 121–2).

The possibility that the medieval houses excavated at Rack Street were further examples of cob building is discussed in EAPIT 2, Chapter 8. Their small rooms dug into sloping ground, with wall-lines indicated simply by upstanding strips of natural deposits, are indeed like those of the cob houses at Cowick Street and Exmouth, and they were initially interpreted as cob structures. Many slates and fragments of a ceramic louver were found in the layers overlying these structures, however, and these suggest the urban tradition of slate and stone.

Roofing materials

The archaeological evidence shows that south Devon roofing slate of the sort first discussed by Jope and Dunning (1954) was in common use from the early 12th century, and slates have been found on every medieval site, or almost every one, excavated in the city (Allan 1984a, 300–3). Their sources are discussed below (see 'Regional trade' below). Medieval Exeter documents repeatedly mention tiled roofs, but clay tiles are unknown in medieval contexts and very rare even in the 17th and 18th centuries; slate roofs must actually be meant.

Although no archaeological evidence for roofing in thatch has been found, a few documentary sources show that thatched houses were once to be seen in the city. In 1262 Adam of Kennford was granted the lease of a straw-thatched house close to St Mary Steps church, with permission to bring in ladders to thatch or repair it and to draw off rainwater from it, the rent being a pair of white gloves or 1d and 3d to Exe Bridge (Staniforth and Juddery 1991b, no. 0472). In 1284 Henry de Coldecote was granted the 1d rent from a thatched house in Smythen Street with permission to take water from the eaves of his neighbour's house (Staniforth and Juddery 1991a, no. 0007). The leases of two city properties record that permission was granted for roofs to be tiled (*i.e.* slated) or thatched but they were not to be of lead (Staniforth and Juddery 1991b, nos 0497, 0500).

Tiled floors

No evidence has been found for the provision of a tiled pavement of the 13th or 14th centuries in any Exeter town houses, apart from the private rooms of the Bishop's Palace (Blaylock 2017, 275). By contrast, plain earthenware floor-tiles are common finds on Exeter sites in the late 15th and early 16th centuries, and it is clear that they were in widespread use. Most are imports – principally redware paviours imported from the Low Countries and their competitors in white earthenware from Normandy. Only one house has been found with tiles of this type still *in situ*: at Preston Street (Site 60) small portions of a floor of Low Countries tiles were exposed. The numerous green-glazed and yellow-glazed tile fragments in the layer over it suggested that it had been a pavement of chequered design. The find of over 100 fragmentary Normandy tiles in a tenement at Frog Street (Site 56) must represent a similar pavement, albeit entirely disturbed.

Building types

Houses with single-room plans

The simplest house type of late medieval Exeter documents, and probably the most common, consisted of a ground-floor shop with a solar above. This house form is presumably represented by the many examples of properties with single-room plans, both of medieval and later date, shown on the 18th and 19th-century maps of the city. Being small, such buildings have been especially vulnerable to clearance, but the most celebrated of the city's medieval houses is one notable survivor: 'The House that Moved', which formerly stood at the junction of Exe Bridge and Edmund Street (Fig. 8.12A). Despite its tiny ground-floor plan (4.6 × 3.7 m), it is a well-built structure with generous use of oak timbers. It illustrates a distinctive form of house suited to street corners; other demolished examples include 186 and 208 High Street (Fig. 8.12B), and two similar houses which stood beside a city gate, probably West Gate (Portman 1966, pl. 6, where they are placed at Water Gate).

Despite their restricted sites, some of these houses had elaborate architectural features. The standing figure of St Peter, dating from *c.* 1500 and now at the Royal Albert Memorial Museum, formerly supported the house at the corner of North Street and High Street. The property at the junction of North Street and Waterbeer Street inherited by Elizabeth Farringdon in 1516 perhaps incorporated another such figure, since it was called 'Our Lady at the Corner' (EAPIT 2, Chapter 4).

Row houses

Row (terraced) houses were clearly numerous in Exeter, as elsewhere. The city's most complete medieval example is the Ship Inn in St Martin's Lane, the subject of detailed building recording in the 1990s, and published more recently (Matthews *et al.* 2011). It consisted of three two-storeyed houses of almost identical plan, with a stone-built rear wall in which the single fireplace in each property was housed on the upper floor, the remainder of the house being timber-framed, each house separated from its neighbour by a truss with jointed crucks (Fig. 8.12C). The colleges for minor clergy in Cathedral Close – the Vicars Choral and annuellars (Fig. 8.5) – were essentially buildings of this sort: single-roomed houses on ground and first floor, but served by a common dining hall. Further examples of such houses outside The Close are known from early topographical drawings (*e.g.* at Frog Street: Fig. 8.13A).

Fig. 8.12 Late medieval houses with single-room plans. (A) The House that Moved, formerly 16 Edmund Street (photo: David Garner; © RAMM). (B) 208 High Street drawn by George Townsend, now demolished (© Devon Heritage Centre P&D06534). (C) Reconstruction drawing of The Ship Inn, St Martin's Lane, a row of three shops, probably of c. *1380–1420 (drawn by Richard Parker; © Devon Heritage Centre P&D 41638)*

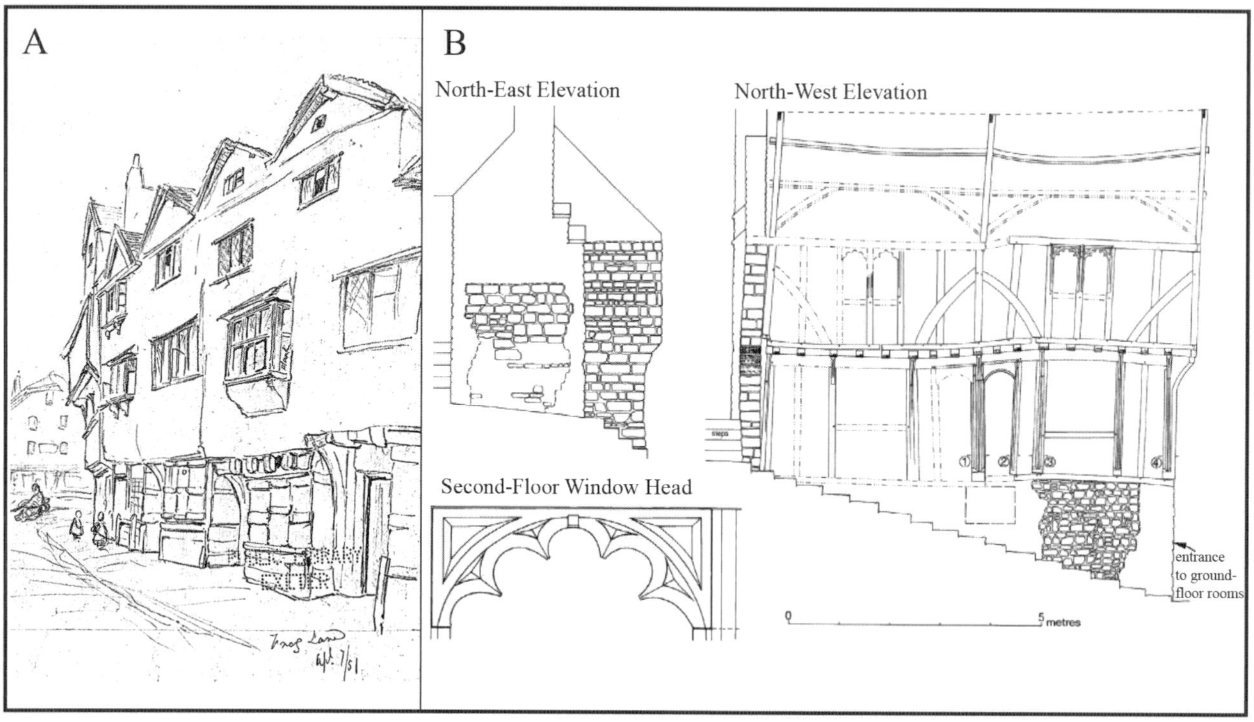

Fig. 8.13 (A) Row of houses in Frog Street, drawn by George Townsend before demolition in 1851 (© Devon Heritage Centre). (B) 1–2 West Street. Note the evidence for two front doorways on the first floor (drawn by John Dunkley and John Allan; © RAMM)

Many more examples are known from documentary evidence, and some of them must have been substantial developments. An early 15th-century property with seven shops and seven solars in Guinea Street was presumably of this form (Portman 1966, 3). It has been argued that William Prince's lease of four shops in Goldsmith Street to four different leaseholders in 1447 refers to a row of buildings, the ground plans of two of which still stand, although they were rebuilt above ground level in the 19th century (EAPIT 2, Chapter 4). This is an instance of the way in which restrictions imposed by cellars and adjoining properties resulted in the retention of medieval house dimensions in the modern city, long after the demolition of the buildings themselves.

1–2 West Street, a two-bay medieval house on a sloping site, provides a good example of the complex domestic arrangements which might obtain, even in these small buildings (Fig. 8.13B). The house is on three floors. At ground level was a shop with a heated room (hall or chamber?) behind. On the first floor, two primary doorways can still be seen in the frame of the side wall, accessed by steps from Stepcote Hill, with chambers on the top floor. The building was evidently designed from the first for multiple occupancy.

Hall houses on the main streets and their development

Number 44 High Street is the only known example of a medieval hall house with a smoke-blackened roof surviving outside Cathedral Close (Fig. 8.14). In its primary form its front block consisted of a tall single-bay chamber overlooking the street frontage, presumably with a shop on the ground floor, behind which rose an open three-bay hall. A small kitchen stood at the back of the tenement, separated from the front block by a small courtyard. The accommodation, then, consisted of four main rooms, with a cellar below.

A later stage in the development of houses on these narrow tenements is illustrated by 36–8 North Street, now demolished (Fig. 8.15; Thorp 2012). They had the same basic arrangement of a three-room front block with a separate kitchen behind a courtyard, but laid out on much longer burgage plots, and with side passages running along one side of each hall. From the first, the hall in each house had a fireplace rather than an open hearth, so their roofs were not smoke-blackened. These and other architectural features suggested a date late in the 15th century, confirmed by dendrochronological analysis (described above).

46–7 High Street illustrate a later stage in the development of houses on these narrow tenement plots: the abandonment of the open hall and its replacement with the post-medieval house with its stacks of rooms on three or more floors each with a front room lit by windows on the street, a rear room lit from the courtyard behind, and a staircase at the centre of the house between the two (Fig. 8.16). The tree-ring date of 1495 × 1515 for this pair of houses (Arnold and Howard 2009) is an important piece of evidence for the timing of this transition.

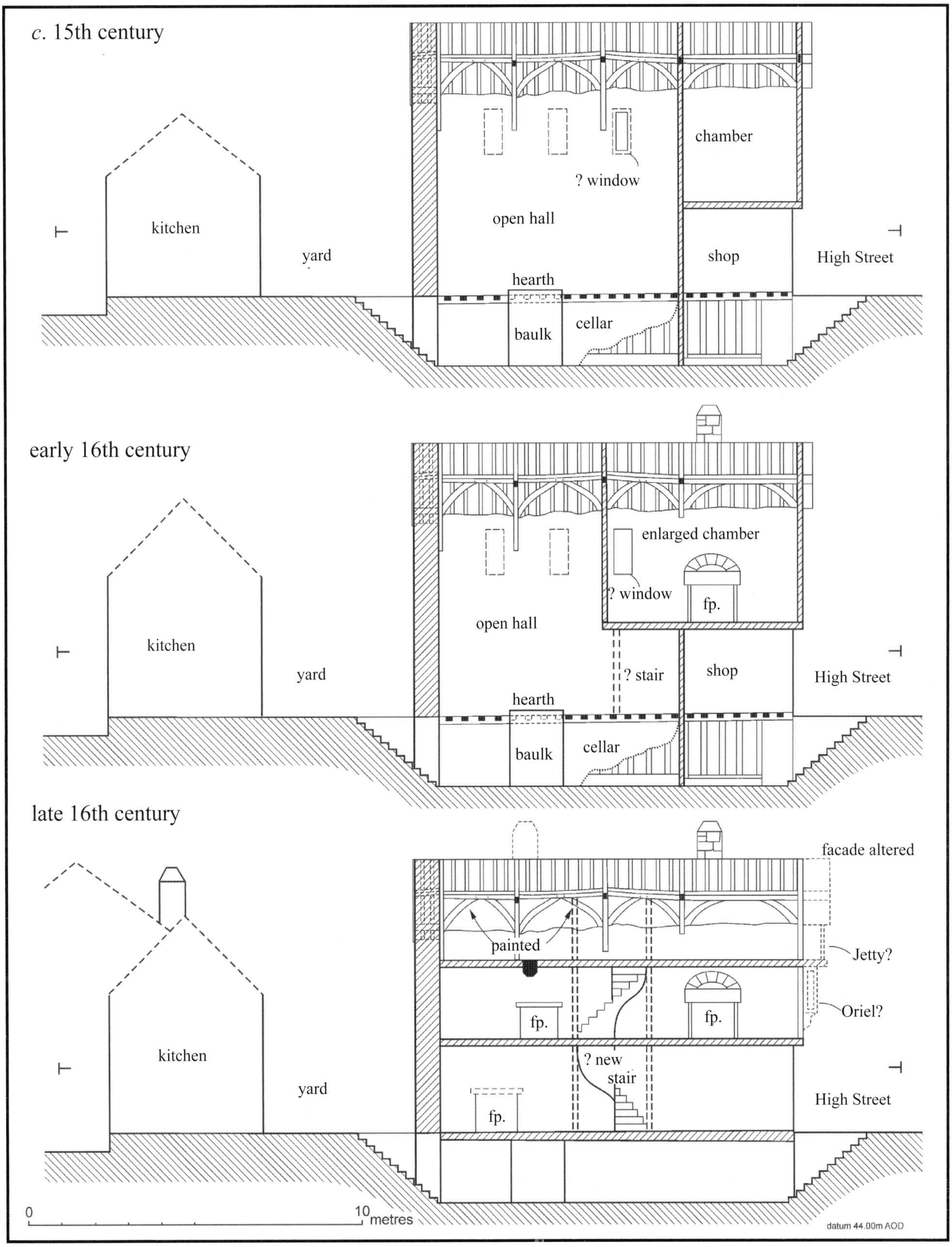

Fig. 8.14 The development of 44 High Street, showing the primary open hall and chamber and their subsequent subdivision (drawn by Richard Parker (Exeter Archaeology Archive © Exeter City Council)

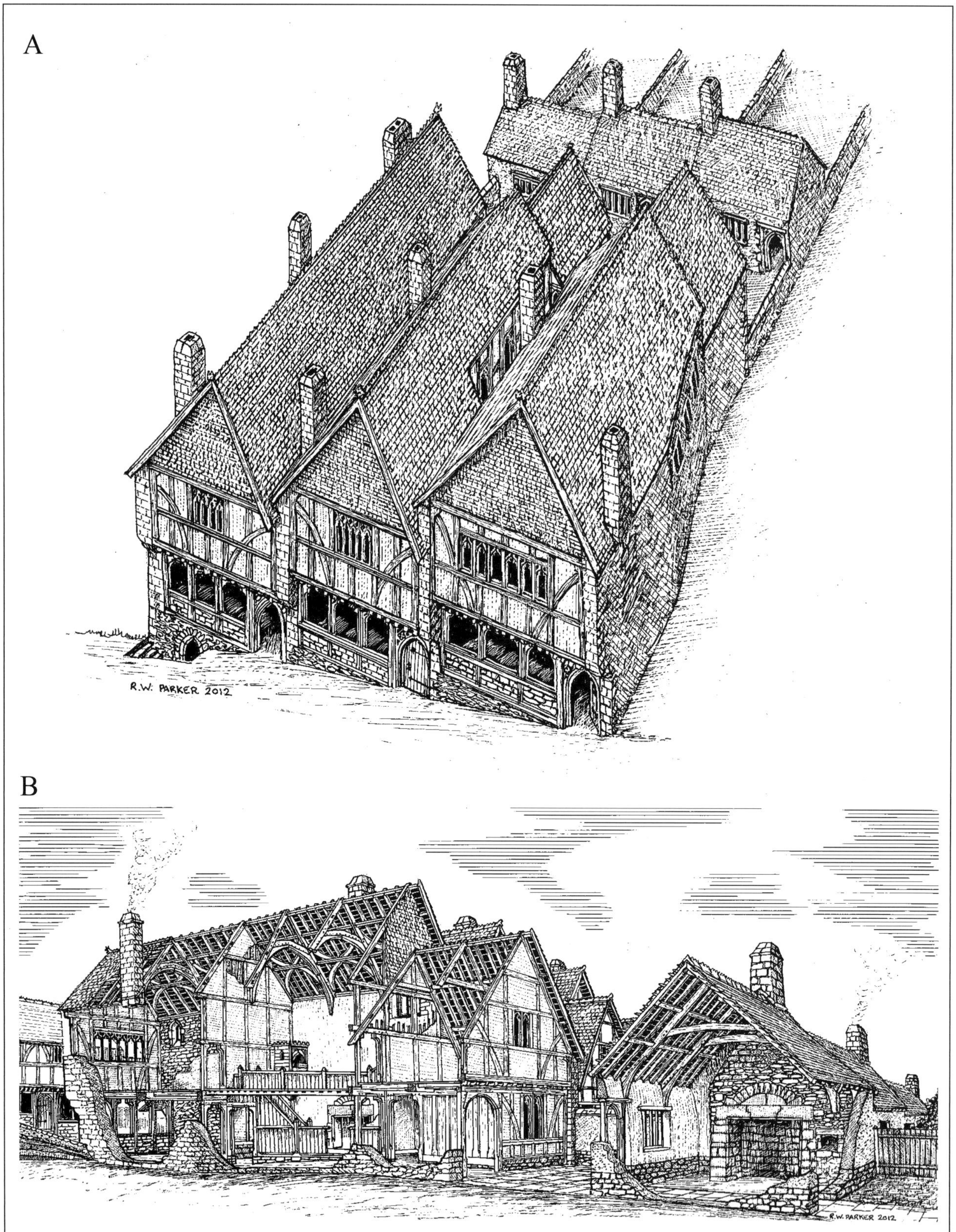

Fig. 8.15 Reconstruction of Nos 36–8 North Street, viewed from the front and rear, c. *1500 (drawn by Richard Parker; © Richard Parker)*

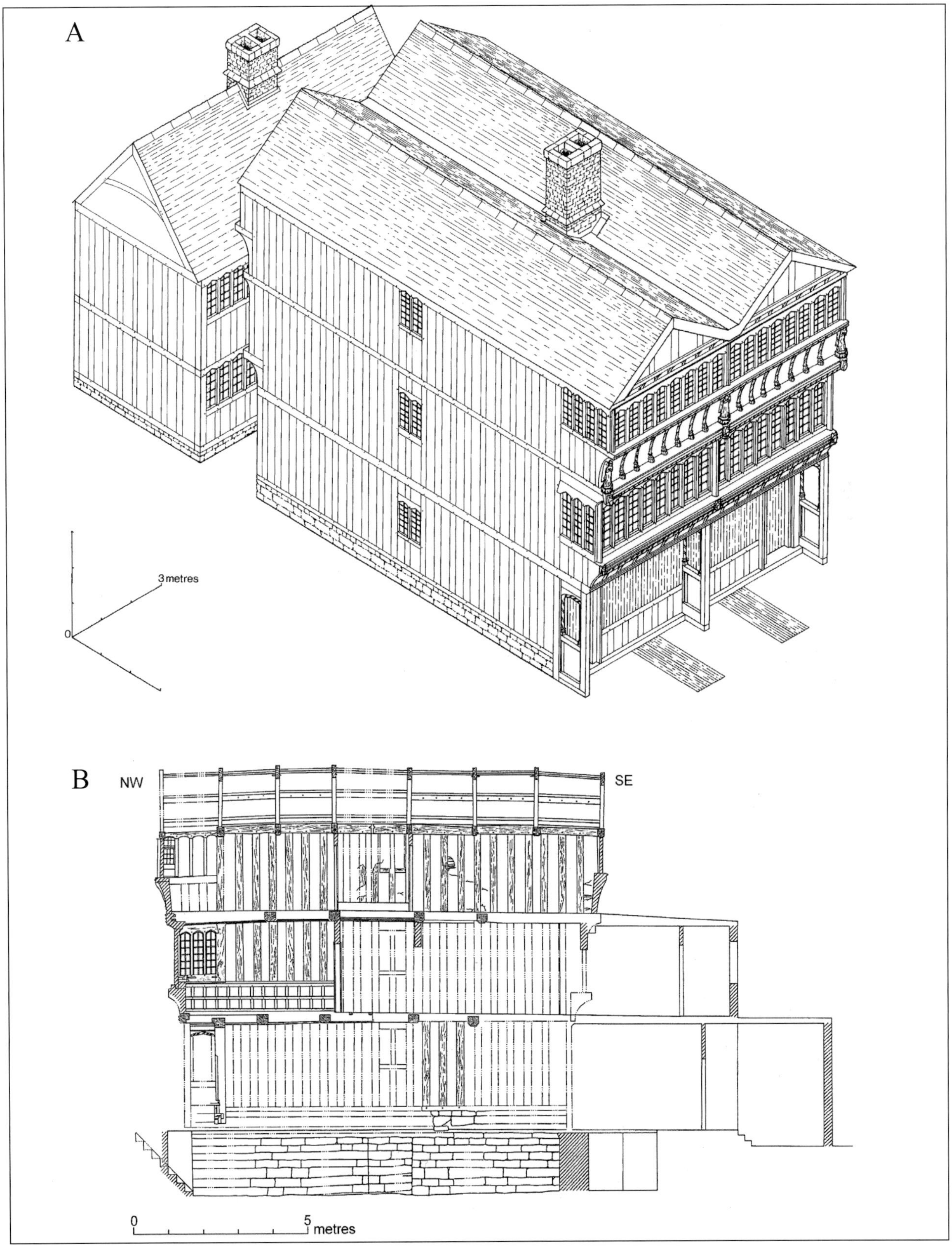

Fig. 8.16 Restoration of the primary form of 46–7 High Street. Most details of the front block survive; the rear range is imaginary (drawn by Keith Westcott; Exeter Archaeology Archive; © Exeter City Council)

Shops and cellars

Shops

The ground floors of old houses on the main streets, and especially their fronts, usually undergo more change than other parts of these structures, so physical evidence for early shops has rarely survived. Here the documentary evidence is more informative. The Exeter shops were commonly described as 'selds'; in this context the word must mean a small booth or stall, rather than the more substantial market hall with several shops known in London and Chester (Keene 1985, 137–8, 1091–2; 1990, 12–13; for selds elsewhere see Leech 2014, 145–6; Brown *et al.* 1999, 137, who conclude that the term was defined by its usage – for selling goods – rather than any specific form of structure). Most or all of the late 14th and 15th-century houses in the central part of High Street examined in the study of St Pancras parish (see EAPIT 2, Chapter 4) had a shop, and commonly two, at the front of the tenement strip, sometimes rented or owned independently of the houses behind them (Fig. 8.19). The continuous pattern of shops extended along Goldsmith Street, a side street at right-angles to High Street, and there were certainly further examples on Waterbeer Street, the back lane at the rear of the High Street houses.

Since the High Street properties were only about 20 feet (6.1 m) wide, and there were sometimes two shops and a passage on the frontage, the shops must have been small. The one acquired by William Caperoun at 200 High Street in 1360 was 21 feet long by 6 feet deep and 9 feet high (6.4 × 1.8 × 2.7 m). Still smaller examples are documented in the late medieval city. Portman (1966, 4) quotes a document of 1336 which mentions a High Street shop measuring 5 feet by 4 feet (1.5 × 1.2 m) in plan, and another beside Broadgate in 1338 measuring 10 feet by × 6 feet (3.0 × 1.8 m). In a dispute of the 1440s between the Cathedral Chapter and the city, the Chapter were accused of encroaching on the High Street by setting up five stalls in front of the New Inn, a property which they owned in St Stephen's parish (Moore 1871, 85). They measured 60 feet by 3 feet (18.2 × 0.9 m) and were therefore on average 12 feet (3.6 m) wide and 3 feet deep.

Cellars

Exeter's cellars have not attracted the attention they deserve from archaeologists, principally because those visible today rarely have distinctive architectural features, but partly because access to them is proving increasingly difficult. Almost all of them have plain party walls of stone and brick, and lie below boarded floors. Stone-vaulted cellars were clearly far less common here than in London, Southampton and Bristol, for example (*cf.* Platt 1973; Schofield 1995; Leech 2014), and none are visible today, but two former vaulted cellars are recorded in the central part of High Street. 'A large and very ancient cellar with groined arches' was recorded in 1825 on the western corner of the High Street and Broadgate (RCC 1909, 53), and on the opposite side of the gate, 1 Broadgate once had at least two 'Early English arches' (Lega-Weekes 1915, 486; Gray 2018, 111, quoting newspapers of 1902–4).

The growth of the city

Urban growth in the 13th and early 14th centuries

The clearest instance of the growth of population within the walled area is in the back streets of the West Quarter – the part of the city between the West Gate and the South Gate – which was notorious for its poverty in post-medieval times. The excavated sites in this area (Sites 52, 60, 63–4) showed little sign of occupation in the Late Saxon and Norman periods. At Rack Street (formerly Rack Lane: Fig. 8.2) the earliest evidence of housing dated from the late 12th century, with more intensive activity from the mid or late 13th century (EAPIT 2, Chapter 8). By the early 14th century one small three-room house was laid out at right angles to the street, suggesting that space was too restricted for houses to spread along the tenement frontage. The late Harold Fox showed that one well-documented adjacent property, partially excavated in the 1970s, had been subdivided into two smaller holdings at this time, again pointing to quite dense settlement in this peripheral part of the walled city (EAPIT 2, Chapter 8; Fox 1986).

The expansion of the city during the 13th century is also evident in the suburbs. The most important extra-mural settlement, outside the East Gate along Sidwell Street, was redeveloped in the 1950s and 1960s without archaeological investigation, but some exploration has been carried out in the suburbs which developed outside the other three gates. Outside the West Gate, the excavations at Exe Bridge showed a rapid build-up of deposits and the laying-out of new tenements on the river bank at Frog Street at the start of the 13th century (Brown 2019), and the impression that this suburb grew quickly in the period around 1200 has been reinforced by the recent recovery of late 12th or early 13th-century occupation from a site much further upstream, on former marshland about 280 m from the West Gate (Site 176). Further early 13th-century ceramics have been recovered from trenches at Cricklepit Mill, about 150 m downstream from the gate (Site 98). It seems likely that the growth of this western suburb was closely related to the construction of Exe Bridge *c.* 1200.

Subsequently a small settlement grew up in the parish of St Thomas on the opposite side of the River Exe. Chris Henderson (pers. comm.) suggested that it may have been a medieval new town in all but name, its Courtenay lords having developed it as a commercial rival to the city, as they did at Topsham (Jackson 1972). By *c.* 1300 settlement on the western side of the Exe had spread to Shooting Marsh Stile on the Alphington Road and to Cowick Street (Sites 79 and 80).

Evidence regarding the extra-mural settlements outside the two other gates is more patchy. In the suburb outside South Gate, rubbish pits show that occupation had spread along the Topsham Road about 150 m from the gate by the late 12th or early 13th century (Chapter 7 above), and large square wattle-lined wells of the late 13th and early 14th centuries, similar to those found on tenements within the walls, were found on the opposite side of the road at the Valiant Soldier site (Site 44). In the suburb outside the North Gate, probably the smallest of the four extra-mural settlements, the land beside the Longbrook was occupied by *c.* 1300; the earliest occupation contained Saintonge polychrome pottery (Site 83).

The impact of the Black Death

Kowaleski (1995, 86–7) has brought together the documentary evidence for the impact of the Black Death at Exeter, concluding that at least one third of the townspeople, and perhaps many more, were killed in the first outbreak of 1348–9. The documentary evidence relating to the excavated area at Rack Street, discussed by Fox (1986), gave a dramatic illustration of the disastrous impact of the plague on tenements in a traditionally poor part of the city; later medieval documents talked of their overthrow or downfall (*casum*) (EAPIT 2, Chapter 8). In this instance the excavated evidence fitted well with the documentary record; the best-preserved of the houses which were examined here was demolished and its site infilled in the early or mid 14th century, and it remained unoccupied until the mid 17th century. The tenement discussed by Fox was turned over to cloth-drying racks, which probably accounted for the numerous postholes at the rear of the excavated properties. Elsewhere, the abandonment of city sites around the mid 14th century is often difficult to recognise in the archaeological record, since it was at about that time that the practice of digging cesspits and rubbish pits in back gardens was largely abandoned, removing the most obvious signs of occupation, even when that occupation continued.

A contrasting picture of continuity emerged from the documentary evidence relating to the highly desirable tenements in the central part of High Street (EAPIT 2, Chapter 4). The sequences of leases for most of these sites indicate an unbroken succession of occupiers. Instances of fresh building work in the generation after the first outbreak of the Black Death may also be noted. In 1377–8 the city received a 2s 8d rent from a vacant plot on the Waterbeer Street frontage, next to the Guildhall. By the end of the following decade the rent was charged 'for a certain tenement new edified behind the garden of the Guildhall', and by the 1420s the same rent was for 'two shops on the eastern side of the Guildhall'. By the 1440s two separate payments of 2s 8d appear in the city accounts, each for two shops at the back of the Guildhall. On the High Street frontage of the same block of tenements, Richard and Denise Tykerigge built two houses at 205 High Street, a property of the Mary Magdalene Hospital,

Fig. 8.17 Vacant properties and building on vacant sites in central Exeter in the late 14th and 15th centuries (research by John Allan, drawn by David Gould)

in 1379. When they did so, the prior of the hospital reduced the annual rent from 20s to 10s because they had built to the hospital's advantage, a suggestion that landowners found it necessary to offer inducements to encourage investment at this time (EAPIT 2, Chapter 4).

Even in this part of the city, however, there were at least five empty plots in Waterbeer Street and one on High Street in the period 1361–82 (Fig. 8.17). Some of them remained vacant long after the Black Death. The desirable corner property at 207 High Street was unoccupied when its sequence of leaseholders can first be traced in 1397, and it was still vacant in 1456 when the city rented it to John Harrys on condition that he build at his own expense a shop on the High Street with solar or solars above (EAPIT 2, Chapter 4). This was presumably the timber-framed building shown on the corner plot in John White Abbot's painting of 1797 (Fig. 8.18). Similarly, the site of St Catherine's Almshouses, behind the opposite side of High Street on the edge of Cathedral Close, was vacant when the almshouses were built *c.* 1450, but fabric analysis showed that they overlay the footings of a 13th- or early 14th-century stone house – presumably still abandoned in the mid 15th century (Parker and Collings 2002, 82, 106–17).

The layout of tenements in High Street in the later Middle Ages

Study of the documentation relating to the 12 High Street properties discussed in the St Pancras parish survey (EAPIT 2, Chapter 4) has concluded that in this central part of High Street the pattern of long narrow tenements evident today has remained little changed since the late 14th century. Not only were all these narrow burgage plots in place by that stage, but the formation of separate properties on Waterbeer Street, carved out of the back of the High Street tenements, was also well advanced, and in one instance this process can be traced back to the mid 13th century. And some of the irregularities visible in the relationships between adjacent properties had arisen by this time. For example, the tenement with 195 High Street on its frontage consisted in the recent past of separate houses on the High Street and Waterbeer Street frontages, whilst the central part of the burgage plot formed part of the adjacent property, 196 High Street. Documentary study shows that this arrangement is evident in the will of John Gist, the wealthy mayor of Exeter in the late 14th century, who lived at 196; his kitchen occupied the middle of the adjacent plot.

Late medieval landowners

The study of St Pancras parish also allowed a partial reconstruction of the pattern of land ownership in this part of Exeter. The fullest picture can be drawn from the Military Survey of 1522, undertaken shortly before the great changes of the Reformation. At that time there were three main groups of landowners in the parish: institutions,

Fig. 8.18 Extract from John White Abbott's view of High Street in 1797, showing the late medieval timber-framed building at 207 High Street, here identified as the pair of houses built by John Harrys in the 1460s (© RAMM)

lay landowners living outside the parish, and people living in the parish. The most important group was the nine institutional owners, which were mainly local religious houses and charitable bodies (EAPIT 2, Chapter 4). Their joint income totalled £15 0s 8d, the largest being that of the cathedral at £5. Most of their properties can be identified; they owned six of the parish's eight valuable burgage plots on the High Street frontage in their entirety, and at least five of its 12 known High Street shops (*ibid.*; Fig. 8.19). The nine lay owners living outside the parish, whose combined annual rents totalled £9 17s 8d, have

Table 8.1 Number of identified specimens (NISP) of mammals in later medieval features (Continued)

	North Quarter						*East Quarter*	*South Quarter*	*West Quarter*			*Extra-mural*			
Total Mammal	**2226**	**3596**	**1078**	**54**	**549**	**997**	**564**	**198**	**416**	**74**	**186**	**176**	**7622**	**2369**	**20105**
Cattle	41.5	35.8	34.7		39.0	44.6	50.3	66.1	51.0		58.3	61.0	49.5	41.9	44.3
Sheep/Goat	47.9	45.7	50.9		51.0	37.7	38.8	27.6	37.8		30.7	25.5	46.1	47.8	45.6
Pig	10.5	18.5	14.4		10.0	17.7	10.9	6.3	11.3		11.0	13.5	4.4	10.3	10.0
Total C+S+P	2130	3408	1027	52	500	937	539	192	400	72	163	141	7518	2358	19437
% S of S+P	82.0	71.2	77.9		83.6	68.0	78.0	81.5	77.0		73.5	65.5	91.3	82.2	81.9
% Horse of C+H	1.9	1.7	2.2		5.8	2.8	2.5	2.3	2.9		2.1	2.3	0.5	0.7	1.4
% Wild	0.9	1.1	1.2		0.9	0.8	1.4	1.0	0.0		1.6	1.7	0.6	0.0	0.7

% S of S+P = percentage of sheep/goat of total sheep/goat and pig
% Horse of C+H = percentage of horse of total cattle and horse
Data for GSI-III, TS and HS adapted from Maltby (1979)
Data for PH adapted from Coles (forthcoming)
Data for BSE, FH, MY, PS, QS and AC adapted from Lauritsen (2019)
Data for EB adapted from Levitan (2015)
Data for PP adapted from Levitan (1987a)
GSI-III = Goldsmith Street
TS = Trichay Street
HS = High Street
PH = Princesshay
BSE = Bartholomew Street East
BSW = Bartholomew Street West
FH = Friernhay Street
MY = Mermaid Yard
PS = Paul Street
QS = Queen Street
EB = Exe Bridge

were lower from sites in the northern quarter than in assemblages from other parts of the city apart from Polsloe Priory (Table 8.1), and these variations do not correlate consistently with the status of the residents of the different sites (see also EAPIT 2, Chapter 9). Other factors such as differential preservation and recovery, variations in disposal practices and variations between features within the same property have all contributed to species fluctuations. For example, Levitan (1987b) demonstrated that more large bones (mainly cattle) were dumped near the kitchens of Polsloe Priory than in other areas.

The relative abundance of different elements of the same species also varied in later medieval and post-medieval deposits in Exeter (Maltby 1979, 18–25; Levitan 1987b; 2015; Lauritsen 2019; Coles forthcoming b). The most spectacular example comes from Exe Bridge where the assemblage was dominated by the 450 horn cores of cattle indicating that large-scale horn-working was taking place in the vicinity during the 13th century (Levitan 1987b; 2015). Similar deposits of horn cores have been found in several other medieval towns (Albarella 2003) including Bristol (Warman 2013, 271–2) and Winchester (Serjeantson 2013, 130–1). Butchery evidence showed continued use of heavy blades for most of the dismemberment. There was an increase in the splitting of the carcasses into equal sides during the late medieval period, probably reflecting an increase in the prominence of professional butchers (Kowaleski 1995). Cattle bones were also heavily exploited for marrow, particularly from sites in the northern quarter (Maltby 1979, 39; EAPIT 2, Chapter 9).

Most of the cattle mandibles came from adults (Maltby 1979, 159; Levitan 2015, tab. 4; Lauritsen 2019; Coles forthcoming b). Most assemblages, however, contained substantial numbers of unfused late-fusing bones (Maltby 1979, 161; Levitan 2015, tab. 2; EAPIT 2, Chapter 9, Fig. 9.4) suggesting that there was a high kill-off of prime beef cattle aged between three and six years. Bones of calves were generally poorly represented, indicating that intensive milk production was not practised. This contrasts with early post-medieval assemblages from the north quarter which included substantial numbers of calf mandibles (Maltby 1979, 162). An increase in the relative abundance of calves is a feature of other late medieval and early post-medieval assemblages, particularly in towns and high status sites (Sykes 2006a, 59–60, 67), reflecting an increase in the importance of the dairy industry and a decrease in the use of cattle as plough animals. Variations in domestic mammal mortality patterns in Exeter that are possibly linked to the social status are discussed further by Lauritsen (2019; EAPIT 2, Chapter 9).

Most cattle from medieval Exeter had short horns (Maltby 1979, 38; Levitan 2015) and continued to be small in stature, and cattle of similar size were found in medieval deposits at Launceston Castle (Albarella and Davis 1996). However, some larger cattle were found in the late medieval assemblages studied by Lauritsen suggestive of size improvements that became more apparent in post-medieval assemblages from Exeter (Maltby 1979, 164–7; EAPIT 2, Chapter 9, Fig. 9.5) and Launceston Castle (Albarella and Davis 1996).

As discussed above, sheep/goat were better represented overall in later medieval deposits compared with previous periods, although percentages varied in assemblages from different sites (Table 8.1). There were also some intra-site variations in the relative abundance of bones from different parts of the skeleton (Maltby 1979, 119–36; Lauritsen 2019). Generally the sheep/goat assemblages were dominated by more robust and/or large bones, although upper limbs were dominant in some deposits, perhaps indicating the acquisition of joints of meat. Bones of lower meat quality were also found in fairly high numbers on most sites indicating that various stages of carcass processing took place within both secular and ecclesiastical sites. This contrasts with the assemblages from the castles at Okehampton and Launceston, where upper limb bones dominated the sheep/goat assemblages (Maltby 1982; Albarella and Davis 1996).

In the intra-mural sites, the vast majority of the diagnostic bones belonged to sheep, which provided over 96% of the sheep/goat metapodials in the medieval assemblages analysed by Maltby (1979, 41). Goats were much better represented by horn cores, particularly amongst the industrial waste derived from horn-working at Exe Bridge (Levitan 2015). In this assemblage, goats provided 94% of the sheep/goat horn cores. Goat horns were widely traded in the medieval period (Albarella 2003).

There is evidence in most assemblages for changes in sheep mortality patterns towards the end of the medieval period. Although many sheep continued to be slaughtered between two and three years of age, there were increases in the percentages of older sheep reflected in the dental and epiphyseal fusion data in several of the 14th century and later assemblages (Maltby 1979, 174–80; Levitan 2015, figs 19–21; EAPIT 2, Chapter 9, Fig. 9.4). This reflects the emergence of the flourishing woollen cloth trade both locally and nationally that meant more sheep were kept alive for longer to supply annual fleeces (EAPIT 1, Chapter 4), a trend that can be seen on all types of settlement (Sykes 2006a, 67–8). The sheep in Exeter, however, generally continued to be small and the majority were horned (Maltby 1979, 181–5; EAPIT 2, Chapter 9, Fig. 9.6).

The percentage of pigs declined in the later medieval deposits in Exeter (Table 8.1), providing only 10% of the NISP counts overall. They were best represented in the Goldsmith Street III assemblage (18%) whereas they provided only 6% of the Mermaid Yard assemblage. The decrease in the percentage of pigs follows the national pattern and could be related to a decline in woodland (Albarella 2006). Throughout the medieval period, pigs are generally better represented on high status sites such as Launceston Castle (Albarella and Davis 1996, 69). It is noticeable, however, that the percentage of pigs (14%) of the total cattle, sheep/goat and pig elements in the late medieval assemblage at Okehampton Castle (Maltby 1982, 116) was no higher than encountered in the extra-mural Acorn Roundabout assemblage and was lower than in the Goldsmith Street III (19%) and Queen Street (18%) assemblages in the north quarter of Exeter (Table 8.1), which may indicate that those sites were associated with residents of higher status.

Ageing data for pigs from this period is limited. As expected, few reached full maturity. There are some indications from epiphyseal fusion data that more pigs were killed during their first year than in the early medieval period (Maltby 1979, 190; Levitan 2015, tab. 23) but the pattern is not consistent and pigs slaughtered in their second and third years remained more common (Maltby 1979, 187; EAPIT 2, Chapter 9, Fig. 9.4). There was a general increase in sty husbandry in the later medieval period and historical records indicate that many pigs were kept in towns (Albarella 2003; Hamilton and Thomas 2012), with the number of wandering pigs attached to each household in Exeter being reported annually by the mayor (Kowaleski 1995, 297). It remains to be established whether the increase in sty husbandry had any effects in improving pig carcass weights in medieval Exeter.

Horses were poorly represented throughout the later medieval assemblages, providing less than 1% of the total mammal NISP counts (Table 8.1). There was only one record of butchery from the Princesshay site (Coles forthcoming b) and two in the Exe Bridge assemblage (Levitan 2015), and horse butchery was not reported from other sites. Nearly all the horse bones came from adults and they continued to serve as working animals, although they were seemingly not commonly employed in ploughteams in Devon until the post-medieval period (Maltby 1979, 62). Most horses found in Exeter were the size of large ponies (Coles forthcoming b).

Bones of dogs and cats were found in small numbers forming 1% and 2% respectively of the mammal NISP counts (Table 8.1). Counts for both species were enhanced by the discovery of several partial skeletons. For example, 21 cat bones came from a Goldsmith Street III pit and two groups consisting of seven and thirteen dog bones were found in Goldsmith Street I–II (Maltby 1979, 118, 124, 131). A partial cat skeleton was also recovered from Paul Street (Lauritsen 2019). Most of these remains were found amongst rubbish deposits but a fairly complete immature male dog skeleton was buried in its own grave (pit 4913) within the Blackfriars' precinct of the Princesshay site (Coles forthcoming b). Cats may have sometimes been skinned (Coles forthcoming b) but these associated groups indicate that most carcasses of these companion animals were not subjected to carcass processing.

Birds formed substantial portions of the late medieval faunal assemblages from most sites. They were particularly abundant in the Friernhay Street deposits forming 47% of the total bird and mammal bones (Lauritsen 2019). They formed 12% of the mammal and bird bones from sites in the north quarter (Table 8.2).

As in previous periods, chickens provided the majority of bird bones, forming over 70% of the avian assemblage in most sites (Table 8.2). About 22% of the chicken bones from the pre-1976 excavations and 18% from Princesshay belonged to immature birds culled for meat (Maltby 1979, 209). Most of the adult birds were hens, many of which would have provided eggs for human consumption. The mortality pattern is typical of later medieval sites (Serjeantson 2006). Most of the chickens were of small stature (Maltby 1979, 67–71).

Bones of domestic geese were also quite common, providing 16% of the bird bones from the north quarter, and 20% from Exe Bridge, but only 7% of the bones from the west quarter (Table 8.2). Their large size has favoured their recovery in hand-collected samples. In contrast to Launceston Castle and Winchester (Albarella and Davis 1996; Serjeantson 2009) only a few bones of goslings have been recorded. It is likely that some of the mallard-sized ducks were from birds kept in captivity, and they were more common in the Exe Bridge assemblage (10%) than on other sites, perhaps reflecting the capture of ducks from the adjacent river. Other captive birds probably included the three hawks found at Friernhay Street that will have been kept for falconry (EAPIT 2, Chapter 9). A single bone of a peafowl was found at Exe Bridge (Levitan 2015) and some of the 16 bones of the pigeon family could have been from birds kept in dovecotes, although these also include bones of wild wood pigeon and stock dove (Maltby 1979, 73).

Although they contributed only small amounts of the bones overall, the late medieval avian assemblage was quite diverse (Table 8.2). A least 25 species were represented including several that as yet have not been recorded in the earlier medieval period (including swan, diver, gannet, grouse, partridge, plovers, chough and buzzard). Woodcock remained the most common gamebird but it now contributed no more than 3% of the bird bones in any of the assemblages. The buzzard and corvids would have scavenged on food waste in the town. Raven bones were the most common but these included bones from several partial skeletons.

The importance of the medieval fishing industry in Exeter remains to be explored further, as only the bones recovered from the pre-1976 excavations and Exe Bridge have been analysed. Wilkinson (1979, 213) identified at least 21 species in medieval deposits and at least 19 species were recorded in the Exe Bridge assemblage (Levitan 2015, tab. 1). Most of these were marine species, many of which would have been preserved by salting and smoking (Locker 2001). The most common species identified is hake, followed by conger, whiting, cod, sea bream and plaice (Wilkinson 1979, 80). The high percentage of hake, which was also prevalent

Table 8.2 Number of identified specimens (NISP) of birds in later medieval features

		North Quarter		*East Quarter*	*South Quarter*	*West Quarter*			*Extra-mural*		
Site Code	*Pre 1976*	*PS*	*QS*	*PH**	*MY*	*BSE*	*BSW*	*FH*	*AC*	*EB*	
EAPIT Site		76	68	156	63	73	47	75	94	56	Total
Chicken	718	27	127	65	1	7	2	131	14	218	1310
Goose (large)	169	5	17		2	3		9		68	273
Goose (small)	1										1
Swan	4										4
Mallard-sized duck	17		3							34	54
Medium-sized duck	2										2
Diver	1										1
Gannet	1										1
Gull										1	1
Woodcock	29		1					2		9	41
Heron		1						1			2
Small wader	1										1
Plover	1										1
Lapwing		2									2
Peafowl										1	1
Red Grouse			1								1
Partridge	2										2
Pigeons	10	1				1			1	3	16
Raven	15		15							1	31
Chough	1										1
Rook/Crow	5		1							4	10
Jackdaw	3										3
Hawk								23			23
Buzzard	1										1
Passerine	2									4	6
Total Bird	**983**	**36**	**165**	**65**	**3**	**11**	**2**	**166**	**15**	**343**	**1789**
% B+M	12.4	6.2	14.2		1.5	2.6	2.6	47.2	7.9	4.3	
% Chicken	73.0	75.0	77.0					78.9		63.6	
Ch:Sh	18.7	9.6	26.5	23.7	1.8	4.4	5.3	72.3	28.0	16.2	14.5

Counts include bones from associated bone groups
* only chicken bones counted. 276 other bird bones from all medieval phases not further identified
% B+M = percentage of total bird and mammal
Ch:Sh = percentage of chicken of total sheep/goat and chicken

at Launceston Castle and in several other medieval assemblages from south-western England (Serjeantson and Woolgar 2006, 115), reflects the proximity of the hake's main fishing grounds. Conger is well represented in many medieval assemblages including some from Bristol (Armitage 2016). Most fish bones in Exeter have been obtained by hand-collection, which has biased the assemblages towards the larger species. This accounts for the absence of herring, which was an important marine fish in medieval Britain (Locker 2001) and the very low number of eel bones. Much higher percentages of herring, eel and other small species have been obtained in sieved samples from Bristol (Armitage 2013; 2016). And while Exeter's proximity to the coast allowed easy access to fish, the consumption of marine fish was by no means confined to coastal or near-coastal places in Devon. The study of the impressive collection of fish remains from Okehampton Castle – the most distant place in Devon from the sea – revealed a very wide range of fish consumed there (Wilkinson 1982).

Overall, the inhabitants of late medieval Exeter relied principally upon cattle and sheep for their meat supply, while pigs were of declining importance. Cattle and sheep were mainly acquired through professional butchers. Some pigs, chickens and geese would also have been brought to Exeter for slaughter but some of these animals were also kept in the town. There is little evidence for significant improvements in the size of any of the domestic stock during the medieval period, and in the case of sheep there was a greater focus on the acquisition of heavy fleeces of wool than attempts to improve carcass weights. There is also evidence for large-scale cattle and goat horn-working. A few of the citizens occasionally acquired venison and, although a wide range of wild birds were caught, they were also rare additions to the diet. Marine fish were probably much more widely and commonly consumed by the city's secular and ecclesiastical residents. As Lauritsen (EAPIT 2, Chapter 9) discusses, there are hints that there were some variations in diet and food preparation between different sectors of Exeter's community, but the bone assemblages have provided much less evidence for conspicuous consumption than those from the castles of Okehampton and Launceston.

Manufacturing

Textiles

Considering that the woollen industry was the economic driver of the revival of Exeter's fortunes in the later Middle Ages and the source of employment of most of the city's workforce throughout the later medieval and early modern periods (Youings 1968, 90), direct archaeological evidence for the cloth industry before *c.* 1550 has proved surprisingly elusive. No clothworkers' premises of this date have been excavated, and few examples of textile workers' equipment have been recognised, an exception being a 'harbick' (shearboard hook) from Bartholomew Street West (Site 47; Goodall 1984, 345, M177).

A partial exception to this general picture has been the recent (2018–19) project arising from Cotswold Archaeology's excavation at Frog Street, a site on the edge of the floodplain of the River Exe, outside the West Gate (Site 176). Documentary research arising from the excavation showed that the concentration of dyers' premises along the Higher Leat, evident in the 18th century, had medieval origins. The study highlighted the dyers' practice of renting 'washing bridges' built over the Higher Leat at the back of these tenements, used by the dyers to wash cloths of noxious substances. Since the leat was city property, the bridges and their rents were recorded on the Chamber Map Book of 1758, on which ten such bridges were shown. It seems clear that many of their sites are ancient, since the annual 'movable rents' from ten washing bridges 'over the weir' are listed in the accounts the bailiff of Exe Island of 1493–4 (Allan and Collings 2019).

One more general piece of evidence regarding the rise of the Devon cloth industry should be noted, however: the pronounced change in the age at which sheep were slaughtered. Maltby (1979, 43–7 and above) has shown that there was a dramatic rise in the number of mature sheep and corresponding decline in the number of immature sheep consumed at Exeter in the 16th century compared with the 13th and 14th centuries, and this almost certainly reflects the rise of sheep farming for wool rather than meat.

Bell-founders

Late medieval Exeter was one of the major West Country centres of bell production, alongside Bristol, Gloucester and Salisbury (Scott *et al.* 2007, 66–85). The documented site of the foundry at this time was in Preston Street (in the West Quarter), then sometimes known as Billeter (*i.e.* bell-founder) Lane, and it was on land behind this area that pits producing bell-founding waste were found at Mermaid Yard in 1977–8 (Site 60). Only limited post-excavation work has been carried out on the site and the finds have not been analysed in detail but summary accounts of the discovery have been published (Blaylock 1996, 74; 2015a, 272–4). The principal evidence consists of clay moulds from the production of bells and domestic cauldrons, recovered from pits dug into the site's natural clay, which presumably provided the raw materials for the moulds; no casting pits were located and no structural evidence encountered. The finds included one large core fragment which was provisionally interpreted as evidence of bell-casting in the manner described by Theophilus, described in Chapter 7 (above). The earliest foundry pits contained pottery of the early to mid 13th century, suggesting that the factory had been established before the earliest documented Exeter founder in the late 13th century. The later foundry pits contained few datable finds but a group of late 15th-century ceramics was found in one deposit. Documentary evidence suggests that production continued into the early 16th century (Blaylock 1996, 74; 2015a, 272–4).

The Billeter Lane foundry appears to have been the place where Robert Norton, the city's best-known medieval founder, operated in the period *c.* 1420–60. Norton's bells have been much admired, both for their beauty of tone and for their clean and precise workmanship (Scott *et al.* 2007, 50–1, 69). In a national context his work displayed some progressive features, such as the use of stock legends, and an innovative way of forming the moulding wires which is not fully understood (*ibid.*, 72). An example of Norton's bells is shown in Fig. 8.23 and is described more fully elsewhere (Allan 2003b, 421).

Fig. 8.23 (A) Tenor or 'Jesus' bell cast by the Exeter founder Robert Norton for Halse church, Somerset, c. *1425–50, with (B–C) his founder's marks: (B) A cross; (C) A bell flanked by his initials, within a rope border (© RAMM)*

Much more extensive evidence for the operation of an Exeter foundry was recovered from Cowick Street, a site in St Thomas parish on the floodplain of the River Exe where the Birdall family of bellfounders is first documented in 1525 and where they cast numerous bells in the following century; the foundry closed *c.* 1624 (Blaylock 2000, 4–8). Much of the evidence, therefore, is rather later than the period reviewed in the present chapter, so only an outline will be offered here. The site was the subject of three main phases of excavation (Sites 66, 79, 143–4) – the last fully published (Blaylock 2000), the earlier ones largely unpublished (but see Egan 1985, 182–3; Blaylock 2000; 2015a). Two reverberatory furnaces were found; they clearly employed the technique of building and baking the core *in situ*, then making a clay model of the bell, as described in Biringuccio's 16th-century treatise (Smith and Gnudi 1959).

Huge quantities of foundry waste were found in the backfill of the many claypits dug in a close of land at the rear of the site; a sample of 1.1 tonnes of waste was processed. This material consisted principally of broken clay moulds discarded from the casting of domestic cauldrons and skillets. A simple observation arose from examination of the relative quantities of the moulds for domestic vessels and bells represented: fragments from the manufacture of cauldrons and skillets were far more common than those from bell-casting, suggesting that by the 16th century the former had become the much more significant aspect of the founders' trade. Detailed reconstructions of the forms of vessel produced here have been published by Blaylock (2000, 39; 2015a, 281). Only a single possible surviving example of a domestic vessel cast by the Birdalls has been identified: a posnet (three-footed cooking vessel with a handle) with a VV mark (probably apotropaic), also seen on foundry waste (Butler and Green 2006, cat. no. 4; Blaylock 2015a, 284; Green 2015b, 310).

Other metalworkers

An extraordinary piece of evidence probably reflects the illicit activities of an Exeter goldsmith: two iron coin dies were found in a stone-lined pit at Trichay Street (Site 42), engraved with the designs of the reverses of gold nobles and half-nobles of the period 1351–1413

(Fig. 8.24A–B; Shiel 1984, 253–4). Careful examination of the letter forms showed that they differed from those used in official coinage (Fig. 8.24C–D). They were clearly made for forging gold coins of these high denominations (6s 8d and 3s 4d).

Finds on four sites close to the centre of the city reflect the production of small cast objects, probably of pewter or other lead/tin alloys (*cf.* examples from London: Egan 1996, 83–6). One half of a pair of stone moulds used in slush-casting barrel-shaped objects (perhaps for casting pilgrim badges connected to St Sidwell's well) was recovered from 189–90 High Street in 1933 (Fig. 8.24G; Montgomerie-Nielson 1933, 67, pl. 1; Allan 1984a, 304, no. 55). A sprue-cup with runners, a waste product from casting a row of small objects using the same technique, was found in an early 16th-century context at Goldsmith Street (Allan 1984a, 346, no. 236; Fig. 8.24E). Other examples of stone moulds found at Trichay Street and Queen Street (Sites 42 and 68) were intended for small-scale casting, either of lead/tin objects or items of copper alloy (*ibid.*, 304, nos 53–4).

Evidence for the manufacture of small items of sheet metal was recovered from a 14th-century deposit in a channel of the River Exe at Exe Bridge (Site 56: Brown 2019, 73). The find consisted of small strips of copper-alloy sheet, some pierced at one end, some cut to regular sizes, with shavings of the same material; it attests the making of small domestic objects (Fig. 8.24F). The context from which the find was recovered lay below the site of a shop fronting onto Exe Bridge on the approach to the city's West Gate.

One further piece of physical evidence shows that altogether more sophisticated metalworking was practised at Exeter at the start of the 14th century. The will of Andrew Kilkenny, Dean of Exeter Cathedral, who died in 1301, provides unique detail about the commissioning of a 14th-century monumental brass, including the purchase of its components and the provision of its design (for the text: Lepine and Orme 2003, 171–202). The Purbeck marble slab of his monument survives in the cathedral's chapel of SS Andrew and Katherine but its inlaid brass has been stripped, leaving only its sunken outline as an indent. John Blair's study of the earliest English brasses has shown that this monument, and the adjacent one to Precentor John Drayton (d. 1302), are local work, albeit closely related to contemporary products of the London marblers. He concludes, 'The fact remains that, between 1302 and 1316, craftsmen in Exeter had the technical skill to make sophisticated and complex brasses' (Blair 1987, 162). There are also strong indications that the enormously elaborate 'pompous marble' to Bishop Bitton (d. 1307), formerly in the cathedral, was a further example of this local group (Binski 1987, 77; Blair 1987, 162). A local workshop seems therefore to have been capable of manufacturing one of the most elaborate brasses in England. In the future its output could perhaps be explored further – for example by XRF analysis which might show that the 'brass' shafts of the cathedral sedilia were related to the scraps of brass lettering remaining in the Drayton monument.

Evidence for the other metalworking trades remains to be studied. No analytical work has been conducted on the numerous but unglamorous finds of ironworking waste from Exeter excavations. In this field too there may be potential for examining ironwork embedded in medieval buildings, such as the cathedral's *ferrementa,* some of which can be related to documented smiths such as William and Stephen Crockernwell, who supplied the cathedral with iron nails, bars and a bell clapper in the period 1316–53 but also supplied iron cramps, picks and wedges for repairs at Exe Bridge (Brown 2019, 130; Erskine 1981, 74; 1983, 291).

Glaziers

Documentary evidence uncovered in the course of the present study has thrown new light on the operation of a glazing workshop at Exeter between the late 13th and the late 15th centuries. It has shown that the first documented glazier who worked at the cathedral, Edward le Verrour, was an Exeter citizen leasing property in High Street in the 1280s, and that his successor, Walter le Verrour, lived and presumably operated in a tenement in North Street beside St Kerrian's church (Fig. 8.25; EAPIT 2, Chapter 4). Walter is a celebrated figure in the history of English glass, since he is the first English glazier whose work can be identified nowadays (Marks 1987, 532). Further research showed that his son leased a tenement on the opposite side of North Street (Allan 2020).

The operation of a glazier's workshop in the late 14th-century city was demonstrated by Brooks and Evans (1988), who showed that Robert Lyen, the glazier who made the beautiful late 14th-century glass in the cathedral's east window, was also an Exeter man. They also demonstrated that a glazing workshop operated in Devon in the mid to late 15th century, supplying a number of parish churches including Doddiscombsleigh and Ashton in the Teign valley and Bratton Clovelly in west Devon, as well as the cathedral. Use of the cathedral fabric rolls provides a near-continuous sequence of glaziers supplying the cathedral from 1300 to 1500, many of them demonstrably local people (Allan 2020); it seems probable that they are the source of most of this glass. No archaeological evidence for these glaziers' activities is known from the city, however.

The building trades: masons and lime-burners

The most significant excavated find regarding the building trades has been the early 13th-century limekiln with its associated lime-slaking pits, found at Trichay Street and discussed in detail in EAPIT 2, Chapter 5. It must have been an unpleasant neighbour in the crowded setting of St Pancras parish.

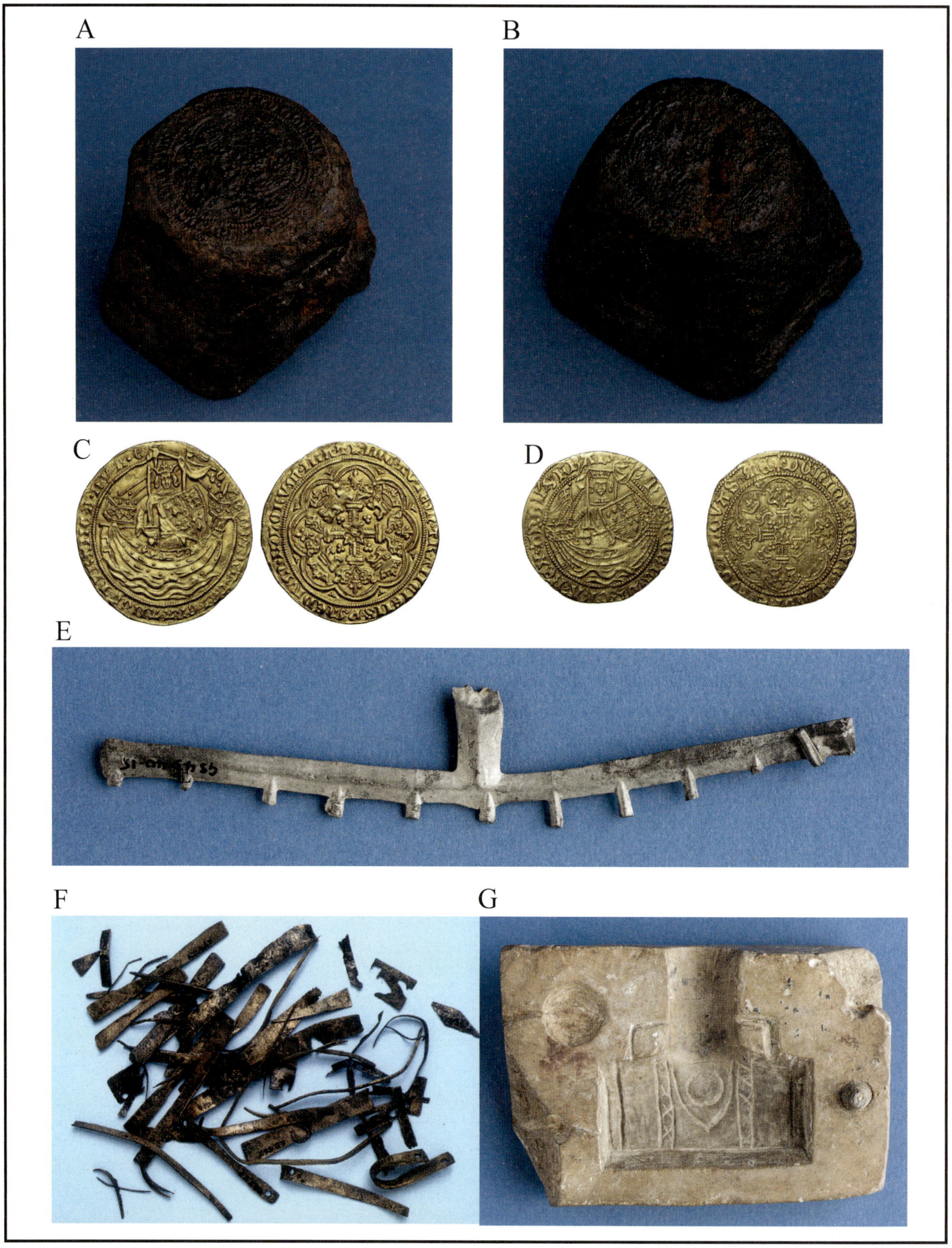

Fig. 8.24 (A–B) Iron dies for striking forged nobles and half-nobles of the period 1351–1413, found in Trichay Street. (C–D) Gold noble and half-noble, showing the coin type imitated by the Exeter forger. (E) Sprue-cup (waste piece) from casting small objects of pewter. (F) Scrap from the production of objects of copper alloy, found at Exe Bridge. (G) A stone mould for casting barrel-shaped objects (photos A–B, E–G © RAMM; C–D (© A.H. Baldwin and Sons)

Fig. 8.25 Examples of work by the Exeter glaziers' workshop from the Great East Window of Exeter Cathedral. (A) By Walter the Glazier, c. *1301–3. (B) Figures by the 'Master of Exeter Cathedral'* c. *1455–65 in earlier canopies (photos: Gary Young; © The Dean & Chapter of Exeter Cathedral)*

No archaeological work has been conducted on the quarries which supplied the city with building stone and roofing slate, although several of them deserve further research. The quarries at Salcombe Regis and Beer, for example, would make excellent subjects for archaeological investigation.

The building trades: carpenters

Surprisingly, carpenters formed the largest sector of the city's building trades in the late 14th century (Kowaleski 1995, 128; the city Murage Tax Roll, for 1377, which records contributions by citizens for work on the city walls, lists 22 carpenters but only seven masons). Some of the leading figures in the trade are known to have worked for long periods for the Dean and Chapter of the cathedral whilst undertaking commissions for other townspeople (Kowaleski 1995, 164–5). It is therefore very likely that the distinctive local group of six 15th-century roofs, five of them surviving in the city with a single outlier at Cadhay in Ottery St Mary parish, represents some of the output of city craftsmen (Fig. 8.26; for a full discussion of the group see Blaylock 2004, 176–89). They reflect a high level of carpentry skill (Fig. 8.26E). Tree-ring studies have shown that the Exeter group spans almost the full 15th century, from about the 1420s until *c.* 1500 (*ibid.*).

Leatherworkers and hornworkers

Kowaleski (1990; 1995, 156–61) has emphasised the prominence of the leather trades in late medieval Exeter, which in the late 14th century accounted for about a sixth of the working population and were among the most prosperous of occupations (Kowaleski 1990; 1995, 156–61). The best physical evidence for the production of leather goods in the medieval city comes from Exe Bridge, where a pair of barrel-lined pits dating from the mid or late 13th century, one of them with laminated residues of lime, almost certainly result from early stages of tanning or tawing, in which skins were soaked in lime to break down hair and fat (Brown 2019, 67–70, 99). A huge collection of horn-cores was recovered from a range of 13th-century deposits at the same site, with a smaller quantity of 14th-century and later material. The question of whether they represent leather- or horn-working is discussed in detail by Levitan (2019, 165–73).

Potters and tile-makers

Petrological analysis of ceramics from Exeter excavations has shown that a pottery industry, principally making decorated wheel-thrown jugs (Exeter fabrics 40 and 42: Allan 1984a), operated close to the city from about

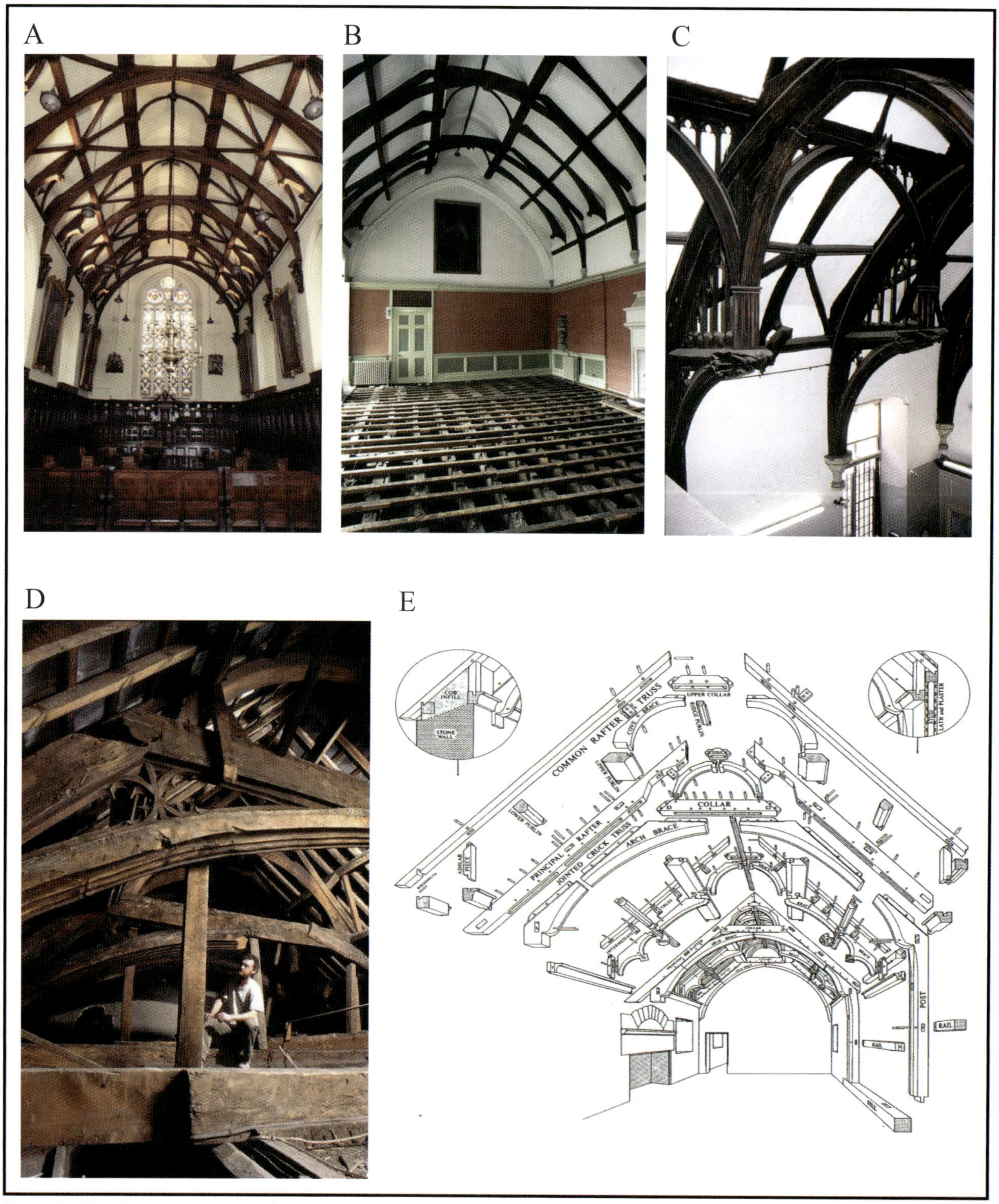

Fig. 8.26 The Exeter group of roofs. (A) Guildhall. (B) The Old Deanery. (C) The Law Library. (D) The Archdeacon of Exeter's house. (E) 'Exploded' view of one of the roofs at Bowhill (drawn by Piran Bishop, reproduced from Blaylock 2004, 152, fig. 7.13; all © Exeter City Council)

the mid 13th to mid or late 15th century, although neither kilns nor wasters have yet been found (EAPIT 2, Chapter 17). Three other ceramic production centres have been found in the city, however. A small kiln with a small circular oven and opposing flues was excavated on the Valiant Soldier site outside the South Gate (Site 44); it produced floor-tiles (some stamped), ridge-tiles and some wheel-thrown pottery, attributable to the early 16th century (Allan 1984a, 242–7). Judging by the wasters, their quality was not high. The finds show several points in common with contemporary kiln waste found at Barnstaple, and it is possible that this represents a short-lived venture by a north Devon potter (Allan and Morris 2017, 317).

A second, potentially more important, find was made by AC Archaeology at 31 Cowick Street (Site 172), where wasters providing clear evidence for the production of early 14th-century tiles of Exeter Series 1 was recovered in a watching brief (for Exeter Series 1: Allan and Keen 1984). The find follows the recovery of a small quantity of medieval floor-tile waste nearby at the Cowick Street foundry site (Allan 2000, 82–3). These two finds are strong indicators that a tilery making inlaid floor-tiles operated close to Cowick Street in the period 1280–1350. Its location on a suburban site, on the floodplain of the Exe where abundant alluvial clays would have been available, would have been very suitable for this purpose. The wasters from an early 16th-century pottery in Goldsmith Street are described below.

Regional trade

The distribution of manufactured goods from Exeter

Kowaleski's (1995) seminal study *Local Markets and Regional Trade in Medieval Exeter* brought together a wide range of documentary evidence for the economic hinterland of Exeter. Archaeology can now make significant contributions to this subject, as the products of Exeter's industries can be identified on a large number of sites across Devon and beyond.

Bells

Bell-founding offers the most complete material evidence for the distribution of one of Exeter's leading late medieval manufactures, since about 280 medieval bells made by the Exeter founders survive today or were documented in the past before they were recast (Scott *et al.* 2007, 77–8). Moreover the tradition of casting bells with inscribed bands which incorporate foundry marks and the symbols and initials of individual founders allows the identification of foundries and individual founders with a confidence which is unusual in the study of medieval artefacts. Figure 8.27A shows the distribution of the Exeter products in the four south-western counties, alongside those of the other foundries represented in Devon. After the 1330s the Exeter foundry was virtually the sole supplier of bells to the churches of Devon (which numbered in total about 500 parish churches and over 1000 chapels) and to Cornwall. It was also the leading supplier to the parishes of west Somerset, but its market range declined sharply in east Somerset, where access to Bristol was easier. Only five Dorset churches, all in the western part of the county, have or had Exeter bells, but they were occasionally marketed beyond the four south-western counties mapped here: Exeter bells survive in Gloucestershire (Brimpsfield), Oxfordshire (Dorchester) and Shropshire (Upton Magna), with four examples on Guernsey (Vale, in St Pierre du Bois) (Scott *et al.* 2007, 77–8). We may note, however, that the map probably shows a mixture of bells cast in the Billeter Lane workshop (see above) with others cast on-site in temporary casting houses set up in the church or churchyard.

The city did not produce all Devon's medieval bells; about 25 examples made by the Bristol founders are known in 18 Devon churches (Fig. 8.27B). Although these are largely in the north of the county, and often near the coast, Bristol bells are occasionally seen in south-east Devon, as at Broadhembury and Woodbury, and there is one example at Luffincott in west Devon, which would have entailed carriage overland of about 45 km if it was carried from the port of Bideford (Scott *et al.* 2007, 77–8). The source of a further group of pre-*c.* 1330 bells is uncertain; they may have been made in London (Fig. 8.27C).

Window glass

A similar picture of a major urban craft operating in Exeter and supplying a sizeable part of South-West England over the later Middle Ages may one day be reconstructed from the evidence for the Exeter glaziers, but far less physical evidence survives, and much work needs to be done, both on the surviving glass and on the associated documentary record, to explore this topic further.

The demand for a regional glazing centre must have been very considerable: the majority of Devon's 500 parish churches have windows in the Perpendicular style, mostly dating between 1400 and 1550, with an average of something like ten windows per church. If we add the windows of the 30 monastic houses in the diocese of Exeter alone, plus hospitals, almshouses, chapels and some secular patrons, there must have been a demand for many thousands of windows. Demand must have been especially high in the period 1450–1550; Mattingly estimates, for example, that 90% of all Cornish churches undertook new building in this century (Mattingly 2005; 2017).

Ceramics

The more humble evidence of the local pottery and tile industry has been examined in more detail in EAPIT 2, Chapter 17 but may be summarised briefly here. The glazed and decorated jugs made in the Exeter area formed only a part of the local ceramics market – around half the vessels at most in any household assemblage. The city itself must have been the potter's most important market by far, but their wares have been found in smaller quantities on sites around the Exe estuary, in east Devon as far to the east as Colyford, and in south Devon places such as Totnes, Buckfast Abbey and Newton Abbot. They are hardly ever seen in mid and north Devon, or on peasant sites on the northern fringes of Dartmoor,

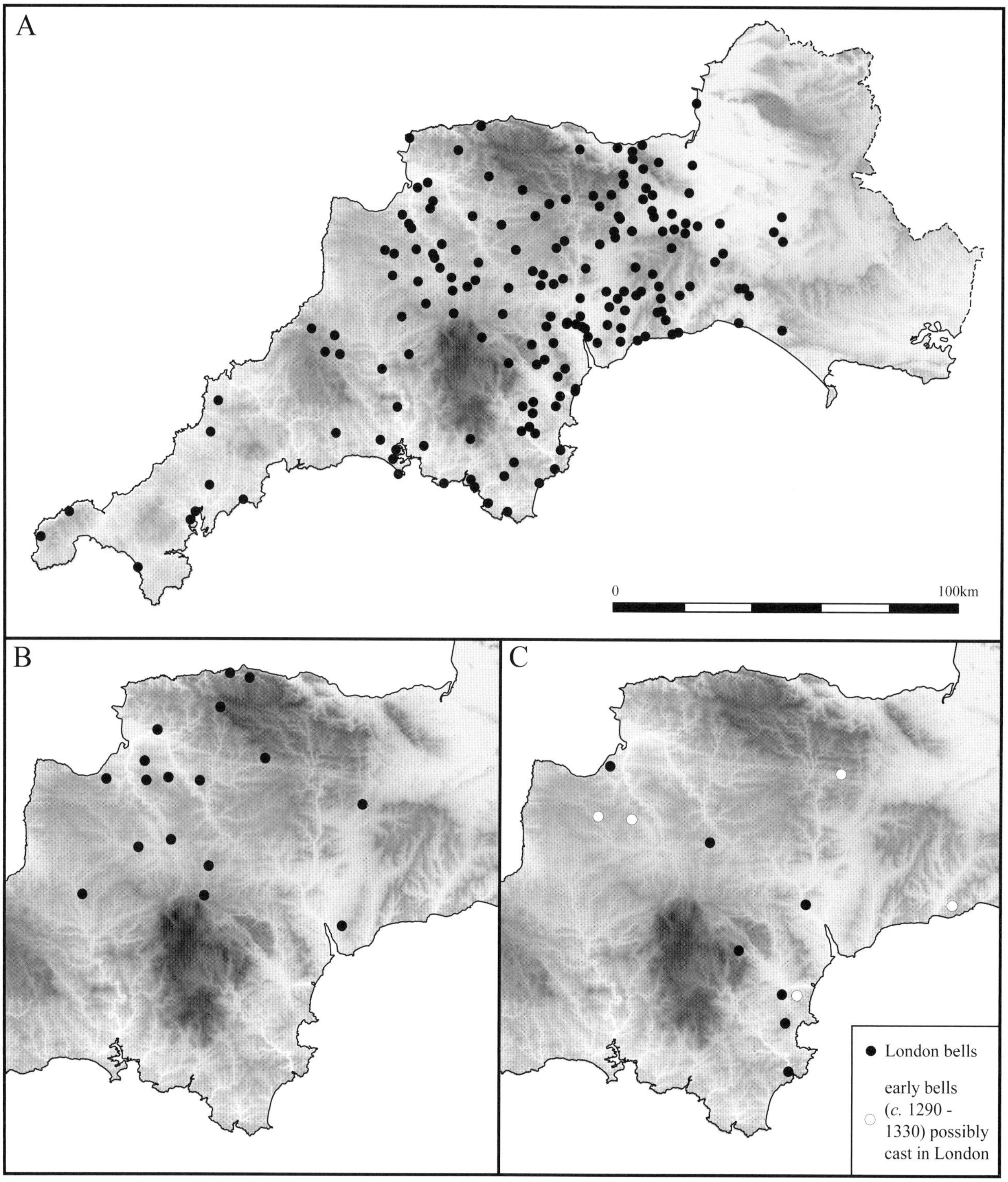

Fig. 8.27 (A) The distribution of Exeter bells, c. *1400–1550. (B) The distribution of Bristol bells in Devon. (C) The distribution of early bells in Devon (*c. *1290–1330), possibly made in London (after Scott* et al. *2007, 77–81; drawn by David Gould)*

where they make up less than 1% of every assemblage. They do, however, feature in the castle assemblages from Okehampton and Launceston, especially the latter, where they may represent goods moving as part of the baggage of aristocratic households. Until recently, Launceston Castle, 68 km to the west of the city, was the most distant findspot known, but recent finds at Truro, and from Tresco Channel on the Isles of Scilly, show that Exeter wares travelled (no doubt by sea) to coastal sites along the entire southern coastline of Cornwall.

The city's market for regional goods

The market in building stone

We have seen that by the late 12th century there was a highly developed market for building stone in Exeter: a mason working in the Late Norman city could choose from a dozen different stone types with a wide range of properties (above). At the cathedral, the city's most prestigious building project, the range of stone types increased a little in the 13th and early 14th centuries, with the introduction of a few specialist materials, such as Ham stone from south Somerset, employed occasionally for roof bosses and steps (Pounds 1990; Allan 1991). Before *c.* 1350, however, the great majority of building work in the city was undertaken in local volcanic trap, sometimes with Salcombe stone dressings.

In the course of the 14th century there were major changes in the market in building stone in the city. First, Beer stone rose quickly in popularity in the period *c.* 1310–50, supplanting Salcombe stone as the cathedral's most favoured material for carved work, and eclipsing the other limestones from Portland and Caen. From the late 14th century, Beer became by far the most popular source of freestone used in south Devon for windows, arcades, doorways and other carved work. It is seen in high-quality secular buildings, where, however, volcanic stone dressings also continued to be popular. Beer stone is a fine-grained white chalk, very suitable for elaborate carving, and its rise can be seen as the success of a beautiful, higher-quality material.

The mid 14th century saw a more fundamental change in stone building in the city: the introduction and rapid rise of Heavitree stone, a red Permian breccia quarried not only at Heavitree and Whipton, now in the city's suburbs, but also at Exminster, to the south of the Exe Estuary. In contrast to volcanic stone, this could be quarried in large blocks which could be dressed to form ashlar walls. Nowadays this material has a poor reputation because it commonly weathers badly after hundreds of years of exposure to Devon's wet weather, but when newly laid this too must have seemed a great advance on the rough angular rubble of most buildings in volcanic trap. The change to Heavitree stone is in fact part of a general rise in building standards over most of Devon and Cornwall in the period *c.* 1350–1450/1500 which saw the use of higher-quality materials suitable for ashlar, such as granite in Cornwall and Dartmoor, and slates and red sandstone in the South Hams. This must have entailed more effort, both in dressing stone and in longer-distance transport.

The market in timber

A large number of timbers from archaeological excavations and standing structures have been dated through dendrochronological analysis, and this sheds light on the sources of the timber (EAPIT 2, Chapter 11). Documentary evidence indicated that much of the timber used in Exeter Cathedral and other buildings within the city was from woodland in Devon, generally close to Exeter (Erskine 1981; 1983; Juddery and Staniforth 1986; Mills 1988), and the dendrochronological evidence supports this. Documentary evidence also shows that as early as the 12th century there was significant importation of European timber into England (*e.g.* Salzman 1952; Dollinger 1970; Kent 1973; Fedorowicz 1980; Clarke 1992), although in Exeter the earliest evidence is in the form of 14th-century vertical oak boards from the Cathedral Song School door and the *c.* 1500 oak ceiling boards at Bowhill that have been identified as of Baltic origin (Groves 2004; Hurford *et al.* 2009). Documentary evidence also shows that there were strong links between the South-West Peninsula and Ireland, such as the Exeter Cathedral accounts which record the use of boards from Ireland (and Wales) in the early 14th century (Erskine 1981, 87, 89, 138). The possible presence of Irish timber at Trichay Street, first suggested by Hillam (1978; 1984a) has been re-assessed by Tyers (EAPIT 2, Chapter 11), who concludes that at least some of these timbers – dating to the late 12th and 13th centuries – are likely to be of Irish origin, probably from the south and east of the island.

The market in roofing materials

The slate roofs of medieval Exeter were quarried from at least five geological formations. The most popular was the Nordon Slate Formation which runs in a band from the Totnes area westward to Plymouth and accounts for about 60% of the large sample from excavations in Exeter (Allan 1984a, 300–1). A second major source, represented by about one third of the same sample, came from the Gurrington Formation, which were quarried around Ashburton and Buckfastleigh. Slates from the Meadfoot Formation, which were worked on a large scale around the Salcombe estuary and could be shipped by coast to Exeter, are surprisingly uncommon in the city (*ibid.*, 300). The sources favoured in the medieval period are different from those in Roman deposits in the city, in which Kate Brook slates are the most common (50% of the collection), followed by White Lias (18%) and Nordon slates (13%: Holbrook and Bidwell 1991, 282).

The ceramics market

The different strands in the ceramics trades are described more fully in EAPIT 2, Chapters 17–18 so will be summarised only briefly here. The central feature of the pottery market at the start of the 13th century was the dominance of wares from the fringes of the Blackdown Hills and south Somerset (the Upper Greensand-Derived wares). With the rise of a market for glazed jugs, however, Exeter householders turned to a range of other sources: the London area (represented by about 20 finds), south Dorset, and occasionally Bristol and south Hampshire. Most of this material will presumably have come to Exeter by coastal trade, and the Dorset and London wares especially have a distinct coastal distribution pattern across the South-West. In the mid 13th century the rise of a local centre making glazed jugs brought an end to the importation of these distant items, but south Somerset continued to supply coarse unglazed cooking pots ('jars') until they were superseded by metal vessels in the 14th century. Cornish wares and north Devon products are both rare in the city. The most distant English wares represented in the Exeter collection are highly decorated jugs from Nottingham, Lincoln and Scarborough. After about 1350, the local potteries and south Somerset account for more than 95% of the city's English pottery. The local industry seems to have closed around the mid 15th century.

Imported goods

The operation of both the foreign and the coastal trade of the port of Exeter is richly documented since its customs accounts survive from as early as the 1260s (Kowaleski 1993). Kowaleski has shown that the port's trade was dominated by coastal shipping; most foreign goods arrived as transhipments from Southampton, Dartmouth and Plymouth, all of which had 'better harbours and more valuable exports to lure vessels directly from continental ports' (*ibid.*, 24). In the early 14th century wine accounted for fully half the cargoes arriving in the port, followed by fish, grain, woad and iron (*ibid*). The trade of late medieval and Tudor Exeter focused on three main areas: Gascony, Normandy and Brittany (*ibid.;* Childs 1992; MacCaffrey 1958; Stephens 1958).

Trade with northern France

Exeter's prominent position in the trade in north French pottery before 1200 has been described in Chapter 7 above, and it is now clear that many or most of these wares came from the Lower Seine valley. With the rise in demand for ceramic tablewares in the late 12th and early 13th centuries, there is a marked increase in the range of sites on which pottery from Normandy is recorded in the region, extending to high-status inland places, especially castles and monastic sites, such as Sherborne Old Castle (Dorset), Glastonbury Abbey (Somerset) and Launceston Castle (Cornwall); nevertheless the finds from Exeter remain much the largest series of such finds in the region (EAPIT 2, Chapter 17).

The picture changes with the rise of the trade in Saintonge pottery, produced in south-western France, from *c.* 1250 which soon brought a sharp decline in the trade in north French pottery. In the late 13th and early 14th centuries documentary evidence records the importation of very large quantities of window glass from Rouen, both white and coloured, for use at the cathedral (Erskine 1981, 98), but the source of the glass now surviving there has not been determined.

North French ceramics re-emerge in Exeter households in the late 15th and early 16th centuries with the arrival of decorated tableware from the Beauvais region, flasks from Martincamp, and white ware floor-tiles, probably from the Lower Seine Valley around Rouen. The distribution of these wares in the region is shown in EAPIT 2, Chapter 17, Fig. 17.19. Some of these products, notably the Beauvais sgraffito wares, are very widely distributed elsewhere in the British Isles (*e.g.* Haggarty 2019, recording these wares along the coast of Scotland). Others, however, show a specific concentration in South-West England. The national distribution of plain white ware floor-tiles shows a pronounced concentration in south Devon, where there are many more finds than in all other parts of the British Isles combined (EAPIT 2, Chapter 17, Fig. 17.34).

The presence in Devon of a group of wooden furnishings which probably reflect the county's late medieval import trade with northern France may also be highlighted here. Crediton church preserves one of the four published examples in England of the richly carved gothic chests made in northern France in the early 16th century with their characteristic panels of flamboyant tracery (Fig. 8.28A; Tracy 2001, 146). It had been on a local farm before being refurbished and donated to the parish church in the 1880s and therefore appears not to have arrived in Devon in the recent past (contra *ibid.*, 146; information at the church). These chests are currently believed to have been made in Normandy, although Christopher Pickvance has emphasised the uncertainty about the specific region where these chests were made and the need for a thorough study (pers. comm. to the writer, 2014).

Since these objects are rare in England, the evidence that further examples of such chests were once in Devon should be noted. A second example was recorded in Exeter Cathedral at the end of the 18th century, although lost subsequently (Fig. 8.28C–D, from Carter MS, BL 29931, f.142), and reused panels of similar gothic tracery, perhaps from further chests of this type, may be seen in the Devon churches of Christow (reused in the pulpit) and Widecombe-in-the-Moor. A final example, now in Holcombe Burnell church close to Exeter and formerly in the neighbouring manor house, is in the same style (Fig. 8.28B), although it has yet to be the subject of detailed examination (Charles Tracy is doubtful about its authenticity: pers. comm. following a visit with the writer in 2017; Christopher Pickvance notes the absence of the lock-plate seen in other chests of this style: pers comm. to the writer, 2019).

Trade with Brittany

Although Exeter had long-standing commercial links with many Breton ports, large and small (Touchard 1967), the archaeological evidence for Breton trade is slight. The examples of ceramics which almost certainly come from Brittany are discussed in EAPIT 2, Chapter 17. Although no specific source can be offered, they are of considerable interest, since they are the largest group of such wares recognised in the British Isles. The examples of late medieval or early 16th-century Breton-style woodwork in Exeter and the surrounding countryside are seen here as the work of immigrant Breton craftsmen rather than imported goods (see 'Ethnicity' below).

Trade with south-west France

A distribution of finds of Saintonge wares in the region is shown in EAPIT 2, Chapter 17, Fig. 17.28. In the late 13th and early 14th centuries the places with the highest proportions of such imports were the new port of Plymouth and the outlying sites on the Isles of Scilly. The quantities at Plymouth are especially impressive: Saintonge wares make up between 25% and 69% of sherds in the major stratified groups recovered from the town, with a number of instances where they form rather less than half the total (figures in Allan 1983b, 193–6; 1994, 46). These are even higher figures than those in the celebrated Southampton collections.

Throughout the British Isles the quantities of imported Saintonge pottery decline sharply outside the ports, and Exeter's noticeably lower proportions of Saintonge wares – about 10–15% of most major groups in the period 1280–1350 (Allan 1983b; 1994) – is likely to reflect the city's distance from the quayside at Topsham and the fact that its economy relied more on its role as a regional market than on foreign trade (Kowaleski 1995, *passim*). Further inland, the quantities of Saintonge imports fall more rapidly, to 1–3% at inland ecclesiastic sites and towns. They are unknown on the peasant sites around the fringes of Dartmoor and on farms in north and west Devon (Allan 1983b, 193–6; 1994).

One other unusual form of evidence which may also reflect the wine trade may be mentioned here. Four examples of medieval pits lined with casks have been recorded in the city. In the first three, from Goldsmith Street and High Street, a single cask was employed after the removal of its heads (Allan 1984a, 312). In the fourth instance, from Paul Street (Site 76), two casks had been placed one above the other to line a deeper well; the lower example was especially well preserved (Fig. 8.29). In each case most of the exterior of the staves was tightly bound with withies, suggesting that they were intended to be watertight and thus suitable for the carriage of liquids including wine. No analytical work has been carried out to seek for traces of the fluids stored in them.

Trade with the Low Countries and northern Europe

A significant feature of the pottery collections of Exeter and other sites in Devon and Cornwall is the striking rarity of stonewares dating before *c.* 1450, notably those from Langerwehe and Siegburg, which form the most abundant archaeological evidence for later medieval trade with the Low Countries elsewhere in England. It is only with the arrival of Raeren-type stonewares in the mid and late 15th century that the market in stoneware develops. This pattern is fundamentally different from that seen in the ports of the eastern coast of England and Scotland, where the market for stoneware was well established in the 14th century and grew markedly through the 15th (*e.g.* Vince 1985; Evans 2019; Haggarty 2019). This distinction surely reflects the fundamentally different direction of Exeter's trade, which was with Normandy, Brittany, south-west France and Iberia, a pattern which continued into the mid 17th century (Stephens 1958; Childs 1992).

The late 15th century saw a major change in the pottery trade at Exeter: stonewares rapidly became the principal class of imported ceramics in the city, and they remained so into the early 18th century. The documentary evidence shows that this change does not reflect a significant reorientation of the city's trading pattern but the development of an indirect trade via London; in the late 16th century fully 90% of the Rhenish stonewares arriving at Exeter had come by indirect trade through the capital (Allan 1983a, 37–40; 1984, 113–26). The scale of the trade was impressive: fragments of more than 500 stoneware vessels dating before 1550 have been recovered (Allan 1984, 103 for more than 333 examples recorded by 1980). Documentary evidence shows that more than one million stoneware pots arrived in the port of Exeter over the post-medieval period (*ibid.*, 125–6).

One other form of physical evidence for the north European trades may be mentioned here. The cathedral fabric rolls record the purchase of 'Riga boards' and 'Estrigge boards' [Baltic oak] in the early 15th century; the 'Dutch wainscot' they also mention was probably the same material, imported through the Low Countries (Bishop and Prideaux 1922, 98–9). Two verified instances of the trade in Baltic oak have arisen from dendrochronological analysis in Exeter. First, a group of 60 boards from the parlour ceiling at Bowhill proved to be entirely of Baltic oak dating from *c.* 1500; they have been described as 'the largest single-phase Baltic assemblage analysed from an archaeological or historic building context, but also from the farthest point west in England' (Groves 2004, 243, 266–7). Second, analysis of the boards forming the door to the cathedral Song School (Hurford *et al.* 2009) showed that the close-grained timbers used for the door's vertical face boards were imported from the Baltic, felled shortly after 1356, whilst the rapidly grown timbers of the inner face are locally sourced. The same pattern of using close-grained high-quality (?Baltic) wood for the facing boards can be seen in at least two other pairs of 15th-century doors at the cathedral (the 'Brewer door' and Chapter House west doors) but these have not been analysed.

Trade with Spain and Portugal

The ceramic evidence for trade with Iberia is discussed fully by Gutiérrez (EAPIT 2, Chapter 18). Briefly, the earliest of the Exeter finds, from late 13th-century deposits, are among the first known in the British Isles, but there are few examples before *c.* 1450. From the mid

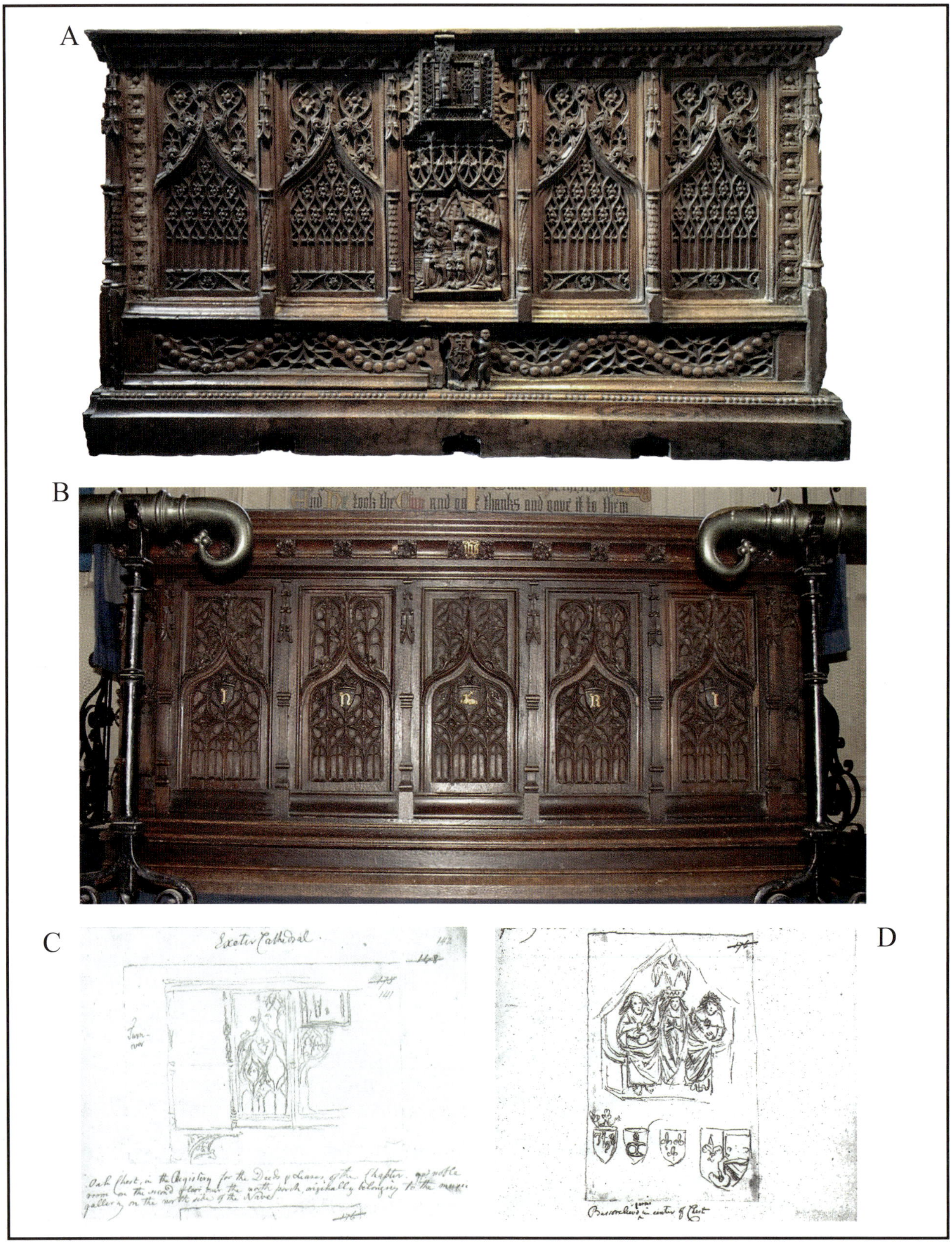

Fig. 8.28 Chests in north French style in the Exeter area, possibly imported from Normandy in the early 16th century. (A) The Crediton chest. (B) Chest now used as the altar table at Holcombe Burnell. (C–D) Sketches by John Carter of a chest in north French style, formerly at Exeter Cathedral (photos A–B © John Allan; C–D BL 29931, f. 142; © the British Library)

Fig. 8.29 A 13th-century cask, reused as the lining of a well, excavated in Paul Street (Site 76), with a detail of its bindings (Exeter Archaeology Archive; © Exeter City Council)

15th century, however, the number of finds increases markedly, and by the early 16th century Spanish pottery had become a common feature of Exeter households, the Morisco wares from Seville being especially numerous. Most household assemblages of *c.* 1500–50 contain a few examples of Spanish tablewares. In the 16th and 17th centuries, however, quantities are far smaller than at Plymouth, and the proportions probably lower than at Dartmouth and Totnes (for a regional survey: Allan 1995).

The possibility that a few pieces of imported glass from Exeter may be of Spanish origin may also be noted here. Robert Charleston raised this possibility in publishing a fine green glass flask, probably of 15th or 16th-century date, from Trichay Street whose form is reminiscent of Islamic glass (Fig. 8.30C; Charleston 1984, 271, G94). It belongs to a group of vessels recently reviewed by Tyson (2019, 37–9, 'glasses with bulges in the neck'), who suggests that either southern Spain or the Middle East are the most likely source.

Trade with Italy

The ceramic evidence for the city's trade with Italy is discussed fully by Blake in EAPIT 2, Chapter 18. It amounts to a total of a dozen vessels of the period 1480–1550. The regional context of these wares has been discussed by Allan (2015), who has shown that these early finds are relatively uncommon in the South-West Peninsula, but that the region became a major importer of Italian ceramics in the period 1570–1630. In considering these modest totals, however, it should be borne in mind that the city's excavated sample of imported ceramics can be estimated to be about 0.1% of the vessels imported (Allan 1984a, 125–6); these finds, therefore, are likely to represent something like 10,000 Italian vessels imported into the city before 1550.

The city's finds of Italian/Venetian glass present a similar picture of relatively low levels of consumption before 1500. About five glass vessels of late 13th and 14th-century date from excavations in the city are probably Italian, some of them possibly from Venice (Fig. 8.30A–B: Charleston 1984, 265–6, G1, G38, G43, G45). The finds become rather more numerous after 1500; there were, for example, five Italian pieces in a single early 16th-century pit on Goldsmith Street (*ibid.*, 268, G49–G53), and at least a dozen such vessels from other contexts (*ibid.*; Willmott 2015, 324–5). They have been reviewed by Willmott (2015) in his survey of the region's vessel glass; he points out that although Exeter has produced the most important collections of such material in the region, the number of vessels is actually relatively modest, and Italian products always make up a small fraction of the total assemblage of glass in every context in the city. For example, there were only two or perhaps three Italian pieces among more than 50 glass vessels of *c.* 1500–30 recovered from Paul Street (*ibid.*).

Since the excavated evidence for the Italian trades is limited, other forms of material evidence reflecting trade in more valuable commodities may be noted. As his will shows, John Grandisson, Bishop of Exeter (1327–69) possessed Italian textiles, and one of them – the Baltimore altar frontal – survives (King 1987, 61; Stratford 1991, 148–9). They were very probably used in Exeter cathedral. Moreover, the textiles he commissioned in England show clear signs of artistic links to Italy, presumably reflecting the imitation of imported Italian textiles (King 1987, 61; Stratford 1991, 148–9). At the more humble level of the city's churches, the two examples of late 15th or early 16th-century vestments surviving from the city's parish churches (the St Petrock's and Mary Arches palls) incorporate pieces of cloth of silk, blue velvet and cloth of gold, all of Italian origin. Before the Reformation many Exeter churches had several such costly textiles, as the Edwardian inventories of the city illustrate (Cresswell 1916).

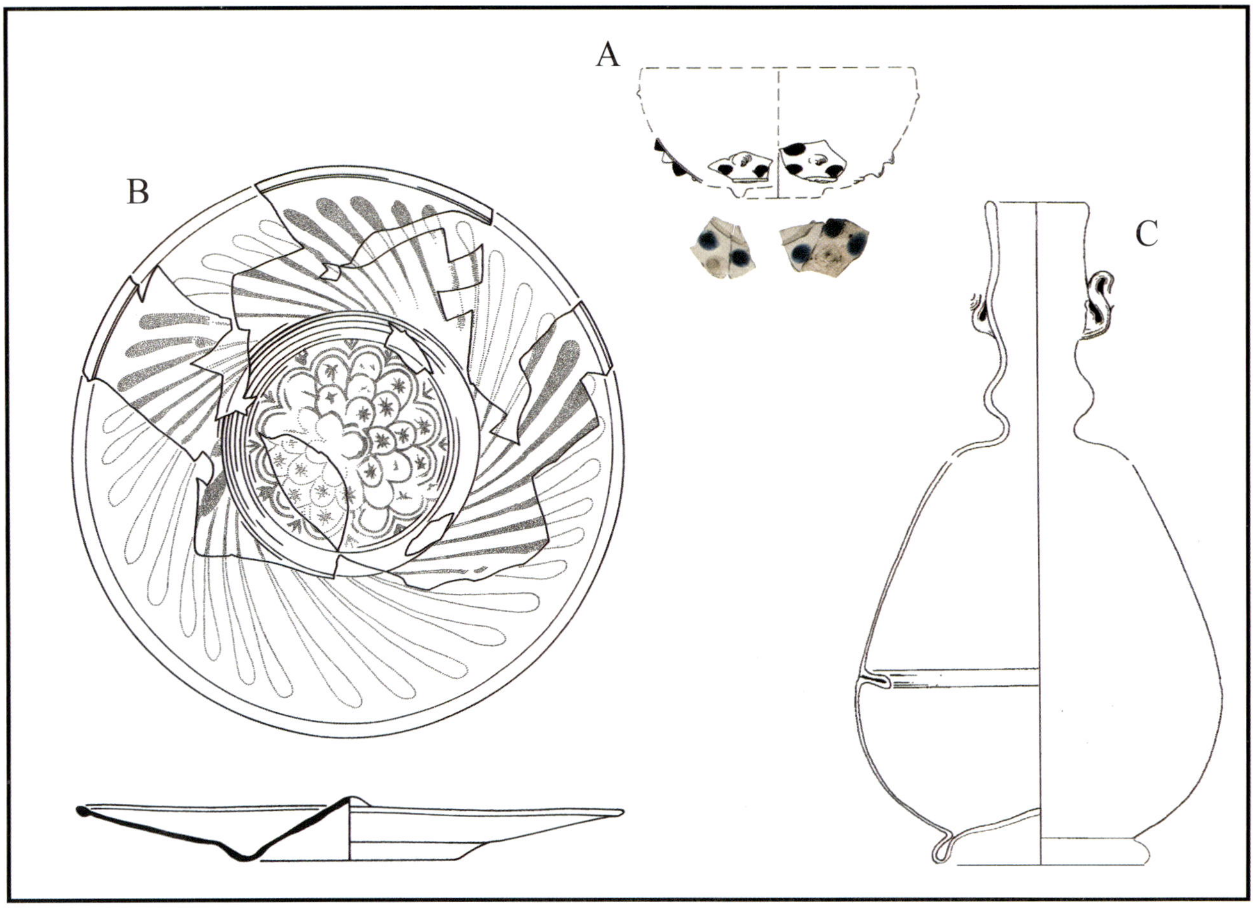

Fig. 8.30 Imported glass at Exeter. (A) Fragments of an early 14th-century bowl from Goldsmith Street, possibly from Venice. (B) Blue glass dish from Paul Street with the ghost of gilded enamelled decoration, probably Venetian. (C) Flask from Trichay Street, perhaps Spanish. Scale 1:3 (line drawings: A, C John Allan, B Jane Read; photo © RAMM)

The evidence for the importation of Italian paper may also be noted. In his study of the earliest examples of paper surviving in the Exeter Cathedral Library and Archive, Jessie Lynch has found that the cathedral adopted the use of Italian paper at a surprisingly early date – by the 1320s – and was certainly using paper from the celebrated north Italian centre of paper-making at Fabriano by the late 14th century. The city adopted the use of paper in the 15th century (Lynch pers. comm., Nov. 2019).

A chest surviving in a north Devon church may illustrate the occasional importation of Italian furniture into the county in the 16th century, although the object and its history have not yet been researched. Tracy (2001, 142–5) published the group of six early 16th-century chests of cypress wood known from sites scattered across England whose source is thought to be North Italian (possibly Venetian); they are believed to have been used as vestment chests. An unpublished chest in Tawstock church, in north Devon, has the characteristic 'woodcut-type' technique of this group, in which the backgrounds to the figures were originally infilled with gesso (white pigment), with added detail in penwork. This is therefore a possible example of this class of object, perhaps reflecting the patronage of the wealthy Bourchier family of the adjacent Tawstock Court. The subject is currently undergoing fresh research. Examples of the type found in Britain appear to span the period from *c.* 1470 until *c.* 1630, and a distinct group found in South-West England belonging to the latter part of this period was probably made in Portugal (Humphrey 2018).

Ethnicity: two case studies

Late medieval Exeter had a substantial immigrant population. As Kowaleski has shown, about 100 strangers were listed in the city in the Alien Subsidy for Devon of 1440 – a smaller total than in some of the other south coast ports such as Sandwich (where there were about 200) and appreciably smaller than Bristol's 701 people, but much the largest such community in South-West England (Kowaleski 2017a; 2017b, 167–8). They came principally from Normandy, Guernsey, France and the Low Countries, with smaller groups of Irish, Bretons and Gascons (*idem.* 2017b, 168). Among them were specialist craftsmen: goldsmiths from France, Prussia and Zealand, glaziers from Brabant, Frisia and Saxony, and an organ-maker from the Low Countries. An appreciable number of these people became freemen of the city, and some took up political office; they seem generally to have been assimilated into the city's life without conflict. Other parts of Devon also saw the arrival of aliens at this time: some 583 were listed elsewhere in Devon, about half of them from Normandy (*ibid.*).

The city's community of strangers seems to have been at least as large in the early 16th century. The fullest record of their numbers, occupations and origins at this time is the Military Survey of 1522, with 89 aliens forming 6.5% of the 1363 people listed in the survey (Rowe 1977, xi, 7–33; Allan 2014, 322; these figures, however, seem to exclude Channel Islanders, who had made up almost a quarter of their number in 1440). Where known, the origins of these people were slightly different from those of the mid 15th century, the most numerous being Bretons, Normans and French in that order, with others from Holland and Flanders, and more distant individuals from Hesse, Cologne, Cleves, Lucca and Lombardy. Among them were shoemakers, hatmakers, a capper, a bookbinder and a carver (Allan 2014). They formed the largest community of immigrants in Devon and Cornwall, but the Lay Subsidies of 1524–7 listed over 400 immigrants elsewhere in the two counties (*ibid*).

Although no evidence for alien households has been recognised in the city's fine assemblages of late medieval and early 16th-century household goods, one archaeological find and one piece of architectural evidence are interpreted as evidence of these immigrant groups. They are of some interest because the identification of immigrant households in medieval and early modern towns in England on archaeological evidence has often proved difficult.

Low Countries potters

In 1972 two pits filled with about 50 kg of wasters of red earthenware were excavated at the rear of a tenement in Goldsmith Street (Site 39; Allan 1984a, 154–9). These finds indicate pottery production in or close to Goldsmith Street, a location surprisingly near the city centre. They are datable to the early 16th century by their association with Raeren stonewares and local wares of that period. The character of the collection will be seen in Fig. 8.31. In almost every regard the forms and techniques of these vessels differ from the pottery produced at this time in the other potteries of South-West England. A far wider range of vessel forms is evident – not only those which were adopted at this time all over the region, such as cups and chafing dishes, but plates, flasks, candlesticks, slipware bowls, tall jars and rectangular dishes. Some of these forms are otherwise unattested in local pottery until the early 17th century. The vessel forms do, however, correspond to those used in the production of red earthenware throughout much of the Low Countries. They include tripod-footed cooking pots with rilled bodies imitating metal forms (Fig. 8.31) which correspond to the *grapen* of the Low Countries, and slipware bowls with broad rims and pulled feet, also closely paralleled in the same tradition (*cf. e.g.* Baart 1994). Specific details such as pulled or pod feet, horizontal rod handles, bands of applied thumbing at the neck, and broad bowl mouths also belong to the Low Countries tradition. For example, van der Leeuw's technical study of the Haarlem pottery illustrated the practice of pinching the base of a pot prior to the application of a pod foot (van der Leeuw 1975); precisely the same feature can be seen on the Goldsmith Street pottery, but it is unknown on other examples of South-West English ceramics. Again, the Low Countries practice of double-firing slipware contrasted with single firing in South-West England; the Goldsmith Street wasters were double-fired.

Are these the work of immigrant potters from the Low Countries or local copies of foreign fashions? The employment not just of the shapes of Low Countries pottery but of specific techniques used there points to the former interpretation. The belief that these wares were made by an immigrant potter is also encouraged by some documentary evidence. The excavated site lies in the parish of St Paul, Goldsmith Street. The Military Survey of 1522 lists three Low Countries immigrants in the parish: Peter Schere born in Holland, Garrett Growning (from Gröningen?) born in Friesland, and James Selond (from Zealand?) a Flemish servant (Rowe 1977, 13).

Since examples of the pottery made in Goldsmith Street have rarely been found outside the tenement in which the wasters were recovered, this was probably a short-lived venture, and there is no sign that other local potteries adopted the new vessel forms and decorative styles introduced there. In a regional context, then, this seems to have been an isolated instance of the operation of a foreign pottery in the 16th century. In a national setting, however, this is an example of a wider phenomenon. The most plentiful evidence comes from London, where pottery in the style of Low Countries redwares forms a considerable proportion of early 16th-century ceramics assemblages (for an overview: Nenk 1999, 243). For example, the late 15th-century and early 16th-century redware wasters from Ferry Approach in Woolwich, London, share many points in common with the Goldsmith Street finds from Exeter, including slipped bowls with pulled feet and horizontal handles and pipkins, costrels, dripping pans and chafing dishes (Pryor and Blockley 1978, 44–9, 83–4), and the same features are seen in the large assemblages of the same date from Guy's Hospital, in London (Dawson 1979). Later 16th-century documentary evidence records Dutch potters at Greenwich, some of them probably redware potters (Edwards 1974, 6). Other instances of immigrant potters working in southern England in the

Fig. 8.31 Early 16th-century pottery wasters from Goldsmith Street, interpreted as evidence of potters from the Low Countries operating in the city (photos by Gary Young; © RAMM)

early 16th century include the pottery at Lower Parrock, in East Sussex, whose potter probably came from the Beauvaisis of northern France (Freke 1979, esp. 86–7).

Breton woodworkers: King John's Tavern

In the later Middle Ages a highly distinctive form of town house evolved in Morlaix, the town on the northern coast of Brittany which was a major trading partner of the Devon ports. It had three components: a stack of rooms on the street frontage, a tall hall behind the front rooms which was open from the ground to the roof, and a further stack of rooms at the rear (Fig. 8.32A). The defining feature of houses of this type, which gives this house type its name – the *maison à pondalez* (*cf. ponts d'aller)* – is the series of superimposed timber galleries running along one side of the hall, linking the front and rear rooms. The galleries were served by a spiral stair rising from the front of the hall, typically with rich linenfold carving and a standing figure on the ground floor; a grand fireplace of granite in the opposing wall is a further characteristic feature.

The remarkably rich collection of timber-framed houses in Morlaix has been studied by Daniel Leloup, who showed that this form of house is specific to the town; when he wrote in the 1990s only a single atypical example was known elsewhere in Brittany. He argued that the house type was designed to serve the minor nobility who traded in Morlaix; the hall provided a grand ceremonial setting for wealthy families – the urban equivalent to the *salle manoriale* of the rural manor house (Leloup 1996; 2002). King John's Tavern, a house which stood in South Street prior to its demolition in 1834 has, however, recently been as identified as an example of a *maison à pondalez* in Exeter (Allan 2014). If this is accepted, it is the only example of this house form recognised so far in England. Much is known about this building despite the early date of its demolition, since its ornate frontage, and the hall with its carved wooden staircase and galleries, attracted the attention of local artists; some of its carved wooden figure sculptures have been preserved and have recently been recognised in the collections of the Metropolitan Museum of New York (*ibid.*). The hall is shown in Fig. 8.32B; it had galleries on two floors, with evidence of a further gallery on the floor above. The form of the stairs and gallery define this as a *maison à pondalez*, and the decoration of linenfold panelling and figure sculpture are closely comparable to examples in Morlaix (*e.g.* Figs 8.32B–C). The frontage likewise shows various features which can be related closely to Morlaix houses, including the figure sculpture, the use of spiral-decorated and pellet-decorated shafts, the arrangement of the beams between the floors and the form of the bracing (Fig. 8.33; details in Allan 2014). Some of the constructional features of King John's Tavern, such as the manner in which the galleries were engaged with the stair, are different from those seen in Morlaix houses of *c.* 1500 but match the many houses surviving in the town centre which were built after the English sack of the town in 1522; a date in or close to the 1520s is probable (*ibid.*).

How might a Morlaix house have been built in Exeter? Whilst portable objects such as chests and panels might have been imported from Brittany, it is highly unlikely that the major structural components of a house were transported for assembly in Exeter, and almost certain that the house would have been constructed on site by immigrant craftsmen from Morlaix (*ibid.*, *cf.* Tracy 1999, 97–100).

There is clear evidence for the activities of other Breton woodworkers elsewhere in rural Devon at this time. The wooden screens in three mid-Devon churches (Coldridge, Colebrooke and Brushford) have long been recognised as examples of the *dentelle* (lacework) style of woodwork which is unique to Brittany (Allan 2014, 331–9). Both stylistic and constructional features which match continental practice and differ from local Devon fashions have been recognised in about twenty early 16th-century works in churches and houses in Devon (mainly in south Devon), and a case has been made for believing that these too are also works of continental craftsmen, although it is more difficult to establish whether they were from Brittany, Normandy or the Low Countries (*ibid.*, 339–49). This body of work consists of church screens, pulpits and other furniture, and domestic panelling and furniture. Documentary evidence records the presence of both Breton and Dutch carvers working in Devon and Cornwall at this time, and it is clear that many of the men practising the craft here were foreigners.

Conclusion

The introduction to this chapter drew attention to the relatively poor survival of stratified medieval deposits in much of Exeter. This is in fact a regional phenomenon arising from the hillslope topography of many towns, large and small, in Devon and Cornwall; the same could be said of the archaeology of Totnes, Plymouth, Bideford and most Cornish towns. This can give the impression that the region's urban archaeology is less rewarding than that of low-lying towns in central and eastern England.

On the other hand, Exeter offers particular opportunities to the student of the English medieval town. First, the same physical character of the region is particularly suitable ground for some forms of archaeological study. The varied geology of the area surrounding Exeter makes it an especially interesting place to examine the complexities in the market in building stone, for example. No fewer than 15 different sources of building stones and six or seven different types of roofing material are represented in the city's medieval buildings, and they changed over time with changes in building practice. The complexities and distinctive features of the local geology can also bring particularly successful results

Fig. 8.32 (A) A maison à pondalez in *Morlaix (drawn by Jean-François Guével; courtesy of the Musée de Morlaix, Morlaix). (B) Edward Ashworth's drawing of the gallery and stairs of King John's Tavern, Exeter (© Devon and Exeter Institution). (C) The gallery and stairs of Anne of Brittany's house, Morlaix (© John Allan)*

Fig. 8.33 (A) Ashworth's reconstruction drawing showing the original form of the frontage of King John's Tavern (© Devon & Exeter Institution). (B) Houses of the 1520s in the Grand'rue, Morlaix (© John Allan)

in petrological analysis of ceramics of all periods, especially when undertaken by experienced local fieldworkers, as Roger Taylor's work has shown (EAPIT 2, Chapter 17). The many analyses undertaken by Michael Hughes on sites in South-West England using ICP and ICP-MS offer the prospect of developing a regional mapping of the chemistry of pottery fabrics which shows particularly promising results in a national context (EAPIT 2, Chapter 17). And for the same reason Exeter is an especially suitable place in which to develop the oxygen isotope analysis of faunal remains undertaken in this project by Müldner and Frémondeau (Chapters 3 and 4 above).

Second, Exeter's unusually rich documentation offers great potential, only partially realised so far. The city's records have been described as 'the best surviving series of civic documents for any provincial city in medieval Britain' (Kowaleski 2019, 1). Much of this documentation awaits transcription and detailed study. Kowaleski has argued for many years that it should be possible to use this huge body of material to locate occupants, leaseholders and owners. A key point arising from the documentary study of St Pancras parish (EAPIT 2, Chapter 4) is the demonstration that this is indeed possible in some parts of the city, and individual tenement histories with remarkable details about specific people can be built up, although the process is laborious. Fox's study of the tenements in Rack Street illustrates how transforming the documentary evidence can be when brought to an excavated site (EAPIT 2, Chapter 8). When the archaeological evidence is viewed with the detailed documentation, this rather unremarkable excavation can be seen as an excellent example of the spread of housing onto a marginal part of the city in the late 12th century, followed by progressively more intensive occupation in the 13th century, leading to subdivision of the property and the provision of small crowded houses in the years around 1300, followed by the calamity of the Black Death and the use of the area for cloth racks in the following centuries.

9

Conclusions: Exeter – A Changing Place in Time

Stephen Rippon, John Allan, Paul Bidwell, David Gould and Neil Holbrook

Introduction

A key character-defining feature of the British landscape is the degree of regional variation in the nature of its towns and their surrounding countryside. Exeter lies at the heart of one of our most distinctive landscapes – the South-West Peninsula – and the history of the city has been inexorably linked with that of the rich agricultural land and mineral deposits within its hinterland, and its location at a nodal point in communication routes between the South-West, the rest of Britain, and mainland Europe. At different times Exeter was one of the most important places in Britain, and at others a sleepy backwater of little significance beyond its immediate region.

During the 1970s Exeter was at the forefront of urban rescue archaeology in Britain through the work of the Exeter Museums Archaeological Field Unit (EMAFU), but from the 1980s it struggled with the problems of post-excavation analysis that bedevilled so many other towns and cities. Such has been the success of developer-funded archaeology in Britain since 1990 – and the resultant upsurge in excavations – that it is legitimate to ask the question 'is it worth dealing with these backlogs of unpublished fieldwork?' The premise behind the *Exeter: A Place in Time* project was that the answer to this question is yes, although the best way of achieving it is through its integration with a wider programme of research. In this particular case the writing up of old excavations was combined with scientific analyses using techniques that had not even been dreamt of when the artefacts were dug out of the ground, along with contextual research into how Exeter developed within its local, regional, national and international hinterlands.

At the times when Exeter was of particular importance, its location was crucial as the Exe Estuary provided a safe harbour for traders from the Mediterranean, Iberia and western France, as well as closer to home. Also crucial to Exeter's economy were the South-West's rich natural resources that most famously included minerals such as tin, but also silver and iron. It is particularly important to recognise that Exeter was also surrounded by good quality farmland and that the South-West Peninsula was not a wholly upland region (cf. Fox 1932; Rackham 1986). The inherent nature of the Peninsula – with open seas on three sides, and the high ground of the Blackdown and Quantock Hills on the fourth – helped shape the character of the communities living there, no doubt contributing to a strong sense of local identity. It was for this reason that when placing Exeter within its wider context a study area was chosen that embraced the historic counties of Cornwall, Devon, Dorset and Somerset, thereby allowing comparisons either side of the Blackdown and Quantock Hills and between two regions in which society developed in different ways during the Roman and medieval periods. It has also become increasingly evident that even within the South-West Peninsula there were marked variations between the eastern region (broadly what was to become Devon) and the areas to the west (that was to become Cornwall).

The conclusions to this volume therefore start with a summary of the development of Exeter, before turning to the consideration of four diachronic themes: the reasons why Exeter was located where it was, and how this contributed to its success; Exeter's role as the South-West Peninsula's major central place in both the Roman and medieval periods; the reasons for its fluctuating fortunes; and the priorities for future research.

The development of Exeter

Pre-Roman antecedents

Exeter (*Isca Dumnoniorum*) was the capital of the *civitas* of the Dumnonii, with Dorchester in Dorset the capital of the *civitas* known either as the Durotriges or Durotraces (Chapter 3). The character of the settlement patterns and material culture of these two areas suggest that there were communities with separate and distinct identities living there during the Late Iron Age reflected, for example, in the distribution of 'Durotrigian Ware' and the near-absence of pottery in Devon apart for the sparse occurrences of Plain Ware. The Blackdown and Quantock Hills appear to have formed a sparsely settled boundary zone between them. The Dumnonii lacked the large nucleated settlements and other traits – such as coin production – of the increasingly centralised societies of central and eastern Britain, and this may account for why the Early–Middle Iron Age port-of-trade at Mount Batten, beside Plymouth Sound, was seemingly less important in the Late Iron Age. Exeter at this time appears to have been open countryside, reflected in the small number of farmsteads that have been excavated beneath the modern city.

The military occupation of the South West, c. *AD 55 to* c. *AD 80*

In the mid AD 50s, during the governorship of Didius Gallus, the foundations of Exeter were laid when a fortress was constructed for the *legio II Augusta* on a low hill overlooking the lowest bridging point of the River Exe (Chapter 5). Exeter was chosen as the site for a legionary fortress as it was obvious from the outset of the military campaigns that the Roman army in the South-West Peninsula would need to be supplied with essential foodstuffs and other materials by sea or by road from the east. It would have been simply impossible to stimulate almost overnight the agricultural economy of the decentralised society in the South-West to supply the needs of 10–15,000 soldiers and dependent civilians. Indeed, to date there is comparatively little evidence for the foundation of new farms in the hinterland of Exeter in the second half of the 1st century AD, or that such settlements persisted after the legion had moved on (although Aller Cross, Hill Barton and Penns Mount, in Kingsteignton, may be examples as they have produced Fortress Wares; EAPIT2, Chapter 12, Fig. 12.6). A base at Exeter also allowed the army to move westwards – both to the north and south of Dartmoor – which would have been a much more difficult proposition if the fortress had been established further west. As part of this military deployment a series of forts was constructed across the Peninsula, and it is likely that the Roman roads that radiated from Exeter also date to this period. Recent fieldwork has significantly improved our understanding of this emerging infrastructure with greater clarity over the course of the Dorchester to Exeter road, confirmation that there was a road south from Exeter to Ipplepen which presumably then headed south around Dartmoor, and the identification of a road heading north from Exeter via the fort at Cullompton.

A reassessment of the available dating evidence has confirmed that the fortress at Exeter was founded *c.* AD 55 (Chapter 5 above, and EAPIT 2 Chapter 15). It has traditionally been thought that this marked the start of the Roman invasion and conquest of the South-West Peninsula, but a series of recent finds of Claudian *sestertii* in southern Devon may suggest an earlier phase of expeditionary activity perhaps under the governorship of Ostorius Scapula (although the coins may have reached there through trade: Chapter 3 above, and EAPIT 2, Chapter 16). Along with Usk, in Monmouthshire, Exeter is the most extensively excavated Claudio-Neronian legionary fortress in Britain, and with a considerable amount of interpolation its plan can now be substantially reconstructed, although this has involved significant modifications to Henderson's (1988) earlier, partly speculative, reconstruction. Excavations have now revealed parts of the legionary baths (Bidwell 1979), barracks, granaries, *fabrica*, *praetorium* (reinterpreting Fox 1952, House 2), streets and defences (Chapter 5 above, and EAPIT 2, Chapter 3.1). The baths at Exeter are amongst the very earliest stone buildings in Roman Britain, and as such mark a major milestone in our architectural history. The legionary fortress at Exeter was just part of a complex multi-faceted military landscape that included two satellite forts – one probably for cavalry at Princesshay, and another recently discovered at St Sidwell's Point – and two outlying fortlets or signal stations at Ide and Stoke Hill. There was also a civilian *canabae* (a civilian settlement outside a legionary fortress) on the *prata legionis* (land belonging to the legion) immediately outside the South-East Gate, a second civilian settlement 2.2 km to the east at St Loye's College that probably lay beyond the land directly controlled by the legion, as well as a possible fort, port and associated settlement on the Exe Estuary at Topsham.

The population of Exeter at this time – the legionary fortress, its associated military satellites and *canabae* (but excluding the St Loye's College settlement and the port at Topsham) – may have been as high as 10,000 – and these communities will have consumed a large amount of food and other resources. The Roman-style architecture within the St Loye's College settlement suggests that it was largely occupied by an immigrant population, in contrast to the later roadside settlements at both Pomeroy Wood near Honiton and Dainton Elms Cross in Ipplepen that saw the construction of native-style roundhouses. The isotopic analysis of animal bones from the fortress suggests that significant numbers of cattle and sheep had grazed on pastures to the east of Exeter – on the Blackdown Hills or even further east – suggesting a supply network that reflects the direction in which the Roman invasion occurred. A tile kiln to the north-east of the fortress was probably under military control, whereas pottery supply to the fortress appears to have been undertaken by civilian industries further away (EAPIT 2, Chapter 13). The most important local pottery industry supplying the military establishment in Exeter was South-Western BB1 that EAPIT has established was produced in the western parts of the Blackdown Hills (EAPIT 2, Chapter 12). Grey Burnished ware (Fabric 81), whose petrology suggests that it was also from the Upper Greensand (*i.e.* the Blackdown Hills), produced copies of BB1 forms and was presumably a local initiative that grew up close to the South-Western BB1 industry. A second local industry supplying the Exeter garrison was a group of fabrics that in the 1970s were called 'Fortress Wares' as it was assumed that they were produced locally; although work carried out as part of EAPIT has shown that they were made from clay found *c.* 20 km to the south in the Teign Valley which may have been transported to Exeter. Fortress Wares comprise a particularly high proportion of the ceramics at sites beyond the fortress (at Lower Coombe Street and St Loye's College) and it appears that the principal market for these wares was not the legion but rather the civilian communities in the *canabae* and in the settlement at St Loye's College. The Fortress Ware potters were surely civilians and various vessel forms suggest that at least some of the potters may have come from northern Gaul. In the post military period Exeter Fortress Wares were extremely well travelled being found in small quantities on military sites as far north as York and Scotland.

Excavations within the legionary fortress and its associated sites have produced far larger amounts of imported pottery than is the case with other contemporary military sites in western Britain – such as mortaria, *terra nigra* and butt beakers from Gaul, and colour-coated wares from Spain – or the later civilian town of Exeter (EAPIT 2, Chapter 12). This suggests that Exeter – or more correctly its port at Topsham – was a major entrepot for goods flowing into Britain from *c.* AD 55 to 80/85 via the Atlantic and Channel seaways. From Exeter, these various imports appear to have been redistributed over land and by sea, for example via the transhipment port at Crandon Bridge on the Parrett Estuary. Ruth Shaffrey's study of the querns from Exeter and the rest of Devon suggests that during the military period most were of Mayen lava imported from the continent (EAPIT 2, Chapter 14). Evidence for metalworking from the legionary fortress includes cupellation of silver (the separation of silver from base metals) and copper-alloy working, while debris from the *fabrica* show evidence for the repair of armour and iron smithing (EAPIT 2, Chapter 10).

As there are, at present, no charred plant remains from Exeter – although it is hoped that when current and recent excavations are published this will change – it is only through the study of animal bones that we can understand the army's food supply (Maltby in Chapter 5 above). Cattle provided the greatest amount of meat, although together more sheep and pigs may have been slaughtered. The very small size of the cattle and sheep suggests that they were local stock, and Gundula Müldner and Delphine Frémondeau's isotopic analysis of the faunal remains from the fortress has shown that a significant proportion of the animals had grazed on lands to the east of the fortress (in contrast to the later city when the livestock had mostly grazed on pasture around Exeter and on the high moorland to the north and west: Chapter 3 above). In addition to new methods of butchery and processing meat, chickens were introduced by the Roman army while some pigs may also have been brought in to bolster local supplies.

The intention may have been for Exeter to be a permanent legionary base with the Exe Estuary as the first port of call for an Atlantic supply route, and this trade with western Gaul and Iberia resulted in patterns of pottery consumption that were very different from those in South-East Britain (*e.g.* London). Around AD 60 the civilian *canabae* and settlement at St Loye's College were defended – an indication of troubled times – and Exeter may have assumed a particular importance in re-establishing control following the Boudican revolt. A second occasion when Exeter was at the centre of Roman politics was when the *legio II Augusta* declared for Vespasian – its former commander – during the struggle for control of the Empire in AD 69.

The Roman town and its hinterland

Around AD 75 a decision was taken to abandon Exeter as a legionary base, and move the *legio II Augusta* to Caerleon in South-East Wales (Chapter 3 above). Although it was traditionally thought that this redeployment was a rapid process it now appears to have taken place over several years with the fortress finally abandoned in the late AD 70s or early AD 80s. Whilst the timber buildings appear to have been dismantled, and large parts of the intra-mural area levelled, some key elements of the legionary fortress were retained as it was converted into a *civitas* capital including the defences, streets and baths (the latter being converted into the basilica: Chapter 4 above). That the fortress site was adopted for the new town, as well as the continuing occupation of the port at Topsham, surely indicates that maritime trade continued to play a part in the economy of Roman Exeter, although the vastly reduced population of the new town rendered supply from the rural hinterland a much more feasible proposition. The military tilery to the north-east of the fortress also appears to have continued in use to supply new public buildings within the civilian town, notably the basilica and forum that appears to date to around AD 90. The civilian settlement at St Loye's College was largely abandoned at this time, with much of the population presumably moving into newly available space within the former fortress, although domestic occupation within Exeter does not appear to have expanded very quickly. There may have been aspirations for Exeter to become a major town as its forum-basilica, at 7,135 m^2, appears to have been the 7th-largest such complex in Britain and larger than either Gloucester (6,750 m^2) or Lincoln (6,545 m^2) (Bidwell 1979, 80, tab. 6; for Lincoln see Steane 2006, 270–1, fig. 14.2; for Gloucester see Hurst 2020, 35, fig. 2.29). Whether it was initially intended to be a *colonia* will never be known, but the tribal suffix to its place-name clearly suggests that it became a *civitas* capital.

It is not known when the public baths – to the east of the basilica/forum – were constructed, but in AD 100–1 a timber aqueduct was constructed across the western part of the town. That this cut diagonally across *insulae* IV and V suggests that they were largely undeveloped at this time, and in the second half of the 2nd century AD these *insulae* were amalgamated which supports a wide range of other excavated and artefactual evidence in suggesting that the development of Exeter was a slow process; not surprisingly there is little evidence for suburban development during the Early Roman period, and it is possible that the sizeable port-town at Topsham inhibited the early commercial development of Exeter.

In the mid 2nd century AD sections of the ditch that ran around the Early Roman town appears to have been re-dug, but in *c*. AD 160–180 the city authorities decided to more than double the size of Exeter from 16.6 ha to 37.5 ha through the construction of a new set of earthen and timber defences extending for 2.3 km. It is difficult to see why this decision was taken since there is little evidence for pressure on space within the town before the new defences were constructed. The subsequent extension of the street system appears to have been less extensive than previously assumed and development within the newly enclosed areas was slow. With an area of 37.5 ha Exeter possessed the 13th-largest urban defended area in Britain, although it was probably not ranked so highly in terms of its actual population.

Exeter's initially earthen and timber defences were heightened and faced with stone in the early 3rd century AD, and refurbishment of the basilica – that when first published was dated to the mid 4th century AD – is now thought to have occurred around the mid 3rd century AD. Various excavations have shown that Exeter's streets were lined with a mixture of building types, including small strip-based *tabernae* (shops) through to well-appointed town houses. Some of the latter were furnished with hypocausts and mosaic pavements which is significant as such features are virtually unknown in the countryside around Exeter. Mosaics are, however, poorly represented in Exeter compared to Dorchester and Ilchester to the east and show a lower level of workmanship. There is some evidence for extra-mural occupation outside the South Gate, but nothing like the extensive suburbs seen around some other *civitas* capitals.

A significant change in the supply of manufactured goods occurred in the 3rd century AD with the decline in several local pottery industries, including South-Western BB1, their place being taken by South Devon Ware and South-East Dorset BB1 (Chapter 6 above, and EAPIT 2, Chapter 12). Ceramic tile was also imported into Exeter from outside the region, although their source is currently unknown (the Solent has been suggested but a continental origin is not out of the question: EAPIT 2, Chapter 13). Oxfordshire Ware – albeit in small amounts – is found right across the South-West Peninsula, although it is striking that New Forest Ware did not find its way down into Cornwall (reflecting how that region retained a distinctive identity throughout the Roman period). The presence of significant amounts of *céramique à l'éponge* from western Gaul, as well as North African and Eastern Mediterranean amphorae, in Exeter is one indication that it remained a significant port on the Atlantic seaboard. There were also significant changes in the tile industry. The relatively centralised Early Roman pattern of production based upon a small number of centres such as the putative 'eastern' and 'southern' tileries appears to have ceased in the later 3rd century AD. It seems to have been replaced by a greater number of smaller-scale tileries scattered across the landscape including Hatherleigh Moor which dates to the 3rd and/or 4th centuries AD (its products have been recognised on a number of sites spread across the Culm Measures north of Dartmoor).

Across most of lowland Roman Britain *civitas* capitals such as Exeter were at the centre of a hierarchy of smaller towns and roadside settlements that have some urban functions, but this happened to only a very limited extent in the South-West Peninsula (Chapter 3 above). Two roadside settlements – Woodbury, in Axminster, and Pomeroy Wood, in Honiton – grew up on the major road between Dorchester and Exeter, both on the sites of conquest-period forts, while it is possible that another roadside settlement developed at Cullompton north of Exeter. To the south and west of Exeter, however, the urban hierarchy was poorly developed with just a small roadside settlement at Dainton Elms Cross, in Ipplepen, and a possible site at North Tawton. The lack of a network of local centres across the whole Peninsula is one of its key character-defining features in the Roman period, as is the scarcity of villas: apart from a small cluster of sites in the immediate hinterland of Exeter, there is just a single definite example in the far west of Cornwall (at Magor) whose isolated location suggests that it may have been the house of an official supervising the tin industry. There was a scatter of other Romanised buildings, some with tiled roofs, but they lacked the other trappings of a Roman villa such as mosaic pavements and underfloor heating: were those same structures to be found in Dorset or Somerset they would be classed simply as farmsteads. Lower down the social scale it is increasingly clear that enclosed farmsteads predominated, as opposed to the complex farmsteads that were typical of lowland areas to the east of the Blackdown and Quantock Hills. These simple enclosures contained mostly circular (in Devon) or oval (in Cornwall) buildings, and lack the rectangular structures prevalent in some other parts of Roman Britain (Smith 2016a, fig. 3.6).

There was also less use of Roman-style material culture in the South-West Peninsula, again with differences between what is now Devon and Cornwall (Chapter 3 above). Whereas the traditional view is that material culture across Roman Britain was relatively homogenised, there is increasing evidence for distinctive regional identities. Right across Cornwall, for example, the locally produced gabbroic ware dominated pottery assemblages throughout the Roman period, whereas it hardly crossed the Tamar Valley to the east of which South Devon Ware dominates in the later Roman period (at least in southern Devon). It is also striking how the Roman period saw new vessel forms, such as tablewares and drinking vessels, introduced into Cornwall through the importation of vessels from outside the area, but that these forms were not usually reproduced in the local gabbroic ware. There is also a suite of other Cornish material culture that appears to have a distribution restricted predominantly to areas west of the Tamar including stone mortars, bowls and weights, and a distinctive type of brooch with a cruciform-shaped bow and fantail foot.

It is difficult to reconstruct patterns of animal husbandry across the South-West Peninsula due to the poor bone preservation, although the far higher proportions of cattle and sheep/goat in Exeter compared to Dorchester suggests that they were more common in the countryside around Exeter than on the chalk downland of Dorset (Chapter 3 above). Müldner and Frémondeau's analysis of stable isotopes derived from the teeth of cattle and sheep/goat demonstrates that the animals eaten within 2nd-century AD Exeter were reared in the Devonian hinterlands of the town, rather than being imported from further east as seems to have occurred to some degree during the period of military occupation (Chapter 3 above). A far clearer picture of regional variation in arable regimes emerges from the study of charred cereal assemblages with far more mixed regimes across the South-West Peninsula (Chapter 3 above). These included significant amounts of oat cultivation in contrast to the lowlands of Somerset where wheat dominated. The slightly greater significance of wheat in the immediate hinterland of Exeter, compared to the rest of the Peninsula, may reflect cultural change (such as food preferences on the part of the urban population) and/or the qualities of eastern Devon's soils. While there clearly were significant areas of arable across the South-West Peninsula it appears to have been a region that contained a greater proportion of pasture compared to many other parts of lowland Roman Britain which is reflected in both the pollen evidence and the relative scarcity of corn drying ovens, querns and ditched field systems.

Although the evidence from excavated buildings and the distribution of casual coin finds suggests that most of Exeter's intra-mural area was still occupied in the 4th century its character appears to have been changing (Chapter 6 above; and EAPIT 2, Chapter 16). We know very little about the fate of the basilica in the 4th century AD although there are suggestions that parts of it were still standing after *c.* AD 340. The presence of a stockyard at nearby Trichay Street suggests once bustling commercial streets were taking on a rather more rural character. The lack of Theodosian coinage suggests little official interest in Exeter by the last decade of the 4th century AD (in contrast to towns such as Caerwent and Cirencester), as does the virtual absence of crossbow brooches and belt sets from Exeter and the rest of the South-West Peninsula.

Late antiquity: the post-Roman/early medieval period

The only evidence for occupation within Exeter between the early 5th and late 9th centuries comes from the Cathedral Close, and elsewhere the Late Roman occupation is sealed beneath a layer of 'dark earth' (Chapter 7 above). Two burials immediately west of the later cathedral radiocarbon dated to the 5th to 7th centuries may relate to a church which pre-dated that attended by the young St Boniface in *c.* 680. A second phase of burials has been dated by radiocarbon to the 8th century onwards and was associated with the Late Saxon minster. The Byzantine coins said to have been found in Exeter can all be dismissed, and the lack of 5th to 6th-century pottery imported from the Mediterranean – that has been found on a series of probable coastal beach markets in Devon, and more widely across Cornwall and Somerset – is striking. This early post-Roman history of Exeter is broadly in keeping with what is seen in former Roman towns across much of Britain, with abandonment followed by initially small-scale reuse as the location for a church: there is no evidence that Exeter was in any sense a central place for the Dumnonian kingdom of the 5th to mid 9th centuries.

Across the wider South-West, however, there appears to have been broad continuity in the countryside, with no evidence for widespread woodland regeneration and a growing number of settlements being recognised through radiocarbon dating of aceramic features containing charred cereal remains (Chapter 4 above). While wheat continued to dominate arable regimes in Somerset, across the South-West Peninsula there were far more mixed cropping patterns (another thread of continuity with the Roman period). Differences between Devon and Cornwall persisted, with a continuous ceramic tradition to the west of the Tamar Valley but Devon being aceramic (except for the 5th or 6th-century imports found on some coastal sites).

If the *Anglo-Saxon Chronicle* is to be believed, the West Saxon kingdom expanded as far as Exeter by the 660s, and this appears to have been followed by the establishment of several minster churches including Exeter. Around the 8th century there was a growing intensity in landscape exploitation, a phenomenon that is seen across southern Britain. In the South-West Peninsula this is apparent in pollen diagrams and the appearance of possible high-status estate centres (such as Berry Meadow, in Kingsteignton, and the Pinn Brook Enclosure, in Pinhoe). There is also palaeoenvironmental evidence for an increased intensity in the exploitation of tin.

Urban revival, c. *900*

The author of *Gesta Stephani* claimed that Exeter was the 4th-ranked town in England in the mid 12th century, and while probably an exaggeration it does reflect the dramatic rise in fortunes that the city saw during the Saxo-Norman period. The absence of datable pottery in Devon until the 10th century makes it difficult to establish when the revival of Exeter began, although the limited number and distribution of pre-10th century coins suggests that there was little occupation within the old Roman walls until the late 9th century (Chapter 7 above). In 875–7 the *Anglo-Saxon Chronicle* described Exeter as a *faestan* (fortress) – suggesting that it was little more than a defensible shell – although in 893 it was described as a *burh* implying that it may have assumed some urban functions. By 895–9, for example, it was one of King Alfred's mints, and in the 970s, under King Æthelred II, Exeter was the 5th most productive mint in England (it ranked 8th for the overall period 973–1066). This production probably reflects the local availability of silver (from the Tamar Valley) as Exeter may only have been the 18th most populous town at the time of Domesday Book. There is, however, archaeological evidence for a wide range of trades including pottery production, textiles and metalworking (including a 12th-century bell foundry). The analysis of Exeter's Saxo-Norman ceramic assemblage reveals that it was already engaging in international trade, particularly with the Lower Seine Valley in northern France but also Brittany, Normandy and the Low Countries (a series of trading links that was similar to Southampton, but very unlike London). The importation of stone from Caen (in northern France), and the names of Exeter's moneyers also reflect its cosmopolitan nature as they include Scandinavian names, while Bedford Garage Ware may have been produced by an immigrant potter(s) from Normandy.

Detailed surveys have shown that more Roman fabric survives in the city wall than was previously supposed, and in Northernhay Gardens a long stretch of rebuilding can be dated to the Late Saxon period. While this Late Saxon masonry is extremely rare in southern England, it is unclear whether it relates to a re-defence of the city as a whole, or just a putative royal enclave at Rougemont. The date when the Late Saxon streets were laid out is also unclear, although they were unrelated to the Roman grid. The distribution of Bedford Garage Ware – produced in the North-East corner of the city – suggests that occupation within the central part of the walled area was extensive, and although peripheral areas were yet to be built on there was some extra-mural occupation outside the South Gate. Several areas appear to have become high status enclaves in the form of the royal enclosure at Rougemont, the area that was to become St Nicholas Priory (that was a comital enclave of the Godwin family known as 'Earlsbury'), and the minster/Cathedral Close. Exeter has traditionally been seen as an example of the impact that Norman lordship had on English towns as Domesday records that 48 houses were 'wasted', whereas if Rougemont – the site of the later Norman castle – was already a royal enclave then the houses may have been part of that royal property (Higham in Chapter 7 above). There were at least four Late Saxon masonry churches in Exeter in addition to the minster, while Saxo-Norman features within the castle gatehouse also reflects this tradition of building in stone; an early engraving records a possible example of another stone building, on Waterbeer Street, for which a 12th-century date may be appropriate.

The later medieval period

The 12th and 13th centuries saw population growth across Britain, and while the rate of increase in the South-West Peninsula appears to have been slower than elsewhere it still led to significant changes (Chapter 4 above). There were particularly significant developments in the urban landscape, with the rapid rise of Bristol – which became the second ranked town in England – alongside a proliferation of new towns across the entire region. Exeter was about the 18th most populous town in England at the time of Domesday, slipping to 27th or 28th in 1334, but it remained the largest town within the South-West Peninsula. There were major changes to Exeter's topography with the creation of several new monasteries (the Blackfriars within the intra-mural area, and the Greyfrairs outside the South Gate), three new hospitals, and a new underground water supply system that was started in the late 12th century (Chapter 8 above). There was also suburban expansion during the 12th and 13th centuries, including that associated with Exe Bridge, but the Black Death appears to have killed around a third of the population which led to the abandonment of some tenements in the more peripheral parts of the city.

Exeter has 'the best surviving series of civic documents for any provincial city in medieval Britain' (Kowaleski 2019, 1), but until EAPIT it had not proved possible to link the tenements referred to in these written sources with physical tenements as recorded on early maps and in some cases preserved within the modern fabric of Exeter. For the parish of St Pancras, John Allan has been able to do not just this but also to relate the written records for individual tenements to the results from archaeological excavations (EAPIT 2, Chapter 4). The result is a fascinating insight into one of the wealthiest parts of Exeter – the central High Street, next to the Guildhall – where some of the city's most prominent residents lived. An example of such a tenement is now 197 High Street whose lease was acquired by Thomas Forbour in 1319 from Henry atte Lane (*de Venella)* excepting two *selds* [shops] on the frontage; his neighbours were William of Chagford to the east and Stephen of London to the west (VC 3027, 3038). Three years later Henry atte Lane also granted Thomas Forbour the two *selds* in High Street at the front of this holding that were described as 'opposite Broadgate (*la Vyshfoldeyete)'* (VC 3037, S&J 0987). The tenement eventually passed to Joan Tuckfield for whom we even have a portrait (Fig. 9.1). The adjacent tenement was later occupied by the prominent Exeter widow and benefactor Elizabeth Flay (Fig. 9.2) who in 1660 leased from the Dean and Chapter 'one shop, four chambers over the shop whereof two of them are no biger then a standing bedstead will stand in them, one little narrow kitching over two payre of stares, one loft over the same' (D&C 4573/2/7a).

A further conclusion emerged from the documentary study: not only could all the main property boundaries of the tenements between High Street and Waterbeer Street be shown to survive from the 14th century, but several of the oddities in their layout, still evident in the 20th century, could also be traced back to the same period. For example, the unusual arrangement in which the central part of the tenement of 195 High Street formed an intruding portion of the neighbouring property explains some features of the will of the celebrated mayor John Gist of 1381, when this part of his holding was occupied by his kitchen. The dimensions of the shop owned by the Dean and Chapter on the street frontage at 200 High Street, recorded in 1360, remained unchanged, and still in separate ownership, in the 18th and 19th centuries. These examples of urban continuity suggest that the bounds of this group of tenements in the wealthy core of the city centre survive little altered from the mid 14th century.

The properties examined in the documentary study preserved little medieval building fabric, as many of the houses had been rebuilt in the early modern period, and most were rebuilt once more in the years after 1800. It was nevertheless very instructive to find that much information relating to the medieval city is still embedded in the modern fabric of these buildings. Of the row of four shops on Goldsmith Street whose leases were sold by the London goldsmith William Prince in 1447, for example, nothing stands above ground today. The plans of these houses may nevertheless be reconstructed from the Victorian buildings which stand on the site of two of them: small roughly square plots over older cellars (now inaccessible) whose presence ensured the survival of the ground plans of the preceding buildings. Similar continuities no doubt arose because the rebuilding of houses on properties hemmed in by neighbours could only be achieved by replicating the ground plan of the preceding building. The survival of embedded information of this sort in more recent buildings seems an unexplored and potentially valuable theme in urban conservation.

Fig. 9.1 Portrait of Joan Tuckfield, who lived at No. 197 High Street in the period 1544–57 (Guildhall collection; © RAMM)

Fig. 9.2 Portrait of Elizabeth Flay, who lived at No, 196 High Street in the period 1640–62 (Guildhall collection; © RAMM)

There is also a wide range of archaeological and documentary evidence for the economy of later medieval Exeter, which included the range of activities that are to be expected in any county town such as pottery and tile production, the minting of coins, the working of textiles, leather and horn, metalworking (including the manufacture of pewter vessels, and a particularly significant bell foundry), and the construction trades (Chapter 8 above). The discovery of two dies for the forging of coins gives us a rare insight into the black economy. Dendrochronology – and its related technique of 'dendroprovenancing' – supports the available documentary evidence in suggesting that most timber used in Exeter came from local Devonian sources, although some of the 12th and 13th-century timbers from Trichay Street are of Irish origin, and 14th-century boards from the Cathedral Song School are from around the Baltic (EAPIT 2, Chapter 11). Detailed analysis of the ceramic assemblage from Exeter has revealed that it lay at the centre of a series of far reaching international trade routes (EAPIT 2, Chapter 18). Trade with France shifted from the Lower Seine Valley to Normandy in the late 12th and early 13th centuries, followed by a shift to Iberia in the later 13th century. There is some evidence for trade with Italy in the 15th century (reflected in ceramics, wooden goods and paper), but less stoneware from the Low Countries than in other English cities until the late 15th century. The cosmopolitan nature of Exeter is reflected by the presence of immigrants from Ireland, Brittany, Normandy, Gascony, France, the Low Countries and Saxony.

The population of any urban centre will have required feeding through the production of an agricultural surplus in the surrounding countryside, and Domesday records that the fertile lowlands of eastern Devon were as densely populated, and had the same density of ploughteams, as lowland areas to the north and east of the Blackdown and Quantock Hills (Chapter 2 above). Rural population growth during the 12th and 13th centuries was, however, modest across the South-West Peninsula and this was accommodated within a landscape characterised by predominantly dispersed settlement patterns and enclosed fields, with just limited open fields associated with mainly small hamlets rather than large villages. The region's large number of small new towns was another distinctive feature of the landscape. The analysis of animal bone and charred cereal assemblages from across the wider South-West supports the documentary sources in suggesting the continuation of some marked regional variation in agricultural practices such as a greater emphasis on cattle and a wider diversity of crops – including oats – in Devon and Cornwall compared to Dorset and Somerset (Chapter 4 above). The late medieval period saw the most important regional specialisation with the rise of the woollen industry that was focussed on Exeter and was a major reason why it rose up the rankings to become England's 6th most prosperous city during the 16th and 17th centuries (based on a wide variety of indicators including the number of taxpayers, the amount of tax paid, and the number of hearths taxed: Table 1.1 in Chapter 1 above). This is reflected in the animals consumed in Exeter with an increase in sheep/goat and a rise in the age at which they were killed. Lauritsen's recent examination of the faunal assemblages that had not been examined during the 1970s and 80s has given several new insights, including the importance of marrow extraction and marked social differentiation between different parts of the city in terms of the meat consumed (EAPIT 2, Chapter 9).

Mandy Kingdom's analysis of the human burials across a series of cemeteries has shown that the health of Exeter's later medieval population was gradually improving compared to the Saxo-Norman period, with a better diet and longer lives (although this meant that more people experienced ill-health associated with older age including dental problems, infections, joint disease and trauma: EAPIT 2, Chapter 19). Exeter's later medieval population was, on average, shorter than in the Saxo-Norman period but the body mass ratio, dietary isotope levels, older age-at-death profile, and increased skeletal indications of affluence indicate at least adequate if not good nutrition. Exeter's population also typically lived longer and had lower levels of disease than that of Winchester.

An eminently well-situated place

By the 16th and 17th centuries Exeter was unquestionably one of the wealthiest and most populous cities in Britain and many of the factors that led to this success were instrumental in its earlier development. The legionary fortress was founded on a sloping spur overlooking the lowest bridging point of the Exe and at the head of the first major estuary encountered after sailing west along the coasts of southern Dorset and eastern Devon (that are otherwise punctuated by just a few minor inlets). The location of the fortress will have been determined by strategic reasoning – there was no significant Iron Age predecessor – and that it was chosen as the location for the *civitas* capital reflects the well-attested practice of establishing major towns on former Roman military sites.

The success of a town usually depended upon the nature of its hinterland, and Exeter was fortunate in lying at the heart of a resource-rich region. Its immediate hinterland – the eastern Devon lowlands – is characterised by soils that afford rich arable and pasture as well as an abundance of meadow on the floodplains of the Exe, Creedy, Culm and Clyst (see Chapter 2 above). Domesday Book provides us with data on the densities of population and ploughteams across the four historic counties of the wider South-West and this shows that the immediate hinterland of Exeter had the highest density of ploughteams and third highest population of all the *pays* within the four south-western counties. Although other parts of the wider South-West were far less suited to arable agriculture – such as the high moorland of Devon and Cornwall – these areas were used as summer grazing by communities living in the surrounding lowlands. The seasonal movement of livestock up onto Dartmoor in the medieval period is well documented (Fox 2012), and the isotopic analysis of cattle and sheep teeth as part of EAPIT has not only yielded archaeological evidence for this but also that it happened in the Roman period. The fortress, town and city of Exeter were therefore very well located within an agriculturally rich area.

Exeter's wider hinterland was also rich in a wide range of other resources. The South-West Peninsula was well-known in the pre-Roman period for its tin, and there is growing archaeological and palaeoenvironmental evidence for peaks in its exploitation during the Roman period and from around the 8th century onwards (see Chapter 2 above). Exeter has produced very little direct archaeological evidence for its involvement in the tin industry, and it is not known whether the military period copper-alloy working within the Trichay Street *fabrica* and at Friernhay Street, and late 2nd-century AD working at Rack Street, was using south-western tin. During the Late Saxon period, however, there is a range of evidence to suggest that Exeter's growth was closely linked to exploitation of its region's mineral resources. From *c.* AD 300 to 1240 South-West England was Europe's only source of tin (Maddicott 1989, 20), and once King Alfred had established a *burh* at Exeter it soon developed central place functions as it became the South-West's only Alfredian mint (Slater 2000, 591). King Æthelstan (924–39) founded a minster and – according to William of Malmesbury – redefended it, but during his reign Exeter had just two moneyers making it of middling importance. Under Æthelred (978–1016), however, Exeter was England's 5th most productive mint and Maddicott (1989) sees the source of this wealth as tin. Henry of Huntingdon, writing *c.* 1130, describes Exeter as '*Excestra clara metallis*' ('bright metal', which is assumed to be tin), although the first direct documentary evidence for tin production in the South-West comes during the second half of the 12th century when Dartmoor was the main source. In 1198 a tax was imposed on the second smelting of tin which specified that it was to take place in either Exeter or Bodmin being 'places where it was customarily done'. Although there is no archaeological evidence for the working of tin in Exeter this documentary evidence suggests that it was a major factor in the growth of the city, and while the earliest firm evidence for the mining of silver in Devon comes from the 13th century it is possible that there were deposits being worked in the 10th century which could explain the high productivity of the mints at Exeter and Lydford (see Chapter 2 above).

There is also some archaeological evidence for the working of precious metals in Exeter during the Roman period (see EAPIT 2, Chapter 10). Military-period crucibles from South Street, excavated during the late 1940s, could not be re-examined as part of EAPIT but from their published description it is possible that they were used for silver refining or assaying (the determination of the quantity of a given metal, normally silver or gold, in an ore or alloy). Also from the military period, two shallow hemispherical crucibles from Friernhay Street were used for cupellation (the separation of silver from base metals), while a fragment of dense, lead-copper rich slag from a late 4th-century AD deposit at Rack Street could be from litharge (a by-product of the cupellation of silver). Crucibles from a 2nd-century AD roadside ditch at Friernhay Street appear to have been used for 'parting' (the process of separating silver from gold), although the presence of copper in the vessels suggests that they were used to recycle artefacts made from mixed precious metals to create pure bullion for use in the imperial economy (copper would not be expected if the vessels were used in the processing of freshly-mined Cornish gold as native gold does not normally contain that metal). During the medieval period there is good documentary evidence for the presence of goldsmiths in Exeter (Kowaleski 1995, 163), although in practice they will have worked primarily in silver, and there is still 'Goldsmith Street' leading off the High Street.

In addition to the mineral-rich areas of Dartmoor and Cornwall, there are several parts of the South-West that – although not associated with industry today – were particularly rich in natural resources. There were important deposits of iron on Exmoor and the Blackdown Hills. It has also been known for some time that the Blackdowns were the location of a major late medieval pottery industry – most famously at Donyatt, in southern Somerset – and recent excavations at Hemyock have revealed a major Late Saxon production centre for the Upper Greensand-Derived wares that are common in Exeter. To this ceramic heritage EAPIT can now add the Early Roman South-Western BB1 industry, that was also exploiting Upper Greensand-Derived clays (EAPIT 2, Chapter 12), and it is possible that Exeter fabric 81 (handmade grey-burnished ware, produced for a few decades in the mid to late 1st century AD) – that had been attributed to a small outcrop of the Upper Greensand south-west of Exeter around Ideford (Holbrook and Bidwell 1991, 163) – was in fact from the Blackdowns. The Blackdown Hills were also a source of querns in the Roman period (EAPIT 2, Chapter 14) and clay used to make tiles (EAPIT 2, Chapter 13)

In addition to widespread awareness of the South-West's rich mineral wealth, there is a perception that it was a 'maritime region', although it is not very clear whether this is an appropriate tag before the late medieval period (see Chapter 2 above). The coastal fishing villages, that are such a distinctive part of the Devon and Cornwall landscape, are no older than the 15th century (Fox 2001) and it is very striking that medieval churches within coastal parishes are invariably located well inland, at the centre of agricultural fields. This suggests that – even for communities whose parishes lay next to the coast – land was their major preoccupation, not the sea. Exeter's involvement with fishing was as the pre-eminent regional centre for trade in marine fish especially from the late medieval period (late 14th century onwards), but it was not itself a fishing port (Kowaleski 1995, 307–24). The main fish traded were initially herring – a large proportion of which came from the North Sea – although over time this was replaced by cod, hake and conger eel fished offshore around the South-West Peninsula and which were brought to Exeter from small fishing ports all around Devon and Cornwall. There was very little trade in freshwater fish. A lack of appropriate recovery strategies (*i.e.* sieving) during Exeter's major excavations mean that we know relatively little about the importance of fish during the Roman and earlier medieval periods.

Having considered the rich resources of the South-West Peninsula, and the significance of its position at the head of the Exe Estuary, there is one further aspect of Exeter's location that was of great importance in its development: the way in which it lay at the nodal point for communication routes in and out of the South-West. The establishment of the legionary fortress at Exeter was associated with the creation of a series of five roads: one ran across the Blackdown Hills from Dorchester in Dorset; another headed south crossing the River Teign near the medieval town at Newton Abbot whereupon it went through Ipplepen and then presumably headed south around Dartmoor towards the natural harbour of Plymouth Sound; the third road headed west of Exeter around the northern side of Dartmoor linking the forts at North Tawton and Okehampton; while the fourth road radiating from Exeter has recently been identified heading north to Cullompton (the fifth road was the short stretch east to Topsham). In places these roads have survived in use, and where this was not the case medieval routes were re-established along very similar lines that are first depicted on 17th and 18th-century small-scale county maps (*e.g.* Fig. 9.3: Batten and Bennett 1996; Down and Webb 2016). These early maps show a series of major routes converging on Exeter from across Devon and Cornwall, and then heading either north over Whiteball Hill to Wellington, Taunton and hence the lowlands of central Somerset, or east to Honiton and then across the Blackdown Hills to Axminster (the modern A35) that was described by Lysons and Lysons (1822, cclxi) as 'the great road from London to Exeter and Plymouth'. Some of these routes are also described in the accounts of early topographical writers such as the routes taken by Thomas Clerk in 1476 and William Worcestre in 1478 (Harvey 1969), John Leland in *c.* 1540 (Toulmin Smith 1964), Celia Fiennes in 1698 (Morris 1982, 192–214), and Daniel Defoe (1742a; b).

At various times in its history Exeter was also a major international port. During the Roman period this was most notably during two periods. The first was the occupation of the legionary fortress, when Exeter was a base for the re-export of continental pottery to northern Britain (Chapter 5 above, and EAPIT 2, Chapter 12). The second was the late 3rd and 4th centuries AD when the relatively large amounts of *céramique à l'éponge* from the Bordeaux region – an assemblage only surpassed in size by *Clausentum* (Bitterne, near Southampton) – demonstrate the strength of trading links with western Gaul, while Exeter has one of the four major concentrations of North African amphorae in Britain (the others being London, Leicester and York); it is very likely that the North African amphorae were brought to Exeter as part of its trade with Bordeaux (Chapter 5 above, and EAPIT 2, Chapter 12). International trade resumed during the Late Saxon period when Exeter was only one of a small number of places in the British Isles with imports from the continent (Chapter 7 above, and EAPIT 2, Chapter 17), and again in the late medieval period when the cloth trade flourished (Chapter 8 above, and EAPIT 2, Chapter 18).

A central place?

Over the course of its nearly 2,000 years of existence Exeter has had various functions, first as a legionary fortress, then a Romano-British *civitas* capital, perhaps as a British Christian church, and finally the Late Saxon, medieval and modern city. With the probable exception of the early 5th to mid 9th centuries it has been widely assumed that Exeter functioned as the most important central place within the South-West Peninsula, although this is based upon the traditional interpretation of the *civitas* capital as also having the attributes of a major town. The character and role of Romano-British towns has, however, recently been questioned (*e.g.* Perring and Pitts 2013; Smith and Fulford 2019) and so this aspect of Exeter's history needs some further consideration. Given the uncertainties concerning the functions performed by towns in the Roman period the discussion will begin in the medieval period when we are on firmer ground.

As discussed in Chapter 4, there has been much debate amongst medievalists as to what constituted a town, and the view taken here is that the key criteria are a mixture of physical, economic and social organisational traits:

- a permanent, densely occupied settlement (with a particularly high density of occupation along the major street frontages), that resulted in a large number of churches.
- major towns were enclosed spaces (as well as being defensive, these walls were of symbolic value in confirming the population's special social status as well as controlling economic traffic).
- the majority of the population was not directly involved in agriculture but instead made their living through manufacturing, retailing or other service provision.

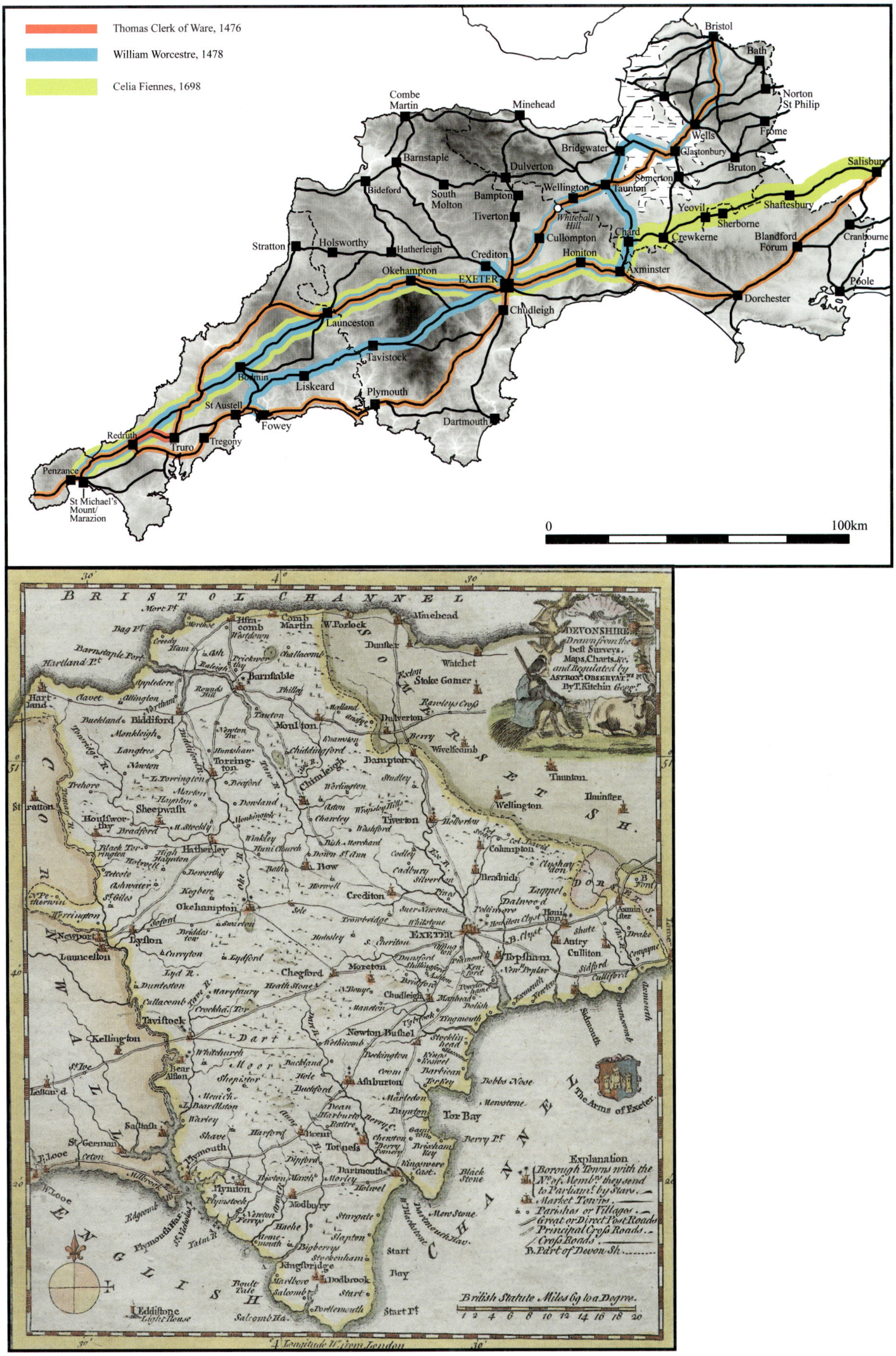

Fig. 9.3 The major 16th to 18th-century roads across the wider South-West as depicted on early small-scale county maps and described in the accounts of early topographical writers such as William Worcestre in 1478 (who also describes the journey of Thomas Clerk in 1476) and Celia Fiennes in 1698 (after Harvey 1969; Morris 1982 (based on John Speed's county maps of 1610, and Thomas Kitchin's county maps of the 1760s such as that of Devon illustrated above; drawn by Stephen Rippon)

- they provided a range of services both to the town's own inhabitants and the surrounding rural population, such as secular and ecclesiastical administration, and marketing (allowing people to buy and sell raw materials and manufactured goods).
- the urban population had a distinct social identity (usually confirmed with the legal status of being a borough that was conferred by the crown).
- a highly stratified society that resulted in a wide range of architecture.

We cannot expect all towns to look the same, and while major towns will have displayed all of these facets there were smaller towns that only had some of them. But what medieval towns all had in common was that they were central places providing goods and services to the surrounding rural communities, articulating a market-based economy, and which drew in food and raw materials from the countryside.

From the late 10th century onwards Exeter was clearly a major town. Archaeological excavations have revealed dense occupation, especially along the major roads but also spreading out into the peripheral parts of the defended area, and surviving fabric within Exeter's churches suggests that many had Saxo-Norman origins. At least one part of Exeter's town walls – at Northernhay – had been refurbished in the Late Saxon period, and the city had become a centre for manufacturing, including the production of coins, pottery, textiles and metal objects. Imported pottery suggests that it was a major local/regional market, and an international port. Exeter went on to become an important centre of political (having a royal castle) and ecclesiastical power (the cathedral having moved there from Crediton in 1050), was the centre of local government (being the county town and home for the justices of the assize; *e.g. Hooker's Chronicle*, 30–1), had its own local governance and officers (*e.g.* Hooker's *Antique Description*, 16–17, 146–92), was home of the social and economic elite (having royal, comital and ecclesiastical enclaves within its walls; see Higham in Chapter 7 above), and saw life in the medieval borough governed by a mixture of custom and legal privilege (MacCaffrey 1958, 26–53). That Exeter had a special social status is also revealed by Domesday Book which records that in the time of Edward the Confessor Exeter only paid geld when London, Winchester and York did (Thorn and Thorn 1985, f. 100a [C4])

When Late Saxon Exeter can first be classed as a town is a little less clear. Astill (2000, 28–36) has argued that the *burhs* across southern England did not acquire the characteristics of towns until the late 10th century, and there is nothing from late 9th-century Exeter to contradict this. While it had a number of high-status secular and ecclesiastical central place functions – the church of probable minster status (from 909 to 1050 the cathedral was at nearby Crediton), the Alfredian mint, and perhaps a royal vill at Rougemont – there is no evidence for other characteristics of towns such as dense occupation, manufacturing and a role as a market. What the creation of the Alfredian mint – the only one within the wider South-West – does show, however, is that Exeter had been identified as the most important political centre in the region (Astill 2000, 36). This status as an important royal vill was confirmed under King Æthelstan who refounded the minster in 932 and used Exeter for a meeting of nobles, bishops and Welsh princes (Orme 2009, 7–10), although such is the lack of datable material culture before the very clear evidence from coinage in the late 10th century that it is unclear whether there was occupation within Exeter that can be truly called 'urban'. Thereafter, Exeter's role as a major regional market centre is clear both through the archaeological evidence (*e.g.* pottery) and documentary sources in that it served much of Devon and southern Somerset (Kowaleski 1995).

Returning now to the Roman period, towns were made up of the major centres of public administration as well as a far greater number of nucleated settlements which varied considerably in size and morphology (all of the major towns were defended but only some of the latter category). These towns are frequently thought to have performed similar functions to their medieval successors, but this view is all too often assumed rather than demonstrated. Indeed the degree to which Romano-British towns served as market centres for their surrounding hinterlands is increasingly being questioned. Nor should we necessarily assume that all towns performed similar functions. For instance, Perring and Pitts (2013) have studied the interaction between the major towns of London and Colchester, as well as sites situated in their hinterlands in Essex and Cambridgeshire, through analysis of ceramics, coins, small finds and animal bones. Their work was hindered by problems of data consistency and compatibility, but their principal contention was that 'the cities of Roman Britain stood apart: they appear as alien places of government where the exercise of power made exaggerated call on available resources' (Perring and Pitts 2013, 250). They argue that their study shows little support for the idea that towns served as market centres, rather that rural surplus was drawn towards them through tribute, rent and taxation, with little reciprocal exchange. In similar vein Fulford (2020, 303) has remarked on how little satellite settlement developed around the major towns of Roman Britain, London being particularly notable in this regard, and wondered whether this indicates that these places did not in fact contain markets that drew people in from the countryside. The situation in those parts of the country where villas and complex farms were prevalent might also have been somewhat different to those parts of the province where these types of rural settlement are only rarely found, if at all. For instance, research around Wroxeter using the techniques of fieldwalking and limited excavation found relatively little material culture at the rural settlements in the hinterland and concluded that 'rural sites in the area betray little evidence for engagement with the Roman city' (Gaffney *et al.* 2007, 280).

It is not straightforward to approach these questions for Exeter and its region. While on the one hand rural settlements in Devon produce considerably fewer artefacts than those in the Essex study area examined by Perring and Pitts, on the positive side the hinterland of Exeter has been subject to much more excavation than that around Wroxeter (see the case study looking at the area east of Exeter in Chapter 3). Foodstuffs should be an important source of evidence in this discussion but unfortunately we are somewhat frustrated. While animal bones are plentiful in Exeter and have been studied in detail and to a high standard, they are rarely preserved at sites in the hinterland due to the acidic ground conditions (Chapter 3 above). Conversely plant macrofossils have been recovered from an increasing number of rural sites due to the implementation of systematic programmes of sampling, processing and analysis. Yet the plant record from Roman Exeter is disappointingly weak because similar programmes of environmental sampling have not been successfully applied at the principal urban sites published to date. Given these caveats, how then are we to assess the degree to which Exeter served as a market centre for its region, if indeed it did?

We can be reasonably confident that there was no halo of villas or complex farms around Exeter which might be regarded as places of maximised agricultural production to feed the urban population. There are hints of slightly more complex rural settlements in the vicinity of Exeter, certainty in comparison with the isolated enclosures known from aerial photography over much of lowland Devon, but they do not possess the plan form or produce the quantity or diversity of artefacts which characterise these settlements further east. We cannot as yet say much about settlement density, although the combined evidence from development-led investigations to the east of Exeter might suggest some intensification hereabouts (Chapter 3). A handful of roadside settlements are known to the west of the Blackdown Hills. Only at Ipplepen can we say much about extent or layout, with little indication that it conforms to the classic pattern of ribbon development along the road so well attested in other parts of the province; rather it has a more sprawling plan and rather blurs the modern artificial division between a large rural settlement and a nucleated roadside one. Our knowledge of the chronological development of these roadside settlements is also weak. Cullompton seems to be predominately Early Roman; the others stretch on into the later Roman period, but when they were abandoned is unclear. They could well have been in decline in the 4th century AD, as has been tentatively suggested for the port at Topsham. Quite what functions these roadside settlements performed beyond servicing life on the road is quite unclear, and it remains to be demonstrated that they served as localized market centres for their hinterlands.

Analysis of ceramic assemblages may be a more fruitful avenue to investigate the relationship of Exeter and its hinterland. In 1991 the prevalence of South Devon Ware at the rural settlements of Hayes Farm and Rewe in the vicinity of Exeter was remarked upon, and a contrast drawn with contemporary pottery groups in Exeter where South-East Dorset BB1 was much better represented. It was suggested that the inhabitants of the rural enclosures might have found it difficult to participate in the cash economy on which the sale of BB1 may have largely depended, and so made use of other wares which could be obtained by socially embedded networks which largely bypassed the town (Holbrook and Bidwell 1991, 21–3). That idea was founded upon a very small amount of evidence, so does it still hold up 30 years later when we now have more available information? Figure 3.24 in Chapter 3 above broadens out the picture considerably compared to 1991, and at sites to the north and east of Exeter South Devon Ware is well represented and, in some cases, forms over half of the total ceramic assemblage. While the lack of chronological precision inherent in rural assemblages is an issue, the prevalence of South Devon Ware does seem to have been a later Roman phenomenon to judge from the available evidence (Table 9.1).

In the earlier Roman period the Bishop's Court assemblage is broadly comparable in terms of its composition of coarse ware fabrics to contemporary groups in Exeter, although it lacks the quantities of fine wares, mortaria and flagons found there (a common discriminator between urban and rural assemblages). From the 3rd century AD onwards South Devon Ware is much more prevalent than in Exeter itself, where the quantity of South Devon Ware relative to SE Dorset BB1 increased throughout the 4th century AD but never exceeded the latter (Bidwell 2016, section 3). A difference in the composition of rural and urban coarse ware pottery assemblages in the later Roman period does therefore appear to have been substantiated by more recent work and lends weight to the notion that rural sites were supplied with ceramics by different mechanisms to the town, an observation that in turn gives little support to Exeter as a market centre for its hinterland. As we have seen Exeter is by no means unique in this respect. Fulford (2017, 359–62) provides other examples and concludes that there was only weak interaction between town and country.

To date there has been comparatively little quantitative analysis of pottery assemblages in and around Exeter by vessel form, and this could be a profitable means of examining differences not only between Exeter and its surrounding rural settlements, but between those farmsteads. It could assist, for instance, in identifying those sites which have a greater variety of vessel types and thus potentially had some higher status or greater integration with the urban economy than those farmsteads where utilitarian forms predominate (as at Hill Barton, for instance, where 80% of identifiable forms were jars or storage jars).

Other specialist analyses undertaken as part of the EAPIT project also lend little support for Exeter's role as a market centre, and thus the source of artefacts found on rural sites in Devon. In her study of the quern stones found in Devon, Shaffrey remarks that there is little evidence that the town functioned as centre for the secondary distribution of querns given that stones deriving from different sources occur in an uneven distribution pattern around Exeter (EAPIT2, Chapter 14). Brown and Moorhead's study of the coins recorded by the Portable Antiquities Scheme in Devon also reaches a similar conclusion (EAPIT2, Chapter 16). They conclude that the currency pool in Devon was not necessarily dependent on, or very closely related to, that of Exeter, and that the town was not a currency nodal-point for the region in the way suggested for *Verulamium*, for instance (Moorhead 2015, 157). We do need to be mindful, however, that we may not be comparing like with like here. The coins from Exeter were recovered predominately through excavation while those in rural Devon are mostly the product of metal detecting. The two assemblages will have different biases in their composition. Machin and Warry also show that the dominance of Exeter as a source of ceramic tiles for buildings in its hinterland had waned by the later Roman period, with a number of new production centres springing up from the 3rd century AD in southern, central and eastern Devon, although the actual site of only one rural kiln site has as yet been firmly recognised (at Hatherleigh Moor). Once again the role of Exeter as a central place seems to have diminished by the later Roman period.

In conclusion, the evidence we have does not support the view that Exeter was a pre-eminent market centre for its region in the Roman period. Rather Exeter appears to have been an administrative centre created by the state which drew in resources from its hinterland. This is best exemplified by the animal bones which demonstrate that throughout the Roman period Exeter was the home of specialist butchers who slaughtered cattle and sheep brought in on the hoof from the surrounding countryside to provide food and other resources for the urban population. We might also envisage other archaeologically invisible resources being drawn into the town such as slaves or peasant workers. While Exeter drew resources in, fewer goods moved in the opposite direction and in the later Roman period at least, Exeter seems not to have been the market where farmers obtained their pottery, querns or coins.

Fluctuating fortunes

A distinctive feature of Exeter's development was that rather than steady growth from humble beginnings to become England's 6th wealthiest city in the 16th century, there were instead very marked fluctuations in its fortunes (Fig. 9.4). When initially founded, the legionary fortress was one of the most important places in Roman Britain with one of its earliest masonry buildings conceived on a grand scale (the bath-house). The size of the forum-basilica complex – the 7th largest that we know about in Roman Britain – suggests that the imperial and/or civil authorities had high aspirations for the development of Exeter as a major urban centre, and the same might be said of the greatly increased area that was defended in the later 2nd century AD. The actual density of occupation within Exeter, however, and the quality of its domestic buildings – as reflected, for example, in the relatively few mosaic pavements – suggest somewhat stifled development. The abandonment of Exeter in the 5th century was in common with virtually all Romano-British towns as they had become socially and economically irrelevant, just as its reuse for an early Christian church was part of a phenomenon seen elsewhere across 7th-century England. Its reuse as a burghal fortress is also not unusual, although King Alfred's establishment of the only royal mint in the South-West Peninsula suggests a particular royal interest. By the late 10th century Exeter was the 5th to 8th most productive mint, but perhaps the 18th most populous town in 1086; it was the 5th to 7th wealthiest town in the 12th century, but just 27th or 28th in 1334 (and the 23rd most populous town in 1377). Its rise to the 6th ranked town in the 16th and 17th centuries was, therefore, momentous.

Exeter's changing fortunes can be attributed to a range of factors that were both internal and external to itself and its hinterland. Its choice as the location for a legionary fortress must surely reflect the strategic significance of Exeter's location, as well as awareness of the region's rich mineral resources. The decision to abandon the fortress presumably reflects both an internal factor – the

Table 9.1 Proportions of three coarse ware pottery fabrics at three rural settlements in the hinterland of Exeter. Hayes Farm was quantified by fabric weight; the other sites by sherd number. For site references see Appendix 3.5

Site	*Period of occupation*	*Total sherds*	*South Devon*	*SE Dorset BB1*	*SW BB1*
Bishop's Court	predominantly Early Roman	617	6%	18%	47%
Hill Barton	pre mid/late C3	587	27%	11%	27%
Rewe Turnspit	C3	339	78%	2%	2%
Hayes Farm	mid C2–C4	(7.6 kg)	47%	12%	3%
Old Park, Pinhoe	predominantly Late Roman	348	53%	26%	2%

successful subjugation of the South-West – as well as the important external factor of the desire to increase the military presence in Wales and the North. Although there may have been high aspirations on the part of the Roman authorities for Exeter to become a major town, a range of local factors appear to have stifled this most notably the lack of engagement on the part of the local population in cultural change (a social conservatism that is seen in the medieval period too). The continued existence of the port at Topsham may also have stifled development of Exeter itself. Exeter's return to importance in the Late Saxon period surely reflects King Alfred's recognition of its strategic and defensible location as well as the value of its tin and perhaps silver and iron deposits. Although there was clearly considerable enthusiasm on the part of the townsfolk to engage with a market-based economy and international trade, it is striking that the pottery produced within the town – Bedford Garage Ware – is not found widely across the Devon countryside, suggesting that Exeter's central place role within its local hinterland was still limited. Exeter's strategic and economic importance continued until the early 13th century when its prosperity was hit by the decline in the South-West's tin industry due to competition from Germany. The impact of this on Exeter was compounded by Cornish production overtaking that of Devon's for the first time, and by the establishment of a series of 'stannary' towns around the edge of Dartmoor (Ashburton, Chagford and Tavistock) that weakened Exeter's control of the industry. Tin was also increasingly exported via other ports such as Dartmouth and Plymouth, and while Exeter's late 13th-century exports did include some tin, its 14th-century exports did not (Maddicott 1989, 20–6; Kowalseski 1995, 233–4, 253, 325).

It is also striking how population growth across the South-West Peninsula was far less than was seen elsewhere in England, suggesting that the region was not sharing in the strong economic development seen elsewhere across the nation (with Devon's annual population growth between 1086 and 1290 being just 0.21% compared to 0.37% in Dorset and 0.32% in Somerset: Broadberry *et al.* 2015, fig 1.03, tabs 1.07 and 1.09). By the late medieval period, however, Devon had a relatively high number of seigneurial boroughs, and its rural economy was highly commercial with its pastoralism based upon on the sale of beef, wool, and dairy products, alongside increased fishing. There was a strong tradition of rural industry, and from the 15th century the production of woollen cloths expanded rapidly and this formed the basis of the new period of prosperity for Exeter. Once again, however, this shows that the economic fortunes of a town were in part determined by factors outside of its residents' control. As Carus-Wilson (1963, 5–6) has commented, 'In the late fourteenth century Exeter was a modest provincial town, of consequence indeed to the people of Devon, but to few others' its trade being 'small, indeed almost insignificant'. A century later Exeter was the 6th wealthiest and most populous city in England, and this can be accounted for by its relatively late involvement in England's export trade in woollen cloth that started to expand during the pause in hostilities with France in the 1430s and 1440s and resumed after a lasting peace was established in 1475. Crucial for Exeter was that demand was shifting from the expensive finely finished broadcloths produced in regions such as Lincolnshire and Flanders to cheaper-priced cloths such as that produced in Devon. The impact of this was dramatic: in the late 14th century Exeter exported around 350 cloths a year which was just 1% of the national total, while around 1440 Exeter exported *c.* 2,000 cloths (nearly 4% of England's total); this fell to *c.* 1,000 cloths in the 1450s and 60s, before rising to 6,000 in 1481–2 and *c.* 8,600 cloths a year in the early 16th century comprising nearly 11% of the national exports. Exports of tin from Exeter even rose during the late 15th century, while the return trade between Exeter and France – wine – also expanded rapidly in the period (Carus-Wilson 1963).

The prosperity of Exeter, and eastern Devon more widely, was not therefore based upon a change in the character of the wool produced by its sheep – that remained relatively coarse – but instead in changing consumer demand across western Europe and the access that English ports had to continental markets which was determined by national politics. Exeter's, and therefore Devon's, economy was also in part determined by the prosperity of other countries, and in particular France: the inter-connectivity of international economies is not a new phenomenon.

Overall, in the development of Exeter we can see how the prosperity and importance of a place is determined by a wide range of factors. Crucially, no individual settlement can be seen in isolation, and the development of Exeter can only be understood within the context of its wider landscape context. Many of the factors that led to Exeter's success were internal to its region. The South-West was rich in a range of easily accessible minerals and is not, contrary to some popular views, a predominantly upland region as eastern and southern Devon in particular have large areas of rich agricultural land. Exeter also became a nodal point within the communication networks of the South-West Peninsula, drawing in the area's produce along a series of roads that radiated from both the Roman town and the medieval city. Exeter was also ideally located for trade with other ports along the Atlantic coast of Europe, although in any market-based economy the success of any one place will be reliant upon the economies of others. This was seen in Exeter during several key periods in its development, including the 13th and 14th centuries when its involvement in the tin industry suffered due to competition to elsewhere.

Just as Exeter's hinterland provides many of the explanations for periods when it developed strongly, it may provide some of the reasons why there were

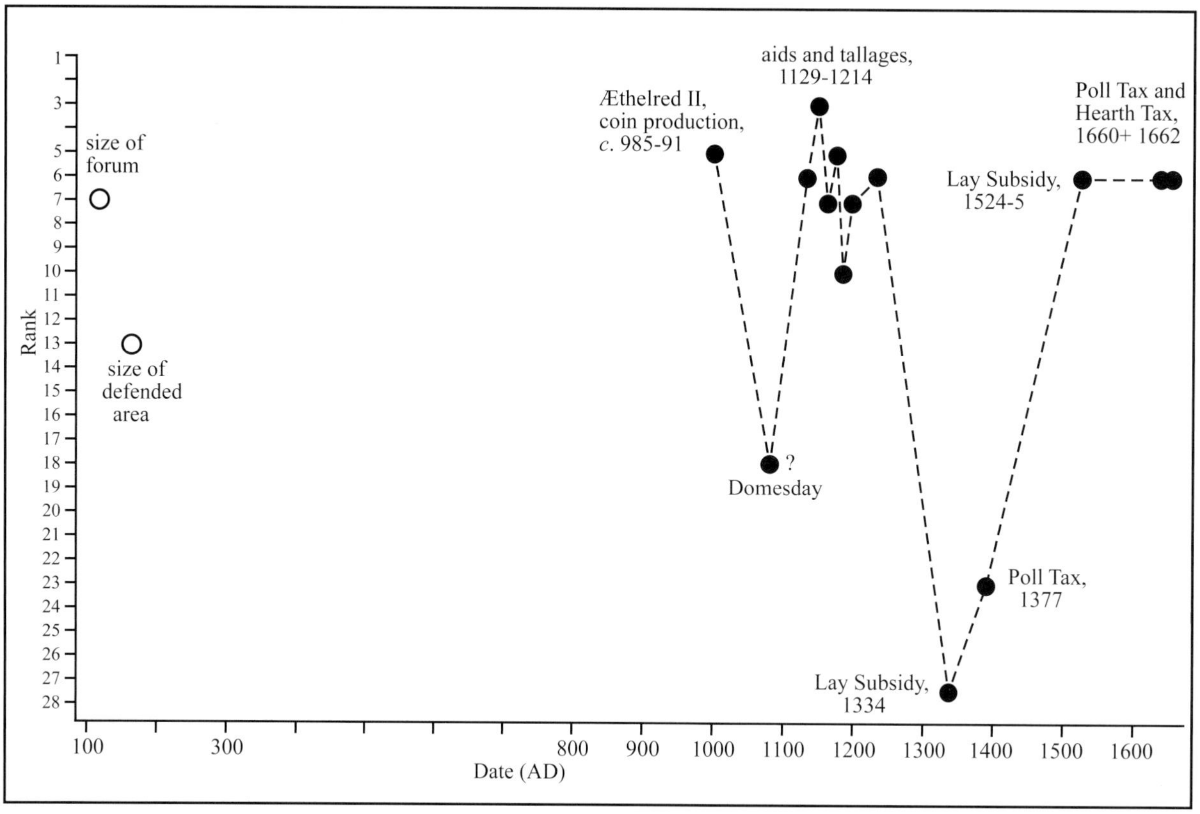

Fig. 9.4 Exeter's fluctuating fortunes in the national ranking of towns (drawn by Stephen Rippon)

periods when it did not. The large size of Exeter's forum-basilica, and the area enclosed by its new defensive circuit in the late 2nd century AD, suggest that the authorities had high hopes for its development as a major town. The actual density of occupation, and the wealth displayed in its townhouses, for example through the numbers and quality of mosaic floors, was however modest, and an explanation for this may once again be found in Exeter's hinterland. Although there were several roadside settlements, a small number of villas, and several possible complex farms within *c.* 20 km of Exeter, Dumnonian society across the South-West Peninsula as a whole did not change to the same degree following the Roman conquest as was seen in regions further east. The boundary between communities that run along the Blackdown and Quantock Hills is a remarkably stable feature within the landscape – evident from the Iron Age through to the early medieval period – with another constant being subtle differences between what were to become Devon and Cornwall. Many of the differences that are archaeologically visible suggest that what we are seeing is communities who chose to live their lives differently: they selected different crops, chose to produce and use different material culture (or in the case of early medieval Devon to use almost no durable material culture), and – in the Roman period in particular – there is also a strong thread of conservatism. This is seen in many ways, but is perhaps most evident in domestic architecture, as to the east of the Blackdown and Quantock Hills people moved to living in rectangular houses quite quickly whereas in the South-West Peninsula they retained their traditional circular (in Devon) and oval-shaped houses (in Cornwall).

Exeter is just one city, in one county, but it illustrates many of the themes that are common to so many archaeological sites in the Roman and medieval periods: the importance of place, politics, economics and society. The foundation of Exeter as a legionary fortress was part of a political and military strategy to conquer new territory, and for two decades it was one of the most important places in Britain. There appear to have been plans for it to become a beacon of *Romanitas* in the far South-West of the newly civilian province, but these ambitions were not quite realised as the Dumnonians did not appear to have been very keen on the idea. Exeter was, however, a very well-placed town for both internal and international trade which is seen both in the Roman and especially the medieval periods with the late 10th–12th and late 15th–16th centuries seeing Exeter ranked within the top ten English cities. We cannot, however, understand this prosperity simply by looking at Exeter itself: we need to understand the rich natural resources of the South-West Peninsula alongside the entrepreneurial Devonians who exploited them.

Future priorities

The vast majority of excavation within Exeter has been, and will be in the future, carried out within the context of urban redevelopment, and as such the location of future work will be determined by the activities and ambitions of landowners and the planning system. The exciting recent discoveries at St Sidwell's Point, St David's Church and St Loye's College remind us of the very high archaeological potential of areas well outside the designated Area of Archaeological Importance (the walled area and immediate suburbs). Even within Exeter's walls there has been more work carried out in some areas than others, with a marked bias towards the central area with its public buildings, major ecclesiastical sites and high-status private residences. Far less work has been carried out in the lower-status neighbourhoods and areas associated with manufacturing most notably the South Quarter.

What EAPIT has revealed, however, is that that are some noticeable gaps in our understanding of Exeter's past that can hopefully be filled. In terms of its chronological development the early medieval period is least understood, including the abandonment of the Late Roman town, the context of the 5th to 7th-century burials in Cathedral Close (a British church?), whether there was any secular domestic occupation contemporary with this or the 7th to 9th-century minster church, and the earliest stages of the Late Saxon urban revival. Palaeoenvironmental sampling and dating of the dark earth sequence is a high priority.

There is a need for more palaeoenvironmental work in general. While many excavations have revealed artefact rich deposits, there are at present almost no plant macrofossil assemblages (although hopefully modern sampling techniques can remedy this). Although there are a series of well-studied faunal assemblages it would be helpful to retrieve more material from the Roman military phase, and there is a particular need for more sampling for, and analysis of, fish bones both in Exeter and other towns. A problem that affects all periods is that some zones within Exeter have seen more excavations than others, which means that we have a better understanding of meat consumption by some communities – notably those of higher status – than others, and this could be addressed as opportunities to excavate in more peripheral parts of the city arise.

EAPIT has shown that the archives left by the EMAFU are of a high quality and can be written up, and hopefully this will happen for more sites. Plans are afoot to publish the Roman phases at Princesshay, Mount Dinham, St Loye's College and the likely *canabae* at Lower Coombe Street outside the South Gate in a Devon Archaeological Society monograph, while the medieval phases at Princesshay are due to be published in the Society's *Proceedings* and a monograph on Exeter Castle is currently being prepared for publication. In designing EAPIT difficult decisions had to me made in order to ensure that the project could be completed on time and within budget, and this meant that some excavations of very high importance could not be written up. The post-Roman sequence in the Cathedral Close – including the Saxon minster – is a particular priority for post-excavation analysis and publication, as is the Roman military to post-medieval sequence at Friernhay Street. The detailed surveys of the city walls – that are currently in the form of unpublished typescript reports (*e.g.* Blaylock 1988; 1995) – also warrant publication, while the considerable amount of excavation that has been undertaken on Exeter's defences are a high priority. The decision to focus on the Roman and medieval periods has also meant that some important post-medieval excavations are still to be published, including those related to the Civil War defences. The study of Exeter's defences could even be taken into the 20th century by studying the nearby Second World War airfields, anti-aircraft gun batteries, and decoy sites. It will also be important to produce an updated synthesis of the work carried out in what was Exeter's rural hinterland to the east of the city where housing and industrial development is continuing at a rapid pace.

Bibliography

Unpublished primary sources

D&C	Dean and Chapter records (in Exeter Cathedral Library and Archive)
DHC	Devon Heritage Centre

Published Primary Sources

Agricola	Tacitus' *Agricola* (Ogilvie and Richmond 1967; translation Birley 1999)
Anglo-Saxon Chronicle	*Anglo-Saxon Chronicle* (Swanton 1996)
Bede	Bede's *A History of the English Church and People* (Latham 1968)
Geography	Strabo's *Geographies* (Jones 1917)
Histories	Herodotus' *Histories* (Godley 1963)
Hooker's Antique Description	John Hooker's *The Antique Description and Account of the City of Exeter* (Brice 1765)
Hooker's Chroncicle	John Hooker's *Chronicle* (Gray 2005)
Worcester's Itineraries	William Worcestre's *Itineraries* (Harvey 1969)

Secondary Sources

DOI Abbreviations

ADS:	Archaeology Data Service
CA:	Cotswold Archaeology
IA:	Internet Archaeology
ORCA:	Online Research at Cardiff University
WA:	Wessex Archaeology

Abdy, R., Brunning, R.A. and Webster, C.J. 2001 'The discovery of a Roman villa at Shapwick and its Severan coin hoard of 9,238 denarii', *Journal of Roman Archaeology* 14(1), 358–73

Abrams, L. 1996 *Anglo-Saxon Glastonbury: church and endowment* Woodbridge, The Boydell Press

AC Archaeology 1996 *An archaeological evaluation of a proposed housing development at Front Street, Portesham, Dorset* AC Archaeology report 2096/2/0 [ADS: https://doi.org/10.5284/1028796]

Agate, A., Duggan, M., Roskams, S. and Turner, S. 2012 'Early medieval settlement at Mothecombe, Devon: the interaction of local, regional and long-distance dynamics', *Archaeology Journal* 169, 343–94

Aitkin, G.M. and Aitkin, G.N. 1990 'Excavations at Whitcombe, 1965–67', *Proceedings of the Dorset Natural History and Archaeological Society* 112, 57–94

Alan Baxter and Associates 2004 *Rougemont castle conservation plan* Unpublished report for Exeter City Council

Albarella, U. 2003 'Tawyers, tanners, horn trade and the mystery of the missing goat', in Murphy and Wiltshire (eds) 2003, 71–83

Albarella, U. 2006 'Pig husbandry and pork consumption in medieval England', in Woolgar *et al.* (eds) 2006, 72–87

Albarella, U. and Davis, S.J.M. 1996 'Mammals and birds from Launceston Castle, Cornwall: decline in status and the rise of agriculture', *Circaea, The Journal of the Association for Environmental Archaeology* 12(i), 1–156

Alcock, L. 1995 *Cadbury Castle, Somerset: the early medieval archaeology* Cardiff, University of Cardiff Press

Alexander, J. and Binski, P. (eds) 1987 *Age of chivalry* London, Royal Academy of Arts

Alexander, M. (ed.) 2016 *Medieval and post-medieval occupation and industry in the Redcliffe suburb of Bristol* Cirencester, Cotswold Archaeology Monograph 8

Allan, J.P. 1981 'The pottery', in Weddell 1981, 128–35

Allan, J.P. 1983a 'Some post-medieval documentary evidence for the trade in ceramics', in Davey and Hodges (eds) 1983, 37–45

Allan, J.P. 1983b 'The importation of pottery to southern England, *c.* 1200–1500', in Davey and Hodges (eds) 1983, 193–207

Allan, J.P. 1984a *Medieval and post-medieval finds from Exeter, 1971–1980* Exeter, Exeter City Council and the University of Exeter

Allan, J.P. 1984b *Medieval and post-medieval finds from Exeter, 1971–1980: Microfiche* Exeter, Exeter City Council and the University of Exeter

Allan, J.P. 1986 'The pottery', in Weddell, P.J., 'The excavation of medieval and later houses at St Margaret's Chapel, Exmouth', *Proceedings of the Devon Archaeological Society* 44, 131–6

Allan, J.P. 1991 'The building stones of the cathedral', in Kelly (ed.) 1991, 10–18

Allan, J.P. 1994a 'Medieval pottery and the dating of deserted settlements on Dartmoor', *Proceedings of the Devon Archaeological Society* 52, 141–8

Allan, J.P. 1994b 'Imported pottery in South-West England, *c.* 1350–1550', *Medieval Ceramics* 18, 45–50

Allan, J.P. 1995 'Iberian pottery imported into south-west England, *c.* 1250–1600', in Gerrard *et al.* (eds) 1995, 299–314

Allan, J.P. 1999 *St Nicholas Priory, Exeter* Exeter, City Museums

Allan, J.P. 2000 'Medieval floor tiles', in Blaylock 2000, 82–3

Allan, J.P. 2002 'The Anglo-Saxon mint at Lydford', *Report and Transactions of the Devonshire Association* 134, 9–32

Allan, J.P. 2003a 'A group of early 13th-century pottery from Sherborne Old Castle and its wider context', *Proceedings of the Dorset Natural History and Archaeological Society* 125, 71–82

Allan, J.P. 2003b 'Tenor ('Jesus') bell', in R. Marks and P. Williamson (eds) *Gothic Art for England 1400–1547* London, V & A Publications, 421

Allan, J.P. 2005a *An introduction to the Roman legionary fortress at Exeter* Exeter, Exeter City Council

Allan, J.P. 2005b 'The college of the Vicars Choral at Exeter', in Hall and Stocker (eds) 2005, 29–43

Allan, J.P. 2008 *Archaeological recording at Tuckers Hall, Fore Street, Exeter* Exeter Archaeology report 08.29

Allan, J.P. 2014a 'The Romanesque cathedral', *Annual Report of the Friends of Exeter Cathedral for 2014*, 13–20

Allan, J.P. 2014b 'Breton woodworkers in the immigrant communities of south-west England, 1500–1550', *Post-Medieval Archaeology* 48(2), 320–56

Allan, J.P. 2014c *Medieval and later pottery from the Lamb site, Totnes,* John Allan Archaeology report 6/2014

Allan, J.P. 2017 *Archaeologist's report on observations following the removal of part of the forecourt outside the west front of Exeter Cathedral, 2017* Unpublished report to the Dean & Chapter

Allan, J.P. 2018 *The archaeological assessment and report on Exeter cathedral and its precinct: quinquennial review* Unpublished report to the Dean & Chapter

Allan, J.P. 2019 *An archaeological assessment of the excavations at St Nicholas Priory, Exeter, 1971–2001* John Allan Archaeology report 94/2019

Allan, J.P. 2020 *An archaeological record of the high eastern gable and great east window of Exeter cathedral, 2015–18. Part 2: the glass* Unpublished report to the Dean & Chapter

Allan, J.P. and Collings, A.C. 2019 'Documentary study', in Austin and Clutterbuck 2019, 29–37

Allan, J.P. and Keen, L. 1984 'The medieval floor-tiles', in Allan 1984a, 323–47

Allan, J.P. and Langman, G. 2002–3 'The pottery', in P. Manning and P. Stead 'Excavation of an early Christian cemetery at Althea Library, Padstow', *Cornish Archaeology* 41–2, 97–104

Allan, J.P. and Morris, B. 2017 'The pottery', in B. Morris 'The missing link – the Exeter Inn, Barnstaple: North Devon pottery in the 16th century', *Proceedings of the Devon Archaeological Society* 75, 284–311

Allan, J.P. amd Silvester, R.J. 1981 'Newenham Abbey, Exminster', *Proceedings of the Devon Archaeological Society* 39, 159–71

Allan, J.P., Henderson, C. and Higham, R. 1984 'Saxon Exeter', in Haslam (ed.) 1984b, 385–414

Allan, J.P., Durrant, J. and Taylor, R. 2009 'Roman tiles in Exminster church', *Proceedings of the Devon Archaeological Society* 66, 69–84

Allan, J.P., Blackmore, S. and Passmore, A.J. 2010 'Archaeological investigations around Crediton parish church', *Proceedings of the Devon Archaeological Society* 68, 113–98

Allan, J.P., Alcock, N. and Dawson, D. (eds) 2015 *West Country households 1500–1700* Society of Post-Medieval Archaeology Monograph 9

Allan, J.P., Henderson, C.G. and Weddell, P.J. 2016 'A summary of the archaeological evidence for the late medieval friary', in Orme 2016, 235–48

Allason-Jones, L. 1991a 'Objects of copper alloy', in Holbrook and Bidwell 1991, 242–63

Allason-Jones, L. 1991b 'Objects of clay', in Holbrook and Bidwell 1991, 274–5

Allason-Jones, L. 1991c 'Objects of bone and antler', in Holbrook and Bidwell 1991, 266–71

Allen, J.R.L. and Fulford, M.G. 1996 'The distribution of South-East Dorset Black Burnished category I pottery in South-West Britain', *Britannia* 27, 223–81

Allen, J.R.L. and Fulford, M.G. 2004 'Early Roman mosaic materials in southern Britain, with particular reference to Silchester (*Calleva Atrebatum*)', *Britannia* 35, 9–38

Allen, J.R.L., Fulford, M.G. and Todd, J.A. 2007 'Burnt Kimmeridgian shale at early Roman Silchester, South-East England, and the Roman Poole-Purbeck complex-agglomerated industry', *Oxford Journal of Archaeology* 26(2), 167–91

Allen, M. 2017 'Pastoral farming', in Allen *et al.* (eds) 2017, 85–141

Allen, M. (ed.) 2019 *The role of zooarchaeology in the study of the western Roman empire* Portsmouth (Rhode Island), Journal of Roman Archaeology Supplementary Series 107

Allen, M. and Lodwick, L. 2017 'Agricultural strategies in Roman Britain', in Allen *et al.* 2017, 142–77

Allen. M. and Smith, A. 2016 'Rural settlement in Roman Britain: morphological classification and overview', in A. Smith *et al.* 2016, 17–43

Allen, M., Abdy, R. and de Jersey, P. 2004 'Coin register', *British Numismatic Journal* 74, 198–229

Allen, M., Blick, N., Brindle, T., Evans, T., Fulford, M., Holbrook, N., Lodwick, L., Richards, J.D. and Smith, A. 2015 *The rural settlement of Roman Britain: an online resource,* [ADS: https://archaeologydataservice.ac.uk/archives/romangl/]

Allen, M., Lodwick, L., Brindle, T., Fulford, M. and Smith, A. 2017 *The rural economy of Roman Britain* London, The Society for the Promotion of Roman Studies Britannia Monograph 30

Anon. 2001 'Christopher George Henderson: an appreciation', *Proceedings of the Devon Archaeological Society* 59, 1–9

Anon. 2019 'Vicus discovered in Devon?', *Current Archaeology* 346, 10

Appleton-Fox, N. 1992 'Excavations at a Romano-British round: Reawla, Gwinear, Cornwall', *Cornish Archaeology* 31, 69–123

Archibald, M. 1984 'Foreign coins', in Allan 1984a, 250–1

Armitage, P.L. 2013 'Fish bone', in Ridgeway and Watts (eds) 2013, 283–8

Armitage, P.L. 2016 'Fish bones', in Alexander 2016, 101–4

Armitage, P.L. 2017 'Fishbone', in Farnell and Rainbird 2017, 61–3

Armstrong, S. forthcoming *Cultural diversity within south-west Britain during the Roman period* Unpublished PhD thesis, University of Exeter

Arnold, A. and Howard, R. 2009 *46 High Street, Exeter, Devon: tree-ring analysis of timbers* English Heritage Scientific Dating Report 71/2009

Arup Associates 1973 *Exeter Roman bath-house. Proposals for the preservation of the remains, feasibility study*

Ashby, T., Hudd, A.E. and Martin, A.T. 1902 'Excavations at Caerwent Monmouthshire on the site of the Romano-British city of Venta Silurum in 1901', *Archaeologia* 58, 119–52

Astill, G. 2000 'General survey 600–1300', in Palliser (ed.) 2000a, 27–49

Aston, M. 1984 'The towns of Somerset', in Haslam (ed.) 1984b, 167–201

Atherton, I., Fernie, E., Harper-Bill, C. and Smith, H. (eds) 1996 *Norwich Cathedral: church, city and diocese, 1096–1996* London and Rio Grande, Hambledon Press

Atkinson, D. 1942 *Report on excavations at Wroxeter (the Roman city of Viroconium) in the county of Salop 1923–1927* Oxford, Birmingham Archaeological Society

Austin, J. 2017 *Westclyst Community Primary School Site, Westclyst, Devon* Cotswold Archaeology report 17067 [CA: https://reports.cotswoldarchaeology.co.uk/]

Austin, J. 2018 *Land at Hollow Lane, Pinhoe, Exeter* Cotswold Archaeology report 18238 [CA: https://reports.cotswoldarchaeology.co.uk/]

Austin, J. 2019 *Playing field off Wear Barton Road, Exeter, Devon* Cotswold Archaeology report 880374_1 [CA: https://reports.cotswoldarchaeology.co.uk/]

Austin, J. and Clutterbuck, J. 2019 *The former Radmore and Tucker site, Frog Street, Exeter: archaeological excavation'* Cotswold Archaeology report EX0031_1

Austin, J. and Massey, R. 2018 *Land off Exeter Road, Topsham, Exeter. Excavation report, incorporating statement of potential and updated project design* Cotswold Archaeology report 889014 [CA: https://reports.cotswoldarchaeology.co.uk/]

Avon Archaeological Unit 2005 *St Mary's CE Va Primary School, Portbury, North Somerset* Avon Archaeological Unit report [ADS: https://doi.org/10.5284/1029155]

Baart, J. 1994 'Dutch redwares', *Medieval Ceramics* 18, 19–28

Baker, A.R.H. 1973 'Changes in the later middle ages', in Darby (ed.) 1973, 186–247

Baker, J. and Brookes, S. 2013 *Beyond the Burghal Hidage: Anglo-Saxon civil defence in the Viking age* Leiden, Brill

Baker, N., Brett, J. and Jones, R. 2018 *Bristol: a worshipful town and famous city* Oxford, Oxbow Books

Balaam, N.D., Levitan, B. and Straker, V. (eds) 1987 *Studies in palaeoeconomy and environment in south west England* Oxford, British Archaeological Reports British Series 181

Balasse, M., Ambrose, S.H., Smith, A.B. and Price, T.D. 2002 'The seasonal mobility model for prehistoric herders in the south-western Cape of South Africa assessed by isotopic analysis of sheep tooth enamel', *Journal of Archaeological Science* 29, 917–32

Bampton, J. 2012 *Land off Langaton Lane, Broadclyst, Devon* Southwest Archaeology report 12.07.31 [ADS: https://doi.org/10.5284/1017716]

Bampton, J. and Morris, B. 2013 *Brayford School, High Bray, Devon* Southwest Archaeology report 130110 [ADS: https://doi.org/10.5284/1026586]

Bampton, J. and Morris, B. 2017 *St Margaret's School, Exeter, Devon* Southwest Archaeology report 171016 [ADS: https://doi.org/10.5284/1048720]

Bampton, J. and Walls, S. 2013a *The Glebe, Tregony, Cornwall* Southwest Archaeology report 130611 [ADS: https://doi.org/10.5284/1025008]

Bampton, J. and Walls, S. 2013b *Land adjacent to Waybrook Cottages, Alphington, Devon* Southwest Archaeology report 130912 [ADS: https://doi.org/10.5284/1022406]

Bampton, J., Morris, B., Walls, S. and Wapshott, E. 2014 *Land at Tredinnick Farm, St Newlyn East, Cornwall. Results of an archaeological evaluation and historic visual impact assessment* Southwest Archaeology report 140220 [ADS: https://doi.org/10.5284/1039640]

Barber, A. 1999 *Cherry Tree Farm, Kingston Seymour, North Somerset* Cotswold Archaeology report 991023 [CA: https://reports.cotswoldarchaeology.co.uk/]

Barber, A. 2000 *Hayes Farm, Clyst Honiton, nr Exeter, Devon. Archaeological excavation phase 1 (1999)* Cotswold Archaeology report 001127 [ADS: https://doi.org/10.5284/1028777]

Barber, A. 2013 *Old Park Farm, Pinhoe, Devon* Cotswold Archaeology report 13078 [ADS: https://doi.org/10.5284/1024483]

Barber, A. 2014 *Shepherd's Farm, Clyst St Mary, Devon* Cotswold Archaeology report 14182 [ADS: https://doi.org/10.5284/1028380]

Barber, A. and Thomas, A. 1995 *Wixenford Bottom, Plymstock, Devon* Cotswold Archaeology report 95276

Barber, J. 1986 'Buildings and quays', in C. Gaskell Brown (ed.) *Plymouth excavations: the medieval waterfronts, Woolster Street: the finds* Plymouth, Plymouth Museum Archaeological Series No. 3, 11–12

Barclay, A., Evans, J., Booth, P., Wood, I., Knight, D. and Brown, D. 2016 *A standard for pottery studies in archaeology* Prehistoric Ceramics Research Group, Study Group for Roman Pottery and Medieval Pottery Research Group

Barlow, F. 1980 'The English background', in Reuter (ed.) 1980, 1–28

Barrowman, R.C., Batey, C.E. and Morris, C.D. 2007 *Excavations at Tintagel Castle, Cornwall 1990–1999* London, Reports of the Research Committee of the Society of Antiquaries of London 74

Bately, J.M. (ed.) 1986 *The Anglo-Saxon Chronicle: a collaborative edition. Volume 3: MS. A: a semi-diplomatic edition with introduction and indices* Cambridge, Brewer

Bateson, J.D. 2007 'Coins', in W.S. Hanson *Elginhaugh: a Flavian fort and its annexe* (2 vols) London, The Society for the Promotion of Roman Studies Britannia Monograph 23, 253–70

Bath, P. and W.G.T. 2019 *Dorset building stone* [http://dorsetbuildingstone.weebly.com/wimborne-minster-interior.html]

Batten, K. and Bennett, F. 1996 *The printed maps of Devon; County maps 1575–1837* Tiverton, Devon Books

Bayley, J. 2001 'Precious metal refining in Roman Exeter', *Proceedings of the Devon Archaeological Society* 59, 141–7

Bayley, J. and Butcher, S. 2004 *Roman brooches in Britain: a technological and typological study based on the*

Richborough Collection London, Society of Antiquaries Research Report 68
Beacham, P. 1990 *Devon building: an introduction to local traditions* Exeter, Devon Books
Beacham, P. 1991 'Rural building: 1400–1800', in Cherry and Pevsner 1991, 62–78
Beacham, P. (ed.) 2017 *Buckfast Abbey: history, art and architecture* London and Buckfast, Merrell
Beagrie, N. 1989 'The Romano-British pewter industry', *Britannia* 20, 169–92
Bedford, J.B. and Hall, M.E.P. 1994 *Archaeological excavations in advance of sewer repairs in The Close, Cathedral Green, Exeter 1994* Exeter Archaeology report 94.99
Bedford, J.B. and Salvatore, J.P. 1992 *Excavations at Mary Arches Street, Exeter, 1975. Part 1: Roman military* Exeter Museums Archaeological Field Unit report 92.40 [ADS: https://doi.org/10.5284/1035191]
Bedford, J.B. and Salvatore, J.P. 1993 *Excavations at Paul Street, Exeter, 1982–85. Part 1: Roman military* Exeter Museums Archaeological Field Unit report 93.23 [ADS: https://doi.org/10.5284/1035213]
Bellamy, P. 2004 *New extension, 49 Blandford Road, Hamworthy, Poole* Terrain Archaeology report 53169.1 [ADS: https://doi.org/10.5284/1038762]
Bellamy, P. 2017 *Upton Park Farm, Poole, Dorset* Terrain Archaeology report 53415/3/2 [ADS: https://doi.org/10.5284/1046605]
Bellamy, P. 2018 *Top o'Town House, Bridport Road, Dorchester, Dorset* Terrain Archaeology report 53490/2/1 [ADS: https://doi.org/10.5284/1049574]
Bellamy, P. and Tatler, S. 2006 *Former Pilkington's tile factory, Shapwick Road, Hamworthy, Poole, Dorset* Terrain Archaeology report 53127/3/1 [ADS: https://doi.org/10.5284/1028817]
Bentley, R.A. 2006 'Strontium isotopes from the Earth to the archaeological skeleton: a review', *Journal of Archaeological Method and Theory* 13, 135–87
Beresford, G. 1979 'Three deserted medieval settlements on Dartmoor: a report on the late E. Marie Minters' excavations', *Medieval Archaeology* 23, 98–158
Beresford, M. 1967 *New towns of the middle ages: town plantation in England, Wales and Gascony* London, Lutterworth Press
Beresford, M. and Finberg, H.P.R. 1973 *English medieval boroughs: a handlist* Newton Abbot, David and Charles
Besly, E. 2003 'The coins', in James 2003, 283–8
Best, J. 2005 *Archaeological recording and excavation at Bray Valley Quarries, Brayford, Devon* Exeter Archaeology report
Best, J. 2006 *Archaeological fieldwalking and trial trenching for the proposed Sherford New Community Development, South Hams, Devon* Exeter Archaeology report 06.44 [ADS: https://doi.org/10.5284/1028758]
Best, J. and Farnell, A. 2007 *Archaeological recording at 38 Gordon Road, Topsham, Exeter* Exeter Archaeology report 07.80 [ADS: https://doi.org/10.5284/1028779]
Bhanji, S. 2013 'Caleb Hedgeland's model of Exeter and the topography of the Georgian city', *Proceedings of the Devon Archaeological Society* 71, 187–209
Biddle, M. 1976a 'Towns', in D.M. Wilson (ed) *The Archaeology of Anglo-Saxon England* London, Methuen, 99–150
Biddle, M. 1976b *Winchester in the early middle ages* Oxford, Clarendon press
Bidwell, P.T. 1979 *The legionary bath-house and basilica and forum at Exeter with a summary account of the legionary fortress* Exeter, Exeter City Council and the University of Exeter
Bidwell, P.T. 1980 *Roman Exeter: fortress and town* Exeter, Exeter Museums Service
Bidwell, P.T. 1982 'Roman occupation?', in R.A. Higham, J.P. Allan and S.R. Blaylock 'Excavations at Okehampton Castle, Devon. Part 2 – The Bailey', *Proceedings of the Devon Archaeological Society* 40, 25–7
Bidwell, P.T. 2002 'Timber baths in Augustan and Tiberian fortresses', in P. Freeman, J. Bennett, Z.T. Fiema and B. Hoffmann (eds) *Limes XVIII: Proceedings of the XVIIIth International Congress of Roman Frontier Studies held in Amman, Jordan (September 2000)*, Oxford, British Archaeological Reports International Series 1084 (I), 467–81
Bidwell, P.T. 2009 'The earliest occurrences of baths at auxiliary forts', in W.S. Hanson *The army and frontiers of Rome. Papers offered to David J. Breeze* Portsmouth (Rhode Island), Journal of Roman Archaeology Supplementary Series 74, 55–62
Bidwell, P.T. 2016 'Fifth century pottery in Devon and North East Cornwall', *Internet Archaeology* 41 [IA: https://doi.org/10.11141/ia.41]
Bidwell, P.T. 2017 'Rural settlement and the Roman army in the north: external supply and regional self-sufficiency', in Allen *et al.* 2017, 290–305
Bidwell, P.T. forthcoming 'The Roman pottery', in J.P. Salvatore, M. Steinmetzer and H. Quinnell forthcoming
Bidwell, P.T. and Boon, G.C. 1976 'An antefix type of the Second Augustan Legion at Exeter', *Britannia* 7, 278–80
Bidwell, P.T. and Speak, S. 1994 *Excavations at South Shields Roman fort, Vol. 1* Newcastle upon Tyne, Society of Antiquaries of Newcastle upon Tyne Monograph Series 4
Bidwell, P.T. and Wild, F.C. forthcoming 'The Roman pottery', in Steinmetzer forthcoming
Billingsley, J. 1797 *A general view of the agriculture of the county of Somerset* London, Board of Agriculture
Binski, P. 1987 'The stylistic sequence of London figure brasses', in Coales (ed.) 1987, 69–132
Birbeck, V. 2002 'Excavations on Iron Age and Romano-British settlement at Cannard's Grave, Shepton Mallet', *Somerset Archaeological and Natural History Society* 144, 41–116
Bird, D. (ed.) 2017 *Agriculture and industry in south-eastern Roman Britain* Oxford, Oxbow Books
Bird, J. (ed.) 1998 *Form and fabric: studies in Rome's material past in honour of B.R. Hartley* Oxford, Oxbow Books
Birley, A.R. 1979 *The people of Roman Britain* London, Batsford
Birley, A.R. 1999 *Agricola and Germany, translated with an introduction and notes* Oxford, Oxford University Press
Birley, A.R., 2005 *The Roman government of Britain* Oxford, Oxford University Press
Birrell, J. 2006 'Procuring, preparing and serving venison in late medieval England', in Woolgar *et al.* (eds) 2006, 176–88
Bishop, H.E. and Prideaux, E.K. 1922 *The building of the cathedral church of St Peter in Exeter* Exeter, Commin
Bishop, M.C. 1991 'Soldiers and military equipment in the towns of Roman Britain', in Maxfield and Dobson (eds) 1991, 21–7
Bishop, M.C. 2012 *Handbook to Roman legionary fortresses* Barnsley, Pen and Sword Military

Bishop, M.C. and Coulston, J.C.N. 2006 *Roman military equipment* London, Batsford

Blackburn, M.A.S. (ed.) 1986 *Anglo-Saxon monetary history: essays in memory of Michael Dolley* Leicester, Leicester University Press

Blackburn, M.A.S. 1990 'Hiberno-Norse coins of the *Helmet* type', in Jonsson (ed.) 1990, 11–24

Blackburn, M.A.S. and Lyon, S. 1986 'Regional die-production in Cnut's quatrefoil issue', in Blackburn (ed.) 1986, 252–72

Blagg, T. and King, A. (eds) 1984 *Military and civilian in Roman Britain* Oxford, British Archaeological Reports British Series 137

Blair, J. 1987 'English monumental brasses before 1350: types, patterns and workshops', in Coales (ed.) 1987, 133–74

Blair, J. and Orme, N. 1995 'The Anglo-Saxon minster and cathedral at Exeter: twin churches?', *Annual Report of the Friends of Exeter Cathedral* 65, 24–6

Blair, J., Rippon, S. and Smart, C. 2020 *Planning in the early medieval landscape* Liverpool, Liverpool University Press

Blaylock, S.R. 1988 *Exeter city defences: excavation and survey on the city walls from the North Gate to the Castle, 1978–88. Part I: Roman* Exeter Museums Archaeological Field Unit report 88.13 [ADS: https://doi.org/10.5284/1035173]

Blaylock, S.R. 1990 'Exeter Guildhall', *Proceedings of the Devon Archaeological Society* 48, 123–78

Blaylock, S.R. 1991 '*St Katherine's Priory, Polsloe: fabric survey of the west range, 1979–80* Exeter Archaeology report 91.57

Blaylock, S.R. 1993 'The building stones of the city wall', in Simpson 1993b, 1–4

Blaylock, S.R. 1995 *Exeter city wall survey* Unpublished report, Exeter Archaeology

Blaylock, S.R. 1996 'Bell and cauldron founding in Exeter', *Historical Metallurgy* 30(2), 72–82

Blaylock, S.R. 2000 'Excavation of an early post-medieval bronze foundry at Cowick Street, Exeter, 1999–2000', *Proceedings of the Devon Archaeological Society* 58, 1–92

Blaylock, S.R. 2004 *Bowhill: the archaeological study of a building under repair in Exeter, Devon, 1977–95* Swindon, English Heritage

Blaylock, S.R. 2015a 'The archaeology of the West Country bronze foundries', in Allan *et al.* (eds) 2015, 271–307

Blaylock, S.R. 2015b *Exeter city wall. Introduction to the series of Exeter Archaeology reports* Exeter City Council, Cotswold Archaeology 2015 [ADS: https://doi.org/10.5284/1035173]

Blaylock, S.R. 2017 'Exeter bishop's palace', in P, Rollason (ed.) *Princes of the church: bishops and their palaces,* 266–84 London and New York, Routledge, 266–84

Blaylock, S.R. forthcoming 'Appendix 4: bell-casting at Princesshay', in Steinmetzer *et al.* forthcoming

Blaylock, S.R. and Higham, R. in preparation 'Exeter castle: history, fabric analysis and excavation'

Blaylock, S.R. and Westcott, K.A. 1989 'Late Saxon fabric in St Martin's church, Exeter', *Proceedings of the Devon Archaeological Society* 47, 119–22

Boon, G.C. 1972 *Isca. The Roman legionary fortress at Caerleon, Monmouthshire* Cardiff, National Museum of Wales

Boon, G.C. 1982 'The coins', in G.C. Boon and M. Hassall *Report on the excavations at Usk 1965–1976. The coins, inscriptions and graffiti* Cardiff, University of Wales Press, 1–42

Boon, G.C. 1991 'Byzantine and other exotic ancient bronze coins from Exeter', in Holbrook and Bidwell (eds) 1991, 38–45

Borlase, M. 2018 *The way of saints: socio-economic and cultural continuity across the Camel/Fowey corridor from the late Iron Age to the post-Roman period* Unpublished PhD thesis, University of Bristol [https://research-information.bristol.ac.uk/en/theses/the-way-of-saints(c90d3e82-4a05-498f-9b7d-02ff86e165a1).html]

Borlase, M. and Wright, M. 2014a 'A late Iron Age and Romano-British settlement at Middle Amble Farm, St Kew', *Cornish Archaeology* 53

Borlase, M. and Wright, M. 2014b 'A Romano-British enclosure at East Leigh, Stratton, Cornwall', *Cornish Archaeology* 53, 209–22

Branigan, K. 1977 *Gatcombe Roman villa* Oxford, British Archaeological Reports British Series 44

Branigan, K. and Miles, D. (eds) 1989 *The economies of Romano-British villas* Sheffield, University of Sheffield, Department of Archaeology

Brannlund, L. and Busby, P. 2015 *Carloggas Farm, St Stephen, St Austell, Cornwall* Cotswold Archaeology report 15093 [ADS: https://doi.org/10.5284/1042667]

Bray, L.S. 2006 *The archaeology of iron production: Romano-British evidence from the Exmoor region* Unpublished PhD thesis, University of Exeter

Brayshay, M. (ed.) 1996 *Topographoical writers in south-west England* Exeter, University of Exeter Press

Brennan, N. and Leivers, M. 2013 'A probable Roman road at Den Brook, North Tawton', *Proceedings of the Devon Archaeological Society* 71, 87–90

Brett, M. 2011 *Project Dixie (phase 1; plot 1), Hayes Farm, Clyst Honiton, Devon* Cotswold Archaeology report 11245 [CA: https://reports.cotswoldarchaeology.co.uk/]

Brett, M. and Mudd, A. 2013 'Prehistoric, Roman and post-Roman discoveries in south Somerset: the archaeology of the Ilchester to South Petherton gas pipeline 2005–6', *Somerset Archaeological and Natural History Society* 156, 74–104

Brewer, R. 2006 *Caerwent Roman town* 3rd edition Cardiff, Cadw

Brice, A. (ed.) 1765 *The antique description and account of the city of Exeter in three parts, by John Vowell, alias Hoker* Exeter, North-gate Street

Brickstock, R.J. 2017 'Continuing the search for an "Antonine gap" on Hadrian's Wall', in N. Hodgson, P. Bidwell and J. Schachtmann (eds) *Roman frontier studies 2009. Proceedings of the XXI International Congress of Roman Frontier Studies (Limes Congress) held at Newcastle upon Tyne in August 2009* Oxford, Archaeopress Roman Archaeology 25, 331–5

Brickstock, R.J. and Casey, P.J. 2002 'Coins', in Webster 2002, 85–9

Bridgwater and District Archaeological Society 2002 *The "Barn", a Romano-British building* Bridgwater and District Archaeological Society report

Brigers, J. 2006 *Little Haven, Church Road, Edington, Somerset: report on an archaeological investigation* unpublished report in the Somerset County Council Historic Environment Record 14452

Brindle, T. 2016 'The south-west', in A. Smith *et al.* 2016, 331–58

Brindle, T. 2018 'Personal appearance in the countryside of Roman Britain', in A. Smith *et al.* 2018, 6–47

Brindle, T., Holbrook, N. and Sausins, T. 2018 'A first-century AD burial plot at Barnwood, Gloucestershire: excavations in 2013–14', *Britannia* 49, 147–77

Brittain, M. 2013 *Excavations at Ham Hill, Somerset (2012)* University of Cambridge Archaeological Unit report 1159 [ADS: https://doi.org/10.5284/1021183]

Britton, K., Grimes, V., Dau, J. and Richards, M.P. 2009 'Reconstructing faunal migrations using intra-tooth sampling and strontium and oxygen isotope analyses: a case study of modern caribou (Rangifer tarandus granti)', *Journal of Archaeological Science* 36, 1163–72

Broadberry, S., Cambpell, B.M.S., Klein, A., Overton, M. and van Leeuwen, B. 2015 *British economic growth 1270–1870* Cambridge, Cambridge University Press

Brooks, C. and Evans, D. 1988 *The great east window of Exeter cathedral* Exeter, Exeter University Press

Brooks, N.P. 1996 'The administrative background to the Burghal Hidage', in D. Hill and A. Rumble (eds) *The defence of Wessex: the Burghal Hidage and Anglo-Saxon fortifications* Manchester, Manchester University Press, 128–50

Broomhead, D. 1998 'Ilchester, Great Yard excavations 1995', *Somerset Archaeological and Natural History Society* 142, 139–91

Broomhead, R.A. 1995 *Masters Yard, Free Street, Ilchester: a report on an archaeological watching brief for Somerset County Council* R.A. Broomhead BA report [ADS: https://doi.org/10.5284/1029107]

Broomhead, R.A. 1998 *Sycamore Lodge, East Brent: an archaeological evaluation* R.A. Broomhead report RAB/20/98 [ADS: https://doi.org/10.5284/1029122]

Broomhead, R.A. 1999 *Yatton and Congresbury Wildlife Action Group: a documentary and archaeological survey of two moorland sites in Yatton and Congresbury* R.A. Broomhead report RAB/15/99

Broomhead, R.A. 2002 *Rossholme School, East Brent: an archaeological evaluation* R.A. Broomhead report RAB/16/02 [ADS: https://doi.org/10.5284/1029117]

Broomhead, R.A. 2006a *Gatcombe Farm, Flax Bourton, North Somerset* R.A. Broomhead report RAB/08/06 [ADS: https://doi.org/10.5284/1029150]

Broomhead, R.A. 2006b *Amulet Way, Shepton Mallet* R.A. Broomhead report RAB/17/06 [ADS: https://doi.org/10.5284/1029067]

Brown, A. 2016 *Sewer bifurcation works, Wear Barton Road, Exeter, Devon* AC Archaeology report ACD1469/2/0 [ADS: https://doi.org/10.5284/1053577]

Brown, A. and Hughes, S. 2018 *2 The Mede, Topsham, Exeter, Devon* AC Archaeology report ACD1717/2/1 [ADS: https://doi.org/10.5284/1057570]

Brown, A., de Figueirodo, P., Grenville, G. *et al.* 1999 *The Rows of Chester: the Chester Rows research project* London, English Heritage Archaeology Report 16

Brown, A., Quinnell, H. and Rainbird, P. 2018 'The excavation of an early medieval site at Park En Venton, Mullion', *Cornish Archaeology* 57, 189–206

Brown A.G., Hawkins C., Ryder L., Hawken S., Griffith F. and Hatton J. 2014 'Palaeoecological, archaeological and historical data and the making of Devon landscapes. I. The Blackdown Hills', *Boreas* 43, 834–55

Brown, L., Hayden, C. and Score, D. 2014 *'Down to Weymouth town by Ridgeway': prehistoric, Roman and later sites along the Weymouth Relief Road* Dorchester, Dorset Natural History and Archaeological Society Monograph Series 23

Brown, R.A., Colvin, H.M. and Taylor, A.J. 1963 *The history of the King's works. Volume II: the Middle Ages* London, Her Majesty's Stationery Office

Brown, S.W. 2005 *Exeter Cathedral archaeological recording: South Quire Aisle and St Gabriel's Chapel (external) 2005* Unpublished report to the Dean and Chapter of Exeter Cathedral

Brown, S.W. 2012 *St Stephen's Church, Exeter. Archaeological fabric recording and excavation during reordering works 2011–2012* Stewart Brown Associates report [ADS: https://doi.org/10.5284/1016683]

Brown, S.W. 2018 *Excavations and building recording at Buckfast Abbey, Devon, 1984*–2017 Exeter, Devon Archaeological Society Occasional Paper 21

Brown, S.W. 2019 *The medieval Exe Bridge, St Edmund's Church, and excavation of waterfront houses, Exeter* Exeter, Devon Archaeological Society Monograph 1

Brown, S.W. and Holbrook, N. 1989 'A Roman site at Otterton Point', *Proceedings of the Devon Archaeological Society* 47, 29–42

Burnham, B.C. and Davies, J.L. (eds) 1990 *Conquest, co-existence and change. Recent work in Roman Wales* Lampeter, Trivium 25

Burnham, B.C. and Davies, J.L. (eds) 2010 *Roman frontiers in Wales and the Marches* Cardiff, Royal Commission on the Ancient and Historic Monuments of Wales

Burrow, I. 1977 'The town defences of Exeter', *Report and Transactions of the Devonshire Association* 109, 13–40

Burrow, I. 1988 'Excavations at 5–9 Fore Street, Taunton, 1979', *Somerset Archaeological and Natural History Society* 132, 95–164

Busby, P. 2016 *Winham Farm, Cullompton, Devon* Cotswold Archaeology report 16251 [ADS: https://doi.org/10.5284/1048925]

Butcher, S. 2014 'The Roman brooches from Nornour, Isles of Scilly', *Cornish Archaeology* 53, 1–80

Butler, R. and Green, C. 2006 *English bronze cooking vessels* Taunton, Somerset County Council

Caine, C. 2015 *Land to the northeast of Stuart Way, Hill Barton Business Park, Clyst St Mary, Devon* AC Archaeology report ACD1118/2/0 [ADS: https://doi.org/10.5284/1032974]

Caine, C. 2016 *Land north of Tithebarn Lane, adjoining the M5 motorway, Tithebarn Lane, Monkerton, Exeter* AC Archaeology report ACD1471/3/1 [ADS: https://doi.org/10.5284/1053107]

Caine, C. 2018 *Land adjacent to Pilton Lane, Pinhoe, Exeter, Devon* AC Archaeology report ACD1827/2/0

Caine, C. and Rainbird, P. 2017 *Land at Creedy Bridge, Crediton, Devon* AC Archaeology report ACD1486/2/0 [ADS: https://doi.org/10.5284/1049682]

Caine, C. and Valentin, J. 2011 'Part of a prehistoric ring ditch and two post-Roman corn drying ovens on land at Oaklands, Cowick Lane, Exeter', *Proceedings of the Devon Archaeological Society* 69, 95–112

Camden, W. 1623 *Britannia: or, a chorographical description of Great Britain and Ireland, together with adjacent lands* (translated into English and revised by Edmund Gibson, 3rd edition) London

Campbell, B.M.S. 2000 *English seigniorial agriculture, 1250–1450* Cambridge, Cambridge University Press

Campbell, B.M.S. and Bartley, K. 2006 *England on the eve of the Black Death: an atlas of lay lordship, land and wealth, 1300–49* Manchester, Manchester University Press

Campbell, E. 1991 *Imported goods in the early medieval Celtic west: with special reference to Dinas Powys* Unpublished PhD thesis, University of Wales College Cardiff.

Campbell, E. 2007a *Continental and mediterranean imports to Atlantic Britain and Ireland, AD 400–800* York, Council for British Archaeology Research Report 157

Campbell, E. 2007b *Imported material in Atlantic Britain and Ireland c.AD400–800* York, Council for British Archaeology [ADS: https://archaeologydataservice.ac.uk/archives/view/campbell_cba_2007/]

Cardelli, M. 2017 *Kingston Buildings, Bath, Bath and North-East Somerset* Cotswold Archaeology report 17301 [ADS: https://doi.org/10.5284/1046878]

Carew, T. 2008 'An early Bronze Age timber structure, a Saxon kiln, and Saxon and medieval occupation at Coppice Street, Shaftesbury, Dorset', *Proceedings of the Dorset Natural History and Archaeological Society* 129, 59–96

Carlyon, P.M. 1982 'A Romano-British site at Kilhallon, Twyardreath: excavation in 1975', *Cornish Archaeology* 21, 155–70

Carlyon, P.M. 1987 'Finds from the earthwork at Carvossa, Probus', *Cornish Archaeology* 26, 103–44

Carr, J. 1985 'Excavations on the Mound, Glastonbury, Somerset, 1971', *Somerset Archaeological and Natural History Society* 129, 37–62

Carruthers, W. 1995 *Charred plant remains from the medieval farmstead at Eckweek, Avon* London, Historic Buildings and Monuments Commission, Ancient Monuments Laboratory report 27/95

Carruthers, W. 2006 *Bestwall Quarry, Wareham: the charred plant remains from Iron Age, Romano-British and later contexts* Unpublished report

Carruthers, W. 2007 *Truro College Playing Fields, Threemilestone, Truro: the charred plant remains* Unpublished report

Carruthers, W. 2008 *Penryn College: the charred plant remains* Unpublished report

Carruthers, W. 2012 'Plant macrofossils', in S.R. Taylor 2012, 143–8

Carruthers, W. forthcoming *Atlantic Road, Newquay* Unpublished report

Carter, D. 2000 *Archaeological investigations at Shepherd's Mead, Hinton Charterhouse (ST 7675 5813)* Bath Archaeological Trust report [ADS: https://doi.org/10.5284/1029141]

Carus-Wilson, E.M. 1963 *The expansion of Exeter at the close of the middle ages* Exeter, University of Exeter

Caseldine, C. 1999 'Environmental setting', in Kain and Ravenhill (eds) 1999, 25–34

Chadwick, A.M. 2012 *An archaeological watching brief and excavation at Beechwood Parc, Truro, Cornwall* John Moor Heritage Services report TRTR11

Chaffey, G., Cooke, N.M., Jones, G., Kendall, M. and Mckinley, J. 2016 *Sherford New Community, Phase 1.1, Plymouth, Devon (Fields 23 and 24). Post-excavation Assessment* Wessex Archaeology report 107560.13 [ADS: https://doi.org/10.5284/1045686]

Charleston, R.J. 1984 'The glass', in Allan 1984a, 258–78

Cherry, B. and Pevsner, N. 1989 *The buildings of England: Devon* London, Penguin

Cherry, B, and Pevsner, N. 1991 *The buildings of England: Devon* 2nd edition London, Penguin

Cherry, J. 1982 'Post-medieval; Britain in 1982' *Post-Medieval Archaeology* 16, 217–29

Chibnall, M. 1969 *The ecclesiastical history of Orderic Vitalis* 2 Oxford Medieval Texts Series, Oxford, Clarendon Press

Childs, W.R. 1992 'Devon's overseas trade in the late middle ages', in M. Duffy,S. Fisher, B. Greenhill, D.J. Starkey and J. Youings (eds) *The new maritime history of Devon. Volume I: from early times to the late 18th century* Exeter, The Bath Press, 79–89

Clark, J., Cotton, J., Hall, J., Sherris, R. and Swain, H. (eds) 2008 *Londinium and beyond: essays on Roman London and its hinterland for Harvey Sheldon* York, Council for British Archaeology Research Report 156

Clark, K. 1995 'The later prehistoric and protohistoric dog: the emergence of canine diversity', *Archaeozoologia* 7, 9–32

Clark, K. n.d. *Compact Farm, Worth Matravers, Dorset* Unpublished report

Clarke, H. 1992 'The Hanse and England: a survey of the evidence for contacts between England and the Baltic in the Middle Ages', *Archaeologia Elbingensis* 1, 135–8

Clarke, P. 2019 *St Sidwell's Point, Exeter Bus Station, Exeter: archaeological excavation fieldwork summary* Cotswold Archaeology report 18554 [CA: https://reports.cotswoldarchaeology.co.uk/]

Claughton, P.F. 1997 'Silver sources in the late 10th century', conference paper available online: [https://people.exeter.ac.uk/pfclaugh/mhinf/vikings.htm]

Clelland, S. 2011 *Lyde Road Yeovil, Somerset* Wessex Archaeology report 71486.04

Clelland, S. and Budd, C. 2010 *Lyde Road, Yeovil, Somerset* Wessex Archaeology report 71484.03 [ADS: https://doi.org/10.5284/1029103]

Clutton-Brock, J. 1976, 'The animal resources', in Wilson (ed.) 1976, 373–92

Coales, J. (ed.) 1987 *The earliest English brasses: patronage, style and workshops 1270–1350* London, Monumental Brass Society

Cobley, G. 2016 *Devon's antiquarians: identifying what has been lost from the archaeological record* Unpublished PhD thesis, University of Exeter [https://ore.exeter.ac.uk/repository/handle/10871/23265]

Coe, D. and Hawkes, J.W. 1994 'Excavations at 29 High Street, Wimborne Dorset, 1990', *Proceedings of the Dorset Natural History and Archaeological Society* 114, 135–44

Coe, D., Davies, S. and Heaton, M. 1990 *Archaeological observations at Poundbury Farm Track, Fordington, Dorchester, Dorset* Wessex Archaeology report W371 [ADS: https://doi.org/10.5284/1030502]

Cole, D., Jones, A.M. and Lawson-Jones, A. 2004–05 'Discoveries along the Mullion to Lizard South West Water pipeline', *Cornish Archaeology* 43–44, 159–64

Cole, M.A. and Linford, N.T. 1993 'The geophysical survey at Woodbury Farm, Axminster', *Proceedings of the Devon Archaeological Society* 51, 135–49

Coles, C. forthcoming a 'The animal bones of Roman Princesshay', in Steinmetzer, Stead *et al.* forthcoming

Coles, C. forthcoming b 'Medieval faunal bone from Princesshay, Exeter', in Steinmetzer, Pearce and Allan forthcoming

Coles, S. and Pine, J. 2009 'Excavation of an Iron Age and Roman settlement and salt production site at Shapwick Road, Hamworthy, Poole, Dorset, 2005–6', *Proceedings of the Dorset Natural History and Archaeological Society* 130, 63–98

Colleoni, F. (ed.) 2016 *Stations routières en Gaule romaine. Architecture, équipements et fonctions*, Gallia 73.1

Collingwood, R.G. and Myres, J.N.L. 1937 *Roman Britain and the English settlements* 2nd edition Oxford, Oxford University Press

Collingwood, R.G. and Richmond, I. 1969 *The archaeology of Roman Britain* 2nd edition London, Methuen

Collingwood, R.G. and Wright, R.P. 1965 *The inscriptions of Roman Britain I* Oxford, Oxford University Press

Collis, J. 1972 *Exeter excavations: The Guildhall site* Exeter, University of Exeter

Colls, K. 2002 *Puriton Level Gas Pipeline, Puriton, Somerset* Cotswold Archaeology report 02083 [CA: https://reports.cotswoldarchaeology.co.uk/]

Cool, H. 1990 'Roman metal hair pins from southern Britain', *Archaeological Journal* 147, 148–82

Cool, H. 2000 'The parts left over: material culture into the fifth century', in T. Wilmott and P. Wilson (eds) *The late Roman transition in the North. Papers from the Roman Archaeology Conference, Durham, 1999*, Oxford, British Archaeological Reports British Series 299, 47–65

Cool, H. 2006 *Eating and drinking in Roman Britain* Cambridge, Cambridge University Press

Cooper, A. 2013 *Pinhoe, Devon* Stratascan report J2359

Cooper, N.H. 1990 *The Exeter area: proceedings of the 136th summer meeting of the Royal Archaeological Institute, 1990* Leeds, Royal Archaeological Institute

Corfield, P.J. and Keene, D. (eds) 1990 *Work in towns, 850–1850* Leicester, Leicester University Press

Corney, M. 2012 *Construction of a new garden store at Hill Close, Studland, Dorset* AC Archaeology report ACW352/2/0 [ADS: https://doi.org/10.5284/1039810]

Cosh, S.R. 2001 'Seasonal dining rooms in Romano-British houses', *Britannia* 32, 219–42

Cosh, S.R. and Neal, D.S. 2005 *Roman mosaics of Britain. Volume II: South-West Britain* London, The Society of Antiquaries of London

Cosh, S.R. and Neal, D.S. 2010 *Roman mosaics of Britain. Volume IV: Western Britain* London, The Society of Antiquaries of London

Costen, M. 2011 *Anglo-Saxon Somerset* Oxford, Oxbow Books

Costen, M.D and Costen, N.P. 2016 'Trade and exchange in Anglo-Saxon Wessex, *c* AD 600–780', *Medieval Archaeology* 60/1, 1–26

Cotswold Archaeology 2000 *Land at Alvington Lane, Brympton, Yeovil, Somerset* Cotswold Archaeology report 001245 [ADS: https://doi.org/10.5284/1029130]

Cotswold Archaeology 2018 *Land off Exeter Road, Topsham, Exeter* Cotswold Archaeology report 18275

Cotter, J. 1997 *A twelfth-century pottery kiln at Pound Lane, Canterbury: evidence for an immigrant potter in the Late Norman period* Canterbury, Canterbury Archaeological Trust Occasional Paper 1

Cottrell, T. 1997 *An archaeological field evaluation of the proposed development of land off Dorchester Road, Straton, Dorset* AC Archaeology report 9396/2/0 [ADS: https://doi.org/10.5284/1028804]

Cox, A. 1998 *Keynsham Cemetery, Durley Hill, Keynsham, Bath and North East Somerset* Avon Archaeological Unit report [ADS: https://doi.org/10.5284/1029136]

Cox, J. and Thorp, J.R.L. 2001 *Devon thatch: an illustrated history of thatching and thatched buildings in Devon* Tiverton, Devon Books

Cox, M. and Gilmour, B. 2013 *Blackdown Hills iron working survey 2013: Interim report* [https://blackdownhillsaonb.org.uk/our-work/document-library/]

Cox, P.W. 1992 'Excavation at the Waitrose supermarket site, Chantry Fields, Gillingham, Dorset 1991–2', *Proceedings of the Dorset Natural History and Archaeological Society* 114, 135–44

Cox, P.W. and Broomhead, R.A. 1993 *The archaeological evaluation of the proposed accommodation facilities at Hinkley 'C' Power Station, Somerset* AC Archaeology report 6693/1/10

Cox, P.W. and Hearne, C.M. 1991 *Redeemed from the heath: the archaeology of the Wytch Farm oilfield (1989–90)* Dorchester, Dorset Natural History and Archaeological Society Monograph Series 9

Cramp, R. 2006 *Corpus of Anglo-Saxon stone sculpture. Volume VII: South-West England* Oxford, Oxford University Press

Crees, G. 2016 *Somerdale, Keynsham, Bath and North East Somerset, New Fry Club and F1 Pitch* Cotswold Archaeology report 15279 [ADS: https://doi.org/10.5284/1047833]

Crees, G. and Thomson, A. 2015 *Somerdale, Keynsham, Bath and North East Somerset, Phase 1* Cotswold Archaeology report 14454 [ADS: https://doi.org/10.5284/1046356]

Creighton, J. 2000 *Coins and power in late Iron Age Britain* Cambridge, Cambridge University Press

Cresswell, B. 1916 *The Edwardian inventories for the City and County of Exeter transcribed from the original documents in the Guildhall* Exeter, Mowbray

Crick, J. 2014 'The charter evidence for Exeter in the twelfth century', *Newsletter of the Friends of Exeter Cathedral for December 2014,* 10–12

Crickmore, J. 1984 *Romano-British urban defences* Oxford, British Archaeological Reports British Series 126

Cripps, L.J. 2007 'Re-situating the later Iron Age in Cornwall and Devon: new perspectives from the settlement record', in C.C. Haselgrove and T. Moore (eds) *The later Iron Age in Britain and beyond* Oxford, Oxbow, 140–55

Crocker, J. 2016a *Elizabethan inventories and wills of the Exeter Orphans' Court. Part 1* Exeter, Devon and Cornwall Records Society New Series 56

Crocker, J. 2016b *Elizabethan inventories and wills of the Exeter Orphan's Court. Part 2* Exeter, Devon and Cornwall Records Society New Series 57

Crockett, A. 1996 'Archaeological sites along the Ilchester to Odcombe Pipeline', *Somerset Archaeological and Natural History Society* 139, 59–88

Crossley, D. 1990 *Post-medieval archaeology in Britain* Leicester, Leicester University Press

Crummy, N. 1983 *The Roman small finds from excavations in Colchester 1971–9* Colchester Archaeological Reports 2, Colchester, Colchester Archaeological Trust

Crummy, N. (ed.) 1987 *The coins from excavations in Colchester 1971–9* Colchester, Colchester Archaeological Report 4

Crummy, N. 2014 'Iron Age and Roman brooches', in E. Durham and M. Fulford *A late Roman town house and its environs. The excavations of C.D. Drew and K.C. Collingwood Selby in Colliton Park, Dorchester, Dorset, 1937–8* London, The Society for the Promotion of Roman Studies Britannia Monograph 26, 156–67

Crummy, P. 1997 *City of victory. The story of Colchester – Britain's first Roman town* Colchester, Colchester Archaeological Trust

Cudlip, D. 2005 *Land at the rear of The Ship Inn, Banwell, North Somerset* Cotswold Archaeology report 05182 [ADS: https://doi.org/10.5284/1029146]

Cunliffe, B. (ed.) 1968 *Fifth report on the excavations of the Roman fort at Richborough, Kent* London, Reports of the Research Committee of the Society of Antiquaries of London 23

Cunliffe B. 1979 *Excavations in Bath, 1950–75* Bristol, Committee for Rescue Archaeology in Avon, Gloucestershire and Somerset Excavation Monograph 1

Cunliffe, B. 1987 *Hengistbury Head, Dorset. Volume I: the prehistoric and Roman settlement, 3500BC–AD500* Oxford, Oxford Committee for Archaeology Monograph 13

Cunliffe, B. 1988 *Mount Batten, Plymouth: a prehistoric and Roman port* Oxford, Oxford University Committee for Archaeology Monograph 26

Cunliffe, B. 2001 *Facing the ocean: the atlantic and its peoples* Oxford, Oxford University Press

Cunliffe, B. 2010 *Iron Age communities in Britain* 4th edition London, Routledge

Cunningham, P. 2009 *Geophysical survey and archaeological excavation at Welcombe Farm, Charles, Devon* Brayford Community Archaeology Group report [ADS: https://doi.org/10.5284/1028757]

Dannell, G.B. 1991 'Decorated samian', in Holbrook and Bidwell 1991, 55–71

Dannell, G.B. 1992 'The decorated samian ware', in Holbrook and Bidwell 1992, 40–50

Darby, H.C. (ed.) 1973 *A new historical geography of England* Cambridge, Cambridge University Press

Darby, H.C. and Welldon Finn, R. 1967 *The Domesday geography of south-west England* Cambridge, Cambridge University Press

Darby, H.C., Glassock, R.E., Sheail, J. and Versey, G.R. 1979 'The changing geographical wealth of England, 1086–1334–1525', *Journal of Historical Geography* 5, 247–62

Darvill, T. and Gerrard, C. 1994 *Cirencester: town and landscape. An urban archaeological assessment* Cirencester, Cotswold Archaeological Trust

Daubney, A. 2010 'The cult of Totatis: evidence for tribal identity in mid Roman Britain', in S. Worrell, G. Edan, J. Naylor, K. Leahy and M. Lewis (eds) *A decade of discovery: proceedings of the Portable Antiquities Scheme Conference 2007*, Oxford, British Archaeological Reports British Series 520, 109–20

Davenport, P. 1991 *Archaeology in Bath 1976–1985* Oxford, Oxford University Committee for Archaeology Monograph 28

Davenport, P. 1999 *Archaeology in Bath: excavations 1984–1989* Oxford, British Archaeological Reports British Series 284

Davenport, P. 2003 *An archaeological evaluation at Avon Valley Country Park, Saltford, Bath and North East Somerset* Bath Archaeological Trust report [ADS: https://doi.org/10.5284/1029135]

Davenport, P., Poole, C. and Jordan, D. 2007 *Excavations at the New Royal Baths (the Spa), and Bellott's Hospital 1998–1999* Oxford, Oxford Archaeology Monograph 3

Davey, P. and Hodges, R. (eds) 1983 *Ceramics and trade. The production and distribution of later medieval pottery in north-west Europe* Sheffield, University of Sheffield

Davies, S.M. 1983 'Excavations at Christchurch, Dorset, 1981 to 1983', *Proceedings of the Dorset Natural History and Archaeological Society* 105, 21–56

Davies, S.M., Bellamy, P.S., Heaton, M.J. and Woodward, P.J. 2002 *Excavations at Allington Avenue, Fordington, Dorchester, Dorset, 1984–87* Dorchester, Dorset Natural History and Archaeological Society Monograph Series 15

Davies Pryce, T. 1938 'The Roman occupation of Britain: its early phase', *Antiquaries Journal* 18, 29–48

Davis, G. 2016 *An archaeological evaluation at Bishops Court Extension, Sidmouth Road, Exeter EX2 7JH* John Moore Heritage Services report 3573

Davis, S.J.M. 1991 *Faunal remains from the late Saxon-mediaeval farmstead at Eckweek in Avon, 1988–1989 excavations* London, English Heritage Ancient Monuments Laboratory Report 35/91

Dawson, G.J. 1979 'Excavations at Guy's Hospital, 1967', *Research Volume of the Surrey Archaeological Society* 7, 27–65

Dean, R. 2008 *Land at Exeter Airport Business Park, Clyst Honiton and Aylesbeare, East Devon* Southwest Archaeology report 081013 [ADS: https://doi.org/10.5284/1018022]

Dean, R. 2011 *Land at Poltimore House, Poltimore, Devon* Substrata report 111007 [ADS: https://doi.org/10.5284/1043599]

Dean, R. 2013a *Addlepool site, Clyst St George, East Devon* Substrata report 130423 [ADS: https://doi.org/10.5284/1043606]

Dean, R. 2013b *Land adjacent to Cumberland Way, Monkerton, Exeter, Devon* Substrata report 130913

Dean, R. 2013c *Land adjacent to Pinhoe Road, Pinhoe, Exeter Devon* Substrata report 130617

Dean, R. 2014a *Land near Cat Copse, Clyst St Mary, Devon* Substrata report 140529 [ADS: https://doi.org/10.5284/1043620]

Dean, R. 2014b *Land at Lodge Trading Estate, Broadclyst, Exeter* Substrata report 141024 [ADS: https://doi.org/10.5284/1043628]

Dean, R. 2014c *Land by Clyst Valley Road, Clyst St Mary, Devon* Substrata report 141129 [ADS: https://doi.org/10.5284/1043635]

Dean, R. 2014d *Land at Blackhorse, Clyst Honiton, East Devon* Substrata report 141211 [ADS: https://doi.org/10.5284/1043637]

Dean, R. 2014e *Land at Countess Wear, Exeter, Devon* Substrata report 141103 [ADS: https://doi.org/10.5284/1043629]

Dean, R. 2014f *Land at Old Rydon Lane, Exeter, Devon* Substrata report 140113

Dean, R. 2016a *Land north of Honiton Road, Clyst Honiton, Devon* Substrata report 1601CLY-R-1 [ADS: https://doi.org/10.5284/1043652]

Dean, R. 2016b *Land at Exeter Golf Club, Newcourt Drive, Exeter* Substrata report 1605EXE-R-1 [ADS: https://doi.org/10.5284/1043662]

Dean, R. 2017a *Land west of Exminster, Devon* Substrata report 1702EXM-R-1 [ADS: https://doi.org/10.5284/1044303]

Dean, R. 2017b *Land at Exeter Golf Club with 2017 additional area, Newcourt Drive, Exeter* Substrata report 1705NEW-R-1 [ADS: https://doi.org/10.5284/1053657]

Dean, R. 2018 *Land off Hollow Lane and Cumberland Way, Exeter, Devon* Substrata report 1801CUM-R- [ADS: https://doi.org/10.5284/1053300]

Defoe, D. 1742a *A tour thro' the whole island of Great Britain. Volume 1* 3rd edn., edited by Samuel Richardson London, Garland Publishing (1975)

Defoe, D. 1742b *A tour thro' the whole island of Great Britain. Volume 2* 3rd edn., edited by Samuel Richardson London, Garland Publishing (1975)

DeLaine, J. 1999 'Baths – the urban', in DeLaine and Johnston (eds) 1999, 159–63

DeLaine, J. and Johnston, D.E. (eds) 1999 *Roman baths and bathing. Proceedings of the First International conference on Roman Baths held at Bath, England, 30 March–4 April 1992* Portsmouth (Rhode Island), Journal of Roman Archaeology Supplementary Series 37

Dickinson, B. 1979 'Samian stamps', in Bidwell 1979, 182–4

Dickinson, B. 1991 'Samian potters' stamps', in Holbrook and Bidwell 1991, 46–55

Dickinson, B. 1992 'The samian potters' stamps', in Holbrook and Bidwell 1992, 50–4

Dickinson, B. forthcoming 'Samian stamps', in Bidwell forthcoming

Dickinson, B. and Bird, J. 2014 'Lincoln samian', in M. Darling and B. Precious *A corpus of Roman pottery from Lincoln* Lincoln Archaeological Studies 6, Oxford, Oxbow Books, 233–9

Dickinson, T. 2011 *Test pitting at Parsonage Farm, Sutton Montis, April 2010* South Somerset Archaeological Research Group report 004 [ADS: https://doi.org/10.5284/1017034]

Diez, V. and King, C. 2004 *Monkton Heathfield, Taunton, Somerset* Oxford Archaeology report 2384 [ADS: https://doi.org/10.5284/1008008]

Digital Atlas of Roman Britain: http://dare.ht.lu.se/

Dinwiddy, K.E. 2017 'Excavation of a medieval farmhouse with an adjacent droveway, at Beaple's Moor Cross, Knowstone', *Proceedings of the Devon Archaeological Society* 75, 135–53

Dinwiddy, K.E. and Bradley, P. 2011 *Prehistoric activity and a Romano-British settlement at Poundbury Farm, Dorchester, Dorset* Salisbury, Wessex Archaeology

Dinwiddy, M. and Mason, C. 2015 *Stonehills Mine, Avalanche Road, Southwell, Portland, Dorset* Wessex Archaeology report 109620.02 [ADS: https://doi.org/10.5284/1042111]

Dodd, M., Cook, I. and Martin, T. 2017 *Camel Creek, Tredinnick, Cornwall* Oxford Archaeology report 6567 [ADS: https://doi.org/10.5284/1049452]

Dolley, R.H.M. 1955 'The Mysterious Mint of "Fro"', *British Numismatic Journal* 28, 504–8

Dolley, R.H.M. 1961a 'An apparently unrecorded class of Hiberno-Norse imitations of the coinage of Æthelred II', *British Numismatic Journal* 30, 277–30

Dolley, R.H.M. (ed.) 1961b *Anglo-Saxon coins: studies presented to F.M. Stenton on the occasion of his 80th birthday* London, Methuen

Dolley, R.H.M. 1966 *The Hiberno-Norse coins in the British Museum* Sylloge of Coins of the British Isles 8, London, British Museum

Dolley, R.H.M. and Blunt, C.E. 1961 'The chronology of the coins of Alfred the Great' in Dolley (ed.) 1961b, 77–95

Dollinger, P. 1970 *The German hansa* Stanford, Stanford University Press

Domesday Book Glossary: http://www.nationalarchives.gov.uk/domesday/glossary/default.htm

Donkin, R.A. 1973 'Changes in the early middle ages', in Darby (ed.) 1973, 75–135

Down, A. 1978 *Chichester excavations. Volume 3* Chichester, Chichester Civic Society

Down, E. and Webb, A. 2016 *Somerset mapped: cartography in the county through the centuries* Wellington, Halsgrove

Driessen, M. 2009 'The early Flavian *castra* and the Flavian-Trajanic stone legionary fortress at Nijmegen (the Netherlands)', in A. Morillo, N. Hanel and E. Martín (eds) *Limes XX. XX Congreso Internacional de Estudios sobre la Frontera Romana* (3 vols), Anejos de *Gladius* 13, 1245–56

Duggan, M. 2018 *Links to late antiquity – ceramic exchange and contacts on the Atlantic seaboard in the 5th to 7th centuries AD* Oxford, British Archaeological Reports British Series 693

Dungworth, D. 2016 'Metals and metalworking', in Millett *et al.* (eds) 2016, 532–54

Dunning, R.W. 1975 'Ilchester: a study in continuity', *Somerset Archaeological and Natural History Society* 119, 44–50

Durham, E. 2012 'Depicting the gods: metal figurines in Roman Britain', *Internet Archaeology* 31 [IA: https://doi.org/10.11141/ia.31.2]

Durham University 2012 *Park Wall Solar Park, Bridgwater, Somerset* Durham University report 2960

Durrant, J. forthcoming 'Roman tile', in Steinmetzer forthcoming

Dyer, A. 2000 'Ranking lists of English medieval towns', in Palliser (ed.) 2000a, 747–70

Dyer, M.J. 1999 *Archaeological observation and recording of a residential development between Peel Close and Orchard Lane, Topsham, Exeter, 1999* Exeter Archaeology report 99.83 [ADS: https://doi.org/10.5284/1028783]

Eagles, B. 2018 *From Roman* civitas *to Anglo-Saxon shire: topographical studies on the formation of Wessex* Oxford, Oxbow Books

Earle, J. 1865 *Two of the Saxon Chronicles parallel* Oxford, Clarendon Press

Earwood, C. 1991 'Objects of wood', in Holbrook and Bidwell 1991, 275–8

Eckardt, H. 2014 *Objects and identities: Roman Britain and the northern western provinces* Oxford, Oxford University Press

Eckardt, H. and Crummy, N. 2008 *Styling the body in late Iron Age and Roman Britain: a contextual approach to toilet instruments* Monographies *instrumentum* 36, Montagnac, Editions Montique Mergoil

Edmonds, E.A., McKeown. M.C. and Williams, M. 1975 *British regional geology: South-west England (Fourth Edition)* London, Her Majesty's Stationery Office

Edwards, C. 2012 *Land at Fosse Lane, Shepton Mallet, Somerset: a post-excavation assessment report* AOC Archaeology Group report [ADS: https://doi.org/10.5284/1019591]

Edwards, J. and Paynter, S. (eds) 2019 *Ceramics and glass: a tribute to Sarah Jennings* London, Medieval Pottery Research Group Occasional Paper 8

Edwards, K. and Kirkham, G. 2008 'Gear and Caervallack, St-Martin-in-Meneage: excavations by Time Team, 2001', *Cornish Archaeology* 47, 49–100

Edwards, M. 2018 *Land at Pocombe Grange House, Pocombe Bridge, Exeter, EX2 9SX* Substrata report 1810POC-R [ADS: https://doi.org/10.5284/1058764]

Edwards, R. 1974 'London potters c. 1570–1710', *Journal of Ceramic History* 6

Egan, G. 1985 'Post-medieval Britain in 1984', *Post-Medieval Archaeology* 19, 159–91

Egan, G. 1996 'Some archaeological evidence for metalworking in London, *c.* 1050 AD–*c.* 1700 AD', *Historic Metallurgy* 30(2), 83–94

Egan, G. and Michael, R.L. (eds) 1999 *Old and new worlds: historical/post-medieval archaeology papers from the societies' joint conferences at Williamsburg and London 1997* Oxford, Oxbow Books

Elks, D. 2005 *Police HQ, Middlemoor, Exeter* Stratascan report J 1970 [ADS: https://doi.org/10.5284/1024827]

Ellis, C. 2012 'The excavation of a late Bronze Age/early Iron Age-middle Iron Age settlement at Home Field, Down Farm, Sixpenny Handley, Dorset', *Proceedings of the Dorset Natural History and Archaeological Society* 133, 77–98

Ellis, C. 2015a *Former Milber Down abattoir, Newton Abbot, Devon* Cotswold Archaeology report 1460 [CA: https://reports.cotswoldarchaeology.co.uk/]

Ellis, C. 2015b *Land at Mosshaye Farm, Pinhoe, Devon* Cotswold Archaeology report 15028 [ADS: https://doi.org/10.5284/1046475]

Ellis, P. 1982 'Excavations at Silver Street, Glastonbury, 1978', *Somerset Archaeological and Natural History Society* 126, 17–31

Ellis, P. 1984 *Catsgore 1979. Further excavation of the Romano-British village* Bristol, Western Archaeological Trust Monograph 7, Committee for Rescue Archaeology in Avon, Gloucestershire and Somerset

Ellis, P. 1987 'Sea Mills, Bristol: the 1965–1968 excavations in the Roman town of Abonae', *Transactions of the Bristol and Gloucestershire Archaeological Society* 105, 15–108

Ellis, P. 1989 'Norton Fitzwarren hillfort: a report on the excavations by Nancy and Philip Langmaid between 1968 and 1971', *Somerset Archaeological and Natural History Society* 133, 1–74

Ellis, P. 2000 *The Roman baths and* macellum *at Wroxeter. Excavations by Graham Webster 1955–85* English Heritage Archaeological Report 9, London, English Heritage

Ellis, P. and Leach, P. 2012 'The Roman settlement at Fosse Lane, Shepton Mallet: the Tesco excavation, 1996–7', *Somerset Archaeological and Natural History Society* 155, 1–38

Enright, D. 1996 *Hayes Farm, Clyst Honiton, nr Exeter, Devon* Cotswold Archaeology report 96368

Erskine, A.M. 1969 *The Devonshire lay subsidy of 1332* Exeter, Devon and Cornwall Records Society

Erskine, A.M. (ed.) 1981 *The accounts of the fabric of Exeter Cathedral, 1279–1353. Part 1: 1279–1326* Exeter, Devon and Cornwall Records Society New Series 24

Erskine, A.M. (ed.) 1983 *The accounts of the fabric of Exeter Cathedral, 1279–1353. Part 2: 1328–1353* Exeter, Devon and Cornwall Records Society New Series 26

Esmonde Cleary, A.S. 1989 *The ending of Roman Britain* London, Batsford

Esmonde Cleary, S. 1996 'Roman Britain in 1995. I. Sites explored: 8, South-western counties', *Britannia* 27, 433–6

Esmonde Cleary, S. 2003 'Civil defences in the west under the high empire', in P. Wilson (ed.) *The archaeology of Roman towns. Studies in honour of John S. Wacher* Oxford, Oxbow Books, 73–85

Evans, D. 2005 *Cade's Farm, Wellington, Somerset* Cotswold Archaeology report 05011 [CA: https://reports.cotswoldarchaeology.co.uk/]

Evans, D. 2017 *Land off Exeter Road, Topsham, Exeter* Cotswold Archaeology report 17441 [CA: https://reports.cotswoldarchaeology.co.uk/]

Evans, D.H. 2019 'Continental ceramic imports into Hull between *c.* 1260 and *c.* 1700', in Edwards and Paynter (eds) 2019, 97–128

Evans, E. 2010 'Bulmore', in Burnham and Davies (eds) 2010, 170–2

Evans, J. 2018 *Biosphere isotope domain map GB (V1): strontium isotope data* British Geological Survey [http://dx.doi.org/10.5285/ba36de6f-5a20-476b-965d-48182166114a]

Evans, J.A., Montgomery, J., Wildman, G. and Boulton, N. 2010 'Spatial variations in biosphere $^{87}Sr/^{86}Sr$'I', *Journal of the Geological Society* 167, 1–4

Exeter Archaeology 1997 *Archaeo-historical assessment of no. 5 The Close, Exeter* Exeter Archaeology Report 97.30

Exeter Archaeology Archive Project 2015 https://doi.org/10.5284/1035173

Exeter City Council 1994 *Archaeological advisory committee report* Exeter, Exeter City Council [ADS: https://doi.org/10.5284/1035173]

Farnell, A.J. 2007 *Archaeological investigations on land at Crosslands, Dainton Elms Cross, near Ipplepen, Devon* Exeter Archaeology report 07.77 [ADS: https://doi.org/10.5284/1004405]

Farnell, A.J. 2009a *An archaeological trench evaluation on land between Hill Barton Industrial Estate and the A3052 Exeter to Sidmouth Road* Exeter Archaeology report 09.110 [ADS: https://doi.org/10.5284/1007822]

Farnell, A.J. 2009b *Archaeological monitoring at Howell Road Fire Station, Exeter* Unpublished report in the Devon Historic Environment Record

Farnell, A.J. 2010a *Archaeological monitoring and recording at North Gate Court, Lower North Street, Exeter* Exeter Archaeology report 10.75 [ADS: https://doi.org/10.5284/1007831]

Farnell, A.J. 2010b *Archaeological evaluation and recording at 48 Beacon Lane, Exeter* Exeter Archaeology report 09.92 [ADS: https://doi.org/10.5284/1022912]

Farnell, A.J. 2014 *Land at Pinhoe Quarry, Exeter* AC Archaeology report ACD617/2/0 [ADS: https://doi.org/10.5284/1029598]

Farnell, A.J. 2015a 'Multi-period settlement, burial, industry and agriculture: archaeological excavations 2007–2012 at Twinyeo Quarry, Chudleigh Knighton', *Proceedings of the Devon Archaeological Society* 73, 185–278

Farnell, A.J. 2015b *Land at Exeter Crematorium, Topsham Road, Exeter, Devon* AC Archaeology report ACD1129/2/1
Farnell, A.J. 2018a *Land off Hill Barton Road, Exeter, Devon* AC Archaeology report ACD1795/1/2
Farnell, A.J. 2018b *Three successive Iron Age roundhouses at Old Park Farm, Pinhoe* AC Archaeology report ACD1121/2/0 [ADS: https://doi.org/10.5284/1047651]
Farnell, A.J. 2018c *23–27 Mary Arches Street and Quintana Gate, Bartholomew Street West, Exeter, Devon* AC Archaeology report ACD1607/1/0
Farnell, A.J. and Fairclough, P. forthcoming *Multi-phase prehistoric activity at Newcourt Drive, Exeter,* draft report from Exeter City HER
Farnell, A.J. and Payne, N. 2016 *Archaeological recording on land north of Wessex Close, Topsham, Exeter, Devon: interim results on archaeological excavation* AC Archaeology report ACD1123/2/1
Farnell, A.J. and Rainbird, P. 2017 *Land north of Wessex Close, Topsham, near Exeter, Devon* AC Archaeology report ACD1360/3/0
Farnell, A.J. and Salvatore, J.P. 2010 *An archaeological trench evaluation on land at Sentry's Farm, Exminster, Devon* Exeter Archaeology report 11.08 [ADS: https://doi.org/10.5284/1019172]
Fedorowicz, J.K. 1980 *England's Baltic trade in the early seventeenth century* Cambridge, Cambridge University Press
Fenwick, C.C. 1998 *The poll taxes of 1377, 1379 and 1381. Part 1: Bedfordshire – Leicestershire* Oxford, Oxford University Press
Fenwick, C.C. 2001 *The poll taxes of 1377, 1379 and 1381. Part 2: Lincolnshire – Westmoreland* Oxford, Oxford University Press
Fenwick, C.C. 2005 *The poll taxes of 1377, 1379 and 1381. Part 3: Wiltshire – Yorkshire* Records of Social and Economic History New Series, 37, London, British Academy
Fernandez, A. 1996 'Bronze studs from Roman Spain', *Journal of Roman Military Equipment Studies* 7, 97–146
Fernie, E. 1979 'Observations on the Norman cathedral plan', in *Medieval Art and Architecture at Ely Cathedral*, British Archaeological Association Conference Transactions 2 (for 1976), 1–7
Ferris, I.M. and Bevan, L. 1993 'Excavations at Maidenbrook Farm, Cheddon Fitzpaine, in 1990' *Somerset Archaeological and Natural History Society* 137, 1–40
Field, N. 1976 'The discovery of a Roman fort at Shapwick near Badbury Rings', *Britannia* 7, 280–3
Finberg, H.P.R. 1954 *The early charters of Devon and Cornwall* Leicester, University College of Leicester
Finberg, H.P.R. 1964 *The early charters of Wessex* Leicester, University College of Leicester
Fincham, G., Harrison, G., Holland. R. and Revell, L. (eds) 2000 *TRAC 1999: Proceedings of the tenth annual theoretical Roman archaeology conference, Durham 1999* Oxford, Oxbow Books
Fitzpatrick, A.P. 2013 'Roman amphora in Iron Age Cornwall: pre Roman, Roman or post-Roman?', *Cornish Archaeology* 52, 233–8
Fitzpatrick, A., Butterworth, C.A. and Grove, J. 1999a *Prehistoric and Roman sites in east Devon: the A30 Honiton to Exeter Improvement DBFO Scheme, 1996–9. Volume 1* Salisbury, Wessex Archaeology [ADS: https://doi.org/10.5284/1028754]
Fitzpatrick, A., Butterworth, C.A. and Grove, J. 1999b *Prehistoric and Roman sites in east Devon: the A30 Honiton to Exeter Improvement DBFO Scheme, 1996–9. Volume 2* Salisbury, Wessex Archaeology [ADS: https://doi.org/10.5284/1007940]
Flaherty, S. 2014 *Twerton Wood railway cutting, Bath* Wessex Archaeology report 102250.01 [ADS: https://doi.org/10.5284/1028920]
Flaherty, S. 2016 *Seabrook Orchards phase 2, Topsham Road, Exeter, Devon* Wessex Archaeology report 106351.01 [ADS: https://doi.org/10.5284/1053075]
Flaherty, S. 2017 *Seabrook Orchards phase 1, Topsham Road, Exeter, Devon* Wessex Archaeology report 106359.02
Flaherty, S., Andrews, P. and Leivers, M. 2017 *A medieval manor house rediscovered: excavations at Longforth Farm, Wellington, Somerset* Oxford, Oxbow Books
Fleming, A. 2008 *The Dartmoor reaves. Investigating prehistoric land divisions* Oxford, Windgather Press
Fletcher-Cutts, M. 2015 *Quab Lane, Wedmore, Somerset: archaeological evaluation trenching* Archaeological Research Services Ltd report 2015/138 [ADS: https://doi.org/10.5284/1042650]
Ford, B.M. and Teague, S. with Biddulph, E., Hardy, A. and Brown, L. 2011 *Winchester – a city in the making.* Oxford, Oxford Archaeology Monograph 12
Förtsch, R. 1996 'Villa und praetorium: zur Luxusarchitektur in frühkaiserzeitlichen Legionslagern', *Kölner Jahrbuch* 28, 617–34
Fowler, P.J. 1968 'Excavation of a Romano-British settlement at Row of Ashes Farm, Butcombe, North Somerset. Interim report 1966–67', *Proceedings of the University of Bristol Spelaeological Society* 11(ii), 209–36
Fowler, P.J. 1970 'Fieldwork and excavation in the Butcombe area, North Somerset', *Proceedings of the University of Bristol Spelaeological Society* 12(ii), 169–94
Fox, A. 1952 *Roman Exeter (Isca Dumnoniorum). Excavations in the war-damaged areas 1945–1947* Manchester, Manchester University Press
Fox, A. 1955 'Some evidence for a Dark Age trading site at Bantham, near Thurlestone, South Devon', *Antiquaries Journal* 35, 55–67
Fox, A. 1964 *The South West* London, Thames and Hudson
Fox, A. 1966 'Roman Exeter (*Isca Dumnoniorum*), origins and early development', in J. Wacher (ed.) *The civitas capitals of Roman Britain* Leicester, Leicester University Press, 46–51
Fox, A. 1968 'Excavations at the South Gate, Exeter, 1964–5', *Proceedings of the Devon Archaeological Society* 26, 1–20
Fox, A. 1969 'Roman settlement in Devon and West Somerset', in F. Barlow (ed.) 1969 *Exeter and its region* Exeter, University of Exeter Press, 137–49
Fox, A. 1973 *South-west England 3500 BC–AD 600* Newton Abbot, David and Charles
Fox, A. 1979 'Foreword: the origin of the excavations in the Cathedral Close', in Bidwell 1979, v–vi
Fox, A. 1995 'Tin ingots from Bigbury Bay', *Proceedings of the Devon Archaeological Society* 53, 11–23
Fox, A. 2000 *Aileen: a pioneering archaeologist* Leominster, Gracewing
Fox, A. and Ravenhill, W. 1959 'The Stoke Hill signal station: excavations 1956–7', *Report and Transactions of the Devonshire Association* 91, 71–82

Fox, A., and Ravenhill, W. 1966 'Early Roman outposts on the North Devon coast, Old Burrow and Martinhoe', *Proceedings of the Devon Archaeological Society* 24, 3–39

Fox, A. and Ravenhill, W. 1969 'Excavation of rectilinear earthwork at Trevinnick, St Kew, 1968', *Cornish Archaeology 8*, 89–96

Fox, A. and Ravenhill, W. 1972 'The Roman fort at Nanstallon, Cornwall', *Britannia* 3, 56–111

Fox, C. 1932 *The personality of Britain: its influence on inhabitant and invader in prehistoric and early historic times* Cardiff, National Museum of Wales

Fox, C. 1956 'The siting of the monastery of St Mary and St Peter in Exeter', in D.B. Harden (ed.) *Dark Age Britain: studies presented to E.T. Leeds* London, Methuen, 202–17

Fox, H.S.A. 1972 'Field systems in the east and south of Devon', *Transactions of the Devonshire Association* 104, 81–135

Fox, H.S.A. 1973 'Outfield cultivation in Devon and Cornwall: a reinterpretation', in M. Havinden (ed.) *Husbandry and marketing in the South-West 1500–1800* Exeter, Exeter University Press, 190–38

Fox, H.S.A. 1975 'The chronology of enclosure and economic development in medieval Devon', *Economic History Review,* 2nd Series, 28, 181–202

Fox, H.S.A. 1986 'Exeter, Devonshire', in R.A. Skelton and P.D.A. Harvey (eds) *Local maps and plans from medieval England* Oxford, Clarendon Press, 164–9

Fox, H.S.A. 1991a 'Occupation of the land: Devon and Cornwall', in Miller (ed.) 1991, 152–74

Fox, H.S.A. 1991b 'Farming practice and techniques: Devon and Cornwall', in Miller (ed.) 1991, 303–23

Fox, H.S.A. 1991c 'Tenant farming and farmers: Devon and Cornwall', in Miller (ed.) 1991, 722–43

Fox, H.S.A. 1996a *Seasonal settlement.* Vaughan Papers in Adult Education No. 39 Leicester, University of Leicester, Department of Adult Education

Fox, H.S.A. 1996b 'Introduction: transhumance and seasonal settlement', in Fox (ed.) 1996a, 1–23

Fox, H.S.A. 1999a 'Medieval farming and rural settlement', in Kain and Ravenhill 1999 (eds), 273–80

Fox, H.S.A. 1999b 'Medieval rural industry', in Kain and Ravenhill 1999 (eds), 322–29

Fox, H.S.A. 1999c 'Medieval urban development', in Kain and Ravenhill (eds) 1999, 400–7

Fox, H.S.A. 2001 *The evolution of the fishing village: landscape and society along the south Devon coast, 1086–1550* Oxford, Leopard's Head Press

Fox, H.S.A. (edited by Tompkins, M. and Dyer, C.) 2012 *Dartmoor's alluring uplands: transhumance and pastoral management in the middle ages* Exeter, University of Exeter Press

France, J. and Nelis-Clément, J. (eds) 2014 *La* statio. *Archéologie d'un lieu de pouvoir dans l'empire romain* Bordeaux, Ausonius Scripta Antiqua 66

Freke, D.J. 1979 'The excavation of a 16th-century pottery at Lower Parrock, Hartfield, east Sussex, 1977' *Post-Medieval Archaeology* 13, 79–125

Frere, S.S. 1967 *Britannia, a history of Roman Britain* London, Routledge and Kegan Paul

Frere, S.S. 1983a 'Roman Britain in 1982. I: sites explored', *Britannia* 14, 280–335

Frere, S.S. 1983b *Verulamium excavations 2* London, Reports of the Research Committee of the Society Antiquaries of London 41

Frere, S.S. 1984 'British urban defences in earthwork', *Britannia*, 15, 63–74

Frere, S.S. 1987 *Britannia. A history of Roman Britain* 3rd edition London, Routledge and Kegan Paul

Frere, S.S. 1991a 'Roman Britain in 1990. I: sites explored', *Britannia* 22, 274–82

Frere, S.S. 1991b *Britannia, a history of Roman Britain* 3rd edition London, Pimlico

Frere, S.S. 1999 *Britannia, a history of Roman Britain* 4th edition London, Folio Society

Friendship-Taylor, D.E. 1984 'The leather', in Allan 1984a, 323–33

Fulford, M.G. 1984 *Silchester defences, 1974–80* London, The Society for the Promotion of Roman Studies Britannia Monograph 5

Fulford, M.G. 1985 'Excavations on the sites of the amphitheatre and forum-basilica of Silchester, Hampshire. An interim report', *Antiquaries Journal* 65, 39–81

Fulford, M.G. 1996 *The Second Augustan legion in the west of Britain. The ninth annual Caerleon lecture* Cardiff, National Museums and Galleries of Wales

Fulford, M.G. 1999 'Veteran settlement in 1st-c. Britain and the foundations of Gloucester and Lincoln', in Hurst 1999a, 177–80

Fulford, M.G. 2001 'Links with the past: pervasive "ritual" behaviour in Roman Britain', *Britannia* 32, 199–218

Fulford, M.G. 2006 'Corvées and civitates', in Wilson (ed.) 2006b, 65–71

Fulford, M.G. 2015 'Retrospect and prospect: advancement of knowledge, methodologies and publication', in Fulford and Holbrook (eds) 2015, 194–211

Fulford, M.G. 2017 'Conclusions', in Allen *et al.* 2017, 358–63

Fulford, M.G. 2020 'The countryside of Roman Britain: a Gallic perspective', *Britannia* 51, 292-306

Fulford, M.G. and Brindle, T. 2016 'Chapter 1: Introduction', in A. Smith *et al.* 2016, 1–16

Fulford, M.G. and Clarke, A. 2011 *Silchester: city in transition. The mid-Roman occupation of insula IX c.AD 125–250/300. A report on excavations undertaken since 1997* London, The Society for the Promotion of Roman Studies Britannia Monograph 25

Fulford, M.G. and Holbrook, N. 2015 *The towns of Roman Britain: the contribution of commerc ial archaeology since 1990* London, The Society for the Promotion of Roman Studies Britannia Monograph 27

Fulford, M.G. and Holbrook, N. 2018 'Relevant beyond the Roman period: approaches to the investigation, analysis and dissemination of archaeological investigations of the rural settlements and landscapes of Roman Britain', *Archaeological Journal* 175(2), 214–30

Fulford, M.G. and Huddlestone, K. 1991 *The current state of Romano-British pottery studies: a review for English Heritage* London, English Heritage Occasional Paper 1

Fulford, M.G. and Timby, J. 2000 *Late Iron Age and Roman Silchester. Excavations on the site of the forum-basilica 1977, 1980–86* London, The Society for the Promotion of Roman Studies Britannia Monograph 15

Fulford, M.G., Rippon, S., Ford, S., Timby, J. and Williams, B. 1997 'Silchester: excavations at the north gate, on the north walls, and in the northern suburbs 1988 and 1991–3', *Britannia* 28, 87–168

Fulford, M.G., Clarke, A. and Eckardt, H. 2006 *Life and labour in late Roman Silchester: excavations in insula IX since 1997* London, The Society for the Promotion of Roman Studies Britannia Monograph 22

Fulford, M.G., Pankhurst, N., Wheeler, D. and Machin, S. n.d. *The Silchester environs project. The Roman tilery and pottery industry at Little London, Pamber 2017* Reading, University of Reading

Fyfe, R.M. and Rippon, S.J. 2004 'A landscape in transition? Palaeoenvironmental evidence for the end of the "Romano-British" period in South West England', in R. Collins and J. Gerrard (eds) *Debating late antiquity in Britain AD300–700* Oxford, British Archaeological Reports British Series 365, 33–42

Fyfe, R.M. and Woodbridge, J. 2012 'Differences in time and space in upland vegetation patterning: analysis of pollen data from Dartmoor, UK', *Landscape Ecology* 27, 745–60

Fyfe, R.M., Brown, A.G. and Rippon, S.J. 2003 'Mid- to Late-Holocene vegetation history of Greater Exmoor, UK: estimating the spatial extent of human-induced vegetation change', *Vegetation History and Archaeobotany* 12, 215–32

Fyfe, R.M., Brown, A.G. and Rippon, S.J. 2004 'Characterising the late prehistoric, "Romano-British" and medieval landscape, and dating the emergence of a regionally distinct agricultural system in South West Britain', *Journal of Archaeological Science* 31, 1699–714

Gaffney, V.L. and White, R.H., with Goodchild, H. 2007 *Wroxeter, the Cornovii and the urban process. Final report of the Wroxeter hinterland project 1994–1997. Volume 1: Reseraching the hinterland* Portsmouth (Rhode Island), Journal of Roman Archaeology Supplementary Series 68

Gahan, A. and McCutcheon, C. 1997 'Medieval pottery', in M.F. Hurley, O.M.B. Scully, R.M. Cleary and S.W.J. McCutcheon (eds) *Late viking age and medieval Waterford: excavations 1986–1992* Waterford, Waterford Corporation, 285–359

Gallant, L., Luxton, N. and Collman, M. 1985 'Ancient fields on the South Devon limestone plateau', *Proceedings of the Devon Archaeological Society* 43, 23–38

Gan, Y.M., Towers, J., Bradley, R.A., Pearson, E., Nowell, G., Peterkin, J. and Montgomery, J. 2018 'Multi-isotope evidence for cattle droving at Roman Worcester', *Journal of Archaeological Science Reports* 20, 6–17

Gandham, G. 2017 *Topsham Library, Nelson Close, Exeter* Cotswold Archaeology report 17516 [CA: https://reports.cotswoldarchaeology.co.uk/]

Gandham, G. and Stubbings. P. 2018 *Exeter Logistics Park, land at Hayes Farm, Devon* Cotswold Archaeology report 18471 [CA: https://reports.cotswoldarchaeology.co.uk/]

Garland, N. 2016a *Land at Hill Barton, Exeter, Devon* Cotswold Archaeology report 16234

Garland, N. 2016b *Pinn Brook Enclosure, Redhayes, Exeter, Devon* Cotswold Archaeology report 16375 [CA: https://reports.cotswoldarchaeology.co.uk/]

Garland, N. 2019 'Prehistoric settlement and burial, early medieval crop processing and a possible early medieval cemetery along the Clyst Valley: investigations south of the Pin Brook, Broadclyst, near Exeter, 2015–2016', *Proceedings of the Devon Archaeological Society* 77, 103–45

Garland, N. and Orellana, J. 2017 *Aldi, Exeter Road, Topsham* Cotswold Archaeology report 16234 [ADS: https://doi.org/10.5284/1043259]

Garland, N. and Orellana, J. 2018 'Prehistoric and Roman occupation along the River Exe: archaeological excavations at the Aldi site, Exeter Road, Topsham, Devon', *Proceedings of the Devon Archaeological Society* 76, 97–114

Garland, N. and Whelan, J. 2016 *Pinn Brook Enclosure, Redhayes, Exeter, Devon* Cotswold Archaeology report 16375 [CA: https://reports.cotswoldarchaeology.co.uk/]

Gaskell Brown, C. (ed.) 1986 *Plymouth excavations: the medieval waterfront, Woolster Street and Castle Street* Plymouth, Plymouth Museum Archaeological Series 3

Gater, J. 2017 *Clyst Road, Topsham, Devon* SUMO Services report 11733

Gem, R. 1990 'The Romanesque architecture of Old St Paul's Cathedral and its late eleventh-century context', in *Medieval Art and Architecture in London* British Archaeological Association Conference Transactions 10 for 1984, 46–63

Gent, H. and Quinnell, H. 1999a 'Excavations of a causewayed enclosure and hillfort on Raddon Hill, Stockleigh Pomeroy', *Proceedings of the Devon Archaeological Society* 57, 1–76

Gent, H. and Quinnell, H. 1999b 'Salvage Recording on the Neolithic Site at Haldon Belvedere', *Proceedings of the Devon Archaeological Society* 57, 77–104

Gent, T. 2007, 'Bronze Age burnt mounds and early medieval wells at Town Farm Quarry, Burlescombe', *Proceedings of the Devon Archaeological Society* 65, 35–45

Geoindex Onshore http://mapapps2.bgs.ac.uk/geoindex/home.html?topic=Minerals

Gerrard, C. and Aston, M. 2007 *The Shapwick Project, Somerset: a rural landscape explored* Leeds, Society for Medieval Archaeology Monograph 25

Gerrard, C., Guiterrez, A. and Vince, A.G. (eds) 1995 *Spanish medieval ceramics in Spain and the British Isles* Oxford, British Archaeological Reports International Series 610

Gerrard, J. 2011 'New light on the end of Roman London', *Archaeological Journal* 168, 181–94

Gerrard, J. 2016 'Economy and power in late Roman Britain', in Millett *et al.* (eds) 2016, 850–67

Gerrard, S. 2000 *The early British tin industry* Stroud, Tempus

Gibson, E. 1695 *Camden's Britannia, newly translated into English; with additions and improvements* London (reprinted by Times Newspapers Limited, 1971)

Gilbert, D. 2007a *An archaeological evaluation of the Lower R.N.S.D. and S.E.F. sites, Topsham Road, Exeter, Devon SX 9535 8974* John Moore Heritage Services report [ADS: https://doi.org/10.5284/1007985]

Gilbert, D. 2007b *An archaeological evaluation of Old Rydon Lane and land adjacent to Newcourt House, south Exeter, Devon* John Moore Heritage Services report [ADS: https://doi.org/10.5284/1008171]

Gilbert, D. 2008 *An archaeological evaluation at land off Topsham Road, Exeter, Devon* John Moore Heritage Services report 1879 [ADS: https://doi.org/10.5284/1024567]

Gilbert, D. 2012 'A Bronze Age enclosure with extramural structures and field system on land to the north of Old Rydon Lane, Exeter', *Proceedings of the Devon Archaeological Society* 70, 67–86

Gilbert, D. 2015 *Pixford Fruit Farm, Ash Priors, Taunton Dean, Somerset, archaeological evaluation* AB Heritage report [ADS: https://doi.org/10.5284/1041627]

Gilchrist, R. and Green, C. 2015 *Glastonbury Abbey: archaeological investigations 1904–79* London, Society of Antiquaries of London

Gillard, M. 2016a *Land south of the A379 (residential site) Exeter* Cotswold Archaeology report 16520 [ADS: https://doi.org/10.5284/1052892]

Gillard, M. 2016b *Roseland Parc Retirement Village, Tregony, Cornwall* Cotswold Archaeology report 16661 [ADS: https://doi.org/10.5284/1042928]

Gillard, M., Morris, B. and Walls, S. 2012 'Excavation of an Iron age roundhouse at middle Burrow Farm, East Worlington', *Proceedings of the Devon Archaeological Society* 70, 107–32

Gillard, M., Jones, G.P. and Garland, N. 2018 *Land south of the A379, Newcourt, Exeter* Cotswold Archaeology report 18207

Glasscock, R.E. 1973 'England *circa* 1334', in Darby (ed.) 1973, 136–85

Glasscock, R.E. 1975 *The Lay Subsidy of 1334* Records of Social and Economic History, New Series II, London, British Academy

Glassburn, C.L., Potter, B.A., Clark, J.L., Reuther, J.D., Bruning, D.L. and Wooller, M.J. 2018 'Strontium and oxygen isotope profiles of sequentially sampled modern bison (Bison bison bison) teeth from interior Alaska as proxies of seasonal mobility', *Arctic* 71(2), 183–200

Godden, D., Grove, J. and Smith, R.J.C. 2000 'Medieval and post-medieval Bridport: excavations at 43 South Street, 1996', *Proceedings of the Dorset Natural History and Archaeological Society* 122, 111–23

Godley, A.D. 1963 *Herodotus with an English translation. Volume II: Books III and IV* Cambridge, Massachusetts, Harvard University Press

Good, O. 2016 *Land at Tithe Barn Green, Monkerton, Exeter, Devon: post-excavation assessment and updated project design* Cotswold Archaeology report 15853 [ADS: https://doi.org/10.5284/1040798]

Good, O. and Massey, R. 2017 'A summary report on the excavation of land at Tithe Barn Green, Monkerton, Devon', *Proceedings of the Devon Archaeological Society* 75, 97–106

Goodall, A. 1984 'Objects of non-ferrous metal', in Allan 1984a, 337–48

Goodchild, R.G. 1937 'The Greek coins from Exeter reconsidered', *Numismatic Chrincicle*, 5th Series, 17, 124–41

Goodchild, R.G. 1946 *Roman Exeter (the city of* Isca Dumnoniorum*)* privately printed

Goodchild, R.G. 1947 'An antiquary in Devon (W.T.P. Shortt, 1800–1881)', *Report and Transactions of the Devonshire Association* 79, 229–55

Goodchild, R.G. 1952 'Structural remains of the Roman period found in Exeter before 1942', in Fox 1952a, 98–104

Goodman, P.J. 2007 *The Roman city and its periphery* London, Routledge

Gossip, J. 2013 'The evaluation of a multi-period prehistoric site and fogou at Boden Vean, St Anthony-in-Meneage, Cornwall, 2003', *Cornish Archaeology* 52, 1–98

Gossip, J. and Jones, A.M. 2007 *Archaeological investigations of a later prehistoric and a Romano-British landscape at Tremough, Penryn, Cornwall* Oxford, British Archaeological Reports British Series 443

Gossip, J. and Jones, A.M. 2009–10 'Excavations at Tremough, Penryn, Cornwall, 2000–6', *Cornish Archaeology* 48–49, 1–66

Gossip, J. and Jones, A.M. 2017 'Later Neolithic pits and an Iron Age and Romano-British settlement at Penryn College', *Cornish Archaeology* 56, 1–44

Gossip, J. and Thorp, C. 2010 *Penwith College, Penzance, Cornwall* Cornwall Council report

Gould, D. 2016 *Rabbit warrens of South-West England: landscape context, socio-economic significance and symbolism* Unpublished Ph.D Thesis, University of Exeter

Govier, E. 2016a *Land to the rear of the Devon Hotel, Old Matford Lane, Exeter, Devon* AC Archaeology report ACD1396/1/0 [ADS: https://doi.org/10.5284/1041645]

Govier, E. 2016b *Land at Bricknells Bungalow, Old Rydon Lane, Exeter* AC Archaeology report ACD1319/2/1

Govier, E. 2016c *Land south of Moonhill Copse, West Clyst, Broadclyst, Devon* AC Archaeology report ACD1068/2/0 [ADS: https://doi.org/10.5284/1039813]

Govier, E. 2017 *Bishop's Court extension, Sidmouth Road, Exeter, Devon. Results of an archaeological excavation* AC Archaeology report ACD1455/2/1 [ADS: https://doi.org/10.5284/1052995]

Govier, E. and Rainbird, P. 2016 *Land at Exeter and Devon Crematorium, Topsham Road, Exeter, Devon: results of an archaeological excavation and proposals for further work* AC Archaeology report ACD1348/2/1

Graham, A. 2006 *The excavation of five Beaker burials, the Iron Age and Romano-British settlements, and the 4th century courtyard villa at Barton Field, Tarrant Hinton, Dorset* Dorchester, Dorset Natural History and Archaeological Society Monograph Series 17

Graham, A.H. and Mills, J.M. 1996 'A Romano-British building at Crimbleford Knap, Seavington St Mary', *Somerset Archaeological and Natural History Society* 139, 119–34

Graham-Campbell, J. 1982 'A middle Saxon finger-ring from the Cathedral Close, Exeter', *Antiquaries Journal* 62, 366–7

Graham-Campbell, J. 1983 'A ninth-century Anglo-Saxon strap-end from the Cathedral Close, Exeter', *Proceedings of the Devon Archaeological Society* 41, 133–5

Grant, A. 1979 'Animal bone, in Cunliffe 1979, 60–70

Grant, A. 1988 'Bone deposition and animal husbandry: the animal bone remains', in Cunliffe 1988, 28–35

Grant, E. (ed.) 1986 *Central places, archaeology and history* Sheffield, J.R. Collis

Grant, L. (ed.) 1990 *Medieval art, architecture and archaeology in London* British Archaeological Association Conference Transactions for 1984, Leeds, British Archaeological Association

Grant, N. 1995 'The occupation of hillforts in Devon during the late Roman and post-Roman periods', *Proceedings of the Devon Archaeological Society* 53, 87–108

Gray, H.L. 1915 *English field systems* Cambridge (Massachusetts), Harvard University Press

Gray, T. 2005 *The chronicle of Exeter* Exeter, The Mint Press

Gray, T. and Jackson, S. 2018 *St Martin's Island: an introductory history to forty-two Exeter buildings* Exeter, The Mint Press

Green, C. 2015a *Old Oak Farm, Back Lane, Curry Rivel, Somerset* Context One report [ADS: https://doi.org/10.5284/1031438]

Green, C. 2015b 'Cast bronze cooking pots in England, 1500–1720', in Allan *et al.* (eds) 2015, 309–20

Green, C. 2016 *The Kings of Wessex Academy, Station Road, Cheddar, Somerset* Context One report [ADS: https://doi.org/10.5284/1049304]

Green, C. and McConnell, R. 2015 *Grimstone Reservoir, Dorchester, Dorset* Context One report [ADS: https://doi.org/10.5284/1041293]

Green, C., Gosden, C., Cooper, A., Franconi, T., Ten Harkel, L., Kamash, Z. and Lowerre, A. 2017 'Understanding the spatial patterning of English archaeology: modelling mass data, 1500 BC to AD 1086', *Archaeological Journal* 174, 244–80

Green, F.J. 2015 *Grain deposits from the 12th century granary, Lydford, Devon* Historic England report 3108

Green, M., Maltby, M. and Perrin, R. 2015 'Excavation of a Romano-British well at Farnham', *Proceedings of the Dorset Natural History and Archaeological Society* 136, 107–43

Greenway, D.E. 2002 *Henry of Huntingdon: the history of the English people, 1000–1154* Oxford, Oxford University Press

Greeves, T. 2017, 'The world of the Dartmoor tinner: an historical context 12th to 20th century', in Newman (ed.) 2017, 27–54

Griffith, F.M. 1984 'Roman military sites in Devon: some recent discoveries', *Proceedings of the Devon Archaeological Society* 42, 11–32

Griffith, F.M. 1986 'Salvage observations at the Dark Age site at Bantham Ham, Thurlestone, in 1982', *Proceedings of the Devon Archaeological Society* 44, 39–57

Griffith, F.M. 1988 'A Romano-British villa near Crediton', *Proceedings of the Devon Archaeological Society* 46, 137–42

Griffith, F.M. and Quinnell, H. 1999 'Iron Age to Roman buildings, structures, coin and other findspots', in Kain and Ravenhill (eds) 1999, 74–6

Griffith, F.M. and Reed, S.J. 1998 'Rescue recording at Bantham Ham, South Devon, in 1997', *Proceedings of the Devon Archaeological Society* 56, 109–31

Griffith, F.M. and Reed, S.J. 2000 *Rescue recording at Bantham Ham, South Devon, in 1997* Exeter Archaeology report 98.85 [ADS: https://doi.org/10.5284/1028769]

Griffith, F.M and Weddell, P.J. 1996 'Ironworking in the Blackdown Hills: results of recent survey', in Newman (ed.) 1996, 27–34

Griffith, F.M. and Wilkes, E.M. 2011 'In the footsteps of pioneering women: some recent work on Devon hillforts', in Pearce (ed.) 2011, 121–38

Grimes, W.F. 1930 *Holt, Denbighshire. The works-depôt of the Twentieth Legion at Castle Lyons* Y Cymmrodor 41, London, Society of Cymmrodorion

Grimm, J. 2008, 'Animal bone', in M. Trevarthen *Suburban life in Roman Durnovaria* online resource: [WA:https://www.wessexarch.co.uk/sites/default/files/projects/dorchester_county_hospital/07_Animal_bone.pdf]

Groves, C. 2004 'Dendrochronological analysis of timbers from Bowhill', in Blaylock 2004, 243–67

Guest, P., Luke, M. and Pudney, C. 2012 *Archaeological evaluation of the extramural monumental complex ('The Southern Canabae') at Caerleon 2011* Cardiff, Cardiff Studies in Archaeology Specialist Report 33 [ORCA: http://orca.cf.ac.uk/37324/7/CSC11%20interim%20compressed.pdf]

Guthrie, A. 1969 'Excavation of a settlement at Goldherring, Sancreed, 1958–1961', *Cornish Archaeology* 8, 5–39

Haarer, F. (ed.) 2014 *AD 410: The history and archaeology of late and post-Roman Britain* London, Society for the Promotion of Roman Studies

Hadley, D.M. and Dyer, C. 2017 *The archaeology of the 11th century; continuities and transformations* Leeds, Society for Medieval Archaeology Monograph 38

Haggarty, G.R. 2019 'French pottery in Scotland *c.* 1250–*c.* 1650: ceramic resource disk', disk held at National Museums of Scotland, Edinburgh

Haines, C. 2013 *Shepherd's Lane, Teignmouth, Devon: archaeological evaluation* Cotswold Archaeology Report 12373 [ADS: https://doi.org/10.5284/1028778]

Haines, C. 2015a *Axe View, Wadbrook, Devon* Cotswold Archaeology report 15605 [ADS: https://doi.org/10.5284/1036533]

Haines, C. 2015b *Staplegrove (West), Taunton, Somerset* Cotswold Archaeology report 15658 [ADS: https://doi.org/10.5284/1041795]

Hall, R. and Stocker, D. (eds) 2005 *Vicars choral at English cathedrals*: cantate domino: *history, architecture and archaeology* Oxford, Oxbow Books

Hallam, H.E. (ed.) 1988a *The agrarian history of England and Wales II 1042–1350* Cambridge, Cambridge University Press

Hallam, H.E. 1988b 'Population movements in England, 1086–1350', in Hallam 1988a, 508–36

Hambleton, E. 1999 *Animal husbandry regimes in Iron Age Britain* Oxford, British Archaeological Reports British Series 282

Hambleton, E. 2008 *Review of middle Bronze Age – late Iron Age faunal assemblages from southern Britain* Bournemouth, Bournemouth University [ADS: https://doi.org/10.5284/1000102/]

Hamilton, D. and Dunbar, E. 2011 'Radiocarbon dating', in Matthews *et al.* 2011, 179–80

Hamilton, J. and Thomas, R. 2012 'Pannage, pulses and pigs: isotopic and zooarchaeological evidence for changing pig management strategies in later medieval England', *Medieval Archaeology* 56, 234–59

Hamilton-Dyer, S. 2008 'Fish bones from selected contexts', in M. Trevarthen *Suburban life in Roman Durnovaria* online resource: [WA:https://www.wessexarch.co.uk/sites/default/files/projects/dorchester_county_hospital/06_Fish_bones.pdf]

Hamlin, A. 1976 'A painting of Norman work at St Stephen's Church, Exeter', *Proceedings of the Devon Archaeological Society* 34, 92–4

Hansen, L. and Wickham, C. (eds) 2000 *The long eighth century: production, distribution and demand* Leiden, Brill

Hanson, J.W. and Orton, S.G. 2017 'A systematic method for estimating the populations of Greek and Roman settlements', *Journal of Roman Archaeology* 30(1), 301–24

Hanson, W.S. 1988 'Administration, urbanism and acculturation in the Roman west', in D.C. Braund (ed.) *The administration of the Roman empire, 241 BC–AD 193* Exeter Studies in History 18, Exeter, University of Exeter, 53–68

Hanson, W.S., Daniels, C.M., Dore, J.N. and Gillam, J.P. 1979 'The Agricolan supply base at Red House, Corbridge', *Archaeologia Aeliana,* 5th series, 7, 1–98

Hanson, W.S., Jones, R.E. and Jones, R.H. 2019 'The Roman military presence at Dalswinton, Dumfriesshire; a reassessment of the evidence from aerial, geophysical and LiDAR survey', *Britannia* 50, 285–320

Harding, P., Mepham, L. and Smith, R.J.C. 1995 'Excavation of 12th and 13th century deposits at Howard's Lane,

Wareham', *Proceedings of the Dorset Natural History and Archaeological Society* 117, 81–90

Hardy, A., Charles, B.M. and Williams, R.J. 2007 *Death and taxes. The archaeology of a Middle Saxon estate centre at Higham Ferrers, Northamptonshire* Oxford, Oxford Archaeology

Harris, D. and Johnson, N. 1976 'Carlidnack Round, Mawnan', *Cornish Archaeology* 15, 73–6

Harry, R. and Morris, C.D. 1997 'Excavations on the lower terrace, site C, Tintagel Island 1990–94', *Antiquaries Journal* 77, 1–143

Hart, J. 2009 *Land at Mendip Avenue, Shepton Mallet, Somerset* Cotswold Archaeology report 09098 [ADS: https://doi.org/10.5284/1007396]

Hart, J. 2010 *Cloakham Lawns, Axminster, Devon* Cotswold Archaeology report 10109 [ADS: https://doi.org/10.5284/1009142]

Hart, J. 2016a *Hinkley Point C associated development: Cannington Bypass, Somerset* Cotswold Archaeology report 16141 [ADS: https://doi.org/10.5284/1042230]

Hart, J. 2016b *Land east of Fulwell Lane, Faulkland, Hemington, Somerset* Cotswold Archaeology report 16627 [ADS: https://doi.org/10.5284/1042925]

Hart, J. and McSloy, E.R. 2018 'A Roman settlement in the Mendip Hills: summary report of archaeological investigations at Fulwell Lane, Faulkland, Hemington 2016', *Somerset Archaeological and Natural History Society* 161, 95–111

Hart, J. and Mudd, A. 2018 *Cannington Bypass Somerset; excavations in 2014* Cirencester, Cotswold Archaeology Monograph 10

Hart, J., Wood, I., Barber, A., Brett, M. and Hardy, A. 2014 'Prehistoric land use in the Clyst Valley: excavations at Hayes Farm, Clyst Honiton, 1996–2012', *Proceedings of the Devon Archaeological Society* 72, 1–56

Hartgroves, S. and Smith, J. 2008 'A second Roman fort is confirmed in Cornwall', *Britannia* 39, 237–9

Hartley, B.R. 1983 'The enclosure of Romano-British towns in the second century AD', in Hartley, B.R. and Wacher, J.S. (eds) *Rome and her northern provinces* Gloucester, Alan Sutton, 84–93

Hartley, B.R. and Dickinson, B.M. 2008–12 *Names on* Terra Sigillata*: An index of makers' stamps and signatures on Gallo-Roman* Terra Sigillata *(Samian Ware)* Bulletin of the Institute of Classical Studies Supplement 102-01-09, London [https://www1.rgzm.de/samian/home]

Hartley, K.F. 1991 'Mortaria', in Holbrook and Bidwell 1991, 189–215

Hartley, K.F. and Tomber, R. 2006 'A mortarium bibliography for Roman Britain', *Journal of Roman Pottery Studies* 13

Hartmann, M. 1986 *Vindonissa. oppidum, legionslager, Castrum* Windisch, Effingerhof

Haselgrove, C. 1987 *Iron Age coinage in south east England* Oxford, British Archaeological Reports British Series 174

Haslam, J. 1984a 'The towns of Devon', in Haslam (ed.) 1984b, 264–83

Haslam, J. (ed.) 1984b *Anglo-Saxon towns in southern England* Chichester, Phillimore

Haslam, J. 2013 'A probable late Saxon burh at Ilchester', *Landscape History* 34(1), 5–22

Hassall, M. 2000 'Pre-Hadrianic legionary dispositions in Britain', in R.J. Brewer (ed.) 2000 *Roman fortresses and their legions* London, Society of Antiquaries, 51–67

Hatcher, J. 1988a 'New settlement: south-western England', in Hallam (ed.) 1988a, 234–44

Hatcher, J. 1988b 'Farming techniques: south-western England', in Hallam (ed.) 1988a, 383–98

Hatcher, J. 1988c 'South-western England', in Thirsk (ed.) 1988, 383–99

Hatton, J. and Caseldine, C. 1991 'Vegetation change and land use history during the first millennium AD at Aller Farm, East Devon as indicated by pollen analysis', *Proceedings of the Devon Archaeological Society* 49, 115–21

Havard, T. 2012 *Land at Island Farm, Ottery St Mary, Devon* Cotswold Archaeology report 12021 [ADS: https://doi.org/10.5284/1028378]

Havard, T. 2013 *Horseworld, Staunton Lane, Whitchurch, Bath and North East Somerset* Cotswold Archaeology report 13486 [CA: https://reports.cotswoldarchaeology.co.uk/]

Haverfield, F. 1912 *The Romanization of Britain* Oxford, Clarendon Press

Haverfield, F. 1924a *The Roman occupation of Britain*, revised by G. Macdonald, Oxford, Oxford University Press

Haverfield, F. 1924b 'Romano-British Cornwall', *Victoria County History of Cornwall V* London, The St Catherine Press

Havinden, M. 1999 'The woollen, line, tanning, and leather-working, and paper-milling industries, *c*.1500–*c*.1800', in Kain and Ravenhill (eds) 1999, 338–44

Hawkes, J. and Cotton, J. 1995 *Mount Batten, Plymouth: archaeological field evaluation of Zone D* AC Archaeology report 7995/1/0 [ADS: https://doi.org/10.5284/1028759]

Hawkins, C. 2005 *Vegetation history and land use change over the past 10,000 years in three study areas of lowland Devon: the Blackdown Hills, the Clyst Valley and Hartland Peninsula* Unpublished PhD thesis, University of Exeter

Hawthorne, J.G. and Smith, C.S. (eds) 1979 *Theophilus: on divers arts* New York, Dover Publications

Haynes, I. 2013 *Blood of the provinces. The Roman* Auxilia *and the making of provincial society from Augustus to the Severans* Oxford, Oxford University Press

Heard, H. 2006 *Water/sewage treatment infrastructure near Exeter Airport, east Devon* Stratascan report J2155 [ADS: https://doi.org/10.5284/1048185 and https://doi.org/10.5284/1048186]

Hearne, C.M. and Seager Smith, R. 1995 'A Middle Iron Age and Roman site at Aller Cross, Kingkerswell, 1993', *Proceedings of the Devon Archaeological Society* 53, 109–120

Hearne, C.M. and Birbeck, V. 1999 *A35 Tolpuddle to Puddletown Bypass DBFO, Dorset, 1996–8, incorporating excavations at Tolpuddle Ball 1993* Salisbury, Wessex Archaeology

Hegarty, C., Knight, S., and Sims, R. 2016 *East and mid Devon river catchments. National Mapping Programme survey: Phases 1 and 2, final report* Historic England Project No. 6634, Document No: ACD613/2/4

Henderson, C.G. 1984a 'Paul Street excavations', in Henderson 1984b, 1–13

Henderson, C.G. (ed.) 1984b *Archaeology in Exeter 1983/4* Exeter, Exeter City Council

Henderson, C.G. 1984c 'The plan of the Roman legionary fortress', *Archaeology in Exeter 1983/4*, Exeter Museums Archaeological Field Unit, 18–21

Henderson, C.G 1988 'Exeter (*Isca Dumnoniorum*)', in Webster (ed.) 1988, 91–119

Henderson, C.G. 1991 'Aspects of the planning of the Neronian fortress of *Legio II Augusta* at Exeter', in Maxfield and Dobson (eds), 1991, 73–83

Henderson, C.G. 1999a 'The city of Exeter from AD 50 to the early nineteenth century', in Kain and Ravenhill (eds) 1999, 482–98

Henderson, C.G. 1999b 'The design of the Neronian fortress baths at Exeter', in Delaine and Johnston (eds) 1999, 164–83

Henderson, C.G. 2001 'The development of the South Gate of Exeter and its role in the city's defences', *Proceedings of the Devon Archaeological Society* 59, 45–124

Henderson, C.G. and Bidwell, P.T. 1982 'The Saxon minster at Exeter', in Pearce (ed.) 1982, 145–75

Henderson, C.G. and Weddell, P.J. 1994 'Medieval settlements on Dartmoor and in west Devon: the evidence from excavations', *Proceedings of the Devon Archaeological Society* 52, 141–8

Henig, M. 1993 *Roman sculpture from the Cotswold Region* CSIR Great Britain 1.7, Oxford, British Academy

Herring, P., Preston-Jones, A., Thorpe, C. and Wood, I. 2011 'Early medieval Cornwall', *Cornish Archaeology* 50, 287–314

Herring, P., Johnson, N., Jones, A.M., Nowakowski, J.A., Sharpe, A. and Young, A. 2016 *Archaeology and landscape at the Land's End, Cornwall* Truro, Cornwall County Council

Hesse, R. 2011 'Reconsidering animal husbandry and diet in the northwest provinces', *Journal of Roman Archaeology* 24, 215–48

Hewitt, I. and Jones, G. 2015 'Preston: Bowleaze Cove Romano-British building', *Proceedings of the Dorset Natural History and Archaeological Society* 136, 88–98

Heywood, S. 1996 'The Romanesque building', in Atherton *et al.* (eds) 1996, 73–115

Higbee, L. 2003 *An assessment of the animal bone from excavations at Bleak Bridge, Huntspill, Somerset* Unpublished report in the Somerset County Council Historic Environment Record

Higbee, L. 2008 *Mendip Avenue, Shepton Mallet: the animal bones* Unpublished report, supplied by Charles and Nancy Hollinrake

Higbee, L. and Mepham, L. 2017 *Living on the edge: archaeological investigations at Steart Point, Somerset* Oxford, Oxbow Books

Higgins, J. 2009 *Archaeological excavations at Nancemere Fields, Truro, Cornwall* Southwest Archaeology report ER975 [ADS: https://doi.org/10.5284/1028747]

Higham, N.J. 1994 *The English conquest: Gildas and Britain in the fifth century* Manchester, Manchester University Press

Higham, N.J. and Ryan, M.J. (eds) 2010 *Landscape archaeology of Anglo-Saxon England* Woodbridge, The Boydell Press

Higham, R.A. 1977 'Excavations at Okehampton Castle, Devon. Part I: the motte and keep', *Proceedings of the Devon Archaeological Society* 35, 35–8

Higham, R.A. 1987 *Security and defence in south-west England before 1800* Exeter, Exeter Studies in History 19

Higham, R.A. 2008 *Making Anglo-Saxon Devon* Exeter, The Mint Press

Higham, R.A. 2013 'William the Conqueror's siege of Exeter in 1068', *Report and Transactions of the Devonshire Association* 145, 93–132

Higham R.A. 2018 'Earlsbury: a comital residence in Exeter', *Proceedings of the Devon Archaeological Society* 76, 141–85

Higham, R.A. and Henderson, C.G. 2011 'Danes Castle, Exeter: excavations 1992–3', *Proceedings of the Devon Archaeological Society* 69, 125–56

Higham, R.A., Allan, J.P. and Blaylock, S.R. 1982 'Excavations at Okehampton Castle, Devon. Part 2: the bailey', *Proceedings of the Devon Archaeological Society* 40, 86–101

Hill, D. 1969 'The Burghal Hidage: the establishment of a text', *Medieval Archaeology* 13, 84–92

Hill, D. 1974 *The Anglo-Saxon town* Unpublished PhD thesis, University of Southampton

Hill, D. 1981 *An atlas of Anglo-Saxon England* Oxford, Blackwell

Hill, D. 1984 *An atlas of Anglo-Saxon England* 2nd edition Oxford, Blackwell

Hillam, J. 1978 *Tree-ring analysis of Trichay Street timbers, Exeter* English Heritage, Ancient Monuments Laboratory Report 2510

Hillam, J. 1984 'Tree-ring analysis of Trichay Street timber, Exeter', in Allan 1984a, 315–18

Hingley, R. 2018 *Londinium. A biography* London, Bloomsbury Academic

Hingley, R. and Willis, S. (eds) 2007 *Roman finds: context and theory* Oxford, Oxbow Books

Hinton, D.A. and Webster, C.J. 1988 'Excavations at the church of St Martin, Wareham, 1985–86, and minsters in south–east Dorset', *Proceedings of the Dorset Natural History and Archaeological Society* 109, 47–54

Hobley, B. 1975 '"The Lunt" Roman fort and training school for Roman cavalry, Baginton, Warwickshire. Final report: excavations (1972–73) with conclusions', *Birmingham and Warwickshire Archaeological Society Transactions* 87, 1–56

Hodder, I. 1974 'Some marketing models for Romano-British coarse pottery', *Britannia* 5, 340–59

Hodder, I. and Orton, C. 1976, *Spatial analysis in archaeology* Cambridge, Cambridge University Press

Hodge, R. 1982 *Dark Age economics: the origins of towns and trade AD 600–1000* London, Duckworth

Hodges, R.A. and Mainman, A. 1984 'The Saxo-Norman imported pottery', in Allan 1984a, 13–18

Hodgson, N. 2008 'The development of the Roman site at Corbridge from the first to the third centuries AD', *Archaeologia Aeliana*, 5th series, 37, 47–92

Hodgson, N. (ed.) 2009 *Hadrian's Wall 1999–2009. A summary of excavation and research prepared for the 13th pilgrimage of Hadrian's Wall* Kendal, Cumberland and Westmorland Antiquarian and Archaeological Society and The Society of Antiquaries of Newcastle upon Tyne

Hodgson, N. 2017 *Hadrian's Wall. Archaeology and history at the limit of Rome's empire* Hale, Ramsbury

Hodgson, N. and Bidwell, P. 2009 'South Shields – Arbeia', in Hodgson (ed.) 2009, 61–72

Holbrook, N. 1987 'Trial excavations at Honeyditches and the nature of the Roman occupation near Seaton', *Proceedings of the Devon Archaeological Society* 45, 59–74

Holbrook, N. (ed.) 1998 *Cirencester: the Roman town defences, public buildings and shops* Cirencester Excavations 5, Cirencester, Cotswold Archaeological Trust

Holbrook, N. 2001 'Coastal trade around the South-West peninsula of Britain in the later Roman period: a summary of the evidence', *Proceedings of the Devon Archaeological Society* 59, 149–58

Holbrook, N. 2008 'Cirencester and the Cotswolds: the early Roman evolution of a town and rural landscape', *Journal of Roman Archaeology* 21, 304–23

Holbrook, N. 2010 'Kingsholm and Gloucester', in Burnham and Davies (eds) 2010, 184–7

Holbrook, N. 2015 'The towns of south-west England', in Fulford and Holbrook (eds) 2015, 90–106

Holbrook, N. 2018 'Discussion', in Brindle *et al.* 2018, 168–73

Holbrook, N. and Bidwell, P. 1991 *Roman finds from Exeter* Exeter Archaeological Reports 4, Exeter, Exeter City Council and The University of Exeter

Holbrook, N. and Bidwell, P. 1992 'Roman pottery from Exeter 1980–1990', *Journal of Roman Pottery Studies* 5(5), 35–80

Holbrook, N. and Fox, A. 1987 'Excavations in the legionary fortress at Bartholomew Street East, Exeter, 1959', *Proceedings of the Devon Archaeological Society* 45, 23–58

Holbrook, N. and Timby, J. 1998a 'The basilica and forum', in Holbrook (ed.) 1998, 99–121

Holbrook, N. and Timby, J. 1998b 'Shops and houses in insula VI. Excavations directed by A.D. McWhirr 1974–6', in Holbrook (ed.) 1998, 230–45

Holden, P. (ed.) 2017 *New research on Cornish architecture: celebrating Pevsner* London, F. Boutle

Holdsworth, C. 1980 'Saint Boniface the monk', in Reuter (ed.) 1980, 47–68

Hollinrake, C. and Hollinrake, N. 1997a *An archaeological evaluation at Perrot Hill School, North Perrot* Charles and Nancy Hollinrake report 104 [ADS: https://doi.org/10.5284/1029075]

Hollinrake, C. and Hollinrake N. 1997b *An archaeological evaluation at Perrot Hill School, North Perrot: fieldwork report* Charles and Nancy Hollinrake report 221 [ADS: https://doi.org/10.5284/1029077]

Holt, R. 2014 *Land at Midsomer Norton, Bath and North East Somerset* Cotswold Archaeology report 14170 [ADS: https://doi.org/10.5284/1046467]

Hood, A. 2007 *Penhale Round, Fraddon, Cornwall* Foundations Archaeology report 541 [ADS: https://doi.org/10.5284/1007654]

Hood, A. 2010 'Later Iron Age and early Roman settlement at Willand Road, Cullompton, Devon', *Proceedings of the Devon Archaeological Society* 68, 61–842

Hood, A. 2013a *Land at Pensipple Farm, Trewidland, Cornwall* Foundations Archaeology report 860 [ADS: https://doi.org/10.5284/1040562]

Hood, A. 2013b *Land at Trequite Farm, Liskeard, Cornwall* Foundations Archaeology report 869 [ADS: https://doi.org/10.5284/1040958]

Hood, A. and King, D. 2019 'Early mesolithic occupation, a beaker ring ditch with probable burials and probable Middle Bronze Age activirty at Cranbrook', *Proceedings of the Devon Archaeological Society* 77, 1–51

Hooke, D. 1994 *Pre-Conquest charter bounds of Devon and Cornwall* Woodbridge, The Boydell Press

Hooker, J. and Horn, H.G. 1987 *Die Römer in Nordrhein-Westfalen* Stuttgart, Theiss

Horner, B. 2018 'Early date for tin-streaming on Crownhill Down', *Devon Archaeological Society Newsletter* 130, 10

Horner, W.S. 1993 'A Romano-British enclosure at Butland farm, Modbury', *Proceedings of the Devon Archaeological Society* 51, 210–15

Horsley, K. 2016 *Land off Wick Lane, Brent Knoll, Highbridge, Somerset* Wardell Armstrong Archaeology report [ADS: https://doi.org/10.5284/1043718]

Hoskins, W.G. 1935 *Industry, trade and people in Exeter, 1688–1800* Manchester, Manchester University Press

Hoskins, W.G. 1960 *Two thousand years in Exeter* Chichester, Phillimore

Hoskins, W.G. 1984 *Local history in England* 3rd edition London, Longman

Hoskins, W.G. and Finberg, H.P.R. 1952 *Devonshire studies* London, Jonathan Cape

Howard, R., Laxton, R. and Litton, C. 2004 'Tree-ring analysis of timbers from four of the Exeter group of medieval roofs', in Blaylock 2004, 267–76

Howard, S. 1989 'Rescue excavation of a Roman enclosure and field system at West Moors, Dorset, 1988', *Proceedings of the Dorset Natural History and Archaeological Society* 110, 99–116

Hudson, A. and Valentin, J. 2001 *Land adjacent to White Pit Farm, Shillingstone, Dorset (centred on NGR ST830106)* AC Archaeology report 8801/1/0 [ADS: https://doi.org/10.5284/1028820]

Hughes, E.G. 1990a *Excavations at Stoke Lane, Wincanton, Somerset: interim statement* Birmingham University Field Archaeology Unit report [ADS: https://doi.org/10.5284/1029096]

Hughes, E.G. 1990b 'Excavations at 9 Bridport Road, Dorchester', *Proceedings of the Dorset Natural History and Archaeological Society* 111, 87–90

Hughes, S. 2011 *Land at 137–137a Cowick Street, St Thomas, Exeter, Devon* AC Archaeology report ACD191/1/2 [ADS: https://doi.org/10.5284/1011912]

Hughes, S. 2013 *Land on the site of the Stable Block and Yard, Oaklands, Cowick Lane, Exeter, Devon* AC Archaeology report ACD304/2/2 [ADS: https://doi.org/10.5284/1047654]

Hughes, S. 2015 'A prehistoric and Romano-British settlement at Aller Cross, Kingkerswell', *Proceedings of the Devon Archaeological Society* 73, 91–184

Hughes, S. 2016a *Land at Pinhoe Shooting Club, Langaton Lane, Pinhoe, Devon* AC Archaeology Report ACD1449/2/0 [ADS: https://doi.org/10.5284/1039976]

Hughes, S. 2016b *Villa Gardens, Cowick Lane, Exeter* AC Archaeology report ACD1242/2/0 [ADS: https://doi.org/10.5284/1047121]

Hughes, S. 2017a *Land at Eleanor's Bower, Follett Road, Exeter, Devon* AC Archaeology report ACD1422/2/0 [ADS: https://doi.org/10.5284/1053667]

Hughes, S. 2017b 'Rescue excavations at Challaborough Beach, South Hams', *Devon Archaeological Society Newsletter* 127, 1–3

Hughes, S. 2018 *Land to the rear of Five Acres, Exeter Road, Topsham* AC Archaeology report ACD1433/2/0 [ADS: https://doi.org/10.5284/1054014]

Hughes, S. 2019 *63 Cowick Street, St Thomas, Exeter, Devon* AC Archaeology report ACD1738/2/2 [ADS: https://doi.org/10.5284/1056363]

Hughes, S. and Allan, J. 2019 *63 Cowick Street, St Thomas, Exeter, Devon: draft publication for the Proceedings of the Devon Archaeological Society* AC Archaeology report ACD1738/3/0 [ADS: https://doi.org/10.5284/1056209]

Hughes, S. and Firth, E. 2010 *Land to the east of Secmaton Lane, Dawlish, Devon* AC Archaeology report ACD182/2/0 [ADS: https://doi.org/10.5284/1008584]

Hughes, S. and Rainbird, P. 2016 *The new Cranbrook watermain, East Devon* AC Archaeology report ACD295/2/0

Hughes, S. and Rainbird, P. 2017 'Late prehistoric and Romano-British activity at Somerton Door, Somerton, Somerset', *Somerset Archaeological and Natural History Society* 160, 1–16

Hughes, S., Payne, N. and Rainbird, P. 2015 *Land at Pyde Drove, near Woolavington, Somerset* AC Archaeology report ACD839/1/1 [ADS: https://doi.org/10.5284/1045907]

Hughes, T. 1979 *Moortown* London, Faber and Faber

Hulka, K. 1998 *Archaeological evaluation report: Glebe Allotments, Church Knapp, Wyke Road, Wyke Regis, Weymouth, Dorset* AOC Archaeology report [ADS: https://doi.org/10.5284/1028806]

Hume, L. 1993 *Site specific archaeological evaluation at Somerdale, Cadbury Limited, Keynsham* Avon Archaeological Unit report [ADS: https://doi.org/10.5284/1029138]

Hume, L. 2001 *Land off Church Road North, Portishead, North Somerset* Avon Archaeological Unit report [ADS: https://doi.org/10.5284/1029149]

Humphrey, N. 2018 'Imported cypress chests in the "long" 16th century', *Regional Furniture History Society Newsletter* 69, 16–17

Hurford, M., Howard, R.E., Arnold, A.J. and Tyres, C. 2009 *Exeter Cathedral, Exeter, Devon. Tree-ring analysis of timbers from the Song School door* Swindon, English Heritage Research Department Report Series 35-2009

Hurst, H.R. 1985 *Kingsholm. Excavations at Kingsholm Close and other sites with a discussion of the archaeology of the area* Cambridge, Gloucester Archaeological Reports 1

Hurst, H.R. 1988 'Gloucester (*Glevum*)', in Webster (ed.) 1988, 48–73

Hurst, H.R. (ed.) 1999a *The coloniae of Roman Britain. New studies and a review* Portsmouth (Rhode Island), Journal of Roman Archaeology Supplementary Series 36

Hurst, H.R. 1999b 'Topography and identity in *Glevum colonia*', in Hurst 1999a, 113–35

Hurst, H.R. 2020 *Gloucester. The Roman forum and post-Roman sequence at the city centre* Cambridge, Gloucester Archaeological Reports 3

Hurst, J.D. and Wacher, J.S. 1986 'A multi-period site at Poxwell, Dorset', *Proceedings of the Dorset Natural History and Archaeological Society* 108, 63–80

Hutcheson, A. and Andrews, P. 2002 'Excavations at the County Hotel, Taunton, 1995–6', *Somerset Archaeological and Natural History Society* 144, 139–63

Ingrem, C. forthcoming *The animal bone from Romano-British deposits at Atlantic Road, Newquay, Cornwall* Unpublished report

Institute of Geological Sciences 1977 *Geological survey ten mile map south sheet first edition (quaternary) scale 1: 625,000* Southampton, Institute of Geological Sciences

Institute of Geological Sciences 1979 *Geological survey ten mile map south sheet third edition (solid) scale 1:626,000* Southampton, Institute of Geological Sciences

Ivleva, T. 2014 'Remembering Britannia. Expressions of identities by "Britons" on the continent during the Roman empire', in B. Alroth and C. Scheffer, C. (eds) *Attitudes towards the past in antiquity. Creating identities. Proceedings of a conference held at Stockholm University 15–17 May 2009* Stockholm, Stockholm Studies in Classical Archaeology 14, 217–31

Jackson, A.M. 1972 'Medieval Exeter, the Exe and the Earldom of Devon', *Report and Transactions of the Devonshire Association* 104, 57–80

Jackson, R. 2007 *A Roman settlement and medieval manor house in south Bristol: excavations at Inns Court, Bristol* Bristol, Bristol and Region Archaeological Services

James, H. 2003 *Roman Carmarthen. Excavations 1978–1993* London, The Society for the Promotion of Roman Studies Britannia Monograph 20

James, T. 2011 *Land at 13 Lyndhurst Road, St Leonard's, Exeter, Devon* AC Archaeology report ACD200/2/1 [ADS: https://doi.org/10.5284/1029591]

Jamieson, E. 2015 *The historic landscape of the Mendip Hills* Swindon, Historic England

Jarvis, K. 1976 'The M5 motorway and the Peamore/Pocombe Link', *Proceedings of the Devon Archaeological Society* 34, 41–72

Jarvis, K. and Maxfield, V. 1975 'The excavation of a first-century Roman farmstead and a late Neolithic settlement, Topsham, Devon', *Proceedings of the Devon Archaeological Society* 33, 209–65

Jarvis, K.S. 1983 *Excavations in Christchurch 1969–1980* Dorchester, Dorset Natural History and Archaeological Society Monograph 5

Jeffrey, E. 2014 *Shudrick Lane, Ilminster, Somerset* Headland Archaeology report SHUD/01 [ADS: https://doi.org/10.5284/1027573]

Jenkins, A. 1806 *The history and description of the city of Exeter* Exeter, P. Hedgeland

Johnson, A.E. 2003 *Exeter school sites, archaeological geophysical (magnetic) survey* Oxford Archaeotechnics report for Exeter Archaeology

Johnson, N. and Rose, P. 2008 *Bodmin Moor. An archaeological survey. Volume 1: The human landscape to c 1800* London, Historic England.

Johnston, D.A., Moore, C. and Fasham, P.N. 1998–9, 'Excavations at Penhale Round, Fraddon, Cornwall', *Cornish Archaeology* 37–8, 72–120

Jones, A.M. 2000–1 'The excavation of a multi-period site at Stencoose, Cornwall', *Cornish Archaeology* 39–40, 45–94

Jones, A.M. 2017 'Excavation of a multi-phased roundhouse at West Northwood Farm, Bodmin Moor, 2017', *Cornish Archaeology* 56, 45–84

Jones, A.M. 2019 *Excavation of later prehistoric and Roman sites along the route of the Newquay Strategic Road Corridor, Cornwall* Oxford, Archaeopress

Jones, A.M. and Quinnell, H. 2014 *Lines of archaeological investigation along the north Cornish coast* Oxford, British Archaeological Reports British Series 594

Jones, A.M. and Taylor, S.R. 2004 *What lies beneath... St Newlyn East and Mitchell* Truro, Cornwall County Council

Jones, A.M. and Taylor, S.R. 2010 *Scarcewater, Pennance, Cornwall: archaeological excavation of a Bronze Age and Roman landscape* Oxford, British Archaeological Reports British Series 516

Jones, A.M. and Taylor, S.R. 2015 'Archaeological investigations of late Iron Age settlement at Sir James Smith's

Community School, Camelford, Cornwall, 2008–9', *Cornish Archaeology* 54, 1–87

Jones, A.M., Taylor, S. and Sturgess, J. 2012 'A Beaker structure and other discoveries along the Sennen to Porthcurno South West Water pipeline', *Cornish Archaeology* 51, 1–68

Jones, B. and Mattingly, D. 1990 *An atlas of Roman Britain* Oxford, Blackwell

Jones, G. 2018 *Land south of the A379, Newcourt, Exeter: archaeological excavation* Cotswold Archaeology report 17442

Jones, H.E. 1917 *The geography of Strabo with an English translation in eight volumes, I* London, William Heineman

Jones, J. 1996 *Charred plant remains from Shapwick Roman villa, Somerset* Unpublished report

Jones, J. 1998 *Waterlogged and charred plant macrofossils from Brean Down* Unpublished report

Jones, J 2001a *Charred plant remains from Gaffers, Membury, Devon* Unpublished report

Jones, J. 2001b *Charred plant remains from Dukes Break, Latton, Wiltshire* Unpublished report

Jones, J. 2003a *Charred plant remains from Bleak Bridge, Somerset* Unpublished report

Jones, J. 2003b 'Charred plant remains', in Lawson-Jones 2003, 86–8

Jones, J. 2004 *Charred plant remains from Parsonage Cross, Littlehemston, Devon* Unpublished report

Jones, M. 1988 'Lincoln (*Lindum*)', in Webster (ed.) 1988, 145–66

Jones, M. 1989 'Agriculture in Roman Britain: the dynamics of change', in Todd (ed.) 1989b, 127–34

Jones, M. and Dimbleby, G. (eds) 1981 *The environment of man: the Iron Age to the Anglo-Saxon period* Oxford, British Archaeological Reports British Series 87

Jones, M.J. 2011 *Roman Lincoln. Conquest, colony and capital* Stroud, History Press

Jonsson, K. (ed.) 1990 *Studies in Late Anglo-Saxon coinage* Stockholm, Numismatiska Meddenlanden 35

Jope, E.M. 1964 'The Saxon building-stone industry in southern and Midland England', *Medieval Archaeology* 8, 91–118

Jope, E.M. and Dunning, G.C. 1954 'The use of blue slate for roofing in medieval England', *Antiquaries Journal* 34, 209–17

Joyce, S. 2011 *Newquay Strategic Route, Newquay, Cornwall* Cotswold Archaeology report 11247 [ADS: https://doi.org/10.5284/1028751]

Joyce, S. 2012 *New inclined borehole, Hot Bath Street, Bath, Bath and North East Somerset* Cotswold Archaeology report 11199 [CA: https://reports.cotswoldarchaeology.co.uk/]

Joyce, S., Reynish, S., Sheldon, S. and Haines, C. 2014 *Hinkley Point C, Somerset* Cotswold Archaeology report 13432 [CA: https://reports.cotswoldarchaeology.co.uk/]

Juddery, J.Z. and Staniforth, P.R. 1986 *Timber supply for public works I, Exeter 1562–1766* Exeter, Exeter Museums Archaeological Field Unit

Juddery, J.Z., Staniforth, P.R. and Stoyle, M. 1989a *Exeter city defences: expenditure on the walls and gates recorded in the Receivers' accounts 1339–1450* Exeter Archaeology report 89.09

Juddery, J.Z., Staniforth, P.R. and Stoyle, M. 1989b *Exeter city defences: expenditure on the walls and gates recorded in the Receivers' accounts 1450–1570* Exeter Archaeology report. 89.10

Kain, R.J.P. 1979 'Compiling an atlas of agriculture in England and Wales from the tithe survey', *Geographical Journal* 145(2), 225–35

Kain, R.J.P. and Ravenhill, W. (eds) 1999 *Historical atlas of south-west England* Exeter, University of Exeter Press

Keen, L. 1984 'The towns of Dorset', in Haslam (ed.) 1984b, 203–48

Keen, L. and Ellis, P. 2005 *Sherborne abbey and school: excavations 1972–76 and 1990* Dorchester, Dorset Natural History and Archaeological Society Monography 16

Keene, D. 1985 *Survey of medieval Winchester. Parts 1, 2 and 3* Oxford, Oxford University Press

Keene, D. 1990 'Shops and shopping in medieval London' in Grant (ed.) 1990, 29–46

Kelly, F.P. (ed.) 1991 *Medieval art and architecture at Exeter Cathedral* British Archaeological Association Conference Transactions XI, Leeds, British Archaeological Association

Kent, H.S.K. 1973 *War and trade in the northern seas: Anglo-Scandinavian economic relations in the mid-eighteenth century* Cambridge, Cambridge University Press

Kerr-Peterson, K. and Passmore, A. 2012 *1-11 Sidwell Street, Exeter, Devon* AC Archaeology report ACD368/2/1 [ADS: https://doi.org/10.5284/1012490]

Keystone Historic Buildings Consultants 2000 *Conservation Plan for the Deanery, Cathedral Close, Exeter* Keystone Historic Building Consultants report

Keystone Historic Building Consultants 2016 *Exeter Cathedral gazetteer* Report to the Dean and Chapter of Exeter Cathedral, copy at Exeter Cathedral Library and Archive

King, A. 1984 'Animal bones and the dietary identity of military and civilian groups in Roman Britain, Germany and Gaul', in Blagg and King (eds) 1984, 187–217

King, A. 1989 'Villas and animal bones', in Branigan and Miles (eds) 1989, 51–9

King, A. 1991 'Food production and consumption – meat', in Jones (ed.) 1991, 5–120

King, A. 1999 'Meat diet in the Roman world: a regional intersite comparison of the mammal bones', *Journal of Roman Archaeology* 12, 168–202

King, A.C. and Grande, C.M. 2015 *Dinnington and Yarford, two Roman villas in south and west Somerset* Winchester, Department of Archaeology, University of Winchester [http://www.academia.edu/13097905/Dinnington_and_Yarford_two_Roman_villas_in_south_and_west_Somerset]

King, D. 1987 'Embroidery and textiles', in Alexander and Binski (eds) 1987, 157–68

King, R. 2015 *Cranbrook extension, Devon* Foundations Archaeology report 1085 [ADS: https://doi.org/10.5284/1053483]

Kingdom, M. 2019 *The past people of Exeter: health and status in the Middle Ages* Unpublished PhD thesis, University of Exeter

Knibb, P. 2009 *What does the excavation at Ford Farm tell us about the settlement there in the Roman period? A re-assessment of the finds* Unpublished dissertation, University of Bristol

Kowaleski, M.J. 1990 'Town and country in late medieval England: the hide and leather trade' in Corfield and Keene (eds) 1990, 57–73

Kowaleski, M.J. 1993 *Local customs accounts of the port of Exeter 1266–1321* Exeter, Devon and Cornwall Records Society New Series 36

Kowaleski, M.J. 1995 *Local markets and regional trade in medieval Exeter* Cambridge, Cambridge University Press

Kowaleski, M.J. 2017a 'The assimilation of foreigners in late medieval Exeter: a prosopographical analysis', in M.W. Ormrod, N. McDonald and C. Taylor (eds) *Resident aliens in later medieval England*, Turnhout, Brepols, 163–79

Kowaleski, M.J. 2017b 'French immigrants and the French language in late-medieval England', in T. Fenster and C.P. Collette (eds) *The French of medieval England: essays in honour of Jocelyn Wogan-Browne* Woodbridge, Boydell and Brewer, 206–24

Kowaleski, M.J. 2019 *A guide to the records of medieval Exeter* Unpublished typescript, circulated privately

Kühlborn, J.-S. 2006 'Haltern', in Reddé *et al.* (eds) 2006, 285–90

L-P Archaeology and AB Archaeology 2017 *Gordano School, Portishead* L-P Archaeology and A.B. Heritage report [ADS: https://doi.org/10.5284/1048826]

Ladle, L. 2012 *Excavations at Bestwall Quarry, Wareham 1992–2005. Volume 2* Dorchester, Dorset Natural History and Archaeological Society Monograph 20

Ladle, L. 2018 *Multi-period occupation at Football Field, Worth Matravers, Dorset: excavation 2006–11* Oxford, British Archaeological Reports British Series 643

Laithwaite, M. 1989 'Town houses: medieval to mid seventeenth century', in Cherry and Pevsner 1989, 78–82

Laithwaite, M. 1990 'Town houses up to 1660', in Beacham 1990, 95–115

Lambacher, N., Gerdau-Radonic, K., Bonthorne, E. and de Tarazago Montero, F.J.V. 2016 'Evaluating three methods to estimate the number of individuals from a commingled context', *Journal of Archaeological Science Reports* 10, 674–83

Lancley, J. 1991 *Empool to Chalbury main* Wessex Archaeology report W446 [ADS: https://doi.org/10.5284/1030500]

Lancley, J. 1993 *Sutton Poyntz water treatment works, Sutton Poyntz, nr. Weymouth, Dorset* Wessex Archaeology report W616 [ADS: https://doi.org/10.5284/1030499]

Lane, R. and Blaylock, S.R. 2017 'Late Saxon and medieval discoveries at the church of St James, Jacobstowe, Devon, in 2015', *Proceedings of the Devon Archaeological Society* 75, 155–20

Latham, A. 2014 *Land south-west of Exeter, Alphington, Devon* Oxford Archaeology report 5794 [ADS: https://doi.org/10.5284/1035770]

Latham, R.E. 1968 *Bede: a history of the English church and people* London, Penguin Books

Laur-Belart, R. 1935 *Vindonissa, Lager und Vicus* Berlin, Römisch-germanische Forschungen 10

Lauritsen, M.L. 2019 *Exeter from fort to city: a faunal perspective* Unpublished PhD thesis, University of Exeter

Lawson-Jones, A. 2003 *Little Quoit Farm, St Columb Major, Cornwall, excavation of a Romano-British smithing site* Cornwall Archaeological Unit report 2003R001 [ADS: https://doi.org/10.5284/1028735]

Lawson-Jones, A. 2013 'Discoveries along the North Land's End pipeline', *Cornish Archaeology* 52, 197–222

Laycock, S. 2008 *Britannia – the failed state: tribal conflicts and the end of Roman Britain* Stroud, The History Press

Leach, P. 1977 'Excavations at North Petherton, Somerset, 1975', *Proceedings of the Somerset Archaeological and Natural History Society* 121, 9–39

Leach, P. 1982a *Ilchester. Volume 1: excavations 1974–75* Bristol, Western Archaeological Trust Monograph 3

Leach, P. 1982b 'Roman pottery', in Leach 1982a, 127–68

Leach, P. 1984 *The archaeology of Taunton: excavations and fieldwork to 1980* Bristol, Western Archaeological Trust Monograph 8

Leach, P. 1994 *Ilchester. Volume 2: archaeology, excavations and fieldwork to 1984* Sheffield, Sheffield Excavation Reports No. 2

Leach, P. 1999 *An archaeological evaluation at Coate's Barn, Greinton* Peter Leach report [ADS: https://doi.org/10.5284/1029071]

Leach, P. 2001 *Excavation of a Romano-British roadside settlement in Somerset: Fosse Lane, Shepton Mallet 1990* London, The Society for the Promotion of Roman Studies Britannia Monograph 18

Leach, P. 2003 'Excavations at Hillyfields, Upper Holway, Taunton', *Somerset Archaeological and Natural History Society* 145, 57–82

Leach, P. and Ellis, P. 2004 'Roman and medieval remains at Manor Farm, Castle Cary', *Somerset Archaeological and Natural History Society* 147, 80–129

Lee, R. 2009 *Production, use and disposal of Romano-British pewter tableware*, Oxford, British Archaeological Reports British Series 478

Leech, R.H. 1977 'Late Iron Age and Romano-British briquetage sites at Quarrylands Lane, Badgworth', *Somerset Archaeological and Natural History Society* 121, 89–96

Leech, R.H. 1982 *Excavations at Catsgore 1970–73: a Romano-British village* Bristol, Western Archaeological Trust Monograph 2

Leech, R.H. 2014 *The town house in medieval and early modern Bristol* Swindon, English Heritage

Leech, R.H., Besly, E.M., Everton, R.F. and Fowler, E. 1981 'The excavation of a Romano-British farmstead and cemetery on Bradley Hill, Somerton, Somerset', *Britannia* 12, 177–252

Leech, R., Henig, M., Jenkins, F., Guido, M., Charlesworth, D, Besly, E.M., Butcher, S.A. and Everton, R.F. 1986 'The excavation of a Romano-Celtic temple and later cemetery on Lamyatt Beacon, Somerset', *Britannia* 17, 259–328

Lega-Weekes, E. 1915 *Some studies in the topography of the Cathedral Close, Exeter* Exeter, Commin

Leloup, D. 1996 *La maison urbaine en Trégor aux XVe et XVIe Siècles* Rennes, Presses Universitaires de Rennes

Leloup, D. 2002 *Maisons en pan-de-bois de Bretagne, histoire d'un type d'architecture urbaine* Rennes, Editions Ouest-France

Leonard, C. 2014 *Kenniford Farm, Clyst St George, Devon* Cotswold Archaeology report 14538 [ADS: https://doi.org/10.5284/1034380]

Lepine, D. and Orme, N. 2003 *Death and memory in medieval Exeter* Exeter, Devon and Cornwall Records Society New Series 47

Letters, S. 2013 *Online gazetteer of markets and fairs in England and Wales to 1516* [https://www.history.ac.uk/cmh/gaz/gazweb2.html]

Leverett, M. and Valentin, J. 2005 *Archaeological evaluation at Dinham Road, St David's, Exeter* Exeter Archaeology report 05.53 [ADS: https://doi.org/10.5284/1028773]

Leverett, M., Manning, P. and Allan, J. 2011 *A guide to the archives of archaeological projects carried out in Exeter, 1970–90* Exeter Archaeology report 11.26 [available on the EAPIT webpage under 'Resources', [http://humanities.exeter.ac.uk/archaeology/research/projects/place_in_time/]

Levitan, B. 1987a 'Medieval animal husbandry in South West England: a selective review and suggested approach', in Balaam *et al.* 1987, 51–80

Levitan, B. 1987b, *Bone analysis and urban economy: examples of selectivity and a case for comparison*, Ancient Monuments Laboratory Report 224/87

Levitan, B. 1989 'Bone analysis and urban economy: examples of selectivity and a case for comparison', in Serjeanston and Waldron (eds) 1989, 161–88

Levitan, B. 2015 *The vertebrate remains from Exe Bridge, Exeter, Devon* Portsmouth, Ancient Monuments Laboratory Report (Old Series) 4236

Levitan, B. 2019 'The animal bones, with special emphasis on the horncore collection', in Brown 2019, 165–73

Light, T. and Ellis, P. 2009 *Bucknowle. A Romano-British villa and its antecedents: excavations 1976–1991* Dorchester, Dorset Natural History and Archaeological Society Monograph 18

Ling, R. 1991 'Sculptural finds', in Holbrook and Bidwell 1991, 230–2

Little, A.G. and Easterling, R.C. 1927 *The Franciscans and Dominicans of Exeter* Exeter, History of Exeter Research Group Monograph 3

Locker, A. 2001 *The role of stored fish in England 900–1750AD; the evidence from historical and archaeological data* Sofia, Publishing Group Ltd

Locker, A. 2007 '*In piscibus diversis*: the bone evidence for fish consumption in Roman Britain', *Britannia* 38, 141–80

Lodwick, L. 2017 'Arable farming, plant foods and resources', in Allen *et al.* 2017, 11–84

Lovell, J. 2006 'Excavation of Romano-British farmstead at RNAS Yeovilton', *Somerset Archaeological and Natural History Society* 149, 7–70

Lucas, R.N. 1993 *The Romano-British villa at Halstock, Dorset: excavations 1967–1985* Dorchester, Dorset Natural History and Archaeological Society Monograph 13

Lyne, M. 2002 'The Late Iron Age and Romano-British pottery production sites at Redcliff, Arne and Stoborough', *Proceedings of the Dorset Natural History and Archaeological Society* 124, 45–100

Lysons, D. and Lysons, S. 1822 *Magna Britannia; being a concise topographical account of the several counties of Great Britain. Volume 6: Devonshire* London, Thomas cadell

MacCaffrey, W.T. 1958 *Exeter 1540–1640: the growth of an English county town* Cambridge (Massachusetts), Harvard University Press

MacCaffrey, W.T. 1975 *Exeter, 1540–1640*: the growth of an English county town 2nd edition Cambridge (Massachusets), Harvard University Press

McConnell, R. and Green, C. 2014a *The Kings of Wessex Academy, Station Road, Cheddar, Somerset* Context One report [ADS: https://doi.org/10.5284/1031436]

McConnell, R. and Green, C. 2014b *The Kings of Wessex Academy, Station Road, Cheddar, Somerset: A programme of archaeological monitoring and recording – phase 2* Context One report [ADS: https://doi.org/10.5284/1043997]

McConnell. R., Hall, N. and Place, C. 2007 *Kings of Wessex School, Station Road, Cheddar, Somerset: an archaeological watching brief* Context One Report

McIntyre, L.J. 2015 'Reconstructing population size in a Romano-British *colonia*: the case of *Eboracum*', *Journal of Roman Archaeology* 28(1), 413–29

McKerracher, M. 2018 *Farming transformed in Anglo-Saxon England* Oxford, Windgather Press

McKinley, J.I. 1998 'Excavations at Ham Hill, Montacute, Somerset 1994 and 1998', *Somerset Archaeological and Natural History Society* 142, 77–138

McKinley, J.I. 2000 'Excavations at Tinney's Lane, Sherborne, Dorset', *Proceedings of the Dorset Natural History and Archaeological Society* 121, 53–68

Mackney, D., Hodgson, J.M., Hollis, J.M., and Staines, S.J. 1983 *Legend for the 1:250,000 soil map of England and Wales* Harpenden, Soil Survey of England and Wales

Mackreth, D.F. 1982 'The brooches', in Leach 1982a, 241–8

Mackreth, D.F. 1991 'Brooches', in Holbrook and Bidwell 1991, 232–41

MacMahon, A. 2003 *Taberna structures of Roman Britain* Oxford, British Archaeological Reports British Series 356

McNicoll-Norbury, J. 2009 *Byways, Cleve and Linden, Bathwick Street, Bath* Thames Valley Archaeological Services report 07/138b [ADS: https://doi.org/10.5284/1010333]

Macphail, R.I. and Courty, M.A. 1985 'Interpretation and significance of urban deposits', in H. Jungner (ed.) *Proceedings of the third Nordic conference on the application of scientific methods in archaeology* Helsinki, Finnish Antiquarian Society, 71–83

McWhirr, A.D. 1979a 'Tile kilns in Roman Britain', in McWhirr 1979b, 97–190

McWhirr, A.D. (ed.) 1979b *Roman brick and tile: studies in manufacture, distribution and use in the western empire* Oxford, British Archaeological Reports International Series 68

Maddicott, J.R. 1989 'Trade, industry and the wealth of King Alfred', *Past and Present* 123, 3–51

Maddicott, J.R. and Palliser, D.M. (eds) 2000 *The medieval state: essays presented to James Campbell* London, The Hambledon Press

Madgwick, R., Lewis, J., Grimes, V. and Guest, P. 2019 'On the hoof: exploring the supply of animals to the Roman legionary fortress at Caerleon using strontium ($^{87}Sr/^{86}Sr$) isotope analysis', *Archaeological and Anthropological Sciences* 11(1), 223–35

Makarewicz, C.A. and Sealy, J. 2015 'Dietary reconstruction, mobility, and the analysis of ancient skeletal tissues: expanding the prospects of stable isotope research in archaeology', *Journal of Archaeological Science* 56, 146–58

Maltby, M. 1979 *Faunal studies on urban sites: the animal bones from Exeter 1971–1975* Sheffield, Exeter Archaeological Reports 2

Maltby, M. 1981 'Iron Age, Romano-British and Anglo-Saxon animal husbandry: a review of the faunal evidence', in Jones and Dimbleby, 1981, 155–204

Maltby, M. 1982 'Animal bones', in Higham *et al.* 1982, 114–35

Maltby, M. (ed.) 2006a *Integrating zooarchaeology: proceedings of the 9th ICAZ Conference, Durham 2002* Oxford, Oxbow Books

Maltby, M. 2006b 'Salt and animal products: linking production and use in Iron Age Britain', in Maltby (ed) 2006, 119–24

Maltby, M. 2007 'Chop and change: specialist cattle carcass processing in Roman Britain', in B. Croxford, N. Ray, R. Roth and N. White (eds) *TRAC 2006: Proceedings of the 16th annual theoretical Roman archaeology conference, Cambridge 2006* Oxford, Oxbow Books, 59–76

Maltby, M. 2010a *Feeding a Roman town: environmental evidence from excavations in Winchester, 1972–1985* Winchester, Winchester Museums

Maltby, M. 2010b 'Zooarchaeology and the interpretation of depositions in shafts', in Morris and Maltby (eds) 2010, 24–32

Maltby, M. 2015 'Commercial archaeology, zooarchaeology and the study of Romano-British towns', in Fulford and Holbrook 2015, 175–93

Maltby, M. 2016 'The exploitation of animals in Roman Britain', in Millet *et al.* 2016, 791–806

Maltby, M. 2017 'The exploitation of animals and their contribution to urban food supply in Roman southern England', in Bird (ed.) 2017, 180–209

Maltby, M. 2019 'From Appendix to integration? A review of the contribution of zooarchaeology to Romano-British studies, 1970–2015', in Allen (ed.) 2019, 11–36

Maltby, M., Allen, M., Best, J., Fothergill, B.T. and Demarchi. B. 2018 'Counting Roman chickens: multidisciplinary approaches to human-chicken interactions in Roman Britain', *Journal of Archaeological Science Reports* 19, 1003–15

Mann, J.C. (ed. Roxan, M.) 1983 *Legionary recruitment and veteran settlement during the principate* London, Institute of Archaeology Occasional Publications 7

Manning, W.H. 1981 *Report on the excavations at Usk 1965–1976. The fortress excavations 1968–1971* Cardiff, University of Wales Press

Manning, W.H. 2010 'Usk', in Burnham and Davies (eds) 2010, 187–92

Margary, I.D. 1955 *Roman roads in Britain. Volume 1: South of the Foss Way – Bristol Channel* London, Phoenix House

Margary, I.D. 1957 *Roman roads in Britain. Volume 2: North of the Foss Way – Bristol Channel (including Wales and Scotland)* London, Phoenix House

Margary, I.D. 1967 *Roman roads in Britain* London, John Baker Publishers Ltd

Marks, R. 1987 'The prophet Isaiah', in Alexander and Binski (eds) 1987, 532–4

Martin, E. 2007 '"Wheare most inclosures be". The making of the East Anglian landscape', in M. Gardiner and S. Rippon (eds) *Medieval Landscapes*, Macclesfield: Windgather Press, 122–38

Martin, E. and Satchell, M. 2008 *Wheare most Inclosures be. East Anglian fields: history, morphology and management* Ipswich, East Anglian Archaeology 124

Marvell, A.G. 1996 'Excavations at Usk 1986–1988' *Britannia* 27, 51–110

Mason, D.J.P. 2010 'Heronbridge', in Burnham and Davies (eds) 2010, 182–3

Mason, D.J.P. 1988 '"Prata legionis" in Britain', *Britannia* 19, 163–89

Mason, D.J.P. 2010 'Chester', in Burnham and Davies (eds) 2010, 172–83

Masson Phillips, E.N. 1965 'Excavation of a Romano-British site at Lower Well Farm, Stoke Gabriel, Devon', *Proceedings of the Devon Archaeological Society* 23, 3–34

Matthews, A.J., Collings, A.G. and Allan, J. 2011 'The Ship Inn: a row of late medieval houses in St Martin's Lane, Exeter', *Proceedings of the Devon Archaeological Society* 69, 157–80

Mattingly, D. 2006 *An imperial possession – Britain in the Roman empire* London, Penguin

Mattingly, D. 2011 *Imperialism, power and pdentity: experiencing the Roman Empire* Princeton, Princeton University Press

Mattingly, J. 2005 'Building into the Reformation: or just how late are Cornwall's medieval churches?', *Journal of the Cornwall Association of Local Historians 2005*, 32–6

Mattingly, J. 2017 'If only Pevsner had started in the Midlands: making sense of Cornwall's perpendicular architecture', in Holden (ed.) 2017, 74–82

Mawer, F. 1995 *Evidence for Christianity in Roman Britain: the small finds* Oxford, British Archaeological Reports British Series 243

Maxfield, V.A. 1981 *The military decorations of the Roman army* London, Batsford

Maxfield, V.A. 1984 'Early Devonians? Cologne tombstone of Dumnonian sailor', *Report and Transactions of the Devonshire Association* 116, 127–33

Maxfield, V.A. 1987 'The army and the land in the Roman South West', in Higham 1987, 1–25

Maxfield, V.A. 1991 'Tiverton Roman fort (Bolham): excavations 1981–1986', *Proceedings of the Devon Archaeological Society* 49, 25–98

Maxfield, V.A. and Dobson, M. (eds) 1991 *Roman frontier studies 1989. Proceedings of the XVth International Congress of Roman Frontier Studies* Exeter, Exeter University Press

Meharg, A.A., Edwards, K.J., Schofield, J.E., Raab, A., Feldman, J., Moran, A., Bryant, C.L., Thornton, B. and Dawson, J.J.C. 2012 'First comprehensive peat depositional records for tin, lead and copper associated with the antiquity of Europe's largest cassiterite deposits', *Journal of Archaeological Science* 39(3), 717–27

Metcalf, D.M. 1981 'Continuity and change in English monetary history c.973–1086 – part 2', *British Numismatic Journal* 51, 52–90

Metcalf, D.M. 1998 *An atlas of Anglo-Saxon and Norman coin finds, 973–1086* Oxford, Ashmolean Museum

Milby, S. 2007 *Warleigh water main replacement, Bath and North East Somerset* Context One report [ADS: https://doi.org/10.5284/1010389]

Miles, H. 1977a 'The Honeyditches villa, Seaton', *Britannia* 8, 107–48

Miles, H. 1977b 'The A38 roadworks 1970–3', *Proceedings of the Devon Archaeological Society* 35, 43–52

Miles, H. 1977c 'Excavations at Killibury Hillfort, Egloshayle, 1975–6', *Cornish Archaeology* 16, 89–121

Miles, H. and Trudgian, P. 1976 'An excavation at Lesquite Quoit, Lanivet', *Cornish Archaeology* 15, 7–10

Miller, E. (ed.) 1991 *The agrarian history of England and Wales 3, 1348–1500* Cambridge, Cambridge University Press

Milles, J. 1782 'Account of some Roman antiquities discovered at Exeter', *Archaeological Journal* 6, 1–5

Millett, M. 1990 *The Romanization of Britain. An essay in archaeological interpretation* Cambridge, Cambridge University Press
Millett, M. 2016 '"By small things revealed"; rural settlement and society', in Millett *et al.* (eds) 2016, 699–719
Millett, M. 2017 'Roman Kent', in J.H. Williams (ed.) *The archaeology of Kent to AD800* Woodbridge, Boydell
Millett, M., Revell, L. and Moore, A. (eds) 2016 *The Oxford handbook of Roman Britain* Oxford, Oxford University Press
Mills, A.D. 1977 *The Dorset lay subsidy roll of 1332* Dorchester, Dorset Record Society
25Mineral Occurrences: http://mapapps2.bgs.ac.uk/geoindex_layer_help/Minerals/All_Regions/Mineral_Occurrences_header.html
Minerals Information Online: https://www.bgs.ac.uk/mineralsuk/maps/maps.html
Ministry of Agriculture, Fisheries and Food 1979 *Agricultural land classification of England and Wales* Pinner, Ministry of Agriculture, Fisheries and Food
Minniti, C., Valenzuela-Lamas, S., Evans, J. and Albarella, U. 2014 'Widening the market. Strontium isotope analysis on cattle teeth from Owslebury (Hampshire, UK) highlights changes in livestock supply between the Iron Age and the Roman period', *Journal of Archaeological Science* 42, 305–14
Mócsy, A. 1974 *Pannonia and Upper Moesia. A history of the middle Danube provinces of the Roman empire* London, Routledge
Montgomerie-Neilson, E. 1933 'Report of the Exeter Excavation Committee: introduction and conclusions', *Proceedings of the Devon Archaeological Exploration Society* 2(1), 55–71
Montgomerie-Neilson, E. and Montague, L.A.D. 1933 'Report on the excavations in the Deanery Garden, Exeter, 1932–3, *Proceedings of the Devon Archaeological Exploration Society* 2(1), 72–8
Montgomerie-Neilson, E. and Montague, L.A.D. 1934 'Reports of the Exeter Excavation Committee. III. Description of the finds, 1932 and 1933', *Proceedings of the Devon Archaeological Exploration Society* 2(2), 84–109
Moon, K. 2013 *Land south-west of Exeter, Alphington, Devon* Oxford Archaeology report 5794
Moore, S.A. 1871 *Letters and papers of John Shillingford, Mayor of Exeter 1447–50* Camden Society New Series 2
Moore, T. 1829 *The history of Devonshire* London, Robert Jennings
Moore, T. 2011 'Detribalizing the late prehistoric past: concepts of tribes in Iron Age and Roman studies', *Journal of Social Archaeology* 11 (3), 334–60
Moorhead, S. 2009 'Early Byzantine copper coins found in Britain; a review in light of new finds recorded with the Portable Antiquities Scheme', in Tekin (ed.) 2009, 263–74
Moorhead, S. 2015 'A Survey of Roman coin finds from Hertfordshire', in K Lockyear (ed.) *Archaeology in Hertfordshire – recent research* Hatfield, Hertfordshire Publications, 135–64
Moorhead, S. forthcoming 'Byzantine coins', in C. Scull *et al.* Rendlesham report
Moorhead, S. and Walton, P. 2014 'Coinage at the end of Roman Britain', in Haarer (ed.) 2014, 99–116
Morris, B. 2014 *Land at Shortlands Lane, Cullompton, Devon. Results of a desk-based assessment and archaeological excavation* Southwest Archaeology report 140815 [ADS: https://doi.org/10.5284/1035617]
Morris, B. and Rohan, B. 2014 *Land off Tiverton Road, Cullompton, Devon* Southwest Archaeology report 140815 [ADS: https://doi.org/10.5284/1035618]
Morris, B. and Walls, S. 2010 *Land at Exeter Airport Business Park, Clyst Honiton and Aylesbeare, Devon* Southwest Archaeology report 100910 [ADS: https://doi.org/10.5284/1018026]
Morris, B., Wapshott, E. and Boyd, N. 2018 *The Barns, Penbro Farm, Breage, Cornwall* Southwest Archaeology report 180322 [ADS: https://doi.org/10.5284/1049111]
Morris, C. 1984 *The illustrated journeys of Celia Fiennes, c.1682–1712* London, MacDonald and Co.
Morris, J, and Maltby, M. (eds) 2010 *Integrating social and environmental archaeologies: reconsidering deposition* Oxford, British Archaeological Reports International Series S2077
Morris, P., Montague, L. and Goodchild, R. 1938 'A Romano-British building at Topsham', *Proceedings of the Devon Archaeological Society* 3(2), 267–82
Morris, R. 1989 *Churches in the landscape* London, Dent
Mudd, A. and Joyce, S. 2014 *The Archaeology of the south-west reinforcement gas pipeline, Devon* Cirencester, Cotswold Archaeology Monograph 6
Mudd, A. and Weavill, T. 2017 'Old Park Farm, Pinhoe', *Proceedings of the Devon Archaeological Society* 75, 107–34
Mudd, A., Cobain, S. and Haines, C. 2018 'A medieval building and its contents at Island Farm, Ottery St Mary, East Devon: excavations in 2014', *Internet Archaeology* 47 [IA: https://doi.org/10.11141/ia.47.4]
Mudd, A., Garland, N. and Brindle, T. 2019 'A Bronze Age ringwork and other prehistoric, Roman and later occupation at Hill Barton, Exeter, Devon. Excavations 2012–2015', *Proceedings of the Devon Archaeological Society* 77, 147–221
Müldner, G., Frémondeau, D., Hughes, M., and Rippon, S.J. 2020 *Exeter: A Place in Time* [data-set]. York, Archaeology Data Service [distributor] https://doi.org/10.5284/1075876
Müldner, G., Frémondeau, D., Evans, J., Jordan, A. and Rippon, S. forthcoming 'Putting southwest England on the (strontium isotope) map: a possible origin for "highly radiogenic" $^{87}Sr/^{86}Sr$ values from Britain', submitted to *Archaeological and Anthropological Science*
Munby, J., Norton, A. and Poore, D. 2019 *Excavations at Oxford Castle 1999–2009* Thames Valley Landscapes Monograph 44, Oxford, Oxbow
Murphy, P. and Wiltshire, P.E.J. (eds) 2003 *The environmental archaeology of industry* Oxford, Oxbow Books
Names on Terra Sigillata *(NoTS)* see Hartley and Dickinson 2008–12
Neal, D.S. and Cosh, S.R. 2002 *Roman mosaics of Britain. Volume I: Northern Britain* London, Society of Antiquaries of London
Nehlich, O. 2015 'The application of sulphur isotope analyses in archaeological research: a review', *Earth-Science Reviews* 142, 1–17
Nenk, B. 1999 'Post-medieval redware pottery of London and Essex', in Egan and Michael (eds) 1999, 235–45
Newman, C. and Morris, E.L. 1999 'Iron Age and Romano-British sites along the Bowden reservoir link pipeline, south-east Somerset', *Somerset Archaeological and Natural History Society* 143, 1–27

Newman, P. 2011 *The field archaeology of Dartmoor* Swindon, English Heritage
Newman, P. (ed.) 2017 *The tinworking landscape of Dartmoor in a European context – Prehistory to 20th Century* Dartmoor Tinworking Research Group
Newton, L. 2018a *Iron Age and Romano-British settlement at Lower Easton Farm, Pylle, Somerset* Wessex Archaeology report [WA: https://www.wessexarch.co.uk/our-work/lower-easton-farm-pylle]
Newton, L. 2018b 'Middle Bronze Age settlement and a Romano-British villa at Queen Camel, Somerset', *Somerset Archaeological and Natural History Society* 161, 49–90
Nicholas, P. and Hartgroves, S. 2018 'The Roman fort at Restormel: geophysical surveys 2007–2009', *Cornish Archaeology* 57, 169–88
Nowakowski, J.A. 2007 *Excavations of a Bronze Age landscape and post–Roman industrial settlement 1953–1961, Cornwall – Assessments of individual key datasets 2003–2006. Volume II* Truro, Cornwall County Council
Nowakowski, J.A. 2016 'Remarkable landscapes of ancient fields – the later prehistoric and Romano-Briutish legacy', in Herring *et al.* 2016, 160–91
Nowakowski, J.A. and Johns, C. 2015 *Bypassing Indian Queens* Truro, Cornwall County Council
Nowakowski, J.A. and Quinnell, H. 2011 *Trevelgue Head, Cornwall: the importance of CK Croft Andrew's 1939 excavations for prehistoric and Roman Cornwall* Truro, Cornwall County Council
Ogilvie, R.M. and Richmond, I. (eds) 1967 *Cornelii Taciti. De vita Agricolae* Oxford, Clarendon Press
Oliver, R., Kain, R. and Gray, T. 2019 *William Birchynshaw's Map of Exeter 1743* Exeter, Devon and Cornwall Records Society Extra Series 3
O'Neil, B.H. St J. 1931 'Roman villa in Cornwall' *Antiquity* 5 (20), 494–5
O'Neil. B.H. St J. 1933 'The Roman villa at Magor Farm, near Camborne, Cornwall', *Journal of the British Archaeological Association* 39, 117–75
Ordnance Survey 1978 *Map of Roman Britain Map* 4th Edition Southampton, Ordnance Survey
Ordnance Survey 2010 *Roman Britain Map and Historical Guide* 5th Edition Southampton, Ordnance Survey
Orellana, J. 2016 *Topsham Library, Nelson Close, Exeter.* Cotswold Archaeology report 16278 [ADS: https://doi.org/10.5284/1053643]
Orellana, J. 2017a *Land at Trevithick Manor Farm (Phase II), Newquay, Cornwall* Cotswold Archaeology report 16571 [ADS: https://doi.org/10.5284/1042932]
Orellana, J. 2017b *Exeter Gateway phase 2, Clyst Honiton, Devon* Cotswold Archaeology report 16734 [ADS: https://doi.org/10.5284/1043298]
Orellana, J. 2018 *Land at Beech Cottage, Old Rydon Lane, Exeter, Devon* Cotswold Archaeology report 18075 [CA: https://reports.cotswoldarchaeology.co.uk/]
Orellana, J. and Evans, D. 2018 'Early medieval iron smelting at Culmstock Road, Hemyock, Devon', *Dannicus: Cotswold Archaeology Staff newsletter* 10, 4
Orellana, J. and Garland, N. 2016 *Aldi, Exeter Road, Topsham, Devon* Cotswold Archaeology report 16234 [ADS: https://doi.org/10.5284/1043259]
Orellana, J. and Massey, R. 2019 *Land North of Culmstock Road, Hemyock, Devon* Cotswold Archaeology report EX0032
Orgill, N. 2014 *Specialization of butchery in the Roman legionary fortress at Exeter* Unpublished BSc dissertation, Bournemouth University
Orme, N. 2009 *Exeter Cathedral: the first thousand years, 400–1550* Exeter, Impress Books
Orme, N. 2011 'Christianity in Devon before 1086', *Reports and Transactions of the Devonshire Association* 143, 1–39
Orme, N.I. 2014 *The churches of medieval Exeter* Exeter, Impress Books
Orme, N.I. 2015a 'St Nicholas Priory, Exeter', *Proceedings of the Devon Archaeological Society* 73, 315–35
Orme, N.I. 2015b 'Polsloe Priory', *Report and Transactions of the Devonshire Association* 147, 185–212
Orme, N.I. 2016 'The Franciscan friars of Exeter', *Proceedings of the Devon Archaeological Society* 74, 217–54
Orme, N.I. and Henderson, C.G. 1999 'Exeter cathedral' in Kain and Ravenhill 1999, 499–502
Orme, N.I. and Webster, M. 1995 *The English hospital, 1070–1570* New Haven, Yale University Press
Ottaway, P. 2017 *Winchester: Swithun's city of happiness and good fortune: an archaeological assessment* Oxford, Oxbow Books
Palliser, D.M. (ed.) 2000a *The Cambridge history of urban Britain. Volume I: 600–1540* Cambridge, Cambridge University Press
Palliser, D.M. 2000b 'Towns and the English state, 1066–1500', in Maddicott and Palliser (eds) 2000, 127–46
Palliser, D.M. 2000c 'Introduction', in Palliser (ed) 2000a, 3–15
Palmer, S. and Reilly, D. 2009 *Excavation of an enigmatic multi-period site on the Isle of Portland, Dorset* Oxford, British Archaeological Reports British Series 499
Papworth, M. 1997 'The Romano-British settlement at Shapwick, Dorset', *Britannia* 28, 354–8
Papworth, M. 1998 'The medieval manorial buildings of Kingston Lacy: survey and excavation results with an analysis of the medieval account rolls 1295–1462, *Proceedings of the Dorset Natural History and Archaeological Society* 120, 45–62
Papworth, M. 2011 *The search for the Durotriges: Dorset and the West Country in the late Iron Age* Stroud, The History Press
Papworth, M. 2013 'Excavations at Thorncombe Beacon, Doghouse Hill and Golden Cap on the Golden Cap Estate, west Dorset', *Proceedings of the Dorset Natural History and Archaeological Society* 134, 205–47
Papworth, M. 2014 'The Romano-Celtic temple at Badbury Rings, Doset', *Proceedings of the Dorset Natural History and Archaeological Society* 135, 242–71
Parker, R.W. 1999 *Archaeological recording at St Olave's Church, Exeter* Exeter Archaeology report 99.67
Parker, R.W. and Allan, J. 2015 'The transformation of the building stock of Exeter, 1450–1700', in Allan *et al.* 2015, 35–67
Parker, R.W. and Collings, A.G. 2002 'St Catherine's Almshouses and the medieval canonry in Catherine Street, Exeter', *Proceedings of the Devon Archaeological Society* 60, 75–205
Parker, R.W. and Collings, A.G. 2006 'The historic buildings and tenurial history of No. 2 Broadgate, Exeter', *Proceedings of the Devon Archaeological Society* 64, 267–342
Parker, R.W., Bishop, P., Collings, A.G. and McNeilage, R. 2013 'No. 18 North Street, Exeter: a 17th-century merchant's

house with painted panelling', *Proceedings of the Devon Archaeological Society* 71, 123–85

Parrington, M. 1978 *The excavation of an Iron Age settlement, Bronze Age ring-ditches and Roman features at Ashville Trading Estate, Abingdon, Oxfordshire 1974–6* London, Council for British Archaeology Research Report 28

Parsons, D. (ed.) 1990 *Quarrying and building in England AD 43–1525* Chichester, Phillimore

Passmore, A.J. 2003 *Archaeological recording at the former Topsham First School, Majorfield Lane, Topsham* Exeter Archaeology report 03.59

Passmore, A.J. 2005 'A Roman enclosure and probable Roman trackway at Newland Mill, North Tawton', *Proceedings of the Devon Archaeological Society* 63, 33–41

Passmore, A.J. 2008 *Archaeological recording at Exton Road, Exeter, Devon* Exeter Archaeology report 08.16

Passmore, A.J. 2011 *Exeter Science Park Drive South, Sowton, Devon: archaeological evaluation.* Exeter Archaeology report 11.56 [ADS: https://doi.org/10.5284/1017973]

Passmore, A.J. 2013a *Discovery Quarter, Mount Dinham, Exeter* AC Archaeology report ACD356/1/2 [ADS: https://doi.org/10.5284/1028784]

Passmore, A.J. 2013b *Earl Richards Road, Exeter, Devon* AC Archaeology report ACD596/3/0

Passmore, A.J. 2015 *Land to the west of Cumberland Way, Monkerton, Exeter, Devon* AC Archaeology report ACD1073/2/1 [ADS: https://doi.org/10.5284/1049203]

Passmore, A.J. forthcoming 'Roman military and later remains at the Discovery Quarter, Mount Dinham, Exeter', in *Roman Exeter,* Devon Archaeological Society Occasional Paper

Passmore, A.J. and Hughes, N. 2014 *Old Matford, Wonford Street, Exeter* AC Archaeology report ACD821/1/1 [ADS: https://doi.org/10.5284/1028440]

Passmore, A.J. and Pink, F. 2011 *Exeter Science Park Drive North, Sowton, Devon, Archaeological investigations 2010–2011* Exeter Archaeology report 11.37 [ADS: https://doi.org/10.5284/1017971]

Peacock, D.P.S. 1969 'A contribution to the study of Glastonbury Ware from south-western Britain', *Antiquaries Journal* 49, 41–61

Pearce, J. 2015 Urban exits: commercial archaeology and the study of death rituals and the dead in the towns of Roman Britain', in Fulford and Holbrook 2015, 138–66

Pearce, P., Steinmetzer, M. and Quinnell, H. 2011 'An early Neolithic pit alignment, grooved ware and Bronze Age field boundaries at the former Royal Navy Stores Depot, Old Rydon Lane, Exeter', *Proceedings of the Devon Archaeological Society* 69, 23–51

Pearce, S. 2004 *South-western Britain in the early Middle Ages* Leicester, Leicester University Press

Pearce, S. (ed.) 2011 *Recent archaeological work in south-western Britain: Papers in honour of Henrietta Quinnell* Oxford, British Archaeological Reports British Series 548

Pearce, S.M. (ed.) 1982 *The early church in western Britain and Ireland: studies presented to C.A. Ralegh Radford arising from a conference in his honour organised by the Devon Archaeological Society and Exeter City Museum* Oxford, British Archaeological Reports British Series 102

Pears, B. 2013a *Land at Pyde Drove, near Woolavington, Somerset* AC Archaeology report ACD806/2/0 [ADS: https://doi.org/10.5284/1045906]

Pears, B. 2013b *Land to the west of Churchside, Clyst Honiton, Devon* AC Archaeology report ACD815/2/0 [ADS: https://doi.org/10.5284/1024209]

Pears, B. and Rainbird, P. 2014 'An Iron Age enclosure and post-Roman activity at Hazard Farm, Harberton, near Totnes', *Proceedings of the Devon Archaeological Society* 72, 57–69

Pears, B. and Rainbird, P. 2017 *Land off Hill Barton Road, Exeter, Devon: interim results of archaeological excavations on phase 1 development area* AC Archaeology report ACD1189/1/1

Pears, B. and Rainbird, P. forthcoming 'Neolithic and Bronze Age activity at Old Rydon Lane, Exeter', *Proceedings of the Devon Archaeological Society*

Pears, B. and Valentin, J. 2013 *Land adjacent to Higher Exeter Road, Teignmouth, Devon* AC Archaeology report ACD773/2/1

Pears, B. and Valentin, J 2015 *Land at Countess Wear, Exeter, Devon* AC Archaeology report ACD971/2/0

Pears, B. and Valentin, J. 2016 *Land adjacent to Sentry's Farm, Exminster, Devon* AC Archaeology report ACD1089/3/0

Pederzani, S. and Britton, K. 2019 'Oxygen isotopes in bioarchaeology: principles and applications, challenges and opportunities', *Earth-Science Reviews* 188, 77–107

Penhallurick, R.D. 1986 *Tin in antiquity* London, Institute of Metals

Perring, D. 2002 *The Roman house in Britain* London, Routledge

Perring, D. 2015 'Recent advances in the understanding of Roman London', in Fulford and Holbrook 2015, 20–43

Perring, D. and Pitts, M. 2013 *Alien cities: consumption and the origins of urbanism in Roman Britain* Portslade, Spoilheap Monograph Series 7

Petersson, H.B.A. 1990 'Coins and weights: late Anglo-Saxon pennies and mints, *c.* 973–1066', in Jonsson (ed.) 1990, 207–433

Pink, F. 2011 *Land at Crealy Adventure Park, Clyst St Mary, Devon* AC Archaeology report ACD294/2/0

Pink, F. and Farnell, A. 2014 *Land at Sandy Park, Newcourt, Exeter, Devon* AC Archaeology report ACD922/1/1

Pitts, L.F. and St Joseph, J.K. 1985 *Inchtuthil. The legionary fortress* London, The Society for the Promotion of Roman Studies Britannia Monograph 6

Pitts, M. 2016 'Rural transformation in the urbanized landsacape', in Millett *et al.* (eds) 2016, 720–40

Place, C. 2008 *Forston contact tank protection, Charminster, Dorset* Context One report [ADS: https://doi.org/10.5284/1028818]

Platt, C.P.S. 1973 *Medieval Southampton. The port and trading community AD 1000–1600* London and Boston, Routledge and Kegan Paul

Platt, C.P.S. and Coleman-Smith, R. 1975 *Excavations in medieval Southampton 1953–1969.* Volume 2 Leicester, Leicester University Press

Plouviez, J. 2008 'Counting brooches: ways of examining Roman brooch assemblages in London and beyond', in Clark *et al.* (eds) 2008, 171–6

Pluskowski, A. (ed) 2007 *Breaking and shaping beastly bodies: animals as material culture in the Middle Ages* Oxford, Oxbow Books

Pluskowski, A. (ed.) *Ecologies of crusading, colonization, and religious conversion in the medieval Baltic: Terra Sacra II* Turnhout, Brepols

Pollard, S.H.M. 1966 'Neolithic and Dark Age settlement on High Peak, Sidmouth, Devon', *Proceedings of the Devon Archaeological Society* 23, 35–59

Pollard, S.H.M. 1967 'Radiocarbon dating. Neolithic and Dark Age settlement on High Peak, Sidmouth, Devon', *Proceedings of the Devon Archaeological Society* 25, 41

Pollard, S.H.M. 1972 'A Romano-British and post-medieval road at Honeyditches, Seaton', *Proceedings of the Devon Archaeological Society* 30, 222–6

Pollard, S.H.M. 1974 'A Late Iron Age settlement and a Romano-British villa at Holcombe, near Uplyme, Devon', *Proceedings of the Devon Archaeological Society* 32, 59–162

Polsue, J. 1868 *A complete parochial history of the county of Cornwall* Truro, William Lake and London, John Camden Hotton

Polwhele, R. 1797 *The History of Devonshire in three volumes. Volume 1* reprinted in 1977 Dorking, Kohler and Coombes

Ponsford, M. 2002 'Excavations at a Saxo-Norman settlement, Bickley, Cleeve, 1982–89', *Somerset Archaeological and Natural History Society* 146, 46–112

Portman, D. 1966 *Exeter houses, 1400–1700* Exeter, Exeter University Press

Potter, K.R. 1976 *Gesta Stephani: the deeds of Stephen (1135–54)* Oxford, Oxford University Press

Pounds, N.J.G. 1990 'Buildings, building stones and building accounts in South-West England', in Parsons (ed.) 1990, 228–37

Powell, A.B. 2015 'The development of properties inside the southern defences of Roman *Durnovaria*: an excavation at Charles Street, Dorchester', *Proceedings of the Dorset Natural History and Archaeological Society* 135, 162–84

Powell, A.B. 2017 'Excavation at 22 and 23 Joy Street, Barnstaple: late medieval to modern cccupation', *Proceedings of the Devon Archaeological Society* 75, 233–70

Powell, B.P., Mepham, L. and Stevens, C.J. 2008 'Investigations of later prehistoric and Romano-British settlement at Huntworth, 2006', *Somerset Archaeological and Natural History Society* 152, 69–82

Powell, J. 2017 'Romano-British and medieval settlement in the vicinity of Brent Knoll hillfort, Somerset', *Somerset Archaeological and Natural History Society* 160, 17–50

Powell, J.A.B, Mepham, L. and Stevens, C.J. 2009 'Investigation of later prehistoric and Romano-British settlement at Huntworth, 2006', *Somerset Archaeological and Natural History Society* 152, 69–81

Powell, K. 2009 'Excavation of a medieval site at West Wick, Weston-super-Mare', *Somerset Archaeological and Natural History Society* 152, 165–88

Prestidge, O. 2016a *Land at Broadoak, Clyst Honiton, East Devon, Devon* Context One report [ADS: https://doi.org/10.5284/1039836]

Prestidge, O. 2016b *Land behind No. 9 Higher Aboveway, Exminster, Devon* Unpublished report in the Devon Historic Environment Record [ADS: https://doi.org/10.5284/1039121]

Price, R. and Watts, L. 1980 'Rescue excavations at Combe Hay, Somerset, 1968–1973', *Somerset Archaeological and Natural History Society* 124, 1–50

Probert, D.W. 2002 *Church and landscape; a study in social transition in south-western Britain, AD c.400 to c.1200* Unpublished PhD thesis, University of Birmingham

Pryor, S. and Blockley, K. 1978 'A 17th-century kiln at Woolwich', *Post-Medieval Archaeology* 12, 30–85

Putnam, B. 2007 *Roman Dorset* Stroud, Tempus

Quinn, G.F. 1995 'A new survey of the prehistoric field system on Kerswell Down and Whilborough Common', *Proceedings of the Devon Archaeological Society* 53, 131–4

Quinnell, H. 1986 'The Iron Age and Roman period in Cornwall', *Cornish Archaeology* 25, 111–34

Quinnell, H. 1993 'A sense of identity: distinctive Cornish stone artefacts in the Roman and post-Roman periods', *Cornish Archaeology* 32, 29–46

Quinnell, H. 2004 *Trethurgy: excavations at Trethurgy Round, St Austell: community and status in Roman and Post-Roman Britain* Truro, Cornwall County Council

Quinnell, H. 2010 'Prehistoric and Roman material from Lundy', *Proceedings of the Devon Archaeological Society* 68, 19–60

Quinnell, H. 2011 'A summary of Cornish ceramics in the first millennium BC', *Cornish Archaeology* 50, 231–40

Quinnell, H. 2015 'The prehistoric pottery', in Hughes 2015, 117–20

Quinnell, H. 2017a 'Prehistoric sites and finds beneath central Exeter', *Proceedings of the Devon Archaeological Society* 75, 1–25

Quinnell, H. 2017b 'Dartmoor and prehistoric to early medieval tinworking', in Newman (ed.) 2017, 27–54

Quinnell, H. and Farnell, A. 2016 'Prehistoric sites in the Digby Area of Exeter', *Proceedings of the Devon Archaeological Society* 74, 171–206

Quinnell, H. and Reed, S. 2012 'Archaeology and the Branscombe to Gatcombe water pipeline, east Devon', *Proceedings of the Devon Archaeological Society* 70, 87–106

RCC 1909 *The report of the commissioners concerning charities: containing that part which relates to the City of Exeter* Exeter, T. Besley

Rackham, O. 1986 *The history of the countryside* London, J.M. Dent and Sons

Radford, C.A.R. 1937 'Report of the Exeter Excavation Committee: the Roman site at Topsham', *Proceedings of the Devon Archaeological Exploration Society* 3(1), 4–23

Rahtz, P. 1969, 'Cannington hillfort 1969', *Proceedings of the Somerset Archaeological and Natural History Society* 113, 56–68

Rahtz, P. 1970 'Excavations on Glastonbury Tor', *Archaeological Journal* 127, 1–81

Rahtz, P. 1979 *The Saxon and medieval palaces at Cheddar* Oxford, British Archaeological Reports British Series 65

Rahtz, P. and Greenfield, E. 1977 *Excavations at Chew Valley Lake, Somerset* London, Her Majesty's Stationery Office

Rahtz, P. and Hirst, S. 1974 *Beckery Chapel, Glastonbury* Glastonbury, Glastonbury Antiquarian Society

Rahtz, P., Woodward, A., Burrow, I., Everton, A., Watts, L., Leach, P., Hirst, S., Fowler, P. and Gardner, K. 1992 *Cadbury Congresbury 1968–73: a late/post-Roman hilltop settlement in Somerset* Oxford, British Archaeological Reports British Series 223

Rahtz, P., Hirst, S. and Wright, S.M. 2000 *Cannington cemetery* London, The Society for the Promotion of Roman Studies Britannia Monograph 17

Rainbird, P. 2013 *Land adjacent to Cumberland Way, Monkerton, Exeter, Devon* AC Archaeology report ACD756/2/0 [ADS: https://doi.org/10.5284/1030655]

Rainbird, P. 2014 *Land to the east of Dean Clarke House, Southernhay, Exeter, Devon* AC Archaeology report ACD584/2/1 [ADS: https://doi.org/10.5284/1028447]

Rainbird, P. 2016 *Land at Plumb Park, Exmouth, Devon* AC Archaeology report ACD1090/2/0 [ADS: https://doi.org/10.5284/1040973]

Rainbird, P. 2020 *The former Exeter Golf and Country Club practice ground, Newcourt Drive, Exeter* AC Archaeology report ACD1430/1/0

Rainbird, P. forthcoming 'A Bronze Age ring ditch and later Iron Age settlement at the former Royal Navy Stores Depot Lower Site, Topsham Road, Exeter', *Proceedings of the Devon Archaeological Society*

Rainbird, P. and Farnell, A. 2019 'A hint of Exeter's hinterland and port: a new large aisled hall building at Wessex Close, Topsham, Devon', *Britannia* 50, 385–93

Rainbird, P. and Passmore, A. 2016 'Prehistoric and Romano-British remains and a post-medieval brickworks at Knowle Lane, Cullompton, Devon', *Proceedings of the Devon Archaeological Society* 74, 171–206

Rainbird, P. and Quinnell, H. 2018 'The excavation of a late Iron Age and Romano-British enclosure at Tews Lane, Fremington, near Barnstaple', *Proceedings of the Devon Archaeological Society* 76, 115–39

Rainbird, P. and Valentin, J. 2014 *Land at Great Court Farm, Totnes, South Hams, Devon* AC Archaeology report ACD868/2/0 [ADS: https://doi.org/10.5284/1049197]

Rainbird, P. and Young, T. 2015 'Saxon iron smelting furnaces at Culmstock Road, Hemyock, Devon', *Proceedings of the Devon Archaeological Society* 73, 279–313

Rainbird, P., Pears, B., Pink, F. and Valentin, J. 2017 'Archaeological investigations of Romano-British settlement at Parkengear, Probus, Cornwall', *Cornish Archaeology* 56, 115–52

Randall, C. 2015 *Land at Barges Close, Litton Cheney, Dorset. Archaeological field evaluation in support of a planning application* Context One report [ADS: https://doi.org/10.5284/1038943]

Randall, C. 2017 *M5 Junction 25 improvement works, Taunton, Somerset* Context One report [ADS: https://doi.org/10.5284/1049781]

Randall, C., Green, C. and McConnell, R. 2016 'On the edge of the chalk: an Iron Age settlement at Grimstone Reservoir, Dorchester, Dorset', *Proceedings of the Dorset Natural History and Archaeological Society* 137, 232–63

Randall, S. and Hughes, S. 2020 Land at Whitehill, Newton Abbot, Devon; post-excavation assessment report AC Archaeology report ACD1842/4/1

Ratcliffe, J. 1995 'Duckpool, Morwenstow: a Romano-British and early medieval industrial site and harbour', *Cornish Archaeology* 34, 80–175

Read, B. 1988 *History beneath our feet* Braunton, Merlin Books

Reddé, M. 2018 'The impact of the German frontier on the economic development of the countryside of Roman Gaul', *Journal of Roman Archaeology* 31, 131–60

Reddé, M., Brulet, R., Fellmann, R., Haalebos, J.K. and Von Schnurbein, S. (eds) 2006 *Les fortifications militaires* Paris, L'architecture de la Gaule romaine, Documents d'archéologie française 100

Reece, R. 1975 'Coins', in Hobley 1975, 23–5

Reece, R. 1987a *Coinage in Roman Britain* London, Seaby

Reece, R. 1987b 'The Roman coins', in Crummy 1987, 17–23

Reece, R, 1991a 'Roman coins from Exeter', in Holbrook and Bidwell 1991, 33–8

Reece, R. 1991b *Roman coins from 140 sites in Britain* Cirencester, Cotswold Studies 4

Reece, R. 1993 'Roman coins', in Woodward *et al.* 1993, 114–16

Reed, S.J. 1999 *Archaeological evaluation of a proposed tipping site at Bray Valley Quarries, Brayford, Devon* Exeter Archaeology report 99.68 [ADS: https://doi.org/10.5284/1028782]

Reed, S.J. 2005 'Evaluation excavations of post-Roman features at Wembury Bay near Plymouth', *Proceedings of the Devon Archaeological Society* 63, 55–64

Reed, S.J. and Bidwell, P. 2007 *Excavation at Bantham, South Devon and post-Roman trade in south-west England* [ADS: https://doi.org/10.5284/1000305]

Reed, S.J. and Collings, A.G. 1996 *Archaeological assessment and evaluation of a proposed development site, at Clapperbrook Lane, Church Road, Alphington* Exeter Archaeology report 96.28

Reed, S.J. and Manning, P.T. 1994 *A30 trunk road Honiton to Exeter improvement archaeological evaluation part 1: Blackhorse, Sowton* Exeter Museums Archaeological Field Unit report 94.101 [ADS: https://doi.org/10.5284/1008156]

Reed, S.J. and Turton, S.D. 2005 'Romano-British structures at Parsonage Cross near Littlehempston', *Proceedings of the Devon Archaeological Society* 63, 43–53

Reed, S.J., Juleff, G. and Bayer, O.J. 2006 'Three late Saxon iron-smelting furnaces at Burlescombe, Devon', *Proceedings of the Devon Archaeological Society* 64, 71–123

Reed, S.J., Bidwell, P. and Allan, J. 2011 'Excavation at Bantham, South Devon, and post-Roman trade in South-West England', *Medieval Archaeology* 55, 82–138

Reuter, T. (ed.) 1980 *The greatest Englishman; essays on St Boniface and the church at Crediton* Exeter, Paternoster Press

Revell, L. 2016 *Ways of becoming Roman: discourses of identity in the Roman West* Oxford, Oxbow Books

Reynish, S. 2015 *Phase 2 Cannington flood defence scheme, Cannington, Somerset* Cotswold Archaeology report 15621 [ADS: https://doi.org/10.5284/1042896]

Reynolds, S. 1977 *An introduction to the history of English medieval towns* Oxford, Clarendon Press

Reynolds, S. 2013 *Archaeological trial trench evaluation of land at Old Rydon Lane and Newcourt Drive, Exeter* Unpublished report in the Devon Historic Environment Record

Rhodes, J. 2006 'The Severn flood plain at Gloucester in the medieval and early modern periods', *Transactions of the Bristol and Gloucestershire Archaeological Society* 124, 9–36

Richardson, I. 2019 'Ley Hill, a deserted medieval site on Exmoor', *Somerset Archaeological and Natural History Society* 162, 9–43

Richardson, T. 2014 *Exeter Road, Topsham, Devon* Stratascan report J6930 [ADS: https://doi.org/10.5284/1048189 and https://doi.org/10.5284/1048190]

Richardson, T. 2015 *The Vines, Gypsy Hill, Monkerton, Devon* Stratascan report J9163 [ADS: https://doi.org/10.5284/1053209]

Richmond, I.A. 1968 *Hod Hill. Volume 2: excavations carried out between 1951 and 1958* London, British Museum

Ridgeway, V. and Watts, M. (eds) 2013 *Friars, quakers, industry and urbanisation: the archaeology of the Broadmead Expansion Project Cabot Circus, Bristol 2005–2008* Cirencester, Cotswold Archaeology Monograph 5/Pre-Construct Archaeology Monograph 6

Rigold, S.E. 1954 'Totnes Castle. Recent excavations by the Ancient Monuments Department, Ministry of Works', *Report and Transactions of the Devonshire Association* 86, 228–56

Riley, H. and Wilson-North, R. 2001 *The field archaeology of Exmoor* London, English Heritage

Riley, M., Harvey, D.C., Brown, T. and Mills, S. 2005 'Narrating landscape: the potential of oral history for landscape archaeology, *Public Archaeology* 4, 15–26

Riley, R. 2014 *Winham Farm, Cullompton, Devon* Cotswold Archaeology report 14199 [ADS: https://doi.org/10.5284/1029671]

Rippon, S. 1997 *The Severn estuary* Leicester, Leicester University Press

Rippon, S. 2000a *The transformation of coastal wetlands* London, British Academy

Rippon, S. 2000b 'The Romano-British exploitation of coastal wetlands: survey and excavation on the North Somerset Levels, 1993–7', *Britannia* 31, 69–200

Rippon, S. 2006a *Landscape, community and colonisation: the North Somerset Levels during the 1st to 2nd millennia AD* York, Council for British Archaeology Research Report 152

Rippon, S. 2006b 'Landscapes of pre-medieval occupation', in R. Kain (ed.) *England's landscape. Volume 3: the South West* London, Collins/English Heritage, 41–66

Rippon, S. 2007 'Focus or frontier? The significance of estuaries in the landscape of southern Britain', *Landscapes* 8 (i), 23–38

Rippon, S. 2008a *Beyond the medieval village* Oxford, Oxford University Press

Rippon, S. 2008b 'Coastal trade in Roman Britain: the investigation of Crandon Bridge, Somerset: a Romano-British trans-shipment port beside the Severn Estuary', *Britannia* 39, 85–144

Rippon, S. 2010 'Landscape change during the "long eighth century" in southern England', in Higham and Ryan (eds) 2010, 39–64

Rippon, S. 2012 *Making sense of an historic landscape* Oxford, Oxford University Press

Rippon, S. 2017 'Romano-British coarse ware industries and socio-economic interaction in eastern England', in Allen *et al.* (eds) 2017, 337–52

Rippon, S. 2018a *Kingdom, civitas and county: the evolution of territorial identity in the English landscape* Oxford, Oxford University Press

Rippon, S. 2018b 'The early medieval territory associated with Cannington', in Hart and Mudd (eds) 2018, 140–2

Rippon, S. forthcoming 'Romano-British settlement on the North Somerset Levels: new evidence from Kingson Seymour', *Somerset Archaeology and Natural History* 163

Rippon, S., Fyfe, R.M. and Brown, A.G. 2006 'Beyond villages and open fields: the origins and development of a historic landscape characterised by dispersed settlement in south west England', *Medieval Archaeology* 50, 31–70

Rippon, S., Claughton, P. and Smart, C. 2009 *Mining in a medieval landscape: the royal silver mines of the Tamar Valley* Exeter, University of Exeter Press

Rippon, S., Wainwright, A. and Smart, C. 2014 'Farming regions in medieval England: the archaeobotanical and zooarchaeological evidence', *Medieval Archaeology* 58, 195–255

Rippon, S., Smart, C. and Pears, B. 2015 *The fields of Britannia* Oxford, Oxford University Press

Rippon, S., Armstrong, S. and Gould, D. 2018 'The Sandy Lane villa: its wider context', in Hart and Mudd 2018, 133–7

Risdon, T. *c.* 1630 *The chorographical description or survey of the county of Devon* (first published in 1811; reprinted Barnstaple, Porcupines, 1970)

Rivet, A.L.F. and Smith, C. 1979 *The place-names of Roman Britain* Cambridge, Cambridge University Press

Rizzetto, M., Crabtree, P. and Albarella, U. 2017 'Livestock changes at the beginning and end of the Roman period in Britain: issues of acculturation, adaptation, and 'improvement', *European Journal of Archaeology* 20(3), 535–56

Roberts, B. and Wrathmell, S. 2000a *An atlas of rural settlement in England* London, English Heritage

Roberts, B. and Wrathmell, S. 2000b 'Peoples of wood and plain: an exploration of national and regional contrasts', in D. Hooke (ed.) *Landscape: the richest historical record* Birmingham, Society for Landscape Studies, 47–62

Roberts, B. and Wrathmell, S. 2002 *Region and place* London, English Heritage

Robertson, A.S. (eds R. Hobbs and T. Buttrey) 2000 *An inventory of Romano-British coin hoards* London, Royal Numismatic Society Special Publication 20

Robinson, D.M. 2017 'The architecture of the medieval Cistercian church and cloister', in Beacham 2017, 33–71

Robinson, S. 2011 *Proposed extension to burial ground at St Nicholas Church, Studland, Dorset* AC Archaeology report ACW350/1/0 [ADS: https://doi.org/10.5284/1030497]

Robinson, S. 2013 *Somerdale Factory, recreation grounds and car park, Keynsham, Bath and Northeast Somerset* AC Archaeology report ACW488/2/0 [ADS: https://doi.org/10.5284/1029142]

Robinson, S. 2016 *Land at Wolvershill Road, Banwell, North Somerset* AC Archaeology report ACW879/2/0 [ADS: https://doi.org/10.5284/1049212]

Rogers, A. 2011 *Late Roman towns in Britain: rethinking change and decline* Cambridge, Cambridge University Press

Roman Amphorae: a digital resource: http://archaeologydataservice.ac.uk/archives/view/amphora_ahrb_2005/index.cfm

Roskams, S. 2001 *Excavation* Cambridge, Cambridge University Press

Rowe, M.M. 1977 *Tudor Exeter: tax assessments 1489–1595 including the Military Survey 1522* Exeter, Devon and Cornwall Records Society New Series 22

Rowe, M.M. and Cochlin, J.J. 1964 *Mayors of Exeter from the 13th Century to the Present Day* Exeter, Exeter City Library

Royal Commission of Historical Monuments of England 1975 *An inventory of the historical monuments of Dorset. Volume 5: East* London, The Royal Commission of Historical Monuments of England

Sabin, D. and Donaldson, K. 2013 *Land at Monkerton, Pinhoe, Exeter: additional survey* Archaeology Surveys Ltd. report 488

Sage, A. 1997 *Archaeological evaluation of land adjacent to Nelson Close, Topsham* Exeter Archaeology report 97.69 [ADS: https://doi.org/10.5284/1028768]

Sage, A. 1999 *Archaeological evaluation at Exeter Road, Topsham, 1999* Exeter Archaeology report 99.37 [ADS: https://doi.org/10.5284/1028770]

Sage, A. and Allan, J. 2004 'The early Roman military defences, late Roman burials and later features at the Topsham School, Topsham', *Proceedings of the Devon Archaeological Society* 62, 1–40

Salvatore, J.P. 1994 *Excavations at Southernhay Gardens, Exeter, 1974. Part 1: Roman military* Exeter Museums Archaeology Field Unit report 94.02 [ADS: https://doi.org/10.5284/1035186]

Salvatore, J.P. 2001 'Three Roman military cremation burials From Holloway Street, Exeter', *Proceedings of the Devon Archaeological Society* 59, 125–40

Salvatore, J.P. 2011 'The Roman military base at Pomeroy Wood: further comment arising from the archaeological investigations north of the A30', *Proceedings of the Devon Archaeological Society* 69, 113–23

Salvatore, J.P. forthcoming 'Roman military activity beyond the *porta principalis sinistra* (South Gate) of the legionary fortress at Exeter', *Proceedings of the Devon Archaeological Society*

Salvatore, J.P. and Knight, M. 1991 'Sections through the Roman road from Exeter to North Tawton', *Proceedings of the Devon Archaeological Society* 49, 99–106

Salvatore, J.P. and Quinnell, H. 2011, 'Excavation of a Bronze Age roundhouse and other prehistoric, Romano-British and early medieval features at the Langage Energy Centre and Park, and the Choakford-Langage pipeline, Sparkwell, South Hams', *Proceedings of the Devon Archaeological Society* 69, 53–94

Salvatore, J.P. and Simpson, S.J. 1992 *Excavations at Bartholomew Street East, Exeter, 1980–81. Part 1: Roman military* Exeter Museums Archaeology Field Unit report 92.33 [ADS: https://doi.org/10.5284/1035210]

Salvatore, J.P. and Steinmetzer, M. 2018 'The recently discovered Roman military supply-base at St Loye's College, Exeter, Devon, South-West Britain: interpretation and significance', *Limes* XXIII, 768–75

Salvatore, J.P., Kaye, S., Stocker, S. and Toller, H. 2019 'Observations on the Roman road between Exeter, North Tawton and Okehampton', *Proceedings of the Devon Archaeological Society* 77, 297–319

Salvatore, J.P., Steinmetzer, M. and Quinnell, H. forthcoming 'The Iron Age settlement, Roman military establishment, Roman civil occupation and mid-late Roman cemetery at the former St Loye's College, Topsham Road, Exeter', in *Roman Exeter,* Devon Archaeological Society Occasional Paper

Salway, P. 1981 *Roman Britain* Oxford, Oxford University Press

Salzman, L.F. 1952 *Building in England down to 1540: a documentary history* Oxford, Oxford University Press

Sampson, J. 2015 'Gothic sculpture and worked stone', in Gilchrist and Green (eds) 2015, 358–82

Sauer, E.W. 2000 'Alchester, a Claudian 'vexillation fortress' near the western boundary of the Catuvellauni: new light on the Roman invasion of Britain', *Archaeological Journal* 157, 1–78

Saunders, A. 1980 'Lydford Castle, Devon', *Medieval Archaeology* 24, 123–86

Saunders, A. and Harris, D. 1982 'Excavations at Castle Gotha, St Austell', *Cornish Archaeology* 21, 109–52

Saunders, C. 1972 'The excavations at Grambla, Wendron, 1972: interim report', *Cornish Archaeology* 11, 50–2

Saunders, K. 2010a *Land adjacent to Junction 24 of the M5, Bridgwater, Somerset* Cotswold Archaeology report 10174 [ADS: https://doi.org/10.5284/1029129]

Saunders, K. 2010b *Land at Haygrove Farm, Bridgwater, Somerset* Cotswold Archaeology report 10204 [ADS: https://doi.org/10.5284/1016834]

Saunders, K. 2010c *Land at Hinkley Point, Somerset: Archaeological evaluation* Cotswold Archaeology report 10049 [ADS: https://doi.org/10.5284/1029128]

Saunders, K. 2011a *Land to the east of Maidenbrook Farm, Taunton, Somerset* Cotswold Archaeology report 11017 [ADS: https://doi.org/10.5284/1007198]

Saunders, K. 2011b *Church Farm, Rode, Somerset* Cotswold Archaeology report 11197 [CA: https://reports.cotswoldarchaeology.co.uk/]

Sausins, D. 2017a *New Kingdom Hall, Keynsham, Bath and North East Somerset* Cotswold Archaeology report 17586 [ADS: https://doi.org/10.5284/1047857]

Sausins, D. 2017b *Roman Baths Museum, Archway Project (Phase 3), York Street, Bath* Cotswold Archaeology report 6185 [ADS: https://doi.org/10.5284/1046883]

Sawyer, P.H. 1968 *Anglo-Saxon charters: an annotated list and bibliography* London, Royal Historical Society

Schofield, J. 1995 *Medieval London houses* New Haven, Yale University Press

Schönberger, H. and Simon, H.-G. 1976 *Römerlager Rödgen* Berlin, Limesforschungen Bd 15

Schulting, R.J., le Roux, P., Gan, Y.M., Pouncett, J., Hamilton, J., Snoeck, C., Ditchfield, P., Henderson, R., Lange, P., Lee-Thorp, J., Gosden, C. and Lock, G. 2019 'The ups and downs of Iron Age animal management on the Oxfordshire Ridgeway, south-central England: a multi-isotope approach', *Journal of Archaeological Science* 101, 199–212

Scott, E. 1993 *A gazetteer of Roman villas in Britain* Leicester, University of Leicester

Scott, J.G.M., Mack, F.D. and Clarke, J.M. 2007 *Towers and bells* of *Devon*, 2 vols Exeter, The Mint Press

Scrivener, R.G. 1979 'Geological report on building materials', in Bidwell 1979, 135

Scull, C., Müldner, G. and Makowiecki, D. 2019 'Carbon and nitrogen stable isotope evidence for animal husbandry and environmental change in the medieval Kulmerland', in Pluskowski (ed.) 2019, 115–29

Seager Smith, R. 2008 'Pottery', in *Suburban life in Roman Durnovaria* online resource: [WA: https://www.wessexarch.co.uk/sites/default/files/projects/dorchester_county_hospital/09_Pottery.pdf]

Seager Smith, R. and Davies, S. 1993 'Roman pottery', in Woodward *et al.* 1993, 202–89

Seetah, K. 2006 'Multidisciplinary approach to Romano-British cattle butchery', in Maltby (ed.) 2006, 109–16

Serjeantson, D. 2006 'Birds: food and a mark of status', in Woolgar *et al.* 2006, 131–47

Serjeantson, D. 2009 'Food, craft and status: the Winchester suburbs and defences in a wider context', in Serjeantson and Rees 2009, 166–83

Serjeantson, D. and Morris, J. 2011 'Ravens and crows in Iron Age and Roman Britain', *Oxford Journal of Archaeology* 30(1), 85–107

Serjeantson, D and Rees, H. (eds) 2009 *Food, craft and status in medieval Winchester* Winchester, Winchester Museums

Serjeanston, D. and Waldron, T. (eds) 1989 *Diet and crafts in towns. The evidence of animal remains from the Roman to the post-medieval periods* Oxford, British Archaeological Reports British Series 199

Serjeantson, D. and Woolgar, C.M. 2006 'Fish consumption in medieval England', in Woolgar *et al.* 2006, 102–30

Sharpe, A. and Smith, R. 2018 *Castle Kayle Farm, Hayle, Cornwall* Cornwall Archaeological Unit report 2018R039 [ADS: https://doi.org/10.5284/1049324]

Sharples, N.M. 1991 *Maiden Castle: excavations and field survey 1985–6* London, Historic Buildings and Monuments Commission for England

Sheail, J. 1972 'The distribution of taxable population and wealth in England during the early sixteenth century', *Transactions of the British Institute of Geographers* 55, 3–20

Sheail, J. 1998 *The regional distribution of wealth in England as indicated in the 1524/5 Lay Subsidy. Volumes 1–2* London, Lists and Index Society Special Series 28

Sheldon, S. 2010 *Land around Pinn Court Farm, Pinhoe, Devon* Cotswold Archaeology report 10185 [ADS: https://doi.org/10.5284/1007400]

Sheldon, S. 2011 *Newquay growth area, Newquay, Cornwall* Cotswold Archaeology report 11267 [ADS: https://doi.org/10.5284/1028750]

Sheldon, S. 2012 *Land at Tithebarn Green (Redhayes), Exeter, Devon* Cotswold Archaeology report 12012 [ADS: https://doi.org/10.5284/1034384]

Sheldon, S. 2013a *Canal Way, Ilminster, Somerset* Cotswold Archaeology report 13517 [CA: https://reports.cotswoldarchaeology.co.uk/]

Sheldon, S. 2013b *Cannington Flood Defence Scheme, Cannington, Somerset* Cotswold Archaeology report 13617 [CA: https://reports.cotswoldarchaeology.co.uk/]

Sheldon, S. 2014 *Sentry's Farm, Exminster, Devon* Cotswold Archaeology report 13689 [CA: https://reports.cotswoldarchaeology.co.uk/]

Sheldon, S. 2015 *Cloakham Lawns, Axminster, Devon* Cotswold Archaeology report 15767 [CA: https://reports.cotswoldarchaeology.co.uk/]

Shiel, N. 1979 'The hoard of 1715', in Bidwell 1979, 167–79

Shiel, N. 1984 'The numismatic finds', in Allan 1984a, 248–57

Shiel, N. 1991 'Coin list', in Holbrook and Bidwell 1991, 24–33

Shiel, N. and Reece, R. 1979 'The coins', in Bidwell 1979, 162–79

Shorter, A.H., Ravenhill, W.L.D. and Gregory, K.J. 1969 *South west England* London, Thomas Nelson and Sons

Shortt, W.T.P. 1841a *Sylva antiqua Iscana, numismatica, quinetiam figulina, or, Roman and other antiquities of Exeter: Being a description and elucidation of the numerous ancient coins, Samian ware, and other relics, lately discovered in that venerable and interesting city* London, J.B. Nichols & Son

Shortt, W.T.P. 1841b *Collectanea curiosa antiqua Dunmonia* London, J.B. Nichols & Son

Silvester, R.J. 1980 'The prehistoric open settlement at Dainton, South Devon', *Proceedings of the Devon Archaeological Society* 38, 17–489

Silvester, R.J. 1981a 'Excavation at Honeyditches Roman villa, Seaton, in 1978', *Proceedings of the Devon Archaeological Society* 39, 37–87

Silvester, R.J. 1981b 'An excavation on the post-Roman site at Bantham, South Devon', *Proceedings of the Devon Archaeological Society* 39, 89–118

Silvester, R.J. and Bidwell, P.T. 1984 'A Roman site at Woodbury, Axminster', *Proceedings of the Devon Archaeological Society* 42, 33–58

Simpson, S.J. 1990 *An archaeological evaluation at Bramble Hill, Seaton Down Hill, Seaton 1990*, Exeter Museums Archaeological Field Unit report 90.14

Simpson, S.J. 1993a *Excavations on the Roman fort and settlement site in Woodbury Great Close, Axminster 1999* Exeter Archaeology report 93.11 [ADS: https://doi.org/10.5284/1020227]

Simpson, S.J. 1993b *Exeter city defences: West Gate to South Gate, survey and excavation in the West Quarter* Exeter Archaeology report 93.73 [ADS: https://doi.org/10.5284/1035173]

Simpson, S.J. and Griffith, F.M. 1993 'Trial excavation at the Roman fort at St Andrew's Hill, Cullompton', *Proceedings of the Devon Archaeological Society* 51, 149–60

Simpson, S.J., Griffith, F.M. and Holbrook, N. 1989 'The prehistoric, Roman and early post-Roman site at Hayes Farm, Clyst Honiton', *Proceedings of the Devon Archaeological Society* 47, 1–28

Sims, R. 2009 *An archaeological strip, map and sample excavation and trench evaluation on land at Matworthy House, Deepdene Park, St Leonard's, Exeter* AC Archaeology report ACD22/2/0 [ADS: https://doi.org/10.5284/1021109]

Sims, R. 2013 *Land to the north of the A3052, Clyst St Mary, Devon* AC Archaeology report ACD611/1/0 [ADS: https://doi.org/10.5284/1031478]

Sims, R. and Valentin, J. 2011 *Archaeological investigation on land off Par lane, Par, Cornwall* AC Archaeology report ACD161/1/1

Sims, R. and Valentin, J. 2012 *Land between Harepath Road and Colyford Road, Seaton, Devon* AC Archaeology report ACD548/1/0 [ADS: https://doi.org/10.5284/1028776]

Slater, A. 2009 *Hamdon Hill, Montacute, Somerset* Cambridge University Archaeological Unit report 880 [ADS: https://doi.org/10.5284/1021182]

Slater, A. and Brittain, M. 2013 *Excavations at Ham Hill, Somerset (2011)* Cambridge University Archaeological Unit report 1101 [ADS: https://doi.org/10.5284/1021188]

Slater, T.R. 2000 'The south west of England', in Palliser (ed.) 2000a, 583–607

Sleap, J. and Lane, A. 2016 *Land at Clapton Farm, Tinkers Lane, Wincanton, Somerset, BA9 8LH* Pre-Construct Archaeological Services report [ADS: https://doi.org/10.5284/1043574]

Smart, C. 2008 *Old County Ground, St Thomas, Exeter: results of archaeological monitoring of environmental trial pits and evaluative gradiometer survey* Exeter Archaeology report 08.74

Smart, C. 2014 *A Roman military complex and medieval settlement on Church Hill, Calstock, Cornwall: survey and excavation 2007–2010* Oxford, British Archaeological Reports British Series 603

Smart, C. 2018 *Industry and the making of a rural landscape: iron and pottery production at Churchill's Farm, Hemyock, Devon* Oxford, British Archaeological Reports British Series 636

Smart, C. and Smart, H. 2014 *Archaeological trench evaluation at Membury Court, Membury, east Devon, June 2013* University of Exeter report SX-05990

Smart, V. 1986 'Scandinavians, Celts and Germans in Anglo-Saxon England: the evidence of moneyers' names', in Blackburn (ed.) 1986, 171–86

Smith, A. 2016a 'Buildings in the countryside', in Smith *et al.* 2016, 44–74

Smith, A. 2016b 'Ritual deposition', in Millett *et al.* (eds) 2016, 641–59

Smith, A. 2017 'Rural crafts and industry', in Allen *et al.* 2017, 178–236

Smith, A. 2018a 'Religion and the rural population', in Smith *et al.* 2018, 120–204

Smith, A. 2018b 'Death in the countryside: rural burial practices', in Smith *et al.* 2018, 205–80

Smith, A. 2018c 'Lifestyle and the social environment', in Smith *et al.* 2018, 48–77

Smith, A. and Fulford, M. 2016 'Conclusions: the rural settlement of Roman Britain', in Smith *et al.* 2016, 385–420

Smith, A. and Fulford, M. 2019 'The defended vici of Roman Britain: recent research and new agendas', *Britannia* 50, 109–47

Smith, A., Allen, M., Brindle, T. and Fulford, M. 2016 *New visions in the countryside of Roman Britain. Volume 1: The rural settlement of Roman Britain* London, The Society for the Promotion of Roman Studies Britannia Monograph 29

Smith, A., Allen, M., Brindle, T., Fulford, M., Lodwick, L. and Rohnbogner, A. 2018 *New visions in the countryside of Roman Britain. Volume 3: Life and death in the countryside of Roman Britain* London, The Society for the Promotion of Roman Studies Britannia Monograph 31

Smith, A.T. and Brown, R. 2006 'Excavation and geophysical survey of the Roman settlement at Charterhouse-on-Mendip, 2005', *Somerset Archaeological and Natural History Society* 149, 79–88

Smith, C.E. 2015 *Puriton landfill solar farm, Somerset* Archaeology Wales report 1339 [ADS: https://doi.org/10.5284/1048890]

Smith, C.S and Gnudi, M.T. (eds) 1959 [1540] *Vannoccio Biringuccio, de la pirotechnia* New York, Dover Publications

Smith, D.J. 1979 'Fragments of mosaic from the legionary baths', in Bidwell 1979, 132–4

Smith, R.J.C. 1993 *Excavations at County Hall, Dorchester, Dorset, 1988* Salisbury, Wessex Archaeology Monograph 4

Smith, R.J.C., Healy, F., Allen, M.J., Morris, E.L., Barnes, I. and Woodward, P.J. 1997 *Excavations along the route of the Dorchester by-pass, Dorset 1968–8* Salisbury, Wessex Archaeology Monograph 11

Smith, W. 2001 *The charred plant remains and charcoal from Sherborne Old Castle, Dorset* English Heritage Centre for Archaeology report 70/2001

Smith, W. 2014 *Yeomans Gardens, Newcourt Road, Topsham, Exeter* AC Archaeology report ACD953/2/1

Smith, W. and Pears, B. 2016 *Land at Penns Mount, Kingsteignton, Devon* AC Archaeology report ACD907/2/0

Smith, W. and Rainbird, P. 2013 *Land adjacent to Chudleigh Road, Alphington, Exeter, Devon* AC Archaeology report ACD668/1/0 [ADS: https://doi.org/10.5284/1024207]

Smith, W and Rainbird P. 2015 *Land at Riverside (east of Steamer Quay Road), Totnes, Devon* AC Archaeology report ACD975/2/1

Soil Survey of England and Wales 1983 *Soils of England and Wales, sheet 5 south west England – scale 1:250,000* Harpenden, Soil Survey of England and Wales

Southwest Archaeology 2007 *4–6 Countess Wear Road, Exeter, Devon. Results of a historic building survey, archaeological evaluation and watching brief* Southwest Archaeology report 071130

Sparey Green, C. 1987 *Excavations at Poundbury. Volume 1: The settlement* Dorchester, Dorset Natural History and Archaeological Society Monograph 7

Stallibrass, S. 1999 'Cattle, culture, status and soldiers in Northern England', in Fincham *et al.* 2019, 64–73

Stallibrass, S. and Thomas, R. (eds) 2008 *Feeding the Roman army: the archaeology of production and supply in northwest Europe* Oxford, Oxbow Books

Stanes, R.G.F. 1964 'A georgicall account of Devonshire and Cornwalle', *Report and Transactions of the Devonshire Association for the Advancement of Science Literature and Art* 96, 269–302

Staniforth, P.R. and Juddery, J.Z. 1991a *Exeter property deeds 1150–1450. Part 1* Exeter Museums Archaeological Field Unit report 91.45

Staniforth, P.R. and Juddery, J.Z. 1991b *Exeter property deeds 1150–1450. Part 2* Exeter Museums Archaeological Field Unit report 91.46

Stead, P.M. 2004 *Archaeological excavation of Southernhay East Car Park, Exeter* Exeter Archaeology report 04.24 [ADS: https://doi.org/10.5284/1028780]

Stead, P.M. and Payne, N. 2013 *Land at and adjacent to Fairfield House, St Loye's, Topsham Road, Exeter, Devon* AC Archaeology report ACD649/3/0 [ADS: https://doi.org/10.5284/1028785]

Steane, K. 2006 *The archaeology of the Upper City and adjacent suburbs* Oxford, Lincoln Archaeological Studies 3

Steinmetzer, M.F.R. 2006a *Trench evaluation at St Pauls Church, Burnthouse Lane, Exeter* Unpublished report in the Devon Historic Environment Record

Steinmetzer, M.F.R. 2006b *Archaeological watching brief at Wonford Methodist Chapel, Exeter, Devon* Unpublished report in the Devon Historic Environment Record

Steinmetzer, M.F.R. 2015a *Historic building recording and archaeological monitoring and recording at Quay Gardens, Monmouth Avenue, Topsham* Oakford Archaeology report 14-07 [ADS: https://doi.org/10.5284/1038682]

Steinmetzer, M.F.R. 2015b *Archaeological evaluation of land at Rosario, Ebford, Devon* Oakford Archaeology report 15-14 [ADS: https://doi.org/10.5284/1035087]

Steinmetzer, M.F.R. 2015c *Archaeological evaluation on land south of 37 Pinn Hill, Pinhoe, Devon* Unpublished report in the Devon Historic Environment Record

Steinmetzer, M.F.R. forthcoming 'A Roman tile production site and post-medieval church at St David's, Queen's Terrace, Exeter', *Proceedings of the Devon Archaeological Society*

Steinmetzer, M.F.R. and Salvatore, J.P. 2011 *Archaeological excavation of an Iron Age enclosure settlement and a Roman military establishment at the former St Loye's College, Topsham Road, Exeter 2010* Exeter Archaeology report 11.39 [ADS: https://doi.org/10.5284/1028781]

Steinmetzer, M.F.R., Pearce, P. and Allan, J.P. forthcoming 'Excavations at Princesshay, Exeter, 1997–2006. Part 2: Saxo-Norman occupation, the Blackfriars and Bedford House', *Proceedings of the Devon Archaeological Society*

Steinmetzer, M.F.R., Stead, P., Pearce, P., Bidwell, P. and Allan, J.P. forthcoming 'Excavations at Princesshay, Exeter, 1997–2006. Part 1: Roman', in *Roman Exeter,* Devon Archaeological Society Occasional Paper

Stephens, W.B. 1958 *Seventeenth-century Exeter. A study of industrial and commercial development, 1625–1688* Exeter, University of Exeter

Stevens, C. 2008 *Suburban life in Roman Durnovaria: additional specialist report – environmental charred plant remains* Wessex Archaeology report [WA: https://www.wessexarch.co.uk/sites/default/files/projects/dorchester_county_hospital/03_Charred_plants.pdf]

Stoyle, M. 2003 *Circled with stone: Exeter's city walls 1485–1660* Exeter, University of Exeter

Stoyle, M. 2014 *Water in the city: the aqueducts and underground passages of Exeter* Exeter, Exeter University Press

Stoyle, M. 2017 'The Western Rebellion of 1549: religious protest in Devon and Cornwall', *Modern History Review 20*(1), 18–21

Stratford, N. 1991 'Bishop Grandisson and the visual arts', in Swanton (ed.) 1991, 144–55

Straker, V., Robinson, M. and Robinson, E. 1984 'Biological investigations of waterlogged deposits in the Roman fortress ditch at Exeter', *Proceedings of the Devon Archaeological Society* 42, 59–70

Straker, V., Brown, A., Fyfe, R. and Jones, J. 2007 'Romano-British environmental background', in Webster (ed) 2007, 145–50

Sturgess, J. and Lawson-Jones, A. 2006 *Post-Roman sites at Gwithian, Cornwall* Truro, Cornwall County Council

Swain, H. and Williams, T. 2008 'The population of Roman London', in Clark *et al.* (eds) 2008, 33–40

Swanton, M. (ed.) 1991 *Exeter Cathedral: a celebration* Exeter, Exeter Cathedral

Swanton, M. (ed.) 1996 *The Anglo-Saxon Chronicle* London, Dent

Swindin, P. 2006 *Archaeological watching brief at Lower Rollestone Farm, Exeter* Unpublished report in the Devon Historic Environment Record

Sykes, N. 2006a 'From *cu* and *sceap* to *beffe* and *motton*', in Woolgar *et al.* 2006, 56–71

Sykes, N. 2006b 'The impact of the Normans on hunting practices in Britain', in Woolgar *et al.* 2006, 162–75

Sykes, N.J. 2007 *The Norman conquest: a zooarchaeological perspective* Oxford, British Archaeological Reports International Series 1656

Symonds, M. 2018 'A composite coastal cordon on Exmoor? Exploring local influence on first-century AD fortlet use', *Britannia* 49, 53–77

Symonds, R.P. and Wade, S. 1999 *Roman pottery from excavations in Colchester, 1971–86* Colchester, Colchester Archaeological Report 10

Tabor, R. 2011 *Stratton House Campus, Dorchester, Dorset* Context One report [ADS: https://doi.org/10.5284/1043985]

Tabor, R. 2012 *Land south of Oil Mill Lane, Clyst St Mary, East Devon* Context One report [ADS: https://doi.org/10.5284/1031429]

Tabor, R. and Johnson, P. 2002 'Sigwells, Charleton Horethoirne: the identification, interpretation and testing of Bronze Age to early medieval landscapes by geophysical survey and excavation', *Somerset Archaeological and Natural History Society* 144, 1–24

Tapply, C. 2017a *Sandy Park Junction, Exeter, Devon* Cotswold Archaeology report 16677 [ADS: https://doi.org/10.5284/1053295]

Tapply, C. 2017b *Devon and Cornwall Police Headquarters, Middlemoor, Exeter, Devon* Cotswold Archaeology report 17563 [CA: https://reports.cotswoldarchaeology.co.uk/]

Tatler, S. and Bellamy, P. 2006 *New fencing, Hengistbury Head, Dorset* Terrain Archaeology report 53207/3/1 [ADS: https://doi.org/10.5284/1046597]

Taylor, A. and Wallace, S. 2006 *Land adjacent to A31, Henbury Park, Sturminster Marshall, Wimborne, Dorset* Thames Valley Archaeological Services report 06/48 [ADS: https://doi.org/10.5284/1041486]

Taylor, H.M. and Taylor, J. 1965 *Anglo–Saxon architecture* (2 vols) Cambridge, Cambridge University Press

Taylor, R. 2012 'Petrology', in Gillard *et al.* 2012, 119–21

Taylor, R. 2016 'Middle and late Iron Age fabrics', in Quinnell and Farnell 2016, 130–2

Taylor, R. forthcoming 'Roman tile: petrographic comment', in Salvatore, Steinmetzer and Quinnell forthcoming

Taylor, S.R. 2012 'Excavations of a Roman and post-Roman site at Penlee House, Tregony: a cremation burial and other burning issues', *Cornish Archaeology* 51, 125–63

Taylor, S.R. and Johns, C. 2015 'Restormel Castle, Cornwall: archaeological recording', *Cornish Archaeology* 54, 89–138

Tekin, O. (ed.) 2009 *Ancient history, numismatics and epigraphy in the Mediterranean world* Istanbul, Ege Yayinlari

Terrain Archaeology 2000a *St John Ambulance Hall, North Square, Dorchester, Dorset* Terrain Archaeology report 5058.1 [ADS: https://doi.org/10.5284/1031867]

Terrain Archaeology 2000b *West Dorset District Council car park, Colliton Street, Dorchester, Dorset* Terrain Archaeology report 5059.1 [ADS: https://doi.org/10.5284/1031404]

Terrain Archaeology 2003 *Dorford Baptist Church, Bridport Road, Dorchester, Dorset* Terrain Archaeology report 53141.1 [ADS: https://doi.org/10.5284/1034298]

Thacker, G. 2012 *Coyte Farm, St Austell, Cornwall* Oxford Archaeology report [ADS: https://doi.org/10.5284/1022374]

Thawley, C.R. 1982 'The animal bones', in Wacher and McWhirr 1982, 211–27

Thirsk, J. 1967a 'The farming regions of England', in Thirsk (ed.) 1967b, 1–112

Thirsk, J. (ed.) 1967b *The agrarian history of England and Wales. Volume IV: 1500–1640*, Cambridge, Cambridge University Press

Thirsk, J. 1984a 'Introduction', in Thirsk (ed.) 1984b, xix–xxxi

Thirsk, J. (ed.) 1984b *The agrarian history of England and Wales. Volume V: 1640–1750, I: regional farming systems* Cambridge, Cambridge University Press

Thirsk, J. 1987 *England's agricultural regions and agrarian history, 1500–1750* Basingstoke, Macmillan Education

Thomas, C. 1966a *Rural settlement in Roman Britain* York, Council for British Archaeology Research Report 7

Thomas, C. 1966b 'The character and origins of Roman Dumnonia', in Thomas (ed.) 1966a, 74–98

Thomas, C. 1981a *Christianity in Roman Britain to AD 500* London, Batsford

Thomas, C. 1981b *A provisional list of imported pottery in post-Roman western Britain and Ireland* Redruth, Institute of Cornish Studies

Thomas, R. 2007 'Chasing the ideal? ritualism, pragmatism and the later medieval hunt in England', in Pluskowski (ed.) 2007, 125–48

Thomas, S. 2018 *On the edge of empire: a new narrative of society in the south-west of England during the first century BC to fifth century AD* Unpublished PhD thesis, University of Cardiff

Thompson, J.D.A. 1956 *Inventory of British coin hoards AD 600–1500* Oxford, Royal Numismatic Society Special Publication 1

Thomson, A., Haines, C., Havard, T. and Holt, R. 2014 *Wales and West Utilities gas main replacement programme 2012–2014 Exeter* Cotswold Archaeology report 14280 [ADS: https://doi.org/10.5284/1046171]

Thorn, F. and Thorn, C. 1985 *Domesday Book: Devon* Chichester, Phillimore

Thordycraft, V., Pirrie, D. and Brown, A.G. 2002 'An environmental approach to the archaeology of tin mining on Dartmoor', in Murphy and Wiltshire (eds) 2002, 19–28

Thordycraft, V., Pirrie, D. and Brown, A.G. 2004 'Alluvial records of medieval and prehistoric tin mining on Dartmoor, SW England', *Geoarchaeology* 19, 219–36

Thorp, J.R.L. 1990 '10 The Close', in Cooper (ed.) 1990, 47–50

Thorp, J.R.L. 2012 'The construction, presentation and development of a merchant's town house c. 1500–1740; 38 North Street, Exeter', *Proceedings of the Devon Archaeological Society* 70, 147–250

Thorpe, C. and Wood, I. 2011 'Early medieval pottery', in Herring *et al.* 2011, 276–80

Threipland, L.M. 1956 'An excavation at St Mawgan-in-Pyder, Cornwall', *Archaeological Journal* 113, 33–81

Thurlby, M. 1991 'The Romanesque cathedral of St Mary and St Peter in Exeter', in Kelly (ed.) 1991, 19–34

Thurlby, M. 1994 'The roles of the patron and the master mason in the first design of the Romanesque cathedral of Durham', in D. Rollason, M. Harvey and M. Prestwich (eds) 1994 *Anglo-Norman Durham 1093–1193* Woodbridge, Boydell, 161–84

Timby, J. 2000 'The pottery', in Rippon 2000b, 174–83

Tingle, M. 2006 'Excavations of a possible causewayed enclosure and Roman site at Membury 1986 and 1984–2000', *Proceedings of the Devon Archaeological Society* 64, 1–52

Tinkley, N. 2010 *Misterton 2008 – watching brief* South Somerset Archaeological Research Group report 04/10 [ADS: https://doi.org/10.5284/1017035]

Todd, M. 1981 *Roman Britain 55 BC–AD 400* London, Fontana Paperbacks

Todd, M. 1985 'The Roman fort at Bury Barton, Devonshire', *Britannia* 16, 49–55

Todd, M. 1987 *The south west to AD1000* London, Longman

Todd, M. 1989a 'The early cities', in Todd 1989b (ed.), 75–89

Todd, M. (ed.) 1989b *Research on Roman Britain 1960–89* London, The Society for the Promotion of Roman Studies Britannia Monograph 11

Todd, M. 1998 'A hilltop enclosure at Rudge, Morchard Bishop', *Proceedings of the Devon Archaeological Society* 56, 133–52

Todd, M. 2002 'The Roman fort and later Roman site at Bury Barton', *Proceedings of the Devon Archaeological Society* 60, 37–58

Todd, M. 2004 'The Claudian conquest and its consequences', in M. Todd (ed.) *A companion to Roman Britain* London, Blackwell Publishing, 42–59

Todd, M. 2007a 'Roman military occupation at Hembury (Devon)', *Britannia* 38, 107–24

Todd, M. 2007b *Roman mining in Somerset. Charterhouse on Mendip: Excavations 1993–5* Exeter, The Mint Press

Toller, H. 2014 'The Roman road from Dorchester to Exeter', *Proceedings of the Devon Archaeological Society* 72, 103–30

Tomber, R. and Dore, J. 1998 *The national Roman fabric reference collection: a handbook* London, Museum of London Archaeology Service

Tomlin, R.S.O. 2016 *Roman London's first voices: writing tablets from the Bloomberg excavations, 2010–14* London, Museum of London Archaeology Monograph 72

Tomlin, R.S.O. 2018 *Britannia Romana. Roman inscriptions and Roman Britain* Oxford, Oxbow Books

Tompsett, I. 2014 *Social dynamics in south-west England AD 350–1150: an exploration of maritime oriented identity* Oxford, British Archaeological Reports British Series 599

Touchard, H. 1967 *Le commerce maritime Breton à la fin du moyen âge* Paris, Les Belles Lettres

Toulmin Smith, L. 1964 *The itinerary of John Leland in or about the years 1535–1543, parts I to III. Volume 1* London, Centaur Press

Toynbee, J.M.C. 1979 'A note on a sculptured torso of a bird', in Bidwell 1979, 130–2

Tracy, C. 1999 'The importation into England of church furniture from the continent of Europe from the late Middle Ages to the present day', *Journal of the British Archaeological Association* 152, 97–149

Tracy, C. 2001 *Continental church furniture in England: a traffic in piety* Woodbridge, Antique Collectors' Club

Trentacoste, A., Lightfoot, E., Le Roux, P., Buckley, M., Kansa, S.W., Esposito, C. and Gleba, M. 2020 'Heading for the hills? A multi-isotope study of sheep management in first-millennium BC Italy', *Journal of Archaeological Science Reports* 29

Trevarthen, M. 2008 *Suburban life in Roman Durnovaria: excavations at the former County Hospital site Dorchester, Dorset 2000–2001* Salisbury, Wessex Archaeology

Trevarthen, M. 2011 *New car park, Redlands Sports Centre, Weymouth, Dorset* Terrain Archaeology report 53346/3/1 [ADS: https://doi.org/10.5284/1046600]

Trevarthen, M. and Bellamy, P.S. 2009 *Scats Countrystore, Grove Trading Estate, Dorchester, Dorset* Terrain Archaeology report 53283/2/1 rev2 [ADS: https://doi.org/10.5284/1030961]

Turner, M.E. (ed) 1982a *Home Office acreage returns (HO 67): list and analysis* London, PRO List and Index Society, Volume 189

Turner, M.E. (ed) 1982b *Home Office acreage returns (HO 67): list and analysis* London, PRO List and Index Society, Volume 190

Turner, M.E. 1982c 'Agricultural productivity in England in the eighteenth century: evidence from crop yields', *Economic History Review*, 35, 489–510

Turner, M.E. (ed) 1983a *Home Office acreage returns (HO 67): list and analysis* London, PRO List and Index Society, Volume 195

Turner, M.E. (ed) 1983b *Home Office acreage returns (HO 67): list and analysis* London, PRO List and Index Society, Volume 196

Turner, M.E. 1984 'Agricultural productivity in eighteenth century England: further strains of speculation', *Economic History Review* 37, 252–7

Turner, M.E. 1986 'Crop distributions, land productivity and English parliamentary enclosure', *Journal of Economic History* 46, 669–92

Turner, S. 2005 *Devon Historic Landscape Characterisation* Exeter, Devon County Council Historic Environment Service [http://www.devon.gov.uk/index/environment/historic_environment/landscapes/landscape-characterisation.htm]

Turner, S. 2007 *Ancient countryside: the historic character of rural Devon* Exeter, Devon Archaeological Society Occasional Paper 20

Turner, S. and Gerrard, J. 2004 'Imported and local pottery from Mothecombe: some new finds amongst old material in Totnes Museum', *Proceedings of the Devon Archaeological Society* 62, 171–6

Tutt, R. 2006 *Cheddar Touring Park, Cheddar, Somerset* Avon Archaeological Unit report

Tyacke, A., Bayley, J. and Butcher, S. 2011 'Romano-British brooches – of Cornish origin?', in Pearce (ed.) 2011 139–49

Tyers, C. 2012 'Dendrochronology', in Thorp 2012, 228

Tyler, K. 2011 *Land at Hill Barton, Clyst Honiton, Devon* AC Archaeology report ACD350/2/0 [ADS: https://doi.org/10.5284/1011335]

Tyson, R. 2019 'Islamic and Byzantine-style medieval and early post-medieval glass from Plantation Place, London', in Edwards and Paynter (eds) 2019, 35–44

Uglow, J. 2000 'Three Romano-British sites in the Lower Exe Valley', *Proceedings of the Devon Archaeological Society* 58, 227–48

Uglow, J., Brown, A.G. and Silvester, R.J. 1985 'The investigation of a cropmark complex in the Lower Exe Valley', *Proceedings of the Devon Archaeological Society* 43, 115–17

Valentin, J. 1996 *An archaeological evaluation of a proposed redevelopment at the Coldstream Dairy, Milborne St Andrew, Dorset* AC Archaeology report 3096/3/0 [ADS: https://doi.org/10.5284/1028798]

Valentin, J. 1999 *An archaeological field evaluation of a proposed new lagoon system near West Creech Farm, Steeple Parish, Dorset* AC Archaeology report 1899/1/0 [ADS: https://doi.org/10.5284/1028803]

Valentin, J. 2003 'Manor Farm, Portesham, Dorset: excavations on a multi-period religious and settlement site', *Proceedings of the Dorset Natural History and Archaeological Society* 125, 23–70

Valentin, J. 2010 *Land at Oaklands, Cowick Lane, Exeter, Devon* AC Archaeology report ACD148/2/0 [ADS: https://doi.org/10.5284/1024197]

van der Leeuw, S.E. 1975 'Medieval pottery from Haarlem: a model', *Rotterdam Papers* 2, 67–87

van der Veen, M. 2016 'Arable farming, horticulture and food: expansion, innovation and diversity', in Millett *et al.* (eds) 2016, 807–33

Vince, A.G. 1985 'Saxon and medieval pottery in London: a review', *Medieval Archaeology* 29, 25–93

Vince, A.G. 2004 *Assessment of the pottery from High Street, Glastonbury (HSG04)* Alan Vince Archaeological Consultancy report 2004/90 [ADS: https://doi.org/10.5284/1005755]

von Petrikovits, H. 1975a *Novaesium. Das römische Neuss* Böhlau, Führer des Rheinischen Landesmuseums in Bonn 3

von Petrikovits, H. 1975b *Die Innenbauten Römischer Legionslager während der Prinzipatszeit* Opladen, Abhandlungen der Rheinisch-Westfälischen Akademie der Wissenschaften, Bd 56

von Schnurbein, S. 1974 *Die römischen militäranlagen bei Haltern* Bodenaltertümer Westfalens 14, Münster, Verlag Aschendorff

Wacher, J. 1974 *The towns of Roman Britain* London, Batsford

Wacher, J. 1995 *The towns of Roman Britain* 2nd edition London, Batsford

Wacher, J. 1998a 'The dating of town walls in Roman Britain', in Bird (ed.) 1998, 41–50

Wacher, J. 1998b 'The *Verulamium* Gate and its related works' in Holbrook (ed.) 1998, 37–46

Wacher, J. and McWhirr, A. 1982 *Early Roman occupation at Cirencester* Cirencester, Cirencester Excavations I

Wacher, J. and Salvatore, J.P. 1998 'The town defences', in Holbrook (ed.) 1998, 35–98

Wakeham, C.S. 2003 *Archaeological recording at Globefield, Topsham, Exeter* Exeter Archaeology report

Wallace, L. and Mullen, A. 2019 'Landscape, monumentality and expression of group identities in Iron Age and Roman East Kent', *Britannia* 50, 75–108

Wallace, P.F. 1986 'The English presence in Viking Dublin', in Blackburn (ed.) 1986, 455–85

Walls, S. 2013 *The Glebe, Tregony, Cornwall* Southwest Archaeology report 130104 [ADS: https://doi.org/10.5284/1025007]

Walton, P.J. 2012 *Rethinking Roman Britain: coinage and archaeology* Wetteren, Collection Moneta 137

Wapshott, E, Webb, P. and Morris, B. 2018 *79 Heavitree Road, Exeter, Devon, EX1 2HZ* Southwest Archaeology report 181002 [ADS: https://doi.org/10.5284/1058729]

Warman, S. 2013 'Animal bone', in Ridgeway and Watts 2013, 268–83

Warry, P. 2006 *Tegulae: manufacture, typology and use in Roman Britain* Oxford, British Archaeological Reports British Series 417

Warry, P. 2017 'Production, distribution, use and curation: a study of stamped tile from Gloucestershire', *Britannia* 48, 77–115

Watts, V. 2004 *The Cambridge dictionary of English place-names* Cambridge, Cambridge University Press

Weale, A. 2015 *Land at Wick Farm, Wick Road, Lympsham, Weston-super-Mare, Somerset* Thames Valley Archaeological Services report 15/178 [ADS: https://doi.org/10.5284/1038770]

Weale, A. 2016 *Hurn Court Farm, Parley Lane, Hurn, Bournemouth, Dorset Phase 5* Thames Valley Archaeological Services report 12/186c [ADS: https://doi.org/10.5284/1044329]

Weavill, T. 2015 *Old Park Farm, Pinhoe, Devon* Cotswold Archaeology report 15292 [ADS: https://doi.org/10.5284/1041796]

Weavill, T. 2017 *Saw Close, Bath, Bath and North East Somerset* Cotswold Archaeology report 16532 [ADS: https://doi.org/10.5284/1046818]

Webster, C.J. (ed.) 2007 *The archaeology of South West England. South West archaeological research framework, resource assessment and research agenda* Taunton, Somerset County Council

Webster, C.J 2008 *The archaeology of South West England. South West Archaeological Research Framework, resource assessment and research agenda* Taunton, Somerset County Council

Webster, C.J., Wilkinson, K.N., King T., Marter, P., Stoodley, N. and Turn A. 2003 *Archaeological investigations at Yarford, Kingston St Mary, Somerset, April–July 2003* King Alfred's College, Winchester School of Humanities and Somerset County Council report [ADS: https://doi.org/10.5284/1029084]

Webster, G. 1958/9 'An excavation at Nunnington Park near Wiveliscombe, Somerset', *Somerset Archaeological and Natural History Society* 103, 81–91

Webster, G. 1966 'Fort and town in early Roman Britain', in Wacher (ed.) 1966, 31–45

Webster, G. 1978 *Boudica, the British revolt against Rome AD 60* London, Batsford

Webster, G. (ed.) 1988 *Fortress into city: the consolidation of Roman Britain first century AD* London, Batsford

Webster, G. (J. Chadderton (ed.)) 2002 *The legionary fortress at Wroxeter. Excavations by G. Webster, 1955–85* London, English Heritage Archaeological Report 19

Webster, J. 2003 'Bronze objects', in James 2003, 289–325

Webster, J. 2001 'Creolizing the Roman provinces', *American Journal of Archaeology* 105, 209–25

Webster, L.E and Cherry, J. 1979 'Medieval Britain in 1978', *Medieval Archaeology* 23, 234–78

Weddell, P.J. 1980 'Excavations at 3–5 Lower Fore Street, Exmouth', *Proceedings of the Devon Archaeological Society* 38, 91–116

Weddell, P.J. 1981 'Excavations at Southgate Cottages, Lydford', *Proceedings of the Devon Archaeological Society* 39, 128–35

Weddell, P.J. 1986 'The excavation of medieval and later houses at St Margaret's Chapel, Exmouth', *Proceedings of the Devon Archaeological Society* 44, 131–6

Weddell, P.J. 1987 'Excavations within the Anglo-Saxon enclosure at Berry Meadow, Kingsteignton, in 1985', *Proceedings of the Devon Archaeological Society* 45, 75–96

Weddell, P.J. 2000 'The excavation of a post-Roman cemetery near Kenn', *Proceedings of the Devon Archaeological Society* 58, 93–126

Weddell, P.J. and Reed, S.J. 1997 'Excavations at Sourton Down Okehampton 1986–1991: Roman road, deserted medieval hamlet and other landscape features', *Proceedings of the Devon Archaeological Society* 55, 39–147

Weddell, P.J., Reed, S.J. and Simpson, S.J. 1993 'Excavation of the Exeter-Dorchester Roman road at the River Yarty and the Roman fort ditch and settlement site at Woodbury, near Axminster', *Proceedings of the Devon Archaeological Society* 51, 33–134

Welfare, H. and Swan, V. 1995 *Roman camps in England. The field archaeology* London, Royal Commission on the Historic Monuments of England

Welldon Finn, R. 1967 'Devonshire', in Darby and Welldon Finn (eds) 1967, 223–95

Wells, W.C. 1923–4 'A hoard of coins of Æthelred II found in Ireland', *British Numismatic Journal* 17, 51–9

Welsh, K. 1997 *Cade's Farm, Taunton Road, Wellington, Somerset. Archaeological evaluation report* Oxford Archaeology report [ADS: https://doi.org/10.5284/1029090]

Wessex Archaeology 1998 *Roweberrow treatment works outfall drain, Shipham, Somerset* Wessex Archaeology report 44525.01 [ADS: https://doi.org/10.5284/1029118]

Wessex Archaeology 1999 *Fisher's Square, 142–6 Cowick Street, Exeter* Wessex Archaeology report 46761.03

Wessex Archaeology 2003a *Green Island, Poole Harbour, Dorset* Wessex Archaeology report 52568.07 [ADS: https://doi.org/10.5284/1039269]

Wessex Archaeology 2003b *Zinch House, Station Road, Stogumber, Somerset* Wessex Archaeology report 52568.14 [ADS: https://doi.org/10.5284/1001082]

Wessex Archaeology 2004a *Myncen and Goldfield Farms, Minchington, Dorset* Wessex Archaeology report 52568.13 [ADS: https://doi.org/10.5284/1028789]

Wessex Archaeology 2004b *Whitestaunton Manor House, Whitestaunton, Somerset* Wessex Archaeology report 52568.12 [WA: https://www.wessexarch.co.uk/our-work/whitestaunton-manor]

Wessex Archaeology 2005 *Picket Farm, Picket Lane, South Perrott, Dorset* Wessex Archaeology report 55575 [ADS: https://doi.org/10.5284/1028790]

Wessex Archaeology 2007a *Land to the north of Poundbury Farm, Poundbury, Dorchester, Dorset* Wessex Archaeology report 60021.02 [ADS: https://doi.org/10.5284/1028794]

Wessex Archaeology 2007b *Blacklands, Upper Row Farm, Laverton, Somerset: assessment and evaluation results* Wessex Archaeology Report 62504.01 [ADS: https://doi.org/10.5284/1030416]

Wessex Archaeology 2008a *Lellizzick, near Padstow, Cornwall* Wessex Archaeology report 65312.01 [ADS: https://doi.org/10.5284/1028748]

Wessex Archaeology 2008b *Ide Park and Ride, Alphington, Devon* Wessex Archaeology report 69871.01 [ADS: https://doi.org/10.5284/1042091]

Wessex Archaeology 2009 *Lake Farm, Wimborne, Dorset* Wessex Archaeology report 72110.02 [ADS: https://doi.org/10.5284/1038779]

Wessex Archaeology 2010a *Exeter Science Park Drive, Exeter, Devon* Wessex Archaeology report 73567.01 [ADS: https://doi.org/10.5284/1046627]

Wessex Archaeology 2010b *Alphington Road, Exeter, Devon* Wessex Archaeology report 73280.03 [ADS: https://doi.org/10.5284/1024856]

Wessex Archaeology 2011a *Langport Ranges, High Ham, Somerset* Wessex Archaeology report 74150.01 [ADS: https://doi.org/10.5284/1026662]

Wessex Archaeology 2011b *Environment Agency Habitat Creation Scheme, Steart Peninsular, Somerset* Wessex Archaeology report 77220.02 [ADS: https://doi.org/10.5284/1048791]

Wessex Archaeology 2011c *Land south of Yeoford Way, Marsh Barton Trading Estate, Exeter* Wessex Archaeology report 77790.03 [ADS: https://doi.org/10.5284/1024858]

Wessex Archaeology 2012a *Steart Farm, Cheddar, Somerset* Wessex Archaeology report 88300.01 [ADS: https://doi.org/10.5284/1027001]

Wessex Archaeology 2012b *Land at Saundercroft Farm, Whimple, Devon* Wessex Archaeology report 87780.01 [ADS: https://doi.org/10.5284/1042094]

Wessex Archaeology 2013a *Land adjacent to Steart Village, Steart Point, Somerset, TA5 2PX* Wessex Archaeology report 77221.12 [ADS: https://doi.org/10.5284/1049173]

Wessex Archaeology 2013b *Shaw's Orchard, Bawdrip, Somerset* Wessex Archaeology report 87260.03 [ADS: https://doi.org/10.5284/1027860]

Wessex Archaeology 2014a *Heritage Court, Glastonbury, Somerset* Wessex Archaeology report 78050.03 [ADS: https://doi.org/10.5284/1047462]

Wessex Archaeology 2014b *Green Pits Lane, Nunney, Somerset* Wessex Archaeology report 102501.03 [ADS: https://doi.org/10.5284/1031014]

Wessex Archaeology 2014c *Land at Wick Farm, Lympsham, Somerset* Wessex Archaeology report 106530 [ADS: https://doi.org/10.5284/1038858]

Wessex Archaeology 2015a *Exeter flood defence scheme, Exeter, Devon* Wessex Archaeology report 105800.09 [ADS: https://doi.org/10.5284/1048280]

Wessex Archaeology 2015b *Sherford New Community – phase 1.1, Plymouth, Devon (RMA 1.1 advanced planting works)* Wessex Archaeology report 107560.04 [ADS: https://doi.org/10.5284/1045354]

Wessex Archaeology 2015c *Sherford New Community – phase 1.1, Plymouth, Devon (RMA 1.1 and NEVS areas 1–10)* Wessex Archaeology report 107560.04 [ADS: https://doi.org/10.5284/1045355]

Wessex Archaeology 2016a *Sherford New Community – phase 1.1, Plymouth, Devon (fields 23 and 24)* Wessex Archaeology report 107560.13 [ADS: https://doi.org/10.5284/1045686]

Wessex Archaeology 2016b *Land at Gatehouse Farm, Dawlish, Devon* Wessex Archaeology report 108011.02 [ADS: https://doi.org/10.5284/1042112]

Wessex Archaeology 2016c *Land off Higher Hoopern Lane, Exeter, Devon* Wessex Archaeology report 113830.01 [ADS: https://doi.org/10.5284/1052721]

Wessex Archaeology 2017 *Land at Pinn Lane, Sandrock, Exeter* Wessex Archaeology report 106671 [ADS: https://doi.org/10.5284/1048776]

Wessex Archaeology 2018 *Sherford New Community – Phase 1.1, Plymouth, Devon (2016 work): post-excavation assessment* Wessex Archaeology report 10756017

Wheeler, R.E.M. and Wheeler, T.V. 1936 *Verulamium. A Belgic and two Roman cities* London, Reports of the Research Committee of the Society of Antiquaries of London 11

Whelan, J. 2015 *Land north and south of Blundell's Road, Tiverton, Devon* Cotswold Archaeology report 15007 [ADS: https://doi.org/10.5284/1042666]

Whelan, J. 2016a *The Mead, Whitchurch, Bristol, Bath and North-East Somerset* Cotswold Archaeology report 16378 [ADS: https://doi.org/10.5284/1046352]

Whelan, J. 2016b *Land at Chickerell, Weymouth, Dorset* Cotswold Archaeology report 16444 [ADS: https://doi.org/10.5284/1042920]

White, R.H. 2010 'Wroxeter', in Burnham and Davies (eds) 2010, 193–6

White, R.H. and Barker, P. 1998 *Wroxeter: life and death of a Roman city* Stroud, Tempus

White, R.H., Gaffney, C. and Gaffney, V.L. 2013 *Wroxeter and the Cornovii. Final report on the Wroxeter hinterland project 1994–1997. Volume 2: Characterizing the city* Oxford, Archaeopress

Whitelock, D. 1955 *English historical documents 1, c. 500–1042* Oxford, Oxford University Press

Wilkes, E.M., Griffith, F.M., Quinnell, H., Allason-Jones, L. and Randall, C. 2012 'Cadbury Castle, Devon, reconsidered', *Archaeological Journal* 169, 237–80

Wilkinson, M. 1979 'The fish remains', in Maltby 1979, 74–81

Wilkinson, M. 1982 'Fishbones', in Higham *et al.* 1982, 135–8

Williams J.H. 1971 'Roman building materials', *Transactions of the Bristol and Gloucestershire Archaeological Society* 90, 95–120

Williams, M. 1969 'The 1801 crop returns for Somerset', *Somerset Archaeological and Natural History Society 113*, 69–85

Williams, R.G.J. 1998 'The St Cuthbert's Roman mining settlement, Priddy, Somerset: aerial photographic recognition', *Proceedings of the University of Bristol Spelaeological Society* 21(2), 123–32

Williamson, T. 2002 *The transformation of rural England* Exeter, University of Exeter Press

Williamson, T. 2003, *Shaping medieval landscapes* Macclesfield, Windgather Press

Willis, A. and Young, A. 2008 *Weston-super-Mare Technical College & School of Art, Hans Price Building, South Terrace, Weston-super-Mare, North Somerset* Avon Archaeological Unit report [ADS: https://doi.org/10.5284/1029148]

Willis, S. 2004 'Samian pottery, a resource for the study of Roman Britain and beyond: the results of the English Heritage funded Samian Project', *Internet Archaeology* 17 [IA: https://doi.org/10.11141/ia.17.1]

Willis, S. 2011 'Samian ware and society in Roman Britain and beyond', *Britannia* 42, 167–242

Willis, S. and Hingley, R. 2007 'Roman finds: context and theory', in Hingley and Willis (eds) 2007, 1–17

Willmes, M., Bataille, C.P., James, H.F., Moffat, I., McMorrow, L., Kinsley, L., Armstrong, R.A., Eggins, S. and Grün, R. 2018 'Mapping of bioavailable strontium isotope ratios in France for archaeological provenance studies', *Applied Geochemistry* 90, 75–86

Willmott, H. 2015 'Table glass in the West Country home, *c.* 1500–1700', in Allan *et al.* 2015, 321–38

Willmott, T. 1982 'Excavation at Queen's Street, City of London, 1953 and 1960, and Roman timber-lined wells in London', *Transactions of the London and Middlesex Archaeological Society* 33, 1–78

Wills, R. 2015 *Land at Wear Barton Road, Exeter, Devon* Cotswold Archaeology report 14253

Wilson, B. 1978 'The animal bones', in Parrington 1979, 110–37

Wilson, D.M. (ed.) 1976 *The archaeology of Anglo-Saxon England* Cambridge, Cambridge University Press

Wilson, R.J.A. 2006a 'Urban defences and civic status in early Roman Britain, in Wilson (ed.) 2006b, 1–47

Wilson, R.J.A. (ed.) 2006b *Romanitas: essays on Roman archaeology in honour of Shepherd Frere on the occasion of his ninetieth birthday* Oxford, Oxbow Books

Wilthew, P. 1986 *Examination of slag from various Roman sites in Exeter* London, Ancient Monuments Laboratory report 44/86

Winfer, J. 2016 *Land at Lower Lane, Ebford, Devon: an archaeological evaluation* Unpublished report in the Devon Historic Environment Record

Winterbottom, N. (ed.) 1978 *Gildas: the ruin of Britain and other documents* Chichester, Phillimore

Wood, I. 2014 'Early-medieval Cornish pottery in Hiberno-Norse Ireland', *Cornish Archaeology* 53, 223–31

Wood, M. 1935 'Norman domestic architecture', *Archaeological Journal* 92, 167–242

Wooding, J.M. 1996 *Communications and commerce along the western sealanes AD400–800* Oxford, British Archaeological Reports British Series 654

Woodley, K. and Thacker, G. 2013 *Land off Station Road, Feniton, Devon* Oxford Archaeology report [ADS: https://doi.org/10.5284/1026505]

Woodward, P.J. 1983 'Wimborne Minster, Dorset: excavations in the town centre 1975–80', *Proceedings of the Dorset Natural History and Archaeological Society* 105, 57–74

Woodward, P.J. 1987 *Romano-British industries in Purbeck: excavations at Norden, and excavations at Ower and Rope Lake Hole* Dorchester, Dorset Natural History and Archaeological Society Monograph Series 6

Woodward, P.J. and Woodward, A. 2004 'Dedicating the town: urban foundation deposits in Roman Britain', *World Archaeology* 36, 68–86

Woodward, P.J., Grieve, D. and Davies, S.M. 1985 'The excavation of a ring-ditch and associated settlement features on the South Dorset Ridgeway, Winterbourne St Martin, Dorset', *Proceedings of the Dorset Natural History and Archaeological Society* 107, 95–100

Woodward, P.J., Davies, S.M. and Graham, A.H. 1993 *Excavations at Greyhound Yard, Dorchester 1981–4* Dorchester, Dorset Natural History and Archaeological Society Monograph Series 12

Woolf, G. 1998 *Becoming Roman* Cambridge, Cambridge University Press

Woolgar, C.M., Serjeantson, D. and Waldron, T. (eds) 2006 *Food in medieval England* Oxford, Oxford University Press

Woolner, D. and Woolner, A. 1954 'Teignbridge and the Haldon Road', *Report and Transactions of the Devonshire Association* 3, 211–27

Worrell, S. and Pearce, J. 2012 'Roman Britain in 2011. II. Finds reported under the Portable Antiquities Scheme', *Britannia* 43, 355–93

Wright, J. 2013 *Land south of the Met Office, Exeter, Devon* Cotswold Archaeology report 12295 [ADS: https://doi.org/10.5284/1024480]

Wyles, S.F. 2017 'Appendix D plant macrofossils report' *Winham Farm, Cullompton, Devon: archaeological excavation* Cotswold Archaeology report 16251 [ADS: https://doi.org/10.5284/1048925]

Wyles, S.F. 2018 'Appendix 7 charred plant remains', Higher Nansloe Farm, Helston, Cornwall Cotswold Archaeology report 18038 [CA: https://reports.cotswoldarchaeology.co.uk/]

Yegül, F., 1992 *Baths and bathing in classical antiquity* New York, The Architectural History Foundation

Yorke, B. 1990 *Kings and kingdoms of early Anglo-Saxon England* London, Routledge

Yorkston, D. 1996 'Excavation of a medieval site at Keynsham Nursery, The Park, Keynsham', *Bristol and Avon Archaeology Journal* 13, 57–77

Youings, J. 1952 'The city of Exeter and the property of the dissolved monasteries', *Reports and Transactions of the Devonshire Ass*ociation 84, 122–41

Youings, J. 1968 *Tuckers Hall, Exeter* Exeter, University of Exeter

Young, A. 2000–1 'Time Team at Boleigh fogou, St Buryan', *Cornish Archaeology* 39–40, 129–45

Young, D. 2007 'Iron Age, medieval and recent activity at Whitegate Farm, Bleadon, North Somerset', *Somerset Archaeological and Natural History Society* 151, 31–81

Young, D. 2009 'Excavation of an early medieval site at Brent Knoll, Somerset', *Somerset Archaeological and Natural History Society* 152, 105–37

Young, D.E.Y. 2002 *Trial excavation on land at Coates Farm, Greinton, Somerset* Avon Archaeological Unit report [ADS: https://doi.org/10.5284/1029101]

Young, D.E.Y. 2003 *Excavation of a Romano-British and medieval site on land at Coates Farm, Greinton, Somerset* Avon Archaeological Unit report [ADS: https://doi.org/10.5284/1029095]

Young, T. 2018 'Iron production in early medieval Britain: possible cultural influences on technological change', in Smart 2018, 211–14

Zant, J.M. 1993 *The Brooks, Winchester, 1987–88. The Roman structural remains* Stroud, Winchester Museums Service Archaeological Report 2

Zienkiewicz, J.D. 1986 *The legionary fortress baths at Caerleon. I, The buildings* Cardiff, National Museums and Galleries of Wales

Zienkiewicz, J.D. 1990 'The early development of the legionary fortress of Caerleon-*Isca* and consequences for Flavian policy in Britain', in Burnham and Davies (eds) 1990, 27–34

Zienkiewicz, J.D., 1993 'Excavations in the *scamnum tribunorum* at Caerleon: the Legionary Museum site 1983–5', *Britannia* 24, 27–140

Zochowski, A. and Holt, R. 2018 *The Kings of Wessex Academy, Station Road, Cheddar, Somerset* Wessex Archaeology report 110970.02 [ADS: https://doi.org/10.5284/1053047]

Index

Numbers in *italic* denote pages with figures, those in **bold** denote pages with tables.